THE PROCESS OF
Social Research

THE PROCESS OF
Social Research

SECOND EDITION

Jeffrey C. Dixon
College of the Holy Cross

Royce A. Singleton, Jr.
College of the Holy Cross

Bruce C. Straits
University of California, Santa Barbara

New York   Oxford
OXFORD UNIVERSITY PRESS

Oxford University Press is a department of the University of Oxford.
It furthers the University's objective of excellence in research, scholarship,
and education by publishing worldwide. Oxford is a registered trade mark of
Oxford University Press in the UK and certain other countries.

Published in the United States of America by Oxford University Press
198 Madison Avenue, New York, NY 10016, United States of America.

Library of Congress Cataloging-in-Publication Data

Names: Dixon, Jeffrey C., author. | Singleton, Royce, author. | Straits,
    Bruce C., author.
Title: The process of social research / Jeffrey C. Dixon, College of the Holy
    Cross, Royce A. Singleton, Jr., College of the Holy Cross, Bruce C.
    Straits, University of California, Santa Barbara.
Description: Second edition. | New York : Oxford University Press, [2019]
Identifiers: LCCN 2018016612 | ISBN 9780190876654 (pbk.)
Subjects: LCSH: Social sciences—Methodology. | Social sciences—Research.
Classification: LCC H61 .D588 2019 | DDC 300.72/1—dc23
LC record available at https://lccn.loc.gov/2018016612

9 8 7 6 5 4 3
Printed by Marquis Book Printing, Canada

Brief Contents

Contents

BOXES

CHAPTER 9   **Field Research and In-Depth Interviews:** Systematic People-Watching and Listening   249

CHAPTER 13   **Qualitative Data Analysis:** Searching for Meaning   406

CHAPTER 14   **Reading and Writing in Social Research:** It's All About
Communication   437

About the Authors

JEFFREY C. DIXON, Associate Professor of Sociology at the College of the Holy Cross, received his PhD from Indiana University, Bloomington, with a minor in research/ quantitative methods, and also holds a BS in Secondary Education from Wright State University. He is the co-editor (with Royce Singleton) of *Reading Social Research: Studies in Inequalities and Deviance*. His research has appeared in such journals as *Social Forces, European Sociological Review, Public Opinion Quarterly, British Journal of Sociology, International Migration Review, Social Science Quarterly*, and *Teaching Sociology*. Currently, his research focuses on job insecurity from a cross-national perspective as well as liberal-democratic values and attitudes in Turkey and the European Union (EU). He has taught research methods courses for about nine years, including a graduate course at Koç University in Istanbul and an undergraduate course at Holy Cross.

ROYCE A. SINGLETON, JR., Professor Emeritus of Sociology at the College of the Holy Cross, received his PhD from Indiana University, Bloomington, with a minor in mathematics. He is a co-author (with Jonathan Turner and David Musick) of *Oppression: A Socio-History of Black-White Relations in America*, co-author (with Bruce Straits) of *Approaches to Social Research*, and co-editor (with Jeffrey Dixon) of *Reading Social Research: Studies in Inequalities and Deviance*. Spanning several methodological approaches and topics, his research has appeared in the *American Sociological Review, Social Forces, Sex Roles*, and *Teaching Sociology* among other journals. Before his retirement, he taught both graduate and undergraduate courses in social research methods, including a course offered at Holy Cross for 32 years.

BRUCE C. STRAITS, Professor Emeritus of Sociology at the University of California, Santa Barbara, received his PhD from the University of Chicago. He is a co-author (with Paul Wuebben and Gary Schulman) of *The Experiment as a Social Occasion* and the co-author (with Royce Singleton) of *Approaches to Social Research*. In addition to research methodology, his research areas include social demography, cigarette smoking and cessation, the social psychology of research settings, and the influence of personal networks on individuals' attitudes and behavior. His research has appeared in the *American Journal of Sociology, Public Opinion Quarterly, Sociology of Education*, and *Social Networks* among other journals. In teaching research methods and social statistics, he has emphasized "hands-on" experience in research design, data interpretation, and analytical reasoning.

Letter from the Authors

DEAR READER:

Of all the courses students take, none may be more important than research methods. Methodology is the heart of the social sciences; more than anything else, it is what distinguishes social science from journalism and social commentary, from the humanities and natural sciences. Understanding social research methods, therefore, should give you a better sense of sociology and related disciplines and of exactly what social scientists do.

Besides deepening your understanding of social science, knowledge of social research is essential for making informed decisions about our daily lives. Social scientific methods and findings influence us in numerous ways. Many government social programs are shaped and evaluated by social research; businesses constantly rely on consumer research for key marketing and management decisions; the popular press daily reports research findings on the most personal aspects of people's lives. One of the goals of this book is to help you understand the logic and limitations of social research so that you can evaluate it effectively.

We also hope to provide enough information about how to do research so that you can conduct your own study. Throughout the book we provide step-by-step guides on how to design and carry out research projects. Studying the process of social research can sharpen your powers of critical thinking and evaluation and enable you to become a more intelligent gatherer of information.

Sincerely,
Jeffrey C. Dixon
Royce A. Singleton, Jr.
Bruce C. Straits

Preface

The Process of Social Research introduces students to the fundamentals of research, from topic selection and research design to data collection, analysis, and interpretation. A unique feature of the book is its emphasis on process. Every chapter contains flowcharts of research processes—for example, the process of measurement, the process of sampling, and the process of planning and conducting a survey—that provide step-by-step guides to conducting social research and evaluating the research of others.

We have tried to make the book student-friendly in many ways: By writing in a conversational style, by illustrating concepts with familiar everyday examples, and by carefully selecting research examples that are culturally relevant to students' lives, such as studies of Facebook and alcohol consumption and grades.

Many chapters revolve around studies that are current, methodologically rigorous, and cover a wide range of cutting-edge topics, including immigration, homelessness, family composition, prosecutorial misconduct, mass incarceration, and social inequality and education. To fully describe study methods, we often contacted the researchers to obtain additional information on methodology that was not contained in their published work. In this way, our readers see how research is sometimes a bumpy road and how researchers negotiate the bumps along the way.

In writing this book, we drew material from Singleton and Straits' *Approaches to Social Research*. Those familiar with *Approaches* will find, however, that this book is almost entirely new. In addition to its more current examples, emphasis on process, and more student-friendly features, *The Process of Social Research* provides a better balance between qualitative and quantitative research and takes a more integrated approach to describing the relationship between theory and research.

ORGANIZATION

The book is organized into 14 chapters, grouped as follows:

Contexts of the Social Research Process

Includes an overview of the research process (Chapter 1) followed by chapters on three important contexts of social research: science, ethics, and politics. Chapter 2 shows how the essence of social research as a scientific enterprise is a constant interplay between theory and data. Chapter 3 considers how research is shaped by ethical and political choices.

Designs for Social Research

Chapter 4 introduces basic terminology as we discuss topic selection and research designs in quantitative and qualitative research. The next two chapters then examine two key considerations in planning or designing a study: measurement (Chapter 5) and sampling (Chapter 6).

General Approaches to Social Research

Chapters 7–10 cover basic approaches to social research: experiments, surveys, qualitative field research and in-depth interviews, and the use of existing data. Chapter 11 presents strategies for combining methods and approaches.

Analyzing and Interpreting Social Research

Chapters 12 and 13 discuss data analysis and interpretation, respectively, for quantitative and qualitative data. The final chapter (14) offers guidance for reviewing the social science literature, writing a proposal, and writing a research report.

FEATURES

The book has several special features that will be useful in teaching and learning about the process of social research.

- **Learning objectives** are listed at the opening of each chapter, previewing key topics being discussed.
- **Flowcharts** illustrate the underlying logic of methods while providing step-by-step guides to conducting social research.
- **Section summaries** highlight the main ideas after each major section of a chapter.
- **Boxes** *assess comprehension of key concepts* (Checking Your Understanding), and provide practical advice to *conduct social research* (Doing Social Research) and to *understand and evaluate research* (Reading Social Research).
- **Key terms** are highlighted and defined in each chapter and also included in the book's comprehensive glossary.
- **Key Points, Review Questions,** and **Exercises** at the end of each chapter reinforce learning objectives.

ANCILLARIES

Oxford University Press is proud to offer a complete supplements package to accompany *The Process of Social Research*.

The **Ancillary Resource Center (ARC)** at **www.oup-arc.com** is a convenient, instructor-focused single destination for resources to accompany this book. Accessed online through individual user accounts, the ARC provides instructors with up-to-date ancillaries while guaranteeing the security of grade-significant resources. In addition, it allows OUP to keep instructors informed when new content becomes available.

The ARC for *The Process of Social Research* contains a variety of materials, prepared by Royce Singleton, to aid in teaching:

- **PowerPoint lecture slides** to aid in the presentation of course material
- An **Instructor's Manual** with lecture and demonstration ideas, exercises, answers to textbook review questions, and answers to selected textbook exercises
- A **computerized test bank** with multiple-choice, true/false, and essay questions.

THE SECOND EDITION

As we tell our students, the key to good writing is revise, revise, revise. Although the first edition went through numerous revisions, the process of revision is endless, and we are fortunate to have the opportunity to make this a better book.

Our revision was guided by responses from reviewers and from Dixon's "Logics of Inquiry" students at the College of the Holy Cross; we thank them for their feedback. Many of the changes are subtle but important. This includes editing every chapter to improve the clarity and flow of the text, updating discussions, and presenting the latest data from the GSS and other sources. These changes are most evident in Chapters 4–6 and 12. More substantive changes include the following:

- We replaced three of the four Facebook studies in Chapter 1 with more current examples, including field research on the use of Facebook in rural Kenya.
- In Chapter 2, Box 2.2, we provide a more sophisticated treatment of how to identify and evaluate deductive and inductive reasoning.
- In Chapter 4, we distinguish between descriptive and explanatory research questions, note reference management software that may help students reference their papers, and include a box on the ecological fallacy, which was moved from Chapter 10 in the first edition.
- In clarifying the sometimes-difficult process of measurement, we reorganized Chapter 5 to reflect better the steps in this process, and we created boxes on the value of composite measurement and the difference between indexes and scales, which were covered in Chapter 11 of the first edition.
- In addition to clarifying key points in the section on principles of probability sampling in Chapter 6, we added a box that applies these principles to the 2016 election polls.
- In Chapter 9, we added an example, previously included in Chapter 13, of how field jottings are transformed into field notes.
- In Chapter 10, we added a box on big data and a research example on the use of IPUMS data.

- We rewrote Chapter 11 by omitting the coverage of composite measurement and focusing on mixed-methods research, which combines two or more approaches. This chapter now begins with an overview of basic approaches to social research covered in Chapters 7–10, followed by four research examples and a discussion of the purposes and design of mixed-methods research. Two of the four research examples, including Dan Clawson and Naomi Gerstel's *Unequal Time*, are new.
- We revised and updated all exercises that required readers to visit the GSS website or to analyze GSS data using the Survey Documentation and Analysis (SDA) website; this includes exercises in Chapters 3 (Box 2.1), 4, 5, 8, and 12.

We welcome comments and suggestions for further improving the book and helping to make it better serve your needs. Just send a message to Jeff Dixon (jdixon@holycross. edu) or Royce Singleton (rsinglet@holycross.edu).

COMPANION WEBSITE

The Process of Social Research is also accompanied by an extensive **companion website** (**www.oup.com/us/dixon**), which includes materials, prepared by Royce Singleton, to help students with every aspect of the course. For each chapter, you will find:

- **Learning Objectives** that identify the concepts that students should understand after reading each chapter
- **Practice quizzes** to help students review the material and assess their own comprehension
- **Additional links** to websites providing supplemental information on the topics covered in each chapter

ACKNOWLEDGMENTS

As sociologists, we know well how much we depend on others. This is certainly true of producing a book. Indeed, we have benefited greatly from the support of so many people that it is not possible to thank everyone to whom we are indebted. Still, several persons deserve special mention. Among Dixon's and Singleton's colleagues at the College of the Holy Cross, Renée Beard provided important input into our discussion of grounded theory; David Hummon commented on Box 13.2, which is a simplified adaptation of his teaching technique; and reference librarian Laura Hibbler (formerly at Holy Cross, now at Brandeis University) helped us refine a set of guidelines for searching databases. Furthermore, we received valuable feedback from Andy Fullerton, Oklahoma State University, on the chapter on quantitative data analysis, and from Johnny Saldaña, Arizona State University, on the qualitative analysis chapter. Within the latter chapter, Don Zimmerman of the University of California–Santa Barbara, commented on an early version of the section on conversation analysis, and Kathleen Blee of the University of Pittsburgh offered comments on the section on narrative analysis. Josh Klugman, Temple University, alerted Dixon to the debate surrounding Mark Regnerus's study on the impact of gay parenting, which became the focal point of our discussion of politics and research. For the second edition, Mary Kraetzer of Mercy College provided useful comments on Laud Humphreys' study and convinced us to incorporate the ASA style guide for citations and references.

As we wrote many of the chapters, we were in contact with the scholars whose research we were highlighting. They not only responded readily to our numerous questions; they read drafts of chapters in which their work was cited and made many helpful suggestions. So, we owe a special note of gratitude to Jessica Calarco of Indiana University (Chapter 4), Jeff Lucas of the University of Maryland (Chapter 7), Brian Powell of Indiana University (Chapter 8), Robert Courtney Smith of City University of New York (Chapter 9), Jessica Vasquez of the University of Oregon (Chapter 9), Melissa Kearney of the University of Maryland and Phillip Levine of Wellesley College (Chapter 10), Andrew Lindner of Skidmore College (Chapter 10), Michael Campbell of the University of California, Irvine, and Heather Schoenfeld of Northwestern University (Chapter 10), Dan Clawson and Naomi Gerstel of the University of Massachusetts at Amherst (Chapter 11), and Leon Anderson of Utah State University (Chapter 13).

We would never have written this book without the encouragement and support of our editor at Oxford University Press, Sherith Pankratz. We also benefited from the expert advice and guidance of our developmental editor Elsa Peterson and from the extraordinary work of assistant editor Katy Albis and assistant editor Grace Li. In constructing several figures, we were fortunate to receive the professional input of graphic designer Kate Singleton Blehar of Blehar Design. Thanks also to John Buckingham of A-V Services at Holy Cross for preparing several high-resolution images of figures, and to Holy Cross graphic designer Sharon Matys for creating the facsimile of the letter to Tuskegee participants. In the Oxford production department, we would like to thank manager of content operations Lisa Grzan, art director Michele Laseau, production editor Keith Faivre, and copy editor Wendy Walker. And last, but by no means least, we would like to acknowledge and thank the Oxford marketing team, including marketing manager Tony Mathias, marketing assistant Jordan Wright, director of marketing Frank Mortimer, and the other hardworking men and women who are getting our book into the hands of the students for whom we wrote it.

We owe a huge debt of gratitude to our spouses. Jeff would like to thank Zeynep Mirza, whose intellectual and emotional support is nothing short of amazing. Zeynep commented on early versions of several chapters, had countless discussions with Jeff about the book, and provided constant encouragement throughout the process of writing. Royce thanks Nancy for her patience and for acting as an indispensable sounding board to numerous ideas and drafts. Bruce would like to thank Cathy Straits for keeping him active, healthy, and happy since meeting her in Iceland 18 years ago.

We also would like to note that the order of authorship is simply alphabetical and is not a measure of the division of labor among the authors.

We would like to extend special thanks to the many instructors who took the time to look over drafts of the manuscript for the first edition:

Robert Adelman, University at Buffalo, SUNY

Francisco Alatorre, New Mexico State University

Michael P. Allen, Washington State University

Mikaila Mariel Lemonik Arthur, Rhode Island College

Dawn Michelle Baunach, Georgia State University

Nick Berigan, East Tennessee State University

Christopher Bradley, President and CEO of Three Rivers Social Research

George W. Burruss, Southern Illinois University Carbondale

Ernesto Castañeda, University of Texas at El Paso

Hannah B. Emery, Mills College

Martie Gillen, University of Florida

Steve Jacobs, Piedmont College

Wesley James, The University of Memphis

Antwan Jones, The George Washington University

Veena Kulkarni, Arkansas State University

Michael A. Long, Oklahoma State University

Matthew T. Loveland, Le Moyne College

Kris Marsh, University of Maryland

John R. Mitrano, Central Connecticut State University

E. Dianne Mosley, Texas Southern University

Lois Ritter, California State University, East Bay

Bryan L. Sykes, University of California, Irvine

Xiaohe Xu, The University of Texas at San Antonio

We also thank those instructors who took the time to offer thoughtful reviews of the first edition:

Daniel Boudon, St. Francis College

Linda Bzhetaj, Oakland University

Ginny Garcia-Alexander, Portland State University

Andrew Martin, Ohio State University

Lauren Jade Martin, Pennsylvania State University

Virginia Adams O'Connell, Moravian College

Summer Roberts, University of South Carolina, Beaufort

Sandra Sulzer, Xavier University of New Orleans

Shalini A. Tendulkar, Tufts University

Introduction

Why Care About Research Methods?

STUDENT LEARNING OBJECTIVES

By the end of this chapter, you should be able to

1. Explain what it means to be a consumer and producer of research evidence.

2. Identify the four major steps in the research process.

3. Describe the major approaches to social research.

▲ Is social media ruining students? That's one of many headlines that question the impact of Facebook and other such forms of online communication.

Launched in 1999 "for students, by students," ratemyprofessors.com claims to be the largest online source of professor ratings. Students visiting the website may rate professors' overall quality and level of difficulty, indicate whether they would take a course with the professor again, determine "hotness" (symbolized with a red chili pepper), and add comments. Students may even select classes based on the "data" reported on this website. But how credible is the website? Can you trust such ratings?

In April 2009, Aryn Karpinski (2009a), then a graduate student at The Ohio State University, presented a research paper at a professional meeting indicating that students who use Facebook have lower grades than those who do not. Karpinski's study generated a media frenzy, triggering such headlines as "Sad but true: Using Facebook can lower your GPA" and "Facebook dumbs you down." Like many students today, you probably spend some time on social media. Should you believe these headlines?

A working knowledge of research methods can help you answer questions like these and many more. The utility of studying research methods begins with our daily exposure to vast amounts of information. As you encounter information on websites, in the news, through advertisements, and from other sources, it is important to know what to believe, for much of this information can be inaccurate, misleading, or conflicting.

Suppose, for example, it's time to select classes again, and you're thinking about a particular course. You're interested in the course topic and the days and times when it meets are compatible with your schedule, but you don't know anything about the professor. So you decide to find out what students think about the professor by going to www.ratemyprofessors.com. According to the posted ratings, your potential professor is clear and helpful. You also read some of the student comments: some say the professor is very challenging. Others complain about the heavy amount of assigned reading and unfair tests. How trustworthy is this information? Should you use it to decide whether to take this professor's course?

The answer: it would be hard to trust ratemyprofessors.com's ratings and make a good decision based on them. The problem is that these ratings are not based on a representative group of students who have taken the professor's course but rather on self-selected students who took the time to go to the website. Very few students choose to rate their professors on ratemyprofessors.com. It is also possible that those few students who visit the website have strong feelings about the professor, either favorable or unfavorable. As a result, you might find that responses fall at the extremes: they rate the professor as either very good or very bad. Thus, it's hard to accurately predict what this professor will be like from these ratings.

Sometimes, faulty or misreported evidence and research can have other consequences, such as causing false alarm. Reports of Karpinski's study of Facebook and grades are an example. Though attention grabbing, the headlines we cited are misleading. To conclude from this type of study that being on Facebook *causes* bad grades violates a cardinal principle of social research: a relationship between two phenomena does not mean that one thing caused the other. To put it more succinctly, association does not equal causation. In fact, Karpinski (2009b) herself was careful to note this limitation: her study merely showed an association between using Facebook and grades; it did not demonstrate that using Facebook *causes* one's grades to drop. To turn the logic around, an equally likely interpretation is that receiving bad grades causes students to become Facebook users. Still another possibility is that there is no causal link between Facebook and grades. Facebook use may be a symptom of procrastination. Or the association could be due to a common factor, such as a student's major. For example, critics of Karpinski's study pointed out that science majors, who were more likely to use Facebook than humanities and social science majors, also might tend to get lower grades, perhaps because of more stringent grading standards in the sciences (Pasek, more, and Hargittai 2009a). Studying research methods will enable you to apply this reasoning as well as identify other limitations of reported research.

It is also not unusual to encounter conflicting information in everyday life and in social science research. One website presents different ways to lose weight, complete with percentages of people who successfully applied each weight-loss method. Another website is filled with stories of those who used the same strategies and *gained weight*. One news report cites studies showing the harmful effects of drinking coffee; another report claims that scientific studies refute most of these effects. Karpinski's study showed a relationship between Facebook use and bad grades. Within a few weeks of her presentation, an article in the online journal *First Monday* (Pasek, more, and Hargittai 2009a) presented new findings. The authors' conclusion: "We find no evidence that Facebook use is related to diminished academic performance." When you come across conflicting information or evidence such as this, knowledge of research methods can help you sort out what is most credible.[1] For an example, see Box 1.1, READING SOCIAL RESEARCH: Critical Evaluation of Facebook Studies.

As you read this book, you will develop the ability to understand and evaluate the accuracy and limits of social scientific research, so that you can draw *your own* conclusions about it. You should find this useful in numerous ways. As a student, you may be required to read published research articles for class or to prepare a term paper or other course project. After graduation, you may need to know the policy implications of research findings or read research reports to keep up in your field. And as an ordinary citizen, you may want to use information from published research to make

---

[1]Conflicting results also may stimulate additional research. In fact, subsequent studies have shown that academic performance is related to time spent on Facebook, multitasking on Facebook, and academic class standing (Junco 2015; Karpinski et al. 2013; Kirschner and Karpinski 2010).

BOX 1.1

READING SOCIAL RESEARCH

Critical Evaluation of Facebook Studies

What, if anything, should you believe about the relationship between Facebook use and grades? As a student of research methods, you will learn to evaluate research, such as the studies on Facebook, by asking tough questions. For example, we can ask who took the surveys, how many people took them, and how were they selected.

Karpinski (2009a) surveyed a relatively small group of 117 graduate students and 102 undergraduate students at a Midwestern university in the US, and most of the undergraduates were third- and fourth-year students. All of the students surveyed were volunteers taking summer and fall classes. By contrast, the follow-up research, which found no association between Facebook use and grades, examined data from three separate samples: 1,060 first-year students at the University of Illinois at Chicago and 1,020 students from two national samples of individuals between the ages of 14 and 22 (Pasek, more, and Hargittai 2009a). The first-year students, like Karpinski's sample, were recruited through classes; however, the classes consisted of nearly all sections of a mandatory first-year course, and 82 percent of the students completed the survey. More importantly, students in the national samples were selected randomly.

This additional information helps us evaluate the Facebook researchers' conflicting conclusions. For example, because Karpinski surveyed student volunteers at one university, her conclusion may hold true only for those students she surveyed. These students, like the students who post ratings on ratemyprofessors. com, do not represent all students at the university, let alone *all* college students. In the second study, one of the samples was representative of all first-year students at one university. Although limited, this is a much more viable sample than Karpinski's and might even be generalizable to first-year students at other similar types of universities. The other samples used in the second study were based on random selection and represented students of different levels of education and at many different schools across the country. This means we can be reasonably sure that among US students aged 14–22 in 2009, Facebook users' grades were no different, on average, from those of their non–Facebook-using peers.

When evaluating research conclusions, you will often find that "the devil is in the details." That is, we need to understand exactly how researchers conducted their studies in order to evaluate their conclusions. This example illustrates only one of many methodological details: the process of selecting respondents, or sampling, which will be discussed throughout this book. (For an interesting exchange between the authors, which draws attention to other limitations of both studies, see Karpinski [2009b] and Pasek, more, and Hargittai [2009b].)

informed decisions or simply evaluate information reported online and in the media every day.

You will learn from this book not only how to evaluate research but also how to conduct it yourself. In this way, you will become both a critical *consumer* of research and an active *producer* of knowledge. Students often enjoy doing their own research. It can be empowering to learn how to find out something *you want to know*, whether about Facebook or some other topic. It can also be fun to "get one's hands dirty" in the research process itself.

Learning how to conduct research also has many benefits. First and foremost, it may be an essential skill for the course you are currently taking. Later in your undergraduate academic career, you may conduct research for another course, a capstone project, or a thesis. If you plan to further your education, knowing how to do research may be a prerequisite for gaining admission to graduate or professional school and successfully completing a postbaccalaureate degree. These and related skills are also quite valuable in the world of work (Hart Research Associates 2015). As instructors, we've had former students ask for our advice on a research project they are working on for their employer. For example, one project consisted of a client survey; in another, the student wanted to assess the effectiveness of an intergenerational program she designed to promote positive attitudes about aging.

Now that you can see how useful it is to study research methods, we want to give you a better idea about the nature and process of social science research. When we say *social* science research, we mean that the topic must have some social aspect such as studying people, interactions, groups of people, social networks, or whole nations. It also means that this research is *scientific*, or based on systematic and verifiable observations. Like all sciences, social research aims to arrive at explanations of the natural world through systematic observations and logical reasoning. In the remainder of this chapter, we provide an overview of the process of social research found in such fields as sociology, anthropology, psychology, and political science.

THE PROCESS OF SOCIAL RESEARCH

We believe that the best way to learn how to do something is to understand the underlying *process*. As an example, consider the process of course registration. The first step in this process is to see which courses are offered. As a next step, you might consult with others, such as an academic advisor, friends, or family, about the courses. (We hope, though, that you now understand the drawbacks of consulting ratemyprofessors.com!) At the same time, you need to consider your schedule and time preferences to ensure there are no conflicts. Once you have decided on your course schedule, the final step is to actually register.

Likewise, if you want to learn how to do social research so that you can evaluate reported studies as well as conduct your own study, you need to understand the research process. Figure 1.1 shows the major steps in this process. As the figure illustrates, research begins with a research question. After posing a research question, you need to determine how best to answer it. That is, you need to devise a plan, called a research design (step 2 in the figure). Step 3 is to carry out your research design by gathering data to answer your research

FIGURE 1.1
The Research Process

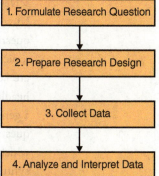

1. Formulate Research Question

2. Prepare Research Design

3. Collect Data

4. Analyze and Interpret Data

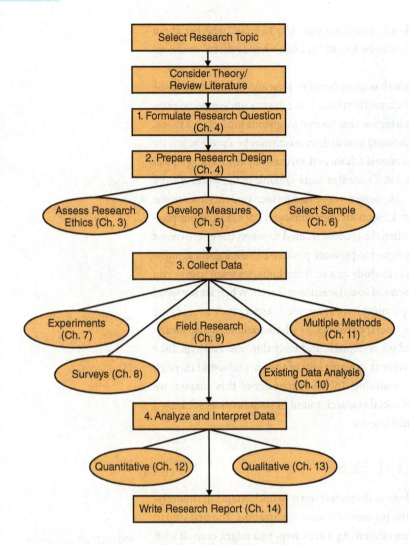

question. Finally, step 4 consists of the analysis and interpretation of your data. This book is organized to follow these steps. After a discussion of the scientific, ethical, and political contexts of research in Chapters 2 and 3, Chapters 4–6 cover steps 1 and 2. Chapters 7–11 cover step 3, and Chapters 12, 13, and 14 cover step 4.

Each major step in a process is often a series of other steps. For instance, there is more to the process of course registration than we described, as you probably know. Consider the step of consulting with others: this may also involve getting course approval from advisors and professors, filling out additional paperwork, and ensuring that all of your fees are paid before you can register. Even these steps are processes themselves. To get approval for the course, for example, you may need to set up an appointment, meet with your advisor or professor, and then get this approval put into the system.

FIGURE 1.2
The Research Process Elaborated

Although we hope it is not as frustrating as the process of course registration (!), the process of social research also involves other steps, which are processes in and of themselves (see Figure 1.2). The chapters of this book describe these steps and their underlying processes. Consider, for example, the first major step of formulating a research question: for beginning researchers, this initially depends on the selection of a *general* topic. Facebook is a timely topic because the effects of social media, including Facebook, are hotly debated. One online blog asked, "Is social media ruining students?" Media headlines, personal interest, and curiosity are all worthwhile motivators for the study of a general topic. However, a general topic must be narrowed to a more specific research question. This narrowing process requires a consideration of theory and prior research, which involves reviewing the literature: locating scholarly books or articles and reading, synthesizing, and evaluating them. Once you've reviewed the literature on, say, Facebook, you can formulate a research question. You might decide that you are interested in how people evaluate each other's Facebook profiles (Walther et al. 2008). You might want to know if there is any benefit to maintaining relationships on Facebook (Ellison et al. 2014). You might ask about people's experiences of using Facebook outside the United States (Wyche et al. 2013). Or you might be curious about whether comments posted on Facebook pages differ from those posted on websites in which the author is anonymous (Rowe 2015).

Finally, whether we are considering course registration, social research, or some other process, one size rarely fits all. While an understanding of the general process will help you to complete the steps, each step in the process will shape those that follow. For example, in designing research to answer your question (step 2), the steps will depend largely on the *type* of research question you ask (see Chapter 4). The question also will shape, in particular, which method you choose to collect data (step 3). Among the numerous methods available, the most essential differences occur among the broad approaches into which these methods can be grouped: **experiments**, **surveys**, **field research and in-depth interviews**, and **existing data analysis**. We discuss the process of doing research with each of these approaches in Chapters 7 through 10. Then we discuss strategies for using a combination of approaches in Chapter 11. Reading these chapters will enable you to decide which approach or combination best answers your research question as well as how to use the approach in your own research. Finally, the process of analyzing data (step 4) varies according to whether your data are in numerical form. We explain how to analyze quantitative (numerical) data in Chapter 12 and how to analyze qualitative (nonnumerical) data in Chapter 13. The end product of the research process is almost always a research report, which we discuss in Chapter 14.

FOUR FACEBOOK STUDIES

Now that you have a general idea of the overall research process, we want to give you a "sneak preview" of this process by describing studies that address each of the questions we posed about Facebook. We chose these questions in part because each is best answered with a different methodological approach. In this way you can see how the specifics of the research process vary depending on the approach.

An Experiment

Have you ever judged people based on the attractiveness of their Facebook friends? To answer this question, Joseph Walther and colleagues (2008) conducted an experiment. If you've ever done a "norm-breaking experiment," where you observe people's behavior before and after you break a social norm (e.g., standing too close to someone in an elevator), you might already understand the general logic of experimentation. An **experiment** is a distinctive methodological approach with two key features: manipulation and

experiment Basic approach to social research that entails manipulating an aspect of the environment to observe behavior under different, controlled conditions.

control. Researchers introduce changes into the environment (manipulation) so that behavior is observed under different conditions, and the conditions are the same except for the manipulation (control).

Wanting to know if people's judgments of Facebook profile owners differ according to the physical attractiveness of their Facebook friends, Walther and colleagues (2008) designed an experiment by manipulating "attractiveness." Specifically, they created "mock" Facebook profiles for people who were neither attractive nor unattractive: they were simply of "neutral" attractiveness. What varied was the attractiveness of the *profile owner's friends*: in one version of the mock profile, posted photos of the profile owner's friends were highly attractive; in another version, the photos of the owner's friends were not attractive. The profile "raters" were 389 college students in communication and telecommunications courses at a public university in the Midwestern United States who volunteered to participate in the study. After viewing mock profiles on the Internet, the participants were asked to what extent they agreed or disagreed with such statements as, "I find this person attractive physically" (Walther et al. 2008:40).

What did the analysis of data reveal? Participants in the experiment rated the same profile owner as more attractive if the profile owner had more attractive Facebook friends. According to Walther and colleagues (2008:41), these ratings seem to be based on the assumption that birds of a feather flock together: attractive people hang out with attractive people and unattractive people associate with unattractive people.

Well-conducted experiments can help us understand the *causes* of human behavior. In Chapter 7 you will learn how they do this effectively. As you will see, more than any other approach, experiments emphasize the design phase of social research. Once you have figured out how to manipulate the causal factor and how to control other factors, data collection and analysis are fairly straightforward. Yet experiments have limitations: you cannot manipulate everything of interest to social scientists, and experiments are usually performed on a select group of people at a certain place and time, such as the communication and telecommunications students at the university where Walther and colleagues conducted their research. Experiments also often involve deception, which raises questions about research ethics (see Chapter 3).

A Survey

Given the media's apparent focus on the negative consequences of Facebook, you may wonder whether there are any positive aspects. Nicole Ellison and colleagues (2007, 2014) have investigated this question in a number of ways, most recently asking whether maintaining relationships on Facebook is related to greater social resources. To answer this question, Nicole Ellison, Jessica Vitak, Rebecca Gray, and Cliff Lampe (2014) conducted an online survey about Facebook. A **survey** involves asking questions, usually of a randomly selected group of people. Ellison and colleagues (2014:859) contacted 2,149 randomly selected nonfaculty staff "at a large Midwestern U.S. university" to

survey Basic approach to social research that involves asking a relatively large sample of people direct questions through interviews or questionnaires.

participate in their survey. Included in the survey were a series of items about how re-spondents maintain relationships on Facebook. Below are these items, which you can also answer by deciding whether you strongly disagree, disagree, neither disagree nor agree, agree, or strongly agree with each statement.

1. When I see a friend or acquaintance sharing good news on Facebook, I try to respond.
2. When I see a friend or acquaintance sharing bad news on Facebook, I try to respond.
3. When I see someone asking for advice on Facebook, I try to respond.
4. When a Facebook friend has a birthday, I try to post something on their wall.
5. When I see someone asking a question on Facebook that I know the answer to, I try to respond. (Ellison et al. 2014:861)

What were your answers? Ellison and colleagues assigned numerical values to every-one's responses and calculated various statistics. They found overall that women were more likely than men to report engaging in the above Facebook relationship mainte-nance activities. Moreover, the researchers found that people who reported engaging in these activities also reported having greater social resources. In other words, they had more "social capital," which in this context refers to "contact with diverse others, feeling part of a broader group, and engaging in reciprocal behaviors with one's com-munity," among other things (Ellison et al. 2014:860). Thus, maintaining relationships on Facebook is associated with some "benefits."

Surveys help researchers to understand patterns and relationships that may be gen-eralizable to a larger group of people. As you will see in Chapter 8, survey researchers take great care in writing questions, designing the questionnaire, and selecting respon-dents. Like experimental data, survey data typically are numerical and thus amenable to quantitative analysis (see Chapter 12). There are drawbacks to the survey method, how-ever. Although the numbers generated by survey responses provide a snapshot of what a generally large group of people has to say, what people *say* may not always be truthful or even predictive of what they *do*. Furthermore, it can be difficult to establish "what causes what" with survey data, especially if the survey is conducted at only one point in time, which is true of Ellison and colleagues' (2014) survey. Another limitation is that surveys may not adequately represent the group under study. Only 29 percent of ran-domly selected nonfaculty staff completed Ellison and colleagues' (2014:860) survey, and some groups were disproportionately represented: compared to a national dataset, for example, women and social network site users were more likely to complete it.

A Field Research Study

You may have noticed that the Facebook studies discussed so far focus on the United States. Susan Wyche, Sarita Yardi Schoenebeck, and Andrea Forte (2013:33) won-dered: "What is the Facebook experience . . . where the social, economic, and technical contexts affecting use differ from the American college campuses where the site was first popularized?" To answer this question, Wyche and colleagues conducted field research in rural Kenya. ***Field research*** involves observing people in their natural settings and often interviewing them. Both field research and *in-depth interviews*, which may be used as a stand-alone method, produce *qualitative* (nonnumerical) data. Although field research is akin to engaging in "people-watching" and deep discussions in everyday life, it is systematic, requiring careful observation, listening, and analytic skills.

Between June and August 2011, Wyche and colleagues (2013) conducted observations in rural areas in central and western Kenya, particularly at cyber cafés, which provide Internet access for a fee. They also interviewed 24 people, including cyber café owners, employees, and customers, more than half of whom actively used Facebook. Noting that infrastructure in rural Kenya is underdeveloped and many rural Kenyans live on only $1.50–$2/day, the researchers found that it can be difficult and expensive for people to use Facebook. One difficulty that the researchers observed is that it is common for the cafés to experience blackouts:

> When touring towns and entering cafés we found dark rooms and unlit monitors on more than one occasion. Café employees rarely knew when power would return. While interviewing a staff member at a café in Bungoma we experienced four blackouts during a six-hour period, each lasting between 10–45 minutes. (Wyche et al. 2013:38)

Another challenge is that Internet bandwidth is limited, which one of the researchers' interviewees dealt with as follows: "When the Internet is a bit slow, I will open two tabs and while Yahoo! loads I am on Facebook browsing, getting updates, and then checking my mails again" (Wyche et al. 2013:38). At cyber cafés, which charge by the minute, time is also money; it can be expensive to do things like uploading photographs that require more bandwidth, particularly given that a 30-minute session "could easily consume about one third of a person's daily expenditures in rural Kenya" (41). Still, participants in the study noted that Facebook connects them to friends, family, and others, including those outside the country. Moreover, the financial costs could be less than an international phone call. Based on these and other findings, Wyche and colleagues (2013) conclude that, despite some similarities, rural Kenyans' experiences with Facebook differ in many ways from those of Facebook users in the United States as reported in prior research.

Field research is distinct from experiments and surveys in several ways. Although both experiments and field research rely on observations, field researchers do not intentionally attempt to change people's behaviors. Rather, field researchers describe what they observe in people's natural settings and try to understand the broader social context of people's behaviors. The interviews used in field research—and in-depth interviews more generally—are distinct from survey interviews because researchers are less interested in the number or percentage of people who provide a certain response than the social meanings and processes behind those responses. Such qualitative research

field research Basic approach to social research that involves directly observing and often interviewing others to produce nonnumerical data.

requires a more open-ended type of inquiry, which, in contrast to other approaches, places less emphasis on design and more on the collection and analysis of data. Thus, early findings from observations and/or interviews tend to shape the direction of the research. The data are reported in ordinary language such as Wyche and colleagues' description of Internet cafés during a blackout. As you'll see in Chapter 13, the analysis of qualitative data requires a different set of tools than the analysis of quantitative data.

Although field research can deepen our understanding of the context and meanings behind behaviors and emotions, conclusions may not apply beyond the sometimes-narrow group being studied. Indeed, a criticism of Wyche and colleagues' research is that their conclusions were based on observations and interviews in selected rural areas of Kenya, which makes it difficult to know how generalizable the findings are—that is, to whom they apply. Moreover, interviews in this form of research are subject to the same criticism as surveys: they capture what people say, but are not necessarily reflective of what people do.

An Analysis of Existing Data

Given the stakes of contemporary political debates about issues such as immigration, same-sex marriage, and gun control, it would not be surprising if some became heated and perhaps even uncivil. Arguing that civility "lies at the heart of democratic society," Ian Rowe (2015:121) wanted to know if comments about political stories were more civil on a Facebook page in which the author's comments could be identified or on a newspaper website in which the author's comments were anonymous. To address this issue, Rowe analyzed existing data. **Existing data analysis** is the analysis of data from sources of information that were not produced directly by the researcher who uses them. In addition to Facebook pages and websites, vast sources of existing data are available for analysis; these include advertisements, books, historical documents, and official statistics.

> **existing data analysis**
> Analysis of data from existing sources of information that were not produced directly by the researcher who uses them.

Using a specific type of existing data analysis called *content analysis* (see Chapter 10), Rowe (2015) analyzed comments on political news stories from the *Washington Post's* Facebook page and its website. After selecting a total of 26 political news stories on various topics from 2013, Rowe randomly selected 1,000 comments on these stories; half of these appeared on the Facebook page and the other half appeared on the website. He then identified comments that were "uncivil," which was defined as a "verbalized threat to democracy," "assigned stereotypes," or "threatened others individuals' rights" (Rowe 2015:128). The following is an example of an uncivil comment:

> Flori-duh is about the dumbest state I have ever lived in. People do not know how to vote because they do not read newspapers or pay attention to the news. They stand in line for voting just to take time off of work. (Rowe 2015:129)

Altogether, Rowe found that only about 4 percent of the comments were characterized as uncivil. However, there was indeed a difference between the data sources: as expected, uncivil comments were more numerous on the anonymous *Washington Post* website than on its Facebook page.

The enormous variety of existing data is limited only by the researcher's imagination. The challenges are to find data that are appropriate to answer the research question and to figure out how to analyze them. In Chapter 10 we examine diverse data sources and some of the major forms of existing data analysis. As you will see, the analysis of existing data often is well suited to studying the past and understanding social structure and social change. Compared with other approaches, a major strength is that existing data analyses tend to eliminate the tendency of research participants to change their behavior in the presence of a researcher. Yet this strength can also be a weakness: the distance between the researcher and the people he or she is studying can be problematic.

SUMMARY

Once you become aware of research findings and other evidence, you will realize that they surround us all on a daily basis. In the news, in everyday life, and even in our college classrooms, we hear: "Research indicates *this*"; "Research shows *that*." We see numerical ratings of professors (e.g., www.ratemyprofessors .com) and even our colleges or universities online (e.g., *U.S. News and World Report*'s rankings, available at www.usnews.com/ rankings). Knowledge of research methods can empower you to become a critical *consumer* of research findings and other evidence by asking tough questions. It can also enable you to pose research questions and answer them yourself, thereby becoming a *producer* of knowledge. The goals of this book are to provide you with the tools to do both.

In order to carry out systematic investigation, social scientists follow a research process. The four major steps in the process are to (1) formulate a research question, (2) prepare a research design, (3) collect data, and (4) analyze/interpret data. Each of these major steps in the process requires taking other steps to complete:

the formulation of a research question, for example, involves selecting a general research topic and reviewing previous research and theory. These steps, in turn, are processes in and of themselves. Reviewing previous research and theory, for instance, requires reading, synthesis, and evaluation. Although this may seem complicated, it's similar to what you do in everyday life. As in registering for courses, the process goes much more smoothly if you know what it is and take it one step at a time.

Like other processes in everyday life, the process of social research provides you with options about how to carry out your study and collect data. We discussed several general methodological approaches: experiments, surveys, field research and in-depth interviews, and existing data analysis. We gave you a "sneak preview" of each of these approaches using specific Facebook examples, some of which we'll return to throughout the book. Each approach has its own set of strengths and weaknesses. The approach you use will depend on your research topic, question, and the available resources at your disposal.

KEY TERMS

existing data
analysis, p. 11

experiment, p. 7

field research, p. 10

survey, p. 8

KEY POINTS

- The study of research methods can enable you to become a more critical consumer of research evidence.
- The study of research methods can enable you to conduct your own research.
- The research process begins with the formulation of a research question and moves to the preparation of a research design, data collection, and data analysis.
- The most basic approaches to social research are experiments, surveys, field research and in-depth interviews, and the analysis of existing data.

REVIEW QUESTIONS

1. What do the authors mean when they say that you can benefit from the study of research methods as both a *consumer* and a *producer* of research evidence?
2. What are the four major steps in the research process?
3. Briefly describe each of the major approaches to social research. What are some strengths and weaknesses of each approach?

EXERCISES

1. Find a story or article in the media (e.g., newspaper, magazine, television) that reports the findings of a social scientific study or of a contention (e.g., an advertising claim) purportedly based on social scientific evidence. What information, if any, is given about the methods of the study or the limitations of the findings? Does the author report where the data came from, how they were collected, or how many observations the findings were based on?
2. Select a recent issue of a major social science journal, such as the *American Sociological Review*, *American Political Science Review*, or *Social Psychology Quarterly*. Based on your reading of the abstracts (the concise summaries on the first page) of each article, identify the basic approach (experiment, survey, field research/in-depth interviews, or analysis of existing data) that is used in each study reported in the issue.

2

Chapter Outline

Science and Social Research

From Theory to Data and Back

STUDENT LEARNING OBJECTIVES

By the end of this chapter, you should be able to

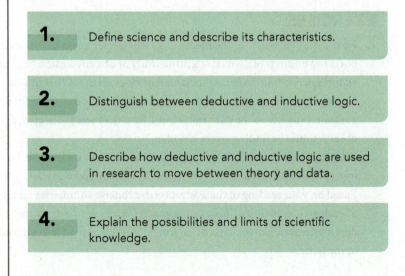

1.   Define science and describe its characteristics.

2.   Distinguish between deductive and inductive logic.

3.   Describe how deductive and inductive logic are used in research to move between theory and data.

4.   Explain the possibilities and limits of scientific knowledge.

When you think of a "scientist," what do you think of? For many years, Royce Singleton asked his sociology methods students this question. If you're like most of Singleton's students, you associate science first and foremost with the natural sciences—chemistry, physics, and biology. Moreover, you probably picture a scientist wearing a white lab coat in a laboratory, surrounded by test tubes and microscopes. Like many other students, you also might think of a scientist as a "researcher" or "experimenter" (Singleton 1998).

These responses suggest two important patterns. First, students rarely think of sociologists or other *social* scientists as "scientists." The American public distinguishes between natural and social sciences in

▲ When you think of a scientist, what do you think of? Most people associate science with natural science and with laboratory research.

a similar way: whereas 71.3 percent of a national sample of American adults thinks that biology is "very scientific," only 10 percent say the same of sociology (Smith et al. 2017). Even though social scientists do not always agree on exactly what science is, their disciplines strive to be scientific (American Psychological Association 2012; American Sociological Association 2012). To understand how they practice their craft, we therefore need to understand how science guides their activities. In this chapter we identify a characteristic process of inquiry that defines and unifies all the sciences—natural and social.

Second, students picture scientists almost exclusively as researchers. Singleton's students also referred to invention, discovery, exploration, and data analysis as other research activities. But they rarely thought of *theorists* when they thought about scientists (Singleton 1998). Neither does the American public: when a national sample of adults was asked in 2016 to express in their own words "what it means to study something scientifically," only 11.9 percent mentioned the "formulation of theory" or "testing hypotheses" (Smith et al. 2017). This is a glaring omission because the best overall characterization of the scientific process is that it involves a continuous interplay between theory and data. This interplay is at the heart of every scientific discipline. It is why, for example, virtually every undergraduate and graduate student in sociology is required to take at least two courses: one in theory and one in research methods (American Sociological Association 2003).

This chapter introduces you to the characteristics and process of science. It also outlines how scientists use logical reasoning to move back and forth between theory and data. This movement is illustrated in Figure 2.1, which shows that theory shapes data just as data shape theory. Lastly, we examine the possibilities and limits of scientific knowledge, which you should keep in mind when reading reports of research and conducting research yourself.

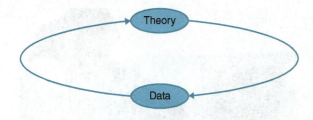

FIGURE 2.1
The Theory-Data
Relationship

THE CHARACTERISTICS AND PROCESS OF SCIENCE

Scientific studies are guided by a cumulative body of knowledge, or *theory*; they also add to this body of theoretical knowledge. As noted in Chapter 1, science is based on *verifiable data* that have been *systematically* collected and analyzed. Scientists use the principles of *logical reasoning* to move back and forth between theory and data. Let's further examine each of these characteristics of science, beginning with theory.

Theory

theory An interconnected set of propositions that shows how or why something occurs.

We all have abstract ideas about how the social world works; a **theory** is no more than a formal statement, or system of statements, of these ideas. Sociologist Robert Merton (1996:41) defines theory as "logically interconnected sets of propositions from which empirical uniformities can be derived." The goal of science is to produce knowledge in the form of theory. If you have taken natural science courses, you're probably familiar with Darwin's theory of evolution, which holds that humans evolved from nonhuman animals through a process of natural selection over many, many years. In your social science courses, you may have encountered numerous theories, including those of Karl Marx, Émile Durkheim, Max Weber, or Sigmund Freud.

As an example, consider a theory that addresses a question you might have asked yourself: in social life, are we "actors on a stage"? In *The Presentation of Self in Everyday Life* (1959), sociologist Erving Goffman puts forward a theory of the self. The theory contains the following propositions, or statements: first, social life does, in fact, resemble a play; second, people often attempt to manage impressions through "performances"; third, people engage in "front-stage" or "back-stage" behavior, depending on their definition of the situation, the setting, and the audience. When people are in a setting defined as formal and with unambiguous roles, they engage in front-stage behavior by looking and acting in a manner consistent with the roles or expectations of the social setting (Goffman 1959:Chapter 1). As a student in a classroom, for instance, you probably dress "like a student" because that is what is expected of you; you probably don't dress up in business clothing. Similarly, you probably don't directly challenge the instructor because that's not expected either. Backstage behavior, on the other hand, is more relaxed, less formal, and associated with ambiguous roles; it is

▼ Front-stage behavior may be very different from that which takes place backstage, as Goffman noted.

"where the impression fostered by the performance is knowingly contradicted as a matter of course" (Goffman 1959:112). For example, students' back-stage performance may involve gossiping about their instructor before he or she enters the room. (Caution for students: some instructors may actually wait outside the door!)

Characteristic of both the natural and social sciences is an emphasis on theory testing and development. That is, theories such as Darwin's or Goffman's *inform* data and *are informed by* data, as illustrated in Figure 2.1. Contrary to popular belief, scientists rarely come up with brilliant ideas themselves and then test them; rather, their research is often guided by theories of their predecessors (Merton 1996). Neither does research end after the collection and analysis of data. The patterns observed by researchers may support an existing theory, modify it, or lead to the generation of a new theory altogether.

In short, theory is integral to science. It both inspires and is inspired by research. Even more, beyond the scientific goal of producing theoretical knowledge, theory underlies the entire research process, from formulation of a research question to choices about how to conduct a study to the interpretation of data. While theory is a fundamental characteristic of science, science also depends on verifiable data.

Verifiable Data

Sometimes referred to as facts or empirical evidence, **data** are another characteristic of science. Their most important quality is to be verifiable. To verify is to check. And for this to be possible, the data must be observable to both the researcher and others in the scientific community. The terms "observable" and "empirical" are interchangeable; they mean that data must be tangible or "sensed" in some way—through sight, hearing, taste, smell, or touch. Evidence that cannot be sensed, such as appeals to authority, tradition, revelation, or intuition, cannot be verified; thus, they are not scientific data.

data Information recorded from observation; may be in numerical or nonnumerical form.

In Chapter 1 we provided several examples of social science data: data from interviews and surveys, Facebook profiles, and student grades. Each of these kinds of data is observable by the researcher and can also be checked by others. For example, we may read research reports containing extensive verbatim statements of people who participated in in-depth interviews. It is possible to verify these data by going back to the transcription or recording of the interview. Likewise, for a research report presenting survey data in numerical form, it is possible to verify these data by reviewing the questionnaires that respondents completed; in the case of available survey data, it is possible to check with the organization that collected these data, as in Box 2.1, READING SOCIAL RESEARCH: Verify This!.

Scientific knowledge is only as good as the data upon which it is based (Lieberson 1985). Even if data are verifiable, they may not be systematically collected and analyzed. This brings us to another characteristic of science: it is systematic.

BOX 2.1

READING SOCIAL RESEARCH

Verify This!

In the introduction, we presented survey data from a national sample of the American public indicating that only 10 percent consider sociology to be "very scientific." We got these results from the 2012 General Social Survey (GSS). The GSS is a widely used source of available survey data, which is collected by the National Opinion Research Center (NORC). By going to a website that houses this datafile, it is possible to verify the statistic we cited. Although this isn't the same as going back to the survey questionnaires, it still illustrates the process of verification. To verify the data we present, just follow the steps below:

- Go to the following website, maintained by the University of California at Berkeley: http://sda. berkeley.edu/sdaweb/analysis/?dataset=gss16

- Toward the top of the screen, under "GSS 1972-2016 Cumulative Datafile," click "Search."

- Once the next screen comes up, type in "Sociology" next to "Variable search term(s)" (we'll define "variable" in Chapter 4), and click "Search."

- The first entry you should see below is "SOCSCI— HOW SCIENTIFIC SOCIOLOGY." Click on "Select" next to this.

- Now, in the upper left corner, beneath "SDA," click "Analysis." When a new page appears, click "Row" beneath "SOCSCI."

- On the right side of the page, opposite "Selection Filter(s)," enter "Year(2012)." And in the row below that, use the dropdown menu to select "No weight."

- At the bottom of the page, click "Run the Table."

The page that comes up provides you with the survey question that a sample of American adults was asked in 2012, and the percentage (in **bold**) and number (beneath the percentage) of people who provided each response. You'll see that 10 percent, or 46 respondents, said that sociology was "very scientific." You can also check the percentage that said biology was very scientific by following the process above, replacing "sociology" with "biology."

This example gives an idea of how to verify something. It also introduces you to the GSS, which is useful for learning what American adults think about science and many other topics. You will very likely make use of it further when you embark on your own research.

Systematic Observation and Analysis

Science is systematic in that it follows a typical process or a series of steps, which we outlined in Chapter 1. This process, which includes the collection and analysis of verifiable data, gives the broader scientific community greater confidence in the knowledge that is produced. Understanding that knowledge is based on a series of steps—and knowing what those steps are—lends credibility, or believability, to the conclusion (Gieryn 1999).

If you have any doubt about the need to be systematic in order to arrive at credible conclusions, think about the grades you receive on the papers you write for your courses. Would your reaction to a grade differ depending on whether it was graded *systematically* or *unsystematically*? Suppose you had worked extremely hard on the paper: you logged long hours at the library, reading whatever you could on the topic; spent many sleepless nights writing and rewriting; and proofread the paper more times than you can remember. A week after you turned in the paper, your instructor returned it with a grade of a "C." You are not happy with a "C," but under which of the following scenarios are you most likely to accept the instructor's conclusion?

In the first scenario, the instructor explains to the class how he graded the papers. First, he developed a grading rubric that weighted certain components of the paper: for example, 10 percent of your grade was based on the clarity of your writing, 25 percent was based on the thesis development, and so on. Then, he read all the papers, marking them up with point deductions and comments explaining the point deductions. After adding up points, your instructor explains, he then reread the papers to check for consistency in how he applied the rubric. Finally, he made sure that he didn't make any calculation errors and determined final grades from the grading scale.

In the second scenario, the instructor does not offer an explanation for how he graded the papers. When one student asks about this, the instructor replies that students' grades are based on their demonstrated knowledge of the material. Another student then asks: "How do you know that *we know* the material?" The instructor says, "I just know based on my reading of the papers."

Our guess is that, even if you're unhappy with the grade in either case, you're more likely to accept the grade as credible under the first scenario, and you're less likely to think that the grade reflects the instructor's personal values or biases. This is because the grading is systematic: the instructor has a process, or series of steps, by which he reads the papers, analyzes them, and ultimately assigns grades. In the second, by contrast, there is no system or method.

Just like the instructor under the first scenario, scientists attempt to be systematic. Being systematic minimizes the influence of scientists' personal values and lends credibility to their conclusions. But in practice, what does it mean to conduct research systematically? In the natural sciences, researchers may follow protocols; these are explicit statements, for example, of which chemicals should be combined in a test tube, how they should be measured, and what should be done next. This can be contrasted with an unsystematic approach, such as that of the second instructor's grading. Like natural scientists, social scientists follow a series of steps in their research, which we further discuss in Chapter 4 and describe in detail throughout the book. However, these steps depend on the specific research approach they use (discussed in Chapters 7–10) and on the logic of their inquiry, which we will now consider.

Logical Reasoning

When you answered the question in the chapter introduction about your mental image of a "scientist," you may have said that you think of a scientist as "logical." Science is often said to follow the principles of logical reasoning, which are also standards by which science is evaluated.

Whenever we reason, we proceed from certain information to conclusions based on that information. One of the true masters of reasoning would have to be Sir Arthur Conan Doyle's famous detective, Sherlock Holmes. In "Silver Blaze," the police investigating a murder identify someone unknown to the victim as the prime suspect. Holmes is certain, however, that this suspect is innocent. To make his point, he draws attention to "the curious incident of the dog in the night-time." When the police inspector protests, "the dog did nothing in the night-time," Holmes utters, "that was the curious incident." The fact that the dog did nothing (i.e., did not bark) shows that the perpetrator was someone the dog knew well. Therefore, the suspect could not have committed the crime (Doyle 1894:22).

We use logic to evaluate the correctness of our reasoning—to determine how justified a conclusion is, based on the evidence. There are two main types of reasoning: deductive and inductive. The primary difference between the two is how certain we are that the conclusion is true based on the evidence. When we use **deductive logic**, we are claiming that the conclusion must be true if the evidence is true. With **inductive logic**, by contrast, the conclusion is uncertain even if the evidence is true because the content of the conclusion goes beyond the evidence.

You are likely familiar with these logics even if you've never formally studied them. Popular books, movies, and television shows, especially involving criminal investigations, often prominently feature them. As described above, for example, Sherlock Holmes reasoned deductively as follows: Dogs bark at strangers. If the intruder were a stranger, the dog would have barked. The dog did not bark. Therefore, the intruder was not a stranger, i.e., he or she was someone known to the dog. This reasoning is said to be deductively valid—that is, correct—because the conclusion must be true if the evidence (or premises) is true.

In everyday life, however, we often use inductive, rather than deductive, logic to make choices about everything from which foods to eat to which course to take. Suppose, for example, you observed a pattern of getting a stomachache whenever you consume a soft drink; therefore, you choose not to drink a carbonated beverage when you're thirsty. Or, you think that you'll enjoy a history course and decide to take it because you always have liked history courses. In neither case does the conclusion necessarily follow if the evidence is true. For it is possible that you won't have stomach pain the next time you drink a soft drink; it is also possible that you might not like the history course.

Unlike deductive reasoning, which may be either valid or invalid, inductive reasoning may be "weak" or "strong," depending on how strongly the evidence supports the conclusion. Thus, the inductive conclusion that you'll get a stomachache

deductive logic
Reasoning in which the conclusion necessarily follows if the evidence is true.

inductive logic
Reasoning in which the conclusion is implied by, but goes beyond, the evidence at hand and, hence, may or may not be true.

from drinking a carbonated beverage in the future would be stronger if this has happened to you 20 times than if it happened only once. To check your ability to reason deductively and inductively, complete the two questions presented in Box 2.2, CHECKING YOUR UNDERSTANDING: Identifying and Evaluating Deductive and Inductive Reasoning.

As we use the terms in this book, deductive and inductive reasoning represent two different ways of moving between theory and data, based on two different *starting points* for conducting social research. On the one hand, deductive inquiry—that is, research based on deductive reasoning—represents a top-down approach, moving from abstract theory to concrete data (refer to the right-hand side of Figure 2.1). Along the way, a scientist *deduces* conclusions, albeit tentative, based on premises or theoretical propositions, which are then tested with data. Inductive inquiry, on the other hand, is a bottom-up approach, moving from data to theory (see the left-hand side of Figure 2.1). Here, a scientist *infers* a generalization or conclusion based on a pattern of observations or data. In the next section we will explain exactly how scientists employ these logics of inquiry.

BOX 2.2

CHECKING YOUR UNDERSTANDING

Identifying and Evaluating Deductive and Inductive Reasoning

If you're thinking of going to law school or graduate school, or even applying for a job, you may have to take a logical reasoning test. These tests gauge people's ability to analyze reasoning. Your success on the tests would be enhanced greatly if you've taken a course in logic, which would provide the tools for identifying and evaluating different types of reasoning. Short of taking a logic course, however, you can learn a few skills that will aid your critical thinking.

The official website of the Law School Admissions Test (LSAT) lists several skills that are central to legal and logical reasoning. The first skill consists of "recognizing the parts of an argument and their relationships" (Law School Admissions Council [LSAC] 2017). The second consists of "recognizing similarities and differences between patterns of reasoning." By examining each of these skills, in turn, we can help you understand a little more about the logic of scientific reasoning and maybe even improve your performance on the LSAT.

1. Recognize the parts of an argument and their relationships. The first skill provides a starting point for logical analysis. In our Sherlock Holmes example, Holmes stated a conclusion along with supporting evidence. He proceeded from certain *continues*

continued
information that he held to be true (the dog didn't bark; dogs don't bark at people they know) to a claim (the suspect is innocent) that he inferred from them. Logical analysis concerns the relation between the evidence and conclusion. It begins when people like Holmes make an *argument*, which is to claim that one proposition (the *conclusion*) follows from one or more other propositions (the evidence, usually referred to as *premises*).

2. Recognize similarities and differences between patterns of reasoning. There are many patterns of reasoning, but two of the most important, which also are central to scientific inquiry, are deduction and induction. Understanding this difference is critical for analyzing reasoning because the evidence (or premises) bears a different relation to the conclusion in each argument type. In a valid deductive argument, if the premises are true, the conclusion is true. In an inductive argument, if the premises are true, the conclusion may or may not be true.

Here is a sample question from the LSAT that tests your ability to evaluate deductive reasoning (https://www.manhattanprep.com/lsat/resources/logical-reasoning-example.cfm):

> Everyone who is compassionate is kind, and someone who has experienced life's challenges is invariably compassionate. Jeremy is kind, so he has experienced life's challenges.
> Which one of the following exhibits a pattern of flawed reasoning most similar to that exhibited above?

(A) Roberta is a highly productive person. Every person who is motivated is highly productive, and every person who is organized is motivated. Therefore, Roberta is very organized.

(B) Nice people are always sympathetic people, and those who have experienced hardships always end up being nice. Betsy is not a sympathetic person, so Betsy has not experienced hardships.

(C) Almost everyone who loves black and white films is a movie buff, and all movie buffs enjoy popcorn. Sasha does not love black and white films, so Sasha probably does not enjoy popcorn.

(D) Patience requires an even temperament, and being a good parent certainly requires patience. James has no patience, so James is not a good parent.

(E) Successful entrepreneurs are either confident or experienced. Yoshi is a successful entrepreneur, and he is not experienced. Therefore, Yoshi is confident.

To determine the correct answer, let's first identify the premises and conclusion of the argument. The word "so" in the last sentence (or proposition) suggests a conclusion.

All other propositions are premises. Now, if we rearrange the premises and conclusion, we can reconstruct the argument as follows:

> Someone who has experienced life's challenges is invariably compassionate.
> Everyone who is compassionate is kind.
> Jeremy is kind, so he has experienced life's challenges.

If the first two premises are true, it follows deductively that "everyone who has experienced life's challenges is kind." Notice, however, that the conclusion of the argument is the reverse of this proposition. Therefore, it is not a valid argument. Were you able to identify the answer that exhibits the same pattern of flawed reasoning? If you reconstruct the argument of each answer, you will see that the answer is A:

> Roberta is a highly productive person.
> Every person who is organized is motivated.
> Every person who is motivated is highly productive.
> Therefore, Roberta is very organized.

Theoretical explanations should be deductively valid, and whenever scientists formulate hypotheses, they use deductive reasoning. It is therefore important to evaluate the reasoning that underlies theoretical arguments. As you can see, this involves identifying the parts of the argument (i.e., the premises and conclusion) and determining if the relation between premises and conclusion is deductively valid.

Other tests of logical reasoning gauge people's ability to reason inductively. Recall that inductive reasoning means that the conclusion is uncertain even if the evidence is true because the content of the conclusion goes beyond the evidence. Often, these tests present people with some sequence of shapes, symbols, or even numbers; test takers are then asked to complete the next part of the sequence. Consider the following example:

> 12, 15, 19, 24, 30

Which of the following numbers best completes the sequence?
- a. 33
- b. 34
- c. 35
- d. 36
- e. 37

For this question, "e" is the best answer. The evidence is the numbers. The answer, or conclusion, is reasonable because there is a (linear) pattern to the order of the numbers: they increase by 3, then 4 (= 3 + 1), then 5 (= 4 + 1), then 6 (= 5 + 1), and finally 7 (= 6 + 1),

continues

continued

making 37 (= 30 + 7) the best answer. However, the conclusion goes beyond the evidence and is by no means certain. For example, who's to say that the rest of the pattern would not be a (circular) repetition of the first, such that the next number might be 12 (a choice not given in the answer)?

Inductive reasoning in science involves the same uncertainty. Scientists use inductive reasoning whenever they attempt to arrive at theoretical generalizations based on observations or data. To evaluate this type of reasoning, you must first identify the parts of the theoretical argument, as in deductive reasoning. However, because inductive conclusions exceed the information contained in the premises, the concept of validity does not apply, and you can only evaluate inductive arguments in terms of their strength or weakness. This amounts to determining the probability or likelihood that the conclusion is true, based on the evidence. One way of strengthening inductive conclusions is to consider additional evidence; imagine, for example, obtaining additional numbers in the sequence 12, 15, 19, 24, 30. As you will see in later chapters, scientists have developed various methods for strengthening conclusions, such as increasing sample size (Chapter 8) and replicating studies (Chapter 7).

SUMMARY

The goal of science is to produce knowledge. Science is characterized by theory, verifiable data, systematic data collection and analysis, and logical reasoning. In the process of moving between theory and data, scientists primarily use two forms of logical reasoning: deductive and inductive. These logics also represent two ways of conducting research.

FIGURE 2.2
Deductive Logic of Inquiry

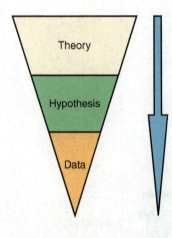

LOGICS OF INQUIRY

Having now examined the characteristics and process of science, including the two different types of logical reasoning, how exactly do we put these logics into practice when conducting research? One way of thinking about deductive and inductive inquiry is to imagine two funnels (see Figures 2.2 and 2.3). At the ends of both funnels, you see familiar terms: theory and data. Reflecting the top-down approach of deductive inquiry, the arrow in Figure 2.2 is pointing down, indicating that this process moves from (broad) theory to concrete data. The arrow in Figure 2.3 is inverted, or flipped, reflecting the fact that inductive inquiry begins with data and moves to theory. In Figures 2.2 and 2.3 you also see other terms, which means that there is more to the process than just theory and data.

Let's first consider the deductive (top-down) logic of inquiry in Figure 2.2: to understand how the world works, a researcher begins with a broad and abstract theory or multiple theories, comprised of interconnected propositions. Recall, for example, Goffman's (1959) theory of the self, which suggests:

- Social life resembles a play.
- People often attempt to manage impressions through "performances."
- People engage in "front-stage" or "back-stage" behavior, depending on their definition of the situation, the setting, and the audience.

From the theory and its propositions, a researcher deduces a **hypothesis**, which is a tentative, but unconfirmed, expectation about the relationship between two or more phenomena. In formulating a hypothesis from a theory, a researcher is using the deductive reasoning described earlier by effectively saying, "*If* theoretical propositions A, B, and C are true, *then* we should expect the following relationship in the data." To return to Goffman's theory and our example of classroom behavior, we might expect students to be less likely to adhere to formal classroom norms of deference when the instructor is out of the classroom than when he or she is in the classroom. As suggested by this example and illustrated by the funnel in Figure 2.2, a hypothesis is a more specific—and less abstract—statement than theory. A hypothesis is then tested with concrete data, which is represented by the narrowest part of the funnel.

hypothesis An expected but unconfirmed relationship among two or more phenomena.

Whereas the "line of sight" is from theory to data in deductive inquiry, it is from data to theory in the bottom-up approach of inductive inquiry (see Figure 2.3). In analyzing the data, a researcher *infers* empirical patterns, which are regularities or uniformities in the data. An **empirical pattern** represents general tendencies based on data, much like the pattern of effects from drinking carbonated beverages, mentioned earlier, or the sequence of numbers in Box 2.2. These patterns are at a higher level of generality or abstraction than individual pieces of data, such as a single experience drinking a carbonated beverage, or in the case of research, a single observation of students' classroom behavior, individual words spoken by interviewees, or a specific answer provided by survey respondents. At the highest level of abstraction is theory, which may be generated from—or "grounded" in (Glaser and Strauss 1967)—data and the empirical patterns that emerge from analysis.

empirical pattern A relationship among phenomena usually inferred from data.

FIGURE 2.3
Inductive Logic of Inquiry

As you will see throughout this book, deductive inquiry is most characteristic of quantitative research such as experiments and surveys, and inductive inquiry is most characteristic of qualitative research. This is true of the next two examples, which illustrate how social scientists use deductive reasoning and inductive reasoning in their research.

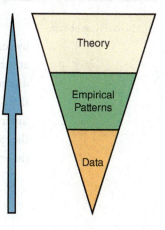

Does Contact Change Stereotypes? An Answer from Deductive Inquiry

Many social scientists are interested in understanding the sources of racial prejudice and how prejudice may change. This was the motivation for a study conducted by Jeffrey Dixon and Michael Rosenbaum (2004). Dixon and Rosenbaum wanted to know whether whites' personal contact with blacks is related to their beliefs about blacks. A simplified version of their study illustrates the process of deductive inquiry.

▲ Jeffrey Dixon

As a first step, Dixon and Rosenbaum (2004) examined the writings of social psychologist Gordon Allport, who put forward a widely cited theory of prejudice in his book *The Nature of Prejudice* ([1954] 1979). According to Allport, people have a tendency to see themselves and those like them as one group (an "in-group") and people with different characteristics as another (an "out-group"). If sociocultural factors, such as history and language, suggest that the out-group is not only different but also "bad" or inferior, then in-group members are likely to form negative perceptions of out-group members. One way to change these perceptions and otherwise reduce group animosity, Allport theorized, is through interpersonal contact between groups, which exposes in-group members to new information. By coming into contact with blacks, for example, whites may encounter evidence that contradicts their negative images of blacks and come to see them more favorably. Whether contact changes whites' views, however, also depends on how intimately whites know blacks, how frequently they interact with them, whites' and blacks' mutual goals and cooperation, and the social setting in which contact takes place, among other conditions (Allport 1979:Chapter 16).

▲ Michael Rosenbaum

Illustrating the move from theory to hypothesis, Dixon and Rosenbaum (2004) deduced hypotheses from Allport's theory about how contact in different social settings may shape whites' negative stereotypes, or beliefs, about African Americans. Specifically, they focused on how stereotypes are affected by contact in the family, schools, and other settings. "Scholars," they wrote, "know relatively little about whether the specific forms of majority-minority contact . . . actually disconfirm . . . negative stereotypes" (Dixon and Rosenbaum 2004:258). They proposed that "because of its high degree of intimacy, relative frequency, and its potentially voluntary nature, family contact should disconfirm negative stereotypes" (261). They further proposed that because contact in schools meets some of the conditions of Allport's theory, this setting also should help to disconfirm stereotypes. They thus hypothesized:

- Whites who have black relatives will be less likely to hold anti-black stereotypes than whites who do not have black relatives.
- Whites who personally know blacks from school will be less likely to hold anti-black stereotypes than whites who do not know blacks from school.

The next step in the research process is to examine data to test hypotheses. Dixon and Rosenbaum's data came from the General Social Survey (see Box 2.1), conducted in 2000. The data consisted of whites' responses to survey questions about whether they personally know any blacks and, if so, whether they know them by family relation (as relatives) and/or from school. As measures of stereotypes, the researchers used questions asking whites to rate blacks' intelligence, work ethic, and family values on a scale ranging from positive to negative.

Based on their data analysis, is contact associated with less negative stereotypes? To their surprise, Dixon and Rosenbaum (2004) found that whites with black relatives were just as likely to express anti-black stereotypes as whites without black relatives. As expected, though, whites who knew blacks from school were less likely to express anti-black stereotypes than whites who did not know blacks in this social setting. Dixon and Rosenbaum indicated that these and other findings (not discussed here) provide only "qualified support for hypotheses derived from contact theory" (270).

Dixon and Rosenbaum's study illustrates deductive inquiry, or the "top-down" approach to research: they began with theory and its propositions, derived hypotheses, and used data to test their hypotheses. Their study thus added to knowledge about the strengths and limits of contact theory as applied to the effects of interracial contact in different social settings.

How Does Class Matter? An Answer from Inductive Inquiry

In her book *Unequal Childhoods*, Annette Lareau (2011:8) writes, "It is a lot of work to get young children through the day, especially for parents. When I embarked on this study, I was interested in understanding that labor process." Focusing on families with grade-school children, Lareau examined the meanings and consequences of social class in their everyday lives. But while informed by theories of social class, she was less interested in testing hypotheses derived from theory than starting with the data themselves.

To understand how class matters, Lareau recruited families after observing their children at schools with different levels of resources. Her data consisted of interviews and field observations of middle-class, working-class, and poor families, divided equally among whites and blacks. In 1990, she and her research assistant interviewed the parents of 31 third-grade children in a public school in the Midwestern United States. Subsequently, they conducted interviews with 57 parents of third-grade children in the Northeast (Lareau 2011:345). From these and other families, they then selected 12 for "intensive observations," which Lareau describes, in part, as follows:

> We generally visited each family about twenty times in and around their home, usually in the space of one month. We followed children and parents as they went through their daily routines, as they took part in school

▲ Annette Lareau

activities, church services and events, organized play, kin visits, and medical appointments. Most visits lasted about three hours; sometimes, depending on the event . . . we stayed much longer. In most cases, we also arranged one overnight visit in each family's home. (Lareau 2011:9)

Faced with mounds of data, Lareau had to organize and analyze them. Reflective of the inductive process of moving from concrete data to theory, she writes, "I tried to link the bits and pieces of data to ideas" (Lareau 2011:360). She got some ideas by identifying themes that ran throughout the data as a whole. One such theme was that of language use. Below are a couple of conversations from the families she studied that illustrate this theme. The first is a conversation between a fourth-grader, Alex Williams, and his mother, Ms. Williams (both pseudonyms):

[Ms. Williams:] I want you to pay close attention to Mrs. Scott [Alex's teacher] when you are developing your film. Those chemicals are very danger- ous. Don't play around in the classroom. You could get that stuff in someone's eye. And if you swallow it, you could die.

[Alex:] Mrs. Scott told us that we wouldn't die if we swallowed it. But we would get very sick and would have to get our stomach pumped. (Lareau 2011:118)

The second is a conversation between Wendy Driver, a fourth-grade student at the time, and her mother, Ms. Driver:

Wendy asks her mother, "Can I put the sticker on? Please?"

[Ms. Driver:] "We aren't going to do that."

Wendy is silent. (Lareau 2011:208)

Each such conversation or observation is thus a piece of data, and in analyzing the data, Lareau inferred several empirical patterns, or general tendencies. One of them is that language use is related to class position. On the one hand, middle-class parents, such as Ms. Williams, frequently reason and negotiate with their children, who sometimes contest their statements. On the other hand, parents in working-class and poor families, such as Ms. Driver, often simply give directives to their children, who tend not to question or challenge these directives (Lareau 2011:31). Other empirical patterns include class differences in the activities in which children participated, in how families viewed institutions (e.g., health care, education), and, ultimately, in whether a child feels entitled or constrained.

On the basis of her data, analysis, and inferred empirical patterns, Lareau used the inductive or bottom-up approach to research to develop a theory of childrearing. She observed that middle-class families typically practice a childrearing strategy she calls "concerted cultivation," in which the "parent actively fosters and assesses [the] child's talents, opinions, and skills" (Lareau 2011:31). In contrast, working-class

Table 2.1 Lareau's Typology of Differences in Childrearing

	Childrearing Approach	
	Concerted Cultivation	Accomplishment of Natural Growth
Key Elements	Parent actively fosters and assesses child's talents, opinions, and skills	Parent cares for child and allows child to grow
Organization of Daily Life	Multiple child leisure activities orchestrated by adults	"Hanging out," particularly with kin, by child
Language Use	Reasoning/directives Child contestation of adult statements Extended negotiations between parents and child	Directives Rare questioning or challenging of adults by child General acceptance by child of directives
Interventions in Institutions	Criticisms and interventions on behalf of child Training of child to take on this role	Dependence on institutions Sense of powerlessness and frustration Conflict between childrearing practices at home and at school
Consequences	Emerging sense of entitlement on the part of the child	Emerging sense of constraint on the part of the child

Source: Table I in Lareau (2011:31).

and poor families often use an approach called "accomplishment of natural growth," which emphasizes caring for the child and allowing him or her to grow without such active participation. In the organization of daily life, middle-class families, generally practicing the strategy of concerted cultivation, encourage and support their children's participation in organized activities supervised by adults (sports, school plays, music, etc.). Working-class and poor families, adopting the natural growth approach, tend not to encourage participation in these activities but rather allow children to "play" on their own or with peers or family. These two approaches are summarized in Table 2.1.

Combining the Logics of Inquiry

There are strengths and limitations to both deductive and inductive inquiry. One advantage of deductive, top-down inquiry is that theory provides researchers with focus. At the same time, researchers must be cautious not to get "funnel vision" or otherwise

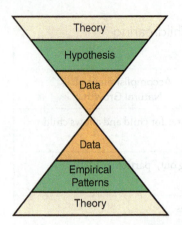

FIGURE 2.4
Combining Logics,
Starting with Theory

let the sides of the funnel depicted in Figure 2.2 blind them to other theoretical insights. As for the inductive, bottom-up approach, development of *new* theory is one of its greatest advantages (Glaser and Strauss 1967). One of inductive reasoning's drawbacks, however, is that the empirical patterns it generates are likely to be subject to multiple (theoretical) interpretations.

In reality, researchers often combine both deductive and inductive logics of inquiry to some extent. This was true of the studies by Dixon and Rosenbaum (2004) and Lareau (2011) just described. The two logics of inquiry may be combined in a way that essentially puts together the funnels in Figures 2.2 and 2.3. On the one hand, researchers may begin with theory, deduce a hypothesis, test the hypothesis with data, infer empirical patterns, and put forth a new or revised theory (see Figure 2.4). On the other hand, they may begin with data, infer empirical patterns, put forth a theory, deduce a hypothesis, and then analyze (still other) data (see Figure 2.5). We next describe a study that illustrates how researchers may combine the logics of inquiry, as depicted in Figure 2.4.

From a Psychological Theory of Suicide to a Sociological One

Suicide is often considered to be a purely psychological phenomenon. However, this interpretation of suicide is somewhat less common today than it was in the late 19th century, when French sociologist Émile Durkheim published his seminal study *Suicide* ([1897] 1951). Not only did Durkheim's study help to establish the *social* factors explaining suicide and the field of sociology more generally, his study illustrates both the deductive and inductive approaches to research. In this case, Durkheim's research started with one theory and ended with another, as in Figure 2.4.

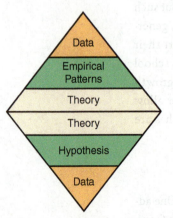

FIGURE 2.5
Combining Logics,
Starting with Data

In the 19th century, existing theories of suicide pointed to its psychological causes. One such theory was that of "mental alienation," which posits that suicide is the result of insanity. According to this theory, individuals may be afflicted with a variety of mental disorders, including mania, depression, anxiety, and nervous system problems. These disorders create the conditions—for example, intense negative feelings, hallucinations, and pain—that ultimately lead to suicide (Durkheim [1897] 1951).

Mental alienation theory thus suggests a relationship between insanity and suicide rates. From this theory, Durkheim further reasoned that if suicide were the result of insanity, the same groups with higher rates of insanity ought to have higher rates of suicide. More specifically, he deduced the following hypothesis:

- As rates of insanity increase, so too will suicide rates.

Given the disproportionate number of women (versus men) and Jews (versus members of other religious groups) in "insane asylums," Durkheim also proposed the following hypotheses:

- Women will have higher rates of suicide than men.
- Jews will have higher rates of suicide than members of other religious groups.

To examine these hypotheses, Durkheim used existing data such as official published statistics for as many as 15 European countries in the mid- to late 19th century. The data on suicides were based on official reports; insanity was measured as the percentage of people in insane asylums. In addition, the data could be broken down in terms of several sociodemographic characteristics of the population in these countries, such as the percentage of women and Jews.

Durkheim's analysis revealed several empirical patterns, all of which were contrary to the hypotheses deduced from mental alienation theory. In contrast to the first hypothesis, European countries with higher insanity rates did *not* also have higher suicide rates; in fact, if anything, the opposite was true. Moreover, men were far more likely than women to commit suicide, which runs counter to the second hypothesis. And the third hypothesis did not receive support, either: Jews had the *lowest* rates of suicide of the religious groups Durkheim examined.

Other empirical patterns from Durkheim's analysis of data helped give rise to a *new* theory of suicide. For example, Durkheim discovered that predominantly Catholic countries and areas of countries with a strong Catholic presence had lower suicide rates than their Protestant counterparts. He attributed this to the fact that Protestantism allows "greater freedom to individual thought" and that it "has fewer common beliefs and practices" than Catholicism (Durkheim 1951:159). Similarly, married people were less likely to commit suicide than unmarried people, and people with children were less likely to commit suicide than people without children. Durkheim concluded that the family provides some "immunity," or otherwise helps to "safeguard" against suicide. Common among these empirical patterns was a *social* aspect of suicide that was central to Durkheim's theory of suicide. That is, in some cases, suicide is due to a lack of social bonds, or what he called *integration*. As Durkheim argued, "suicide varies inversely with the degree of integration of the social groups of which the individual forms a part" (209). Or, put simply, the weaker the integration, the greater the chance for suicide. Although Durkheim's study is not without criticism, which we discuss below, it is a good illustration of the continuous process of deductive and inductive reasoning and going "from theory to data and back."

▲ Émile Durkheim
(1858–1917)

SUMMARY

Scientists may use a deductive logic of inquiry, which provides researchers with theoretical focus; however, deductive logic may blind researchers to other theoretical insights. In contrast, an inductive logic of inquiry has the advantage of generating new theory but may be especially subject to multiple theoretical interpretations. Researchers may combine the logics of inquiry in one of two ways: they may move from "theory to data and back," as Durkheim did, or they may start with data, move to theory, and then go back to new data. The constant interplay of theory and data over time and across many studies best characterizes science as a whole. Each study is part of a continuous, unending cycle of inquiry.

EVALUATING SCIENCE: POSSIBILITIES, CAUTIONS, AND LIMITS

Scientific knowledge is advanced through the process of moving between theory and data. As such, science has an amazing potential to offer new knowledge that might not be gained through other means. It can help to dispel "common-sense" notions that may not be true; conversely, it can help to confirm information that we long believed was true but weren't sure of (Berger 1963). Science can help us to make choices in our everyday lives, ranging from which beverages are safe to drink to recognizing the potential dangers of simply following an authority's orders (Milgram 1974). Equipped with the latest scientific knowledge, scientists and others can improve the human condition with new treatments or social programs. For example, studies of suicide inform treatment of its causes (Wray, Colen, and Pescosolido 2011). In the 1950s, research on the positive effects of interpersonal contact between racial groups helped inform the US Supreme Court's decision to desegregate schools (*Brown v. Board of Education of Topeka* 1954).

Yet, just as we need to critically evaluate other forms of knowledge, we need to critically evaluate scientific knowledge. Despite the possibilities that science presents, it also has limits that we need to be aware of when we read scientific studies or conduct research ourselves; we also need to be cautious about putting too much weight on what we know now.

Tentative Knowledge

The goal of science, as we noted, is to produce new knowledge. This also means that our *current* scientific knowledge is *tentative*. Regardless of how good scientists' theories are, how systematically scientists collect and analyze data, or how logical scientists' reasoning is, we must always remember that scientific knowledge changes. Today's knowledge may be tomorrow's "old news"; yesterday's knowledge may be today's "old news." New discoveries may be made that change scientific knowledge (Popper [1959] 1992) or even the very nature of science (Kuhn 1970).

The reason scientific knowledge is tentative is that patterns inferred from data may not recur and inevitably are open to alternative theoretical interpretations. This is clearly demonstrated in continuing research on suicide. Since Durkheim conducted his study in the late 19th century, research into the early 21st century has tested hypotheses derived from his theory. Some of the patterns Durkheim found continue to hold today: for instance, men continue to have higher rates of suicide than women (Wray, Colen, and Pescosolido 2011). However, some of Durkheim's interpretations and other findings have been challenged. You might also recall Durkheim's finding that suicide rates in areas with a large concentration of Catholics were lower than in areas with a large concentration of Protestants. In the United States in the late 20th century, suicide rates in areas heavily populated with certain Protestant groups, such as evangelical Protestants, paralleled those in areas with large concentrations of Catholics (Pescosolido 1990; Pescosolido and Georgianna 1989). In this ongoing process of scientific inquiry, research has confirmed elements of Durkheim's theory or findings, qualified other elements including its applicability outside Europe, and directly challenged still others.

Science, then, is a double-edged sword. On the one hand, the tentative nature of scientific knowledge is suggestive of endless possibilities for theory and research. On the other hand, the tentative knowledge that science produces cautions us against putting too much faith in a single study, including our own. We also have to be realistic about the scientific process.

The Ideal and Reality of the Scientific Process

The process of moving back and forth between theory and data is an idealized version of how science operates. It is not unusual for scientists to deviate from this ideal. Scientists may, for example, begin with a theory, deduce hypotheses from it, and find that the data do not support the hypotheses. Then, they may start with another theory, repeat the process, and find support for a different hypothesis. It is also possible that scientists will discover something through intuition, by making an educated guess (Popper [1959] 1992), or by chance, which Merton (1996) calls the **serendipity pattern**.

An example of the reality of the scientific process—and, more specifically, the serendipity pattern—comes from the famous Hawthorne studies, so named after the Western Electric Hawthorne plant in Cicero, Illinois, that F. J. Roethlisberger and William J. Dickson (1939) studied. Roethlisberger and Dickson wanted to know how changes in working conditions would affect workers' productivity in a controlled experiment. In one of these studies, six women with the task of assembling a telephone part were placed in a special test room for observation. Then, changes in the working conditions were introduced over a period of time.

To the astonishment of Roethlisberger and Dickson (1939:86), however, the workers' productivity increased uniformly, no matter what the change. After questioning the women, Roethlisberger and Dickson concluded that the workers' increased productivity

serendipity pattern
Unanticipated findings that cannot be interpreted meaningfully in terms of prevailing theories and, therefore, give rise to new theories.

▲ Assembly line workers at the Western Electric Hawthorne plant, the site of a study that suggested people's behaviors change when they are being observed.

was a response to the special attention they received as participants in what was considered an important experiment. The fun of the test room and the interest of management simply made it easier for the women to produce at a higher rate. This chance, or "serendipitous," finding came to be known as the **Hawthorne effect**, which generally refers to the tendency of research participants to change their behavior as a result of their awareness of being studied. This study is but one example of research that does not strictly follow the deductive logic of inquiry, and, interestingly enough, it is also an example of *tentative knowledge* in science. Although many other studies showed how researchers' mere presence could change the behavior of study participants, later analyses showed that Roethlisberger and Dickson's conclusions were unsupported by the evidence (Carey 1967).

In short, the scientific process of reasoning between theory and data that we outlined in this chapter is an ideal. While many scientists likely strive toward this ideal (and so can we), we must also realize that it may be difficult to achieve in practice—and for social and historical reasons, too.

Hawthorne effect A change in behavior, such as an improvement in performance, that occurs when research participants know they are being studied.

The Sociohistorical Aspect of Science

Science does not occur in a vacuum. Rather, it is a product of the society and culture in which scientists live. Discoveries, disciplines, and even scientific revolutions are themselves products of the times (Kuhn 1970). When we evaluate research and conduct it ourselves, we need to be aware of its broader sociohistorical context. When social scientists study the "problems of their times," they may have an understanding of those problems that an outsider lacks (Merton 1996). However, it is also possible that the broader sociohistorical context may bias research interpretations and findings.

In fact, Durkheim's study on the social causes of suicide may have been strongly influenced by social and historical factors. At the time of Durkheim's study in the late 19th century, sociology was a fledgling field throughout Europe; psychology was the dominant social science. Durkheim's study, according to critics, may have been more of an attempt to legitimize the field of sociology than to fully understand the factors leading to suicide (Phillips, Ruth, and MacNamara 1994). And by emphasizing social causes of suicide, Durkheim may have downplayed psychological factors (Wray, Colen, and Pescosolido 2011).

There are other, more insidious ways in which science is a product of its times. One of the foremost examples is research on racial and ethnic minorities. Undoubtedly influenced by waves of immigration and the prejudiced environment of the time, as well as spurred by Darwin's theory of evolution, some scientists in the late 19th and early 20th century looked for "proof" that African Americans and other racial and ethnic minorities were "inferior." Their research ran the gamut of examining facial features of prisoners (and concluding that "black" features were associated with criminality) to applying culturally biased IQ tests (and concluding that the low scores of minorities "proved" their intellectual inferiority). Ignoring the widespread discrimination against minorities as well as the cultural bias in IQ tests, this research had the unfortunate consequence of perpetuating prejudice and racism. While less prominent today, this kind of "science" is still around (Zuberi 2003; Zuberi and Bonilla-Silva 2008).

Scientific knowledge is thus a product of social and historical factors, sometimes quite harmful ones. This should give us pause as we evaluate and conduct research.

The Human Element of Science

Behind every scientific study is an imperfect human. If you think that scientists don't make mistakes, let us quickly dispel you of that notion. Moreover, scientists have their own motivations, values, and interests that may shape their research.

An example of a mistake comes from the data used in a study on social networks and isolation. Sociologists Miller McPherson, Lynn Smith-Lovin, and Matthew Brashears (2006) wanted to know if and how Americans' social networks had changed between the mid-1980s and 2004. Using GSS data, they analyzed responses to a question indicating how many people respondents discussed "important matters" with over the past six months. They found that the percentage of people that did not discuss important matters with anyone—"social isolates," as they call them—increased nearly threefold between 1985 and 2004. On the basis of these and other findings, they concluded that Americans are growing increasingly isolated.

Two years after this study, the National Opinion Research Center (NORC), which runs the GSS, officially announced that it misclassified some respondents in the 2004 social network data. Forty-one respondents were mistakenly classified as not having anyone with whom they discussed important matters (and therefore defined as social isolates by McPherson and colleagues). When McPherson and colleagues (2008) published a correction to their original article, they noted that correcting this data misclassification did not fundamentally change their conclusion: Americans were still more isolated in 2004 than in the mid-1980s.

Subsequently, however, a debate ensued about the validity of the study's conclusions. This debate highlights how science attempts to correct itself. Sociologist Claude Fischer (2009:657) argued that "scholars and general readers alike should draw no inference from the 2004 GSS as to whether Americans' social networks changed; they probably did not." To begin, he contended, there is no "plausible sociological *theory* for such a drastic social change" (659, our emphasis). Other *verifiable data* that Fischer analyzed do not indicate a drastic change in social isolation, if any at all. Moreover, among other factors that may have affected the conclusion, it is possible that even more data were misclassified.

In the face of Fischer's critique, McPherson and colleagues (2009) maintained the credibility of their conclusion. After the correction, they pointed out that they reanalyzed the 2004 GSS data with the same and different methods, which led to the same conclusion. Reflective of the ongoing cycle of inquiry, however, a subsequent analysis of the 2004 GSS data on social networks showed that "some interviewers obtained highly improbable levels of social isolation," apparently due to inadequate interviewer training and fatigue (Paik and Sanchagrin 2013:1). Thus, for now, inferences about declining social connectivity may be mistaken or, at least, depend on more accurate data.

Scientists are not perfect, and this must be borne in mind when we evaluate and conduct research. However, before you dismiss science, consider a question that we sometimes ask our students: Would you dump a romantic partner because they're not perfect? Probably not, we'd guess. Similarly, we need to give some leeway to scientists and the process as a whole because science has its own set of checks that ensure greater accuracy over time, as illustrated in the debate over social isolation.

SUMMARY

Through the never-ending process of scientific inquiry, science produces new knowledge that can be useful in our everyday lives and in society as a whole. Scientific knowledge is tentative and subject to revision; it doesn't always strictly follow the scientific process; it is shaped by sociohistorical factors; and, it is—after all—produced by imperfect humans. Thus, it should be critically evaluated and treated with caution. These are by no means fatal flaws, however, as science can better itself through its own checks. Indeed, the ability of science to critique itself is one of its major strengths.

KEY TERMS

data, p. 17

deductive logic, p. 20

empirical pattern, p. 25

Hawthorne effect, p. 34

hypothesis, p. 25

inductive logic, p. 20

serendipity pattern, p. 33

theory, p. 16

KEY POINTS

- The constant interplay between theory and data best characterizes science as a whole.

- Science involves theory, verifiable data, systematic data collection and analysis, and logical reasoning (deductive and inductive).
- Deductive and inductive reasoning are used in research to link theory and data.
- A deductive logic of inquiry represents a "top-down" approach to research, whereby researchers deduce hypotheses from theory and then test these hypotheses with data.
- An inductive logic of inquiry represents a "bottom-up" approach to research, whereby researchers infer empirical patterns from observations, and empirical patterns form the basis of theory.
- Researchers often use both logics of inquiry, sometimes starting from theory and sometimes starting from data.
- Science produces new knowledge that may be used to improve the human condition.
- Scientific knowledge is tentative, shaped by sociohistorical factors, and subject to human error.

REVIEW QUESTIONS

1. What is the relationship between theory and data in scientific inquiry?
2. Describe how data in science should be (a) verifiable and (b) systematically collected and analyzed.
3. Describe deductive and inductive logic or reasoning and provide an example of each.
4. Why are deductive and inductive inquiry described, respectively, as "top-down" and "bottom-up" approaches to scientific research?
5. From this chapter, identify two examples each of *theories* and *empirical patterns*.
6. How is scientific knowledge (a) tentative, (b) shaped by sociohistorical factors, and (c) subject to human error?

EXERCISES

1. Indicate whether each of the following inferences represents *deductive* or *inductive* reasoning.

   (a) A pollster interviews 2,500 randomly chosen US adults and finds that 69 percent of them say they are in favor of capital punishment. He concludes that 69 percent of the US adult population favors capital punishment.

   (b) The presence of others strengthens people's dominant (prevalent or most likely) responses. If the dominant response is correct, people will perform better in the presence of an audience than when they perform alone. (This is called the "social facilitation effect.") Assuming these statements are true, it follows that good pool players will make a higher percentage of their shots when an audience is watching them play than when they are shooting pool by themselves.

(c) Research with University of Hawaii students found that women, Asians, and students living at home were less likely to smoke marijuana than men, non-Asians, and students not living at home, respectively. Noting that each of the former groups has more to lose (e.g., is likely to experience more disapproval) from smoking marijuana, the researcher concluded that the more social constraints a student has, the less likely he or she will smoke marijuana.

2. Select a recent issue of a major social science journal, such as the *American Sociological Review*, *American Political Science Review*, or *Social Psychology Quarterly*. Find an article that reports the results of empirical research. Read the first part of the article to see how the researcher(s) presents the theory underlying the research. What theory or theories does the researcher present? What hypotheses, if any, does the researcher derive from theory?

The Ethics and Politics of Research

Doing What's "Right"

STUDENT LEARNING OBJECTIVES

By the end of this chapter, you should be able to

1. Explain the four major ethical issues in the treatment of research participants: potential harm, informed consent, deception, and privacy invasion.

2. Use federal regulations and professional guidelines concerning the ethical treatment of research participants.

3. Apply the process of ethical decision-making to your own research.

4. Discuss the relationship between politics and social research.

5. Describe how ethics and politics may be related in social research.

"Let's talk about sex," sang the music group Salt-N-Pepa (1991) in their classic hit of the same title. Well, that's easier said than done. It can be difficult for people to "talk about sex" because they may view it as a private matter. The topic of sex is also politically charged, evoking ideological and religious values in debates over public issues ranging from abortion to same-sex marriage, parenting, and adoption. In social science research, sex is among the most ethically and politically sensitive topics, according to sociologist Janice Irvine (2012).

Sex research has a tumultuous history in each of these respects. During the 1960s, Laud Humphreys conducted a study of male–male sexual encounters in public restrooms by posing as an undercover voyeur and "watch queen," whose job was to warn men of intruders as they engaged in oral sex. He recorded the license plate numbers of these men, traced their identities through the Department of Motor Vehicles by misrepresenting himself as a market researcher, and later interviewed them in their homes after changing his appearance so that he would not be recognized (Humphreys [1970] 2009). Widely considered to be ethically indefensible, Humphreys's study was "referenced regularly in deliberations" that led to the development of several ethical principles and guidelines for research in place today (Irvine 2012:30).

The politics of sex is yet another matter. In the middle of the 20th century, Alfred Kinsey and colleagues (1948, 1953) shocked the nation with findings from a controversial, methodologically flawed study on male and female sexuality. Critics feared that Kinsey and colleagues' findings would "break down the moral order" (Michael et al. 1994:20). Among these findings were that a third of men "had a sexual experience with another man" at some point in their lives; moreover, half of married men and a quarter of women had extramarital sex. Members of Congress felt that the latter finding would lower the morale of men fighting in the Korean War (Michael et al. 1994:20–21). When Edward Laumann and colleagues (1994) sought federal funds for a truly scientific survey on sex in the late 1980s, they were greeted with opposition in Congress that echoed the opposition Kinsey and colleagues had faced years earlier. For example, even though the proposed study was intended to help fight AIDS by providing information about its transmission, Senator Jesse Helms argued:

> The real purpose [of sex surveys] is to compile supposedly scientific facts to support the left-wing liberal argument that homosexuality is a normal, acceptable life-style. . . . As long as I am able to stand on the floor of the U.S. Senate, . . . I am never going to yield to that sort of thing, because it is not just another life-style; it is sodomy. (Helms quoted in Fausto-Sterling 1992:30)

In the end, Laumann and colleagues did not receive federal money, but they were able to conduct the survey.

These controversial studies of sex illustrate the twin topics of this chapter: ethics and politics. Both topics further establish the broader context of social research. Just as research is guided by the elements of scientific inquiry, as discussed in Chapter 2, it also is shaped by moral and political considerations. The first part of this chapter will sensitize you to ethical issues in research. Later in the chapter we consider how politics enters into research. Finally, we discuss a case study that illustrates the intersection of ethics and politics of social research.

OVERVIEW: ETHICS

As a subject matter, **ethics** consists of standards of conduct that distinguish between right and wrong. When you were a child, you probably were told that honesty is right and lying is wrong. In the world of research, there are similar ethical standards. Researchers are expected, for example, to make sure that their data are trustworthy by honestly and accurately conducting and reporting their research. They are also expected to give proper credit when they use others' ideas, to accept authorship of a paper only when they have made a significant contribution to it, and to guard against the improper application of their research findings.

ethics Standards of moral conduct that distinguish right from wrong.

Most of the ethical standards that guide social research are derived from the larger society; some standards are enshrined in professional codes of conduct and in federal regulations. Generally, these standards are not hard-and-fast rules by which researchers are expected to abide but rather depend on the situation and are subject to multiple interpretations. Is it necessarily wrong, for example, to deceive a research participant? By an absolutist standard, the answer is yes: because deception is a form of lying, it should not be tolerated. Yet, according to professional organizations such as the American Psychological Association (APA 2017) and the American Sociological Association (ASA 1999), the answer to this question is "it depends." What it depends on are the risks posed to the rights and welfare of research participants, the benefits of the research, and the steps taken to protect participants' rights.

In discussing ethics, we focus on issues regarding the treatment of research participants, as in our example of deception. Every social scientist has a personal and professional obligation to protect the rights and welfare of research participants. It is important to become aware of these ethical issues and how to address them, whether you are evaluating the research of others or conducting your own research. First we consider how scientific research may violate participants' rights and welfare. Next we review federal and professional ethical guidelines for protecting participants. Then we briefly outline an ethical decision-making process intended to guide you in carrying out research.

ETHICAL ISSUES IN THE TREATMENT OF RESEARCH PARTICIPANTS

Which specific issues are at stake as we consider research participants' rights and welfare? Four issues have been identified most often regarding the ethical treatment of human participants: potential harm, lack of informed consent, deception, and privacy invasion (Diener and Crandall 1978). It is considered a violation of basic human rights to harm others, to force people to perform actions against their will, to lie or mislead them, and to invade their privacy. To illustrate these ethical issues, we cite several studies, including landmark cases of unethical or ethically questionable research, some of which were instrumental in the development of current ethical standards.

Potential Harm

The first right of any research participant is the right to personal safety. Atrocities committed in World War II (1939–1945), which came to light in the Nuremberg Trials (1945–1946), brought attention to this issue. During the war, Nazi scientists used prisoners in experiments that resulted in pain, suffering, and even death. In one experiment, subjects were kept naked outdoors in below-freezing temperatures until parts of their bodies froze; in others, they were infected with malaria, typhus, poisons, and bacteria in deliberately inflicted wounds (Katz 1972). This research clearly violated the most fundamental right of research participants: that they should not be harmed by their participation.

Research that would endanger the life or physical health of a human subject is simply not acceptable in the scientific community. But harm is not only physical. Participants in social research may experience anxiety, the loss of self-esteem, feelings of embarrassment or humiliation, or even the loss of trust. These forms of harm often are difficult to anticipate and may occur despite researchers' best intentions. An example is a prison simulation study conducted at Stanford University by Philip Zimbardo and colleagues (1973; Haney, Banks, and Zimbardo 1973). To examine how the roles of "prison guard" and "prisoner" influence behavior, these investigators created a mock prison in the basement of a campus building in which male student volunteers played the roles of a "prison guard" or "prisoner." The study was scheduled to run for two weeks; however, it had to be terminated after only six days because guards physically and psychologically abused prisoners and prisoners broke down, rebelled, or became submissive and apathetic. The participants got so caught up in the situation, became so absorbed in their roles, that they began to confuse role-playing and self-identity.

▼ Student participants in the Stanford Prison simulation study, shown here, quickly absorbed the roles of guard and prisoner. Reactions were unexpectedly intense and pathological, with the potential for harm so great that the study was prematurely stopped after only six days.

In another example, some participants in Lareau's (2011) field study, discussed in Chapter 2, felt hurt, embarrassed, or betrayed. Recall that Lareau and her assistants conducted interviews and "intensive observations" with 12 families. In following up with the families 10 years later, Lareau discovered that some were upset about how they were portrayed in the research: one family felt it had been "misused" (Lareau 2011:318); one of the now grown-up children in the study was embarrassed by Lareau's portrayal of her family's class position (320–21); and, some of the families were so unhappy that they cut ties with Lareau. "You slurred us, Annette; you made us look like poor white trash," wrote one mother (312), whose other family members also seemed "very, very hurt," according to Lareau (323).

Informed Consent

The second ethical issue arises from the value placed on freedom of choice. The significance and meaning of this ethical principle are illustrated by the Tuskegee study of syphilis, a sexually transmitted and life-threatening disease, conducted over the course of four decades by the US Public Health Service. The research participants consisted of about 600 African-American men, many of whom were uneducated sharecroppers. Of these men, about two-thirds had the disease when the study began in 1932; the other third did not. The men were told that they had "bad blood" (see Figure 3.1), which could include a range of illnesses not limited to syphilis; they agreed to participate on the promise of medical care for "minor ailments," burial insurance, and other benefits (Jones 1981, Chapter 1; US Centers for Disease Control and Prevention 2016). For those who had syphilis, though, "there was nothing to indicate that . . . [they] knew they were participating in a deadly serious experiment," according to historian James H. Jones (1981:7). The purpose of the study was to follow the course of untreated syphilis. When penicillin was accepted as a treatment in the late 1940s and early 1950s, the men were not given it. It wasn't until 1972 that the study was exposed and terminated (Jones 1981; US Centers for Disease Control and Prevention 2016).

Both the atrocities committed by Nazi scientists and the Tuskegee study raised the issue of **informed consent**. "Informed" means that research participants must be given enough information about the research, including its risks and benefits, to make a rational decision about whether to participate. In the case of Tuskegee, participants were given incomplete and misleading information (i.e., "bad blood"), and they did not know that treatment for their true underlying condition would be withheld. "Consent" refers to *voluntary* participation, a principle established at the military tribunal at Nuremberg (Katz 1972). Nazi prisoners were, by definition, not free to consent. To volunteer is to have the freedom to choose to participate and to discontinue participation; however, firsthand accounts indicate that the men at Tuskegee were discouraged from seeking treatment, and they would lose benefits if they withdrew from the study (Jones 1981:5–7).

Two controversial social science studies also violated the principle of informed consent. The first is Stanley Milgram's (1974) shock experiment, which was designed to study obedience to authority. Participants in this study volunteered to take part but

Macon County Health Department

ALABAMA STATE BOARD OF HEALTH AND U.S. PUBLIC HEALTH SERVICE COOPERATING WITH TUSKEGEE INSTITUTE

Dear Sir:

Some time ago you were given a thorough examination and since that time we hope you have gotten a great deal of treatment for bad blood. You will now be given your last chance to get a second examination. This examination is a very special one and after it is finished you will be given a special treatment if it is believed you are in a condition to stand it.

If you want this special examination and treatment you must meet the nurse at_____ on

_____ _____at_____ M. She will bring you to the Tuskegee Institute Hospital for this free treatment. We will be very busy when these examinations and treatments are being given, and will have lots of people to wait on. You will remember that you had to wait for some time when you had your last good examination, and we wish to let you know that because we expect to be so busy it may be necessary for you to remain in the hospital over one night. If this is necessary you will be furnished your meals and a bed, as well the examination and treatment without cost.

REMEMBER THIS IS YOUR LAST CHANCE FOR SPECIAL FREE TREATMENT. BE SURE TO MEET THE NURSE.

Macon County Health Department

FIGURE 3.1

This letter to participants in the Tuskegee study, from the National Archives, shows how the participants were enticed to participate and were not informed about the true purpose of the study.

informed consent The ethical principle that individuals should be given enough information about a study, especially its potential risks and benefits, to make an informed decision about whether to participate.

were not given enough information to make an *informed* decision to participate. They were told beforehand that they would be administering harmless electrical shocks to another human being as part of a learning experiment. However, they were *not* told that being in this position could be highly stressful and that they might experience great stress and anxiety.

Another example is Laud Humphreys's ([1970] 2009) study on male–male sexual encounters, described at the beginning of this chapter. Humphreys observed men in *public* places, which generally doesn't require participants' consent. Many critics point out, however, that his observations *could have* posed a risk—of blackmail, for example— to participants if they were exposed (Glazer [1972] 2009; Von Hoffman [1970] 2009; Warwick [1973] 2009). Furthermore, when Humphreys went back to interview many of these men in their homes, he *misinformed* them about the nature of the study: Not knowing that they previously had been observed, they believed that they had been selected to participate in a survey on social and health behavior (Warwick [1973] 2009). Thus, research participants did not consent in the early stage of the study; then, in a later stage, they consented on the basis of false information (Glazer [1972] 2009).

Deception

Both Humphreys's and Milgram's studies involved deception: Humphreys lied and disguised himself; Milgram misled participants in several ways. Volunteers in Milgram's experiment agreed to participate in what they thought was a learning experiment but was actually a study on obedience. When the research participants arrived at the setting, they chose a card designating whether they would be the "teacher" or "learner." In reality, the drawing was rigged, with "teacher" written on both cards. Thus, research participants ended up playing the "teacher" role, whereas an actor, who was a confederate of the experimenter, played the role of "learner." Participants were then told they would be reading word pairs to the learner, and when the learner responded incorrectly, they were to shock him by pressing a lever on a "shock generator." The shocks, the experimenter told the research participants, could be extremely painful but would not cause permanent damage; however, the learner never actually received any shocks. More than 60 percent of participants in Milgram's initial experiment obeyed the experimenter by administering these fake shocks.

▼ Teacher (left) and learner (right) in Milgram's obedience study. The study involved several experimental conditions. In this condition, the teacher forces the learner's hand down on a shock plate.

While these examples of deception raise serious concerns, it is important to realize that researchers rarely give complete information about the purpose of their research and that this is not in itself considered deceptive. Deception in social research involves intentionally misleading or misinforming participants about aspects of a study (Sell 2008). As we noted earlier, deception is allowed in social research in certain circumstances, but its use is controversial. On the one hand, some scholars argue that deception is sometimes necessary to place research participants in a mental state where they will behave naturally. Had Milgram informed research participants that he was studying obedience, they almost certainly would have disobeyed. Only by deceiving them about the true purpose of his research could he observe their naturally obedient behavior. Karen Cook and Toshio Yamagishi (2008:216) further write that "a ban on deception would make it impossible or extremely difficult to investigate non-rational aspects of behavior," as many social scientists do.

On the other hand, many social scientists oppose deception on moral and pragmatic grounds. For some, the most telling argument is that lying is immoral. Similarly, some critics contend that deception invariably violates participants' rights to informed consent, because consent obtained by deceit, by definition, cannot be informed (Baumrind 1985). Although social scientists debate this position, most agree that Milgram's and Humphreys's use of deception went too far, as both investigators misled participants about the *potential risk of harm*, thereby clearly violating the principle of informed consent. Critics who argue against deception on pragmatic or scientific grounds contend that it may make participants suspicious and not produce the spontaneous behavior it intends (Baumrind 1985; Hertwig and Ortmann 2008). Evidence about the impact of suspicion generally fails to support this position, however, with recent research showing that exposure to deception does not affect the validity of experimental results (Barrera and Simpson 2012).

Invasion of Privacy

Social research also presents many possibilities for invading the privacy of research participants, as evidenced in Humphreys's study. Another dramatic case is the 1954 Wichita Jury Study (Vaughan 1967). In an effort to understand and perhaps even improve the operations of juries, researchers secured the permission of judges to record six actual jury deliberations in Wichita, Kansas, without the knowledge of the jurors. When news of the study became known, it was roundly criticized by columnists and commentators across the country and investigated by a Senate subcommittee, which ultimately led to the passage of a law prohibiting the recording of jury deliberations. The argument against this study was that jury deliberations must be sacrosanct to protect the inalienable right to trial by impartial jury. Surveillance such as that used in the study "threatens impartiality to the extent that it introduces any question of possible embarrassment, coercion, or other such considerations into the minds of actual jurors" (Vaughan 1967:72).

The right to privacy is the individual's right to decide when, where, to whom, and to what extent his or her attitudes, beliefs, and behavior will be revealed. New forms of technology and social media make privacy invasion in research a major concern today. As an example, Kevin Lewis and his colleagues (2008) downloaded the Facebook profiles of more than 1,600 first-year students at a private university and linked profile data to information about students' roommates in order to study people's social networks and cultural tastes. The dataset, which was released for a period of time to other interested researchers, thus included students' demographic characteristics (race, gender, etc.), information about their friends, students' cultural tastes (e.g., preferences in music, film, and books), their hometowns or high schools if provided, and their Facebook activity. In addition to keeping the college anonymous, the researchers note that "student privacy was assured by converting all names to numerical identifiers and promptly removing or encoding all other information that could be traced back to individual students" (Lewis et al. 2008:331).

Still, some critics are uneasy about Lewis and colleagues' study. Michael Zimmer (2010), for one, contends that this study is a case of privacy invasion because the college and some students' identities could be inferred from the data (e.g., size of school, school housing characteristics, majors offered, as well as students' hometowns and nationalities). To illustrate how it may be possible to identify specific participants in data sets, Box 3.1, READING SOCIAL RESEARCH: Privacy Invasion in the Public Identification of Participants, describes a hypothetical example related to the concerns raised about Lewis and colleagues' study.

BOX 3.1

READING SOCIAL RESEARCH

Privacy Invasion in the Public Identification of Participants

Consider the data in Table A from a hypothetical online survey on voting among US college professors. In the columns from left to right, you see identification numbers for these professors as well as data on whether they work at the College of the Holy Cross (= 1) or not (= 0), whether they are sociologists/anthropologists (= 1) or not (= 0); whether they identify as male (= 1) or not (= 0), their hometowns, and whether they voted in the 2016 election (= 1) or not (= 0).

You can see from these data how it might be possible to identify professor #3. The table indicates that this professor works at the College of the Holy Cross, is in the Sociology and Anthropology Department, identifies as a male, and hails from Dayton, Ohio. After going to the department's home page through Holy Cross http://www.holycross.edu/academics/programs/sociology-and-anthropology) and looking at the faculty profiles, you see that one (male) professor was "born and bred in good ole' Dayton, Ohio": Jeffrey C. Dixon, one of the authors of this book. Knowing this, you also now know that Dixon voted in the 2016 election. This is not very sensitive information, but if Dixon did not want his voting behavior to be publicly revealed, you can see how this would raise privacy concerns.

Table A Hypothetical Data on Professors' Voting

ID	Holy Cross	Sociology/ Anthropology	Male	Hometown	Voted '16
1	0	1	0	Chicago	1
2	0	1	1	L.A.	1
3	1	1	1	Dayton	1
4	0	0	1	Dallas	1
5	0	0	0	New York	0

SUMMARY

Ethics consists of standards of conduct that distinguish between right and wrong. Researchers are expected to act ethically in conducting their studies and in their treatment of research participants. The four most commonly identified ethical issues concerning the welfare and rights of research participants are potential harm, lack of informed consent, deception, and privacy invasion. Some unethical and ethically questionable studies concerning these issues have led to the development of federal and professional standards to protect participants' rights and welfare.

FEDERAL AND PROFESSIONAL ETHICAL GUIDELINES

Now that you are aware of the four main areas of ethical concern in scientific research with human subjects, let's examine the measures that should be taken to protect participants' rights and welfare. In general, ethical practices are set forth in codes of ethics that were established in response to the worst abuses, such as the Nazi experiments and Tuskegee Syphilis Study. In the United States, congressional hearings on the Tuskegee Study led to the National Research Act (1974), which created a commission charged with the task of making recommendations for the protection of human subjects.

In 1979 the commission issued the *Belmont Report* (National Commission 1979), which presented three broad, unifying ethical principles that formed the basis for specific regulations: respect for persons, beneficence, and justice. **Respect for persons** means that researchers must treat individuals as "autonomous agents" who have the

respect for persons
The Belmont principle that individuals must be treated as autonomous agents who have the freedom and capacity to decide what happens to them, and researchers must protect those with diminished autonomy.

freedom and capacity to decide what happens to them. It also requires that researchers protect those with diminished autonomy, such as children, prisoners, and the mentally disabled. **Beneficence** requires researchers to consider the welfare of participants so that they "maximize possible benefits and minimize possible harms." Included in this consideration are longer-term benefits that may result from the advancement of knowledge and betterment of humankind. **Justice** means that the benefits and burdens of research should be fairly distributed (National Commission 1979). In particular, the burdens of research should not fall upon one group, while the benefits accrue to another. The exploitation of unwilling prisoners by Nazi scientists is an extreme example of injustice.

Based largely on the *Belmont Report*, federal regulations for protecting research participants were put into place and have been revised several times (Code of Federal Regulations, Title 45, Part 46 [CFR] 2009).[1] Subpart A of these regulations, known as the **Common Rule,** provides information about the application of regulations and presents criteria for approval of research. The Common Rule applies to all research conducted or funded by a federal department or agency; it also applies to all research, regardless of funding, conducted at nearly every college and university in the United States.

Professional organizations' ethical codes articulate general principles and rules that apply to research situations often encountered in a particular discipline. They are designed at once to protect the welfare of the individuals with whom scientists work and to guide researchers in making ethically responsible choices. Some examples include the American Psychological Association's *Ethical Principles of Psychologists and Code of Conduct* (2017), the American Sociological Association's *Code of Ethics* (1999), the *Statement on Ethics: Principles of Professional Responsibility* of the American Anthropological Association (2012), and *A Guide to Professional Ethics in Political Science* of the American Political Science Association (2012). Below we highlight portions of these codes as they relate to federal regulations and the four issues concerning the ethical treatment of participants.

Evaluating Potential Harm

Federal regulations specify two main criteria for evaluating potential harm: (1) the level of risk to research participants and (2) the risks of the research in relation to the benefits (CFR 2009:46.111). With respect to the first criterion, the level of risk should be "minimized" by using sound research procedures that "do not unnecessarily expose subjects to risk." To distinguish studies in which special precautions should be taken, the Common Rule creates a criterion of "minimal risk": "The probability and magnitude of harm or discomfort anticipated in the research are not

beneficence The Belmont principle that researchers have an obligation to secure the well-being of participants by maximizing possible benefits and minimizing possible harms.

justice The Belmont principle that the benefits and burdens of research should be fairly distributed so that the group selected for research also may benefit from its application.

Common Rule Label given to the federal policy for the protection of human subjects.

[1] These regulations were revised in 2017, but at the time of this writing, have not gone into effect and largely will not go into effect until 2018 (for the text of these regulations, see https://www.gpo.gov/fdsys/pkg/FR-2017-01-19/pdf/2017-01058.pdf). Our discussion thus focuses on the regulations as of this writing.

greater in and of themselves than those ordinarily encountered in daily life" (CFR 2009:46.102). Surveys, for instance, often involve no more than minimal risk because the researcher is asking questions of respondents that they may encounter in everyday life (e.g., "What is your age?"). But when a study poses more than minimal risk (e.g., on a sensitive topic, particularly if participants may be identified) or involves special populations (e.g., children or prisoners), researchers need to take greater precautions to minimize risks.

The second criterion, derived from the principle of beneficence, is that "risks to subjects are reasonable in relation to anticipated benefits" (CFR 2009, 46.111[a][2]). If there is little to no scientific value from a study that knowingly exposes participants to harm, the study should not be done, no matter how small the harm. But if a study has considerable scientific merit, some degree of potential risk may be justified.

Assessing the costs and benefits of social research is difficult. Unlike biomedical research, where participants may benefit directly from a new drug or treatment, the main benefit to participants in social research is simply what they may learn—about the research or themselves—from their experience. The primary benefits accrue to others: investigators gain knowledge that may contribute to professional success and recognition; the profession advances scientific understanding, which may lead to the betterment of humanity. In addition, costs and benefits may be hard to predict. Philip Zimbardo and colleagues (1973) did not foresee the emotional costs to participants in their prison simulation study; neither were they likely to have anticipated the study's contribution to ethical and scientific knowledge. The same can be said for Lareau's field study. While she anticipated some discomfort in her participants, she writes, "the families and I were *both* surprised by the level of pain, hurt, and dismay . . . that the book created for many" (Lareau 2011:327).

Although difficult, conducting a cost-benefit analysis is an important first step in evaluating the ethics of a proposed study. In addition to assessing risk of harm as well as costs and benefits, the following guidelines also help to minimize harm:

1. Researchers should *inform* participants of any reasonable or foreseeable risks or discomforts before the study begins and should give participants sufficient opportunity to consider. This is an important part of informed consent, which is mandated by federal regulations and discussed in the next section.

2. Where appropriate, researchers should screen out research participants who might be harmed by the research procedures. In the prison simulation study, the investigators gave several personality tests to the student volunteers in order to select participants with "normal" personality profiles and thereby minimize the possibility of harm (Zimbardo 1973). By contrast, another criticism of Milgram's research is that he did *not* screen participants to see if they could withstand the stress that they would experience. In effect, participants were placed in a highly stressful conflict situation: Should they obey the experimenter in administering

the shocks, or should they refuse to continue in the experiment? The participants showed many obvious signs of stress; indeed, one person had a convulsive seizure that made it necessary to terminate his participation.

3. If stress or potential harm is likely, measures also should be planned to assess harm after the study and, if necessary, provide resources to ameliorate it. To this end, researchers conducting laboratory experiments or doing interviews on sensitive topics should probe participants' feelings and reactions immediately after the study (see discussion of debriefing below). After discussing such feelings, the researcher may ask participants if they want to talk more and then provide contact information for people or groups who are trained to help, such as counselors and medical professionals.

Informed Consent Procedures

The Belmont principle of respect for persons underlies the ethical requirement of informed consent. According to federal regulations, to make an *informed* decision about whether to take part in a study, research participants must be given adequate information about the study, including foreseeable risks of participating. Furthermore, obtaining their *consent* must minimize "coercion or undue influence" (CFR 2009:46.116), which means participation must be voluntary. Even greater protections should be taken when working with special populations, such as children and prisoners. Children, for example, cannot directly give their informed consent; rather, their parent or guardian needs to do so (CFR 2009:46.117). In a study on students' help-seeking behavior, which we discuss in Chapter 4, Jessica Calarco (2011) sought and obtained parents' consent to observe children in their elementary school. On the other hand, school-aged participants may be required to give their *assent*—that is, agreement to participate in the research—if they are deemed capable of doing so, as determined by their "ages, maturity, and psychological state" (CFR 2009:46.408).

Federal regulations generally dictate the use of a *written* consent form, *signed* by the participant or the participant's legal guardian. This not only protects participants, it also protects the researcher. Participants are protected from harm by being able to make up their own minds about the risks of participation; researchers are protected legally by obtaining a record of participants' explicit voluntary agreement. The exception to this rule is that a signed informed consent agreement is usually not necessary and may be waived in research involving minimal risk. In most surveys, for example, it is sufficient to read or have participants read a consent statement and then ask them if they wish to continue with the survey (Citro 2010).

What should an informed consent statement include? Federal regulations spell out in detail the basic elements of informed consent statements. As applied to social research, these elements include the following (CFR 2009:46.116):

1. A statement that the study involves research
2. An explanation of the purposes of the research

3. The expected duration of the participant's participation
4. A description of the procedures to be followed
5. A description of any reasonably foreseeable risks or discomforts to the participant
6. A description of any benefits to the participant or to others which may reasonably be expected from the research
7. A statement describing how, if applicable, the confidentiality of records identifying the participant will be maintained
8. An explanation of whom to contact for answers to pertinent questions about the research and research participants' rights and whom to contact in the event of a research-related injury to the participant
9. A statement that participation is voluntary, refusal to participate will involve no penalty or loss of benefits to which the participant is otherwise entitled, and the participant may discontinue participation at any time without penalty or loss of benefits

All of this information, according to federal regulations (CFR 2009:46.116), needs to be conveyed in clear and understandable language; anything less undermines participants' ability to make an *informed* decision. In Chapters 7 and 8 we provide sample informed consent statements from a laboratory experiment and a survey, respectively (see Box 7.2 and Box 8.3).

Deception Ground Rules

Federal regulations do not make reference to the use of deception in research. The ethical codes of the American Sociological Association and American Psychological Association permit deception, but these codes also refer to deception as a method of "last resort" (Hertwig and Ortmann 2008:223). For instance, the APA Code of Ethics states:

> Psychologists do not conduct a study involving deception unless they have determined that the use of deceptive techniques is justified by the study's significant prospective scientific, educational, or applied value and that effective nondeceptive alternative procedures are not feasible. (APA 2017:8.07[a])

At the same time, these codes highlight the anticipated *benefits* of a study as a standard by which the use of deception is evaluated, and they establish "ground rules" for studies that use deception.

The first ground rule is that deception is banned when there is substantial *risk* of harm or stress. According to the APA, "Psychologists do not deceive prospective participants about research that is reasonably expected to cause physical pain or severe emotional distress" (APA 2017:8.07[b]). In this case, researchers should undertake a different research design that does not involve deception.

A second ground rule is that researchers must "come clean" about the true nature of their study. According to the ASA Code of Ethics, "When deception is an integral feature of the design and conduct of research, sociologists attempt to correct any misconception that research participants may have no later than at the conclusion of the research" (ASA 1999:12.05[c]). Debriefing is the practical implementation of this requirement.

debriefing A session at the end of a study in which an investigator meets with a participant to impart information about the study, including its real purpose and the nature and purpose of deception (if used), and to respond to questions and concerns.

Debriefing consists of a short interview that takes place between an investigator and research participants after they have finished their participation. Ideally, debriefing should occur in all studies with human participants, not just in studies involving deception, as it serves methodological and educational as well as ethical purposes. By interviewing participants after their participation, researchers may gain valuable information about participants' interpretation of research procedures; furthermore, by understanding the nature of the study, participants can gain a greater appreciation for their research experience. If participants are deceived, however, the debriefing session becomes critically important to reveal the nature and purpose of the deception.

The nature of the debriefing depends on the topic, type of study, and, if deception is used, the extent of the deception. For surveys on nonsensitive topics, it is generally sufficient to answer any questions that respondents may have. Researchers also may provide a brief written statement of the purpose of the research and offer to send a summary of findings. For mild forms of deception (e.g., recall the study from Chapter 1 in which participants were asked to judge false Facebook profiles), it may be enough to answer participants' questions and briefly inform them of the deception, pointing out its purpose and necessity.

If deception is more extensive or likely to cause discomfort, however, the debriefing should be more thorough and probing. In such cases, it is essential to make sure that participants (1) fully understand how they were misinformed and (2) do not leave the experiment feeling worse about themselves than before they began (Kelman 1968). Milgram was obligated, for example, to convey the truth about his procedures—that he was really studying obedience, the drawing was rigged, the shock apparatus was phony, and so forth; he also needed to explain why it was not unusual or abnormal for participants to follow the commands of an experimenter to administer shocks to the learner. To his credit, Milgram carried out his debriefing slowly and sensitively, eliciting participants' reactions, acknowledging that he had placed them in a difficult position, and having the "learner" enter the laboratory so that the participant could see that he was not harmed (Milgram 1974).

Privacy Protection: Anonymity and Confidentiality

Private information, according to federal regulations (CFR 2009:46.102), is that which makes the participant "individually identifiable"; that is, his or her identity can be ascertained from the information. The ASA Code of Ethics helps to clarify the distinction between private and public information: "Information is private when an individual can reasonably expect that the information will not be made public with personal identifiers" (ASA 1999:11.01[g]).

Federal regulations state that researchers need to ensure that "there are adequate provisions to protect the privacy of subjects and to maintain the confidentiality of data" (CFR 2009:46.111). Moreover, the informed consent statement should explain to participants *how* their privacy would be protected. There are two forms of protection: anonymity and confidentiality.

Anonymity means that participants cannot be identified. Of the two means of protecting participants' privacy, anonymity is the highest standard, but it is also the most difficult to achieve. Often at least the investigator can identify participants. Examples of research that provides anonymity include self-administered surveys without names or identifying information attached as well as some existing data.

anonymity Ethical safeguard against invasion of privacy in which data cannot be identified with particular research participants.

Confidentiality means that data obtained from participants are not shared with others without their permission. Because investigators can usually identify individuals' responses, the principal means of protecting participants' privacy is to ensure confidentiality. The researcher can do this in a variety of ways: by conducting research (especially surveys and in-depth interviews) in a private place, by removing names and other identifying information from the data as soon as possible, by keeping the data in a secure place, by not disclosing individuals' identities in any reports of the study, and by not divulging the information to persons or organizations requesting it without research participants' permission.

confidentiality Ethical safeguard against invasion of privacy by which data obtained from participants are not shared with others without their permission.

Field research usually requires ingenuity to safeguard confidentiality. The traditional approach is to use fictitious names for individuals, groups, and locations, which is what Lareau did in her field study. She assigned pseudonyms for each of the families, such as the "Taylors" and the "Garringers." She also masked the true identities of the schools by calling them "Swan" and "Lower Richmond." And she reported that these schools were located in the Midwest and Northeast United States, broad geographical areas that do not allow for the possibility of identification (Lareau 2011).

Yet it may not be possible to guarantee complete confidentiality. Unlike physicians, lawyers, and the clergy, social scientists are *not* generally shielded by laws that allow them to keep their data secret if they are subpoenaed (Palys and Lowman 2002; Scarce 2005). Participants have a right to know about the limits of confidentiality (ASA 1999:11.02), which should be included in the informed consent statement.

Having now read about federal guidelines on privacy and other issues of concern, can you apply this knowledge? Box 3.2, CHECKING YOUR UNDERSTANDING: Ethics Practice Questions, provides the opportunity to do so.

BOX 3.2

CHECKING YOUR UNDERSTANDING

Ethics Practice Questions

The National Institutes of Health (NIH) offers a free online course on research ethics, which covers the *Belmont Report* and federal guidelines concerning the major ethical issues discussed in this chapter (http://phrp.nihtraining.com/users/login.php). If tests from the course are completed successfully, participants get a certificate; indeed, successful completion is mandatory for researchers who pursue NIH funding. The Collaborative Institutional Training Initiative (CITI) offers similar courses, but at a fee, although your institution may already have a paid subscription (see https://about.citiprogram.org/en/homepage/). Below are three test questions, modeled after those in the NIH tests, which you should be able to answer based on your reading of this chapter.

1. With respect to potential harm, the Common Rule states:
    a. There should be no risk of harm to research participants.
    b. The risk of harm should be no greater than the risks encountered in daily life.
    c. Risks should be reasonable in relation to benefits.
    d. Those who take the risks should also receive the benefits.

2. To obtain informed consent, a researcher must do all but which one of the following?
    a. Inform participants that their participation is voluntary.
    b. Forewarn participants about potentially harmful effects of participating.
    c. Fully disclose his or her research objectives or hypotheses.
    d. Forewarn participants about how their rights might be threatened.

3. In studies in which research participants' identities are known to the researcher, the principal way to protect their privacy is to
    a. ensure anonymity.
    b. ensure confidentiality.
    c. ensure both anonymity and confidentiality.
    d. back up the data.

Answers: 1. c; 2. c; 3. b.

SUMMARY

Federal regulations and professional ethical guidelines help clarify researchers' ethical responsibilities and provide measures that should be taken to protect participants' rights and welfare. Potential harm is evaluated by the risks it poses to participants and the risks relative to the benefits. Research participants should be informed of these risks and the nature of the research and should be assured that their participation is voluntary. Deception is considered a method of last resort, but when it is employed, research participants need to be debriefed about the nature of the study; debriefing should ideally occur in all research and especially in research that may pose risk. Finally, researchers need to protect participants' privacy through anonymity or confidentiality.

THE PROCESS OF ETHICAL DECISION-MAKING

What do you need to do to make sure, so far as possible, that you are protecting the rights and welfare of research participants? Figure 3.2 outlines a process of ethical decision-making as it applies to the treatment of research participants. The first step, reviewing federal regulations and professional codes, will sensitize you to potential problems and means of addressing them. Then, as you select a topic and design your research, you should consider the costs and benefits of proposed methods and identify and address areas of ethical concern. If you are conducting your own research, you likely will have to submit a proposal to a college- or university-wide committee called an **Institutional Review Board,** or **IRB**. To ensure compliance with federal regulations, the Common Rule requires that all applicable institutions, including nearly every college and university in the United States, establish an IRB to review and approve research involving human (and animal) subjects. Finally, researchers have an ethical responsibility to secure participants' rights in collecting and analyzing data. Let's examine each of these steps in greater detail.

Institutional Review Board (IRB) A committee formed at nearly all colleges and universities that is responsible for reviewing research proposals to assess provisions for the treatment of human (and animal) subjects.

Review Federal Regulations and Professional Ethics Codes

Having read the previous section of this chapter, you are well on your way to completing the first step in making ethically responsible decisions. We recommend that you also read the *Belmont Report,* Common Rule, and the professional code of ethics of the discipline within which you are working. Box 3.3, DOING SOCIAL RESEARCH: Web Resources on Research Ethics, provides links to federal regulations and several other useful resources as you prepare to conduct your research.

FIGURE 3.2
The Process of Ethical Decision-Making

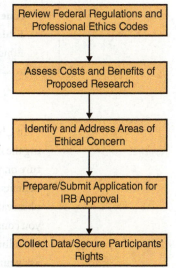

Assess Costs and Benefits of Proposed Research

Ethical considerations should begin with the selection of your research topic, for this is a good starting point for analyzing the potential costs and benefits of research. The potential for doing harm is greatest in social research that investigates negative aspects of behavior, such as aggression, cheating, and obedience to malevolent authority. Research on sensitive topics such as sex and drug use also poses risks. There is potential harm, for example, in surveys that ask questions about illegal behavior such as drug abuse, which could prove embarrassing or put participants at risk for criminal prosecution if the information is disclosed.

BOX 3.3

DOING SOCIAL RESEARCH

Web Resources on Research Ethics

If you are preparing a research proposal or if you simply want to become more familiar with ethical codes and guidelines for conducting social research, there are many valuable online resources at your disposal. These include links to the following.

Belmont Report: http://www.hhs.gov/ohrp/humansubjects/guidance/belmont.html

You also can watch a short video clip (Belmont Report Educational Video) or a longer video (25th Anniversary of the Belmont Report) on the *Belmont Report* at https://videocast.nih.gov/summary.asp?Live=11524&bhcp=1

Code of Federal Regulations: http://www.hhs.gov/ohrp/humansubjects/guidance/45cfr46.html

American Sociological Association Code of Ethics: http://www.asanet.org/images/asa/docs/pdf/CodeofEthics.pdf

Ethical Principles of Psychologists and Code of Conduct: http://www.apa.org/ethics/code/ethics-code-2017.pdf

American Anthropological Association Statement on Ethics: Principles of Professional Responsibility: http://ethics.americananthro.org/category/statement/

American Political Science Association's *A Guide to Professional Ethics in Political Science*: http://www.apsanet.org/portals/54/Files/Publications/APSAEthics Guide2012.pdf

American Association of Public Opinion Research (AAPOR) Code of Professional Ethics and Practices: http://www.aapor.org/Standards-Ethics/AAPOR-Code-of-Ethics.aspx

---

In Chapter 4 we discuss the first few stages of research, from topic selection to reviewing the literature to creating a plan or design to carry out research. As you read the literature on your topic, you are likely to get a better understanding of the potential costs and benefits of doing research on this topic by examining the methods (e.g., deception, covert observation) and samples used in previous research (e.g., children, prisoners). Then, as you consider your research design, we recommend that you solicit opinions from others, including your faculty supervisor and potential participants. Ultimately, too, you should ask yourself, "How would *I* feel if I were a participant in my own research?"

Identify and Address Areas of Ethical Concern

The next step is to go through your research design carefully to determine areas of ethical concern and how you will address them. The best place to start is to review the requirements of an informed consent agreement. As we noted earlier, the agreement should describe foreseeable risks and benefits, indicate how you will maintain confidentiality, and assure participants that their participation is voluntary.

You also should devise a plan for debriefing participants. For research not involving deception, this may be no more than a written statement that describes more fully the nature of the research and reminds participants whom to contact if they have questions about the research or their rights. If the study involves deception, you will need a more elaborate protocol: the debriefing should probe participants' suspicions about the study, fully describe all deceptive elements and why deception is necessary, and explain the true purpose of the study. After the debriefing, APA ethical guidelines further dictate that you give participants the opportunity to withdraw their data (APA 2017:8.07[c]). The debriefing, in effect, fully informs participants about the study so that they are truly in a position to give their informed consent.

Prepare and Submit Application for IRB Approval

Once you've devised means of protecting participants, the next step is to prepare and submit a proposal to your school or organization's IRB, if required. Students engaged in research should complete this step in consultation with a faculty advisor, who is responsible for reviewing and, ordinarily, signing off on all IRB applications. Generally, you must complete a form that describes the proposed research and specifies how participants' rights are to be protected. Although IRB forms vary across educational and other institutions, you should expect at least to address the following issues:

1. Is there the possibility of harm? Is the potential risk to participants beyond what they would experience in everyday life ("minimal risk")? What measures are you taking to mitigate risk and monitor the safety of participants?
2. What are the benefits of the research? Are risks reasonable in relation to the benefits?
3. How will participants be selected? Is the selection equitable; that is, are there sound ethical and scientific reasons for including some types of participants and excluding others?
4. What steps are you taking to gain the informed consent of participants?
5. Does the research involve deception?
6. What steps will be taken to debrief participants?
7. How is the privacy of participants going to be protected? What strategies are being used to secure the confidentiality of data?

When you submit your proposal, initially the IRB will decide whether the proposed study is *exempt*. Social research that is exempt from federal regulations includes the collection of existing data in which participants cannot be identified, research involving normal educational practices and educational testing, and the observation of public behavior when recorded information cannot be linked to individuals (CFR 2009:46.101). Exempt research does not require IRB review; however, it is up to the IRB, not the investigator, to decide if the research qualifies as exempt (Shamoo and Resnick 2009:257). If the research is subject to review but presents no more than minimal risk to participants, it may be given an "expedited review" performed by either the chairperson or one or more designees (CFR 2009:46.101). Otherwise, the full committee will review it. In any case, the IRB may approve, disapprove, or require modifications to secure approval.

Collect Data and Secure Participants' Rights

Once the IRB has approved your proposal, all is not said and done. The final step is to secure participants' rights. For the most part this consists of implementing the procedures presented in your IRB proposal. As you carry out your research, however, it is important to realize that your ethical responsibility to protect the rights and welfare of participants is ongoing, extending throughout and sometimes beyond the research process.

Consider, for example, potential harm. Although it may be sufficient to implement the means you have devised to protect participants from harm, it is possible that the research can unexpectedly threaten participants' welfare. This was the case in Zimbardo and colleagues' prison simulation study. The investigators had devised means to safeguard participants' welfare, such as screening for psychological problems; however, they did not anticipate the study's adverse effects. Because "guards" behaved inhumanely toward "prisoners" and "prisoners" showed signs of depression and extreme stress, Zimbardo and colleagues (1973:45) took additional steps to secure participants' welfare. Not only did they terminate the experiment eight days earlier than planned, they also conducted encounter sessions immediately after the experiment to allow participants to vent their feelings and reflect on the moral issues they had faced. And to assess longer-term effects, they carried out follow-ups via questionnaires, personal interviews, and reunions.

Lareau's field study provides another example. Recall that when Lareau (2011) interviewed participants 10 years after the study, she recognized that some participants were uncomfortable with their portrayal. She attempted to rectify this in several ways. First and foremost, Lareau listened to participants' stories, paying particular attention to expressions of discomfort. She also let participants read and edit what she wrote, and she even published participants' own writing (Lareau 2011).

Finally, circumstances may require additional means of securing participants' confidentiality if something unforeseen happens. For example, when Lewis and colleagues (2008) realized that it was possible to identify people in their Facebook data, they took the dataset down from the Web.

Some researchers have gone to great lengths to protect participants' privacy when confronted with a potential breach. When Laud Humphreys ([1970] 2009:58, 229–30) realized there was a possibility that the confidentiality of his data would be compromised, he took his records out of his locked safe and burned them and vowed to plead the Fifth Amendment rather than divulge the identity of a single man whom he observed. Sociologist Rik Scarce spent 159 days in jail when he refused to testify about conversations he may have had with an animal-rights activist. He had met the activist in the course of research for his book, *Eco-Warriors: Understanding the Radical Environmental Movement*. Scarce (1999:981) believed that sociologists should "treat confidential information as confidential *no matter what*." (You can read more about this on Scarce's website: http://www.skidmore.edu/~rscarce/rsbio.htm.)

SUMMARY

By reviewing federal and professional ethical guidelines and assessing the costs and benefits of our research, we become more familiar with exactly what we should do to protect research participants. On the basis of this knowledge, we can then take action, devising means to protect participants' rights, submitting a proposal to the IRB if required, and then securing participants' rights.

POLITICS AND SOCIAL RESEARCH

At the outset of the chapter, we noted that politics also enters into social research. Underlying the influence of both ethics and politics is the concept of values. Values refer to guiding beliefs about what is good, important, useful, and desirable. As outlined earlier, values of respect, beneficence, and justice guided the creation of federal ethical codes that constrain social research. Similarly, values stimulate the influence of politics in social research, for politics essentially concerns the bargaining, negotiation, and compromise that occur in the pursuit of *valued* outcomes, such as the formation of policy (Pielke 2007:37). Whenever you debate social and political issues, you unavoidably base your position on your personal values, especially your *political ideology*, which refers to the set of values and beliefs associated with a political system or party.

Politics may influence the research process at an individual and a structural level. At the individual level, a researcher's personal values and ideology may shape his or her choice of what or whom to study. However, Max Weber (1949), one of the founders of sociology, believed that personal values should not influence the *collection and analysis of data*. Otherwise, social scientists' findings will not be seen as credible and valid but rather as a projection of their personal beliefs. Although many social scientists today embrace what has come to be known as the "value-free" doctrine, there is disagreement about whether social science can and should be value-free, as you will see.

▲ Max Weber
(1864-1920)

At the structural level, various groups in society, including the scientific community, professional associations, and local, national, and international political systems also may exert pressures that influence the course of the research (Sjoberg 1967:xiii). Earlier in the chapter we described a very important source of political influence at the structural level: namely, the government regulation of scientific research as set forth in policies on research ethics and the protection of human subjects. In the remainder of this chapter we touch on individual and structural influences as we consider how politics enters into each step in the research process, from topic selection to the application of findings. As we discuss politics, we return to research on sexuality, one of the most politically charged topics in the social sciences (Irvine 2012).

Topic Selection, Political Ideology, and Research Funding

Research begins with the selection of a topic. In Chapter 4 we discuss factors that influence topic selection, including personal motivations of the researcher and the current state of scientific research and theory. Politics also enters into the equation, in terms of personal values and institutional support for social research.

Although Weber argued that personal values should not influence how researchers design and conduct their research, he acknowledged that researchers' values do shape their research topics and questions. This is unavoidable, for, as we pointed out in Chapter 2, science is always a product of the culture and times. But the impact of values on topic selection especially applies in sociology and the other social sciences, which justify their work largely on its value relevance to human concerns. The most eminent sociologists of the 19th and early 20th centuries—people like Émile Durkheim, Karl Marx, Max Weber, W. E. B. Du Bois, and Robert Park—concerned themselves with issues emanating from great social upheavals of their day, such as the French and Industrial revolutions, urbanization, and massive foreign immigration to the United States. Their sympathies lay with the victims of these changes, and they focused their attention on social problems such as alienation, inequality, deviance and crime, urban crowding, and racism.

The progressivism of the discipline of sociology and other social sciences has continued to the present day. Driven by the causes of civil rights and racial and sexual discrimination, much contemporary sociological research is devoted to class, race, and gender inequality. For example, many social scientists have chosen to study the impact of same-sex parenting on children because of its relevance to the issues of gay adoption and gay marriage. They also may do this research out of personal convictions regarding gay rights.

Topic selection also may be hindered or promoted by the politics of research funding. Practically all social research requires financial support; so major funding sources exert considerable control over what gets studied (Leavitt 2001). In the United States, sources of funding for scientific research include the federal government, corporations, private foundations, and professional organizations. The biggest single supporter of social science research is the federal government, which awards grants through agencies such as the National Science Foundation (NSF) and National Institutes of Health (NIH). The NSF's Social, Behavioral, and Economics Sciences Directorate "provides approximately 68 percent of the federal funding for basic research at U.S. academic institutions in the social, behavioral, and economic sciences" (NSF 2017:2).

Funding sources influence topic selection in various ways. In allocating resources, funding agencies establish priorities for research on particular topics. During the AIDS epidemic in the 1980s, for example, several government agencies supported the idea of a national survey of sexual practices (Michael et al. 1994). Knowing that AIDS was infectious and one of the ways it was transmitted was through sex, scientists realized that they needed better information on sexual practices and who was most at risk for getting the disease through sexual contact. In response to a request for proposals from the National Institute of Child Health and Human Development, Edward Laumann and his associates (1994) proposed the study that we described at the beginning of the chapter. When Laumann's team was awarded the contract to design the study, however, they encountered political pressures of another sort. Many government officials resisted allowing the researchers to ask questions about sexual behavior, even if these might shed light on the spread of AIDS. And, despite narrowing the focus of the survey, Laumann and colleagues' study was denied research funding because of political opposition to research on sexuality.

When scientists submit proposals for grant support, they must justify the value of their research. Laumann and colleagues (1994) argued that their study would advance scientific understanding of human sexual behavior, and to this end they presented theoretical foundations for their research. But grant proposals generally are expected to do more than describe the intellectual merits of the research. The NSF, for instance, specifies that proposals also must be evaluated in terms of how the research will benefit society and contribute to desired societal outcomes, which is a matter of political preferences.

The contemporary impact of politics on research funding is clearly illustrated in an amendment to the 2013 US spending bill. Senator Tom Coburn inserted language into the bill that restricts NSF funding in political science to research that the agency's director "certifies as promoting national security or the economic interests of the United States" (Mervis 2013:1510). Passed by Congress, the amendment elicited strong reactions from members of the academic community. The American Political Science Association (APSA) said in a formal statement:

> Adoption of this amendment is a gross intrusion into the widely respected scholarly agenda setting process at NSF that has supported our world-class national science enterprise for over sixty years. . . . While political science research is

most immediately affected, at risk is *any and all* research disciplines funded by the NSF. The amendment makes all scientific research vulnerable to the whims of political pressure. (APSA 2013)

Critics of the bill argued that the United States has benefited greatly from a government/science partnership that relies on sound scientific criteria in awarding grants (Farrell 2013; Prewitt 2013). The amendment sets a precedent that may lead politicians to "make sure that the research they like gets money, while the research they dislike does not" (Farrell 2013).

Although the Coburn amendment presents new challenges, science has been a part of the political process by which the government allocates research funding for many years. When threatened with the loss of federal funding in the 1980s, the social sciences created the Consortium of Social Science Associations (COSSA), an organization that promotes funding for social research (Silver 2006). And in 2013, the APSA hired a lobbying firm to endeavor to prevent the continuation of the Coburn language in future legislation (Stratford 2014). In fact, the Coburn language was not included in a spending bill passed in early 2014, but as Michael Stratford (2014) writes, "advocates for social science researchers say the battle isn't over."

Data Analysis and Interpretation and Political Ideology

Aside from topic selection, the doctrine of value-free social science holds that the rest of the research process—that is, the collection, analysis, and interpretation of data—should not be influenced by one's personal beliefs and values. The following chapters of this book, in fact, present numerous methods by which social scientists attempt to control for investigator bias. In addition to these methods, all sciences have structural safeguards "to protest against the persistence of false, inaccurate, or misleading data and interpretations" (Leavitt 2001:27). Experts are called upon to evaluate grant proposals, so that only the most well-designed studies typically are funded. The best studies are published in refereed journals, in which reviewers judge whether the research is worthy of publication. And, over time, consistent results increase the credibility of data, and failed replications lead to the correction of misleading information (Leavitt 2001). Still, despite these efforts, a researcher's political ideology can affect the way in which data are collected and interpreted. While we hasten to add that it is difficult to find direct instances of this, sociologists Judith Stacey and Timothy Biblarz (2001) uncovered an example in research on differences in children raised by homosexual versus heterosexual parents.

Research on same-sex parenting has generated a great deal of ideological debate. At the beginning of the 21st century, some states explicitly or implicitly prohibited the adoption of a child by a same-sex couple. In court cases and in drafting legislation, advocates have used research evidence to support their causes. This research generally shows no notable differences between children raised by homosexual parents and children raised by heterosexual parents. However, opponents of same-sex adoption question the validity of this research and cite other studies indicating the harmful effects of homosexual parenting (Stacey and Biblarz 2001).

In this context, Stacey and Biblarz (2001) reviewed studies of the effects of homosexual versus heterosexual parenting, asking, "(How) does the sexual orientation of parents matter?" At first, they point out how researchers' political beliefs affect their selection of evidence and interpretation of findings. For example, researchers with political views hostile to homosexual adoption report that gay parents subject their children to disproportionate risks for a variety of negative outcomes. Among other issues, Stacey and Biblarz (2001:162) note that this research has extrapolated inappropriately "from studies of single-parent families to portray children of lesbians as more vulnerable to everything from delinquency [and] substance abuse . . . to teen pregnancy [and] . . . suicide." By contrast, research seemingly motivated by political views sympathetic to homosexual parenting has emphasized the consistent absence of differences in children raised by homosexual and heterosexual parents, even though such a finding is theoretically puzzling and unlikely. In effect, Stacey and Biblarz argue, the broader political and social climate has put sexuality researchers on the defensive. Because differences between children of homosexual versus heterosexual parents are assumed to be *deficits*, scholars who support gay rights may ignore differences.

When Stacey and Bilblarz analyzed 21 of the better studies as of 1998, they found that researchers frequently downplayed differences, especially regarding children's gender and sexual preferences and behavior. Some studies showed, for example, that children of homosexual parents were less likely to engage in traditional sex-typed behavior in dress and play than children of heterosexual parents. Such findings raise important theoretical questions. Most of the differences, Stacey and Biblarz (2001) contend, are likely due to the effects of parental gender rather than sexual orientation. For example, children of co-mother parents "should develop in less gender-stereotypic ways than would children with two heterosexual parents" (177). Furthermore, some differences may be due not to parenting practices but to other factors associated with the stigma of homosexuality, which makes gay parents more likely to be older, urban, highly educated, and in less stable relationships.

Stacey and Biblarz's analysis makes the influences of political ideology on same-sex parenting research seem obvious and avoidable. However, avoiding biases in the use and interpretation of evidence may be easier said than done, and some critics of the value-free ideology suggest that researchers "hide behind" the veil of "value-free" research when their research is anything but value-free. One way to address this criticism is to admit one's values and biases up front and allow others to evaluate the research with that information in hand. Stacey and Biblarz (2001:161) agree, noting that especially for ideological and emotional subjects such as gay parenting, it is "incumbent on scholars to acknowledge the personal convictions they bring to the discussion." Thus, they stated in their article that they "personally oppose discrimination on the basis of sexual orientation or gender" (161).

Acknowledging personal and political sympathies is especially important in sociological studies of the marginalized, who are outside the societal mainstream, such as deviants, the poor, and racial/ethnic and sexual minorities. Charles Ragin and Lisa Amoroso (2011:114) point out that field research often is undertaken and is best suited to give voice to these groups, whose views are rarely heard by mainstream audiences and whose lives are often misrepresented. In trying to understand reality from the perspective of the marginalized, field researchers may become sympathetic with their point of view. The way to deal with this, sociologist Howard Becker (1967) argues, is to adhere to the standards of good scientific work but also carefully consider and acknowledge "whose side we are on." Doing this clarifies the limits of a study and how its findings should be applied. Part of this "sociological disclaimer," Becker (1967:247) believes, should be a statement

> in which we say, for instance, that we have studied the prison through the eyes of the inmates and not through the eyes of the guards or other involved parties. We warn people, thus, that our study tells us only how things look from that vantage point—what kinds of objects guards are in the prisoner's world—and does not attempt to explain why guards do what they do or to absolve the guards of what may seem, from the prisoners' side, morally unacceptable behavior.

Dissemination of Research Findings: Science, Politics, and Public Policy

Another way in which science and politics relate to one another is in the use of scientific knowledge to inform public policy. The authority of science is undeniable in settling many questions about the physical world, such as the efficacy of medical treatments and effects of pollution. In such cases, scientists are likely to share the values of the decision-makers and play the role of impartial experts, providing information to others without engaging directly in the politics of policymaking. However, when scientific knowledge is uncertain, and the policy options are based on different values, the role of scientists is more complicated. Scientists may be forced to take sides or to become advocates for particular policies, and science itself may become a tool of political debate (Pielke 2007).

When it comes to public policy, it is especially difficult for *social scientists* to play the role of the pure and impartial scientist. As noted earlier, the problems researchers choose to study often have immediate relevance to people's lives and are inherently value-laden. Therefore, social scientists must not only be aware of the possible influence of personal values and political views on their research, they also must consider the practical implications of their research and how others may use their findings. Once again, research on same-sex parenting illustrates the politicization of social research.

Stacey and Biblarz were well aware of the implications of their findings and how others may use them. They knew that opponents of same-sex marriage and parenting interpret differences as deficits; therefore, they were careful to point out that their analysis showed no differences between the children of homosexual and heterosexual parents in the key areas of psychological well-being and cognitive functioning. And while they did find differences in some areas, they "unequivocally" concluded, "social science research provides no grounds for taking sexual orientation into account in the political distribution of family rights and responsibilities" (Stacey and Biblarz 2001:179).

Yet the Stacey and Biblarz article was reported almost immediately in the mainstream media and was used by both legal opponents and proponents of gay rights. On July 18, 2001, Foxnews.com, for example, ran an article with the following lead: "Dozens of studies about gay parents were mischaracterized for political reasons so as not to draw the ire of homosexual activists or encourage anti-gay rhetoric, a new report suggests" (Foxnews.com 2001). *Slate* journalist Ann Hulbert (2004) found it ironic that as an advocate of gay marriage, Judith Stacey would produce "the most incisive critique of the claim that research has proved there are no differences between kids raised by gay and straight parents." In 2004, legal opponents of same-sex marriage drew on the Stacey and Biblarz article in a case in Ontario, Canada.

In the Ontario case, Stacey was also called as an expert witness in *defense* of same-sex marriage (Burawoy 2004). In fact, it is not unusual for social scientists to offer expert testimony. In the 1960s, '70s, and '80s, many social scientists, driven by their staunch support for racial integration and civil rights, testified in cases involving desegregation, busing, and affirmative action. Similarly today, social scientists lend their expert judgments in cases involving sexual discrimination, sexual harassment, and gay rights.

At times, professional associations also may serve as knowledge brokers. The American Sociological Association (ASA), for example, has "a long history of presenting the consensus research findings of sociologists to American courts for their use in evaluating evidence and legal issues" (Brief of ASA 2013:1). In February 2013, the ASA filed an amicus brief with the US Supreme Court in two cases involving same-sex marriage. One case challenged the federal Defense of Marriage Act (DOMA); the other challenged Proposition 8, a California law that revoked the right of same-sex couples to marry. One issue in these cases concerned the well-being of children raised by same-sex parents. Groups defending DOMA and Proposition 8 asserted that children with same-sex parents fare worse than children of opposite-sex parents. Contrary to this claim, the ASA brief concluded, based on abundant social science research, that positive child well-being is related to stability in the relationship between two parents and greater socioeconomic resources. "Whether a child is raised by same-sex or opposite-sex parents has no bearing on a child's wellbeing" (Brief of ASA 2013:3).

SUMMARY

The doctrine of value neutrality holds that researchers should not mix science and politics. As we have seen, however, it is inevitable that social scientists make value judgments about what and whom to study, for these choices are a product of the culture and times. Politics and its underlying values can also influence every stage of the research process. In conducting research, social scientists should identify and acknowledge their values and strive to eliminate personal biases from the collection, analysis, and interpretation of data. And when they present their research, social scientists should consider the practical implications of their findings and how others may use them.

THE INTERSECTION OF ETHICS AND POLITICS IN SOCIAL RESEARCH

Ethics and politics are often connected to one another in social research. We mentioned federal ethical regulations as one example of this connection. In this final section of the chapter, we expand the intersection of ethics and politics in social research by returning to research on homosexual parenting and adoption. We present a highly politicized study that has been questioned on ethical grounds.

A Case Study: Research on Same-Sex Parenting

The backstory of the 2013 ASA amicus brief reveals much about both the ethics and politics of social research. It is safe to say that filing the brief was a political action strongly supported by the ASA membership. It was filed on behalf of respondents endorsing gay rights, which the vast majority of members advocate. According to a 2004 survey of 2,394 members, 79 percent opposed a constitutional amendment defining marriage as between a man and a woman; only 9 percent supported (the remainder abstained or did not answer the question) (ASA 2004).

The political position of ASA members, however, does not fully account for the decision to file the brief. For as it turned out, that decision was made in the 11th hour, only a few months before oral hearings on the Supreme Court cases. Apparently, it was precipitated partly by public use of a study published in spring 2012 in the journal *Social Science Research*. The study by sociologist Mark Regnerus had been cited in federal court cases as providing evidence of harm to children raised by homosexual couples. Prior to the annual meetings of the ASA, in August 2012, several members and sections of the ASA, including the Family Section, asked the ASA leadership to clarify through legal action that the Regnerus study did not support the conclusions that were being drawn from it (ASA 2012; Cohen 2012). And so, the ASA submitted its brief, in which 7 of 31 pages contain a refutation of this study. To understand how the study provoked the ASA response and how it relates to the politics and ethics of social research, we first need to describe its methods and findings.

Mark Regnerus's study (2012a:755) focused on young adults, asking, "Do the [adult] children of gay and lesbian parents look comparable to those of their heterosexual counterparts?" To address this question, he conducted an online survey of a relatively large, random sample of adults between the ages of 18 and 39. The survey asked about a broad range of psychological, social, and economic outcomes as well as for information about the respondents' families of origin. Based on the latter information, Regnerus comprised eight comparison groups, which he labeled as intact biological families (in which mother and father are still married), lesbian mothers, gay fathers, adopted, divorced, stepfamily, single parent, and others. The key screening question used to identify children of lesbian mothers or gay fathers was the following: "From when you were born until age 18 (or until you left home to be on your own), did either of your parents ever have a romantic relationship with someone of the same sex?" Respondents who answered "yes" were placed in the lesbian mother or gay father groups.

According to the published results, compared to young adults who grew up in intact biological families, young adults with a "lesbian mother" differed significantly on 25 of 40 outcomes and those with a "gay father" differed significantly on 11 outcomes. For example, children of *both* lesbian mothers and gay fathers were more likely to report being depressed, being unemployed, having trouble in a current relationship, and receiving welfare while growing up (Regnerus 2012a:761–62). Based on these findings, Regnerus concluded that the "empirical claim . . . of no notable differences must go" (766).

The Regnerus study was highly controversial. Immediately after its publication and for a very long period, it was widely featured in the media. Google "Regnerus" and "same-sex" today and you'll get over 40,000 hits. Supporters of gay marriage denounced the study, opponents praised it, and pundits and social scientists attacked Regnerus, his methodology, and his conclusions.

In addition to its political ramifications, the study involved questions of methodology and ethical issues concerning propriety in the publication review process. You can read about these matters in the November 2012 issue of *Social Science Research*, which contains several commentaries. Many social scientists found fault with the study's methodology (Gates et al. 2012; Perrin, Cohen, and Caren 2013; Sherkat 2012); in fact, subsequent research re-examining Regnerus's data has challenged his findings and conclusions on methodological and other grounds (Cheng and Powell 2015; Rosenfeld 2015). However, others pointed out the study's strengths, especially in comparison with previous research on same-sex parenting (Johnson et al. 2012; Schumm 2012; Smith 2012). Still others raised two issues with the study that link politics to research ethics: conflict of interest and social responsibility in the presentation and use of research findings.

Conflict of Interest

A **conflict of interest** occurs in social research when the professional goal of producing "objective" value-free knowledge conflicts with other motives such as financial gain, professional advancement, or political interests. For example, a scientist doing research on the health effects of passive smoking has a conflict of interest if a tobacco company funds the research. Many professional ethical codes have statements about conflict of interest. According to the ASA Code of Ethics:

> Sociologists maintain the highest degree of integrity in their professional work and avoid conflicts of interest and the appearance of conflict. Conflicts of interest arise when sociologists' personal or financial interests prevent them from performing their professional work in an unbiased manner. (ASA 1999:9)

The ASA code also states that sociologists must disclose sources of financial support "that may have the appearance of or potential for a conflict of interest" (ASA 1999:9.03).

The question of conflict of interest arose in the Regnerus study because it was funded—to the tune of $795,000 (Sherkat 2012)—by two very conservative foundations, the Bradley Foundation and the Witherspoon Institute. Documents cited by an investigative journalist show that officials of these organizations expected the study to produce results vindicating "the traditional understanding of marriage" and that they were hoping to have these results before the Supreme Court heard the cases on same-sex marriage (Resnick 2013). Consistent with the ASA ethical code, Regnerus disclosed his funding sources. Furthermore, he claimed that these "sources played no role at all in the design or conduct of the study, the analyses, the interpretation of the data, or in the preparation of this manuscript" (Regnerus 2012a:755). Yet scholars remain skeptical (Massey 2012; Sherkat 2012). To some, it isn't enough to disclose funding sources. Rather, researchers should avoid relationships that might even give the appearance of undermining the integrity of their work, which may explain why at least two social scientists declined Regnerus's invitation to become paid consultants on his study (Resnick 2013).

Social Responsibility

A second issue in Regnerus's study concerns social scientists' responsibility to be aware of and provide direction to how others use their findings. The ethical codes of professional associations often contain statements about "social responsibility." Principle E of the ASA Code of Ethics states: "Sociologists are aware of their professional and scientific responsibility to the communities and societies in which they live and work. They apply and make public their knowledge in order to contribute to the public good" (ASA 1999). The Code of Ethics of the American Anthropological Association (AAA) further stipulates: "Anthropological researchers . . . must consider carefully the social and political implications of the information they disseminate. They must do everything in their power to insure that such information is well understood, properly contextualized, and responsibly utilized" (AAA 2009:III.C.1).

Whether Regnerus violated the ethic of social responsibility in reporting his study revolves around his definition of same-sex parents, which has been called the "single biggest weakness" of the study (Perrin, Cohen, and Caren 2013:331). Recall that Regnerus's research question asks if children of homosexual parents differ from their heterosexual *counterparts*. Given that his heterosexual comparison group consisted of children raised by parents who were continuously married, their homosexual counterparts should be children raised by same-sex couples in a continuous relationship. Instead, he examines children who recalled that one of their parents had a "same-sex romantic relationship" while they were growing up. By this definition, as Regnerus (2012a:757) notes, the majority of the respondents labeled by him as having been raised by a "lesbian mother" or "gay father" were the offspring of a biological parent who subsequently had a same-sex relationship. Far from being raised in a same-sex household, most of the young adults in the "lesbian mother" and "gay father" groups spent some of their childhood living in heterosexual and single-parent households; a minority reported living with a parent while the parent was in a same-sex relationship. In short, Regnerus cannot separate the impact of having a parent who had a same-sex relationship from the impact of experiencing a divorce, living with a single parent, or living in multiple family forms (see also Cheng and Powell 2015; Rosenfeld 2015). By virtue of how he defined the homosexual parenting groups, his study makes, as the ASA brief argues, "inappropriate apples-to-oranges comparisons" (Brief of ASA 2013:17).

Although Regnerus discusses the limitations of his definition of homosexual parents, he frames his research question as if his data can speak to previous research showing "no differences" between same-sex and opposite-sex parents. Then he uses the labels "lesbian mother" and "gay father" throughout his presentation and discussion of findings. In this way, as sociologist Don Barrett (2012:1355) points out, Regnerus "misrepresents" the scope of his findings and "creates misleading understandings." Barrett believes that the presentation of research is particularly important when it touches on a sensitive topic, and he concludes that Regnerus did not take "into sufficient consideration the manner in which research is consumed."

In responding to criticisms of his research, Regnerus (2012b:1368) acknowledged that his use of inappropriate labels is a "reasonable criticism" and that "in hindsight," he wished he had labeled the lesbian mother and gay father groups differently. Still, his response to the criticism of comparing "apples to oranges" has been to emphasize the instability of same-sex relationships and to treat instability as a causal explanation of why such relationships result in poorer outcomes for children. In an article published in *Slate* (Regnerus 2012c), Regnerus states that the political message of his research is unclear: on the one hand, it could be argued that gay and lesbian couples should be extended the security afforded by marriage; on the other hand, allowing same-sex marriage may undermine the "stable, two-parent biological married" household, which is "the safest place for a kid."

During the first few months after his study was published, Regnerus emphasized that his views were not political and was careful to clarify the limitations of his research, especially in regard to the gay marriage debate. Eventually, however, he took sides. In January 2013, he co-signed a brief prominently citing his research that supported the defendants of DOMA and Proposition 8 in the Supreme Court cases (Brief of Social Science Professors 2013). Few social scientists would dispute Regnerus's right to become an advocate or the ethics of his decision to do so. Indeed, the 2009 AAA *Code of Ethics* states that whether a researcher "chooses to move beyond disseminating research results to a position of advocacy . . . is an individual decision, but not an ethical responsibility" (AAA 2009:III.C.3). Still, Regnerus's value position on same-sex marriage seems to underlie the ethical and political issues raised about his research.

As we have argued, virtually all research, especially in the social sciences, is value-driven. So, Regnerus cannot be faulted for having a value position. It seems very likely, too, that his research would never have been scrutinized and politicized to a very great degree if his findings had been different (see Redding 2013). As sociologist Christian Smith (2012) stated in the *Chronicle of Higher Education*: "In today's political climate, and particularly in the discipline of sociology—dominated as it is by a progressive orthodoxy—what Regnerus did is unacceptable."

In the end, however, it is precisely because he did research on a politically controversial topic and published results that challenged both the findings of abundant prior research and the prevailing political view of social scientists that Regnerus's study warranted the level of critical scrutiny that it got. Based on his sources of research funding, he was walking an ethical tightrope to begin. It is questionable that he gave due consideration to how his results might be used. And he could have been more careful in how he framed his research question, defined and labeled same-sex parents, and presented his findings.

SUMMARY

One of the most politicized and critically scrutinized studies in the social sciences in recent years is Mark Regnerus's study comparing the impact on young adults of growing up with a parent who had a same-sex relationship or growing up with stable opposite-sex parents. Reporting that the offspring of same-sex parents fare worse on several outcomes, Regnerus challenged both previous research and dominant political views. Among the critical responses, scholars raised two ethical issues: conflict of interest and social responsibility. The question of conflict of interest was raised because of the conservative agendas of the foundations that funded Regnerus's study. The issue of social responsibility for how one's research is used by others arose because of alleged misuses of the study's findings.

KEY TERMS

anonymity, p. 53

beneficence, p. 48

confidentiality, p. 53

Common Rule, p. 48

conflict of interest, p. 68

debriefing, p. 52

ethics, p. 41

informed consent, p. 43

Institutional Review Board (IRB), p. 55

justice, p. 48

respect for persons, p. 47

KEY POINTS

- Ethical standards of right and wrong guide the conduct of scientific research.
- Four common ethical issues in the treatment of research participants are potential harm, informed consent, deception, and privacy invasion.
- Risk of harm violates a person's right to safety; this risk arises in social research when procedures may result in physical pain, anxiety, loss of self-esteem, feelings of embarrassment, and so forth.
- Informed consent protects freedom of choice; consent is not informed if participation is involuntary or individuals have insufficient information to make a rational decision to participate.
- The use of deception in social research is controversial; some social scientists believe that without it, participants may not act spontaneously, while others question its use ethically and methodologically.
- Privacy may be invaded in social research when participation results in the revelation of personal information that the participant wishes to remain private.
- Federal regulations state that the risk of harm to research participants should be minimal and the benefits of participation should outweigh the risks.
- Federal regulations require informed consent, usually in written form.
- The APA and ASA permit the use of deception, provided there is no substantial risk of harm and participants are informed of the deception immediately after the study.
- Federal regulations require provisions to protect privacy, which may involve collecting data anonymously or taking steps to ensure confidentiality.
- The steps in ethical decision-making include assessing costs and benefits, identifying areas of concern and making provisions to meet those concerns, submitting a proposal to an IRB, and securing participants rights.
- According to the doctrine of value-free science, values should not influence data collection, analysis, and interpretation.
- Values and politics may influence topic selection, data analysis and interpretation, and the dissemination of research findings.
- In social research, ethics and politics may result in conflicts of interest and issues of social responsibility in the use of research findings.

REVIEW QUESTIONS

1. How does an analysis of costs and benefits apply to the ethical conduct of social research? What considerations are involved in conducting a cost-benefit analysis?

2. What are the basic ingredients of informed consent? How did Milgram violate this principle in his research on obedience to authority?

3. Briefly describe the arguments for and against the use of deception in social research. What are the conditions for its use?

4. How is research participants' right to privacy typically secured in (a) surveys and (b) field research?

5. What are Institutional Review Boards (IRBs)? What part do they play in the process of doing ethically responsible research?

6. Give examples of how values may enter into (a) topic selection, (b) the analysis and interpretation of data, and (c) the dissemination of research findings.

7. What obligations do social scientists have regarding the use of the knowledge they generate? How is this obligation an example of the intersection of ethics and politics in social research?

EXERCISES

1. Discuss the ethical problems raised in the following hypothetical research examples.

   (a) A criminologist meets a professional fence through an ex-convict he knows. (A *fence* is someone who buys and sells stolen goods.) As part of a study, the researcher convinces the fence to talk about his work—why he sticks with this kind of work, what kind of people he deals with, how he meets them, and so forth. To gain the fence's cooperation, the researcher promises not to disclose any personal details that would get the fence in trouble. However, when subpoenaed, he agrees to reveal his informant rather than go to jail. Has the researcher violated an ethical principle in agreeing to talk to legal authorities?

   (b) A researcher gains access to a clinic serving AIDS patients by responding to a call for volunteers. While working at the clinic, she makes a record of patients' names and later approaches them, identifies herself as a social scientist, fully explains the nature of her research, and asks them to participate in her in-depth survey of AIDS victims. Most patients agree, although some react negatively to the request. What aspects of the researcher's strategy are ethically problematic?

2. Ethical issues arise when the pursuit of a research question or application of research procedures conflicts with general ethical principles. In a fascinating account
in *The Journal of Contemporary Ethnography* (39 [2010]:554–68), Arlene Stein
reflects on ethical dilemmas she faced and ethical questions that were raised by
community reaction to her published study of a small town in Oregon. The article
shows how a researcher's ethics may be questioned in spite of her best intentions to
conduct research ethically. Read Stein's article and address the following questions:
(a) What ethical dilemma did Stein confront in writing about the townspeople?
(b) Why did Stein's use of pseudonyms fail to protect the privacy of the people she
interviewed? (c) How did she deceive her informants, and do you think this deception was justified?

4

Research Designs

It Depends on the Question

STUDENT LEARNING OBJECTIVES

By the end of this chapter, you should be able to

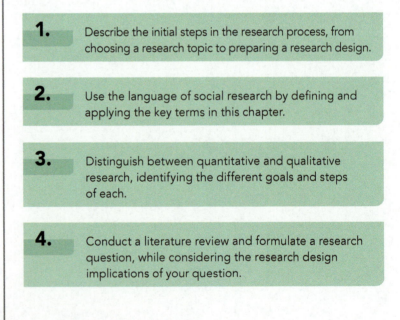

1.   Describe the initial steps in the research process, from choosing a research topic to preparing a research design.

2.   Use the language of social research by defining and applying the key terms in this chapter.

3.   Distinguish between quantitative and qualitative research, identifying the different goals and steps of each.

4.   Conduct a literature review and formulate a research question, while considering the research design implications of your question.

Having considered the scientific, ethical, and political contexts of research, we are ready to focus on the process of social research. The authors have embarked on this process many times. As a graduate student in the 1960s, Royce Singleton was casting about for an idea for his master's thesis. With an interest in race relations, he noticed that changes were beginning to occur in the televised images of African Americans. Prior to the 1960s, blacks were rarely seen on television, and when they appeared, it was nearly always as subservient, stereotypic characters. But suddenly there were several breakthroughs; for example, Bill Cosby costarred in the immensely popular show *I Spy*, and Mal Goode and Bob Teague became television news reporters. Singleton wondered if the greater visibility of African Americans on television would change viewers' racial attitudes.

When he examined research and theory on mass communication, however, Singleton discovered that this idea was untestable. Even if he found that changes in racial attitudes followed changes in blacks' roles on television, he could not say for sure that one change caused the other. It simply was not possible to separate out the effects of changing television images from other social influences on racial attitudes. Did this mean that Singleton needed to give up his interest in television and racial attitudes? Thankfully, no. While it was impossible to say with certainty how changes in television images affected racial attitudes, it was possible to address the following question: What are the effects of racial attitudes on television viewing?

To answer this question, Singleton prepared a **research design**, or overall research plan. In this chapter we introduce the basic terminology of social research as we consider the first few steps from topic selection through the preparation of a research design. Figure 4.1 presents these steps.

research design The overall plan of a study for collecting data.

While the initial steps of conducting research are similar across different forms of research, research design depends on the research question asked and thus the type of understanding of the social world that the researcher hopes to achieve. Singleton's question asked about the relationship between racial prejudice and television viewing patterns. Based on his review of the literature, he derived hypotheses from mass communications theory, following the deductive logic of inquiry discussed in Chapter 2. Research and theory indicated that both exposure to and perception of communications is selective: people tend to expose themselves to communications, such as television programs, that are consistent with their attitudes and beliefs, and their interpretation of what they see also tends to fit their attitudes and beliefs. Singleton therefore hypothesized that white viewers with prejudicial attitudes toward blacks would be less likely to watch programs starring black actors, and would rate such programs less favorably than nonprejudiced white viewers. To test his hypotheses, he collected survey data and conducted quantitative analyses (Singleton 1969).

FIGURE 4.1
The Research Process: from Topic Selection to Research Design

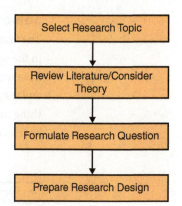

Select Research Topic

Review Literature/Consider Theory

Formulate Research Question

Prepare Research Design

Other research, such as Annette Lareau's (2011), discussed in Chapter 2, is more concerned with the meanings and processes underlying phenomena than with testing explicit hypotheses. This form of research, which is more likely to follow an inductive logic of inquiry, calls for a different research design to uncover how people and social groups interpret the social world. Recall that Lareau was interested in understanding the lives of families with elementary school–aged children. As she carried out interviews and intensive observations of a small set of families, she asked: Does social class make a difference in child-rearing? Based on the patterns that emerged in her data, she concluded that it does, and she went on to develop an influential theory of child-rearing practices.

This chapter discusses the initial steps in the general research process leading to the formulation of a research question and development of a research design. As we point out, different questions call for different research designs with correspondingly different steps. We illustrate these steps with two featured studies: the first is Beckett Broh's (2002) study on sports participation and academic performance, which shares the general design features of Singleton's research; the second is Jessica McCrory Calarco's (2011) research on social class and help-seeking behavior, which shares the general design features of Lareau's (2011) study.[1] Like you, Broh and Calarco were students—albeit graduate students—when they conducted their research, which should give you hope as you design your own research!

INITIAL STEPS IN THE RESEARCH PROCESS

Singleton's research on racial attitudes and television followed the research process outlined in Chapter 1: as initial steps, he selected a general research topic; next, he considered theory and narrowed his topic through a review of the literature; then, he posed a research question; and finally, he prepared a research design. Let's examine these initial steps in detail.

Select Research Topic

The first step in the research process is the selection of a general topic. What topic areas in the social sciences are you most curious about? Are there subject areas in which you have some knowledge but want to know more? Have you ever studied a social problem and realized that its causes are not well understood? Or have you lived through something that makes you want to better understand your personal experience? All of these are motivations for choosing a general topic to research.

---

[1]This chapter draws heavily on additional detailed information that Beckett Broh (personal communication 2003) and Jessica McCrory Calarco (personal communication 2013) provided about their studies.

To begin, social scientists often select topics suggested by the organization of their discipline and by the ongoing development of theory and research. Sociologists, for example, frequently investigate sources of inequality such as social class, race, ethnicity, gender, and sexuality, as well as aspects of various institutions, including education, religion, politics, health care, and the family. Jessica Calarco, for example, was motivated to pursue graduate work in sociology by her interest in how social class affects educational inequality (personal communication 2013). Her research was greatly influenced by Annette Lareau's (2011) work; in fact, Lareau served as Calarco's PhD dissertation supervisor.

You may have been attracted to the social sciences because of their historic focus on social problems. As noted in Chapter 3, many of the founders of sociology concerned themselves with social problems wrought by changing social conditions such as urbanization, the Industrial Revolution, and massive foreign immigration. Many of these problems—urban crowding, alienation, deviance and crime, inequality, racism—have remained major research topics ever since. Similarly today, changing social conditions such as globalization, technological development, and the Information Revolution continue to stimulate topic selection. Some of the studies on Facebook, discussed in Chapter 1, are examples.

▲ Beckett Broh

Finally, your selection of a research topic may be affected by your personal background and experiences. This was certainly true of Beckett Broh's (2002) study, which examined the effect of sports participation on high school academic achievement. Broh herself was a high school athlete, and after her collegiate athletic career was cut short by an injury, she turned to coaching middle and high school basketball in Michigan and Ohio. These experiences sparked her interest in sport and education as a PhD student in sociology, which led her to test her ideas about the impact of athletes' network of relationships on their academic performance (Broh personal communication 2003).

▲ Jessica Calarco

Choosing a topic isn't always easy, but we can offer you a bit of advice: first and foremost, you should choose a topic of interest to you, something that will *sustain* your interest for a period of time. You may be conducting research on the topic for weeks or months in the case of an undergraduate project, years in the case of a master's thesis or doctoral dissertation, and perhaps a lifetime in the case of an academic career. Second, the topic should be practical, which involves a whole series of considerations discussed below.

Review the Literature/Consider Theory

Once you have selected a general topic, the second step in the research process is to conduct a literature review (see Figure 4.1). The "literature" includes theory and prior

▲ The literature review is like navigating a maze in search of a question.

research on your general topic, which will inform your current research. To contribute to scientific knowledge, which is the ultimate goal of social research, we need to know the major theories, key research findings, and unresolved issues in an area of study. In addition, by reviewing prior research you will learn the methods that others have used to study a topic, which should be helpful in designing your research.

As you read the literature and learn about the current state of knowledge on your topic, you should have two related objectives in mind. First, how can I transform my topic into one or more questions that are amenable to research? Second, how can I contribute to ongoing research and theory on the topic? Beckett Broh's research on the effects of sports participation illustrates both of these objectives.

As a high school coach, Broh was struck by the strong support many athletes received from their families, and she wondered if this support might contribute to athletes' success in the classroom. When she reviewed the literature on sports participation, she indeed found several studies showing that students who participated in interscholastic athletics got better grades, on average, than other students. Narrowing her focus on this research, she found that relatively few studies had examined the relationship between grades and other extracurricular activities, such as participating in a music group, vocational club, or student council. Even fewer studies had attempted to test theoretical explanations of how sports participation enhances educational achievement. Consequently, she decided to conduct research to address these gaps in the literature.

Conducting a literature review is easier said than done, and we want to be frank with you: searching the literature can sometimes make you feel like you're in a maze trying to find your way out. You may find a path or a "gap" in the literature, just as Broh found an unanswered question in an ongoing line of inquiry. Be prepared to encounter a few dead ends, including irrelevant and questionable studies. You also may have to reroute your topic, as you may find that it is not amenable to research. Recall that Singleton found that he could not assess the impact on racial attitudes of the increasing visibility of blacks on television; therefore, he decided instead to examine the effect of racial attitudes on viewers' exposure to and perception of television shows with black stars. Further, you need to be flexible enough to realize that there is more than one path. For example, you may decide to recast your topic to fit a particular research strategy or some other need, such as the time you have to undertake a study. Box 4.1, DOING SOCIAL RESEARCH: How to Search the Literature, provides specific pointers to help you with the process of finding theory and research on your topic. In addition, Chapter 14 provides information on how to take notes and write up the results of your review.

BOX 4.1

DOING SOCIAL RESEARCH

How to Search the Literature

The object of a literature review is to grasp the current state of knowledge on a particular topic. More than likely there will be a lot of information on the topic you choose; therefore, you must (a) identify the relevant social science literature and (b) decide which parts of this literature to read. Below is a set of guidelines to help you search the literature.

1. *Start your search by using the library's online resources.* The library's online resources usually include an online catalog and databases. This is where you will find references to books and scholarly articles, in which social science research is most likely to be reported. Beware, however, that the online catalog may only list the library's holdings. In addition, the most current information may be found in journal articles rather than in books.

2. *Conduct a subject or keyword search of the library's electronic databases,* which will enable you to find relevant journal articles as well as books, book chapters, technical reports, and other written materials. Of particular value for social scientists are discipline-specific databases such as Sociological Abstracts, SocIndex, and PsycINFO. Also of great use is the JSTOR database, which can be searched by discipline, and WorldCat.org, which provides a listing of library holdings for "more than 10,000 libraries worldwide," according to its website.

3. *View initial results with the aim of narrowing your topic.* It is not unusual for initial searches to yield results numbering in the thousands. If this occurs, the topic is probably too broad, and you will need to refine your search. By looking at a few of the initial screens, you can quickly see what kind of research is being done and then choose a term to add to the search in order to narrow the results. You can narrow your search by inserting the operators AND or NOT between search terms or by enclosing exact phrases in quotation marks. For example, "sports participation AND grades" is much more limited than just "sports participation." Also be aware that the words you choose can make a difference—decreasing or increasing the number of relevant citations; so, try different words—"well-being" and "happiness," "grades" and "academic performance."

4. *Locate relevant references by reading titles and abstracts.* It is usually impossible—and, fortunately, unnecessary—to read the full text of every article, book chapter, or other citation you find in your search. Rather, it will be sufficient to locate relevant literature by reading titles and, if available, abstracts, which are concise summaries of the content of an article. Once you have begun to narrow your topic and have identified relevant articles, you should read the full text. Fortunately, databases usually indicate whether the "full text" of an article is available online; if the article is not available

continues

continued

online, you'll need to see if the library has a print copy of the journal or order a copy of the article through interlibrary loan.

5. *Read the most recent literature first and then work backward.* Given that all researchers place their work in the context of prior research and theory, the latest articles will provide the most up-to-date references. Citations in many databases are listed in reverse chronological order or can be listed by date, which makes it easy to find the latest published research. In addition, some databases, such as Google Scholar, indicate which studies have cited a reference, so that you can trace a line of inquiry back or forward in time. The search images here illustrate this for the topic of "hooking up," showing that Kathleen Boggle's book, *Hooking Up: Sex, Dating, and Relationships on Campus* (2008) is the most widely cited reference in Figure A; selected literature that cites this book is shown in Figure B. (Be aware, though, that not everything in Google Scholar has been published nor are all publications of the same quality.) Finally, if the full text of an article is available online, citations in the text may be hyperlinked. By examining these additional articles and books for further references, you can "reference-hop" your way through the literature, which should enable you quickly to gain a command of research and theory on the topic.

6. *Search for review articles that summarize the literature on the particular topic*, as these are the best source of information on existing research and theory. Database results will include several types of references. Most articles will consist of reports of empirical research; a few will present a new theory or theoretical synthesis; a few others will consist of commentaries. In addition, there are serial publications such as the *Annual Review of Sociology* that specialize in review articles. You may want to do a keyword search that combines your topic with the term "review" or "annual review."

7. *Use database information to evaluate the quality and importance of a citation.* Some databases indicate whether a journal publication is *peer-reviewed*—that is, subject to the

BOX 4.1 FIGURE A
Google Scholar search for "hooking up."

BOX 4.1 FIGURE B
Google Scholar search for "Hooking up: Sex, dating, and relationships on campus."

evaluation of fellow academics and researchers—an important distinction between scholarly and popular publications. Some databases also indicate the number of times an article has been cited by other references in the database. This could be very useful information as it might indicate the significance of the reported study.

8. *Use the Internet sparingly and selectively.* Although in today's world students are understandably inclined to start any quest for information by searching the Internet, it is important to recognize that the Internet has limited utility for reviewing the social science literature. Internet searches tend to yield extremely large lists of citations or "hits," many of which will be irrelevant to your interests. It is also necessary to evaluate Internet search results carefully because authorship can range from grade-school students to government agencies to political interest groups to profit-making businesses that seek to promote a given viewpoint or body of knowledge. On the other hand, once you have narrowed your topic, the Internet has many valuable resources to help you conduct your research. For instance, one of the largest depositories of social science data is the Inter-university Consortium for Political and Social Research (ICPSR), found at http://www.icpsr.umich.edu/icpsrweb/landing.jsp. The website of the General Social Survey (GSS) offers datafiles, codebooks, and other documentation available to download or order. You also can obtain data online from numerous US government and international agencies, which are outlined in Chapter 10.

9. *Organize your references, perhaps with reference management software.* Although the authors of this textbook are "old school" in that we simply download references to folders on our computers, there are a variety of programs, such as EndNote, Zotero, Mendeley, and RefWorks, that not only allow you to store bibliographic files but also create reference pages from these files.

Formulate Research Question

Once you choose a general topic, you must state it in researchable terms. This involves translating the topic into one or more research questions. A scientific research question is one that is answerable through the systematic collection and analysis of verifiable data. By way of contrast, some questions cannot be answered because they are beyond the realm of science (e.g., Does God exist? Is capital punishment morally wrong?).

Social scientists ask research questions for different purposes. One purpose is description. *Descriptive* research questions seek basic information, which may begin with questions of Who? What? When? Where? Descriptive research questions about the topic of capital punishment might include: What is capital punishment? When was it first implemented? Where is it practiced today? In this case, the answers define and describe the history and contemporary variation in capital punishment: capital punishment is the legal practice of killing people who commit serious crimes; it dates back to biblical times; and it is carried out in more than 50 countries today, including the United States, North Korea, and Iran (Smith 2016).

All research must accurately describe the phenomenon under investigation, and some surveys and field research may have this as their primary purpose. More often, though, researchers want to go beyond description to develop theory by *explaining* how the social world works. *Explanatory* research questions ask why and how phenomena occur. For example, why is capital punishment practiced in the United States today but not in many European countries? Why does the majority of the US population support capital punishment? How and why has support for capital punishment in the United States changed over time?

Whether descriptive or explanatory, what makes for a good research question? First, research questions should be "interesting," according to Glenn Firebaugh (2008). What Firebaugh means is that beyond being interesting to you, research questions should contribute to ongoing conversations in a scientific field of study. Based on her literature review, Beckett Broh formulated three unanswered research questions:

- Why does sports participation boost students' achievement? Does sports participation benefit students' development and social networks, and are these the mechanisms that link participation to educational outcomes?
- Are the educational benefits of sports participation unique to sports, or do non-sports extracurricular activities also promote achievement?
- Do nonsports extracurricular activities benefit students' development and social networks? (Broh 2002:73)

Broh's research questions were "interesting" because they extended prior research in new directions. (Also of interest, albeit much less common, are research questions that challenge well-established findings.) Her questions extended research in two ways: by broadening the question to include participation in nonsports activities as well as interscholastic sports and by identifying theoretical links to account for the influence of sports participation on grades.

Second, good research questions should be focused. To pursue the topic of social class in educational institutions for her dissertation research, Jessica Calarco (2011) had to narrow her focus and formulate a question that could be answered empirically. Focusing on student–teacher interactions, Calarco asked, "What role do children play in educational stratification?" and "Does children's social class background encourage classroom behavior that creates different learning opportunities?" Then, as her research unfolded, she concentrated on a more specific form of classroom behavior, asking: "Do students from different social class backgrounds differ in how they seek help in the classroom?"

Finally, research questions must be manageable or feasible in terms of time, available resources, and other considerations. For example, if you were working on a term project, it clearly would be impractical to pose a research question that would require 6 months of fieldwork. Broh and Calarco were graduate students when they conducted their research, which meant that they had relatively limited access to resources. Broh discovered, however, that her research questions could be answered through the analysis of available survey data. Calarco was able to secure funding for her research.

Prepare Research Design

Having formulated your research question, you are ready to plan your research. The overall plan, called the research design, should carefully spell out how you will answer your question: what kind of data you will gather, and how you will gather and analyze the data. Of course, we cannot expect you to be able to fully prepare a research design at this point; to do so requires a more complete understanding of the research process, something you will gain from reading the whole book. Therefore, our objective in this chapter is to orient you to the design process by introducing the basic options for gathering and analyzing appropriate data. As we outline these options, we also will familiarize you with the language of social research.

In discussing issues of research design, we focus on explanatory research questions. Although the variety of explanatory research questions that could be asked is endless, many of them can be subsumed under two "ideal" types: quantitative and qualitative. Social scientists commonly use these labels to describe two broad methodological approaches to social research: a quantitative approach that tends to produce numerical (quantitative) data and a qualitative approach that results in nonnumerical (qualitative) data. However, the data and the methods used to generate them flow from the types of questions that are asked. Since each type has very

quantitative research question A question that asks about the relationship between two or more variables.

qualitative research question A question that asks about social processes or the meaning and cultural significance of people's actions.

different implications for research design, we discuss them separately in detail in the following sections. In brief, **quantitative research questions** ask: Is there a relationship between X and Y, controlling for other factors? To answer the question, X and Y must be carefully defined and measured *before* the researcher gathers data. **Qualitative research questions** ask about the meaning and cultural significance of social phenomena. They also ask if patterns or relationships exist in people's lives, but they focus on the social processes that produce these patterns and on what the patterns mean to the actors themselves and to the larger society. Unlike quantitative questions, qualitative questions do not necessarily specify relationships or define concepts before data collection and analysis.

SUMMARY

The initial steps in the process of social research are choosing a topic, narrowing the topic through a literature review, formulating a research question, and preparing a research design. The selection of a research topic may be influenced by the ongoing development of theory and research, a concern with social problems, and/or one's personal background and experiences. A literature review not only helps to narrow the research topic, it also situates the proposed study in the context of ongoing research and theory. Knowing what has and has not been done on your research topic allows you to ask a specific research question, which should be "interesting," focused, and practically manageable. The research design is a detailed plan for how the research question will be answered: what kind of data will be gathered, how they will be gathered, and how they will be analyzed. The type of research question influences what kinds of research designs are appropriate. Quantitative and qualitative research questions are two main types.

DESIGNING RESEARCH TO ANSWER QUANTITATIVE QUESTIONS

Social researchers addressing quantitative questions assume that the social world operates according to the same kind of universal laws found in the natural world. Such laws generally take the form of a functional relationship between phenomena. One example is Newton's second law of motion: Force = Mass × Acceleration. The force with which a bowling ball strikes pins is equal to the ball's mass times how fast the ball is rolled. Similarly, from a quantitative perspective, scientific understanding amounts to uncovering general relationships. Much of the research on quantitative questions follows the deductive model of inquiry and has the immediate aim of testing hypotheses.

You might remember that a hypothesis is an expected but unconfirmed relationship between two or more phenomena; it is essentially a tentative answer to a research question. Much of the time, the goal of quantitative research is to identify one or more **causal relationships**. For example, Beckett Broh asked whether there is a relationship between participation in interscholastic athletics and academic performance. Assuming that participation *causes* athletes to receive higher grades than nonathletes, she also asked how this could occur: Do athletes benefit educationally from their development and social networks?

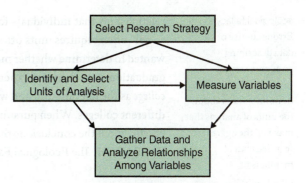

FIGURE 4.2
Steps to Consider in Designing Research to Answer Quantitative Questions

To answer quantitative questions, what do you need to do? Because you want to establish *general* patterns, you need to examine data across many cases and then determine whether the phenomena of interest (e.g., athletic participation and grades) are related to one another. To determine whether a relationship exists, you need to produce numerical data that can be analyzed statistically. Figure 4.2 shows the steps you will need to consider to gather and analyze this kind of data.

Select a Research Strategy

The first step is to select a data-collection strategy or approach. Your primary choices are to design an experiment, conduct a survey, or analyze existing data. Specifics of when and how to employ each of these data-collection methods will be discussed in later chapters. Beckett Broh analyzed data from the National Educational Longitudinal Survey (NELS). She chose this dataset because it contained abundant information on high school students' participation in extracurricular activities as well as their grades and standardized test scores.

Identify and Select Units of Analysis

After selecting a research strategy, you need to define your unit of analysis. **Units of analysis** are the cases or entities you study; they are the things you describe and compare. Social scientists study a variety of units, including individual people; a wide range of social groupings such as families, organizations, and cities; and various social artifacts such as books, periodicals, and television programs. Selecting a unit generally depends on the object of study. In Broh's study, the unit of analysis was *individuals* or, more precisely, individual high school students, for it is individual students who participate in sports and receive grades.

In much social research, however, social scientists are less interested in individual differences than in the impact of the social context on people in general, the social

causal relationship
A relationship in which it is theorized that changes in one variable produce or bring about changes in another variable.

units of analysis The entities such as people, nations, and artifacts that are studied, which are described and compared in terms of variables.

ecological fallacy
Erroneous use of
data describing
an aggregate unit
(e.g., organizations) to
draw inferences about
the units of analysis that
make up the aggregate
(e.g., individual
members of
organizations).

relationships that individuals form, and large-scale social processes. To analyze "the social" often requires units other than individuals. For example, suppose a researcher wanted to determine whether more expensive colleges (in terms of tuition) have higher graduation rates than less expensive ones. In this case, the researcher would treat the *college* as the relevant unit and would gather data on the tuition and graduation rates of different colleges. When pursuing a question like this, however, researchers need to be careful about the conclusions they draw, as discussed in Box 4.2, READING SOCIAL RESEARCH: The Ecological Fallacy.

BOX 4.2

READING SOCIAL RESEARCH

The Ecological Fallacy

As a general rule, researchers should restrict their conclusions to the units of analysis to which their data pertain. Otherwise, they risk committing a logical fallacy. One such fallacy that seems to occur often in everyday life is called the "fallacy of division": assuming that what holds true of a group also is true of individuals within the group. Knowing that Sally attended a college in which the average graduation rate was relatively low, you would commit this fallacy if you assumed that Sally herself did not graduate.

The fallacy of division is quite similar to what social scientists call the **ecological fallacy**. This can occur in social research when relationships between properties of groups or geographic areas are used to make inferences about the individual behaviors of the people within those groups or areas (Robinson 1950). In the past, criminologists analyzed the relationship between neighborhood crime rates and other characteristics of these neighborhoods in order to draw conclusions about characteristics of individual criminals. A typical erroneous conclusion might be that foreign-born persons commit more crimes than native-born persons because the crime rate is higher in areas with greater proportions of foreigners. But such a conclusion is

clearly unwarranted because the data do not tell us who actually committed the crimes—foreign or native-born persons. In fact, studies in the United States consistently show that immigrants are less likely to commit crimes than the native-born (Hagan and Palloni 1998; Martinez and Lee 2000; see also Kubrin and Desmond 2015:346). Similarly, Durkheim's classic study of suicide was subject to the ecological fallacy by inferring that Protestants commit more suicides than Catholics from the observation that suicide rates were higher in predominantly Protestant nations than in predominantly Catholic ones.

It is not always wrong to draw conclusions about individual-level processes from aggregate or group-level data. Social scientists have identified conditions under which it is reasonable to make such inferences (Firebaugh 1978), although it is often difficult to determine if these conditions are met. The implications of the ecological fallacy, however, are clear: when reading research, pay attention to the unit of analysis and ask whether it matches the conclusions. If you are interested in individuals but only group-level data are available, then be sure to recognize the possibility of an ecological fallacy.

For studies of social and cultural change, especially of the distant past, investigators often make creative use of social artifacts as units of analysis. To examine how changes in the cultural images of African Americans from the mid- to late 20th century were related to racial conflict in the larger society, Bernice Pescosolido, Elizabeth Grauerholz, and Melissa Milkie (1997) used two different units of analysis: US children's picture books and *New York Times* articles. Analyzing the portrayal of blacks in over 2,400 children's picture books between 1937 and 1993, the researchers were able to show an increase in the visibility of black characters. By counting the number of *New York Times* articles reporting instances of racial conflict, they also showed how the shifting visibility of black characters was linked to patterns of social conflict.

Once you have identified the type of unit to study, you must decide how many of such units to choose and how to choose them—that is, what method of selection to use. Because Broh was using available survey data, she did not have to design a sampling procedure; nonetheless, it was an important aspect of the data she used. In many surveys that address quantitative research questions, units are chosen randomly from a specified population through some form of probability sampling. This was true of the NELS, which randomly selected students from the nearly 40,000 high schools nationwide. In Chapter 6 we describe sampling in depth.

Measure Variables

Once you've identified your unit of analysis, you are ready to consider the measurement of variables. We devote an entire chapter (Chapter 5) to this aspect of research design. For now, you need to understand what variables are and the different types of variables that appear in a quantitative research design.

WHAT IS A VARIABLE?

Measurement is the bridge between theory and research; it is the means by which social scientists translate abstract concepts into concrete variables. **Concepts** are the building blocks of theory; they are the terms scientists use to group together phenomena that have important things in common. In Émile Durkheim's theory of suicide, the key concepts were suicide and social integration. Broh's research linked the concepts of sports participation and academic achievement. A **variable** is a *measured* concept that varies from one case to the next or over time within a given case. For example, individuals may differ with respect to age, sex, and class year (first, second, third, fourth); and a given individual may change in age, level of education (first grade, second grade, etc.), or income (dollars earned per year). One way Broh measured academic achievement was by examining students' grades, specifically focusing on their English grades. This variable varies across students, as Figure 4.3 shows: for example, Student #1 got a C; student #2 got a B; student #3 got

concept Terms scientists use to group together phenomena that have important things in common.

variable A measured concept that may vary across cases or across time.

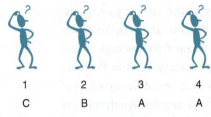

Student #	1	2	3	4
English grade	C	B	A	A

FIGURE 4.3
Variation in English Grades among Four Students

dependent variable
The variable that the researcher tries to explain or predict; the presumed effect in a causal relationship.

independent variable
A presumed influence or cause of a dependent variable.

extraneous variable
A variable that is not part of a hypothesized relationship.

antecedent variable
A variable that occurs before, and may be a cause of, both the independent and dependent variables in a causal relationship.

intervening variable
A variable that is intermediate between two other variables in a causal relationship; it is an effect of one and a cause of the other.

an A; and student #4 got an A. Note, too, that individuals may have the same value on a variable, just as students #3 and #4 both got an "A." Now, can you imagine what Broh's data look like for more than 10,000 students?

Take care not to confuse variables with the attributes or categories they consist of. "Political party" (in the United States) is a variable consisting of categories such as Democrat, Republican, and so forth; "Democrat" and "Republican" by themselves are not variables but simply specific categories that distinguish persons who belong to different political parties. Likewise, "divorced" is not a variable but a category of the variable "marital status." To keep this distinction clear, note that any term you might use to describe yourself or someone else (e.g., sophomore, sociology major) is an attribute or category of a variable (academic class, major), not a variable in itself.

TYPES OF VARIABLES

In designing research to answer quantitative research questions, you need to know the differences among several types of variables. The most important distinction is between independent and dependent variables. A **dependent variable** is the outcome that one is interested in explaining or predicting. It is the variable that is thought to *depend on* or be influenced by other variables. The variables that do the influencing are **independent**. (Here is one way to remember this: **I**ndependent = **I**nfluences and **D**ependent = influence**D**.) For example, when Broh hypothesized that sports participation enhanced academic achievement, her independent variable consisted of whether students reported that they participated in interscholastic sports and a dependent variable was grades in English. Figure 4.4, which is an elaboration of Figure 4.3, helps you to visualize this.

Quantitative research questions are concerned with the relationship between independent and dependent variables. But as you design your research, you also need to consider the relevance of **extraneous variables,** which are other variables that are not specified in your question or hypothesis. Especially important are extraneous variables that may affect the independent variable, the dependent variable, or both. For example, can you think of anything that might explain why students participate in sports or get good grades? In relation to specific independent and dependent variables, extraneous variables may be *antecedent* or *intervening*. An **antecedent variable** occurs prior in time to both the independent and dependent variable. Antecedent variables in Broh's study were parents' income and a student's race and sex; each of these variables can affect both sports participation and grades. An **intervening variable**, on the other hand, is one that is both an effect of the independent variable and a cause of the dependent variable. A key intervening variable that Broh considered was a measure of students' social capital, a concept related to one's social network. Sports participation could affect students' social capital, which in turn could affect a student's academic performance. Figure 4.5 depicts these examples of antecedent and intervening variables. Each arrow in the figure represents causal direction. Thus, "Parents' income → Participation in interscholastic sports" means that parents' income influences or causes students' sports participation, and the absence of an arrow means that one variable does not cause another.

Extraneous variables also may be either controlled or uncontrolled. Controlled or, more commonly, **control variables** are held constant, or prevented from varying during the course of observation or analysis. One aim of quantitative research design is for researchers to identify potentially relevant extraneous variables and then control as many as is feasible, often with the goal of ruling out these variables as possible explanations of the hypothesized relationship. Experiments, discussed in Chapter 7, control extraneous variables by creating experimental and control groups that are the same in all respects except for the independent variable. In nonexperimental studies, quantitative researchers attempt to measure and then *statistically* control for extraneous variables. This is what Broh did. Using quantitative data analysis techniques discussed in Chapter 12, she statistically controlled for numerous extraneous variables, including parents' income, students' race and sex, and school size. This enabled her to test the influence of these variables on the relationship between sports participation and academic achievement. As we discuss below, a researcher can only control what can be observed and measured, meaning that some variables in survey and other research may be uncontrolled due to their exclusion from the analysis.

You are now in a position to test your understanding of variables and units of analysis. Box 4.3, CHECKING YOUR UNDERSTANDING: Quantitative Research Questions, Units of Analysis, and Variables, is designed to help you do this.

Gather Data and Analyze the Relationships Among Variables

Selecting units of analysis and measuring variables are the key design elements for gathering data to address quantitative questions. But to properly design research, you also must anticipate how you will

	Student #	1	2	3	4
Dependent Variable:	English grade	C	B	A	A
Independent Variable:	Interscholastic Sports Participation	No	Yes	Yes	Yes

FIGURE 4.4
Dependent and Independent Variables in Broh's (2002) Study

control variable A variable that is not allowed to vary or otherwise held constant during the course of data collection or analysis.

FIGURE 4.5
Antecedent and Intervening Variables

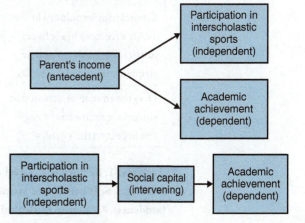

BOX 4.3

CHECKING YOUR UNDERSTANDING

Quantitative Research Questions, Units of Analysis, and Variables

Take a look at Table A. The first column presents six quantitative research questions or hypotheses; the second and third columns identify the relevant units of analysis and variables. For the sample research question in the first row ("Are older people more afraid . . ."), note that the unit of analysis is "Individuals" and the variables are "Age" and "fear of crime." Fill in the numbered blanks for the remaining questions and then check your responses against the answers at the bottom of the table.

Table A Fill in the Blanks

Research Question/ Hypothesis: What One Wants to Know	Unit of Analysis: Entities That Are Described and Compared	Variables: Characteristics in Terms of Which Entities Are Described and Compared
Are older people more afraid of crime than younger people?	Individuals	Age, fear of crime
The higher the proportion of female employees in a factory, the lower the wages.	1._____	Proportion of employees who are female, average wage
Does economic development lower the birth rate?	Nations	2._____, birth rate
The longer the engagement period, the longer the marriage.	3._____	Length of engagement, 4._____
Comic strips introduced in the 1930s were more likely to emphasize powerful heroes than strips introduced in the 1920s.	Comic strips	Whether main characters in strip were powerful, 5._____
Does the amount of alcohol that students consume have a negative impact on their grades?	6._____	7._____, grade-point average

Answers: 1. Factories. 2. Level of economic development. 3. Couples. 4. Length of marriage. 5. When comic strips were introduced (1920s or 1930s). 6. Individuals (students). 7. Amount of alcohol consumed.

analyze the data you collect. As we noted, one of the main goals of quantitative research is to identify causal relationships. So, what kind of evidence is necessary to infer that one variable causes another? In everyday terms, a *cause* is something that makes something else happen or change. It seems obvious that a rock thrown against a window will *cause* the glass to shatter. However, in contrast to this implicit understanding of causality that seems to exist in everyday life, the meaning of the concept of "cause" has been hotly debated by philosophers and scientists for centuries (Hume [1748] 1951). Although social scientists have continued to debate the notion of causality (Blalock 1964; Bunge 1979; Pearl 2010), researchers generally agree that at least three kinds of evidence are needed to establish causality: association, direction of influence, and nonspuriousness.

ASSOCIATION

The first criterion to establish causality is association. Two or more variables are associated, or form a relationship, to the extent that changes in one are accompanied by systematic changes in the other(s): if one variable changes, the other variable changes, and if one variable does not change, the other does not change. Suppose, for example, that you wanted to examine the relationship between a person's race and 2016 presidential vote choice. The kind of data you need could be gathered in a survey, where the units of analysis are individual respondents or voters. In fact, on Election Day, November 8, 2016, exit polls conducted across the country asked respondents to fill out questionnaires as they left voting stations. In addition to whom they voted for, respondents were asked about their sex, age, race, and ethnicity among other questions. Table 4.1 provides answers for four hypothetical respondents. Notice that these data form a perfectly consistent pattern: if one variable changes (from white to black), the other variable changes (from Donald J. Trump to Hillary Clinton); if one variable remains the same, as race does for the first and second respondents, both of whom are white, the other variable remains the same (i.e., both voted for Trump).

Of course, in real life we never see perfect relationships; so, researchers have devised statistics for determining whether there is an association between two variables. To understand how these statistics work, let's examine actual data from

Table 4.1 Answers for Four Hypothetical Respondents

Respondent	Race	Vote for President
1	White	Donald J. Trump
2	White	Donald J. Trump
3	Black	Hillary Clinton
4	Black	Hillary Clinton

Table 4.2 Vote for Presidential Candidate by Race, 2016 President Exit Polls

Candidate	Voter Race	
	White	Black
Hillary Clinton	39.4%	91.7%
Donald J. Trump	60.6%	8.3%
Total	100.0%	100.0%
Number of voters	(16,390)	(2,859)

Source: National Election Pool 2016 Presidential Election Exit Poll; based on results reported by CNN (http://edition.cnn.com/election/results/exit-polls).

the 2016 presidential election exit polls, conducted by Edison Research. Table 4.2 presents the data for the 19,249 respondents who identified themselves as either black or white and as voting for either Clinton or Trump (excluded are other races, other candidate choices, and those who didn't respond). As the table shows, 39.4 percent of whites as compared with 91.7 percent of blacks voted for Clinton; therefore, blacks were more likely to vote for Clinton. The difference in vote choice for Clinton between blacks and whites is 52.3 percent (91.7–39.4), which represents a crude measure of association called the "percentage difference." The larger the percentage difference, the more likely that an association exists. In fact, another statistic, called a *test of statistical significance,* indicates that the difference is so large that, given the sample size, it is unlikely to have occurred at random or by chance. We have much more to say about statistics in Chapter 12, on quantitative data analysis. Read Box 4.4, READING SOCIAL RESEARCH: How to Interpret Correlations and Tests of Statistical Significance, to better understand the meaning of statistics commonly reported in the social science literature.

DIRECTION OF INFLUENCE

The second criterion needed to infer a causal relationship is direction of influence. The direction of influence should be from cause to effect. Thus, if A is a cause of B, then changes in A should bring about changes in B, and not vice versa. For many relationships in social research the direction of influence between variables is easily determined by their *temporal order*—that is, which variable comes first in time. For example, characteristics fixed at birth, such as a person's age, come before characteristics developed later in life, such as a person's education or political party preference, and it is hard to imagine how changes in the latter could influence changes in the former.

BOX 4.4

READING SOCIAL RESEARCH

How to Interpret Correlations and Tests of Statistical Significance

As you read reports of quantitative studies as well as Chapters 5–11 in this book, you will encounter two kinds of statistics that indicate whether an association exists between variables: measures of degree of association and tests of statistical significance. Both kinds of statistics are explained in detail in Chapter 12. For now, we want to give you enough information to understand how to interpret study findings.

Many statistics are available for determining the degree of association between variables. Which statistic is used depends largely on the types of variables being analyzed. The "percentage difference" in Table 4.2 may be applied to two variables with nonnumerical categories, such as race and vote for presidential candidate. For variables with numerical categories, such as age and income, the most common statistic is the Pearson product-moment correlation coefficient, or *correlation coefficient*—often represented by the symbol *r*. Correlation coefficients vary from 0 to 1 (or −1), where 0 indicates that there is no association and 1 (or −1) indicates that there is a perfect association. (The correlation coefficient, including the meaning of the sign, + or −, is explained further in Chapter 12.) Analyzing data from the NELS, Beckett Broh found a correlation of .74 between students'

senior-year English and math grades. This is a strong correlation, and it indicates that students who earned higher grades in English tended to earn higher grades in math.

In Broh's study, this coefficient was **statistically significant**, which means that the association is unlikely to have occurred at random or by chance. In research reports or articles, you may read that an association is "statistically significant at $p < .05$." The lowercase *p* stands for "probability"; "$p < .05$" means that the probability is less than .05, or 5 in 100, that the association could have occurred randomly, assuming that there is no relationship in the larger population from which the sample was drawn. With odds this low, we can be confident that the result would not have occurred by chance and that there is an association between the variables in the larger population.

When we applied a test of significance, *chi-square*, to the sample data in Table 4.2, the relationship between 2016 presidential vote choice and race was statistically significant; therefore, we can be confident that this relationship exists among the larger population of all voters in the 2016 election. Similarly, Broh found that an association between athletic participation and high school grades was statistically significant.

Direction of influence is not always so easy to determine, however. Recall, for example, our discussion of the racial contact hypothesis in Chapter 2. Analyzing data from a survey in which individuals were questioned at one point in time about their beliefs and their contact with people of different races, Dixon and Rosenbaum (2004) found some associations between stereotypes and interracial contact: the more contact a person has with members of other races, the less likely he or she is to hold certain negative stereotypes. One possible interpretation is that racial contact increases familiarity and contradicts stereotypes, thereby reducing prejudice. An equally plausible interpretation

statistical significance The likelihood that the results of a study, such as an association between variables, could have occurred by chance.

is that prejudiced people will avoid contact while tolerant people will readily interact with other races, so that racial prejudice influences racial contact. Without information on temporal ordering, it is difficult to know the direction of influence or, in other words, which variable is the cause and which the effect.

Direction of influence was an issue in the Broh study. An association between sports participation and grades could mean that playing sports has educational benefits, but it also could mean that higher-achieving, "good" students are more likely to choose or be selected to play sports than other students. Because Broh hypothesized that sports participation had a positive influence on grades, it was important for her to rule out the possibility that superior academic performance leads to sports participation. She accomplished this in part by examining the association between sports participation in the 10th and 12th grades with grades received in the 12th grade, so that continuous participation preceded the measurement of academic performance. As we discuss in later chapters, the timing of observations is an important dimension of research design. As you will see, experiments (Chapter 7) and longitudinal survey designs (Chapter 8) provide direct evidence of temporal ordering.

NONSPURIOUSNESS (NO COMMON CAUSE)

The final criterion for inferring causality is that two variables that are associated statistically should have no common cause. If two variables happen to be related to a common extraneous or third variable, then a statistical association can exist between the original two variables even if there is no inherent link between them. Therefore, to infer a causal relationship from an observed correlation, there should be good reason to believe that there are no "hidden" factors that could have created an accidental or spurious relationship between the variables. When an association between variables *cannot* be explained by an extraneous variable, the relationship is said to be *nonspurious*. When an association has been produced by an extraneous third factor and neither of the variables involved in the association has influenced the other, it is called a **spurious relationship**.

spurious relationship
A noncausal statistical association between two variables produced by a common cause (i.e., an antecedent variable).

The idea of spuriousness is obvious when we consider a popular example in the social sciences. Surprisingly, there is a positive correlation in Europe between the number of storks in a geographic area and the number of births in that area (Wallis and Roberts 1956:79): As the number of storks in an area increases, so too does the number of births. Does this mean that storks bring babies? This correlation might explain how the legend that storks bring babies got started, but it hardly warrants a causal inference. Rather, the correlation is produced by the size of the population. Storks like to nest in the crannies and chimneys of buildings, so as the population and thus the number of buildings increases, the number of places for storks to nest increases. And as the population increases, so does the number of babies. In short, the original relationship is an incidental consequence of a common cause: an antecedent extraneous variable. The size of the population accounts for *both* the number of storks and the number of births, as depicted in Figure 4.6.

In actual research, spurious relationships are much less apparent, and the possibility often exists that an unknown variable may have produced an observed association. To infer that a relationship is nonspurious, researchers must identify and control for extraneous variables that might account for an association. Circumstances seldom allow for the control of all variables; therefore, researchers attempt to control the effects of as many as possible. The greater the number of variables controlled without altering a relationship, the greater the likelihood that the relationship is not spurious.

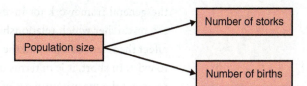

FIGURE 4.6
Example of a Spurious Association

Recall that Broh statistically controlled for several variables, including students' race and sex. This is a very common practice in the analysis of survey data. The major drawback to this method is that one can control statistically only for those variables that have been observed or measured as part of the research. Hence, the effects of any unknown or unmeasured variables cannot be assessed. A stronger test of nonspuriousness is provided in experiments through a process called *randomization*. When participants in an experiment are randomly assigned to an experimental or "control" group, it is assumed that the groups are equivalent—that is, all extraneous variables have been controlled. We discuss randomized experiments in Chapter 7; we discuss causal analysis techniques involving statistical manipulation of nonexperimental data in Chapter 12.

CAUSATION, INTERVENING VARIABLES, AND THEORY

In addition to association, direction of influence, and nonspuriousness, the specification of an intervening mechanism or variable can strengthen causal inferences. Though not a necessary causal criterion, intervening variables are nonetheless an essential part of scientific inquiry. Often, in fact, this is what the development and testing of theory is all about. For example, Durkheim's theory of suicide stipulated the intervening causal mechanism—social integration—for a number of relationships. The reason that fewer suicides are found among Catholics than among Protestants and that there are fewer suicides among married than among single people, according to the theory, is that being a Catholic and being married each engenders a greater sense of social integration. This greater sense of social integration, in turn, reduces the likelihood that anyone within the group will commit suicide.

In her research, Broh specifically tested the effects of several intervening variables derived from theory. Having found that participation in interscholastic sports benefits students' academic performance, she also showed that this relationship was best explained by developmental and social capital theories. High school athletes develop a greater work ethic and sense of control over their lives than do nonathletes, and their athletic participation generates stronger ties among students, parents, and teachers, all of which have positive effects on academic performance.

By specifying intervening variables, theories render a more complete understanding of the causal processes that connect events. Equally important, theories provide the general framework for investigating the nature of all relationships. Theories tell the researcher which relationships to observe, what extraneous variables are likely to affect the relationships, and the conditions under which a causal relationship is likely to exist. In short, it is in terms of some theory that the researcher can determine how to assess the meaningfulness of a "weak" association and how to test for direction of influence and nonspuriousness. Thus, we see again the importance of the interplay between theory and research in science. Theory guides research, and research provides the findings that validate and suggest modifications in theory.

SUMMARY

Quantitative research questions focus on relationships between variables, often with the explicit aim of establishing *causal* relationships, in which the independent variable is the presumed cause and the dependent variable is the presumed effect. Designing research to answer quantitative questions involves selecting a research strategy (e.g., experiments, surveys, or existing data analysis), selecting units of analysis, specifying and deciding how to measure variables, and considering how the data will be analyzed. Three criteria are assumed to be requisites of a causal relationship: association, direction of influence, and nonspuriousness. In addition, the specification of an intervening variable or mechanism can strengthen causal inferences. Theory plays an important role in quantitative research not only in specifying intervening variables but also in shaping the overall research design.

DESIGNING RESEARCH TO ANSWER QUALITATIVE QUESTIONS

FIGURE 4.7
"Snow"?

One way in which the social sciences differ from the natural sciences is that, unlike nonliving things, plants, and lower animals, humans can interpret and interact with the world around them. To fully understand *human* action, therefore, we must take into account the actor's point of view (Simmel 1972; Weber [1905] 1998). Qualitative questions take this perspective; they ask about the meaning and purpose of human actions, both for individuals and for social groups (Schwartz-Shea and Yanow 2012). They also examine the social processes and interactions that produce patterns in society. The aim is to develop theory and deepen understanding by providing in-depth knowledge.

Recall that Jessica Calarco (2011) asked if children's social class background encourages classroom

behavior that creates different learning opportunities. To address this question, she focused specifically on how children seek help from their teachers. In doing so, she examined the meaning and process of children's help-seeking actions—how teachers interpret them, how children profit from them, and how they translate into educational inequalities. (We should add that her research also ultimately addressed a quantitative question about a relationship between variables: How do different forms of help-seeking differ by social class?)

The importance of understanding meaning—and how one thing can mean quite another depending on people's interpretations of it—is evident when we consider a popular example from anthropology (Boas 1911): When you look at the photograph in Figure 4.7, what do you see? Whereas some people may see "snow," others may see something entirely different. In fact, Boas (1911) wrote that the Inuit group he studied had about 50 words for "snow." The different words reflect different types of precipitation that the Inuit experience living in extremely frigid areas: wet snow, salt-like snow, hard-falling snow, and so forth. These interpretations also have consequences for action. Wet snow (*matsaaruti* in local dialect), for example, helps to ice the runners on one's sleigh (Krupnik and Müller-Willie 2010; Robson 2013).

Developing an in-depth understanding of human thought and action requires researchers to "get inside" the individual—to discover his or her interpretations, experiences, intentions, and motives (Schwarz and Jacobs 1979). To represent this inside view, researchers tend not to count or assign numbers to observations but rather to produce data in the form of ordinary language consisting of quotations and detailed descriptions. Unlike research on quantitative questions, research on qualitative questions is more open-ended, as researchers generally aim to develop rather than test theory. Therefore, the research design is more flexible. Typically, researchers begin by carefully selecting a few research sites or cases, keep a record of observations, and then code, analyze data, and develop theoretical concepts throughout the process of data collection. Figure 4.8 depicts the steps you will need to consider in designing research to answer qualitative questions.

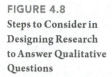

FIGURE 4.8
Steps to Consider in Designing Research to Answer Qualitative Questions

Select Research Strategy

Just as in research designs for quantitative questions, the first step is to select a data-collection strategy. However, the strategies suitable for exploring qualitative questions are quite different. Researchers asking qualitative questions may conduct field research, carry out in-depth interviews, read and interpret archival records, or use some combination of these strategies. The research question will determine which strategy is most appropriate.

Calarco's interest in linking inequality to classroom interaction led her to do field research in a public elementary school, where she observed students' behaviors and teachers' responses. In addition to observing classrooms,

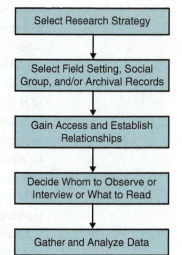

Calarco (2011:866) interviewed the teachers at her field site, "asking about their expectations for students and about students' home lives, academic strengths and weaknesses, and progress over time." We explain when and how to do field research and in-depth interviews in Chapter 9.

Archival records are a form of existing data used in both quantitative and qualitative research, but the types of archival records used vary. Max Weber, for instance, combed through diaries, religious sermons, and other written materials to understand how the religious tenets of Protestantism fostered a personal work ethic conducive to the development of capitalism (Weber [1905] 1998). Kai Erikson (1966) analyzed court records and personal journals to study three crime waves in Puritan New England, including the famous witchcraft hysteria in colonial Salem. Our discussion of qualitative research design focuses here primarily on observations and interviews from field research, but we make mention of archival records below and discuss one method of analyzing archival records in Chapter 10.

Select Field Setting, Social Group, and/or Archival Records

In order to gain an in-depth understanding, qualitative researchers generally select a relatively small number of cases or often a single setting to extract the meaning of, or describe the processes shaping, people's actions in a given context. Qualitative research questions thus tend to be connected with a particular setting, time period, or group or with some combination of these (Schwartz-Shea and Yanow 2012). To return to the "snow" example, you might see how a quantitative concern with the relationship between temperature and the amount of snowfall all over the world would obscure the local differences in the very meaning of snow and its consequences.

To see how the research setting is chosen to fit the question, let's consider Calarco's study. Inspired by the work of Annette Lareau (2011), whose research had shown social class differences in parent–student interactions in two different schools, Calarco (personal communication 2013) wondered if Lareau's findings would be different if she had studied middle- and working-class families in the same school: "Would students and parents learn from the knowledge and experiences of their peers from other class backgrounds? Or would the tendency of people to associate with similar others prevent such exchanges or even reinforce differences between these groups?" Initially, she looked for a research site that would allow her to observe middle- and working-class students interacting together in the same school setting. Eventually, she located a school in which a majority of students were middle class but a substantial minority (approximately 25 percent) came from working-class families.

Qualitative research making use of archival records must make similar decisions about what to analyze. To get a true "insider's view," diaries and personal journals, such as those used by Weber and Erikson, have traditionally been popular choices. More recently, researchers have begun using Facebook profiles, tweets, and other forms of social media, as illustrated in the studies in Chapter 1.

Gain Access and Establish Relationships

The second step is to gain access to the particular setting or group that the researcher has chosen to study, to decide how to interact and to present oneself, and to establish a working relationship with the observed or interviewees. Calarco was familiar with the school because one of her relatives was a district employee. She had to seek permission from school administrators and teachers, as well as secure parental consent for all the children in the classrooms she observed. In the classrooms she was primarily an observer, listening and watching while she sat in empty seats or walked around the classroom (Calarco 2011:866). Gaining access and securing permission involves ethical issues, discussed in Chapter 3, as well as technical issues that are addressed in Chapter 9.

To both students and teachers, Calarco presented herself as a researcher and graduate student; to students, she explained: "I am a student like you, but instead of studying math and language, I study how kids interact at school" (personal communication 2013). To understand behavior from the actor's point of view and describe the processes that shape this behavior, it is important for qualitative researchers not to disturb the naturalness of the setting and to develop trust and rapport with people in the setting. To gain the students' trust, Calarco told them that she "would not 'tattle' or 'tell on' them unless someone's life was in danger" (personal communication 2013). She also believes that her status "as a young white woman (like many of the teachers) . . . seemingly increased the comfort and trust of students, teachers, and families" with whom she interacted (Calarco 2011:866).

Decide Whom to Observe or Interview or What to Read

Reflecting the difference in the understandings they hope to achieve, quantitative and qualitative research typically select cases in different ways. Qualitative research is not usually concerned with statistically generalizing findings to a larger population; rather, it is concerned with gaining an in-depth understanding of particular individuals or social groups, which may lead to a more complete theoretical understanding of the meanings and processes being examined. This calls for a more flexible approach to selecting cases. Thus, beyond choosing an appropriate site or social group to observe and/or interview, qualitative researchers often decide what and whom to observe after they begin to gather data. Initial contacts in the field may suggest who will provide the best or most relevant information; then, as researchers observe and begin to analyze their data, they may choose to gather information that they believe will advance their theoretical understanding. Similarly, in archival research, as researchers develop theoretical insights, their exposure to initial texts or other materials may lead to still others.

Calarco had worked out some of the details of case selection prior to her data collection. Once she had gained access to a socioeconomically diverse elementary school, she chose to observe students in grades three through five. For over two years, she visited the school two times a week for about three hours per visit. To maximize her exposure to various activities, she divided her "time equally between four classes in each grade and rotated days and times [she] observed each class" (Calarco 2011:866).

In contrast to the probability sampling often used in quantitative research, qualitative research tends to rely on nonprobability sampling because of the different understanding it hopes to achieve. We discuss both forms of sampling in depth in Chapter 6.

Gather and Analyze Data

Qualitative researchers, seeking to understand the lived experience of those they study, tend not to fully specify concepts before they embark on their research. Instead, they assume that key concepts and their meaning will emerge in the study setting or will be captured in written words stored in archives (Schwartz-Shea and Yanow 2012). Thus, rather than move from abstract concepts to observable variables, as in quantitative research, qualitative researchers are more likely to infer concepts from observations. In Chapters 9 and 13, we discuss the process of coding observations to extricate their larger meaning. This inductive process has several implications for research design.

When data are not generated to test a specific hypothesis, qualitative researchers understand that the direction of their research may be altered once they begin to gather and analyze data—indeed, this can be a major strength of qualitative research. For example, Calarco changed her research question after the first few months of observation (personal communication 2013). She initially decided to study student interactions and cross-class friendships, hoping to understand the impact of these friendships on students' school experiences and outcomes. However, observing the dynamic of social class in elementary students' friendships turned out to be more challenging than she anticipated. After collecting data on students' class backgrounds, she noticed an interesting divergence in student–teacher interactions along class lines. These differences were particularly evident in terms of students' seeking help, which is where she shifted the focus of her research.

▼ Whether and how students seek help, such as by raising their hand, may depend on their social class background.

Two other aspects of data collection in field research facilitated this shift. First, the shift was made possible in part by the scope of the data that Calarco collected. Like many field researchers, she observed and recorded as much as possible that was happening within the setting. For example, she captured interactions not only between students and their peers but also between students and teachers. In notes quickly jotted in real time during her observational sessions, she kept track of these interactions, noting who was participating, how long the interactions lasted, and what type of exchange was involved, as well as recording key dialogue. On the basis of these jottings, Calarco recorded detailed field notes at the end of each observational session. Also typical of field research, she complemented this information with other data drawn from interviews with the teachers and surveys of parents, which provided information about students' families that helped her to determine their social class backgrounds (Calarco 2011).

Second, Calarco's analysis of the data she gathered was ongoing. Unlike quantitative research, in which analysis follows data collection, qualitative research involves constantly analyzing the data as they are collected. Thus, it was while analyzing student–teacher interactions after collecting data on students' class backgrounds that Calarco noticed the class divergence in terms of help-seeking.

One of the greatest strengths of qualitative research is that its design lends itself to the generation of new theoretical insights, which stems from a very different interplay between theory and data than in quantitative research. Following the deductive logic of inquiry, quantitative researchers conduct literature reviews to assess the state of theoretical knowledge. Once they have devised their question or hypothesis, based on existing theory, they expect the data to provide a definitive answer or test—to support or reject the underlying theory—or to suggest ways to revise it. The research literature also informs qualitative research, identifying the issues that inform a research question and providing information about the setting where the research will be conducted (Schwartz-Shea and Yanow 2012). But just as data are generated to understand actors' experiences, theorizing emerges in the process of data analysis to deepen one's understanding. In evaluating qualitative research, we can ask to what extent the theory, concepts, and data provide new and/or more complete understandings of the specific phenomena under investigation.

Calarco's study illustrates this process. In describing her findings, Calarco points out that teachers provided students with very little guidance on how they should seek help when needed. Although teachers encouraged students to ask for help, calling for questions about assignments or reminding them "to let me know when you get stuck," they did not give clear directions about how to do this. Thus, it was left to the students "to choose whether and how to seek help." As it turned out, requests for help were common, and the requests of middle-class children "were more frequent, diverse, and proactive than those of their working-class peers" (Calarco 2011:868). For example, Calarco often observed middle-class children turning to their teachers, even interrupting them, when they needed help, while working-class children rarely admitted that they were struggling.

Although these patterns were evident in Calarco's field notes, she supplemented this information by systematically coding and counting students' classroom interactions during the last six months of her field work. Her primary data, however, consisted of detailed descriptions of her observations, which enabled her to identify help seeking as a salient aspect of classroom interactions, to examine its meaning, and to understand the processes by which class differences in student help-seeking contributed to inequalities. As she sought to understand the meaning of children's behavior, Calarco turned to the theory of cultural capital, which suggests that class cultures equip individuals with different knowledge and skills, which can be used to their advantage in various situations. As she explained (Calarco 2011:869):

> Because teachers expected students to seek help when they were struggling, and because they legitimated these efforts (providing students with help), middle-class students' help-seeking propensities became a form of cultural capital that allowed them to generate meaningful profits in the classroom. These profits included completing work quickly and correctly and deepening their understanding of key concepts.

By contrast, the reluctance of working-class students to seek help "hindered teachers' awareness" of their "needs, preventing teachers from stepping in to help." Consequently, working-class students often failed to get "the help they needed to complete assignments and activities correctly, promptly, and without incident" (870).

SUMMARY

Qualitative research questions focus on achieving an in-depth understanding of meaning, action, and motive, particularly from an "insider's perspective." To do so, qualitative researchers begin by selecting a research strategy, such as field research or in-depth interviews, or the analysis of existing data such as archival records. Then they select a field setting, social group, and/or archival records; gain and establish relationships, if applicable; decide whom to observe or interview or what to read; and proceed to gather and analyze data. One of the greatest strengths of qualitative research is its potential to develop theory.

KEY TERMS

antecedent variable, p. 88

causal relationship, p. 85

concept, p. 87

control variable, p. 89

dependent variable, p. 88

ecological fallacy, p. 86

extraneous variable, p. 88

independent variable, p. 88

intervening variable, p. 88

qualitative research question, p. 84

quantitative research question, p. 84

research design, p. 75

spurious relationship, p. 94

statistical significance, p. 93

units of analysis, p. 85

variable, p. 87

KEY POINTS

- Research begins by choosing a topic, narrowing it through a literature review, and formulating a research question.
- Good research questions should be focused, contribute to ongoing research and theory, and be manageable in terms of time and other resources.
- Research designs differ according to the type of research question, which reflects the type of understanding researchers hope to achieve.
- Quantitative research questions aim to test hypotheses and establish general causal relationships.
- Qualitative research questions aim to establish context-specific meaning and contribute to the development of theory.
- Designing research to answer quantitative questions involves selecting a research strategy, selecting units of analysis, and specifying and determining how to measure variables.
- The objective of quantitative research is to generate data necessary to infer a causal relationship—that is, evidence of association, direction of influence, and nonspuriousness (or the absence of a common cause).
- Designing research to answer qualitative questions involves selecting a research strategy; selecting a field setting, social group, and/or archival records; gaining and establishing relationships, if applicable; and deciding whom to observe or interview or what to read.
- In gathering and analyzing data, the objective of qualitative research is to develop theories and concepts that make sense of one's observations.

REVIEW QUESTIONS

1. Explain and give an example of how a review of the scientific literature can help a researcher to narrow the focus of a research topic.
2. Explain the difference between quantitative and qualitative research questions. What is the scientific objective of each type of question? How is each related to deductive and inductive inquiry (discussed in Chapter 2)?
3. Give one example, other than those mentioned in the text, of (a) a positive and (b) a negative association between two quantitative variables.
4. What are the necessary criteria for establishing causal relationships in quantitative research?
5. Explain the function of intervening variables in establishing causal relationships.
6. Give an example of how research design in qualitative research is more "open-ended" than in quantitative research.
7. How did Calarco's process of gathering and analyzing data enable her to shift the focus of her research?

EXERCISES

1. Choose one of the following general research topics, conduct a literature review, and then formulate an appropriate research question related to the topic: (a) alcohol use, (b) income/earnings inequality, or (c) crime.

2. In this chapter and throughout the book, we will ask you to examine data from the General Social Survey (GSS), introduced in Chapter 2 (see Box 2.1). GSS data may be accessed and analyzed by visiting a website maintained by the University of California at Berkeley: http://sda.berkeley.edu/sdaweb/analysis/?dataset=gss16. Go to this website and conduct the following analyses.

   (a) First, opposite "Row:" enter DRUNK; opposite "Column:" enter SEX; and opposite "Selection Filter(s):" enter YEAR (1994); and, opposite "Weight:" choose "No weight." Click on the "Output Options" tab and under "Cell Contents," you will see "Percentaging": check "Column" if it is not already checked; below you will see "Other options," and there you should check "Summary Statistics" and "Question text." Finally, click "Run the Table." The numbers in bold are the percentages in each column. Compare the percentages in the first row of the table. Who is more likely to say that they sometimes drink more than they think they should?

   (b) Second, at the top of the page, click on "Correl.matrix." Under "Variables to Correlate:" enter EDUC and CONRINC; opposite "Selection Filter(s)," enter YEAR(2016) and, opposite "Weight:" choose "No weight." Under "Output Options," click "Question text"; then, at the bottom of the page, click "Run Correlations." What is the correlation between highest year of education completed and annual income?

3. For each of the following statistical associations, identify a relevant extraneous (antecedent) variable and explain how it could create a spurious association.

   (a) A 1950s study showed that male graduates of Ivy League schools (e.g., Harvard, Yale, Princeton) were more successful in their professional careers, as measured by annual earnings, than those who graduated from other colleges and universities (Kendall 1986).

   (b) A study shows that as ice cream sales increase, so do incidences of burglary.

4. Referring back to the topics in Exercise #1, identify a field setting/social group that you could study to better understand the meanings and processes underlying each of these topics.

5

Measurement

Linking Theory to Research

STUDENT LEARNING OBJECTIVES

By the end of this chapter, you should be able to

1. Describe the measurement process by identifying its major steps.

2. Apply your knowledge of measurement to operationalize a concept.

3. Distinguish between manipulated versus measured operations and among types of measured operational definitions.

4. Identify and apply your knowledge of different levels of measurement.

5. Define reliability and validity and describe their relationship to each other.

6. Identify the forms of reliability and validity assessment.

7. Explain the "feedback loops" in the measurement process, particularly how data can inform the development and refinement of concepts.

Number/label	To whom/what does it apply?	What does it represent?
3 (stars) / ⭐⭐⭐	Movie (=unit of analysis)	Quality

FIGURE 5.1
The Measurement of a Movie's Quality

Have you ever "liked" something on Facebook? Rated a professor's level of difficulty as "easy" on ratemyprofessors.com? Given a movie three out of four stars? Or simply stepped on a scale to find out how much you weigh? If you've done any of these things, you're already familiar with measurement. Each of these examples contains the essentials of measurement: labels or numbers ("like," "easy," "three stars," a pointer reading on a scale) are assigned to people, objects, or events (Facebook postings, professors and others, a movie) to represent properties (likability, level of difficulty, the overall quality of a movie, weight) (see Figure 5.1).

There is a difference, of course, between these everyday examples of measurement and measurement in social research. In the examples, the meaning of things such as likability are taken for granted, and the rules for assigning labels or numbers to units of analysis are more or less intuitive (e.g., you either like something or you don't). In social research, however, we often need to define the concepts we intend to measure and we must spell out the rules in detail for how we will measure them. Scientific norms require that we fully describe our methods and procedures so that others can repeat our observations and judge the quality of our measurements. In this chapter, we outline the measurement process, provide several examples of measurement in social research, discuss criteria for evaluating the nature and quality of measurements, and consider how data analysis and inductive inquiry may refine concepts and measurement.

OVERVIEW: THE MEASUREMENT PROCESS

Measurement is the process of assigning numbers or labels to units of analysis (people, objects, events, etc.) to represent their conceptual properties. The measurement process reflects the cyclical nature of science as a whole, in which theory informs data and data inform theory. In research addressing quantitative questions, the measurement process generally follows the deductive logic of inquiry, whereby theory leads to hypotheses and guides the collection and analysis of data. It begins as the researcher reviews the literature and formulates a research question. Recall from Chapter 4 that Beckett Broh (2002) asked whether extracurricular involvement promotes academic achievement, and if so, why. Broh hypothesized that extracurricular activities increase social capital, which in turn enhances academic achievement. This hypothesis involves three concepts: "extracurricular activities," "social capital," and "academic achievement." But what do these theoretical concepts mean and how could we see them at work in "real life"? Measurement consists of defining and clarifying each concept, coming up with concrete ways of observing them, applying these observations to produce data (the actual measures), and assessing the quality of the fit between conceptual definitions and data.

conceptualization
Defining and clarifying the meaning of concepts.

Figure 5.2 presents the steps in this process; research addressing quantitative questions tends to follow the steps in this order. The first two steps, called **conceptualization**, consist of defining and clarifying the meaning of a given concept. First, you must consider the concept's meaning by reviewing how it has been defined in the social science literature. As you invariably will encounter multiple definitions, you then must select or create an appropriate **conceptual,** or **theoretical, definition,** one that fits the theoretical framework of your research. The next two steps, called **operationalization,** involve identifying ways of observing the concept in real life and spelling out the procedures for applying these "indicators" when you carry out your research. The "final" steps in the process involve data collection and validation, which entail actually measuring the concept and assessing how well your measure represents the underlying concept.

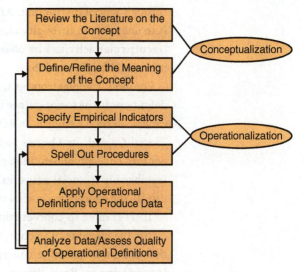

FIGURE 5.2
The Measurement Process

We put the word final in quotes because, like all scientific inquiry, these steps are not really final, but rather part of an ongoing process of theory development. Reflective of inductive inquiry, there often are feedback loops in the measurement process, as represented by the arrows in the figure pointing upward. Thus, research addressing qualitative questions often undertakes these steps in a different order—beginning with data collection/analysis and ending with conceptualization—in hopes of developing a *new* theoretical concept (Glaser and Strauss 1967). In addition, research addressing qualitative questions may refine existing concepts or operational definitions. In this chapter we also discuss research representing these feedback loops, including Jessica Calarco's (2011) study of classroom help-seeking, described in Chapter 4.

CONCEPTUALIZATION AND OPERATIONALIZATION

In this section we examine more closely conceptualization and operationalization.

Conceptualization

The first step in addressing quantitative questions is to define and clarify the meaning of the concepts embedded in your research question with words or examples. Recall from Chapter 4 that a concept is an abstraction that groups together phenomena with important things in common. The main goal of conceptualization is to make this abstraction more specific and ready to be measured. For simpler concepts such as age and class year, researchers may rely on common understandings. For example, Broh does not define—and seems to take for granted—the meaning of academic achievement, which generally refers to the attainment of skills and knowledge

conceptual definition The meaning of a concept expressed in words that is derived from theory and/or observation. Also called *theoretical definition*.

operationalization The process of identifying empirical indicators and the procedures for applying them to measure a concept.

through school instruction. Another strategy researchers use for simpler concepts is to define them through examples. Broh, for instance, clarifies the meaning of extracurricular activities by offering examples such as interscholastic sports, drama, music, and academic clubs.

For more complex concepts, on the other hand, it is important to review existing definitions in the social science literature (step #1 in Figure 5.2). The concept of "social capital" in Broh's study is an example. Citing an article by Alejandro Portes (1998)— "Social Capital: Its Origins and Applications in Modern Sociology"—Broh derived her own conceptual definition of social capital: "the ability to accrue benefits through membership in social networks" (Broh 2002:72). By providing a definition of social capital, the concept becomes less abstract and more "real."

There is more to conceptualization, however, than offering definitions. To further clarify the meaning of a concept (step #2 in Figure 5.2), researchers often distinguish the concept from similar concepts and ideas. Drawing on the analyses of Portes and James Coleman, Broh differentiates social capital from human capital. According to Coleman (1990:304), social capital is "embodied in the relations among persons," whereas human capital is "embodied in the skills and knowledge acquired by an individual." To put this more simply, social capital is related to *who* you know, while human capital is related to *what* you know. This was an important distinction to make in Broh's study because—as you can probably imagine—both "who you know" and "what you know" are likely to affect your academic achievement.

As part of step #2, researchers may also break their main concept down into various *dimensions* and *types* to make it more manageable and concrete. Dimensions and types, as we use the words here, are progressively smaller and less abstract groupings of the concept in question. According to Broh's literature review, social capital can be broken down into two major groupings—or, dimensions—based on where it is acquired: Coleman (1988) argued that the family is a primary site of social capital, while Portes (1998) pointed to nonfamilial social networks as another important dimension of social capital. Within each of these dimensions of social capital (family and nonfamily), social capital can be further broken down. Taking into account these theories, Broh identified four different types of social ties—parent–child, parent–teacher, student–teacher, and student–student—in which the social capital of students is grounded.

Through conceptualization, researchers (1) refine and elaborate the theoretical foundation of their research and (2) provide a basis for linking theory to data. Theoretically, Broh (2002:72) contended that "participation in sports and other extracurricular activities may serve to create social capital within the family by providing opportunities for increased social interaction between the parents and the child"; moreover, these activities create social capital outside the family "by offering opportunities for the formation and intensification of social ties among students, parents, and the school." Operating through these networks, social capital promotes academic achievement in two ways: it exerts social control over students by encouraging them to comply with school norms and values, and it provides channels for students to acquire important educational information and resources.

Having provided examples of extracurricular activities and specified different dimensions and types of social capital, Broh also could generate more precise statements of her hypotheses that could be linked more easily to data. Thus, beginning with the general theoretical relationship between the extracurriculum and social capital, Broh concentrated on the less abstract relationship between participation in interscholastic athletics and social ties among parents, students, and teachers. In this way, the measurement process moves from the abstract to the concrete, and the language shifts from "concepts" to "variables."

Operationalization

In clarifying the meaning of a concept, the researcher begins the process of operationalization: identifying ways of observing variation (Figure 5.2). If you've already done good conceptual work, this process is a straightforward application of that work. To answer quantitative questions, you first need to find ways of indicating the concept in question. Second, you need to spell out the procedures by which you will apply these indicators. How you observe variation, though, depends on your research question and overall research strategy.

SPECIFY EMPIRICAL INDICATORS

Now that you know what your concept is, how would you recognize it if you saw, heard, or otherwise observed it? One way you'd know is through one or more of its characteristics, as suggested by the popular saying, "If it walks like a duck and quacks like a duck, it's probably a duck." Walking style and quacking are **empirical indicators** of a duck. An empirical indicator is an observable characteristic of a concept.

Defining a concept and specifying its dimensions and types should point you in the direction of appropriate indicators. With respect to social capital, ask yourself: What sorts of relationships or social networks might be beneficial? For adults, one possibility is whether someone is a member of LinkedIn, which describes itself as "the world's largest professional network." Another indicator may be how many LinkedIn contacts people have. Still other indicators of social capital include whether people are members of social clubs or organizations, how many clubs or organizations they are involved in, and how often they participate (Putnam 2000).

Recall that Broh was interested in different dimensions and types of social capital among high school students, such as student–teacher interaction. Broh (2002:75) decided to indicate this form of interaction by determining whether students talk to their teachers outside of class about their schoolwork. Note how this "Talks with teacher . . ."

empirical indicator A single, concrete proxy for a concept such as a questionnaire item in a survey.

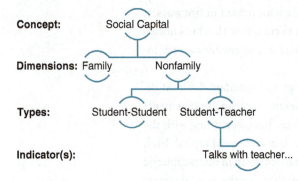

Concept: Social Capital

Dimensions: Family   Nonfamily

Types: Student-Student   Student-Teacher

Indicator(s):   Talks with teacher...

FIGURE 5.3
**From Concept to
Indicator: The Case of
Social Capital**

empirical indicator follows from the concept of social capital and its different dimensions and types, as illustrated in Figure 5.3.

A single empirical indicator of a concept may be inadequate, however, for two reasons: (1) it may contain errors of classification and (2) it is unlikely to capture all the meaning of a concept. We would probably make errors in determining whether an animal is a duck based on the sole indicator of quacking; after all, doesn't "squawking" (as in the sound made by certain cranes, cockatoos, parrots, etc.) sound a lot like quacking? And, just as the saying goes, there's more to a duck than quacking. Similarly, in Broh's study, whether talking to a teacher outside class is a good indicator of social capital depends on *why* students speak with their teacher. Are they doing so for disciplinary reasons at the insistence of the teacher or because they seek guidance on an assignment? And, of course, there are many types of social capital other than student–teacher relations, including students' relations with other students, students' relations with parents, and parent–teacher relations.

Because of the imperfect correspondence between indicators and concepts, researchers often choose to rely on more than one indicator when operationalizing a concept. Sometimes several indicators of a given concept are analyzed separately, yielding multiple tests or crosschecks of a hypothesis. At other times, distinct indicators are combined to form a new variable. Combining several indicators into a composite measure generally provides a better overall representation of the concept. The simplest and most common procedure is to create an **index** by adding or taking an average of the scores of the separate items.

index A composite measure of a concept constructed by adding or averaging the scores of separate indicators; differs from a scale, which uses less arbitrary procedures for combining indicators.

Combining indicators is particularly useful in operationalizing complex concepts like social capital. To operationalize social capital between *children* and *parents*, for example, Broh (200:75) decided to create an index by summing responses (0, 1, 2) to the following three questions from the NELS (National Educational Longitudinal Study):

How often have you discussed the following with either or both of your parents or guardians?

	Never	Sometimes	Often
1. Selecting courses or programs at school?	0	1	2
2. School activities or events of particular interest to you?	0	1	2
3. What classes I take in school?	0	1	2

This should give you an idea of how Broh used multiple empirical indicators, some of which she decided to combine into an index. We have more to say about the use of multiple indicators later in this chapter (see Box 5.3), but for now, we turn to the next step: spell out procedures.

To see how indexes can improve the quality of measurement, read Box 5.1, DOING SOCIAL RESEARCH: Improving Measurement with Composite Measures.

BOX 5.1

DOING SOCIAL RESEARCH

Improving Measurement with Composite Measures

Not only do single indicators rarely capture all the meaning of a concept, but each indicator is likely to have distinctive sources of error or bias. By combining several indicators into a composite measure or index, we generally get a better overall representation of the concept and the errors tend to cancel each other out. This advantage of indexing may be illustrated as follows. Suppose the value of each observed measure (X) is equal to a true score corresponding to the concept being measured (C) and an error score (e); thus, $X = C + e$. Now suppose that we have four different measures and pretend we know the true and error scores for a particular survey respondent, as shown in Table A.

TABLE A. Hypothetical Observed Scores (X), True Scores (C), and Errors (e) on Four Items

Measure	Observed Score (X)	True Score (C)	Error Score (e)
Item 1	2	4	−2
Item 2	3	2	+1
Item 3	7	5	+2
Item 4	5	8	−3
Total	17	19	−2

For each separate item, at least 30 percent of the observed score represents error. If the error tends to be random (or in different directions for the separate items), the error scores tend to cancel out when we sum over the items. Consequently, if we form an index by summing the four items, we obtain a greatly improved measure. For the particular respondent shown in Table A, the index score would be 17 units, only a small fraction of which represents error (2 units).

SPELL OUT PROCEDURES

The next step in the measurement process involves spelling out procedures for applying empirical indicators when you carry out your research. With an indicator in mind, what specific observations will you make or what questions will you ask? Will you use more than one? If so, how will you combine them? In answering these questions, you are formulating an **operational definition**. The counterpart of a conceptual definition, an operational definition describes the exact procedures used to observe the categories or values of a variable.

operational definition
A detailed description of the research procedures necessary to assign units of analysis to variable categories.

Operational definitions must provide enough detail that others can replicate as well as assess what researchers have done. To see how this works, let's consider a simple illustration from everyday life. Suppose you have an idea of what a carrot cake tastes like; in this case, the carrot cake is analogous to a concept like "social capital." Your friend bakes you a delicious carrot cake, so you ask your friend how he made it because you would like to make one. Your friend says, "Oh, you take some carrots, flour, sugar, eggs, and so forth, add some nuts, bake it, and voilà!—you have a carrot cake." Would you be able to make an identical cake with these directions? Not likely.

What you need is an operational definition of your friend's concept of "carrot cake." You would need to have details, such as all of the ingredients, the amount of each ingredient to use, the steps necessary to combine the ingredients, the oven temperature, and baking time. In short, your friend's operational definition should look like an ordinary recipe. Using the recipe (operational definition), you should be able to produce a very similar cake.

For Broh, spelling out the procedures to formulate her operational definitions amounted to identifying questions from the 1988 NELS and, where she used more than one question, indicating how she combined them. To operationally define the student–teacher type of social capital, she used a single item that asked students whether they talked to their teacher outside of class about schoolwork. As we noted above, she operationally defined the "child–parent" type of social capital by adding the responses to three questions to create an index. Similarly, she used multiple items to operationalize each of the other two types—parent–teacher and student–student ties. Thus, her complete operational definition of social capital consisted of the specification of indicators from the 1988 NELS and how she combined them for each of the four types of social capital.

In research as in cooking, many operational definitions are possible. In the end, you have to decide for yourself which to apply to produce data (see Figure 5.2). To do so, you first need to be familiar with how operational definitions differ in the procedures they specify and in the variable categories or values they produce. In the next section, we illustrate how operational definitions vary with respect to the general research

Recipe for Carrot Cake

INGREDIENTS

Cake

- 1 20-ounce can crushed pineapple
- 2 cups whole wheat pastry flour
- 2 teaspoons baking soda
- 1/2 teaspoon salt
- 2 teaspoons ground cinnamon
- 3 large eggs
- 1 1/2 cups granulated sugar
- 3/4 cup nonfat buttermilk
- 1/2 cup canola oil
- 1 teaspoon vanilla extract
- 2 cups grated carrots (4–6 medium)
- 1/4 cup unsweetened flaked coconut
- 1/2 cup chopped walnuts, toasted

Frosting

- 12 ounces reduced-fat cream cheese (Neufchâtel), softened
- 1/2 cup confectioners' sugar, sifted
- 1 1/2 teaspoons vanilla extract
- 2 tablespoons coconut chips or flaked coconut, toasted

Operationalization is like a recipe. The ingredients correspond to empirical indicators, which are combined, following instructions, to create the final "concept."

Preparation

1. To prepare cake: Preheat oven to 350°F. Coat a 9-by-13-inch baking pan with cooking spray.
2. Drain pineapple in a sieve set over a bowl, pressing on the solids. Reserve the drained pineapple and 1/4 cup of the juice.
3. Whisk flour, baking soda, salt and cinnamon in a medium bowl. Whisk eggs, sugar, buttermilk, oil, vanilla, and the 1/4 cup pineapple juice in a large bowl until blended. Stir in pineapple, carrots, and 1/4 cup coconut. Add the dry ingredients and mix with a rubber spatula just until blended. Stir in the nuts. Scrape the batter into the prepared pan, spreading evenly.
4. Bake the cake until the top springs back when touched lightly and a skewer inserted in the center comes out clean, 40 to 45 minutes. Let cool completely on a wire rack.
5. To prepare frosting and finish cake: Beat cream cheese, confectioners' sugar, and vanilla in a mixing bowl with an electric mixer until smooth and creamy. Spread the frosting over the cooled cake. Sprinkle with toasted coconut.

approaches: experiments, surveys, field research, in-depth interviews, and existing data analysis. Then we describe how variable categories provide different kinds of information with which to describe and compare units of analysis.

SUMMARY

To answer quantitative questions, the measurement process initially follows the deductive logic of inquiry in which theory informs hypotheses and guides the collection and analysis of data. The first major step is conceptualization, which includes reviewing the literature on a concept and defining/refining its meaning. The second major step is operationalization, which involves specifying empirical indicators of a concept and spelling out procedures by which these indicators will be applied.

VARIATIONS IN OPERATIONAL DEFINITIONS: DATA SOURCES

Our discussion of the process of operationalization, which focused on how Broh operationalized the concept of social capital, emphasized one data source, surveys, in which people are asked questions. As we now consider other data sources, we distinguish between manipulated and measured operations and among sources of measured operations.

Manipulated Versus Measured Operations

There are two general types of operational definitions in social research: manipulated and measured. *Manipulation operations* are designed to change the value or category of a variable, whereas *measurement operations* estimate existing values or categories.

Both types of operational definitions are illustrated in a study that asked the question: Does having a criminal record reduce a person's chances of getting a job? Embedded in this question are two concepts: criminal record and employment opportunities. To investigate their relationship, Devah Pager (2003) used two pairs of male confederates, or "testers" (accomplices who carried out the experiment). These "testers" applied in person for 350 job openings advertised in Milwaukee, Wisconsin. All four of the testers were 23-year-old college students who were similar in physical appearance, and all presented nearly identical information about themselves in applying for the jobs. The difference was a manipulated independent variable: one member of each pair presented himself as having a criminal record and the other did not. Pager carefully spells out the operations involved in manipulating an applicant's criminal record. The "record" consisted of a felony drug conviction (possession with intent to distribute cocaine), for which the offender had served 18 months in prison. In most of the job application procedures encountered by the testers, the applicant was able to convey this information on the application form, in answer to the question, "Have you ever been convicted of a crime?" When the application form did not ask about criminal history, the tester provided two pieces of evidence indicating that he had spent time in prison. First, he reported work experience obtained while in a correctional facility; second, he listed his parole officer as a reference.

To operationalize the dependent variable, employment opportunity, Pager used a measured definition: whether the applicant received a callback for an interview. To determine callbacks, voice mailboxes were set up for each applicant to record responses. The hypothesis was confirmed: 22.6 percent of the applicants without a criminal record received callbacks, compared with 10.3 percent of those who had reported having a criminal record.

Manipulation of an independent variable is by definition experimental, and we have a good deal more to say about this in Chapter 7. In that chapter we describe Pager's study in full detail, including her manipulation of a second variable, race.

Sources of Measured Operational Definitions

There are three primary sources of measurement operations: verbal reports, observation, and archival records. Generally, these sources correspond respectively to surveys and in-depth interviews, field research, and the analysis of existing data. As in Pager's experiment, however, a given approach may use more than one data source.

VERBAL REPORTS

One way of measuring a concept—by far the most common form of social measurement—is to simply ask people questions. **Verbal reports**, or **self-reports**, consist of replies to direct questions, usually posed in surveys or in-depth interviews. Self-reports provide simple and generally accurate measures of background variables such as age, sex, marital status, and education. They also are used extensively to measure subjective experiences, such as knowledge, beliefs, attitudes, feelings, and opinions.

verbal report An operational definition based on respondents' answers to questions in an interview or questionnaire. Also called *self-report*.

Most of the variables in Beckett Broh's study were operationalized by means of self-reports. For example, she used a single item from the first year of the NELS survey to measure parents' income: "What was your total family income from all sources in 1987?" She also used a single survey question to measure participation in interscholastic sports, which was one of her primary independent variables. And as described earlier, to measure different types of social capital, she combined items from the NELS to create indexes.

Verbal reports also are elicited with pictures and diagrams, which can simplify complex issues. To measure attitudes toward residential integration, for example, Maria Krysan and Reynolds Farley (2002) showed respondents five cards with diagrams depicting neighborhoods containing 14 homes (see Figure 5.4). Each card shows a different interracial mixture ranging from all-black to all-white with three racially mixed neighborhoods. Respondents "were asked to imagine that they had been looking for

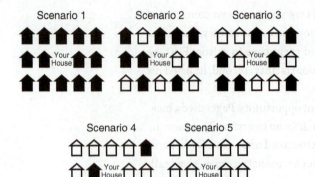

FIGURE 5.4
Neighborhood Cards
Used to Measure
Residential Preferences

a house and found a nice one they could afford" (Krysan and Farley 2002:945). Then respondents were asked to rank the cards from the most to least attractive and to indicate whether they would be unwilling to move into any of the neighborhoods.

OBSERVATION

Another means of measuring a concept is through observation. Pager measured employment opportunity by direct observation of behavior: she observed whether employers called job applicants back for an interview. Observational measures such as this often are used in experiments. They also are common in field research. For example, in the last six months of her field study of elementary school classrooms, Jessica Calarco (2011) measured students' requests for help from their teacher. As a first step, she defined four types of help-seeking (Calarco 2011:872):

1. Assistance: Direct ("Can you help me?") and indirect ("I don't get this") requests for help to resolve problems students are having with projects and assignments.
2. Clarification: Questions ("What does this mean?") about general instructions or directions for specific activities and questions on tests and assignments.
3. Checking-of-Work: Requests ("Can you check this?") for teachers to look over or judge the accuracy of their work.
4. Information: Requests for teachers to provide additional knowledge or instruction (e.g., "Did they find water on the moon?" "How do you use a protractor to draw 420 degrees?").

Based on these categories, Calarco carefully counted students' help-seeking during 16 class periods, each devoted to various subjects and activities. As part of the record, she also recorded the name of the student who engaged in each form of help-seeking. Then, after identifying students' social class backgrounds, she compared the number and types of requests made by children from middle-class and working-class families. Across all classrooms and activities, she found a consistent pattern: middle-class children were more likely to make all types of requests than working-class children.

Observation provides direct and generally unequivocal evidence of overt behavior, but it also is used to measure subjective experiences such as feelings and attitudes. For example, one could measure interpersonal attraction by observing and recording the physical distance that two people maintain between themselves, with closer distances indicative of greater liking. Similarly, Zick Rubin (1970) operationally defined "romantic love" by observing the length of time couples spent gazing into one another's eyes.

Besides direct, firsthand observation, technologies such as video recording, audio recording, and counters are commonly used to observe and measure variables. To measure which television programs people watch, the Nielsen Company attaches an electronic monitoring device to the television set of each household in their sample, which automatically records "a snapshot of consumer viewing." Similarly, as an indirect means of observing everyday activities, social researchers have used time diaries, in which research participants are asked to report all their activities, usually for the previous day (Robinson and Godbey 1997). To compare the time that husbands and wives devote to housework, Yun-Suk Lee and Linda Waite (2005) used the Experience Sampling Method (ESM), a diary-like method in which respondents wear specially programmed wristwatches for one week. The watches "beep" eight random times during waking hours each day, at which point participants are asked to report their activities (Lee and Waite 2005:329). Based on ESM data, Lee and Waite found that wives in their sample did about 8 more hours of housework per week than husbands.

ARCHIVAL RECORDS

Archival records, which refer to existing recorded information, provide another invaluable source of measurement. The various types of archival data include statistical records, public and private documents, and mass communications. We have much more to say about the use of archival records in Chapter 10; here we focus on them in the context of operationalization.

An example of an operational definition based on statistics is the dissimilarity index, which measures residential segregation and can be used to compare the level of residential segregation across areas and over time. The dissimilarity index[1] indicates the degree to which two groups (e.g., blacks and whites) are evenly spread throughout a given geographical area such as a city; more precisely, it gives the percentage of either group that would have to move to produce zero segregation. An index of 0 for a city would indicate that the percentage of blacks living in each neighborhood is the same as the percentage living in any other, so no one would have to move. An index of 100 indicates that blacks live in exclusively black neighborhoods and whites in exclusively white neighborhoods, so that 100 percent of either group (blacks or whites) would have to move to a different neighborhood for the groups to be spread evenly throughout the city. Values below 30 are considered low, and values above 60 are considered high (Logan and Stults 2011:25).

archival records A source of operational definitions that consists of existing documents and institutional records.

---

[1]The formula for the Index of Dissimilarity measuring the segregation of whites from blacks in a city is

$$\tfrac{1}{2} \, \Sigma |(b_i/B) - (w_i/W)|, \text{ where}$$

b_i = the black population in the ith neighborhood
B = the total black population of the city
w_i = the white population in the ith neighborhood
W = the total white population of the city

When the dissimilarity index was calculated for blacks and whites using the most recent US Census data (2010), the most segregated metropolitan area with 500,000 or more population was Milwaukee, Wisconsin, with an index of 81.5; the least segregated was Provo, Utah, with an index of 21.9 (Frey 2012). According to John Logan and Brian Stults (2011), segregation peaked for blacks and whites around 1960 or 1970, with an average dissimilarity index across all metropolitan regions of 79. Since then, racial segregation has declined slowly and steadily, but as of the 2010 census, the average dissimilarity index remained relatively high at 59. Although less segregated than African Americans, Hispanics and Asians have maintained the same segregation levels for the past 30 years; in 2010, the average dissimilarity index was 48 for Hispanics and 41 for Asian Americans.

Two other examples of operational definitions derived from archival records, specifically mass media, come from a study by Bernice Pescosolido and colleagues, which related changes in the cultural images of African Americans in the 20th century to racial conflict in the larger society (Pescosolido, Grauerholz, and Milkie 1997). To operationalize various aspects of the image of African Americans, the researchers examined blacks' representation in a sample of over 2,400 children's picture books. As a measure of blacks' visibility, for example, they recorded whether at least one black character was portrayed in text or illustrations. To measure racial conflict, they counted the number of racial conflict events reported in event summaries listed in the *New York Times Index*. According to their careful operationalization, an event counted as racial conflict if the summary "described an unambiguous instance of public racial strife." This included "conflicts (involving violence, physical confrontation, or arrest), protests (actions related to racial tensions that did not involve direct confrontation), and legal actions (particularly Black-initiated lawsuits)" (Pescosolido, Grauerholz, and Milkie 1997:447). The data showed, among other results, an increase in the visibility of blacks in the last third of the century and a rise and fall in racial conflict that corresponded, respectively, to decreases and increases in blacks' visibility.

SUMMARY

There are two main sources of operational definitions: manipulated operations and measured operations, the latter of which include self/verbal reports, observation, and archival records. Each of these data sources typifies a general research approach. Experiments always involve manipulated operations; surveys and in-depth interviews involve self-reports, or replies to direct questions; field research involves direct observations of behavior; and the analysis of existing data may include a range of archival records.

VARIATIONS IN OPERATIONAL DEFINITIONS: LEVELS OF MEASUREMENT

Operational definitions specify procedures for sorting units into different categories (Davis 1971), such as African American or white (as in Pager's study) and never speak with parents about courses, sometimes speak with parents, or often speak with parents (as in Broh's study). Aside from the number of categories, an important way in which categories vary is in terms of their level of measurement. The four general levels usually identified are nominal, ordinal, interval, and ratio measurement. These levels indicate the kind of inferences you can make when you compare units (people, objects, or events) in different variable categories, which determines how the variables may be analyzed. As we explain in this section, for example, it makes a difference whether you operationalize social capital by having students indicate (1) whether they talked to their teacher outside class or not or (2) the number of times the student talks with a teacher outside class.

Nominal Measurement

The lowest level, **nominal measurement**, is a system in which cases are classified into two or more categories on some variable. As you may recall, Broh classified students into two categories as one indicator of social capital: those who talked with their teachers outside of class about schoolwork and those who didn't. Other examples of variables that typically have a nominal level of measurement include race, religious preference, and political party preference.

In nominal measurement, the numbers are assigned to the categories simply as labels or codes for the researcher's convenience in collecting and analyzing data. For example, Broh assigned the number "1" to students who talked with their teachers outside of class about schoolwork and the number "0" to students who didn't. Similarly, political party preference might be classified as:

1. Democrat
2. Republican
3. Independent
4. Other
5. No preference

Since we are merely using numbers as labels, no mathematical relationships are possible at the nominal level. We cannot say that 1 + 2 = 3 (Democrat plus Republican equals Independent) or that 1 < 2 (Democrats are "lower" on political preference than Republicans). We can say, however, that all 1s share the same political preference and that 1s differ from 2s in their political preference. With nominal measurement, the empirical rule for assigning cases to categories is that cases placed in the same category must be equivalent.

nominal measurement
A level of measurement in which numbers serve only to label categories of a variable.

exhaustive The measurement requirement that a measure includes all possible values or categories of a variable so that every case can be classified.

Nominal measurement has two characteristics that apply to all levels of measurement: variables must be both exhaustive and mutually exclusive. To be **exhaustive** means that there must be sufficient categories so that virtually all persons, events, or objects being classified will fit into one of the categories. The following set of categories for the variable "religious preference" does not meet the exhaustiveness criterion:

1. Protestant
2. Catholic

You can probably think of other categories that would need to be added to make this measure exhaustive: Jewish, Muslim, Hindu, Buddhist, some other religions, or no religious preference at all. Even if one expected few non-Catholic or non-Protestant respondents, one would at least need to add the categories "None" and "Other" to cover all the possibilities.

mutual exclusivity The measurement requirement that each case can be placed in one and only one category of a variable.

The criterion of **mutual exclusivity** means that the persons or things being classified must not fit into more than one category. Suppose that a researcher hastily came up with the following categories for the variable "place of residence":

1. Urban
2. Suburban
3. Rural
4. Farm

You can see that some persons would fit into both categories 3 and 4. The following set of categories would be an improvement:

1. Urban
2. Suburban
3. Rural, farm
4. Rural, nonfarm

Ordinal Measurement

ordinal measurement A level of measurement in which different numbers indicate rank order of cases on a variable.

In **ordinal measurement**, numbers indicate the rank order of cases on some variable. Psychologist S. S. Stevens (1951), who developed the idea of measurement level, used hardness of minerals as an example of ordinal measurement. We can determine the hardness of any two minerals by scratching one against the other: harder stones scratch softer ones. By this means we could number a set of stones, say five, from 1 to 5 according to their hardness. The numbers thus assigned, however, would represent nothing more than the *order* of categories. We could not say how much greater (or harder) one category is than another.

Many survey items that Broh used had ordinal levels of measurement. Recall that students were asked about how often they talked to their parents or guardians about courses or programs at school, with the following numbers assigned to the categories:

1. Never
2. Sometimes
3. Often

The numerical "ranking" here simply refers to the frequency of this form of student–parent interaction: smaller numbers indicate less interaction and greater numbers indicate more.

One virtue of ordinal measurement, as Julian Simon and Paul Burstein (1985:208) note, is "that people can often make an accurate judgment about one thing *compared to another,* even when they cannot make an accurate *absolute* judgment." The ability of human observers to make comparative judgments permits a wide range of reasonably accurate social measurements at the ordinal level—for example, measures of socioeconomic status, intelligence, political liberalism, various preference ratings, and attitude and opinion scales. On the other hand, ordinal measurement is still rather crude. At this level, we cannot perform most mathematical (statistical) operations in analyzing the data. We cannot add, subtract, multiply, or divide; we can only rank things: 1 < 2, 2 < 3, 1 < 3.

Interval Measurement

Interval measurement has the qualities of the nominal and ordinal levels plus the requirement that equal distances or intervals between "numbers" represent equal distances in the variable being measured. An example is the Fahrenheit temperature scale: the difference between 20°F and 30°F is the same as the difference between 90°F and 100°F—a difference of 10°. We can infer not only that 100°F is hotter than 90°F but also how much hotter it is. What enables us to make this inference is the establishment of a standard measurement unit, or metric. For Fahrenheit temperature, the metric is degrees; similarly, time is measured in seconds, length in feet or meters, and US income in US dollars. When numbers represent a metric, the measurement is "quantitative" in the ordinary sense of the word. Thus, we can perform basic mathematical operations such as addition and subtraction.

However, we cannot multiply or divide at the interval level. We cannot say, for example, that 100°F is twice as hot as 50°F or that 20°F is one-half as hot as 40°F. The reason is that interval measures do not have a true or absolute zero but an arbitrary one. That is, the zero point on the scale does not signify the absence of the property being measured. Zero degrees Fahrenheit does not mean that there is no temperature; it is simply an arbitrary point on the scale. Its arbitrariness is illustrated by comparison with another interval scale designed to measure the property of temperature: 0°F equals about –18°C (Celsius or centigrade), and 0°C equals 32°F.

Although social researchers may aim to create interval measures, most of what passes for this level of measurement is only a very rough approximation. IQ score, for example, is sometimes treated as an interval-level measure, even though it makes no sense to add IQ scores or to infer that equal numerical intervals have the same meaning. (Is the difference between IQ scores of 180 and 190 equal to the difference between 90 and 100?)

interval measurement
A level of measurement that has the qualities of the ordinal level plus equal distances (intervals) between assigned numbers.

Pure interval-level measures are hard to find in the social sciences, which is why we used temperature as an example. Most variables in the social sciences with equal intervals between numbers have ratio measurement.

Ratio Measurement

ratio measurement
The highest level of measurement, which has the features of the other levels plus an absolute (nonarbitrary) zero point.

The fourth level, called **ratio measurement**, includes the features of the other levels plus an absolute (nonarbitrary) zero point. The presence of an absolute zero makes it possible to multiply and divide scale numbers meaningfully and thereby form ratios. The variable income, measured in US dollars, has this property. Given incomes of $20,000 and $40,000, we can divide one into the other (i.e., form a ratio) to signify that one is twice (or one-half) as much as the other.

Many measures in social research have a well-defined metric and a zero point that meaningfully signifies none of the property being measured. Besides income, other examples are age in years, number of siblings, and years of employment. Ratio-level measures often are obtained by simply counting—for example, number of callbacks for interviews, number of siblings, number of people in a social network. Also, aggregate variables, which characterize collectivities of people, frequently are measured at this level by counting and then dividing by a population base. Some examples are crude birth rate (number of births per 1,000 people in the total population), divorce rate (number of divorces per 1,000 existing marriages), percentage of labor force unemployed, and percentage Democrat.

To test your understanding of measurement levels and gain practice in inferring the level from operational definitions, see Box 5.2, CHECKING YOUR UNDERSTANDING: Inferring Level of Measurement from Operational Definitions.

BOX 5.2

CHECKING YOUR UNDERSTANDING

Inferring Level of Measurement from Operational Definitions

How do you infer the level of measurement of a variable? You should keep in mind two important points. First, measurement level depends on the operational definition, because a given variable may be measured at more than one level. A field researcher may form an ordinal measure of age, for example, by using people's appearance, manner, and other observed characteristics to classify them as "children," "young adults," "middle-aged," and "seniors." Or date-of-birth information might be used to measure age as a ratio scale.

Second, measurement level depends on the kinds of inferences that can be made when comparing units in different variable categories. Consider income. A common way of operationalizing this variable is to ask respondents, "How much money did you earn last year from all sources—that is, before taxes or other deductions?" and then present them with a set of categories, such as the following:

1. Less than $25,000

2. $25,000 to $49,999

3. $50,000 to $74,999

4. $75,000 to $99,999

5. $100,000 to $149,999

6. $150,000 to $199,999

7. $200,000 to $299,999

8. $300,000 or more

Now, what kind of inferences can you make if you compare people in different categories, say 3 and 5? (Think about this before reading further.) Clearly, you can infer that (1) they have different incomes and (2) one earns more than the other. But can you infer precisely how much more the person in Category 5 earns than the person in Category 3? No. Because of the range of possible incomes in each category, the difference could be as low as $25,001 ($100,000–$74,999) or as high as $99,999 ($149,999–$50,000). Therefore, this operational definition signifies ordinal measurement.

Below is a list of variables together with possible operational definitions based on self-reports. To check your understanding of level of measurement, identify the level of each. Be sure to think about what kind of inferences you could make when you compare persons or units in different categories.

a. *Educational attainment*: Ask respondents to check one of the following categories: 8th grade or less; 9th–11th grade; high school graduate; some college; college graduate.

b. *Religious preference*: What is your religious preference? Is it Protestant, Catholic, Jewish, some other religion, or no religion?

c. *Attitude toward corporal punishment*: Do you strongly agree, agree, disagree, or strongly disagree that it is sometimes necessary to discipline a child with a good, hard spanking?

d. *Television viewing*: On the average day, about how many hours do you personally watch television?

e. *Educational attainment*: How many years of formal education have you completed?

Answers: a. ordinal; b. nominal; c. ordinal; d. ratio; e. ratio.

Table 5.1 Information Provided by the Four Levels of Measurement

Information provided	Nominal	Ordinal	Interval	Ratio
Classification	X	X	X	X
Rank Order		X	X	X
Equal intervals			X	X
Nonarbitrary zero				X

SUMMARY

An important variation in operational definitions is their level of measurement. Operational definitions may produce four different levels: nominal, ordinal, interval, and ratio. The four levels themselves form an ordinal scale with regard to the amount of information they provide. Each level has the features of the level(s) below it plus something else.

Table 5.1 illustrates this. In most social science research, however, the distinction between interval and ratio levels of measurement is not very important compared with the differences between the interval and nominal or ordinal levels. Indeed, Chapter 12 distinguishes statistical analyses appropriate for nominal/ordinal versus interval/ratio measures.

SELECT AND APPLY OPERATIONAL DEFINITIONS TO PRODUCE DATA

Now that you are familiar with sources of operational definitions and levels of measurement, how do you decide on an appropriate operational definition? Ultimately, the most basic requirement is to select an operational definition that fits the concept well, although this is often easier said than done. Recall the carrot cake example: How could you be certain that your friend's recipe represents an authentic carrot cake? Are walnuts really an essential ingredient, as the recipe indicates? Suppose you used two large eggs instead of three. Would you still have a carrot cake? What if you set the oven temperature to 400° instead of 350°? In the end, you would find that there is no correct recipe. Instead, you would have to decide for yourself whether your friend's operational definition (recipe) corresponded to your concept of what a carrot cake is.

Similarly in social research, no operational definition can capture a concept's meaning perfectly or completely. However, this does not license the researcher to select just any measure. It is still desirable to get the best possible fit between concept and measure, and the best way to do this is by carefully considering the meaning of the concept as it relates to the theory in which it is embedded.

An example of a study in which theory guided the selection of an appropriate operational definition is Albert Pierce's test (1967) of Durkheim's (1951) hypothesis that suicide rates increase in periods of rapid economic change independently of the direction of change (boom or bust). Durkheim theorized that marked economic changes can disturb the existing goals and norms toward which people orient their lives, can thrust individuals into new social settings which they are ill suited to manage, and hence can increase the probability of suicide. Pierce examined data for white males during the peacetime years 1919 to 1940. At first, he correlated the suicide rate with various objective measures of economic change, based on income, percentage of labor force unemployed, and housing construction, with indecisive results. Finally he struck upon the notion of using a measure—the "index of common stock prices"—that would reflect the public definition of the economic situation, which is more in tune with Durkheim's theory. That is, rapid fluctuations of stock market prices may be viewed as indicators of public economic uncertainty, resulting in disruption or discontinuities in perceived goals and norms. Pierce's analysis revealed that suicide rates correlated highly with the rate of change in the public definition of economic conditions as operationally defined by the index of stock market prices.

An example of a relatively poor fit between theoretical and operational definitions comes from Pamela Paxton's (2000) critique of the measurement of democracy. A defining characteristic of democracies, according to most scholars, is universal adulthood suffrage—that is, the right to vote for every adult citizen. However, in multiple studies, operational definitions of democracy are limited to male adulthood suffrage, thus excluding women as political participants. These operational definitions of democracy thus capture half of the characteristic in question, given that women constitute about 50 percent of the world's adult population.

Though theory should guide your selection of an operational definition, selecting an operational definition also depends on your general research approach (experiments, surveys, field research, in-depth interviews, or existing data analysis). Some approaches may use more than one data source; for example, experiments use a combination of measures—verbal reports and/or observation in addition to manipulation procedures, and field research often supplements observations with verbal reports and archival records. But the approach you choose will determine the primary source of data and measurement.

Once you have selected a particular approach, another consideration is the number of variable categories and their level of measurement. Using survey data from the NELS, Broh had limited options. For example, there were three questions on child–parent relations, each of which had the response categories "never," "sometimes," and "often." Therefore, she could analyze this type of social capital in terms of frequency of communication, which she did, or analyze it in terms of whether students talked to their parents (= "sometimes" AND "often") or not (= "never").

If you are creating your own operational definitions, you need to determine how precise your measures need to be. As a general rule, we recommend creating a set of categories that will produce as much information as possible. More information often means greater precision and a higher level of measurement, which enables researchers to apply more powerful methods of data analysis. For example, it is usually better to ask respondents when they were born, which creates a ratio measure of age (current date – date of birth) than to provide a list of categories such as under 20, 20–29, 30–39, and so on, which creates an ordinal measure. However, survey researchers sometimes sacrifice precision to form questions that are clearer and more likely to be answered accurately. In operationalizing personal income, for example, research shows that respondents are less likely to answer questions requesting the exact amount that they earned than questions that provide a range of income categories (as in the example in Box 5.2) (Yan, Curtin, and Jans 2010).

Once you have decided on a theoretically appropriate operational definition in the context of your research approach, applying this definition to produce data creates *measures*. In the next section, we discuss methods of analyzing the measures to assess the quality of measurement.

SUMMARY

Researchers try to select operational definitions that best capture the meaning of the concept being measured. How you choose to operationalize a concept also depends on the data source or general methodological approach and the desired level of measurement.

ASSESS THE QUALITY OF OPERATIONAL DEFINITIONS

In deductive inquiry, the final step in the measurement process is to assess the quality of one's operational definitions. Initially, assessment is subjective, based on the investigator's personal judgment of how well an operational definition fits the theoretical meaning of the relevant concept. And, sometimes, as in the case of variables like sex and age, this may be satisfactory. But once you have applied an operational definition to generate data, there are more objective ways to evaluate its quality. Social scientists apply two criteria in evaluating measurement: reliability and validity.

reliability The stability or consistency of an operational definition.

Reliability is concerned with questions of stability and consistency: Is the operational definition measuring "something" consistently and dependably, whatever that "something" may be? Do you get the same results each time you apply the operational definition under similar conditions? If the operational definition is formed from a set of responses or items, are the component responses or items consistent with each other?

An example of a highly reliable measuring instrument is a steel tape measure. When you use it repeatedly to measure the length of a piece of wood 20 inches long, you will get, with negligible variation, 20 inches every time. Further, someone else measuring the same object should get the same results you do. A cloth tape measure would be somewhat less reliable because it may vary with humidity and temperature and you can expect some variation in measurements depending on how loosely or tightly the tape is stretched. Even less reliable would be an "eyeball measure"—that is, an estimate based on sight; chances are that two individuals could come up with widely different eyeball estimates of an object's length.

Measurement validity refers to the congruence or "goodness of fit" between an operational definition and the concept it is purported to measure. Does this operational definition truly reflect what the concept means? Are you measuring what you intend to measure with this operational definition? If so, you have a valid measure. An example of a valid measure is amniocentesis, a prenatal test performed in some pregnancies that reveals information about the health of the unborn child. Although generally used to detect genetic disorders, amniocentesis also reveals the baby's sex. It is a valid measure of biological sex because it indicates with virtually perfect accuracy whether the unborn child will be a male or a female. At one time, a number of invalid "measures" of the unborn child's sex existed in the form of folk wisdoms. One belief, for example, involves tying a string to the pregnant woman's wedding band and holding the band suspended over her abdomen. If the band swings in a circle, the baby will be a girl; if the band swings back and forth, it will be a boy.

Of the two criteria for assessing measurement quality, validity is more critical. Reliability is important; indeed, it is a necessary condition for validity. That is, a highly unreliable measure cannot be valid—how can you measure something accurately if the results fluctuate wildly? But a very reliable measure still may not be valid, because you could be measuring very reliably (consistently) something other than what you intended to measure. To take a facetious example, let us suppose we decide to measure the "intelligence" of students by standing them on a bathroom scale and reading the number off the dial (Davis 1971:14). Such an operational definition would be highly reliable, as repeated scale readings would yield consistent results. However, this obviously would not be a valid measure of an individual's intelligence.

The relationship between reliability and validity is illustrated in Figure 5.5, which displays a target. Measurement is an attempt to hit the bullseye, which represents the theoretical definition of the concept. A tight pattern, irrespective of its location on the target, reflects a reliable measure because it is consistent. Validity is a reflection, however, of how closely the shots cluster about the bullseye.

measurement validity
The goodness of fit between an operational definition and the concept it is purported to measure.

FIGURE 5.5
Analogy of Target to Reliability and Validity

Low reliability
Low validity

High reliability
Low validity

High reliability
High validity

Researchers have devised several ways to assess the reliability and validity of operational definitions. To illustrate these forms of assessment, we'll frequently reference Morris Rosenberg's (1965) Self-Esteem Scale, which Broh (2002) and many other researchers have used. Broh (2002) operationalized self-esteem by combining seven items from Rosenberg's Self-Esteem Scale that were included in the NELS. Each item is actually a statement, to which respondents are asked to indicate their level of agreement, as shown here.

	Strongly agree	Agree	Disagree	Strongly disagree
1. I feel good about myself.	[ ]	[ ]	[ ]	[ ]
2. I feel I am a person of worth.	[ ]	[ ]	[ ]	[ ]
3. I am able to do things as well as most other people.	[ ]	[ ]	[ ]	[ ]
4. On the whole, I am satisfied with myself.	[ ]	[ ]	[ ]	[ ]
5. I feel useless at times.*	[ ]	[ ]	[ ]	[ ]
6. At times I think I am no good at all.*	[ ]	[ ]	[ ]	[ ]
7. I feel I do not have much to be proud of.*	[ ]	[ ]	[ ]	[ ]

*Indicates an item that is a negative statement about the self.

Notice that the first four items are positive statements about the self, and the last three items, indicated by an asterisk, are negative. Agreement with positive statements suggests "high" self-esteem, whereas agreement with negative statements indicates "low" self-esteem. To take this into account, values between 1 and 4 are assigned to the response categories, with a 4 representing strong agreement with a positive statement about the self (or, conversely, strong disagreement with a negative statement). For example, for item 1, "strongly agree" = 4, "agree" = 3, "disagree" = 2, and "strongly disagree" = 1; for item 5, "strongly agree" = 1, "agree" = 2, and so forth. An individual's responses to these seven questions are then added together to produce a single scale score that could range from 7 (low self-esteem) to 28 (high self-esteem). (If you wish, you can also take the full, 10-question Rosenberg self-esteem survey online. From some websites, you will receive a score. At least one website, however, also asks you for consent to use your score for research purposes; see http://personality-testing.info/tests/RSE.php.)

You may notice that what we are describing seems a lot like an index, defined earlier, but we refer to it as a **scale**. To understand why, see Box 5.3, READING SOCIAL RESEARCH: Indexes, Scales, and Scaling Techniques.

Is the Rosenberg Self-Esteem Scale reliable? Is it a valid measure of "self-esteem"? As you will see, numerous studies provide answers to these questions.

unidimensionality
Evidence that a scale or index is measuring only a single dimension of a concept.

scale A composite measure of a concept constructed by combining separate indicators according to procedures designed to ensure unidimensionality or other desirable qualities.

BOX 5.3
READING SOCIAL RESEARCH

Indexes, Scales, and Scaling Techniques

As we have noted, researchers frequently combine indicators to create an index or scale. Scales and indexes condense or reduce the data generated by multiple indicators into a single number or scale score. This not only simplifies the analysis but also increases precision and provides a means of assessing the quality of the measurement.

There is a difference, however, between an index and a scale. An index usually refers to the arbitrary combination of indicators, such as when we simply add together the responses to separate items without regard to what each actually contributes to the measurement of the underlying concept. The chief problem with an index is that it may be measuring more than the intended concept. In other words, it lacks **unidimensionality**. Recall Broh's index of parent–child social capital, which contained three items asking how often students have discussed their courses/programs, activities/events, and classes with their parent(s). Although this may measure social capital, it is possible that it also measures the extent to which a child is an extrovert or an introvert, whether the child is too busy to talk, whether the parents are too busy to talk, and so forth.

A **scale**, on the other hand, combines indicators according to theoretical or empirical criteria that are ordinarily designed to reflect only a single dimension of a concept. Rosenberg's Self-Esteem Scale is an example: it is designed to only measure self-esteem. The construction of scales assumes that a concept can be understood in terms of an underlying continuum; in the case of an attitude, the continuum may range from favorable to unfavorable or positive to negative. It is further assumed that scores on individual items and composite measures represent specific points along the relevant continuum

(or "scale"). Each score, in other words, should uniquely reflect the strength or degree of something, such as an individual's self-esteem. But whereas these assumptions are implicit in an index, scaling procedures make them explicit and are designed to test their validity.

Various scaling procedures have been developed. Some capitalize on each item's placement with regard to an underlying continuum, whereas others capitalize on the inherent pattern among a set of items. One scaling technique, *summated ratings*, assumes that each scale item reflects the entire range of the underlying continuum to the same degree. For many summated ratings scales, the response options for each item vary from "strongly agree" to "strongly disagree." Each item thus constitutes a separate rating, and an individual's score consists of the sum of his or her ratings (hence the label "summated ratings"). The Rosenberg Self-Esteem Scale, as operationalized by Broh in her study, is an example of this scaling technique.

To illustrate another scaling technique, *cumulative scaling*, we will describe the approach developed by Louis Guttman (1974). A cumulative scale is designed so that each item represents a particular point on the underlying dimension. Because the set of items is ordered and *cumulative*, an individual's total scale score not only denotes a place on the underlying dimension but also reveals his or her responses to each and every item. For example, suppose we measure people's reading ability by testing their reading comprehension of items ordered in terms of difficulty, such as portions of a third-grade reader, a ninth-grade textbook, and a college textbook. Participants would be tested on each item starting with the easiest, and the item at which

continues

continued

someone changed from "passing" to "failing" the reading tests would indicate the subject's position on a scale of reading ability. Four response patterns are expected if the items form a perfect Guttman scale: (1) flunk each item, (2) pass only at the third-grade level, (3) pass all but the college text, and (4) pass all reading tests. Other response patterns, such as passing the ninth-grade test and flunking the other two, are called "nonscale" or "mixed types." By selecting a set of items that minimize the proportion of "nonscale" response patterns, the Guttman approach attempts to ensure a unidimensional scale.

Forms of Reliability Assessment

The three principal methods of reliability assessment are test-retest reliability, internal consistency, and inter-coder reliability.

TEST-RETEST RELIABILITY

test-retest reliability
The association between repeated applications of an operational definition.

The simplest way of assessing the reliability of operational definitions is **test-retest reliability**, which involves measuring (or "testing") the same persons or units on two separate occasions. For example, a researcher might administer the self-esteem scale to the same group of students on consecutive days. One then calculates the statistical correlation between the sets of "scores" obtained from the two measurements, and the resulting value serves as an estimate of reliability. Such correlations range from 0 (indicating a completely unreliable measure) to 1.00 (indicating a perfectly reliable measure—that is, each student's score on the first day was the same as his or her score on the second day). Table 5.2 presents hypothetical data for five people on Rosenberg's Self-Esteem Scale, with scores recorded over two days.

For the test-retest procedure, correlation tends to be high, with anything less than .80 considered dangerously low for most measurement purposes. In the hypothetical data in Table 5.2, the correlation is .84. Test-retest reliability checks of the self-esteem scale have produced correlation coefficients of .82 to .88 for 1- and 2-week intervals (Gray-Little, Williams, and Hancock 1997; Rosenberg 1979). However, test-retest reliability coefficients for this scale are much lower for longer periods of 6 months (.63) and 1 year (.50) (Gray-Little, Williams, and Hancock 1997).

Table 5.2 Self-Esteem Scores Among Five People

Person	1	2	3	4	5
Self-Esteem Score (Monday)	25	20	13	10	18
Self-Esteem Score (Tuesday)	19	22	13	12	18

Although it is simple in principle, the test-retest method is seldom used for several reasons. First, either the persons responding to questions or the persons recording observations may remember and simply repeat the responses they gave the first time, thereby inflating the reliability estimate. Second, real change in the concept being measured may occur in the interim between the two "tests." In attitude measurement, new experiences or new information may result in a shift in attitude. For example, positive or negative experiences between administrations may raise or lower a respondent's self-esteem; the loss of a job may change one's attitude toward unemployment insurance or social welfare programs. Because such true changes are inseparable from test-retest inconsistency, they falsely lower the reliability estimate. Third, the test-retest method often is impractical, as researchers rarely have the time or resources to apply a measure more than once to the same group of respondents.

INTERNAL CONSISTENCY

The second method of reliability assessment, **internal consistency**, avoids the practical problem of repeating applications of the same operational definition; however, this method only applies to composite measures based on multiple items, such as the self-esteem scale. Rather than obtain a stability estimate based on consistency over time, as in test-retest reliability, this method estimates the agreement or equivalence among the constituent items of a multi-item measure. If we assume that each item represents the same underlying concept, a lack of agreement among the items would indicate low reliability. Table 5.3 illustrates the basic notion of internal consistency among seven items in the self-esteem scale for five people.

Like the test-retest estimate, internal consistency estimates yield coefficients that run from 0 to 1.00. The most common estimate of internal consistency reliability is **Cronbach's alpha**, which is based on the average of the correlations among the responses to all possible pairs of items. Numerous studies have reported Cronbach's alpha for the self-esteem scale, ranging from a low of .72 for a sample of men 60 years or older to a high

internal consistency
A form of reliability assessment; the consistency of "scores" across all the items of a composite measure (i.e., index or scale).

Cronbach's alpha
A statistical index of internal consistency reliability that ranges from 0 (unreliable) to 1 (perfectly reliable).

Table 5.3 Internal Consistency Among Responses to Seven Items

	Item #1	Item #2	Item #3	Item #4	Item #5	Item #6	Item #7	Total Score
Person #1	4	3	4	4	3	4	3	25
Person #2	3	2	3	3	3	3	3	20
Person #3	2	3	2	2	2	1	1	13
Person #4	1	3	1	2	1	1	1	10
Person #5	4	1	2	4	2	2	3	18

of .88 for a group of college students (Gray-Little, Williams, and Hancock 1997). For the hypothetical data in Table 5.3, Cronbach's alpha = .94.

INTER-RATER RELIABILITY

inter-rater reliability
The extent to which different observers or coders get equivalent results when applying the same measure. Also called *inter-coder reliability*.

A third method of reliability assessment, **inter-rater reliability** (also called **inter-coder reliability**), examines the extent to which different observers or coders using the same instrument or measure get equivalent results. This method often is used to assess the reliability of observational and archival measures, where it is important to show that the data are not affected by the subjectivity of observers or raters. The assumption is that no matter who applies an operational definition, they should get the same scores or values. If two or more observers disagree, this suggests that the measure is unreliable. When Pescosolido, Grauerholz, and Milkie (1997) measured the cultural image of African Americans by coding characteristics (i.e., variables) in children's picture books, they checked the inter-rater reliability of their coding scheme by having more than one researcher code a sample of the books. They reported acceptable levels of agreement "in the 85-percent range" for all variables (447).

IMPROVING RELIABILITY

Partly because of the impracticality of applying the same measure twice to the same group of cases, the reliability of single-item self-reports is seldom checked. However, for composite measures such as the self-esteem scale, researchers usually perform checks on internal consistency. It also is the norm in social research to check for inter-rater reliability whenever it is possible to have more than one observer or rater apply an operational definition. This was easily carried out in the study by Pescosolido and colleagues; however, it often is not possible in field studies in which a single individual is doing the research, such as Calarco's observation of elementary school classrooms.

▼ Inter-rater reliability in action: Any given bird sighting might have everyone agreeing on what kind of bird they saw, or one or more members of the party disagreeing.

What, then, can you do to create the most reliable measures? First, if possible, you should conduct preliminary interviews with a small sample of persons similar to those you intend to study in order to find out whether your measures are clearly understood and interpreted similarly by respondents. The need for preliminary work with actual respondents before the final form of an instrument is completed cannot be overstated. Indeed, it is a topic we will consider again in relation to experiments and survey research. Second, it is not at all necessary to try to "re-invent the wheel" when it comes to measuring most variables. For many common background characteristics (age, level of education, income) and national statistics (economic growth, unemployment rate, poverty rate), survey organizations and the federal government have established standard indicators. And since your research inevitably will build on that of others, you should carefully consider the measures used in prior research. Each of these recommendations also applies to finding the most valid measures.

Forms of Validity Assessment

Validity assessment is much more difficult than reliability assessment. You can assess the stability and consistency of a measure without regard to what is actually being measured. By contrast, in assessing validity, the researcher is concerned precisely with what is being measured—with what a concept means theoretically and whether a given operational definition faithfully represents this meaning or something else. In addition, unlike the observation of consistency and stability, validity cannot be assessed directly—if we knew the value of a variable independent of a given measure, then there would be no need for the measure. Thus, validity assessment is indirect, and it generally boils down to one of two methods: convergent validation and construct validation (Adcock and Collier 2001).

CONVERGENT VALIDATION

Suppose you had a perfectly valid, established measure of a concept. Assessing validity would simply be a matter of checking to see whether the scores obtained with your new operational definition correspond with the scores obtained with an existing one. If we invented a new measure of length, for example, we could easily check its validity by determining whether we get the same results with standard instruments—tape measure, yardstick, transit, and so on—for measuring length. Although there are few standardized measures in the social sciences, there may be alternative measures of the phenomenon under study. **Convergent validation** consists of examining the association between alternative measures of the same concept. An association between different measures is validating because it suggests that the two measures agree, or converge on, the same meaning—namely, the meaning conveyed by the underlying concept.

There is abundant evidence supporting the convergent validity of the Rosenberg Self-Esteem Scale. For example, based on a sample of 9th- and 10th-graders, David Demo (1985) showed that scores on Rosenberg's scale were positively associated with scores on another popular scale, the Coopersmith Self-Esteem Inventory, and with peer ratings of each individual's self-esteem. Other studies similarly have found positive associations between the Rosenberg Self-Esteem Scale and the Lerner Self-Esteem Scale (Savin-Williams and Jaquish 1981) and with an indicator of general self-regard (Fleming and Courtney 1984).

convergent validation Measurement validation based on the extent to which independent measures of the same concept are associated with one another.

The strongest evidence of convergent validity occurs when one of the alternative measures is a well-established, *direct* measure of the concept. A good example is a study that assessed the validity of a new method of measuring physical activity. Research linking exercise to obesity and other health issues has been limited by the inaccurate measurement of physical activity. To remedy this problem, Sandra Hofferth and her colleagues (2008) proposed a time-diary method that asks participants to record the time spent in all activities during one 24-hour period, beginning and ending at midnight on the diary day. Throughout the day, the participant records start and stop times consecutively for all their activities as well as other information describing each activity, such as its location and intensity. To assess the validity of this record, Hofferth and colleagues asked 92 children between the ages of 9 and 14 both to keep a time diary and to wear an Actigraph accelerometer, which looks like a wristwatch, throughout the diary day. Considered the "gold standard" for measuring activity, an accelerometer collects objective information about physical activity by means of "an electronic motion sensor that responds to acceleration in activity and limb movement" (Hofferth et al. 2008:136).

When the researchers estimated the amount of energy expended minute by minute, the correspondence between the time diary and accelerometer was good for determining how much time the children devoted to active pursuits, but it was less satisfactory for determining the intensity of activities. Although the results support the validity of time-diary estimates of activity time, the researchers suggest that using both methods may provide the most comprehensive data on "the social and spatial context of physical activity" (Hofferth et al. 2008:152).

Convergent validation is enhanced in two related ways: by using multiple alternative measures and by using measures based on different operational methods (e.g., self-reports and observations). Because different methods are likely to be subject to different sources of bias, one of the most convincing signs of validity is a correspondence of results when a concept is measured in different ways. For example, self-reports of time spent on physical activity may be biased by the tendency to overestimate socially desirable behavior, but no such bias exists in accelerometer readings of physical activity. Therefore, a correlation between the two measures provides strong evidence of validity. To learn more about the social desirability bias and other sources of inaccurate measurement, see Box 5.4, READING SOCIAL RESEARCH: Measurement Error and the Social Desirability Effect.

CONSTRUCT VALIDATION

According to the logic of **construct validation**, the meaning of any scientific concept is implied by its theoretical relations with other concepts. To validate an operational definition, therefore, you must first examine the theory underlying the concept being measured. In light of this theory, researchers formulate hypotheses about variables that

measurement error A lack of correspondence between a concept and measure that is due to problems with an operational definition or with its application.

social desirability effect A tendency of respondents to bias answers to self-report measures so as to project socially desirable traits and attitudes.

construct validation Measurement validation based on an accumulation of research evidence indicating that a measure is related to other variables as theoretically expected.

BOX 5.4

READING SOCIAL RESEARCH

Measurement Error and the Social Desirability Effect

Validity refers to the accuracy of a measurement. An operational definition that does not match the true value of the concept it is intended to measure results in **measurement error**; this is equivalent to not hitting the bullseye in the target shown in Figure 5.5. A clock that is slow would produce error by overestimating time. Different methods of measurement tend to be subject to different sources of measurement error. Self-report questions may result in error if they are ambiguous or if they are worded in such a way as to encourage agreement rather than truthful answers. Observational measures may be in error if the observations are made at inappropriate places and times.

One particularly vexing source of error in self-reports occurs when respondents are asked about socially approved or disapproved behavior. When asked, "How often do you attend church?" or "Do you exercise regularly?" respondents may inflate their estimates to feel better about themselves or to project a favorable image. And when asked how often they have received a traffic ticket or how often they drink alcoholic beverages, they may underestimate the frequency for the same reasons. This tendency, called the **social desirability effect**, has been demonstrated in numerous studies (Tourangeau, Rips, and Rasinski 2000).

In the early 1990s, for example, Kirk Hadaway, Penny Long Marler, and Mark Chaves (1993) questioned the validity of survey questions measuring attendance at worship services. Many Americans view worship attendance favorably. To gauge how much respondents' reports of worship attendance were inflated, Hadaway and colleagues compared survey-based estimates with observed attendance. For example, in one county in northeastern Ohio, they asked respondents their religious preference (Protestant, Catholic, Jewish, etc.) and whether they had attended church or synagogue in the last seven days. Then they obtained counts of average attendance for all Protestant churches in the county. According to their estimates of Protestants and their attendance counts, 19.6 percent of the Protestants attended church during an average week. By comparison, their survey-based estimate was 35.8 percent, and a national Gallup poll was even higher at 45 percent. Such evidence demonstrates the wisdom in evaluating the validity of self-reported behavior.

should be (and should not be) related to measures of the concept. Then one gathers evidence to test these hypotheses. The more evidence that supports the hypothesized relationships, the greater one's confidence that a particular operational definition is a valid measure of the concept.

An example of construct validation is Rosenberg's validation (1965) of his self-esteem scale. Self-esteem refers to an individual's sense of self-respect or self-worth: those with high self-esteem have self-respect; those with low self-esteem lack it. Rosenberg (1965:18) reasoned that, if his "scale actually did measure self-esteem," then scores on it should "be associated with other data in a theoretically meaningful way." He then tested several theoretical hypotheses. Let's examine two of them:

1. Students with high self-esteem scores will be chosen more often as leaders by classmates than students with low self-esteem scores. This hypothesis follows from the sociological theory that an individual's self-identity is determined largely by what others think of him or her (Cooley 1912; Mead 1934). To test the hypothesis, Rosenberg asked 272 high school seniors, who had completed the self-esteem scale, to identify the person in their English class whom they would be most likely to vote for as the class leader. In support, 47 percent of those with high self-esteem scores received two or more choices as a leader, as compared with 32 percent of those with medium self-esteem scores and 15 percent of those with low self-esteem scores.

2. People with low self-esteem will display more depressive feelings. Supporting the theoretical link between self-esteem and depression, Rosenberg found a strong association when the self-esteem scale and a depression scale were administered to a random sample of 2,695 high school students in New York State. Only 4 percent of the students who were highest in self-esteem but 80 percent of those who were lowest in self-esteem were identified as "highly depressed."

These and other findings from Rosenberg's study helped to support the construct validity of his self-esteem scale.

Construct validity is not established, however, by confirming one or more hypotheses in a single study. Rather, "construct validation ideally requires a pattern of consistent findings involving different researchers using different" theories to test a range of hypotheses (Carmines and Zeller 1979:24). By 1990, 25 years after it was first reported in the literature, Rosenberg's Self-Esteem Scale had been used in more than 1,000 research studies (Blascovich and Tomaka 1991). Many of these studies showed expected associations between self-esteem and other variables. Furthermore, they showed, as predicted, no significant correlations between self-esteem and gender, scores on the Scholastic Aptitude Test (Reynolds 1988), age, and work experience (Fleming and Courtney 1984). This lack of association also supports the construct validity of the scale because there is no theoretical connection between self-esteem and any of these variables. Table 5.4 summarizes the logic of construct validation as applied to Rosenberg's Self-Esteem Scale.

You can understand the importance of accumulated evidence for establishing construct validity when you consider what would happen if data failed to support a theoretically derived prediction (Carmines and Zeller 1979). One interpretation is that the operational definition is not a valid measure of the concept. But it also is possible that (1) the theoretical hypothesis is incorrect or (2) the measurements of one or more other variables in the hypothesis lack validity. The logic of construct validation thus depends on solid theoretical predictions and well-measured external variables. And we become increasingly confident in the validity of a measure as repeated tests of theoretical hypotheses are confirmed.

Table 5.4 Construct Validation of Rosenberg's Self-Esteem Scale

Self-esteem should be related to . . .	Self-esteem should NOT be related to . . .
Peer group ratings of leadership	Gender
(Relative lack of) depressive feelings	SAT scores
	Age
	Work experience

SUMMARY

One criterion by which the quality of an operational definition is assessed is reliability, which refers to the consistency or stability of a measurement. The three major forms of reliability assessment are test-retest reliability, internal consistency, and inter-rater (or inter-coder) reliability. Another criterion by which the quality of an operational definition is assessed is validity, which refers to whether the operational definition is accurately measuring the concept in question. Compared to reliability assessment, validity assessment is more difficult and is often indirect. Two major forms of validity assessment are convergent and construct validation. Both reliability and validity can be improved through repeated tests and by refining operational definitions through data analysis, discussed next.

THE FEEDBACK LOOP: FROM DATA BACK TO CONCEPTS AND MEASUREMENT

The measurement process we have outlined so far follows the deductive model of inquiry, providing the critical link between theory and data. In this model, data analysis represents the last stage in answering our research questions and providing evidence of the validity of our operational definitions. But, as we have emphasized, social science is inevitably cyclical, with data also informing theory. In this way, data analysis may contribute to the measurement process by leading to the development of concepts and by refining operational definitions.

In inductive inquiry, researchers don't necessarily decide in advance what concepts to study and how to measure them; rather, they use data from observations and in-depth interviews to develop or refine important concepts. When Jessica Calarco (2011) began her field research, she observed and recorded, as far as possible, the full extent of interactions among elementary school children and their teachers. Based on these data, she was able "to identify help-seeking as an important component of classroom interactions" (Calarco 2011:867) and to conceptualize it as contributing to the educational advantage of middle-class children. Data from her observations also enabled her to "recognize help-seeking patterns, and determine which behaviors counted as help-seeking" (867), so that she could develop the operational definition of help-seeking that we described earlier. Armed with this operational definition, in the last six months of her research, she moved from theory back to data by counting help-seeking behavior and relating these counts to children's class background.

Another study shows how in-depth interviews may be used to explore the meaning of questions used in the US Census and other government surveys to measure the concept of race. In the 2010 census, respondents were asked the following question: "What is this person's race? Mark one or more boxes." The options are "White," "Black, African American, or Negro," "American Indian or Alaska Native," nine different choices of Asian or Pacific Islander, and "Some other race." In addition, a separate question asked if the respondent is of "Hispanic, Latino, or Spanish origin." Recently, the validity of the race question has been challenged, especially as it applies to Hispanic Americans. For many Hispanics, who identify racially with their ethnic group (e.g., Puerto Rican or Mexican) or identify as Hispanic or Latino, the question does not seem to capture how they think about race (Roth 2010).

To explore Hispanics' understanding of race and how they answer questions about race, Wendy Roth (2010) conducted in-depth interviews with 60 Dominican and Puerto Rican migrants in the New York metropolitan area. During the course of the interviews, she asked several questions, including the US Census question, designed to measure different aspects of racial identity. Many of her respondents found the census question ambiguous, leading them to answer it in varying ways. For example, a Dominican remarked, "This question is very interesting because, one, I'm not totally Black, and then I'm not White. So I'm in the middle. And I'm not Indigenous. So in this case I have to put Hispanic . . ." (Roth 2010:1299). Similarly, a Puerto Rican identified his race as *trigueño*, a term meaning wheat-colored or brown skin. Yet, he believed that most Americans saw him as nonwhite, so he checked "white" on the census question, explaining:

> Yes, I am Puerto Rican but I don't consider myself White. Obviously, the options that the questionnaire gives don't have anything like mixed. Don't have anything like *trigueño*, which is what I consider myself. And the options that are given me make me fill out what is closer to what I consider myself. . . . (Roth 2010:1299)

Roth also found that the respondents' answers to the census question often did not reflect a person's "observed race," which she classified as white, black, or Hispanic based on her impression of each individual's appearance. For Hispanics, in short, answers to the census question had a variety of meanings, making it difficult to discern exactly what it is measuring and how it should be used in social research.

Researchers may also use quantitative analysis to refine operational definitions. Some statistical techniques are specifically designed to do this by helping to identify the underlying dimensions of a set of indicators such as the items making up the Rosenberg Self-Esteem Scale. For example, despite the evidence supporting the validity of the self-esteem scale, researchers have debated whether the set of items represents one or two dimensions (Owens 1993, 1994). One position is that Rosenberg's scale measures "global self-esteem," or a generally positive or negative attitude toward the self. The other position is that the scale actually consists of two subscales, one measuring self-deprecation and the other measuring positive self-worth. Applying a method called "factor analysis," Timothy Owens (1993) found support for the two-dimensional interpretation. His research also showed that the use of these two dimensions revealed "nuances previously overlooked" when the self-esteem scale was treated as unidimensional (Owens 1994:403). For example, self-deprecation was much more strongly related to depression than either positive self-worth or global self-esteem, and positive self-worth had a bigger impact on school grades than negative self-feelings.

SUMMARY

Whereas the first major steps in the measurement process, conceptualization and operationalization, largely follow the deductive logic of inquiry, concepts and operational definitions may emerge and be refined through data analysis, reflective of the inductive logic of inquiry. Researchers may develop concepts from data; assess the quality of measures by using in-depth interviews; and modify operational definitions and refine their meaning through statistical analysis.

KEY TERMS

archival records, p. 117

conceptual (or theoretical) definition, p. 107

conceptualization, p. 106

construct validation, p. 134

convergent validation, p. 133

Cronbach's alpha, p. 131

empirical indicator, p. 109

exhaustive, p. 120

index, p. 110

inter-rater reliability (inter-coder reliability), p. 132

internal consistency, p. 131

interval measurement, p. 121

measurement error, p. 135

measurement validity, p. 127

mutual exclusivity, p. 120

nominal measurement, p. 119

operational definition, p. 112

operationalization, p. 107

ordinal measurement, p. 120

ratio measurement, p. 122

reliability, p. 126

scale, p. 129

social desirability effect, p. 135

test-retest reliability, p. 130

unidimensionality, p. 129

verbal report (self-report), p. 115

KEY POINTS

- The measurement process may follow the deductive logic of inquiry in which theory informs data collection and analysis, but there may be "feedback loops" in this process, which reflect an inductive logic of inquiry.
- In research addressing quantitative questions, the measurement process begins with conceptualization, in which the meaning of a concept is defined and refined based on a careful review of the scientific literature.
- Following conceptualization, concepts are operationalized by specifying empirical indicators and spelling out the procedures to gather data.
- To measure a concept, a researcher may use manipulation operations, which are by definition experimental, or measured operations, which include verbal reports, observation, and the use of archival records.
- An important consideration in operationalization is the level of measurement. Four levels of measurement—nominal, ordinal, interval, and ratio—indicate the meaning of numbers or labels assigned to variable categories and provide progressively more information.
- Concepts are operationalized based on the data source and desired level of precision with the aim of providing the best possible fit between concept and measure.
- Operational definitions may be assessed on the basis of their reliability and validity.
- Reliability may be assessed by calculating the correlation between repeated applications of an operational definition (test-retest reliability), examining the consistency of responses across the items of a composite measure (internal consistency reliability), or observing the correspondence between different coders or raters applying the same operational definition (inter-rater reliability).
- Validity may be assessed by examining the correlation between alternative measures of a concept (convergent validation) or by examining the pattern of associations between an operational definition of a concept and other variables with which the concept should and should not be related (construct validation).
- Analyzing data and assessing the quality of measures may lead to the generation of new concepts and the refinement of operational definitions.

REVIEW QUESTIONS

1. What does it mean to say that measurement moves from the abstract to the concrete? How does this reflect the difference between conceptualization and operationalization in research addressing quantitative questions?
2. Explain the difference between manipulated and measured operational definitions. Which general research approach uses both? What are the three types of measured operational definitions?

3. Rank the four levels of measurement, from least to most, in terms of how much information they provide.

4. What is the relationship between reliability and validity? Is it possible for an operational definition to be valid but unreliable? Reliable but invalid?

5. Which of the three methods of reliability assessment discussed in the text is seldom applied in social research? Which method applies to composite measures? Which method may be used with operational definitions based on observation?

6. Explain the difference between convergent and construct validation.

7. How can data analysis lead to the development of concepts and refinement of operational definitions?

EXERCISES

1. Suppose you were conducting a campus survey of altruism. According to one conceptual definition, altruism refers to helping behavior that is motivated purely by a desire to help others without anticipation of personal rewards. Helping behavior provides some benefit to or improves the well-being of another person. Give examples of at least two empirical indicators of altruism.

2. Suppose you want to test the following hypotheses with data from the General Social Survey (GSS). For each hypothesis, identify the independent and dependent variables, and then find an appropriate GSS question to measure each variable. (Go to the website https://gssdataexplorer.norc.org/variables/vfilter and do a keyword search or filter variables by subject.)

   (a) Men are more likely than women to say that they sometimes drink more than they should.

   (b) People who have completed high school or the equivalent are less likely to smoke than those who haven't.

   (c) People who own a gun are more likely to support stiffer sentences for lawbreakers than people who do not own a gun.

   (d) As education increases, personal income increases.

3. One problem with many studies of domestic violence, including child abuse, is that they have relied upon self-reports. Because domestic abuse is socially stigmatized and can result in criminal charges, individuals may be tempted to underreport abusive conduct. What effect would this have on the reliability and/or validity of such self-report measures?

4. Suppose you want to create a composite measure of altruism in which you ask respondents whether they engaged in several different altruistic actions during the past year (e.g., giving money to charity, helping carry a stranger's belongings, and

giving food or money to a homeless person). How would you assess the reliability and validity of your composite measure?

5. Suppose you were interested in studying students' interactions with each other on your campus. To do so, you conducted field observations at as many campus settings and during as many times as possible, taking copious notes of everything you observed. You are struck by a recurring pattern in your notes: students interacted more often with media and technology—cell phones, headphones, and the like—than face to face with each other. Discuss how you might operationalize this media/technology interaction if you were to go back into the field to see how such interaction varies across social settings. (Hint: You will need to identify and define various observational categories.)

6

Sampling

Case Selection as a Basis for Inference

STUDENT LEARNING OBJECTIVES

By the end of this chapter, you should be able to

1. Describe the steps in the sampling process for probability and nonprobability sampling.

2. Identify the principles of probability sampling and explain how they form the basis for making statistical inferences from a sample to a population.

3. Distinguish between a target population and a sampling frame.

4. Distinguish among probability sampling designs, such as simple random sampling, stratified sampling, and cluster sampling.

5. Identify the factors to consider in determining an appropriate sample size.

6. Distinguish among nonprobability sampling designs, such as convenience sampling, purposive sampling, snowball sampling, and theoretical sampling.

7. Explain the kinds of inferences possible from probability and nonprobability sampling.

Inference is so common in everyday life that we hardly ever take note of it. For example, when you overhear two students saying they find a course "interesting," you might infer that you will find it interesting too. If you see a premed student studying on a Friday night, you may infer that this is the norm for premeds. If you see two students sitting close to one another in the cafeteria, you might infer that they are friends. In each of these examples, the inference is a conclusion or generalization based on an observation. The inference may be true, but it also may be refuted by additional observations.

In general, our confidence in our inferences depends on how many and what particular observations we make. Sometimes we gain confidence by increasing the number of observations; for example, knowing 10 students found a course interesting is likely to strengthen your inference that you will find it interesting. At other times, we enhance our confidence by virtue of the observational context. You probably would be more likely to believe studying on a weekend night is the norm for premeds if you observed this happening in the middle of the semester rather than at the end of the semester during final exams. And, it seems safe to say, you are not likely to infer that two students are friends if you merely observed them sitting next to one another on a crowded subway.

In a similar fashion, social scientists make inferences from systematic observations about the social world. Chapter 5 described methods for determining *what* to observe and *how* to carry out and record one's observations. These methods assume, however, that you have selected the cases—persons, objects, or events—to which you apply your operational definitions. Sampling is the process of selecting cases. This chapter outlines methods for selecting cases and establishing a basis for making inferences.

As with other elements of research design, sampling methods depend on the research question as well as practical considerations. To begin, we discuss the sampling process, focusing on how the research question gives rise to two broad types of sampling design: probability and nonprobability. Then we consider the principles, methods, and process of sampling within each type. In subsequent chapters we discuss sampling in relation to each of the major approaches to social research; this chapter introduces basic sampling concepts that will help you to understand our later discussions.

OVERVIEW: THE SAMPLING PROCESS

probability sampling
Sampling based on a process of random selection that gives each case in the population an equal or known chance of being included in the sample.

Figure 6.1 depicts the steps in the sampling process. As the figure shows, the process begins with the research question, which indicates the kind of inferences we wish to make. The research question dictates the research strategy (e.g., an experiment, survey, field research, in-depth interview, use of existing data) as well as the unit of analysis (e.g., individual people, families, nations, television programs). Together, these two choices shape whether the researcher samples cases at random or by some other means. Sampling methods in which cases are selected randomly and have a known probability of being selected are referred to as **probability sampling**. Methods of nonrandom selection are called **nonprobability sampling**. Much of this chapter is devoted to the steps in drawing probability and nonprobability samples.

The purpose of probability sampling is to make inferences from a sample to a population (see Figure 6.2). A **population** consists of a complete set of persons, objects, or events that share some characteristic, such as all students enrolled in your methods class, all residents of the city of Chicago, or all children's books published in the first half of the 20th century. A **sample** is simply a subset of a population.

For the purpose of estimating population characteristics, probability sampling offers two major advantages over nonprobability sampling. The first is that it removes the possibility that investigator biases will

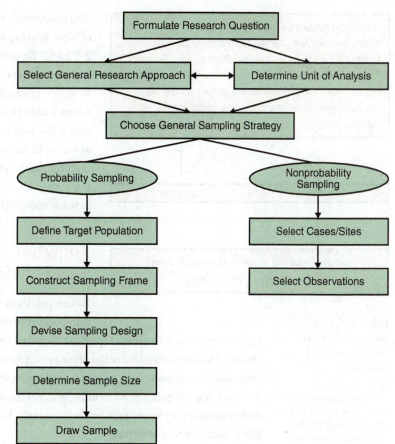

FIGURE 6.1
The Sampling Process

affect the selection of cases. The second advantage is that, by virtue of random selection, the laws of mathematical probability may be applied to estimate the accuracy of the sample. These advantages lend themselves well to certain kinds of research. Survey researchers almost always use probability sampling, and it is a common method in some kinds of existing data research, such as content analysis. Probability sampling works best in sampling individual people or particular artifacts such as periodicals, television programs, and songs. It also may be possible and appropriate for sampling groups or aggregates such as married couples, organizations, and cities.

Probability sampling may not be desirable or possible, however. If you want to understand the meaning of people's actions in a particular context or explain a social movement or historically significant event, it is best to use nonprobability sampling. These research objectives necessarily involve the intensive study of a very small number of cases or events. And as the study unfolds, selecting additional observations will depend on how these may add to one's theoretical understanding. As you will see, probability sampling is less reliable with small samples; it also is inappropriate when sampling is intended to enhance

nonprobability sampling Methods of case selection other than random selection.

population The total membership of a defined class of people, objects, or events.

sample A subset of cases selected from a population.

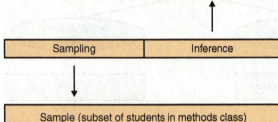

Population (students in methods class)
Aileen, Andrés, Ann, Audrey, Brad, Bruce, Carmen,
Cynthia, Dietrich, Diop, Dwayne, Edward, Elin, Emma,
Felicia, Fred, Garvey, Gayle, Gerry, Guangli, Hal, Heath,
Hector, Heidi, Helene, Isamu, Ivy, Jamal, James, Jane,
Jessica, Joel, John, Jonathan, Julia, Katie, Keith,
Kyle, . . . [etc.]

| Sampling | Inference |

Sample (subset of students in methods class)
Ann, Dwayne, Joel, . . . [etc.]

FIGURE 6.2
**Making Inferences
from a Sample to a
Population**

▼ Drawing names from a
hat is often used to convey
the meaning of random
selection. An analysis
of the 1970 draft lottery
indicated, however, that
manual methods such as
this might not give every
case an equal chance of
being selected.

"the researcher's exposure to different understandings of what is being studied" (Schwartz-Shea and Yanow 2012:85). To gain different understandings, field researchers generally use nonprobability sampling both to select research settings and to sample events or actors within those settings. Nonprobability sampling also is the rule in research using in-depth interviews as well as historical and comparative research. Finally, nonprobability sampling may be necessary when a population is unknown or is not readily identifiable, as in many sociological studies of deviance.

PRINCIPLES OF PROBABILITY SAMPLING

Before you learn the steps in probability sampling, it is important to understand how this form of sampling enables researchers to estimate population characteristics based on the results of a single sample. This requires a discussion of the principles of probability sampling and statistical inference. As you probably (pun intended) know, whole courses are offered in statistics; however, you can gain a good intuitive grasp of the statistical principles underlying probability sampling by knowing a few key concepts. We begin with the concepts of "probability" and "random selection."

Probability and Random Selection

Probability refers to the odds or chances that something will occur. If your instructor puts the names of all 20 students in your class in a hat (with each name presumably on the same-size slip of paper) and selects one at random, the probability that you or any other student will be drawn is 1 in 20, or 5 percent. We know that this is the probability because the selection process—drawing a name from a hat—is random. Statistical inference in probability sampling is based on random selection.

Sometimes we hear students say that they "randomly" met someone; implicit in this everyday understanding of "randomness" is that the meeting occurred by *chance*. Technically speaking, **random selection** refers to a process that gives each element in a set, such as each student in your methods class, a known and independent chance of being chosen. To begin, we need to know what the chance of selection is. By your instructor's method, the chances of randomly choosing one student, say James or Audrey, are 1 in 20. If there were 5 men and 15 women enrolled in the class and your instructor randomly selected one woman and one man, the chances of choosing James would be 1 in 5 and the chances of choosing Audrey would be 1 in 15. Although the chances (or probabilities) differ, selection is random because the probability of selection is *known*.

To be *independent*, the chances of choosing one student should not affect the chances of choosing another. Suppose your instructor divided the class in half and selected one student from the left side of the room and one student from the right side. If James and Audrey were seated on the same side of the room, the selection would not be random because choosing James would mean that Audrey could not be chosen.

If for any reason the selection process favors certain cases or if the selection of one case increases or decreases the likelihood that another case will be selected, then the selection is *biased*. By this definition, your circle of friends clearly would be a biased sample of the student population at your college. So, too, would a number of other samples, such as the students enrolled in your methods course, students who live in your residence hall, and students who pass in front of the student union at a given time. To satisfy the condition of randomness, researchers cannot simply pick cases haphazardly or in any hit-or-miss fashion; subtle and often unconscious bias invariably will enter into the selection process. Rather, mechanical or electronic aids should be used to ensure that chance alone dictates selection. One such aid is described in Box 6.1, DOING SOCIAL RESEARCH: How to Select Things Randomly.

probability The likelihood that something will occur, which may vary from 0 to 100 percent.

random selection A selection process that gives each element in a population a known and independent chance of being selected.

BOX 6.1

DOING SOCIAL RESEARCH

How to Select Things Randomly

If your instructor put each student's name on a slip of paper, placed all the slips in a hat, stirred the slips around with her fingers, and then drew out one slip of paper, would the drawing be random? You might think so, but a well-known example of the failure of physical mixing to achieve randomness suggests that it is probably not. During the Vietnam War, a lottery was conducted, using birthdates, to determine the order in which men (women were not eligible) would be selected for the military draft. Each date was recorded on a slip of paper, each slip was placed in a cylindrical capsule, and the capsules were put first in a box and then poured into a large bowl. Although the box was shaken several times, analyses showed that the order of selection was nonrandom. Capsules were placed in the box in order of the month of birth, beginning with January; as a consequence, those with birthdays in later months of the year had lower lottery numbers, and hence were more likely to be drafted (Fienberg 1971).

continues

continued

BOX 6.1 FIGURE A
The Random Integer Generator at RANDOM.ORG

To make sure that selection is random, you need a mechanism that eliminates physical mixing and human judgment from the selection process. Nowadays, researchers generally use a variety of computer programs that generate random numbers. If all population elements are listed in an Excel spreadsheet, for example, you can use the Excel random number generator to draw a random sample. We recommend one of the easy-to-use, free online services such as RANDOM.ORG or Research Randomizer.

Figure A is a window from RANDOM.ORG for randomly selecting whole numbers. You can use this program to draw a sample or hold a drawing or lottery. If you're drawing a random sample, you'll first need to number all the cases in the population. In Part 1 you enter the sample size in the first box, indicate the size of the population in the third box, and choose a format—one or more columns—for listing the selected random numbers in the last box. Then you click on "Get Numbers." If you want to start over, you click "Reset Form"; and if you want to refine your choice of numerals and output format, you click "Switch to Advanced Mode."

As the note at the bottom of the RANDOM.ORG screen indicates, the numbers generated are "picked independently of each other (like rolls of a die)," which is a requirement of random selection. Consequently, the numbers may "contain duplicates." In other words, each random number is generated from the same range of numbers (the population size). The reason for this is that random selection generally assumes an equal probability of selection. If your instructor were to select two students instead of one, she would probably select one name, set it aside, and then select another. But in doing this, the probability of selection would change. For the first selection, the chances of a student being chosen are 1 in 20, or 5 percent, whereas for the second selection, the chances are 1 in 19, or 5.26 percent. The procedure of removing a case from the population once it is selected is called **sampling without replacement**. By contrast, RANDOM.ORG uses **sampling with replacement**.

In social research and in most real-life applications, we don't want duplicates. After all, we don't want to interview the same person twice! Therefore, sampling with replacement is rare. Fortunately, sampling without replacement has no practical effect on statistical estimates when the population is large and the sample is a small fraction of the population, which is most often the case in social research. If the sample size is a large fraction of the population size (say a half or more), researchers use a correction formula to increase the accuracy of the results.

sampling without replacement A sampling procedure whereby once a case is selected, it is NOT returned to the sampling frame, so that it cannot be selected again.

sampling with replacement A sampling procedure whereby once a case is selected, it is returned to the sampling frame, so that it may be selected again.

Probability Distribution and Sampling Error

To return to our opening example, when your instructor draws one name randomly from a hat containing 20 names, you might imagine two possible outcomes: your name either will or will not be selected. The probability that it will be selected is 1 in 20 or .05; the probability that some other name will be chosen is 19 in 20 or .95. Together, the probability of these two outcomes constitutes a **probability distribution**. Another example is flipping a fair coin. The probability distribution consists of the probabilities of flipping a head (.50) or a tail (.50).

Similarly, in social research we can construct the probability distribution for a single variable. Suppose, for instance, to measure the variable "romantic involvement of students," we interviewed the entire population of 50,000 students at a university and asked them: "Are you intimately or romantically involved with someone at this time?" Table 6.1 presents hypothetical data showing the distribution of responses to

probability distribution A distribution of the probabilities for a variable, which indicates the likelihood that each category or value of the variable will occur.

Table 6.1 Romantic Involvement of Students, University X, Hypothetical Data

Romantically Involved	Number	Percentage	Probability
Yes	21,500	43	.43
No	28,500	57	.57
Total	50,000	100	1.00

this question. The second column shows the number of students who answered "yes" or "no." The third column shows the percentage of students who answered "yes" or "no"; note that 43 percent said they were romantically involved. The last column is the probability distribution. We form the probability distribution by calculating the proportion of "yes" and "no" answers, dividing each number in the second column by the total number of students at University X (50,000). These proportions are equivalent to probabilities; thus, if you were to draw a student at random from this university, the probability that he or she would say "yes" is .43.

It would be very expensive and time-consuming to interview everyone in this population. Just think of all the interviewers you would need to hire and the time required to track down all 50,000 students! Indeed, the cost factor is a major reason for drawing a sample.

Let's assume, then, that we obtain enough funds to draw a sample of 500. Table 6.2 shows a hypothetical distribution of responses to the same question for this sample. Notice that 45 percent of students in the sample answered "yes." Using this as an estimate of the population percentage, we would be off by 2 percent (45% − 43%). This difference is called the **sampling error**. In actual research, we don't know the sampling error (i.e., how far off our estimate is) because we don't know the distribution of the population (as shown in Table 6.1). That's why we're drawing a sample. Therefore, we need some way of knowing how much sample estimates are likely to vary and how confident we can be in a single estimate based on a sample of a given size. Such information is provided by a sampling distribution.[1]

sampling error The difference between an actual population value (e.g., a percentage) and the population value estimated from a sample.

Sampling Distributions

Sample results naturally vary from one sample to another. Table 6.2 shows that 45 percent of the sample answered "yes" to a survey question asking if they were romantically involved, but as you might imagine, other random samples of 500 students might yield estimates such as 39 or 44 or 48 percent. A **sampling distribution** tells us the probability of obtaining each of these estimates; based on probability

sampling distribution A theoretical distribution of sample results for all possible samples of a given size.

Table 6.2 Romantic Involvement of Students, University X, Sample of 500

Romantically Involved	Number	Percentage
Yes	225	45
No	275	55
Total	500	100

---

[1]Our discussion of sampling distributions is modeled after Alan Johnson's (1988) coverage of statistical inference in his excellent textbook *Statistics*.

Table 6.3 Sampling Distribution for a Population
Percentage of 43 and Sample of 500

Sample Estimate (Percentage of "Yes" Responses)	Probability
<39	.021
39	.036
40	.072
41	.120
42	.162
43	.178
44	.162
45	.120
46	.072
47	.036
>47	.021
Total	1.00

sampling theory, it is a distribution of sample results for all possible samples of a given size. Table 6.3 and Figure 6.3 help to illustrate the most important features of this concept. Both the table and figure show the sampling distribution for a population percentage of 43 with a sample size of 500. (To simplify things, we have rounded off the estimates to the nearest point; thus, an estimate of 44.6 = 45.) At the top of the table and on the left-hand side of the figure, for example, you see that there is a .021 probability—or, stated differently, about a 2 in 100 chance—of obtaining a sample estimate of less than 39 percent. This means that, given a population value of 43 percent of students who are romantically involved, there is only a very slim chance (about 2 in 100) of drawing a sample of 500 students in which less than 39 percent are romantically involved.

As you examine the table and figure, keep in mind the difference between a sample distribution and a sampling distribution. A sample distribution shows the results of *individual responses* in a single sample, as in Table 6.2 (i.e., the percentage of students who

FIGURE 6.3
Sampling Distribution for Population Percentage = 43 and Sample Size = 500

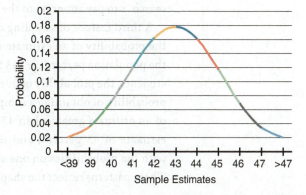

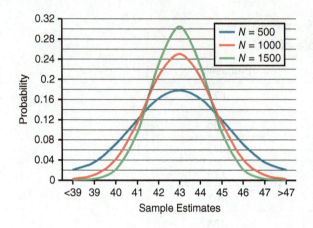

FIGURE 6.4
Sampling Distribution for Population Percentage = 43 with Different Sample Sizes

standard error A statistical measure of the "average" sampling error for a particular sampling distribution, which indicates how much sample results will vary from sample to sample.

are romantically involved in a sample of 500 at University X). A sampl*ing* distribution shows the probability distribution of a *sample statistic*, such as a percentage, for all possible samples, as in Table 6.3 and Figure 6.3 (i.e., the probability of obtaining sample estimates of 39, 44, or 48 percent, for example, across all possible samples of 500 students in the same university). In reality, the number of possible samples of size 500, each drawn randomly from a population of 50,000, is infinitely large. This is why we say that the sampling distribution is theoretical, as derived from probability sampling theory.

Certain features of a sampling distribution provide the basis of statistical inference. First, note in the table and figure that the single most probable estimate is 43 percent. As you might infer, this is also the average value or, in statistical jargon, the *mean* of the sampling distribution. A crucial feature of the sampling distribution of a percentage is that the mean of all sample estimates is always equal to the population value we're estimating, which is 43 percent.

The second feature pertains to how sample estimates vary. Although the single most probable sample estimate (43%) will hit the population value (43%) right on the nose, most sample estimates will miss the population value. By how much will they miss it? The average distance of sample values from the population value is measured by the **standard error**. The standard error for the sampling distribution in Table 6.3 is 2.2. The most fundamental principle of probability sampling theory is *the standard error decreases as the sample size increases*. You can see this in Figure 6.4, which overlays the sampling distributions for samples of 500 (shown in Figure 6.3), 1,000, and 1,500. Notice that for larger samples, sample estimates are more tightly clustered around the population percentage of 43, and therefore have smaller standard errors. For samples of 1,000 and 1,500, the standard errors are 1.6 and 1.3, respectively. Thus, one way of controlling the amount of sampling error as you design your research is to pay attention to the size of the sample.

A third feature of sampling distributions is their distinctive pattern. Notice that the probability of an estimate declines as the difference between the estimate and the population percentage (43 percent) increases. Thus, for a random sample of 500 students, the probability of our sample estimate of 45 percent (.120) is less than the probability of obtaining a sample estimate of 44 percent (.162), and the probability of an estimate greater than 47 percent (.021) is far less than the probability of an estimate of 45 percent, and so on. In addition, the distribution is symmetrical, with the probabilities on one side of the mean exactly equal to those on the other. These patterns reflect the shape of the distribution, for as it turns out, the sampling distribution of a percentage is a "bell-shaped" curve called the **normal curve** or **normal distribution**.

Finally, in a sampling distribution, predictable percentages of sample estimates fall within measurable distances of the population value we're estimating. Figure 6.5 shows the probability (or percentage) of sample estimates in a normal distribution that lie within plus or minus 1, 2, and 3 standard errors of the mean. Notice the chances are 34.13 percent that the sample estimate will be between 0 and 1 standard error above the mean, 47.73 (34.13 + 13.60) percent that it will be

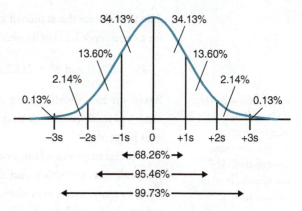

FIGURE 6.5
Standard Normal Distribution

between 0 and 2 standard errors above the mean, and so on. To apply this knowledge, we must first express a given distance from the population value, not in the property we're measuring, but in terms of the standard error. Thus, instead of saying that a sample percentage of "yes" answers to the survey question, say 46, is 3 percentage points above the mean, we say that it is 3/2.2 = 1.36 standard errors above the mean. This is just like translating one set of units into another, such as converting US dollars to British pounds or temperature in degrees Fahrenheit to temperature in degrees centigrade (Johnson 1988:286). The probability of getting a sample percentage that is between 0 and 1.36 standard errors above the mean, which can be extrapolated from Figure 6.5 (or obtained from a table of areas under the normal curve), is .413, or 41.3 percent.

normal curve A bell-shaped distribution of data that characterizes many variables and statistics, such as the sampling distribution of a proportion or mean. Also called *normal distribution*.

Statistical Inference

Now, let's return to our hypothetical sample in Table 6.2 to see how statistical inference works in probability sampling. Our random sample is but one of the nearly infinite number of samples we could have drawn of all possible samples of 500 students. We don't know the percentage of students at University X who answered "yes" to the question about romantic involvement, but we would like to estimate what this percentage is. Our best guess is the sample estimate of 45 percent; however, short of interviewing all 50,000 students, we cannot determine whether this is equal to the actual population percentage. To get around this problem, rather than using a single point estimate, like 45 percent, statisticians construct *interval estimates*. Knowing the sampling distribution, we can determine how confident we are that the population value lies within some range of a sample estimate. Level of confidence is a function of how many standard errors we add and subtract from the sample estimate. For example, based on the normal distribution, we are confident that 95 percent of the time, selecting a random sample of 500 students will result in a sample estimate that is within two standard errors of the population value (see Figure 6.3). Using the 500-student sample data to estimate the standard error, we come up with the following interval estimate for a confidence level of 95 percent:

$$45 - 2(2.2) \text{ and } 45 + 2(2.2) = 40.6 \text{ to } 49.4$$

confidence interval
A range (interval) within which a population value is estimated to lie at a specific level of confidence.

Based on this result, called a **confidence interval**, we could conclude that we are 95 percent confident that the actual population value falls between 40.6 and 49.4 percent.

In social surveys and opinion polling, it is common practice to select random samples, calculate statistics, and then use theoretical knowledge of sampling distributions to make inferences about population characteristics. Pollsters usually do not report the "confidence level" or make reference to "confidence intervals." Instead, they present "margins of error" that are equivalent to the 95 percent confidence interval. For example, on July 26, 2017, Gallup reported, based on telephone interviews with 1,500 adults, that the percentage of Americans who approved of the job Donald J. Trump is doing as president was 39 percent, plus or minus 3 percentage points. Now you know what this means. Gallup is claiming that they are 95 percent confident that the percentage of all Americans who approve of the job Trump is doing lies between 36 and 42 percent.

Gallup's margin of error of plus or minus 3 percentage points is smaller than the margin of error for our sample of 500 students (plus or minus 4.4), because it is based on a larger sample (1,500 versus 500). This confirms what we inferred from Figure 6.4: the standard error decreases as the sample size increases. As you'll see, how big a sample you choose to draw depends partly on how precise your sample estimates need to be. Smaller margins of error are more precise.

To check your understanding of the principles of probability sampling and also learn more about the accuracy of pre-election polls in the 2016 US presidential election, see Box 6.2, CHECKING YOUR UNDERSTANDING: The Principles of Probability Sampling as Applied to the 2016 Pre-election Polls.

SUMMARY

Based on random selection and statistical inference, all probability sampling follows a unified framework for making inferences from a sample to a population: researchers calculate statistical estimates from a random sample; then, they use knowledge of the sampling distribution of the statistic to establish a confidence interval, which indicates the level of confidence that a population value falls within a specified range.

continued

BOX 6.2

CHECKING YOUR UNDERSTANDING

The Principles of Probability Sampling as Applied to the 2016 Pre-election Polls

Just days before the 2016 US presidential election, between November 2 and 6, a poll conducted on behalf of CBS News asked a sample of respondents who they would vote for. Based on a probability sample of 1,753 adults in the United States, the poll showed that 47 percent of 1,426 "likely voters" supported Hillary Clinton and 43 percent supported Donald J. Trump; the remainder supported other candidates (5 percent), wouldn't vote (1 percent), or did not know or did not answer the question (4 percent). Excluding the last two categories, the poll's best sample estimates were that Clinton would receive 49.5 percent and Trump would receive 45.3 percent of the vote, with a margin of error of plus or minus 3 points (for details, see http://www.cbsnews.com/news/cbs-news-poll-state-of-the-race-the-day-before-election-day/).

Let's use this poll and another to check your understanding of the principles of probability sampling.

1. According to the sample results, what is the probability that a "likely voter" will vote for Clinton in the 2016 election? What is the probability that a "likely voter" will vote for Trump? (Be sure to use the best sample estimates.)
2. For the CBS News poll, what would be the confidence interval for the estimate of the percentage of the vote Clinton will receive? What is the confidence interval for the estimate of the percentage of the vote Trump will receive?
3. The final results of the 2016 election showed that Clinton received 48.2 percent and Trump received 46.1 percent of the total US vote. Based on these results, what would be the mean (i.e., average) percentage of votes for Clinton for a sampling distribution with samples = 1,500 (about the size of the CBS News poll)? Is this percentage within the margin of error (or confidence interval) of the CBS News poll?
4. Based on the percentage of the national vote, what is the sampling error for the CBS News poll with respect to the Clinton vote?

Around the same time (between November 3 and 6), Monmouth University conducted a poll of a random sample of 802 registered voters. Among likely voters, the results were very similar to the CBS News poll: 50 percent supported Clinton, 44 percent supported Trump, and the remainder supported other candidates or were undecided, with a margin of error of plus or minus 3.6 points (Monmouth University Poll 2016).

continues

continued

5. Based on the principles of probability sampling, why is the margin of error greater in the Monmouth University poll than the one conducted on behalf of CBS News?

Given similar results in numerous other pre-election polls, experts predicted that the chances of Clinton's winning the election were about 90 percent (American Association for Public Opinion Research [AAPOR] 2017). Consequently, when she lost, "there was . . . widespread consensus that the polls failed" (AAPOR 2017:2). Let's examine the legitimacy of this claim as we consider the answers to the above questions.

1. The probability, or proportion of voters who said they would vote for Clinton, is .495 and the probability of likely voters supporting Trump is .453.
2. The confidence interval for the Clinton vote is 49.5 percent plus or minus 3 points, or 46.5 to 52.5 percent; the confidence interval for the Trump vote is 42.3 to 48.3.
3. The mean of the sampling distribution, equal to the mean of the population, is 48.2 percent for Clinton, which is within the confidence interval.
4. The sampling error, or difference between the sample estimate (49.5) and population value (48.2), is 1.3 percent.
5. As sample size increases, the standard error and, therefore, the margin of error decreases. Hence, the CBS News poll, based on a larger sample (1,426) than the Monmouth poll (802), had a smaller margin of error (plus or minus 3 versus 3.6).

As you can see, these two polls were reasonably accurate in estimating the popular vote. That is, the actual percentage of votes each candidate received was well within the margin of error of both polls. Furthermore, an analysis of national polls completed within 13 days of the election showed, on average, that Clinton would win the popular vote by about 3.2 percentage points (AAPOR 2017). That she won by 2.1 points indicates that taken together the polls were fairly accurate.

So, why do people believe that the polls failed? Part of it has to do with the fact that the winner of the popular vote does not necessarily determine who wins the presidency. Over 90 percent of the time the winner of the popular vote is elected president. But focusing on the popular vote, as this election proves, can be misleading. Also feeding erroneous conclusions, pre-election polls showed Clinton leading in three key states—Pennsylvania, Michigan, and Wisconsin—that Trump won by a very slim margin. In a thorough analysis of 2016 pre-election polling, a committee commissioned by AAPOR concluded that the under-estimation of Trump support in these states was due, in part, to changes in Trump support in the last week of the campaign. The committee also pointed out that "greater caution is needed in predicting" the outcome of the Electoral College given the uneven quality of state-level polls, which tend to be smaller in size and of lesser quality than national polls (AAPOR 2017).

STEPS IN PROBABILITY SAMPLING

Armed with an understanding of probability sampling theory and statistical inference, we are ready to review the steps in probability sampling. Before you draw a random sample and calculate sample estimates, you must identify the set of cases from which to draw your sample. This involves the first two steps in probability sampling: defining and then operationalizing the population to which you wish to generalize (see Figure 6.1). These steps should sound familiar to you, as they parallel the steps in defining (conceptualizing) and operationalizing concepts in the process of measurement.

Define Target Population

Probability sampling is intended "to describe or make inferences to *well-defined populations*" (Groves et al. 2009:69; our emphasis). Thus, the first step in drawing a probability sample is to clearly identify the **target population**, that is, the population to which the researcher would like to generalize his or her results. To define the target population, the researcher must specify the criteria for determining which cases are included in the population and which cases are excluded. The relevant criteria depend on the type of unit, the research topic, and pragmatic considerations. With individual people, some combination of locale and selected demographic variables such as gender, race, employment status, and age may be used. For example, in a series of campus surveys carried out in his methods classes, Royce Singleton and his students defined the target population as "all students currently enrolled and on campus (i.e., not studying abroad) during the current semester." Only on-campus students were targeted because the interviews were conducted in person. In a study of aging and religion, Stephen Ainlay, Royce Singleton, and Victoria Swigert (1992:180) restricted the target population to "noninstitutionalized residents of Worcester, Massachusetts, who were 65 years of age or older." For practical reasons, the researchers excluded "institutionalized" residents in nursing homes or other facilities where access was limited.

> **target population** The population to which the researcher would like to generalize his or her results.

For the National Education Longitudinal Study (NELS), which Beckett Broh (2002) used to analyze the relationship between extracurricular activities and academic achievement, the target population for the base year, 1988, consisted of students enrolled in "all public and private schools containing eighth grades in the fifty states and District of Columbia" (Spencer et al. 1990:6). This definition was clarified further by taking into account several pragmatic considerations:

> Excluded . . . are Bureau of Indian Affairs (BIA) schools, special education schools for the handicapped, area vocational schools that do not enroll students directly, and schools for dependents of U.S. personnel overseas. The student

population excludes students with severe mental handicaps, students whose command of the English language was not sufficient for understanding the survey materials (especially the cognitive tests), and students with physical or emotional problems that would make it unduly difficult for them to participate in the survey.

Construct Sampling Frame

sampling frame An operational definition of the population that provides the basis for drawing a sample; ordinarily consists of a list of cases.

The next step is to find a way of identifying all the persons or cases in the population. This involves constructing a sampling frame. The **sampling frame** denotes the set of all cases from which the sample is actually selected. Because the term can be misleading, please note that the sampling frame is *not a sample*; rather, it is an *operational definition of the population* that provides the basis for sampling.

There are two ways of constructing a sampling frame: (1) listing all cases from which a sample may be drawn and (2) defining population membership by a rule that provides a basis for case selection. For example, in a city telephone survey, the sampling frame could consist of the city phone book (a listing) or telephone numbers within targeted telephone exchanges (a rule). In survey research, establishing a sampling frame often amounts to obtaining an adequate listing—either of the population as a whole or of subgroups of the population. But listing is not always possible or preferable. As long as cases can be identified, a rule procedure usually can be devised for finding and selecting cases. Suppose you want to interview people attending a concert. You obviously cannot obtain a list in advance of the concert; however, the fact that everyone must arrive at (and may leave) the concert at a particular time allows you to establish a rule based on time of arrival (or departure). Thus, stationing interviewers at points of entry or exit, you could randomly select one attendee in every ten.

FIGURE 6.6
Relationship among Target Population, Sampling Frame, and Sample

For relatively small populations such as members of a local school, church, or some other institution, lists are often available. The sampling frame for the campus surveys conducted by Singleton and his students consisted of a complete list of students in an Excel file obtained from the school's registrar. Many small and midsize US cities have population and household directories. For the aging and religion study, the sampling frame was derived from a computer tape of the 1989 Worcester city census, which was culled to include only people 65 years of age or older.

For many populations, though, especially at the national level, lists are unavailable. To sample national populations, researchers generally

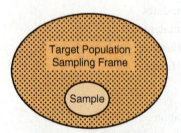

A. Perfect Correspondence between Target Population and Sampling Frame

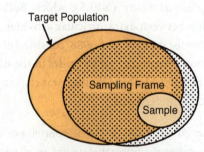

B. Imperfect Correspondence between Target Population and Sampling Frame

break the target population down into natural groupings for which lists (or sampling frames) are available or can be constructed at low cost. We discuss this sampling strategy further under "Sampling Designs."

Figure 6.6 shows the relationship among the target population, sampling frame, and sample. To make accurate inferences from a sample to a target population, the sampling frame should be identical to the target population, as in Figure 6.6A. However, existing frames often are incomplete, as suggested by the imperfect overlap between the target population and sampling frame in Figure 6.6B. Although the Worcester city census provided a reasonably accurate frame, it was nonetheless flawed. Not only was it likely that many people were not counted in the census, but through deaths and migration in and out of Worcester, the target population was bound to have changed somewhat by the time residents were interviewed. This mismatch between the sampling frame and target population is called **coverage error**. It is a particular problem in telephone surveys, which we discuss in Chapter 8.

Once you have defined the target population and obtained or constructed a sampling frame, you are ready to draw a random sample. Probability sampling always involves random selection, but how random selection is implemented depends on the type of sampling design.

coverage error The error that occurs when the sampling frame does not match the target population.

Devise Sampling Design

The defining characteristic of a probability sample is that each case has a *known, non-zero probability* of being selected. For some types of probability samples, the chance or probability of selection is equal. But for others, it is not. Whether the probability of selection is equal or not is one of the ways that probability-sampling designs differ from one another. In this section, we discuss three probability-sampling designs: simple random sampling, stratified random sampling, and cluster sampling.

SIMPLE RANDOM SAMPLING

We begin with the most basic design, a **simple random sample**, in which not only does every case in the sampling frame have an equal probability of being selected, every possible *combination* of cases has an equal chance of being included in the sample. If your instructor put every student's name in a hat and randomly selected two students, one after the other, she would produce a simple random sample because all combinations of two students would have an equal chance of being selected. But if she put female students in one hat and males in another, and randomly selected one name from each hat, she would not have a simple random sample because many combinations, such as any two females or any two males, could not be drawn.

Singleton and his students used simple random sampling to select the sample for their campus surveys. Having obtained an Excel file with a complete list of currently enrolled students from the registrar (the sampling frame), they used Excel's random

simple random sample A probability sampling design in which every case and every possible combination of cases has an equal chance of being included in the sample.

number generator to select N students (the sample size N was different in each survey). In fall 2004 and spring 2005, the topic of the campus surveys was relationships. In both semesters, the researchers asked students: "Are you intimately or romantically involved with someone at this time?" The average percentage of "yes" answers across the two surveys was—you guessed it—43 percent. As you also might have guessed, from fall to spring, this percentage increased, from 39 to 48 percent; moreover, there was a marked increase, from 20 to 70 percent, in the percentage of romantic partners who were other students at the college.

Simple random sampling requires a complete list of the population; however, as we noted earlier, such a list may not exist (and may be prohibitively expensive to construct). In addition, very often there are more effective ways of applying probability sampling than drawing a simple random sample, to which we now turn.

STRATIFIED RANDOM SAMPLING

stratified random sample A probability sampling design in which the population is divided into strata (or variable categories) and independent random samples are drawn from each stratum.

In the religion and aging study, Ainlay, Singleton, and Swigert (1992) wanted to compare residents in three age groups: 65–74, 75–84, and 85 or older. For this purpose, they had two choices in drawing a sample. The first choice was to select a simple random sample that was large enough to include an adequate number of residents in each group. The drawback to this choice, however, is that they would need a very large sample if the proportion of the population in one or more of these age groups was very small. In fact, in the sampling frame of older Worcester residents, 45 percent of the residents were 65–74, 40 percent were 75–84, and only 15 percent were 85 or older. So, a simple random sample of 200, for example, would have yielded, on average, only 30 residents in the oldest age group.

proportionate stratified sampling A sampling procedure in which strata are sampled proportionately to population composition.

The second strategy, which the researchers chose, was to break down the sampling frame into the three age groups and draw a simple random sample within each of these subpopulations. When combined, the three subsamples form what is called a **stratified random sample**. The word "strata" refers to the subpopulations into which the sampling frame is divided. Stratification can be based on categories of any one or a combination of relevant variables, but it requires that you identify the stratum of each person (or object) being sampled and that you know the size of each stratum in the population. The strata in the aging and religion study were age groups (65–74, 75–84, and 85 or older), which the researchers knew from date-of-birth information listed in the sampling frame.

disproportionate stratified sampling A sampling procedure in which strata are sampled disproportionately to population composition.

There are two types of stratified random samples, which differ based on whether the proportion of people sampled in each stratum is equal to the proportion of people in each stratum of the population. In **proportionate stratified sampling**, the sample proportions equal the population proportions of each stratum; by contrast, in **disproportionate stratified sampling**, the sample proportions do *not* equal the population proportions of each stratum. Table 6.4 shows the number and proportion of

Table 6.4 Number and Proportion of Older Worcester Residents for Population and Sample*

Age group (= stratum)	Population		Proportionate Stratified Sample		Disproportionate Stratified Sample	
	Number	Proportion	Number	Proportion	Number	Proportion
65–74	11,250	.45	225	.45	150	.30
75–84	10,000	.40	200	.40	150	.30
85+	3,750	.15	75	.15	200	.40
Total	25,000	1.00	500	1.00	500	1.00

Numbers have been rounded to simplify the illustration.

residents in each age group for the population as a whole and for two potential stratified random samples of 500 older Worcester residents. Notice that in a proportionate stratified sample, the proportion in each group is the same for the sample and population; for example, 45 percent of the older *population* is between 65 and 74 years of age and 45 percent of the *sample* is in this age group. In a disproportionate stratified sample, however, the proportion in each group is different for the sample and population; for example, 45 percent of the older *population* is between 65 and 74 years of age, but 30 percent of the *sample* is in this age group.

Whereas a proportionate stratified sample produces a representative sample of the population on the basis of the stratifying variable, a disproportionate stratified sample does not. To obtain unbiased estimates of population characteristics, researchers therefore make a statistical adjustment, called **weighting**, which takes into account the disproportionality of the sample. The religion and aging study ultimately used a disproportionate stratified random sample (see the last two columns in Table 6.4), in which each person in the sample was given a weight inversely proportional to his or her probability of selection.

weighting A procedure that corrects for the unequal probability of selecting one or more segments (e.g., strata) of the population.

Compared to simple random sampling, stratified random sampling can be advantageous in two ways: by (1) ensuring a sufficient number of cases in each stratum and (2) reducing the standard error. First, stratified random sampling was more efficient in the aging study because, in comparison with a simple random sample, a much smaller overall sample was necessary to obtain an adequate number of residents in each age group. It would have taken a simple random sample of 1,000 to get around 150 residents who were 85 years of age or older; ultimately, though, a stratified sample one-half this size (500) contained no less than 150 residents in any one group.

By reducing the standard error of the sample, stratified random sampling also provides more precise estimates of population characteristics. In addition to sample size, the standard error depends on the amount of variation in the population: the greater the variability, the higher the standard error. Stratified sampling controls for this variability by dividing the population into strata that are relatively homogeneous on key variables. In the aging and religion study, for example, people in each age group should be more similar to one another than to people in the other age groups on several variables, such as physical health, number of living close friends, and number of grandchildren or great-grandchildren. Consequently, the standard error for each sampled age group will be lower than the overall standard error, based on a simple random sample.

Compared to simple random sampling, the only way in which stratified random sampling is less efficient is that you must divide the sampling frame into the relevant strata and draw separate samples from each stratum. The next design we discuss offers different gains in efficiency by reducing the costs of data collection.

CLUSTER SAMPLING

Both simple random sampling and stratified random sampling assume that a complete list of the population is available. What do you do, however, when your target population is so large that it is either impossible or impractical to list all its members? The only lists of the current US population—income tax forms and census forms filed every 10 years—are confidential and not available to the public. Lists of most city and all state populations simply do not exist, and it would be too expensive to compile lists of these and other very large populations. In such instances, researchers often are able to obtain a sample in stages, using a method called **cluster sampling**.

cluster sampling A probability sampling design in which the population is broken down into natural groupings or areas, called clusters, and a random sample of clusters is drawn.

In cluster sampling, the population is broken down into groups of cases, called "clusters." Clusters consist of natural groupings such as colleges and churches or geographic areas such as states, counties, cities, and blocks. The first step in drawing a cluster sample is to randomly select a sample of clusters. The second step is to obtain a list of all cases within each selected cluster. If all the cases in each sampled cluster are included in the sample, the design is called a *single-stage cluster sample* in that sampling occurs once—at the cluster level.

multistage cluster sampling A sampling design in which sampling occurs at two or more steps or stages.

More frequently, cluster sampling involves sampling at two or more steps or stages, hence the term **multistage cluster sampling** (see Figure 6.7). An example of a two-stage cluster sample comes from the NELS 1988 base year survey (Spencer et al. 1990). Although a single list of all eighth-grade students does not exist and would be difficult and extremely costly to compile, all eighth-graders (except for the homeschooled) attend schools. Therefore, the NELS used a complete and accurate list of public and private *schools* in the United States maintained by Quality Education Data, Inc. From the nearly 40,000 schools nationwide in this database, the researchers selected a random sample of 1,057 schools (first stage); then, from each participating school, they obtained a list of all eighth-graders and randomly selected 26 students (second stage).

Cluster samples differ from stratified random samples in a few important ways. First, in terms of population breakdown, strata consist of *variable* categories, whereas clusters are geographical units or natural groupings formed by existing social arrangements, such as schools, churches, and city blocks. Second, in a stratified sample, every stratum is included in the sample because sampling occurs within every stratum; in a cluster sample, however, not all clusters are included in the sample because clusters are randomly selected. Third, while stratified random sampling is used either to increase sample precision or to provide a sufficient number of cases in small strata, the principal reason for cluster sampling is to reduce the costs of data collection. In face-to-face interview studies of large, widely scattered populations, two major costs are interviewer travel and the listing of population elements. Compared to simple random and stratified random sampling methods, clustering concentrates interviews within fewer and smaller geographical areas, thereby spreading the travel costs over several cases and reducing the costs of any one interview. Moreover, since the listing of population elements is a prerequisite for simple random and stratified random methods, clustering also can reduce costs by limiting the compilation of lists of cases to selected clusters rather than compiling a list of the entire population.

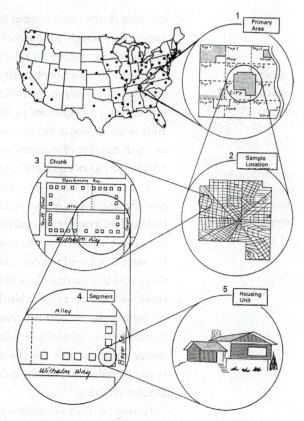

FIGURE 6.7
A Multistage Cluster Sample

Multistage sample designs may involve either simple random or stratified random sampling at each stage of the design. In other words, we can stratify clusters just as we stratify individual units. The NELS stratified clusters, dividing schools into several strata according to four variables: school type (public, Catholic private, other private), region of the country, urbanicity (whether the school's location was urban, suburban, or rural), and percent minority. A number of schools were then selected within each stratum.

One problem with cluster sampling is that natural clusters often vary considerably in the numbers of cases they contain. This, in fact, was true of the schools in the NELS. There are two ways of handling this problem in order to reduce potential sampling error. First, clusters can be stratified *by population size*. In this way, a relatively few clusters with extremely large populations can be sampled from a separate stratum to guarantee that they are represented in the sample. Otherwise, one runs the risk of not selecting clusters that account for a major proportion of the population. When clusters vary in size, though, a more common solution is to equalize the probability of selecting individuals by making the selection of clusters proportionate to the size of the cluster. This method, called **probability proportionate to size sampling**, was applied to the selection of schools in the NELS. Essentially, each cluster was assigned a probability of selection proportionate to the number of cases in the cluster. Thus, a school with 1000 students would be twice as likely to be selected as a school with 500 students. If an equal number of students are selected from each school, then each student in the population has an equal probability of being selected.[2]

A second problem with cluster samples is that, even though they are more *cost*-efficient, they are less precise, size for size, than either simple random or stratified random samples. The main reason for this is that variation within clusters tends to be much smaller than variation between clusters. For example, people who live on the same block tend to have similar incomes and other socioeconomic characteristics; those who live on one block may differ markedly on these same characteristics from those who live on another block. Consequently, because we select a random sample of clusters, the variability across clusters can be relatively large, which increases the standard error. In addition, sampling errors are associated with each stage of a multistage cluster sample. So, the sampling error (or standard error) in the total sample is compounded and can be quite large relative to the error produced by one simple random selection.[3]

Having carefully defined the target population, obtained a good sampling frame, and come up with a sampling design, the researcher finally must determine an appropriate sample size.

Determine Sample Size

When our students are designing a survey, one of the first questions they ask is, "How big should my sample be?" Like so many issues in social research, the short answer is, "It depends." A variety of factors shape optimal sample size, many of which are beyond the scope of this book. However, we can provide a good idea of how informally to "calculate" an appropriate sample size because much of the time it boils down to two primary considerations: desired precision and available resources.

probability proportionate to size sampling The selection of cases in cluster sampling so that the probability of selection is proportionate to the size of (i.e., the number of cases in) the cluster.

---

[2] The following example illustrates how the probabilities are equal. Suppose that the total number of students in the population is 500,000 and that 100 schools are selected. The probability of selecting school A, with 1,000 students, is 100 × 1,000/500,000, or .20. The probability of selecting school B, with 500 students, is 100 × 500/500,000, or .10. If 50 students are selected from each school, the probability of selecting a student from school A is .20 × 50/1,000, or .01, which is the same as the probability of selecting a student from school B (.10 × 50/500 = .01).

[3] One way of handling the first problem is to increase the number of clusters that are selected; however, this also increases costs. Because stratifying tends to reduce the standard error, another method is to stratify clusters. Indeed, most large-scale surveys, such as the NELS, use complex sampling designs combining both cluster and stratified sampling.

DESIRED PRECISION

If you were planning to meet a friend for lunch, would you prefer he say that he'll be there between 11 a.m. and 1 p.m. or between 12 p.m. and 12:15 p.m.? Most of us probably would say the latter because it is more precise (and thus we can better plan the day). Just as we may want a higher level of precision in our everyday lives, researchers value a high level of precision in their sample estimates, which is influenced by the sample size.

To understand how desired precision enters into calculations of optimal sample size, we need to return to probability sampling theory. As noted earlier, precision is a function of the margin of error in a sample estimate, which determines the size of the confidence interval. Confidence intervals of different sizes reflect different levels of precision. Thus, it is more precise to say that the percentage of students who are romantically involved is likely to fall between 41 and 45 than to say that the percentage is likely to fall between 37 and 49. Of course, the larger the sample, the smaller the standard error and size of the confidence interval. Therefore, it follows that the larger the sample, the greater the precision of the sample estimate.

Two facts about this relationship are especially noteworthy because they defy intuition to a certain extent. First, ordinarily *the absolute size of the sample rather than the proportion of the population sampled determines precision*. As long as the population is relatively large, the proportion of the population sampled has a negligible effect on precision. For example, in 2010 the population of Vermont was a little over 600,000 and the population of Massachusetts was over 6.5 million. Now, if one were to take a simple random sample of 2,000 residents in each of these states, the proportion of the total population in the sample would be about 1 of every 300 persons in Vermont and about 1 of every 3,250 persons in Massachusetts. Yet, based on these samples, an estimate (say, of average income) would be just as precise for Massachusetts as for Vermont.

Although precision is governed primarily by the absolute numerical size of the sample rather than by the proportion of the population sampled, *the sample need not be enormous in size to yield very precise results*. This is the second crucial fact about precision and sample size. The sampling error tends to be quite small for samples of size 2,000 to 3,000, and increasing the sample size beyond this number decreases the error by so little that it usually is not worth the additional cost.

The mathematical explanation for both of these facts about sample size and precision can be found in the formula for the standard error:

$$\text{S.E.} = \frac{\sigma}{\sqrt{N}}$$

The Greek letter σ (sigma) stands for a statistical measure of variability in the population known as the *standard deviation*; N is the sample size. Thus, the standard error increases as the standard deviation of the population increases, and it goes down as the *square root* of the sample size goes up. This formula applies to populations of theoretically infinite size and simple random samples. Finite populations and more complex designs require more elaborate formulas.[4]

Because of the square root function in the formula, each time we wish to decrease the standard error by one-half we must increase the sample size fourfold. At this rate, the precision gained with increased sample size reaches a point of minute, diminishing returns after a few thousand cases. Consider, for example, how sample size affects the standard error of a percentage, such as the estimated percentage of the vote a candidate will receive in an election. With two candidates and an evenly split vote, the standard error will be 5.0 percent for a sample size of 100. As Table 6.5 shows, this error decreases to 2.5 percent when the sample reaches 400 and to 1.0 percent when the sample reaches 2,500. To get the error down to 0.5 percent would require a sample size of 10,000.

You should now understand how election forecasters make accurate predictions using samples of a few thousand out of millions of voters. The huge size of the *population* has no effect on the precision of sample estimates. And a sample size of 2,000 to 3,000 is generally large enough to predict accurately all but the closest elections.

We hasten to add that 2,000 to 3,000 should not be regarded as *the* standard size for reliable sample results, as studies vary considerably in the amount of precision that is required. In general, desired precision is based on how the data will be analyzed and how it will be applied. At one extreme, 20–25 cases may be sufficient for pretests and pilot studies to evaluate procedures and feasibility. For experiments comparing only two groups, researchers may use as few as 30 research participants, although this small a number risks not detecting a relationship when it actually exists. At the other extreme, large-scale continuing studies that provide input for major policy decisions may require samples in the tens of thousands (Sudman 1976). For example, the Current Population

Table 6.5 Standard Error of a Percentage of 50 Percent, Broken Down by Sample Size

Sample Size	Standard Error (percent)
100	5.0
400	2.5
2500	1.0
10,000	0.5

[4]For example, the formula for the standard error should be multiplied by a correction factor equal to $\sqrt{1-f}$, where f is the *sampling fraction*, or proportion of the population included in the sample. Notice, however, that if the sampling fraction is near zero, then the correction factor becomes $\sqrt{1}$, or 1, which has no effect on the standard error. Most often in social research, the population is so much larger than the sample that f is extremely small—near zero—and the correction factor can be ignored.

Survey, which is the primary source of labor force statistics for the US population, requires a sample of about 60,000 housing units, so that "a difference of 0.2 percentage points in the unemployment rate for two consecutive months [would] be statistically significant at the .10 level" (US Census Bureau 2006:3–1).

Calculating an appropriate sample size based on how the data will be analyzed is an advanced topic beyond the scope of this book. (Gerald van Belle [2008] provides some statistical rules of thumb for the advanced student.) For statistical estimates of a population percentage, several online tools are available to calculate how large a sample is needed to get results of a specified precision and to find the level of precision for an existing simple random sample. See, for example, "Sample Size Calculator" from The Survey System, located at http://www.surveysystem.com/sscalc.htm. If you're doing a survey as a class project, we recommend at least 25 cases to estimate a single population characteristic and double that number to examine a relationship between two variables. Of course, factors other than statistical precision enter into determinations of sample size. Chief among these factors are time and cost.

AVAILABLE RESOURCES

As you know now, in probability sampling, the larger the sample the smaller the error. So, we are tempted to say that you should draw as large a sample as you can afford. The reality, however, is that money and time must enter into the equation for determining sample size. Suppose, for example, that your university just won a grant for $10,000 to conduct a face-to-face survey on attitudes toward crime in the city. The university wants to hire students with knowledge of research methods (i.e., you!) to collect and analyze the data. One rule of thumb in survey research is to allocate one-half of both money and time to data collection and the other half to data analysis (Sudman 1976:88). Once the data-collection method is specified, the sample size can be determined on a time- and cost-per-case basis. Thus, if student interviewers were hired at the very low rate of $20 per interview and $5,000 were allocated to data collection, the sample size would be 250.

The resource of time may be the most important consideration for student projects, as it was in the campus surveys conducted by Singleton's methods classes. Because this was a class project in which students enrolled in the course conducted the survey interviews, monetary cost was not a factor. But to design, carry out, and analyze the survey during a single semester, only about three to four weeks could be devoted to data collection. And during this period each student could be expected to complete only a limited number of interviews. Based on the time necessary to set up and carry out each interview, Singleton and his students agreed to assign 10 interviews per student. Therefore, sample sizes for the campus surveys were equal to 10 times the number of students enrolled in the course. With 26 students enrolled in fall 2004, the projected sample size was $10 \times 26 = 260$. Assuming all 260 students would be interviewed, Singleton and his students calculated an expected margin of sampling error (or confidence interval) of about 6 percent.

Draw Sample

The final step in the sampling process is to draw the sample. Like the assessment of reliability and validity in measurement, samples should be evaluated for their accuracy following data collection. Up to this point, we have limited ourselves to one kind of error produced by random selection: sampling error, or the difference between a sample estimate and the true population value. This error can be estimated and can be reduced by increasing the size or efficiency of one's sample. But there are other sources of *nonrandom* sampling error present in surveys, where probability sampling is the norm: coverage error and nonresponse error.

Coverage error, which we mentioned earlier in the chapter, is due to incomplete sampling frames; **nonresponse error or bias** is due to incomplete data collection. The problem of nonresponse bias arises when, through refusals to cooperate, unreturned questionnaires, missing records, or some other means, the sample turns out to be a fraction of the number of cases originally selected for observation. The crux of this problem is that nonobservations may differ in systematic ways from observations. For example, in face-to-face interview surveys (discussed in Chapter 8), respondents who live in densely populated urban areas are less likely to cooperate than respondents in less densely populated areas (Groves and Couper 1998). Also, those who feel most strongly about the topics or issues of a study are more likely to respond than those in the middle (Groves, Presser, and Dipko 2004).

Of these two sources of error, the problem of coverage error tends to be addressed prior to data collection, when additional sampling frames may be used to provide more complete coverage (see Chapter 8). Nonresponse error may be reduced by improving the process of data collection, but survey nonresponse is always present to some degree, and various methods have been used to assess its impact on sample quality. A few of these methods are briefly described in Box 6.3, READING SOCIAL RESEARCH: Assessing Nonresponse Bias and Overall Sample Quality.

nonresponse error
In survey sampling, the error that occurs when nonrespondents (sampled individuals who do not respond or cannot be contacted) differ systematically from respondents. Also called *nonresponse bias.*

BOX 6.3

READING SOCIAL RESEARCH

Assessing Nonresponse Bias and Overall Sample Quality

The most frequently cited indicator of nonresponse bias is the *response rate* (Dixon and Tucker 2010), which refers to the proportion of cases sampled from whom data are collected. The conventional wisdom has been that nonresponse bias declines as the response rate increases. It seems plausible, for example, that a sample with a 95 percent rate of response would be more representative of the population than a sample with a 10 percent response. Recent evidence suggests, however, that the response rate may not be the best indicator of sample representativeness (Groves 2006), and researchers have devised other means for assessing the quality of a sample.

In relatively rare instances, it be may be possible to assess survey nonresponse bias by obtaining data from the pool of nonrespondents. For example, in a mail survey of "binge" drinking among college students, the researchers sent a short form of the questionnaire to students who failed to return their questionnaires (Wechsler et al. 1994). They found that "the rate of binge drinking among these nonresponders did not differ from that of respondents to the original survey" (1673–74).

Another method, also applied in the alcohol survey, is to use late responders to a survey (say, the last 5 percent) to approximate noncontacts (Dixon and Tucker 2010). The assumption is that these late respondents would have been noncontacts if a concerted effort were not made to convince them to participate. For example, arguing against nonresponse bias, the alcohol researchers found no significant differences between early and late responders in the percent of nondrinkers, nonbinge drinkers, and binge drinkers (Wechsler et al. 1994).

A common method of assessing nonresponse bias and the general representativeness of a sample is to compare the composition of the sample on key variables with other surveys, known population characteristics, or existing administrative data. For example, Singleton showed that respondents in his campus surveys were similar to the college population in terms of the percentages of men and women, whites and nonwhites, Catholics and Protestants, and so on. Similarly, in a survey study of Americans' sexual practices and beliefs mentioned in Chapter 3, the researchers compared the distribution of several variables, including age, marital status, and race, with data from the Current Population Survey and other surveys of high quality (Laumann et al. 1994). Finding the data were almost exactly the same on these variables convinced them that their sample was representative of the housed US population aged 18–59.

SUMMARY

Probability sampling should begin with a careful definition of the population to which inferences are to be made. The second step is to construct a sampling frame, usually by locating one or more available lists. If a complete list is available, it is possible to draw a simple random sample or, to increase sampling efficiency, draw a stratified random sample. When a complete list is unavailable, multistage cluster sampling may be used. Determining sample size usually involves striking a balance between desired precision and available resources such as time and monetary cost. Besides the measurable error produced by random selection, probability sampling is subject to coverage error and nonresponse error.

NONPROBABILITY SAMPLING

In contrast to probability sampling, nonprobability sampling involves methods of selecting cases other than random selection. Before we examine various methods of nonrandom case selection, let's examine how nonprobability sampling is integral to social research. As we point out, not only is it often a practical necessity in social research, it also complements probability sampling in important ways.

Overview of Nonprobability Sampling

Probability sampling assumes a great deal of knowledge about the target population and the variables to be measured, but researchers may lack the necessary information to draw a probability sample. For example, when studying past events, the archaeologist or historian often finds only a fraction of relevant materials available. Similarly, in contemporary societies, certain individuals or institutions may be inaccessible. Under these circumstances, the researcher must adopt a nonprobability method of case selection or abandon the study altogether. Nonprobability sampling also is a necessity if an adequate sampling frame cannot be obtained or constructed. If the target population is unknown or hidden, such as undocumented immigrants, homosexuals, or intravenous drug users, only nonprobability methods of selection are possible. Likewise, if the population is rare (e.g., elderly caregivers, persons with AIDS, Vietnam War veterans) it may be too costly to compile a list or to use probability sampling to screen for members of the target population.

Yet, nonprobability sampling is not dictated by practical necessity alone. The decision to use nonprobability sampling, like probability sampling, depends on the research question, units of analysis, and methods of data collection. Nonprobability sampling is commonly used when the aim is to develop a holistic understanding of complex social units such as a fraternity, nursing home, or ethnic community. To arrive at a comprehensive understanding, researchers usually elect to study a single unit or a small sample of units, in which case probability sampling is inappropriate and it is better to leave the selection of cases to expert judgment (in other words, nonrandom selection). Similarly in field research, once the researcher is in the field, the choice of whom to observe and interview is usually based on how likely the people are to enhance the researcher's insight and understanding. "Choosing someone at random," as Martin Marshall (1996:523) writes, "would be analogous to randomly asking a passerby how to repair a broken-down car, rather than asking a garage mechanic." Asking the mechanic "is likely to be more productive."

Steps in Nonprobability Sampling

In field research and in some other studies addressing qualitative research questions, the researcher may select a single case or research site in which to carry out observations, and then choose what to observe within the site. Therefore, we begin by discussing the selection of cases or research sites; then we turn our attention to nonrandom methods of selecting units of observation within sites. Note, however, that it is possible for researchers, especially those using in-depth interviews as a stand-alone method, to only complete the second step in this process.

SELECT CASES OR RESEARCH SITES

Researchers seeking an in-depth knowledge of social patterns and processes may conduct case studies or select a single setting in which to carry out their research. A **case study** consists of the holistic analysis of a single person, group, or event by one or more methods (Thomas 2011). Cases and research sites may be selected for several reasons. They may (1) be conveniently located, (2) fit the research topic, (3) provide relevant theoretical comparisons, or (4) represent extreme or deviant cases.

For example, William Foote Whyte (1993) chose an Italian neighborhood for his classic study *Street Corner Society* partly because of its convenience—it was located in the city where he lived—but also because it was a good example of what he wanted to study. Similarly, in a well-known case study, Diane Vaughan (1992, 1996) investigated the decision to launch the ill-fated Space Shuttle *Challenger* that exploded shortly after liftoff because it was a good example of organizational misconduct, which she had studied in other venues.

In addition to being convenient to the researcher and fitting the research topic, cases may be chosen for the purpose of comparison. All social research involves some form of comparison (Lieberson 1985). In studying the impact of social class on educational achievement, for example, it is not enough to examine achievement for only one social class. Rather, one needs to compare achievement among children from different social classes. Two studies discussed earlier in the book, by Jessica Calarco (2011) and Annette Lareau (2011), illustrate the selection of research sites, in this case schools, for comparative purposes. Both researchers were interested in the impact of social class on educational inequality. To compare social class differences in children's classroom behavior, Calarco chose an elementary school that served children from middle- and working-class backgrounds. Lareau's research began with the observation of children in two schools, one serving predominantly middle-class families and the other predominantly working-class families. Her research then expanded to interviews and observations of families with children from these schools.

Calarco's and Lareau's choices of schools made it possible to observe and/or interview *individual* students and their parents from those schools. In historical and field research, researchers analyze larger social units such as organizations, neighborhoods, or nations as whole entities. To understand historical processes, they are interested in identifying similarities and differences among these units (Ragin 1987); so, they select cases that provide important bases of theoretical comparison. In the Comparative Neighborhood Study, for example, William Julius Wilson and Richard Taub (2006) investigated the reactions of urban neighborhoods in Chicago to looming changes such as the increase in Latino residents in the 1990s. For over two years, they conducted field research in selected neighborhoods to understand how racial and ethnic tensions affect neighborhood social organization and stability. To capture the ethnic diversity of the city, they chose four working- and middle-class neighborhoods: a white neighborhood,

case study The holistic analysis of a single person, group, or event by one or more research methods.

a neighborhood in transition from white to Mexican, a predominantly Mexican neighborhood, and an African-American neighborhood.

Finally, a time-honored strategy throughout the sciences is to analyze cases that are extreme or special in some way, such as persons who survived ordinarily terminal illnesses, unusually successful businesses, or schools in low socioeconomic areas with high graduation rates. Such "deviant" cases may provide evidence that challenges or extends existing theory. For example, according to demographer John Caldwell (1986), abundant data have shown a correlation between a nation's economic living standards and the life expectancy of its inhabitants. When Caldwell examined these data, however, he found three outliers, or exceptions to this pattern, all with high life expectancies but low average income: Kerala, Sri Lanka, and Costa Rica. For example, in 1984 the Indian state of Kerala had a gross domestic product per person of $160, which was the fifth lowest in the world; but it had a life expectancy of 66 years, equal to that of many Western industrialized nations at the time. To understand what contributed to the unusual longevity in these three poor nations, Caldwell conducted case studies, drawing on a variety of data and field experiences. One of the most important factors, he found, was the position of women in society. Among other effects, with increased autonomy and education, women are more likely to take action with sick children. Consequently, as education increases, infant mortality decreases; and infant mortality reduces average life expectancy.

SELECT OBSERVATIONS

For many researchers, the selection of a research site is the first step in the sampling process. The next step concerns who or what to observe within the site. This step may involve probability sampling, such as randomly choosing places and times to record observations. In many observational or interview studies, however, deciding what to observe or whom to interview involves one or more methods of nonprobability sampling. In this section, we consider four of the most common methods: convenience, purposive, snowball, and theoretical sampling.

convenience sampling
The selection of cases that are conveniently available.

CONVENIENCE SAMPLING As the name implies, **convenience sampling** consists of selecting a requisite number of conveniently accessible cases. If you were doing a brief survey for your methods class, for example, you might seek volunteers to interview among students who are exiting the cafeteria, who live in your residence hall, or who are studying in the library. Many online surveys are directed to whoever visits a particular website; television stations sometimes tap public opinion by providing a telephone number to call; newspaper reporters may interview conveniently available commuters or shoppers. Such methods of case selection are easy, quick, and inexpensive. If the research is at an early stage, they may be perfectly appropriate. However, with convenience sampling there is no way of determining to whom, other than the sample itself, the results apply. A major limitation of laboratory experiments, discussed in Chapter 7, is that they almost always are based on convenience samples.

PURPOSIVE SAMPLING Researchers may also rely on their expert judgment to select cases. Known as **purposive** or **judgmental sampling**, this method applies to the selection of research sites as well as other units of observation. Calarco's and Lareau's selection of schools are examples of purposive sampling; so, too, is Wilson and Taub's selection of Chicago neighborhoods. This method has its broadest application in field research and in-depth interviews, in which observations and interviews are necessarily limited. In this kind of research, it is important to carefully select informants and interviewees who can best help to answer the research question. To decide whom to select, researchers may use their developing knowledge of the research setting as well as a variety of sources of information.

A good example of purposive sampling comes from Kathleen Blee's (2002:3) study of organized racism, defined as "groups and networks that espouse and promote openly racist . . . views and actions." To understand how organized racism recruits and retains its members, why people join, and how it affects them, Blee chose to conduct in-depth interviews with women members of racist groups. Probability sampling was impossible because there are no lists of organized racists. Indeed, except for a few prominent leaders, most organized racists prefer to keep their racist identities hidden from public view. Prior to Blee's research, the few studies of organized racists had focused on a single racist group or geographic area and had interviewed a small number of members known by or personally referred to the researcher.

To create a broadly representative sample of women racists, Blee engaged in a painstaking process of purposive selection. She spent a year combing the media for every piece of recorded information she could find that was generated or distributed by a racist organization in the United States. She identified these groups through several sources, including personal contacts with self-proclaimed racists, citations in the scholarly literature, lists maintained by major antiracist monitoring and activist organizations, and archival collections on right-wing extremism. With information gathered from more than 100 different groups, Blee selected 30 racist groups from among those that had active women members or leaders. In addition, to account for characteristics that might affect recruitment and commitment to the group, she selected groups from every region of the country and which varied in their ideological emphasis and form of organization.

To identify the women members of the selected groups to be interviewed, Blee drew upon personal referrals and contacts, locating many women racists through "parole officers, correctional officials, newspaper reporters and journalists, other racist activists and former activists, federal and state task forces on gangs, attorneys, and other researchers" (Blee 2002:200). Finally, because a woman's position in an organization may affect her identification

purposive sampling
Sampling that involves the careful and informed selection of typical cases or of cases that represent relevant dimensions of the population. Also called *judgmental sampling.*

▼ Kathleen Blee

and commitment to it, Blee was careful to select women in various leadership positions as well as rank-and-file members. In the end, she persuaded 34 women from a cross-section of racist groups to talk to her "at length about themselves and their racist activities" (7). What she learned debunked popular beliefs about racist women as poor, uneducated, and abused, who followed their husbands and boyfriends into racist groups. Instead, she found that most of the women she interviewed had good jobs, were educated, were not abused as children, joined racist groups on their own, and often developed their extreme views through their participation in the hate movement. We have more to say about Blee's methods and findings in Chapter 13.

SNOWBALL SAMPLING Another set of sampling methods has been developed specifically for sampling target populations that make up small subgroups of the larger population (Sudman and Kalton 1986; Sudman, Sirken, and Cowan 1988): for example, laid-off workers, persons with AIDS, or members of a minority ethnic group that are widely dispersed in a larger population. A common method of reaching these populations is **snowball sampling**, which uses a process of chain referral: when members of the target population are located, they are asked to provide names and addresses of other members of the target population, who are then contacted and asked to name others, and so on.

A basic assumption of snowball sampling is that members of the target population often know each other. This technique has been used to create sampling frames (Sudman and Kalton 1986). It is also sometimes associated with probability sampling, but most applications involve nonprobability methods of selection (Hancock and Gile 2011). For example, D. Michael Lindsay (2008) used snowball sampling to examine the role of public leaders and elite actors in the American evangelicalism movement. Initially, he interviewed 157 religious and nonprofit leaders from a diverse group of organizations within the movement; then, at the end of each interview, he asked these informants to identify other leaders who shared their religious commitments. Thus, with the help of the early informants, he contacted and interviewed a total sample of 360 elites.

Snowball sampling is particularly applicable to studies of deviant behavior, where "moral, legal, or social sensitivities surrounding the behavior in question ... pose some serious problems for locating and contacting potential respondents" (Biernacki and Waldorf 1981:144). In these studies, members of the population are usually socially invisible by virtue of their illicit, clandestine activities. Their characteristics, therefore, are unknown, and drawing a probability sample is virtually impossible. Often the best that one can do is to use all available means to find eligible respondents and start referral chains. The quality of the sample ultimately depends on the researcher's ability to develop initial contacts and referral chains that represent a range of characteristics in the target population.

THEORETICAL SAMPLING The final nonprobability method, theoretical sampling, applies to research with the explicit purpose of developing theory. According to Kathy

snowball sampling A sampling procedure that uses a process of chain referral, whereby each contact is asked to identify additional members of the target population, who are asked to name others, and so on.

Charmaz (2006:97), **theoretical sampling** "means seeking and collecting pertinent data to elaborate and refine categories in your emerging theory." Charmaz illustrates this strategy with Jane Hood's research on working-class and lower-middle-class families in which both husband and wife had full-time jobs outside the home (Hood 1983).

Initially, Hood was interested in the self-concepts and friendship networks of women returning to work after having children. As she began to interview women who had returned to work, however, she discovered a recurring pattern: these women, who were working because they really wanted to, weren't getting much help from their husbands with housework. This led Hood to ask: How do couples negotiate childcare and housework? And, as she describes, "I began to wonder whether women who were working because they *had* to and whose income was really valued by their husbands might get more help." Because she initially sought to interview women

> going back to work after having been home full-time . . . [they] tended to be people who wanted to tell me how wonderful it was to work. I wasn't getting people who were going to work more reluctantly because they had to. But since I was really interested in how women who returned to work kind of bargained with their spouses about getting help with childcare and housework, it was critical that I look at people with a little more bargaining power, who went to work because their husbands really needed them to work. (Hood as quoted in Charmaz 2006:97–98)

This insight led Hood to interview women who were working because they had to; in other words, she applied theoretical sampling by seeking data to elaborate and refine her emerging theory. When she coded the reasons that women gave for going back to work, she found that women who worked out of economic necessity developed a more equal division of household labor in their marriage than women who returned to work for self-fulfillment.

Making Inferences from Nonprobability Samples

Our example of theoretical sampling brings us back to where the chapter began. Sampling, we noted, is about selection and inference. Just as Hood selected women to interview in order to expand and generalize her emerging theory, researchers select cases and observations that will provide reasonable inferences pertinent to their research question. But different sampling methods allow for different inferences, and we must be careful about the kind of inferences we can make.

Unlike probability samples, nonprobability samples provide no basis for making *statistical inferences* from a sample to a well-defined population. Based on a purposive sample such as Blee's, for example, we cannot estimate the percentage of women members of racist organizations who grew up in poverty, were raised in abusive families, or followed their husbands and boyfriends into the racist movement. But because of Blee's

theoretical sampling
A sampling process used in qualitative research in which observations are selected in order to develop aspects of an emerging theory.

careful sampling strategy, she could make reasonable inferences about the impact of these factors on attracting women to organized racism. As with all social research, it remains for subsequent studies to expand and test Blee's nascent theory.

The tentative conclusions researchers draw from nonprobability samples are consistent with all scientific inquiry, for social scientists ultimately want to make *theoretical inferences* about the social world. They are not interested merely in students enrolled at University X, older residents of a midsize North American city, or US voters; rather, they want to understand humankind. To make universal generalizations, no single probability sample, bound by place and time, is adequate. In this sense—within the context of societies around the world—a single probability sample is a nonprobability sample of the theoretical population (Sjoberg et al. 1991).

Finally, determining an appropriate sample size is based on very different criteria when making statistical versus theoretical inferences. The impact of sample size on statistical inference can be estimated mathematically in probability sampling; and so, as discussed earlier, researchers determine sample size based on how many cases they need to achieve a desired level of precision, given finite resources. There are few guidelines, however, for determining appropriate sample sizes for theoretical inferences. According to the most common guideline, sample sizes in purposive and theoretical sampling should be determined inductively, based on the concept of **saturation** (Charmaz 2006; Glaser and Strauss 1967; Guest, Bunce, and Johnson 2006). That is, researchers should continue to sample cases until little or no new information can be extracted from the data. Hood ended up interviewing 16 women, equally divided between those working out of necessity and those working for self-fulfillment. Based on an empirical analysis of 60 in-depth interviews, Greg Guest, Arwen Bunce, and Laura Johnson (2006) found that 70 percent of the variability in the dataset was identified within 6 interviews and 88 percent was identified after 12 interviews. Therefore, they recommend 6 to 12 interviews per subgroup as minimally adequate.

saturation In purposive and theoretical sampling, the point at which new data cease to yield new information or theoretical insights.

SUMMARY

Nonprobability sampling involves nonrandom selection. It is useful for studying populations to which researchers have limited access or cannot construct sampling frames, and is appropriate for studying a small number of cases or deciding what to observe and whom to interview within a research setting. Nonprobability sampling typically occurs in two stages: selecting cases or research sites and selecting observations within selected sites. Four common methods of selecting units of observation within sites are convenience sampling, purposive sampling, snowball sampling, and theoretical sampling. Although nonprobability samples should not be used to make precise statistical inferences, they can be used effectively for developing and generalizing theories.

KEY TERMS

case study, p. 171

cluster sampling, p. 162

confidence interval, p. 154

convenience sampling, p. 172

coverage error, p. 159

disproportionate stratified
  sampling, p. 160

multistage cluster
  sampling, p. 163

nonprobability sampling, p. 145

nonresponse error
  (nonresponse bias), p. 168

normal curve (normal
  distribution), p. 153

population, p. 145

probability, p. 147

probability distribution, p. 149

probability proportionate to size
  sampling, p. 164

probability sampling, p. 144

proportionate stratified
  sampling, p. 160

purposive sampling (judgmental
  sampling), p. 173

random selection, p. 147

sample, p. 145

sampling distribution, p. 150

sampling error, p. 150

sampling frame, p. 158

sampling with replacement, p. 149

sampling without replacement,
  p. 149

saturation, p. 176

simple random sample, p. 159

snowball sampling, p. 174

standard error, p. 152

stratified random sample, p. 160

target population, p. 157

theoretical sampling, p. 175

weighting, p. 161

KEY POINTS

- The two general strategies for selecting cases or observations are probability sampling and nonprobability sampling.
- Based on random selection, probability sampling is used to make precise statistical inferences from a sample to a population.
- To make statistical inferences, researchers use theoretical knowledge of the sampling distribution of a sample statistic to determine the confidence interval, or margin of error.
- The steps in probability sampling consist of defining the target population, selecting a sampling frame, devising the sampling design, and determining the sample size.
- The most basic probability sampling design, simple random sampling, gives each case in a sampling frame an equal chance of being selected.
- Stratified random sampling divides the frame into strata (variable categories) and samples within each stratum; multistage cluster sampling divides the population into a succession of clusters (natural or geographic groupings), first sampling across clusters and then within each selected cluster.
- In probability sampling, the two primary considerations in determining an appropriate sample size are desired precision and available resources.
- Surveys using probability sampling may be subject to two sources of sample bias: coverage error and nonresponse error.

- Based on nonrandom selection, nonprobability sampling may be used when the target population cannot be readily identified, a sampling frame cannot be obtained or easily constructed, and research goals seek a holistic or in-depth understanding of a small number of cases.
- Nonprobability sampling may occur at two stages: when choosing one or a few cases or research sites and when choosing whom or what to observe within selected sites.
- Cases and research sites may be selected because they are conveniently located, fit the research topic, provide theoretical comparisons, or represent deviant cases.
- Nonprobability methods of selecting interviewees or observations consist of convenience sampling, purposive sampling, snowball sampling, and theoretical sampling.
- Probability sampling provides a basis for statistical inference; nonprobability sampling generally is intended to provide a basis for theoretical inference.

REVIEW QUESTIONS

1. Explain the difference between probability and nonprobability sampling. When is it appropriate to use each of these sampling strategies?
2. According to the textbook, four features of sampling distributions provide the basis of statistical inference. What are these four features?
3. Explain the difference between a sample and a sampling frame. Which of these concepts is associated with coverage error? Which is associated with nonresponse error?
4. Explain how simple random sampling is incorporated into both stratified random sampling and multistage cluster sampling.
5. Consider the following guideline for determining sample size: draw as large a sample as time and other resources allow. Explain whether this applies to probability sampling or nonprobability sampling.
6. Give an example from the textbook of the purposive sampling of (a) research sites and (b) interviewees.
7. What kind of inferences may be drawn from probability and nonprobability sampling?

EXERCISES

1. This exercise will help familiarize you with some types of probability sampling. First, using the "A" section of the latest issue of your campus directory as a starting point, draw up a sampling frame composed of the first 50 names listed.

   (a) *Simple random sample.* Select a random sample of 10 names using the Random Integer Generator in RANDOM.ORG (http://www.random.org/integers/).

(See Box 6.1 for instructions on how to use this site.) List all the random numbers you select, and then list the 10 names in your sample. Repeat this procedure in drawing a random sample of 5 names.

(b) *Stratified random sample.* Divide the names in your sampling frame into strata on the basis of an identifiable characteristic, such as class year. Now, using RANDOM.ORG again, select a sample of 5 names within each stratum. List the names that you obtain. Is your sample proportionate or disproportionate? Explain.

2. Each election year, the media rely on exit polls to forecast and analyze election outcomes. Exit polls are surveys of voters immediately after they have cast their votes at their polling places. The polling places (or precincts) are randomly selected to represent each state and, for national polls, the nation as a whole. Interviewers give selected voters a questionnaire that takes only a couple minutes to complete. It asks for whom they voted, about important issues, and about demographics such as gender, age, and race. Participation is voluntary and anonymous. Interviewing starts when the polls open and continues throughout the day until about an hour before they close at night.

In one national election exit poll, voters were selected in the following way. Within each state, a complete list of precincts was obtained. The precincts were divided up into counties, and within each county, precincts were selected randomly so that the odds of being selected were proportionate to the number of people who typically voted in that precinct. At each selected precinct, one or two interviewers stood outside and randomly selected roughly one hundred voters during the day as they exited from voting. The interviewers accomplished this task by counting voters as they left the polling place and selecting every voter at a specific interval (say, every third or fifth voter). The interval was chosen so that the approximately 100 interviews were spread evenly over the course of the day. (Note that the selection of voters at polling places approximates simple random sampling.)

(a) What is the overall sampling design? (Be specific. This is a complex design, involving more than one sampling method.)

(b) What sampling frame was used in the design?

(c) Is stratification incorporated into the design? If so, what was the stratifying variable?

(d) Some journalists and commentators would like to obtain midday numbers or estimates from the exit polls. Why would the midday numbers have a much larger margin of error than the numbers compiled when the polls are closed at the end of the day? Give *two* possible reasons, one involving random sampling error and the other involving sampling bias.

(e) Evaluate the sampling strategy with respect to coverage error, assuming that the target population is all voters in the national election.

3. Suppose that you want to draw a sample from each of the following populations. Devise a sampling plan for each by (1) indicating the unit of analysis, (2) clearly defining the target population, (3) constructing the sampling frame, and (4) selecting and justifying an appropriate sampling design (e.g., simple random sampling, stratified random sampling, purposive sampling).

(a) Students enrolled in US colleges and universities (to study alcohol use).

(b) Residents of Chicago who work night shifts (to study their lifestyles).

(c) Conversations in public places on campus (to study what people talk about in various social settings).

(d) Campus graffiti (to study gender differences).

(e) College employees at a specific college (for a study of factors—pay, hours, working conditions, and so forth—that affect job satisfaction).

4. Because of your developing methodological expertise, someone who is about to conduct a random sample survey asks you, "What proportion of the population should I sample to give me adequate precision?" How would you respond to this question?

Experiments
What Causes What?

STUDENT LEARNING OBJECTIVES

By the end of this chapter, you should be able to

1. Explain the logic of experimentation with respect to how experiments effectively meet the criteria for establishing causality.

2. Describe variations in experimental design related to the timing and measurement of the dependent variable as well as the number of independent variables manipulated.

3. Describe variations in experimental context by distinguishing among laboratory, field, and survey-based experiments.

4. Describe the steps in the process of planning and conducting an experiment and apply them to a research topic.

5. Evaluate experiments as a method of data collection, identifying their strengths and weaknesses.

If you're like us, you have conducted "experiments" of your own in everyday life. For example, you may have intentionally broken a social norm and observed people's reactions. In fact, whole websites are devoted to this. Type "50 fun things to do in an elevator" into your search engine, and you'll see what we're talking about. A classic elevator norm-breaking "experiment" is to stand very close to people who enter the elevator and observe their reactions. Most likely, they'll move away, because in mainstream North American culture people tend to prefer at least a few feet of personal space between a stranger and themselves.

Social science experiments are conducted in a similar but more systematic way. Researchers observe people's behavior under different conditions, such as a *control* condition in which people act "normally," and an *experimental* condition, in which a norm is broken. With the exception of the manipulated factor (acting normally or elevator norm breaking), everything else is the same. Consequently, if we observe a change in people's behavior, such as moving away from a person who stands too close to them in the elevator, we can be pretty sure that the manipulated factor caused the change.

More than any other methodological approach, experiments help social scientists to understand whether one factor *caused* a change in another. Because they provide the strongest possible evidence of cause and effect, experiments are an ideal model for answering quantitative research questions. Even when it is impractical or impossible to do an experiment and some other approach must be used, the logic of experimentation serves as a standard by which other research strategies are judged.

We begin this chapter by describing a typical laboratory experiment as found in social research. Using this example, we introduce the essential features and causal logic of experiments. Then, we discuss variants of the experimental approach, including designs that manipulate two or more variables and experiments conducted outside the laboratory. Again using our introductory example, we outline the process of conducting or "staging" an experiment. Finally, we discuss the strengths and limitations of the experimental approach.

INTRODUCTORY EXAMPLE: MISCONDUCT IN CRIMINAL PROSECUTION

The basic features of an experiment are nicely illustrated by a study of the impact of crime severity on prosecutorial misconduct (Lucas, Graif, and Lovaglia 2006). In criminal trials in the United States, prosecuting attorneys are supposed to turn over to the defense any evidence that might pertain to a defendant's guilt or innocence. Not to do so is illegal and is defined as misconduct. Scholars have noted that cases involving serious crimes, such as rape and murder, are more likely to result in erroneous convictions than other kinds of cases. To account for these findings, Jeffrey Lucas, Corina Graif, and Michael Lovaglia (2006:97) theorized that prosecutorial misconduct might be more likely in serious cases because "prosecutors succumb to increased pressure to convict." Feeling pressure, they use their belief in the defendant's guilt as justification for misconduct by withholding evidence that may help prove the defendant's *innocence*. Based on this theory, Lucas and associates derived three hypotheses. One hypothesis was that misconduct will be more likely to occur in cases involving more severe crimes than less severe crimes.

To test this hypothesis and others, the researchers carried out a laboratory experiment at a Midwestern university. The study design called for research participants to play the role of prosecutor in a criminal case, read a "Police Report" and other materials describing either a murder or an assault, and perform duties in preparation for a trial.

▲ Jeffrey Lucas

After setting up the experiment, the researchers recruited undergraduate students to participate and paid them $10 for their participation. Before the volunteers arrived at the laboratory, they were randomly assigned to either a "murder" or an "assault" condition (described further below). When they arrived, each participant was told that

> he or she would be acting as a defense attorney, a prosecuting attorney, or a judge in a contrived criminal trial. The participant then was asked to draw one of three slips of paper from a hat to determine his or her role in the study. All of the slips, however, contained the word *prosecutor*, so participants always acted as prosecuting attorneys. . . . (Lucas et al. 2006:100)

▲ Corina Graif

All participants then were asked to read the police report, which described a crime in which police responded to a report of a missing person. When police arrived at the residence of the person reported as missing, they found a man's body in the front hallway and immediately called emergency medical personnel. Depending on the condition to which they were assigned in the experiment, participants then read that either (a) the victim was pronounced dead at the scene (murder condition) or (b) the victim fully recovered from his injuries (assault condition). The report further revealed that the police had apprehended a male ex-felon, who was indicted for either (a) murder or (b) assault, depending again on the experimental condition.

After reading the police report, participants read two forms. The first form contained detailed information about the case, most of which implied the guilt of the defendant. The second form carefully explained the duties of the prosecuting attorney. The form describing the prosecutor's job emphasized the responsibility to present the case against the defendant, but also the legal obligation to "turn over to the defense all materials that might point to the defendant's guilt or innocence" (Lucas et al. 2006:101).

▲ Michael Lovaglia

Finally, participants were asked to perform several tasks. The first of these was to read a set of interviews obtained by police officers, and then "compile a list of questions from the interviews to turn over to the defense." Although the interview information "generally pointed to the defendant's guilt," four questions contained "information identifying the victim's wife as a potential suspect" (Lucas et al. 2006:101). The measure of misconduct consisted of the number of these four questions that participants withheld from the defense. As hypothesized, participants in the murder condition (average = 2.15) withheld more questions than participants in the assault condition (average = 1.50).

Using this study as an illustration, we focus on the logic of experimentation in the next section. First we identify those essential features that make experiments a model for testing causal relationships; then we relate these features to the criteria for inferring causality.

THE LOGIC OF EXPERIMENTATION

What basic features of an experimental design are illustrated in the foregoing experiment? Notice, first, that Lucas and associates' hypothesis concerns the relationship between two variables: crime severity and prosecutorial misconduct. In an experiment, a *manipulated* independent variable (the severity of the crime) is *followed by* a measured dependent variable (prosecutorial misconduct). There are at least two groups or conditions, represented by the categories of the independent variable (murder versus assault). And except for this experimental manipulation, all groups are treated *exactly alike*. Finally, participants are *randomly* assigned to one group or the other.

How do these features meet the requirements of causal inference? Although we can never prove beyond all doubt that two variables (say, X and Y) are causally related, recall from Chapter 4 that certain types of empirical evidence are regarded as essential for causal statements: (1) association (i.e., evidence that X and Y vary together in a way predicted by the hypothesis); (2) direction of influence (evidence that X affected Y rather than Y affected X); and (3) the elimination of plausible rival explanations (evidence that one or more variables other than X did not cause the observed change in Y). The first two kinds of evidence show that X could have affected Y; the third kind shows that the relation between X and Y is nonspurious—that other variables are not responsible for the observed effects. Let us refer back to Lucas and associates' experiment to see how these types of evidence were provided.

1. *Association.* It was found, as hypothesized, that the independent variable, severity of the crime, was associated with the dependent variable, misconduct as measured by the number of questions pointing to another suspect that were withheld from the defense. That is, participants in the murder condition withheld more questions than participants in the assault condition.

2. *Direction of influence.* Evidence that the independent variable (X) influenced the dependent variable (Y) and not the other way around is based on time order in experiments: Y cannot be the cause of X if it occurred after X. In the experiment, we know that misconduct could not have caused the severity of the crime because participants were told first either that the victim died (murder) or survived his injuries (assault).

3. *Elimination of rival explanations.* What might be plausible reasons why participants in the murder condition withheld more questions than those in the assault condition? One possibility is that participants in the two conditions differ systematically in terms of personal qualities such as honesty or intelligence or attention to detail. For example, if participants in the murder condition were less careful in performing their duties, they may simply have supplied fewer questions, irrespective of their content, to the defense. Such extraneous variables are controlled, however, by randomly assigning participants to the two conditions. **Random assignment** means that the procedure by which participants are assigned (in this case, tossing a coin) ensures that each participant has an equal chance of being in either group. By virtue of random assignment, individual characteristics or experiences that might confound the results will be about evenly distributed between the two groups. Thus, there should be just about as many participants who are honest or dishonest, motivated or unmotivated, and so forth, in one condition as in the other. To clarify an important point about random assignment, see Box 7.1, CHECKING YOUR UNDERSTANDING: The Difference Between Random Sampling and Random Assignment.

random assignment
The assignment of research participants to experimental conditions by means of a random device such as a coin toss.

In addition to controlling pre-experimental, individual differences through random assignment, the researcher makes every attempt to treat both groups exactly alike during the experiment except for the experimental manipulation. Lucas and colleagues took care to ensure that the laboratory where the research took place, all of the instructions and materials, and the tasks that participants were asked to perform were the same for both groups. An example of a violation of this principle would have been if participants in the assault condition had additional information provided by the victim after he recovered. Such information (which is often included in real criminal trials) obviously would not be available if the victim is deceased.

In an airtight experimental design, there is only one rival explanation: The results could have occurred by chance. This would mean that the process of randomly assigning persons to the experimental and control groups resulted, by chance, in an unequal distribution between the groups on variables such as honesty, intelligence, or how carefully they attended to instructions—variables that could affect their performance on the tasks they were given. As we noted, for example, participants in the murder condition might have supplied fewer questions to the defense than participants in the assault condition because they generally were less careful in performing their duties.

BOX 7.1

The Difference Between Random Sampling and Random Assignment

As we pointed out in Chapter 6, researchers apply the word "random" to processes that give each element in a set, such as all students at your college or university, a known and independent chance of being selected. Probability sampling, also called "random sampling," is based on random processes of selection. So, too, is random assignment of participants in an experiment. It is important to note, however, that random sampling and random assignment refer to distinct methods that occur at different points in the research process and serve different purposes (see Figure A).

Sampling occurs first, when you select the participants for your study. Surveys often use random sampling to select respondents, thus giving every person in the target population a known and independent chance of being selected. This allows researchers to make statistical estimates of population characteristics. Did Lucas and colleagues use random sampling to select their sample of participants? No, they did not. As is typical of laboratory experiments, they selected a convenience sample of students who volunteered to participate.

But once they had their sample of participants, the experimenters randomly assigned each participant to one of the two experimental conditions, murder or assault. In this way, participants had an equal chance of being in either condition, which ensured that the groups were approximately equal on all uncontrolled variables. As we discuss below, this enabled the researchers to use a test of statistical significance to determine whether there was a difference between the two groups.

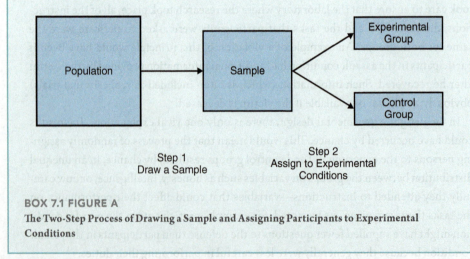

Step 1
Draw a Sample

Step 2
Assign to Experimental
Conditions

BOX 7.1 FIGURE A

The Two-Step Process of Drawing a Sample and Assigning Participants to Experimental Conditions

Table 7.1 Lucas and Associates' Experimental Results

	Mean (SD)	t	p
NUMBER OF EXCULPATORY QUESTIONS WITHHELD FROM DEFENSE			
Murder condition	2.15 (1.51)		
Assault condition	1.50 (1.45)		
Hypothesis: Murder condition > Assault condition		1.96	.027

Source: Adapted from Table 1 in Lucas et al. (2006:103).

To assess the likelihood that the results of an experiment occurred by chance, experimenters use a test of statistical significance. Recall from Chapter 4 that significance tests indicate the likelihood or probability that an association is due to random processes. Such tests express this probability in decimal form. So, when you read that the results of an experiment were found to be significant at the .05 level, this means that only about 5 percent of the time, or 5 times in 100, would differences this large between the experimental conditions occur by chance when the experimental variable actually has no effect. With such a low probability, it would be reasonable to rule out prior differences uncontrolled by the randomization process as a plausible explanation of the experimental results. To illustrate, Table 7.1 presents results from Lucas and associates' experiment. Consistent with their hypothesis, participants in the murder condition withheld more "exculpatory" questions (questions that may help prove the defendant's innocence) from the defense, on average, than participants in the assault condition. And according to the *t*-test statistic, the probability ("*p*" in the table) that this difference is due to chance is less than .05 (.027 to be exact).

On the other hand, if the results were not found to be statistically significant, it would not be reasonable to rule out differences due to chance assignment, and we could not have much confidence that the experimental manipulation caused the effects. In short, a statistical test of significance assesses the likelihood that the observed difference between the groups is real (significant) and not of a magnitude that would occur frequently by chance.

SUMMARY

Experiments provide the ideal model for testing hypotheses and inferring causal relationships. To determine association, experiments compare outcomes in two or more groups or conditions, representing categories of the independent variable. To establish direction of influence, the *manipulated* independent variable (the cause) always precedes the *measured* dependent variable (the effect). And to control for variables that might produce a spurious association, participants are *randomly assigned* to conditions, and everything except the experimental manipulation remains the same throughout the experiment.

VARIATIONS ON THE EXPERIMENTAL METHOD

Now that you have learned the essential features of experiments and have seen how experiments offer strong evidence of cause and effect, let's examine additional research examples that illustrate how these features may be extended to more complex study designs and to contexts outside the laboratory.

Variations in Experimental Design

As you can see, scientific experiments such as the misconduct study contain certain basic requirements. Studies that meet these basic requirements are sometimes called "true experiments." If we let "X" represent the independent variable, "Y" the dependent variable, and "R" random assignment, we can diagram the basic elements of an experimental design as follows:

$$R \begin{cases} X_1 \quad Y \\ X_2 \quad Y \end{cases}$$

Thus, in the misconduct study, each participant was randomly assigned (R) to one of two conditions, murder (X_1) or assault (X_2), after which participants' level of misconduct (Y) was measured. Within these baseline requirements, however, experimental designs may vary in two principal ways: the timing and measurement of the dependent variable and the number of independent variables that are manipulated.[1] As we review these variations, notice that each variant contains the basic design elements as diagrammed above.

TIMING AND MEASUREMENT OF THE DEPENDENT VARIABLE

The misconduct study is called a **posttest-only control group design** because the dependent variable was measured (or "tested") *after* the manipulation of the independent variable. In some experiments, however, the dependent variable is measured *both* before *and* after the manipulation. As diagrammed below, this is called a **pretest-posttest control group design**.

$$R \begin{cases} Y_1 \quad X_1 \quad Y_2 \\ Y_1 \quad X_2 \quad Y_2 \end{cases}$$

Aside from pretests, experiments may apply multiple operational definitions of the dependent variable, such as more than one measure of misconduct. In order to determine when and how long an effect occurs, experiments also may contain multiple posttests at varying points in time. Or, they may test the impact of the independent variable

posttest-only control group design
The most basic experimental design in which the dependent variable is measured after the experimental manipulation.

pretest-posttest control group design
An experimental design in which the dependent variable is measured both before and after the experimental manipulation.

---

[1]Another variation is the within-subjects design in which research participants receive both treatments X_1 and X_2. This design is not discussed in this chapter; the interested reader can learn more about it in Singleton and Straits (2018:235–37).

on more than one dependent variable. In the misconduct study, for example, Lucas and associates administered a questionnaire to participants after they had prepared their case. Included among the questions were measures of two other dependent variables: how strongly participants believed that the defendant was guilty and how important it was to them to attain a conviction. These variables provided a test of two additional hypotheses that were part of the researchers' theory: participants would feel greater pressure to attain a conviction and would be more likely to believe in the defendant's guilt when the crime was more serious.

NUMBER OF INDEPENDENT VARIABLES MANIPULATED

A second variation in the basic design is to manipulate more than one independent variable. Given that social events often are caused by a number of variables, it makes sense to study several possible causes, or independent variables, at the same time. When two or more independent variables are studied in a single experiment, they are referred to as *factors*, and the designs are called **factorial designs**. Let's examine an experiment that manipulated two factors.

factorial design
An experiment in which two or more variables (factors) are manipulated.

Numerous studies have demonstrated the effect of *stereotype threat*: a phenomenon in which confronting people with a negative stereotype of their group can have a detrimental impact on their performance. For example, subjecting women to the negative stereotype that "women are bad at math" tends to inhibit their ability to solve math problems. Robert Rydell, Allen McConnell, and Sian Beilock (2009) hypothesized that providing a positive self-relevant stereotype, such as "college students are good at math," can eliminate the impact of stereotype threat. To test this hypothesis, they conducted a series of experiments in which they manipulated participants' exposure to both stereotypes.

In one experiment, Rydell and colleagues asked female undergraduates to solve 15 math problems modeled after those on standardized tests. Before they performed this task, the participants were randomly assigned to four conditions, in which they were given different information about the purpose of the study. In one condition, the researchers activated a negative gender stereotype by informing participants that abundant research "indicates that males consistently score higher than females on standardized tests of math ability" (Rydell et al. 2009:954). In a second condition, the researchers activated a positive college student stereotype by informing participants that "the research was investigating why college students are better at math than those who are not in college" (954). A third condition presented neither "stereotype"; and a fourth condition presented both. Finally, the measurement of the dependent variable consisted of the number of math problems answered correctly.

The overall design of this study thus manipulated two factors, "negative gender stereotype" and "positive college student stereotype," each with two categories or levels (present or absent). When a design has two independent variables, each having two levels, it is called a 2 × 2 (two by two) factorial design. A design that has three levels of one variable and two levels of another variable would be a 3 × 2 factorial design having six conditions. Following the notation we introduced, we could diagram this experiment as follows, where each subscript represents a variable (negative or positive stereotype) and the number (1 or 2) of the subscript represents the level (presence or absence of the stereotype). (Thus, X_{11} signifies that in this condition, participants were exposed to both stereotypes.)

$$
R
\begin{cases}
X_{11} & Y \\
X_{12} & Y \\
X_{21} & Y \\
X_{22} & Y
\end{cases}
$$

Factorial designs such as this provide evidence of the impact of each factor as well as the joint effect of the factors. In the stereotype threat experiment, the researchers found that participants who were given only the gender stereotype had significantly fewer correct answers than participants in the three other conditions. Moreover, performances in the three other conditions did not differ from one another. This suggests a joint effect: mentioning a positive group stereotype can offset the negative impact of a gender-based stereotype threat.

Like the misconduct study, the stereotype threat experiment took place in a laboratory. Experimental design methodology also may be applied in settings outside the laboratory, to which we now turn.

Variations in Experimental Context

laboratory experiment An experiment conducted in a controlled environment.

Although **laboratory experiments** have a long tradition in scientific research, investigators increasingly have moved outside the lab to apply the experimental approach. Below we discuss two variations in experiments outside of the traditional lab context: field experiments and survey-based experiments.

FIELD EXPERIMENTS

field experiment An experiment conducted in a natural setting.

A study that has all the features of a true experiment (manipulation of independent variable, random assignment, etc.) but is carried out in a natural, real-world setting is called a **field experiment**. A good example is Devah Pager's (2003) study of job discrimination, described briefly in Chapter 5. Let's take a closer look at this study to examine the unique advantages and disadvantages of doing experiments "in the field."

audit study A study that examines racial and other forms of discrimination by sending matched pairs of individuals to apply for jobs, purchase a car, rent an apartment, and so on.

To examine job discrimination, Pager conducted a special type of field experiment, known as an **audit study**, in which matched pairs of confederates ("testers") applied for real job openings. The testers were similar in physical appearance and job qualifications, but differed in other characteristics. Pager varied two characteristics: race and criminal record. She manipulated race by having two pairs, one black and one white; and within each same-race pair, one tester presented himself as having a criminal record and the other did not (see Figure 7.1). Thus, this is a 2 × 2 factorial design. As the testers applied for jobs, employment opportunity was measured by recording whether an applicant received a callback for an interview. Pager found evidence of discrimination on both counts: blacks received fewer callbacks than whites, and men with criminal records received fewer callbacks than their counterparts without criminal records.

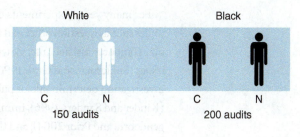

C   N   C   N
150 audits   200 audits

FIGURE 7.1
Pager's Study Design.
"C" refers to criminal record; "N" refers to no criminal record

One advantage of a field experiment over a lab experiment is that behavior is observed in a real-life setting in which the individuals—employers in this case—are unaware that they are participants in a study. As a consequence, their behavior should be more "natural." In addition, a field experiment more closely mirrors reality. For example, unlike role-playing "prosecutors" in the misconduct study, individuals in the audit study applied for real jobs with real employers.

On the other hand, field experiments afford less control in design and implementation. In the laboratory, for example, it would be relatively straightforward to manipulate whether a job applicant has a criminal record; but in the field, an applicant's criminal status is more difficult to convey. As we pointed out in Chapter 5, Pager used various means to draw attention to an applicant's criminal record, including direct responses on application forms, reporting work experience obtained in a correctional facility, and listing a parole officer as a reference. Field experiments also raise ethical and legal issues, as the ordinary means of protecting participants' rights, such as informed consent and debriefing, are usually impossible to implement.

SURVEY-BASED EXPERIMENTS

In addition to natural settings, experiments may be incorporated in surveys. For example, numerous **survey-based experiments** have investigated the effects of slight changes in the wording of a question during an interview. Generally, as part of a larger survey, a mini-experiment is conducted by directing a question with one wording to a randomly selected subsample of respondents and a differently worded question to the remaining respondents. For instance, since 1984 the General Social Survey has included two versions of a question on government spending (Smith 1987; Smith et al. 2017). One version asks the following:

> We are faced with many problems in this country, none of which can be solved
> easily or inexpensively. I'm going to name some of these problems, and for each
> one I'd like you to tell me whether you think we're spending too much money on
> it, too little money, or about the right amount. Are we spending too much, too
> little, or about the right amount on welfare?

In the other version, people were asked the same question, except that the phrase "assistance to the poor" replaced the word "welfare." The experiment consistently has shown that people are much less likely to support spending on welfare than spending on assistance to the poor. Apparently, for many respondents the word "welfare" brings to mind images of liberal social policies for "undeserving" groups of poor people (Appelbaum 2001).

survey-based experiment An experiment embedded in a survey in which respondents are given different, randomly assigned versions of survey questions.

For many years, experiments embedded in surveys tended to focus on methodological topics such as question order and wording; however, innovations in survey design, in particular computer-assisted interviewing, have stimulated experiments on broader substantive issues (Sniderman and Grob 1996). Survey experiments have proven particularly useful for investigating determinants of public opinion on social policies such as affirmative action (Kinder and Sanders 1996), immigration (Hainmueller and Hiscox 2010; Sniderman, Hagendoorn, and Prior 2004), and the US war in Afghanistan (Kriner and Shen 2012).

For example, to examine the effects of different types of news coverage on Americans' attitudes toward war, Douglas Kriner and Francis Shen (2012) conducted an online survey in which they asked respondents to read a short news story describing the death of a hypothetical soldier in the war in Afghanistan. The survey began with basic background questions, including a question about the state where the respondent currently resides. Then, after some unrelated questions, "respondents were randomly assigned to one of four versions of the news story, which varied along two dimensions": whether the fallen soldier was from the respondent's home state, and whether the news story focused on the military's larger strategy or on more personal information as typically presented in local coverage of casualties (Kriner and Shen 2012:765). Finally, all respondents were asked to indicate how strongly they supported or opposed the US war in Afghanistan.

Table 7.2 presents the percentage of respondents who said they opposed the war. The results show that regardless of type of news coverage (local versus national), respondents were significantly more likely to oppose the war when the fallen soldier hailed from the respondent's home state than when he was from a different state. This finding supports the theory of "differential processing," which predicts that citizens place more weight on local casualties than nonlocal casualties when forming their opinions.

One advantage of embedding experiments in surveys is that the study can be carried out with a much larger and generally more diverse set of respondents than in laboratory experiments. The General Social Survey, in which the welfare wording experiment is embedded, is based on a national probability sample of 1,500–3,000 respondents. Kriner and Shen's survey was administered to 849 participants who were recruited online. Although not nationally representative, their sample was much larger and far more diverse than the 80 undergraduate students who participated in the misconduct experiment.

Table 7.2 Percentage Opposed to War in Afghanistan by Home State Connection and Type of Media Coverage

	National story	Local story
Casualty from home state	62%	62%
Casualty from non-home state	53%	50%

Source: Table 2 in Kriner and Shen (2012:767).

A survey also was an appropriate context for Kriner and Shen's experiment because the dependent variable was a measure of public opinion, which is the focus of many surveys. On the other hand, the focus on opinions—and more generally on self-reports—is also a limitation of survey experiments. For social researchers often want to know how people act or behave, which must be observed in the lab or in the field.

SUMMARY

Experiments vary in design and context. Experimental designs may measure the dependent variable after the manipulation of an independent variable (in a posttest-only control group design) or both before and after the manipulation (in a pretest-posttest control group design); and they may measure more than one dependent variable. Designs also may include two or more independent variables (called factors) in a factorial design. Finally, experiments may be conducted outside the traditional lab context, such as "in the field" (field experiments) or embedded in surveys.

THE PROCESS OF CONDUCTING EXPERIMENTS

Now that you know the logic of, and key variations in, the experimental approach, let's examine more closely how experiments are carried out. As with all social research, the process of conducting a study begins with the formulation of a research question. Thereafter, however, the process of designing research and collecting data vary depending on the unique features of each major approach.

Figure 7.2 shows the key points in planning and conducting an experiment. The first stage consists of designing the experiment, or deciding on the context and principal elements of the design, such as the number of manipulated variables. Based on this overall plan, the ensuing steps are much like producing a play. There are "scripts" to write and rewrite; a sequence of "scenes," each contributing something vital to the production; a "cast" of experimental assistants to recruit and train; "props" and "special effects"; and "rehearsals." And once the stage is set, the experimenter must publicize the experiment and sell potential participants, for without an audience there can be

FIGURE 7.2
The Process of Planning and Conducting an Experiment

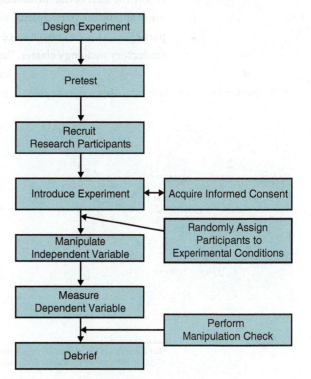

no play. We make reference to this metaphor as we describe in greater detail how Lucas and colleagues' (2006) misconduct experiment was carried out.[2]

Pretesting

pretest A trial run of an experiment or survey instrument to evaluate and rehearse study procedures and personnel.

Like the script of a play, the production of an experiment follows a set of procedures that implement the overall experimental design. After the development of a preliminary "script" of experimental procedures, the next step is to conduct a **pretest** in which the procedures are applied to a few participants, preferably similar to those who will participate in the final production of the experiment, to see how well the "script" is working. Feedback from pretest participants is often used to modify procedures.

In the misconduct experiment, Lucas and associates made several changes as a result of pretesting (Lucas, personal communication 2013). One change involved enhancing participants' motivation. During pretesting, participants were told that they would earn $10 for participating in the experiment. However, when the pretest showed that participants were not very invested in "winning" the case, the researchers decided to tell them that they would receive $10 if they lost the case and $15 if they won. They also made an important change in the language of the script of the study in an effort to make attaining a conviction more important to participants.

Participant Recruitment and Informed Consent

Before the start of the "production," participants must be recruited and the investigator must obtain the participants' informed consent to participate. Lucas and associates' participants were a convenience sample of college students who were recruited from introductory sociology classes. Participants had two incentives to sign up: they would receive extra credit from their sociology instructor, which is a common practice, and they would be paid.

▼ The production of an experiment is like a script of a play.

Once a participant signed up, he or she received an e-mail briefly describing the nature of the study, how long it would take, and available times. Then, when participants arrived at the laboratory, the experimenter repeated the brief study description—that they were doing a study on how people reach decisions on legal matters—and immediately asked them to sign an informed consent form. For an abridged copy of the form used in the Lucas and associates' study, see Box 7.2, DOING SOCIAL RESEARCH: Informed Consent Form for an Experiment.

---

[2]The discussion of the misconduct experiment in this section relies on additional information graciously provided to us by its principal investigator Jeff Lucas (February 2013).

INTRODUCTION TO THE EXPERIMENT

Continuing the theatrical production metaphor, we might say that the first "scene" of an experiment consists of some sort of introduction to the study. Basically, this involves an explanation of the purpose or nature of the research, together with instructions to the participant. As we noted, the researchers initially told participants that they were interested in how people reach legal decisions. After signing the informed consent agreement, participants were informed that there would be three people completing the study as part of the participant's group—a defense attorney, a prosecuting attorney, and a judge—and that the three people might complete the study at different times. Then they were asked to draw one of three slips of paper to determine their role—but, as explained earlier in our description of the experiment, they were actually all given the role of prosecutor (i.e., without their knowledge, all three slips of paper indicated "prosecutor" so it did not matter which slip they chose). Next they received the police report and other materials and were instructed to prepare a list of questions for the defense and to write a one-page closing argument that would be read by the judge.

All research participants are likely to want to understand what the study is about, and they will expect to be given some sort of explanation. But this explanation is especially important in a laboratory experiment. More so than in a survey or in field research, participants are acutely aware that they are participating in a scientific study, that they are being observed, and that certain behaviors are expected of them. Thus, they are in a sense "on stage" and will be very sensitive to any cues about how they should perform. If participants are told the actual hypothesis, then instead of behaving as they ordinarily would, they may behave as they think they should to fulfill the researchers' expectations. On the other hand, participants need to be given some explanation; otherwise, they may try to guess the hypothesis and "help" the experimenter by behaving in a way that confirms whatever they guess the hypothesis may be.

BOX 7.2

DOING SOCIAL RESEARCH

Informed Consent Form for an Experiment

Figure A is an abridged copy of the informed consent form used by Lucas and colleagues (2006). This form contains key elements of informed consent that we outlined in Chapter 3. In particular, it (1) explains the experimental procedures and potential risks and benefits to the participants or to others and (2) informs them that their participation is voluntary and that they have the right to leave the experiment at any time without penalty.

continues

continued

Project Title: Criminal Prosecution and Defense

Project Investigator: Jeffrey W. Lucas, PhD

This study involves research. The purpose of the research is to examine the procedures followed in using evidence to build cases in criminal trials. You are here today because you indicated interest in participating in this study. If you agree to participate in the study, you will be reading a pamphlet of materials and playing an imaginary role in a court case.

Foreseeable risks, discomforts, or inconveniences to you include (1) the time commitment (should you elect to participate, the study takes about an hour and a half to complete), (2) potential anxiety (you will have to read through material describing a violent crime and make decisions about how the criminal case should be handled), and (3) possible frustration (all of the information that you might like to have in making your decisions will not be available to you).

There may be no personal benefit to you for participating in the study, aside from pay. However, we will learn a great deal about the factors that affect the decisions people make in assembling and evaluating criminal cases. This may help researchers better understand individual behavior.

A record of your participation in this research will be maintained, but it will be kept completely confidential. The records of your participation will be in the form of an identification number and your name will not be retained in the record of your participation.

Questions about this research are encouraged and will be answered by:

[Jeff Lucas and the Director of the Office of Research]*

Your participation is voluntary. No penalty or loss of benefits to which you are entitled will occur if you decide not to participate. You may discontinue participation at any time without penalty or loss of benefits to which you are entitled. You will be compensated for time and inconvenience involved in participating in the research in the amount of $10.00. This payment will be in addition to any extra credit you may receive for participation. Compensation will be pro-rated if you withdraw before the research is completed.

Subject's Name (please print): _____

_____   _____

(signature of subject)   (date)

I have discussed the above points with the research participant, using a translator when necessary. It is my opinion that the subject understands the risks, benefits, and obligations involved in participation in this project.

_____   _____

(signature of investigator)   (date)

---

*This information has been modified and abridged by the book authors for reasons of confidentiality. The latter's name is not displayed and contact information for both parties has been redacted.

BOX 7.2 FIGURE A
Abridged Consent Form from Lucas et al.'s study

The challenge, then, is to provide a believable explanation that will encourage participants to behave naturally. Therefore, a false explanation, or **cover story**, such as Lucas and associates offered, is thought to be necessary to prevent preoccupation with the true purpose of the study. A good cover story must make sense to participants; that is, it must be understandable and believable. The first scene, including the cover story, also should have enough impact on the participant to arouse interest. For if the participant is not paying attention to the directions or to the events being staged, experimental "findings" will be worthless.

cover story An introduction presented to research participants to obtain their cooperation while disguising the research hypothesis.

Experimental Manipulation and Random Assignment

The "second scene" of the experiment is the manipulation of the independent variable. This is the point when some stimulus or set of stimuli is introduced, which serves as an operational definition of the independent variable. The major independent variable in the misconduct study was the severity of the crime, assault versus murder. To randomly assign participants to these conditions, the experimenter flipped a coin before each participant arrived (Lucas, personal communication 2013). (Random assignment may occur at any time before the experimental manipulation.) As we described earlier, crime severity was manipulated by indicating in the police report that (1) the victim either died and the defendant was indicted for murder or (2) the victim recovered from his injuries and the defendant was indicted for assault.

Manipulation Checks

To obtain evidence that the manipulation of the independent variable was experienced or interpreted by participants in the intended way, the experimenter may incorporate some sort of **manipulation check** into the experiment. This might involve asking participants, either directly or by means of a written instrument, what they felt or thought during or immediately after the experimental manipulation. A manipulation check also may be used to determine whether participants understood or recalled essential directions or facts related to the manipulation.

manipulation check Procedure used to provide evidence that participants interpreted the manipulation of the independent variable in the way intended.

As we noted earlier, Lucas and associates asked participants to complete a brief questionnaire after the study ostensibly was over. Because they hypothesized that the severity of the crime would affect degree of misconduct, it was important to know if participants perceived murder as a more serious crime than assault. To check the validity of this manipulation, therefore, the post-study questionnaire included an item that asked participants to rate the severity of the crime on a scale from 1 (very severe) to 7 (not at all severe). As expected, the average rating of participants in the murder condition (1.28) was significantly lower than the average rating of participants in the assault condition (3.03).

Researchers may assess the validity of a manipulation at varying points in an experiment. Whereas Lucas and associates performed their manipulation check *after* the experiment ostensibly was over, a manipulation check might be performed after the independent variable is manipulated but before the dependent variable is measured.

The advantage here is that the manipulation is still fresh and the participant's memory of it has not been distorted by later events. At this point, however, it may not be feasible and it could alter participants' subsequent behavior (the dependent variable) by calling attention to or emphasizing the manipulation.

Alternatively, researchers may establish the validity of an experimental manipulation through pretesting. For example, some studies of racial discrimination have manipulated the race of target persons by using racially connected names, such as "Tyrone" for blacks and "Todd" for whites. In one experiment (Ford 1997), the validity of this manipulation was checked, before the experiment was performed, by asking 45 respondents who did not take part in the experiment to indicate the race that was likely to be associated with a list of 25 names, including "Tyrone" and "Todd." All of the respondents reported that the name "Tyrone" implied African American and "Todd" implied white European.

Measurement of the Dependent Variable

The dependent variable, which always follows the introduction of the independent variable, is measured in experiments with either self-reports or observations of behavior. Lucas and associates used observation to measure their dependent variable, level of misconduct. Their operationalization consisted of the number of questions forwarded to the defense attorney that pointed to the possible guilt of the victim's wife (and thus the possible innocence of the defendant). In the Pager study of employment discrimination, a behavioral measure of the dependent variable—number of callbacks for an interview—also was used.

In addition to their observational measure of misconduct, Lucas and associates included a self-report measure of whether participants withheld relevant information from the defense. Specifically, participants were asked on the post-study questionnaire to rate the extent to which they believed that they had "turned over all the relevant evidence to the defense" (1 = definitely turned over all relevant facts; 7 = definitely did not turn over all relevant facts). Consistent with the results for the observational measure, participants in the murder condition had a higher average rating (2.70) than participants in the assault condition (1.93), which suggests that "participants in the murder condition made conscious decisions to withhold exculpatory evidence" (Lucas et al. 2006:104).

The use of verbal versus observational measures of the dependent variable is a controversial point among experimenters. Our examples notwithstanding, verbal reports are common, even though they often contain serious weaknesses. Verbal measures have the advantage of being easy to devise, allowing for more numerous and varied assessments of the dependent variable. There are two major problems with such self-reports, however. First, participants may censor their responses, especially when they construe the "truth" to reflect negatively on themselves. Second, research consistently has shown differences between what people do and what they think and say they will do (e.g., Deutscher, Pestello, and Pestello 1993; Pager and Quillian 2005).

With observations of behavior, on the other hand, participants tend to be less aware or even unaware of the measure. Behavioral measures also can be more precise, as in counting the number of questions submitted to the defense or the number of callbacks for interviews. Finally, when a specific behavior (e.g., misconduct or discrimination) is of interest, it is better to get a direct measure of that behavior than an indirect measure of how participants *say* they will behave.

Debriefing

The closing scene of the experiment is a debriefing session in which the experimenter discusses with the participant what has taken place. When participants have been deceived, it is ethically imperative that they be told at this point about the nature of and reasons for the deception and that their feelings about being deceived be explored fully (see Chapter 3). The experimenter also may try to learn what the participant experienced throughout the experiment: Did the participant understand the directions? If a cover story was used, did the participant believe it? Why did the participant respond as he or she did to the experimental manipulation? Did the participant experience psychological stress or discomfort? How does the participant feel about the experiment as a whole?

The experimenter should be aware that the manner in which the debriefing session is conducted may make a great deal of difference in the feelings of the participant about being deceived (if the participant has been deceived), about this research and researcher, and about social science research in general. Thus, the experimenter should explain the real purpose of the research and why it is of importance. If deception has been used, he or she should inform the participant of this in a sensitive manner and carefully explain the reasons it was necessary. If the deception aroused the participant's emotions, the experimenter should further justify these feelings and make every effort to relieve a participant's discomfort. In general, participants should be encouraged to ask questions and to share any negative feelings toward the study, so that these questions and feelings can be openly discussed.

The debriefing protocol in Lucas and associates' study began with a series of questions that asked participants how they felt about the case and their experiences during the study. The experimenter asked participants what they thought the purpose of the study was. Then he told them its true purpose and carefully explained why deception was necessary to test their hypothesis. To ascertain that participants had positive feelings about their participation, the experimenter asked if they were satisfied with this explanation and had any further questions. Finally, he asked them not to talk to other potential participants about the study (Lucas, personal communication 2013).

This final request in the debriefing session is important because potential participants frequently are acquainted with one another. Certainly, experiments requiring deception will not yield valid results if participants coming to the experiment have been informed of its true purpose. Even experiments not requiring deception will usually suffer if participants previously have been told the hypothesis or what the experimental manipulation is. If the debriefing process has been an open, satisfying experience for the participant up to this point, he or she is very likely to respect the researcher's wishes in regard to secrecy.

SUMMARY

The process of conducting a laboratory experiment generally involves all of the steps we have just described: pretesting, recruiting participants and acquiring informed consent, introducing the experiment, randomly assigning participants to conditions/groups and manipulating the independent variable, checking the manipulation of the variable, measuring the dependent variable, and debriefing participants. If part of a series of experiments, though, later experiments may not be pretested; and if the validity of the experimental manipulation is well established, an experiment may not contain a manipulation check.

In experiments outside the laboratory, some steps routinely are eliminated.

Because participants in a field experiment are unaware that they are actually in an experiment, it is not possible to acquire their informed consent, to provide an introduction to the study, and to debrief them. These stages also are excluded in surveys that incorporate experiments. Excluding some stages, such as informed consent and debriefing, can raise ethical issues, which is a weakness of some field experiments. As we now turn our attention to the strengths and weaknesses of experiments relative to other approaches to social research, we will note how these strengths and weaknesses may depend on the experimental context.

STRENGTHS AND WEAKNESSES OF EXPERIMENTS

Besides knowing *how* to conduct an experiment, you also need to know *when* it is appropriate to use experimentation as opposed to some other research strategy. Understanding the unique strengths and weaknesses of the experimental approach will enable you to answer the *when* question. It also will help you to evaluate experiments, which is in keeping with our twin goals of making you both an informed consumer and producer of research evidence.

Internal Validity

The main reason to conduct an experiment is based on its principal strength: More so than other approaches, experiments provide sound evidence of a causal relationship. As you will see, most social scientific studies offer evidence of an *association* between variables, and some non-experimental studies can clearly establish *direction of influence*. But only experiments effectively rule out the possibility that extraneous variables, rather than the manipulated independent variable, are responsible for observed changes in the dependent variable. Studies that provide such evidence are said to be high in **internal validity**; studies that fail to control adequately for extraneous variables lack internal validity.

The strength of experiments in testing causal hypotheses extends to their use in evaluating research designs more generally. To determine how well a study tests a causal

internal validity
Evidence that rules out the possibility that factors other than the manipulated independent variable are responsible for the measured outcome.

hypothesis, social researchers often compare its design to that of an experiment. Study designs that are deficient suffer from one or more common **threats to internal validity**. Such threats refer to uncontrolled extraneous variables that may account for study results. For example, the threat of **selection** is present in any study that has all the ingredients of an experiment except for random assignment. Without random assignment, it is possible that the comparison groups will differ in ways that affect the outcome of the study; in other words, the "selection" of the groups may be biased. Suppose, for example, that participants in the misconduct study were told that they could *choose* whether to prosecute a defendant indicted for murder or assault. This raises the possibility that participants in the two conditions differ systematically. For instance, perhaps participants choosing the "murder condition" are more inclined to commit misconduct than participants choosing the "assault condition."

Knowing the elements of experimental design can be a powerful tool in helping you to evaluate the trustworthiness of research evidence. Indeed, now that you understand *how* experiments provide sound evidence of cause and effect, you can apply this knowledge to assess the internal validity of almost any study. To test your understanding of these ideas, see Box 7.3, READING SOCIAL RESEARCH: Thinking Critically About Research Designs and Threats to Internal Validity.

> **threats to internal validity** Types of extraneous variables that pose alternative explanations of an experimental outcome, thereby threatening the validity of the experimental manipulation.

> **selection** A threat to internal validity that is present whenever participants are not randomly assigned to experimental conditions.

BOX 7.3

READING SOCIAL RESEARCH

Thinking Critically About Research Designs and Threats to Internal Validity

Assessing internal validity is particularly suitable for studies designed to evaluate the effectiveness of a social program, as they often incorporate elements of experimental methodology. The first step is to identify the study design; the second step is to consider alternative explanations to the researcher's causal inference (threats to internal validity) that are posed by inadequate designs.

To understand how this works, consider research on Drug Abuse Resistance Education (DARE), a school-based program designed to increase students' knowledge of drugs and their resistance to drug use and violence. Taught by a police officer who visits the classroom, DARE is intended for children in their last year of elementary school (5th or 6th grade), although it has been used with children in kindergarten through 12th grade. This program depends on public support and receives millions of dollars annually in public funding (Rosenbaum 2007). Its effectiveness has been extensively evaluated, but many of the earliest studies were inadequate. Below are two types of studies that can be found in the literature. As you read these, begin by identifying the study design; then, consider alternative explanations to the causal inference (threats to internal validity) that are posed by inadequate designs.

continues

continued

Knowing that DARE is being administered in all sixth-grade classes in the local school district, a researcher randomly selects 10 classes. At the beginning of the school year, he measures attitudes toward drug use among all students in the ten randomly chosen classes. Then, at the end of the year, after the children have been exposed to the DARE program, he measures their attitudes toward drug use again. The data show that students have more negative attitudes toward drug use at the end of the year than they did at the beginning.

Were you able to identify the study design? The investigator has measured the dependent variable, attitude toward drug use, before and after students participated in the DARE program. Using the notation we introduced earlier in the chapter, we could represent the study as follows, where Y is the measurement of the dependent variable, attitude toward drug use, at times 1 and 2, and X stands for DARE:

$$Y_1 \quad X \quad Y_2$$

This is called a "pretest-posttest design." One problem with this design is that it lacks a comparison group, such as sixth-grade students who did not go through the DARE program (recall the pretest-posttest *control group* design). And, without a comparison group, there can be no random assignment to experimental conditions. (Beware that randomly selecting classes from the local school district is a way of drawing the sample; it has nothing to do with randomly assigning research participants to experimental conditions. See Box 7.1.)

Now that you know how this design is inadequate, can you come up with alternative explanations of the study results? That is, what else, besides the DARE program, could account for the more negative attitudes toward drug use at the end of the year? The problem with this design is that children's attitude toward drugs may change between the pretest and posttest even if they weren't exposed to DARE. Methodologists have identified two principal threats to the internal validity of studies with this design.

The first threat is called **maturation**, which refers to psychological or physical changes taking place within participants over time. Maturation may account for the results insofar as the children develop psychologically, becoming more aware of their bodies and of the unhealthy effects of ingesting drugs. A second threat is **history**; this refers to events in the participants' environment other than the experimental manipulation. Perhaps events outside the DARE program, in the school or community, influenced the children's attitude toward drugs. For example, a fellow student may have been arrested or suffered serious effects from drug use or an anti-drug campaign may be undertaken in the media.

Now, let's turn to the second example:

A researcher discovers that the DARE program is administered in the local school district but that it is not administered in an adjacent school district. So, with the permission of school administrators and parents, at the end of the school year she has students in all sixth-grade classes in the two districts complete a survey that asks them about their attitudes toward drug use. The data show that students exposed to the DARE program have more negative attitudes toward drug use than those who were not exposed to the program.

Is this study design internally valid? First, let's consider its design. We could represent the design as follows, where Y is the dependent variable, attitude toward drug use, X_1 represents exposure to DARE, and X_2 represents no exposure to DARE:

$$X_1 \quad Y$$
$$X_2 \quad Y$$

This design, called a "static group comparison," lacks an essential feature for establishing a causal connection between X and Y: random assignment. Without it, we cannot be sure that students exposed to DARE are similar in all respects to students who were not exposed to DARE. In fact, we bet you can think of many possible differences between students in the two districts that may affect students' attitude toward drugs. Any one of these differences signifies the internal validity threat of selection.

There are many other threats to internal validity in addition to selection, maturation, and history. You can learn more about these in the classic treatment by Donald Campbell and Julian Stanley (1963). For a briefer treatment, also see Singleton and Straits (2018:226–230).

External Validity

Although the primary concern in designing experiments is to make sure that they provide a sound test of a causal hypothesis, social researchers have the broader scientific goal of applying their findings beyond the specific situations they study. In addition to internal validity, therefore, researchers are also concerned with **external validity**. External validity refers to the question of generalizability, or what the experimental results mean outside the particular context of the experiment.

The researchers in the experiment on prosecutorial misconduct were careful to acknowledge that generalizing the results of their laboratory experiment "to naturally occurring situations is not advisable" (Lucas et al. 2006:104). They simply could not assume that working prosecutors handling actual criminal cases would behave similarly to undergraduate students performing the role of prosecutor in a contrived court case. The laboratory and real-world situations differ in numerous ways, including that many other factors may influence a prosecutor's wrongdoing. For example, as Lucas and associates point out, prosecutors who engage in misconduct may be punished, so

> . . . fear of punishment may make misconduct less likely in cases involving more severe crime. The opposite effect also could occur: the greater rewards and opportunities for advancement earned by obtaining convictions in serious, high-profile cases may increase pressure to engage in wrongdoing. (Lucas et al. 2006:105)

How, then, can we apply the results of this experiment—or any other experiment—to the real world? In other words, how can we enhance external validity? Let's examine four answers to this question that are pertinent not only to experiments but also to other research strategies.

1. Because the least generalizable experiments take place in the artificial environment of the laboratory, one way to enhance external validity is to conduct field experiments. By carrying out a study in a natural social setting, the events in the

maturation A threat to internal validity that refers to psychological or physiological changes taking place within participants.

history A threat to internal validity that refers to events other than the manipulation of the independent variable.

external validity The extent to which experimental findings may be generalized to other settings, measurements, populations, and time periods.

experiment are more similar to everyday experiences. We are relatively more certain, for example, about the applicability of research findings when we send out testers to apply for real jobs with real employers, as in Pager's field experiment on job discrimination, than when we ask undergraduate students to play the role of prosecutor in a contrived court case.

2. All experiments—indeed, all social scientific studies—involve a particular group of participants and take place at a specific time and setting with a certain set of procedures and researchers. Because all these aspects limit external validity, the best strategy for increasing the generalizability of findings often is **replication**, or repetition of the experiment. Replication may be carried out by the same investigator or by another investigator, who conducts the research in a different setting, with slightly different procedures, or with a different sample of participants. In fact, the strongest argument for generality is that widely varying experimental tests, or replications, have produced similar results.

   One limitation to the external validity of Pager's field experiment, for example, was that it was carried out in a single city, Milwaukee. Although similar to many other US metropolitan areas, Milwaukee had two unique features at the time of the study that may have limited its representativeness: it was the second most segregated city in the country, and it had the third largest growth in incarceration rates (and highest rate of incarceration for blacks). Pager speculates that a high level of segregation may strain race relations and that statewide incarceration rates may reflect a punitive approach to crime, which could affect employers' openness to hiring blacks and ex-offenders. As she further notes, "the only way to directly address these issues is through replication in additional areas" (Pager 2003:966). When Pager replicated her audit study in other cities (Pager, Western, and Bonikowski 2009; Pager, Western, and Sugie 2009), she found similar results, which enhanced the external validity of her findings.

3. A third way to increase external validity is through research design. The best examples of this apply to sample selection. One of the most persistent criticisms of experiments is that they are short on external validity because they tend to rely on convenience samples of college students (Henry 2008; Sears 1986). Because experimental manipulation often involves a laboratory setting and/or elaborate staging, it is usually impractical either to sample participants over wide areas or to utilize a large number of participants. As a consequence, experimenters tend to use small samples drawn from readily available populations. And because most experimentation is done in universities, the participants often are college students. How often? In social psychology, a discipline based heavily on experimental research, analyses of three major journals showed that between 1990 and 2005 over 90 percent of the articles reported studies with college student samples (Henry 2008).

   College students differ from people in general on several dimensions, including socioeconomic level, age, occupational goals, education, and interests. Given these

replication The repetition of a study using a different sample of participants and often involving different settings and methods.

and other differences, it is important to broaden the participant population (Sears 1986). One way to do this is to draw the sample from a more diverse population, such as residents of the town where a university is located. Because surveys are based on much larger (and typically random) samples, another method is to embed an experiment within a survey, as we saw in the experiment on support for the war in Afghanistan.

4. Finally, a fourth means of increasing external validity (as well as internal validity) is to extend the methods of replication and improved design by using different re-search strategies to test the same hypothesis or study the same phenomenon. As is true in experiments as much as other forms of research, each approach to social research has unique strengths and weaknesses. By combining them and using them in complementary ways, the strengths of one approach may offset the weaknesses of another. In testing causal hypotheses, for example, surveys provide weaker evidence of cause and effect than do experiments. On the other hand, surveys are almost always based on larger and more representative samples than experiments. We dis-cuss the use of multiple methods in Chapter 11, where we describe a study that com-bined an experiment and a survey.

In the end, all studies are limited to some extent with regard to external validity. The value of an experiment therefore rests largely on how well it validates the underlying theory that is being tested. If it offers strong support, then it provides a useful guide for future research.

Reactive Measurement Effects

Another weakness of laboratory experiments, specifically, is related to the process of measurement. As we noted earlier, participants in an experiment are acutely aware that they are being observed. When this awareness affects how participants behave, it is called a **reactive measurement effect**. Just as people behave differently alone than in front of an audience, or with friends than with strangers, they may react differently when in a research setting. For example, survey respondents who are asked about so-cially approved behavior may over-report how much they engage in the behavior to project a favorable image. As described in Box 5.2, respondents often overestimate how often they attend church. This sort of self-censoring is present to varying degrees in survey and field research, but it is most problematic in laboratory experiments.

reactive measurement
effect An effect in
which participants'
awareness of being
studied produces
changes in how they
ordinarily would
respond.

Reactive effects tend to occur in experiments for one of two reasons. First, knowing that they are taking part in a scientific study, many participants are determined to be helpful by acting in accord with the experimenter's hypothesis. Secondly, participants are very likely to want to project a favorable image of themselves. Although they know it is normative not to be told the true nature of the experiment, they nonetheless will look for cues about the study's hypothesis and about how they should act to "help" the experimenter and/or to "look good." This is why it is important in an experiment to divert participants' attention from the actual hypothesis by presenting a convincing cover story. Imagine, for example, that participants in the misconduct study had known or guessed that the real purpose of the experiment was to observe their level of misconduct. We can be sure that, with this knowledge, participants would have forwarded *all* the questions implicating another suspect to the defense attorney.

It is often difficult for experimenters to gauge the extent to which participants are reacting to cues about how they should respond or are acting as they would ordinarily. One place to try to learn this is the debriefing session. In fact, it is not unusual for experimenters to eliminate from their results the data pertaining to participants who correctly guessed the hypothesis.

One way in which participants may learn how they should respond is through their interaction with the experimenter. When experimenters know which experimental condition a participant is in, they may unconsciously and subtly communicate how the participant should act. Medical researchers have long known that a physician's belief in the efficacy of a drug or treatment may have as much to do with a patient's recovery as the treatment itself. Similarly in social research, it is possible, especially in evaluating a new social program, that staff members may convey their enthusiasm to participants. An effective way to control for such effects is to keep experimenters *blind* to the participants' condition. This would have been possible in the misconduct study, for example, if the research assistant had not known whether participants were in the murder or assault condition. An even more effective control, commonly used in medical research, is a **double-blind experiment**, in which neither the participants nor the experimenter know which experimental condition a participant is in.

double-blind experiment An experiment in which neither research participants nor research personnel know participants' treatment condition during the running of an experiment.

Content Restrictions

Experiments provide an ideal model for testing causal hypotheses. Yet, despite the social scientific goal of establishing causal explanations, social scientists often choose some other research strategy. The primary reason is that the requirements for an experiment limit what is feasible and practical to study. Many of the variables of interest to social scientists, such as race, gender, age, and socioeconomic status, cannot be manipulated. It often is impossible to randomly assign people to different conditions. And, social scientists often study units of analysis (e.g., cities and whole nations), institutions (e.g., religion, family, politics), and social and historical processes (migration, desegregation, social movements) that simply are not amenable to experimentation or must be studied in their entirety.

SUMMARY

The primary strength of an experiment lies in its ability to establish causal relationships; well-conducted experiments tend to be high in internal validity by ruling out extraneous variables that may produce a spurious association between the independent and dependent variables. One weakness of laboratory experiments, in particular, is that they tend to be low in external validity, but external validity may be increased through replication, by doing a field experiment, by selecting a broader range of participants, and/or by combining different approaches. Experiments are also subject to reactive measurement effects, but there are ways to check for these potential problems (e.g., asking participants) and to control for them (e.g., double-blind experiments). Despite their strengths and the flexibility that different experimental designs offer in overcoming weaknesses, experiments are nevertheless limited by content restrictions, as it is not possible to manipulate many phenomena in social life.

KEY TERMS

audit study, p. 190

cover story, p. 197

double-blind experiment, p. 206

external validity, p. 203

factorial design, p. 189

field experiment, p. 190

history, p. 203

internal validity, p. 200

laboratory experiment, p. 190

manipulation check, p. 197

maturation, p. 203

posttest-only control group design, p. 188

pretest, p. 194

pretest-posttest control group design, p. 188

random assignment, p. 185

reactive measurement effect, p. 205

replication, p. 204

selection, p. 201

survey-based experiment, p. 191

threats to internal validity, p. 201

KEY POINTS

- The primary features of an experiment are two or more groups or conditions to which participants are randomly assigned, manipulation of the independent variable(s), measurement of the dependent variable(s), and keeping conditions the same except for the manipulation.
- Experiments meet all three requirements for inferring cause and effect: association, direction of influence, and nonspuriousness.
- Experimental designs vary in whether the dependent variable is measured before or both before and after an experimental manipulation, and whether one or more independent variables is manipulated.
- Although traditionally carried out in a laboratory setting, experiments also may be performed "in the field" (field experiments) or embedded in surveys.
- Similar to the steps in producing a play, the process of conducting experiments often begins with pretesting to see how well the "script" of the experiment works.
- The researcher "gets an audience" by recruiting participants and acquiring informed consent.

- The "opening act" is the introduction of the experiment, which is intended to pique participants' interest through a compelling cover story.
- The "second scene" includes the random assignment of participants and experimental manipulation.
- Following the manipulation of the independent variable, the next "scene" consists of the measurement of the dependent variable(s) and, sometimes, a manipulation check.
- The "closing act" is the debriefing, which informs participants of the true nature of the study and attempts to minimize any discomfort that may have resulted from deception.
- Whereas the principal strength of experiments is high internal validity, experiments may be less generalizable than other studies, are subject to reactive measurement effects, and are limited in the topics that they can address.

REVIEW QUESTIONS

1. Explain how experiments offer sound evidence of cause and effect.
2. Explain two ways in which experimental designs may differ from one another.
3. What are the relative advantages and disadvantages of laboratory experiments as compared with experiments conducted outside the laboratory?
4. Explain the purpose(s) of the following experimental procedures: (a) cover story; (b) manipulation check; and (c) debriefing.
5. Briefly distinguish between internal and external validity. Identify two threats to internal validity.
6. What are the major strengths and limitations of experiments in social research?

EXERCISES

1. About the same time as Pager's field experiment on the mark of a criminal record, another study was done on racial discrimination in the labor market (Bertrand and Mullainathan 2004). Rather than use "live" auditors, the investigators sent resumes in response to help-wanted ads in Chicago and Boston newspapers. They sent a carefully matched pair of resumes to each ad, with one resume randomly assigned a very white-sounding name (e.g., "Todd Baker" or "Anne Kelly") and the other a very African-American–sounding name (e.g., "Tyrone Jackson" or "Ebony Jones"). Then, they recorded whether an applicant received a phone or e-mail callback for an interview.

   (a) Does this study have all the features of a true experiment? Carefully explain.

    (b) What is the independent variable in this study? How is it manipulated?

    (c) What is the dependent variable?

2. In our brief description of the study in Question 1, we omitted one feature of the study design. In addition to the names assigned to each résumé, the investigators varied the quality of the resumes, with high-quality résumés more likely to have degrees, foreign-language and extra computer skills, and awards and honors. Thus, for each ad, two high-quality and two low-quality résumés were sent, with one résumé in each pair randomly assigned a white name and the other an African-American name.

    (a) What type of experimental design is this? Be specific.

    (b) In discussing the weaknesses of the study, the investigators note that (1) newspaper ads represent only one channel for job searches and (2) there are other measures of racial discrimination that they could not use, such as whether applicants got a job and the wage they were offered. Explain whether these criticisms pertain to the *internal validity* or *external validity* of the study.

3. Have you ever tried to borrow your roommate's car, sell something at a yard sale, or solicit a donation to a charitable organization? This is a short list of the attempts to get others to accede to requests that occur every day. Social psychologists refer to agreeing to a request as *compliance*. Not surprisingly, given the prevalence of compliance in everyday life, a great deal of research has examined the effectiveness of numerous tactics in producing compliance (Cialdini 2009; Cialdini and Goldstein 2004). One tactic that people seem to find intuitively compelling is the use of compliments. Yet very little research has evaluated the impact of compliments on compliance (Grant, Fabrigar, and Lim 2010). Suppose you want to test the hypothesis that people who are complimented are more likely to agree to a request than people who are not complimented. How would you test this hypothesis in a *laboratory* experiment? As you develop your study design, address each of the following questions:

    (a) How will you manipulate the independent variable?

    (b) What kind of request will you make and how will you measure compliance?

    (c) How will you recruit research participants and obtain their informed consent?

(d) What will be your cover story?

(e) What will you say to research participants during the debriefing?

4. Now address the following questions as you design a *field* experiment to test the same hypothesis as in Exercise 3.

(a) Why would it be better to conduct your study in the field than in the laboratory?

(b) If you cannot obtain participants' informed consent or debrief them, how can you justify your experiment ethically? (See Chapter 3.)

Surveys
Questioning and Sampling

STUDENT LEARNING OBJECTIVES

By the end of this chapter, you should be able to

1. Describe the three general features of surveys.

2. Explain variations in survey designs by distinguishing between cross-sectional and longitudinal designs.

3. Compare the strengths and weaknesses of face-to-face, telephone, paper-and-pencil, computer-assisted, and mixed modes of data collection.

4. Describe the steps in the process of planning and conducting a survey and apply them to a research topic.

5. Evaluate surveys as a method of data collection, identifying their strengths and weaknesses.

You probably know what surveys are. Maybe you've called to get customer service for some product only to be asked by an automated recording if you would be willing to participate in a survey after the call. Perhaps you've had e-mail requests to participate in online surveys on your health or political views, sometimes with an incentive—such as a gift card for coffee or music downloads—to encourage you to participate. Opening your "snail mail" one day, you may have received a questionnaire from a political organization or from the US Census Bureau.

Even if you have never participated in a survey, you almost certainly have heard or read news headlines about survey results:

- "It's Too Easy to Buy Guns, A Majority of Americans Say" (Gorman 2017)
- "White evangelicals voted overwhelmingly for Donald Trump, exit polls show" (Bailey 2016)
- "US Support for Gay Marriage Edges to New High" (McCarthy 2017).

These examples contain the essential elements of survey research: asking a sample of people a predetermined set of questions in order to estimate characteristics of the population from which the sample was drawn. As you saw in Chapter 6, such estimates are based on random sampling. And if you've taken a survey, you may have been told that you were randomly selected to participate. At their best, surveys produce accurate quantitative data that not only describe the attitudes, opinions, and behavior of a target population but also reveal how social characteristics, such as gender, race/ethnicity, class, and age, are related to people's responses. As such, surveys are widely used in social science research addressing quantitative questions (Wright and Marsden 2010).

We begin this chapter by describing a typical telephone survey. Based on this survey, we discuss the primary features of survey research. Next, we describe major variations in surveys, including designs that gather data at more than one point in time and different modes of collecting data such as face-to-face interviews, telephone interviews, and self-administered questionnaires. We then outline the process of conducting a survey. Finally, we discuss the strengths and weaknesses of survey research.

INTRODUCTORY EXAMPLE: THE CONSTRUCTING THE FAMILY SURVEY

At the beginning of the 21st century, academic and public discourse on the meaning of family had become intense. Challenging the standard definition of "family" as consisting of a mother, a father, and children, many social scientists were expanding family studies to include same-sex couples. In several states, heated debate accompanied the enactment of laws that restricted adoption to heterosexual couples, banned same-sex marriage, or recognized same-sex marriage. This discourse showed that how people define a family matters a great deal. In response to this ongoing controversy, sociologist Brian Powell and his associates (2010) designed the Constructing the Family Survey

(CFS) to address a fundamental question: Which living arrangements do Americans count as family?[1]

To answer this question, Powell and his collaborators carried out the CFS using the resources of the Center for Survey Research (CSR) at Indiana University. In 2003 and again in 2006, 2010, and 2015, they made telephone calls to US adult residents asking for their participation in the survey. CSR staff randomly selected telephone numbers, and at each residential telephone number, randomly selected a household member to interview. Typical of many social surveys, the interview addressed not only the core research question—how Americans define family—but also a variety of related topics, including attitudes toward gay men and lesbians, marital name changes, and the relative importance of biological and social factors in child development. Moreover, the interview included questions on background characteristics such as education, age, gender, race, religion, and marital status. In this way, the researchers could examine how views of family are related to an individual's background, life experiences, and social attitudes.

▲ Brian Powell

In the most direct question about how people define family, interviewers read a list of living arrangements and asked respondents whether they personally thought that each arrangement "counts as a family." There were 11 arrangements in all, beginning with "a husband and wife living together with one or more of their children." Table 8.1 shows the percentage of the 712 respondents in the 2003 CFS who identified each arrangement as a family.

Based on these and other data, the researchers concluded that nearly all Americans agree that the presence of children in the home *and/or* a legal heterosexual relationship count as family. Interviewees were less likely to identify a cohabiting couple with children as a family (78.7 percent), followed by same-sex parents with children (55.0 and 53.6 percent), and then cohabiting and same-sex couples without children (31.1 percent or less). Finally, only about 1 in 10 interviewees identified nonromantic friends living together as family.

In a second stage of their analysis, Powell and associates identified commonalities among the numerous combinations of responses to the various living arrangements, excluding nonromantic friends. Using a statistical technique called latent class analysis, they found three classes or "ideal types" that best captured the way most Americans define family: Exclusionists, moderates, and inclusionists. Exclusionists (45.3 percent of the sample) tended to restrict a family to legal heterosexual marriages and were ambivalent about including a cohabiting heterosexual couple with children; moderates (29.3 percent of the sample) "extended family status to any arrangement with children" (Powell et al. 2010:26); and inclusionists (25.4 percent of the sample) defined each of the 11 living arrangements as a family.

---

[1]This chapter draws heavily on Powell and colleagues' book, *Counted Out: Same-Sex Relations and Americans' Definitions of Family* (2010), as well as information Powell generously provided to us (personal communications 2013 and 2017).

Table 8.1 Which Living Arrangements Count as Family?

	Percentage
A husband and wife living together with one or more children.	100.0
A man living alone with one or more children.	94.2
A woman living alone with one or more children.	94.0
A husband and wife living together who have no children.	93.1
A man and woman living together as an unmarried couple, with one or more of their children.	78.7
Two women living together as a couple with one or more of their children.	55.0
Two men living together as a couple with one or more of their children.	53.6
A man and a woman living together as an unmarried couple who have no children.	31.1
Two women living together as a couple who have no children.	26.8
Two men living together as a couple who have no children.	26.2
Two people living together as housemates who are not living as a couple and have no children.	9.9

Source: Adapted from Figure 2.1 in Powell et al. (2010:21).

When the researchers related background variables and social attitudes to these types, they found important differences. For example, compared with exclusionists and moderates, inclusionists were more often women than men, were more likely to be college educated, and were less religious. Furthermore, the views of the three groups differed sharply with respect to family policy issues: fewer than 10 percent of exclusionists expressed support for either same-sex marriage or adoption by same-sex parents; by contrast, more than 85 percent of inclusionists strongly or somewhat supported these policies.

GENERAL FEATURES OF SURVEY RESEARCH

The Constructing the Family Survey illustrates three features that surveys have to varying degrees:

1. A large number of respondents chosen to represent a population of interest.
2. Structured questionnaire or interview procedures that ask a predetermined set of questions.
3. The quantitative analysis of survey responses.

Let's examine more carefully each of these features with reference to the CFS and to other studies that illustrate variations in the general rule for each feature.

Large-Scale Probability Sampling

Professional surveys make use of large samples chosen through scientific sampling procedures to ensure accurate estimates of population characteristics. Although much larger than the typical experiment, the number of interviewees in the CFS was relatively small in comparison with many surveys: 712 adults in 2003 and 815 in 2006. National opinion polls typically number around 1000 respondents, and the General Social Survey (GSS) has had sample sizes ranging from 1,372 (in 1990) to 4,510 (in 2006). Surveys of national samples can be much larger. In the National Educational Longitudinal Study (NELS), for example, the probability sample in 1988 consisted of 24,599 eighth-graders from 1,052 public and private schools.

Sample accuracy is a function of two factors: sample design and sample size. It is only possible to estimate sample accuracy with probability samples, which involve random selection; and when cases are chosen randomly, the larger the sample, the more accurate the sample estimates of population characteristics. Both of these factors, however, require considerable resources—time, money, and personnel—that may be beyond the capacity of independent researchers or small research teams. Many surveys, therefore, involve smaller samples drawn from state or local populations. In addition to the CFS, the Indiana University Center for Survey Research has carried out many other surveys that have targeted the Indiana state population as well as the populations of cities and counties in Indiana. To address issues of health care reform, for example, the Quality of Life and Health Survey (Pescosolido and Long 2000) involved interviews with 298 randomly selected adult residents of Indianapolis.

Although large-scale probability samples are the ideal, surveys vary considerably in sample size and sampling design. There are legitimate reasons for doing a small-scale survey, particularly if you have a low budget or some specialized or applied research purpose. In fact, you can conduct your own low-budget research if you have a research problem that can be studied appropriately with a brief questionnaire survey of the home campus or a telephone survey of the local dialing area.

Structured Interviews or Questionnaires

Surveys gather data by asking people predetermined questions following standardized procedures that are designed to enhance the reliability of the data. This epitomizes the **structured interviews** that were used in the CFS: the survey objectives were very specific; all the questions were written beforehand and asked in the same order for all respondents; and interviewers were highly restricted in the use of introductory and closing remarks, transitions or "bridges" from topic to topic, as well as supplementary questions to gain a more complete response (probes).

By contrast, an **unstructured interview** has broad research objectives and involves a wide-ranging discussion in which individual questions are developed spontaneously in the course of the interview. Between the two extremes, the **semi-structured interview**

structured interview A type of interview with highly specific objectives in which all questions are written beforehand and asked in the same order for all respondents, and the interviewer's remarks are standardized.

unstructured interview A type of interview guided by broad objectives in which questions are developed as the interview proceeds.

semi-structured interview A type of interview that, while having specific objectives, permits the interviewer some freedom in meeting them.

would have specific objectives, but the interviewer would be allowed some freedom in meeting those objectives. The scope of the interview would be limited to certain sub-topics, and key questions probably would be developed in advance. Unstructured and semi-structured interviews are often used in qualitative research; we have more to say about these types of interviews in Chapter 9.

Surveys can contain many types of questions and question formats, but they almost always include **closed-ended questions**, which require respondents to choose a response from those provided, much like a multiple-choice test. For example, CFS respondents who were not currently married were asked: Are you (1) living with a partner, (2) widowed, (3) separated, (4) divorced, or (5) never married? In a series of questions about marital name changes, CFS respondents also were asked to indicate their level of agreement or disagreement with the following statement: "It is generally better if a woman changes her last name to her husband's name when she marries. Do you: (1) strongly agree, (2) somewhat agree, (3) somewhat disagree, or (4) strongly disagree?" (Powell 2003).

As a follow-up to this closed-ended question, in 2006 respondents who strongly or somewhat agreed were asked an **open-ended question**, which required them to answer in their own words: "Why do you think it's better for a woman to change her name?" Or, if they disagreed, they were asked: "Why don't you think it is better for a woman to change her name?" Over 70 percent of the respondents agreed strongly or somewhat that it is better if a woman changes her name. When asked why, a near majority saw the name change as part of the process of prioritizing women's identity as wives and mothers.

One reason that survey researchers prefer closed-ended questions is that they produce data that lend themselves well to the kinds of quantitative analysis that drives survey research. In contrast, open-ended questions are adopted when the research purpose is not to derive precise quantitative descriptions but to understand respondents' interpretations and experiences, as in qualitative research. In these approaches, open-ended questions provide flexibility in meeting broad research objectives and in developing theory. To weigh the pros and cons of closed- and open-ended questions using another example from the CFS, see Box 8.1, READING SOCIAL RESEARCH: Open-Ended Versus Closed-Ended Questions in Survey Research.

Quantitative Data Analysis

Data-analysis techniques depend on whether the survey's purpose is descriptive, explanatory, or a combination of the two. Surveys that are primarily **descriptive**, such as many opinion polls, make use of simpler forms of data analysis to describe the distribution of certain characteristics, attitudes, or experiences within a population. **Explanatory surveys**, on the other hand, require more sophisticated data-analysis techniques to investigate relationships between two or more variables and attempt to explain these in cause-and-effect terms.

closed-ended question Survey questions that require respondents to choose responses from those provided.

open-ended question A survey question that requires respondents to answer in their own words.

descriptive survey A survey undertaken to provide estimates of the characteristics of a population.

explanatory survey A survey that investigates relationships between two or more variables, often attempting to explain them in cause-and-effect terms.

BOX 8.1

BOX 8.1

READING SOCIAL RESEARCH

Open-Ended Versus Closed-Ended Questions in Survey Research

To examine people's definition of family, the CFS began with a closed-ended question, asking respondents to answer "yes" or "no" to whether they considered each of a series of living arrangements to be a family. After asking about all 11 arrangements, the CFS posed the following open-ended question: "In thinking about your answers to the past few questions about what counts as a family, what determines for you whether you think a living arrangement is a family?"

By revealing respondents' logic or thought processes, answers to this question both corroborated and elaborated the typology based on the closed-ended question. One of the key distinctions among exclusionists, moderates, and inclusionists, for example, was their relative emphasis on structure versus function. Structure refers to the legal and genetic relationship among people living together; function refers to what families actually do to meet the needs of their members. Exclusionists emphasized structure: the most common theme in their responses was the primacy of marriage—an explicit legal arrangement, followed by "blood" ties between parents and children. They rationalized giving family status to a single parent with children by assuming that the parent was divorced or widowed—that is, was formerly in a legal relationship. Inclusionists, by contrast, rarely mentioned structure, focusing instead on the emotional and instrumental ties that bring people together. Thus, two or more people constitute a family if they love and are committed to each other, and/or if they are working together—financially and physically—to create a household. Consistent with their closed-ended responses, the majority of moderates saw the presence of children as the defining feature of a family. Beyond children, some moderates followed exclusionists by requiring marriage for family status, while others mentioned emotional bonds or instrumental qualities favored by inclusionists.

Open-ended questions provide a wealth of information that can clarify and deepen the researcher's understanding of a topic. However, open-ended questions pose several problems that limit their use in survey research. Summarizing and analyzing rich and varied (and sometimes irrelevant and vague) responses is a time-consuming and costly process. Respondents may be reluctant to reveal detailed information or socially unacceptable opinions or behavior. And open-ended questions require more effort to answer; indeed, they often are left blank—and therefore should be used sparingly—in self-administered questionnaires or Web surveys, where respondents must write or type rather than speak.

The CFS involved both descriptive and explanatory analysis. Table 8.1, which reports the percentage of respondents who counted each living arrangement as family, is descriptive. Because the CFS was based on a random sample of US adults, these percentages are reasonable estimates of the percentage of *American adults* who count each arrangement as family.

When the investigators turned their attention to the influence of demographic and other variables on what counts as family, the analysis was explanatory. As noted earlier,

Table 8.2 Family Definitions, by Gay-Lesbian Social Networks, 2003

	Exclusionist	Moderate	Inclusionist
No Gay Friends or Relatives	50.3	29.5	20.3
Gay Friends or Relatives	34.9	30.8	34.3

Source: Adapted from Figure 4.7 in Powell et al. (2010:93).

for example, the investigators found that beliefs about family were related to gender, education, and religious views. This analysis was *multivariate*, examining relationships while statistically controlling for key socioeconomic variables; it also included tests of statistical significance. Consistent with the contact hypothesis, which suggests that interpersonal contact between groups reduces prejudice, the researchers found a statistically significant relationship between whether people have gay friends or relatives and how they generally define family. Furthermore, this relationship holds after statistically controlling for gender, age, race, and education. Table 8.2 shows the predicted probabilities—that is, the expected chance—of being an exclusionist, moderate, or inclusionist, based on whether people had gay friends or relatives. Each row in the table adds up to 100 percent when rounded. Comparing the percentages in the top and bottom rows of this table, you can see that people are less likely to be exclusionists, for example, if they have gay friends or relatives than if they don't have gay friends or relatives. Conversely, people are *more* likely to be inclusionists if they have gay friends or relatives than if they don't.

In addition to these quantitative analyses, Powell and associates also performed qualitative analyses of the responses to open-ended questions. However, as in virtually all surveys, the primary data from the CFS were quantitative.

SUMMARY

There are three general features of surveys. First, a large number of respondents are chosen, usually through probability sampling, to represent a population of interest. Second, surveys tend to use structured questionnaire or interview procedures that ask a predetermined set of closed-ended rather than open-ended questions. Third, surveys involve quantitative analysis of responses, which may be descriptive (to describe a population), explanatory (to test hypotheses), or both.

VARIATIONS IN SURVEY DESIGNS AND MODES

Like experiments, surveys vary in research design and context. The research design specifies the overall structure or plan by which a study will address the research question(s). The context refers to the setting in which the data are collected. Let's take a closer look now at the CFS and other research examples to understand variations in survey design and the mode of data collection.

Survey Research Designs

The basic idea of a survey is to measure variables by asking people questions and then to describe the distribution of responses to single questions or examine the relationships among responses to multiple items. The major design decision is whether to ask the questions just once or to repeat the questions over time.

CROSS-SECTIONAL DESIGNS

The most commonly used survey design by far is the **cross-sectional design**, which involves a sample or "cross-section" of respondents chosen to represent a particular target population. Cross-sectional data are gathered at essentially one point in time. By "one point in time" we do not mean that respondents are interviewed or that self-administered questionnaires are collected simultaneously (although this might be the case with some questionnaire studies). Rather, the data are collected in as short a time as is feasible. Each iteration of the CFS was a cross-sectional survey. For the 2003 CFS, it took almost two months, between May and July, for 26 interviewers to complete interviews with 712 respondents (Powell et al. 2010).

LONGITUDINAL DESIGNS

Because cross-sectional designs call for collection of data at one point in time, they do not always show clearly the direction of causal relationships. Moreover, they are not well suited to the study of process and change. To provide stronger inferences about causal direction and more accurate studies of patterns of change, survey researchers have developed **longitudinal designs**, in which the same questions are asked at two or more points in time. The questions may be asked repeatedly either of independently selected samples of the same general population or of the same individuals. This results in two main types of longitudinal designs: trend studies and panel studies.

A **trend study** consists of a repeated cross-sectional design in which each survey collects data on the same items or variables with a new, independent sample of the same target population. This allows for the study of trends or changes in the population as a whole. Examples of trend studies are the monthly government surveys used to estimate unemployment in the United States (target population) and repeated public-opinion polls of candidate preferences among registered voters (target population) as an election approaches.

Each CFS consisted of an independent cross-sectional design; conducting a second CFS in 2006 created a trend study. When the investigators compared the results from 2003 and 2006, they found a decrease in the percentage of exclusionists (from 45.4 to 38.1 percent) and an increase in the percentage of inclusionists (from 25.4 to 32.4 percent). This led them to conclude that "it is just a matter of time before

cross-sectional design The most common survey design, in which data are gathered from a sample of respondents at essentially one point in time.

longitudinal design Survey design in which data are collected at more than one point in time.

trend study A longitudinal design in which a research question is investigated by repeated surveys of independently selected samples of the same population.

same-sex couples are no longer counted out" (Powell et al. 2010:15). The findings thus foretold changes in public opinion that ultimately would be reflected in changes in public policy, most notably the 2013 Supreme Court decision that struck down part of the federal Defense of Marriage Act that defined marriage as a legal union between a man and a woman (*United States v. Windsor* 2013). To continue to track changes in public opinion on this issue, Powell and associates conducted a third CFS in 2010 and a fourth survey in 2015. By 2015, the percentage of exclusionists had fallen to 30 and the percentage of inclusionists had risen to 40 percent of the respondents (Powell, personal communication 2013 and 2017).

> **panel study** A longitudinal design in which the same individuals are surveyed more than once, permitting the study of individual and group change.

Whereas a trend study identifies which *variables* are changing over time, a **panel study** can reveal which *individuals* are changing over time because the same respondents are surveyed again and again. Paul Lazarsfeld, Bernard Berelson, and Hazel Gaudet's (1948) classic study of voter behavior, *The People's Choice*, exemplifies the panel method. Before the 1940 presidential election, 600 persons were interviewed repeatedly between May and November. The analysis revealed that persons who expressed a clear preference for the Democratic or the Republican candidates at the first interview were unlikely at the second interview one month later to remember having seen or heard any campaign propaganda from the party of the opposing candidate. Because of this phenomenon of selective attention, few voters changed their preferences over the course of the study. See Table 8.3 for the similarities and differences between trend and panel studies.

Panel studies of any duration were a rarity in the social sciences until the late 1960s, when the federal government began conducting large-scale longitudinal studies. A good example is the National Educational Longitudinal Study (NELS), which surveyed a sample of eighth-graders in 1988 and then did follow-up surveys of these same respondents in 1990, 1992, 1994, and 2000. The longest-running household panel survey in the world is the Panel Study of Income Dynamics (PSID), conducted by the Survey

Table 8.3 Similarities and Differences between Trend and Panel Studies

Trend Study	Panel Study
Survey questions are repeated to understand change over time	Survey questions are repeated to understand change over time
A different independent sample of respondents, representative of the same target population (e.g., US adults), is asked the same questions in each survey	The initial sample of respondents is asked the same questions each time the survey is administered
Data show how *the population* changes over time	Data show how *individuals* change over time

Research Center in the Institute for Social Research at the University of Michigan. The PSID has collected data on a sample of US households annually from 1968 to 1997 and biennially beginning in 1999. As of 2009, nearly 6,000 of the original participants from 1968 were still living and had participated in every survey (McGonagle et al. 2012).

Two drawbacks to studies of this magnitude are that they are very expensive and take considerable time. Therefore, cross-sectional and trend designs are far more common. But irrespective of the survey design, surveys also differ in how the data are collected.

Data-Collection Modes

A critical aspect of survey research is the mode of asking questions: interviewer-administered (face-to-face or telephone surveys), self-administered (paper-and-pencil or computer-assisted questionnaires), or some combination of these modes. Figure 8.1 lists the four basic data-collection modes along with typical computer-based variations. The modes may be conceptualized as falling along a continuum from the most to the least interactive. At one end of the continuum, involving all channels of communication, is the face-to-face interview; this is followed, in turn, by telephone interviews, various computer-assisted self-interviews, and autonomous self-administered questionnaires. Although we focus primarily on the four basic modes, recent technological developments have rapidly expanded the options and encouraged the use of multiple modes of data collection within the same study. Therefore, we discuss mixed-mode data-collection strategies after comparing the modes shown in Figure 8.1. Each mode, as you will see, has its distinctive advantages and disadvantages; the choice depends on many considerations, including research objectives, quality of measurement, and available resources such as time and money. We discuss each of these considerations as we introduce each mode.

FACE-TO-FACE INTERVIEWS

The oldest and most highly regarded method of survey research is the **face-to-face (FTF) interview**, which involves direct, in-person contact between an interviewer and interviewee. The General Social Survey (GSS) is an FTF interview survey. From 1972 until 2002, GSS interviewers circled or recorded answers in writing on questionnaires, but in 2002, the GSS shifted to **computer-assisted personal interviewing (CAPI)**. With CAPI, interviewers carry out the survey through a laptop computer, which they

Most Interactive

Face-to-Face (FTF) Interviews
    Computer-Assisted Personal Interviewing (CAPI)

Telephone Interviews
    Computer-Assisted Telephone Interviewing (CATI)

Computer-Assisted Self Interviews
    Internet (Web) Surveys
    Computer Self-Administered Questionnaires (CASI)
    Interactive Voice Response (IVR) Surveys
    E-mail Transmission of Questionnaires

Paper-and-Pencil Questionnaires

Least Interactive

FIGURE 8.1
Survey Data-Collection Modes

face-to-face (FTF) interview A type of interview in which the interviewer interacts face-to-face with the respondent.

computer-assisted personal interviewing (CAPI) A software program, usually on a portable computer, that aids interviewers by providing appropriate instructions, question wording, and data-entry supervision.

▲ Computer-assisted personal interviewing (CAPI) is now the standard for conducting large-scale face-to-face interview surveys, nationally and internationally as shown in this photo from the Yemen Polling Center.

response rate In a survey, the proportion of people in the sample from whom completed interviews or questionnaires are obtained.

FIGURE 8.2
FTF Visual Aid. GSS interviewers hand respondents a card similar to this one when they ask, "Which of the categories on this card come closest to the type of place you were living in when you were 16 years old?" (Smith et al. 2017).

1. In open country but not on a farm
2. On a farm
3. In a small city or town (under 50,000)
4. In a medium-size city (50,000–250,000)
5. In a suburb near a large city
6. In a large city (over 250,000)

bring to the respondent's home. The computer screen prompts the interviewer with instructions and questions; the interviewer reads the questions and then enters the respondent's answers. CAPI makes the interviewer's job easier, reduces mistakes, and saves time and cost since the data are entered directly into a computer file and do not have to be entered manually. It is not surprising, therefore, that it has become the standard for large-scale survey research in the United States.

FTF interview surveys offer many advantages. The presence of an interviewer permits a great deal more flexibility than is possible with a self-administered questionnaire. If the research objectives call for open-ended questions, interviewers can probe for more complete responses; they can also clarify or restate questions that the respondent does not understand. The **response rate**, the proportion of people in the sample who completed interviews (or questionnaires), is typically higher than in comparable telephone or mail surveys (de Leeuw 2008:128–29), although response rates in all three modes have been declining in recent years. Between 1975 and 1998, the average response rate for the GSS was 77 percent; the GSS rate dipped to 70–71 percent between 2000 and 2012 and has fallen below 70 percent since then, with a low of 61.3 percent in 2016 (Smith et al. 2017, Appendix A, Table A.8).

By sustaining respondents' attention and motivation, the FTF mode is generally the best choice when long interviews are necessary. In fact, FTF interviews of one hour's length are common, and they sometimes go much longer. GSS interviews take about 90 minutes for completion of some 400 questions. With the FTF technique, one can use visual aids such as photographs and drawings in presenting the questions, as well as cards that show response options (see Figure 8.2). The cards may be useful when response options are difficult to remember or when it is face-saving for respondents to select the option or category on the card rather than to say the answer aloud.

The greatest disadvantage to the FTF method is cost. Compared to telephone interviews, the research budget for an FTF survey must provide not only for recruiting, training, and supervising personnel but also for interviewer wages and travel expenses, including lodging and meals in some cases. Moreover, it takes much longer to complete each interview in an FTF survey; therefore, the cost per interview is much greater. Robert Groves and associates (2009:173) estimate that national FTF surveys cost 5 to 10 times as much as telephone surveys. The full cost of the 2014 GSS, from sampling through release of the data to the public, was about $1,350 per completed interview (T. W. Smith, personal communication 2016).

TELEPHONE INTERVIEWS

In the last quarter of the 20th century, **telephone interviews** became the most popular survey method in the United States and western Europe. Virtually all opinion polls are telephone surveys. The CFS was a telephone survey conducted by trained staff using **computer-assisted telephone interviewing (CATI)**, the telephone counterpart to CAPI. The primary reason for the widespread use of the telephone survey is its substantial savings in cost and time. We already noted that telephone surveys cost substantially less than FTF surveys; Powell estimates that the 2010 CFS cost about $80 per respondent (personal communication 2013). Compare this to the cost cited above for the 2014 GSS in-person interviews! In addition, survey research organizations like the Center for Survey Research, which have a permanent staff, can complete a telephone survey very rapidly. Even those researchers who must hire and train interviewers can complete a telephone survey in less billable time than one requiring FTF interviews or mailed questionnaires.

Besides savings in cost and time, another major advantage of telephone interviewing is the opportunity for centralized quality control over all aspects of data collection (Lavrakas 2010), including question development and pretesting, interviewer training and supervision, sampling and callbacks, and data entry. Administration and staff supervision for a telephone survey are much simpler than for an FTF interview survey.

Still, telephone surveys have their limitations. Without the benefit of visual aids, the questions in a telephone survey must be simpler, with fewer response options, than in an FTF interview. And without face-to-face contact, it is more difficult for interviewers to establish trust and rapport with respondents, which may lead to higher rates of nonresponse for some questions and underreporting of sensitive or socially undesirable behavior (Aquilino 1994:211, 214; Groves et al. 2009:170; Holbrook, Green, and Krosnick 2003). Overall response rates also tend to be lower than in FTF interview surveys; and conducting a telephone interview longer than 20 to 30 minutes increases the risk of nonresponse and mid-interview termination (de Leeuw 2008). The 2003 CFS, with an average length of 44 minutes, was unusually long for a telephone survey; the 2006 CFS was shorter, at 28 minutes. Perhaps partly because of survey length, the response rates for the CFS were relatively low: 32.5 percent in 2003 and 31.3 percent in 2006 (Powell, personal communication 2013).

You may need to look no farther than your hand, your pocket, or your purse to guess the most serious problems facing telephone surveys. The rapid proliferation of mobile

telephone interview
A type of interview in which interviewers interact with respondents by telephone.

computer-assisted telephone interviewing (CATI)
A set of computerized tools that aid telephone interviewers and supervisors by automating various data-collection tasks.

telephones and the growth of the cell phone–only population has made it difficult to reach respondents and has necessitated dual-frame sampling—of mobile and landline telephones—that raise complex methodological, statistical, legal, and ethical issues (Lavrakas et al. 2007). Response rates for many federal telephone surveys declined from around 70 percent in the 1990s to 50 percent by 2005 (Dixon and Tucker 2010), and rates for private US survey organizations are even lower, with most telephone surveys between 20 and 50 percent (Holbrook, Krosnick, and Pfent 2008). Factors contributing to the plunging telephone response rates include the growth of caller ID call-screening and call-blocking technologies, heightened privacy concerns in the face of increased telemarketing calls, and the increase in cell phone–only households (Curtin, Presser, and Singer 2005; Dixon and Tucker 2010). In short, many people do not answer their phone, be it landline or cell, unless they recognize and wish to speak to the caller. In light of these mounting obstacles to telephone surveys, some foresee an increasing reliance on self-administered questionnaires (Couper 2011; Dillman 2007), which we discuss next.

PAPER-AND-PENCIL QUESTIONNAIRE

paper-and-pencil questionnaire survey A survey form filled out by respondents.

Occasionally, the site of a **paper-and-pencil-questionnaire survey** is a school or organization, where the questionnaire may be hand-delivered and filled out in a group or individually. Most often, however, the setting is the home or a workplace, to which a self-administered questionnaire is mailed to respondents. An interesting example of a *mail survey* is the College Alcohol Study (CAS; Wechsler and Nelson 2008), a widely cited national survey of American college students' drinking habits and other health issues. The CAS was conducted four times: in 1993, 1997, 1999, and 2001. In each of the four surveys, the researchers found that two in five students who responded were binge drinkers, operationally defined as the consumption of five or more drinks in a row for men and four or more drinks in a row for women during the two weeks prior to the survey. Binge drinkers, especially those who frequently binged, were far more likely than nonbinge drinkers to experience a variety of alcohol-related and other health problems, such as engaging in unprotected and unplanned sex, getting in trouble with campus police, damaging property, and getting hurt or injured.

There are several advantages of using a mail survey. A mail survey is less expensive than interview surveys, with costs estimated at 20 to 70 percent less than telephone surveys (Groves et al. 2009:173). No interviewers or interviewer supervisors are needed; there are no travel or telephone expenses; and very little office space is required. The time needed to complete the data-collection phase of the survey is greater than that for telephone surveys but usually less than that for FTF surveys. The sample size may be very large, and geographical dispersion is not a problem. The 1993 CAS, for example, surveyed a random sample of 17,592 students at 140 colleges in 39 states and the District of Columbia (Wechsler et al. 1994). There also is greater accessibility to respondents with this method since those who cannot be reached by telephone or who are infrequently at home usually receive mail. Finally, in contrast to interview surveys, mail surveys can provide respondents with anonymity, which is important in investigating sensitive or threatening topics, such as college drinking or illicit drug use. Anonymity protects respondents' privacy, and research has shown that respondents are more likely to admit to undesirable behavior with self-administered than with interview-administered surveys (Groves et al. 2009:170; Tourangeau and Yan 2007; see Krumpal 2013 for a review).

Despite these advantages, especially its lower cost, the mail questionnaire survey method is inferior to FTF and telephone interview surveys in several ways. Although the response rate for the 1993 CAS was 69 percent, the response rate for mail surveys tends to be much lower, with rates of 50 percent or lower common (Shih and Fan 2008). Certain groups of people, such as those with little writing ability and those not interested in the topic, are less likely to respond to a mailed questionnaire than to a personal interview request. More questions are left unanswered with self-administered questionnaires than with interview methods. And without an interviewer, there is no opportunity to clarify questions, probe for more adequate answers, or control the conditions under which the questionnaire is completed or even who completes it.

Still, the mail survey may serve the research purposes well with specialized target groups who are likely to have high response rates, when very large samples are desired, when costs must be kept low, when ease of administration is necessary, and when moderate response rates are considered satisfactory.

COMPUTER-ASSISTED SELF-INTERVIEWS

Researchers have developed a variety of computer-mediated surveys that are self-administered. In **computer-assisted self-administered interviewing (CASI)**, the questionnaire is transmitted on a computer program that may be sent to respondents (e.g., as a link in an e-mail) or provided by the researcher on a laptop. Whereas computer-assisted personal and telephone interviewing (CAPI and CATI) make the interviewer's job easier, CASI replaces the interviewer. Examples of CASI include emailed questionnaires, interactive voice response (IVR) surveys, computerized self-administered questionnaires, and Internet (Web) surveys (Figure 8.1). E-mail and Web surveys are conducted over the Internet. Both involve computer-to-computer transmission of a questionnaire; in e-mail surveys, the questions are sent as the text of an e-mail message or in an attached file, whereas in Web surveys the questionnaire is accessed on specially designed Web pages. IVR surveys are conducted by telephone as respondents listen to prerecorded, voice-read questions and then use touch-tone data entry or give verbal answers, which are recorded (Steiger and Conroy 2008). Of these methods, we focus here on Web surveys, which have have had the broadest application and have increased dramatically in recent years (Dillman, Smyth, and Christian 2009).

computer-assisted self-administered interviewing (CASI) An electronic survey in which a questionnaire is transmitted on a computer disk mailed to the respondent or on a laptop computer provided by the researcher.

An example of a Web survey is Reynol Junco and Shelia Cotten's (2012) study of the relationship between multitasking and academic performance. To examine this relationship, the researchers conducted a Web survey at a public university in the Northeastern United States. They sent all students a link to a survey hosted on an online survey site through students' university-sponsored e-mail accounts. The measure of multitasking consisted of a series of questions asking how often students engage in various activities at the same time they are doing schoolwork. The measure of academic performance was a student's overall grade-point average (GPA), obtained with permission from students' academic records. Controlling for background variables, high school GPA, and Internet skills, the researchers found that overall college GPA was negatively correlated with using Facebook and with texting while doing schoolwork. However, college GPA was not correlated with multitasking involving searching online, e-mailing, and talking on the telephone. Junco and Cotten (2012) explained the different correlations in terms of how students used these technologies: whereas Facebook and texting are more likely to be used for socializing with friends, e-mailing and searching online tend to be used for academic purposes, and students seldom talk on the telephone while doing schoolwork.

Among the advantages of Web surveys such as this one, the greatest is reduced cost. Compared to self-administered questionnaires, the cheapest of the traditional modes, Internet surveys eliminate the costs of paper, postage, assembly of the mailout package, and data entry (Dillman 2007). The principal costs are computer equipment and programming support, questionnaire development and testing, and Internet service provider fees. For faculty and students, some of these costs are eliminated. And for all researchers, the development of online survey software and questionnaire tools such as SurveyMonkey®, Survs, and QuestionPro™ has facilitated questionnaire construction and delivery. A related advantage is time savings. Web surveys require much less time to implement than other survey modes; compared to mail surveys, which may take weeks or months for questionnaires to be delivered and returned, Web surveys may be completed in only a few days. Finally, Web surveys can substantially reduce the cost of increasing sample size because once the electronic questionnaire has been developed, the cost of surveying each additional person is far less than in an interview or mail survey (Dillman 2007). Thus, it is easy to understand why Junco and Cotten sent their survey to *all* 3,866 students rather than to a sample of students at the university where they conducted their study.

Another advantage of Web surveys, one they share with other computer-mediated methods, is flexibility in the questionnaire design. As Don Dillman (2007:354) points out, the questionnaire can be designed "to provide a more dynamic interaction between respondent and questionnaire" than is possible in a paper-and-pencil survey. Web questionnaires can incorporate pop-up instructions for individual questions, drop-down boxes with lists of answer choices, feedback on possibly incorrect answers (e.g., birth date "1839"), pop-up word definition screens, and automatic fill-ins for later answers. They can use a great variety of shapes and colors and can add pictures, animation, video clips, and sound (Dillman 2007:458). When designed carefully, Web survey options and features may be used to motivate and assist respondents and otherwise substitute for the role that an interviewer plays (Couper, Traugott, and Lamias 2001; Manfreda and Vehovar 2008:276–81).

At this point, the great practical advantages and enormous design potential of Web surveys for social research are offset by some major weaknesses. Response rates to Web surveys tend to be lower than to other modes—generally about 10 percent less than mail surveys (Manfreda et al. 2008; Shih and Fan 2008). The response rate for the multitasking survey was 46 percent, but this is actually high for a Web survey. Another issue is coverage error, the error produced when the sampling frame does not include all members of the population. This error derives from two related problems: the proportion of the general population who are Internet users and the lack of a sampling frame to sample users. By 2015, 73 percent of US households were using the Internet at home. However, a "digital divide" remains, with nonusers being more likely to be black or Hispanic, poorly educated, older, and with less income than those with Internet access (Morris 2016). The second problem is the absence of a good frame for sampling Internet users. For example, there is no list available and no means of generating a list of all US households with Internet service. Researchers often address this problem by limiting their Web surveys to special populations having membership lists and Web access, such as college students, certain professionals, or employees of an organization.

To summarize our discussion of modes thus far, Table 8.4 compares the principal survey modes on five criteria. It is important to know the relative strengths and weaknesses of these modes before we consider the final option: how modes can be combined effectively in a single survey.

Table 8.4 Comparison of Survey Modes on Five Criteria

	Cost	Time	Response rate	Population coverage	Quality of measurement
Best	Web	Web	FTF	FTF	FTF
↑	Mail	Telephone	Telephone	Mail	Telephone
	Telephone	Mail	Mail	Telephone	Web
Worst	FTF	FTF	Web	Web	Mail

MIXED-MODE SURVEYS

Choosing a data-collection mode is difficult when none of the primary modes seems optimal for the intended research. An alternative solution is to design a **mixed-mode survey**, which uses more than one mode, either sequentially or concurrently, to sample and/or collect the data. In this way, the weaknesses of one mode may be offset by the strengths of another mode. For example, since 1970 the US decennial census has combined less expensive mail surveys followed by more expensive in-person interviews with people who do not return the mail questionnaires.

The proliferation of modes, among other developments, has fueled a marked increase in mixed-mode designs in the 21st century (Couper 2011; Dillman et al. 2009). Modes may be combined in many different ways for a variety of reasons. Here we briefly mention three of the most common ways of mixing survey modes (de Leeuw 2005; Dillman et al. 2009).

1. Use one mode to recruit, screen, or contact respondents and another mode to administer the survey. For example, to increase response to a Web survey, Royce Singleton initially contacted respondents with a letter sent by mail. The letter explained the purpose of the survey, provided a link to the Web page where respondents could complete the survey, and included a $2 incentive to respond. As another example, a researcher might use an inexpensive telephone survey to screen and locate specialized populations, such as people with a rare disease, for a study requiring expensive FTF interviews.

2. Use a second mode to collect data on a subset of questions from the same respondents. A mode shift to self-administered questionnaires—paper-and-pencil or CASI—often is used in FTF surveys to increase privacy in the collection of sensitive information. Typically, an interviewer administers the largest part of the interview but then provides the respondent with either a paper questionnaire to be sealed in an envelope or a CASI laptop to complete the self-administered portion that requests the most sensitive information. In this way, respondents are less susceptible to social desirability biases, which are more likely when questions are administered by an interviewer. An early application of this strategy occurred in the 1992 National Health Interview Survey–Youth Risk Behavior Supplement, which used an audio questionnaire to collect sensitive information from adolescents about drug use, sexual intercourse, cigarette smoking, and other unhealthy behaviors (Willard and Schoenborn 1995). Teens listened to the questions on a portable audio headset and recorded their answers on an answer sheet that did not contain any information by which parents or other household members would know the questions being answered.

3. Use different modes to survey different respondents. One solution to the coverage problem in Web surveys, for example, is a respondent-specific approach whereby

those without Web access are surveyed in person or by mail. Another example would be increasing the response rate of the sampled population by conducting telephone or FTF interviews with those who did not respond to an initial mail questionnaire, as in the decennial census.

The first two mixed-mode designs have been common practice for some time; their advantages in reducing cost, increasing response rates, and improving data quality are well established. The recent surge of interest in mixed-mode surveys is due mainly to the third design, in which different modes are used with different respondents during the data-collection process (Couper 2011). The major weakness of this design is the uncertainty as to whether the data from respondents surveyed by different modes are comparable. As the various modes may differ in coverage, sampling, nonresponse, and measurement quality, merging the mode subsamples to statistically estimate the target population is a difficult and uncertain undertaking.

SUMMARY

Surveys vary in their design and modes of data collection. Surveys using a cross-sectional design ask a sample of people questions at one point in time, while surveys using a longitudinal design ask people questions at two or more points in time. Of the two major types of longitudinal designs, a trend study asks the same questions of independent samples of people, whereas a panel study asks the same questions of the same sample of people at multiple points in time. Surveys collect data through face-to-face interviews, telephone interviews, paper-and-pencil questionnaires including mail surveys, computer-assisted self-interviews, or some combination of these modes (mixed-mode surveys). Each mode has strengths and limitations related to its costs, the time it takes to administer the survey, the response rate, the population coverage, and its quality of measurement. Face-to-face interviewing is considered to be the best (and most interactive) mode, but its costs and time investment can be prohibitive.

THE PROCESS OF PLANNING AND CONDUCTING A SURVEY

Once you've decided to do a survey, your research purposes (e.g., descriptive or explanatory) and available resources will determine two key decisions: the measurement of variables (shown on the left side of Figure 8.3) and the selection of the sample (on the right side of Figure 8.3). Survey measurement occurs by asking questions, and the wording and complexity of the questions will depend, first, on the survey mode. Having selected the mode, you must then construct and pretest the survey questionnaire.

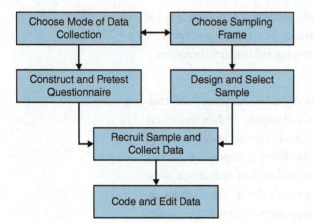

Drawing a sample involves finding or creating an appropriate sampling frame, and then selecting cases based on the sampling design. With the survey instrument ready and the sample drawn, the process of conducting the survey converges by contacting eligible respondents and administering the questionnaire. The data then must be coded and edited before they are analyzed to answer the research questions.

As we examine the steps of planning and conducting a survey in Figure 8.3, we focus on how each was carried out in the CFS. At the same time, we discuss additional studies, based on other modes, which used somewhat different procedures in the survey process.

Choose Mode of Data Collection

The first step in the process of planning and conducting a survey is to choose a mode of data collection, considering the strengths and limitations of each. This choice depends on the goals of the research and the resources available.

The CFS sought to determine how Americans define family and to examine how definitions of family are related to social background and other variables. In addition, the investigators wished to explore more deeply the thought processes behind people's views of family by asking several open-ended questions. Thus, the study required a national sample and a survey mode that would make it more likely for respondents to answer open-ended questions and to answer them more fully. An FTF interview survey best met these requirements, but its cost was prohibitive. Therefore, a telephone survey was the best option, especially given the resources of the Center for Survey Research. The Center had conducted many telephone surveys, had a CATI system in place, and had a well-trained staff of interviewers.

If you're doing a small-scale survey, say, for a class project, it is unlikely you'll have the resources that Powell and associates had. As we noted earlier, a Web survey is the least costly mode of data collection in terms of both time and money. Therefore, we recommend that you consider this mode, provided that it meets your research goals.

Construct and Pretest Questionnaire

To construct the survey instrument, the researcher should first outline the question topics to be covered in the interview or questionnaire. When addressing quantitative research questions with the purpose of explanation or hypothesis-testing, these topics should cover your independent and dependent variables as well as extraneous variables that may affect the hypothesized relationships. For the 2003 CFS, the main topics included definitions of family, rights associated with marriage and other relationships, maternal and paternal responsibilities, causes of child behaviors and traits, and gay marriage and adoption. With these topics as a guide, the researchers had to come up with an appropriate set of questions and organize them into a meaningful sequence.

For a few topics and most background questions, Powell and his associates adopted questions used in previous research, such as in the GSS. There are many advantages to this well-established practice: it shortcuts the measurement process, capitalizes on others' expertise (assuming the questions are from credible sources), and enables researchers to compare results across studies. Lest you be concerned about the ethics of using another person's questions, the norms "of social science in general and survey research in particular not only permit but encourage the repetition of questions" (Sudman and Bradburn 1982:14).

The CFS also explored topics, such as definitions of family, for which the researchers had to compose new questions. Writing questions is a challenge. How questions are written depends on the question topic and whether you are asking about factual events and behaviors or subjective states such as knowledge, perceptions, feelings, and judgments (Fowler 1995). The survey researcher must choose between question forms, such as open and closed, and the number and type of response categories.

As you're designing a survey, you need to pay particular attention to language, as even slight changes in the wording of a question can greatly affect responses. For example, a question might be written, "What is your annual income?" or "What is your total annual income from all sources?" A person answering the first item might neglect to consider income from such sources as interest on stocks or savings, sale of stocks, and rental income. As Jean Converse and Stanley Presser (1986:10) note, "writing sufficiently clear and 'simple' questions is hard-won, heavy-duty work for survey researchers." Part of the work involves carefully examining the language of the items. In general, you want to use questions that (1) respondents understand in a consistent way, so that they would give the same answer if they were asked the same question again (AAPOR 2017b), (2) mean the same thing to all respondents, and (3) have the same meaning for respondents as they do for the researcher. For more specific tips on how to write good survey questions, see Box 8.2, DOING SOCIAL RESEARCH: Writing Survey Questions.

ORGANIZING THE QUESTIONS

Once researchers have developed the questions, the next steps are to decide the order in which to ask them and to write an introductory statement as well as appropriate transitions from topic to topic. The introduction used in the CFS was fairly standard: the interviewer gave his/her name, identified the survey sponsor, and briefly stated the general purpose of the study—that they were interested in what people "have to say about American families and family practices." Deciding how to order the questions after this introduction involved several considerations.

Writing Survey Questions

Through research and experience, researchers have developed guidelines for designing survey questions. These guidelines are so numerous that we cannot review them adequately here (for a more extensive discussion, see Singleton and Straits, 2018, Chapter 10). An excellent resource is Floyd Fowler's (1995) *Improving Survey Questions: Design and Evaluation*; another is Jon Krosnick and Stanley Presser's chapter, "Question and Questionnaire Design," in *The Handbook of Survey Research*, 2nd ed. (2010). In addition, there are many useful guides to survey design online. Based on these and other sources (AAPOR 2017b; Krosnick and Presser 2010) as well as our own experience, we offer the following brief tips for writing good survey questions.

Avoid ambiguous or imprecise words.

Clarity and precision are essential qualities of well-worded items. At times, an item that appears perfectly clear to the designer may be very confusing or carry a different meaning to someone with a different background and point of view. The point is easily illustrated by the question, "How many years have you been living here?" To one respondent, "here" may mean the present house or apartment; to another, the city; and to another, the country.

Especially troublesome are indefinite words such as "usually," "seldom," "many," "few," "here," and "there"; these will have different meanings to different respondents. Following are two alternative items illustrating the problem. The second item, from the CFS, is an improvement over the first because the responses are specific and thereby have the same precise meaning for both researcher and respondent.

How often do you attend religious services? Would you say:

( ) often

( ) occasionally

( ) seldom, or

( ) never

How often do you attend religious services? Would you say:

( ) every day

( ) more than once a week

( ) once a week

( ) two or three times a month

( ) once a month

( ) a few times a year, or

( ) once a year or less

Use "not" or "non" sparingly.

Items should be easy to read or hear accurately. Some respondents will skip over or tune out the negative word in an item and respond the opposite of the way the question is actually intended, so it is best to avoid the use of negative words such as "not." And it is not generally advisable to have two negatives in the question (AAPOR 2017b).

Use simple, familiar words, not technical jargon.

For a national survey such as the CFS, the vocabulary must be kept extremely simple. For example, in the CFS, the investigators asked a series of questions about which factors respondents believed were most important in a child's development of various traits, such as personality, aggressive behavior, and school performance. One trait they were interested in was "sexual identity"; however, this is a technical social science concept that many people may not understand. Therefore, they chose a wording more appropriate for a sample of American adults: "how masculine a boy acts" (and "how feminine a girl acts"), which was further clarified as "how much he acts like a typical boy should act" (and "how much she acts like a typical girl should act").

Limit the question to a single idea, not two or more issues at once.

A **double-barreled question** is one in which two separate ideas are presented together as a unit. An example might be, "What factors contributed to your decision to marry and have children?" The researcher seems to assume that marrying and having children is a single act or decision, whereas in fact there are two questions being asked here. It is a good idea for the survey designer to examine all questions with the word "and" or "or" in them to be sure that they are not double-barreled.

double-barreled question A question in which two separate ideas are presented together as a unit.

Avoid emotionally loaded words and other sources of bias.

Emotionally loaded words and phrases, such as "racial preferences," "pro-life," "cops," or "the president's statement," may evoke responses that have little to do with the real attitudes or opinion of the respondent regarding the issue the researcher is attempting to address. In general, try to word questions in a neutral way, and avoid identifying a statement

continues

continued

or position with any controversial or prestigious person or group. Notice the loaded words ("union czars," "forcing," "knuckle under") in the following question (Sudman and Bradburn 1982:2):

> *Are you in favor of allowing construction union czars the power to shut down an entire construction site because of a dispute with a single contractor, thus forcing even more workers to knuckle under to union agencies?*

leading question
A question in which a possible answer is suggested, or some answers are presented as more acceptable than others.

Another source of bias is **leading questions**. Leading questions suggest a possible answer or make some responses seem more acceptable than others. The question "How often do you smoke marijuana?" may seem to imply that everyone indulges at least occasionally. A question that begins "Do you agree . . ." may suggest to some persons that they ought to agree. The generally accepted practice is to balance attitudinal questions by using such phrases as "agree or disagree," "favor or oppose," and "satisfied or dissatisfied" (Sudman and Bradburn 1982). In asking about attitudes toward gay rights, for example, Powell and associates asked respondents to "Please tell us how much you agree or disagree with each statement."

Ensure that response options are exhaustive and mutually exclusive.

In our experience as survey respondents, we find it very frustrating to read a question that we cannot answer because none of the possible answers applies to us or because more than one answer applies. Questions like this, moreover, are almost impossible to interpret. Therefore, when a question is closed-ended, (1) the list of response options should include all reasonable responses so that every person is capable of answering it (the list is exhaustive), and (2) the response options should provide clear choices so that only one answer is possible (the options are mutually exclusive).

Recall from Chapter 5 that exhaustive and mutually exclusive are requirements of all levels of measurement. An example of a closed-ended question, with ordinal level measurement, that is not exhaustive is the following:

> *What is your grade-point average (GPA)?*
>
> 1. 2.00–2.33
> 2. 2.34–2.66
> 3. 2.67–3.00
> 4. 3.01–3.33
> 5. 3.34–3.66
> 6. 3.67–4.00

Can you tell what is missing? The set of categories omits GPAs below 2.00. In addition, if you are answering this question and happen to be in your first semester in college, even this additional category would not apply to you. Therefore, if a question like this is directed to students without an established GPA, it also should have a category such as "Does not apply." Below is a question, also directed to college students, that violates the principle of mutual exclusivity:

What is your age?

1. Less than 18 years old
2. 18–20
3. 20–22
4. 22–24
5. Greater than 24 years old

Did you catch the error? What category would you circle if you were 20 or 22 years old?

First, the opening question should be relatively easy to answer. Starting with a difficult question may discourage respondents and make them feel inadequate to fulfill their role as respondents. Imagine yourself taking an exam that starts out with a really difficult question—it might make you feel so intimidated and anxious that you have a hard time with the rest of the exam, even if the other questions are easier! To avoid this type of problem, the CFS began with a series of questions asking about marital status, including whether the respondent had ever been married and how long he/she had been married, the age of the respondent and spouse when first married, and so forth (Powell 2003). Following these warm-up questions, the CFS then shifted to more demanding questions that required more thought, asking respondents for their opinions about what counts as family. After asking about 11 different living arrangements, the CFS interviewer then posed an even more challenging open-ended question: "In thinking about your answers to the past few questions about what counts as a family, what determines for you whether you think a living arrangement is a family?" (Powell 2003).

A second consideration is the placement of background questions. Although we have seen many surveys that begin with background items such as gender, age, religious preference, and so on, it is much better to place such uninteresting routine questions at the end of the survey. A good strategy is to start with an interesting question at the beginning that is congruent with respondents' expectations: it should be a question they might reasonably expect to be asked, on the basis of what they have been told by the interviewer about the study. For the most part, this was true of the CFS. The CFS questions about marital status were consistent with what they were told; and these questions were followed in short order by the interesting set of questions on what counts as family.

A third consideration is the placement of sensitive questions, which in the CFS included several items about same-sex issues. Powell and associates knew that many respondents would be uncomfortable talking about same-sex issues. Indeed, in the interviews, many respondents appeared hesitant saying such words as "gay," "lesbian," or "homosexual," according to Powell (personal communication 2013). Asking sensitive questions prematurely may embarrass or upset respondents, possibly leading them to terminate the interview or question the researcher's motives. Therefore, the CFS questions about same-sex issues were not asked until after the interview was well under way and the respondent had invested time and effort and possibly developed trust toward the research and/or interviewer. Following the family definition items, the interviewer asked a few questions about the rights of people in different living arrangements, starting with unmarried couples. The interviewer began:

> Please indicate whether you strongly agree, somewhat agree, somewhat disagree, or strongly disagree that people living in the following arrangements should have certain rights.
>
> A man and woman living together as an unmarried couple who have no children should be able to file joint income tax returns. Do you . . . ? (Powell 2003)

After several items about unmarried opposite-sex couples, interviewers logically transitioned to the rights of gay and lesbian couples by saying, "Now we're going to talk about another living arrangement, that of two men living together as a couple or two women living together as a couple, who have no children." Because the researchers were concerned that having too many questions in a row regarding gay issues would alienate some respondents and make them resistant to complete the survey, they also split these questions up, according to Powell (personal communication, 2013). As a general rule, however, questions on the same topic should be grouped together.

To improve the flow of the interview and enhance respondent understanding and motivation, the CFS also contained several transitions indicating that one topic was completed and another topic was to be discussed. Transitions focus the respondent's attention on the new topic, and may be used to explain briefly why the new topic will be discussed or how it relates to the research purposes. The following are examples of topic transitions from the CFS:

> "People these days have differing opinions of what counts as a family. Next, I will read you a number of living arrangements and I will ask you . . ."
>
> "The next set of questions is about traits that children develop."
>
> "In the last few years there has been a public debate about rights for gays and lesbians. People these days have very different opinions; what we are looking for in this section is YOUR personal opinion."

PRETESTING

With these considerations in mind, Powell and associates constructed a draft of the instrument that interviewers would use to administer the survey. In interview research, this instrument is called an **interview schedule**, whereas in self-administered surveys it is referred to as a questionnaire. The next step is to pretest the interview schedule by trying it out and evaluating its effectiveness before the main survey. Experience has shown that pretesting can greatly improve the ease with which data may be analyzed and the quality of results. For no matter how carefully a researcher may follow guidelines for best practices, it is still possible that a large number of respondents misunderstand the meaning of a question or resist answering some questions. And once the study has been conducted, it is too late to benefit from this information.

Survey pretesting may involve a variety of methods. The survey researcher may ask colleagues or experts in the field to critique the questions, apply formal schemes or computer software to identify question-wording problems, or administer the survey to a small sample of respondents (Krosnick and Presser 2010). The federal government and many survey organizations often pretest specific items in a laboratory setting, where respondents are asked in various ways to reveal their thought processes in answering survey questions. The usual method, however, is **field pretesting**, which involves trying out the survey instrument on a small sample of persons having characteristics similar to those of the target group of respondents.

Powell and associates field pretested the CFS by administering a draft of the CFS to 21 randomly selected respondents using the same sampling methods applied in the main survey (Powell, personal communication 2013). To analyze the questions, the researchers transcribed the interviews and examined how long different sections of the interview were taking and where people seemed to be having trouble understanding or answering the questions. Indicators of problems included respondents asking interviewers to repeat or clarify, interviewers probing to follow up on inadequate answers, and interviewers incorrectly reading or skipping a question. In addition, the researchers examined the distribution of answers to each question; knowing, for example, that 100 percent of the respondents chose the same response option, such as saying that a particular living arrangement was not a family, might imply that an item was uninformative and unnecessary. Similarly, pretesting can be done for an on-campus student research project by asking randomly selected students on campus to respond to an initial draft of the survey.

The pretesting was instructive in many ways. For example, one set of items asked respondents to rank order the importance of several factors in explaining the development of personality traits. In pretesting, the researchers discovered that this task was much too complicated, so they simplified the items by asking people to identify just the most important factor. The draft questions about what counts as family also included a much larger set of living arrangements than the final interview, such as households with adults and foster children, siblings living together, and extended family members living

interview schedule
A survey form used by interviewers that consists of instructions, the questions to be asked, and, if they are used, response options.

field pretesting An evaluation of a survey instrument that involves trying it out on a small sample of persons.

together. However, because the interview was much too long, the researchers deleted some of these items as well as several others (Powell, personal communication 2013).

On the basis of pretesting, Powell and associates revised the survey instrument and were ready to launch the survey. Of course, to do so they needed a sample of potential respondents. In fact, as the researchers were developing their survey instrument, they also were designing and selecting a sample.

Choose Sampling Frame/Design and Select Sample

Recall from Chapter 6 that a sampling frame denotes the set of all cases from which the sample is actually selected. For most surveys, the sampling frame consists of an available listing of all units in the target population. As Figure 8.3 indicates, the selection of the survey mode and the sampling frame are interdependent. Face-to-face interviews require a listing of residences, mail surveys need mailing addresses, telephone surveys need telephone numbers, and Web surveys need e-mail addresses. If a sampling frame fails to provide adequate coverage of the target population, a researcher may switch modes or resort to a mixed-mode strategy.

The target population in the CFS consisted of adults (persons aged 18 years or older) living in US households. To draw a probability sample of this population, the researchers used **random-digit dialing** (**RDD**). In the simplest RDD design, telephone prefixes (exchanges) within the target geographic area are sampled and then the last four digits of the telephone number are randomly selected. The CFS used more complex "list-assisted" RDD procedures (Kalsbeek and Agans 2008). This type of sampling design provides more efficient coverage in RDD sampling by eliminating nonresidential numbers and by including unlisted numbers in the sampling frame. The frame is created from a national database containing telephone numbers for all households with listed numbers. This information is then used to "assist" in creating a frame that will enable researchers to select random telephone numbers that will include *both* directory-listed and nonlisted numbers.

Once someone answers the telephone in a randomly selected household, the interviewer must randomly select an eligible person to interview. There are a variety of ways of doing this; next we describe how it was done in the CFS.

Recruit Sample and Collect Data

Collecting the data in a survey is itself a multi-step process. In an interview survey, if mailing addresses are known, the process may begin by sending respondents a cover letter in advance of being contacted. Then, the interviewer must contact a household member, select an eligible person to interview, obtain his or her agreement to participate, and conduct the interview. And if no one answers a doorbell or dialed telephone number, the interviewer must make additional attempts to reach someone at that address or number. Let's consider each of these steps, in turn, as they were carried out in the CFS.

random-digit dialing (RDD) A sampling-frame technique in which dialable telephone numbers are generated (sampled) randomly.

In RDD surveys, it is not possible to notify respondents about the survey in advance. The process of collecting data thus began in the CFS when someone answered a dialed number. Initially, the interviewer used the introduction that we described earlier. Research has shown that incentives can enhance response rates in all kinds of surveys (Church 1993; Singer 2002). Therefore, to encourage cooperation, the interviewers continued: "We appreciate you taking the time to participate in this study, so we are mailing each person who completes an interview a 120-minute calling card." Finally, to facilitate the random selection of an eligible household member, the interviewer ascertained that the contact was at least 18 years old and a member of the household and then said, "To find out which adult in your household I need to speak with, I need to ask how many people age 18 or older, including yourself, currently live in this household?" If the contact is the only one eligible, that person is interviewed. If more than one person is eligible, the interviewer keys in this information, the CATI software randomly selects a number and, if necessary (when more than two people are eligible), prompts the interviewer to ask for a complete listing of everyone in the household.

After randomly selecting a household member to interview, the interviewer must gain his or her cooperation. To do this, interviewers are trained to make a positive impression and to memorize the introduction and scripts for addressing respondents' reluctance to participate (e.g., "I'm not good at answering surveys," "I'm too busy," "You are invading my privacy") or other concerns (Gwartney 2007). Finally, before the first question is asked, interviewers must read an informed consent statement and ask for permission to begin the interview. For an example of an informed consent statement, see Box 8.3, DOING SOCIAL RESEARCH: Informed Consent Statement in the Constructing the Family Survey.

A concerted effort is made in all surveys to gain the cooperation of nonrespondents. If no contact was made initially, interviewers in the CFS called up to 20 or more times, varying the times and days of the week when they called. In FTF interview surveys, interviewers also may leave notes or ask neighbors when people are usually at home. In mail surveys, respondents are sent follow-up mailings. Respondents in the CAS, for example, received four separate mailings, approximately 10 days apart: the initial mailing of the questionnaire, a postcard thanking those who had completed the questionnaire and urging those who had not to do so, a mailing with another copy of the questionnaire again appealing for its return, and a second reminder postcard (Wechsler et al. 1994).

For telephone and FTF surveys, the major problem is dealing with refusals to participate. In many surveys, more experienced interviewers or supervisors are used to try to gain the respondent's cooperation on the second try. In response to a clear refusal, however, one follow-up call or visit should be the limit to avoid respondent feelings of harassment. The policy of the CSR, which oversaw the CFS, is to attempt to convert each refusal twice: when the person first refuses and then once more after a few days (Powell et al. 2010:220).

BOX 8.3

DOING SOCIAL RESEARCH

Informed Consent Statement in the Constructing the Family Survey

Before we begin, let me tell you that this study is sponsored by Indiana University. It is being conducted by the IU Center for Survey Research. The results will be used by researchers to understand the thoughts and opinions of [FILL STATE] residents.

Let me assure you that this interview is anonymous and all your answers will be kept completely confidential. Your telephone number was randomly generated by a computer. No identifying information will be connected to your individual responses. Your participation is voluntary, and if there are any questions you don't feel comfortable answering, please let me know and we'll move on. The interview generally takes about 30 minutes, depending on your responses. If you need to go at any point, we can finish the interview later to fit your schedule. Portions of this interview may be recorded for quality control. Now, if I have your permission, we'll begin.

[From Powell (2003).]

The process of recruiting respondents is simpler in computer-assisted self-interviews, such as Web surveys, which is one of the reasons for their appeal. If the survey is of individuals, the researcher only needs to send out separate e-mails to potential respondents once a sampling frame of e-mails has been created; the researcher does not need to select individuals within households or families. Further, it is easy to follow up with e-mail remainders.

Code and Edit Data

Like the analysis of experiments, survey analysis is quantitative; that is, the results are presented in numerical form. But survey data require much more extensive preparation (or processing) for data analysis. Survey respondents' answers must be coded (transformed into numbers), entered into a datafile, and checked and corrected for errors. Some correcting for errors, called editing, occurs during survey data collection. We briefly describe coding and editing here, although we have more to say about them in Chapters 12 and 13, where we cover quantitative and qualitative analysis.

coding The sorting of data into numbered or textual categories.

Coding answers for closed-ended questions is straightforward. You simply assign unique numbers to each response category. For the CFS, the first information coded was the respondent's sex; a code of 1 was assigned to "male" and a code of 2 for "female." The particular codes were arbitrary and were specified directly on the interview schedule. The coding of textual responses to open-ended questions, on the other hand, is much more complicated. Because the number of unique responses may number in the hundreds, the researcher must develop a coding scheme that does not require a separate code for each response but that adequately reflects the full range of responses. This is typically done with computer software; Powell and associates (2010:272) report that they "used a variety of analytical techniques ... including Atlas.ti" to analyze the open-ended question about what living arrangements count as family.

Editing a survey involves checking for errors and inconsistencies in responses. Examples of errors would be multiple responses to a single item or a response with a code outside the range of numbers allowed (e.g., a code of "3" for respondent's sex). Inconsistencies occur when responses to certain questions are not related in plausible ways to particular other items. For example, it would be unreasonable, and therefore an indication of an error, to find a respondent who is married and age five or a medical doctor with three years of formal schooling.

editing Checking data and correcting for errors in completed interviews or questionnaires.

Researchers edit and, when possible, correct responses to mail surveys manually by going over completed questionnaires; however, most editing is programmed into computer-assisted interviewing and online surveys. The CATI program used in the CFS, for example, flagged responses that were outside the acceptable limits and prompted interviewers with follow-up questions for apparent inconsistencies. Thus, in many surveys, editing (as well as coding and data entry) occurs during the process of data collection.

SUMMARY

The process of planning and conducting a survey involves choosing a mode of data collection, constructing and pretesting the questionnaire, choosing a sampling frame, designing and selecting the sample, recruiting the sample and collecting data, and coding and editing data, which are then analyzed. Each of these steps involves additional steps or considerations. Choosing a mode of data collection depends on the researcher's goals and the resources available. Constructing and pretesting the questionnaire depends on the mode of data collection, and researchers should strive to write unambiguous

and neutral questions, present them in a logical order, and get feedback on question drafts. Likewise, choosing a sampling frame, selecting and recruiting a sample, and collecting data depend on the mode of data collection. At the minimum, this involves ensuring that the sampling frame is as close to the target population as is possible; selecting respondents randomly; clearly explaining the purposes of the survey to potential respondents and their rights; and attempting to gain their cooperation. Once the data are collected, they need to be coded and edited before being analyzed.

STRENGTHS AND WEAKNESSES OF SURVEYS

Surveys are the "method of choice for much data collection in the [social sciences]" (Wright and Marsden 2010:10), especially in sociology and political science. Yet, the use of surveys outside the scientific community is even more extensive. Media opinion polls, marketing research, and government surveys shape major decisions by politicians, businesspeople, and government officials. Even a good deal of our everyday knowledge comes from the reported results of surveys (Igo 2007). For example, we know from survey results that the majority of Americans support the death penalty, and that nationally there are more registered Democrats than Republicans. Because surveys carry so much weight in our knowledge and decision-making, we all need to know something about their strengths and weaknesses: What can surveys tell us better than other methods of social research? And what are their limitations?

Generalization to Populations

Whereas experiments are used for explanatory, hypothesis-testing research, surveys are used extensively for both descriptive and explanatory purposes. Among all approaches to social research, surveys offer the most effective means of social description. By using probability sampling, survey researchers can be certain, within known limits of sampling error, of how accurately the responses to a sample survey can be generalized to the larger target population.

Versatility

The effectiveness of surveys also is reflected in their versatility. The topics covered and the questions that may be included in surveys are wide ranging. Topics of studies cited in this chapter range from what counts as family to the consequences of alcohol consumption to multitasking and academic performance. Many surveys, such as the GSS, cover numerous topics in the same survey. The following questions from the GSS suggest the broad scope of possible survey questions (see Schuman and Kalton 1985):

1. Social background information (e.g., What is your religious preference? Do you usually think of yourself as a Republican, Democrat, Independent, or what?)
2. Reports of past behavior (e.g., On the average day, about how many hours do you personally watch television? During the last seven days, did you go to see a doctor or receive medical treatment at a clinic or hospital?)
3. Attitudes, beliefs, and values (e.g., Do you believe there is a life after death? Do you agree or disagree that homosexual couples should have the right to marry one another?)
4. Behavior intentions (e.g., If your party nominated a woman for President, would you vote for her if she were qualified for the job? Would you yourself have an abortion if there were a strong chance of a serious defect in the baby?)
5. Sensitive questions (e.g., About how often did you have sex during the last 12 months? Have you ever, even once, used "crack" cocaine in chunk or rock form?)

For categories 1, 2, and 5, which pertain to behavior and personal characteristics, the information may be verifiable from records or observer reports. However, it is often impractical, unethical, or even illegal to obtain it from sources other than the individuals themselves. For subjective phenomena such as categories 3 and 4, the information can be directly known, if at all, only by asking the individuals themselves.

Efficiency

Their versatility makes surveys, in some ways, a very efficient data-gathering approach. While an experiment usually will address only one research hypothesis, numerous research questions can be covered by a single large-scale survey. Furthermore, the wealth of data typically contained in a survey may yield unanticipated findings or lead to new hypotheses. Adding to their cost effectiveness, data from many large-scale surveys such as the GSS are made available to the public. Such data are usually of high quality, and the cost of obtaining the data for analysis is a small fraction of the cost of collecting the data. It is a common practice, called **secondary analysis**, for social scientists to analyze publicly accessible survey data. Beckett Broh's study, reported in Chapter 4, consisted of the secondary analysis of NELS data. According to the GSS website, "the GSS is widely regarded as the single best source of data on societal trends," and analyses of GSS data can be found in over 27,000 scholarly publications (National Opinion Research Center 2017).

secondary analysis
Analysis of survey or other data originally collected by another researcher, ordinarily for a different purpose.

Establishing Causal Relationships

A major disadvantage of surveys relates to their use in explanatory research. Beyond association between variables, the criteria for inferring cause-and-effect relationships cannot be established as easily in surveys as in experiments. For example, the criterion of directionality—that a cause must influence its effect—is predetermined in experiments by first manipulating the independent (or causal) variable and then observing variation in the dependent (or effect) variable. But in most surveys (i.e., cross-sectional designs) this is often a matter of interpretation since variables are measured at a single point in time. Although a longitudinal design may address this limitation, surveys are also problematic in meeting the criterion of eliminating plausible rival explanations. Whether using cross-sectional or longitudinal designs, surveys must first anticipate and measure relevant extraneous variables in the interviews or questionnaires and then exercise statistical control over these variables in the data analysis. Thus, the causal inferences from survey research generally are made with less confidence than inferences from experimental research.

Measurement Issues

Another inherent weakness of surveys is their reliance almost exclusively on self-reports of behavior rather than observations of behavior. As a consequence, validity and reliability may be undermined by respondents' lack of truthfulness, misunderstanding of questions, inability to recall past events accurately, and instability of opinions and attitudes. Like experiments, surveys also are susceptible to reactive measurement effects produced by participants' awareness of being studied. A good example of this, noted in Chapter 5, is the tendency of respondents to give socially desirable answers to sensitive questions; this is particularly likely to occur in interview surveys. Finally, a brief encounter for the purpose of administering a survey does not provide a very good understanding of the impact of the context on behavior. For that understanding, social researchers turn to field research, which we discuss in Chapter 9.

SUMMARY

The major strengths of surveys lie in their ability to provide reasonably accurate estimations of population characteristics, their versatility in speaking to a wide range of topics, and their efficiency. However, surveys are limited in their ability to establish causal relationships and in their reliance on self-reports of human behavior and in the quality of measurement. Finally, it is important to note several problems that have surfaced in the past quarter-century, which are making it increasingly difficult and costly to conduct surveys, forcing some researchers to seek alternative approaches to social research. These include access impediments such as "walled subdivision, locked apartment buildings, telephone answering machines, [and] telephone caller ID," declining response rates, increasing costs due to "increased effort to contact and interview the public," and telephone survey coverage issues created by the increase in mobile phones (Groves 2011:866).

KEY TERMS

closed-ended question, p. 216

coding, p. 240

computer-assisted personal interviewing (CAPI), p. 221

computer-assisted self-administered interviewing (CASI), p. 225

computer-assisted telephone interviewing (CATI), p. 223

cross-sectional design, p. 219

descriptive survey, p. 216

double-barreled question, p. 233

editing, p. 241

explanatory survey, p. 216

face-to-face (FTF) interview, p. 221

field pretesting, p. 237

interview schedule, p. 237

leading question, p. 234

longitudinal design, p. 219

mixed-mode survey, p. 228

open-ended question, p. 216

panel study, p. 220

paper-and-pencil questionnaire survey, p. 224

random-digit dialing (RDD), p. 238

response rate, p. 222

secondary analysis, p. 243

semi-structured interview, p. 215

structured interview, p. 215

telephone interview, p. 223

trend study, p. 219

unstructured interview, p. 215

KEY POINTS

- The primary features of surveys are relatively large probability samples, structured questioning, and quantitative analysis.
- Structured interviews address specific objectives with mostly closed-ended questions, whereas unstructured interviews address broad objectives with mostly open-ended questions.
- Quantitative analysis of surveys may be descriptive and/or explanatory.
- Survey designs may ask questions at one point in time (cross-sectional) or may repeat the same questions at multiple points in time (longitudinal).
- Survey data-collection modes include face-to-face interviews, telephone interviews, paper-and-pencil questionnaires, computer-assisted self-interviews, as well as combinations of these modes (i.e., "mixed mode" surveys).
- Survey data-collection modes vary in their costs, the time they take to complete, their response rates, their population coverage, and their quality of measurement.
- The process of planning and conducting a survey involves key decisions about how to measure variables and how to select a sample.
- Measuring variables entails choosing a mode of data collection and constructing and pretesting a questionnaire.
- Selecting a sample involves choosing an appropriate sampling frame, drawing a probability sample, and, in interview surveys, randomly selecting respondents within households.
- Following recruitment of respondents and administration of the questionnaire, survey responses are coded, edited, and analyzed.
- The strengths of surveys are their versatility, efficiency, and ability to produce accurate generalizations about targeted populations, but surveys offer relatively weak inferences about causality, are limited to self-reports, and are susceptible to reactive measurement effects.

REVIEW QUESTIONS

1. What are the three general features of survey research?
2. Contrast the objectives of structured, unstructured, and semi-structured interviews.
3. What is the difference between (a) cross-sectional and longitudinal survey designs and (b) trend and panel surveys?
4. Compare FTF interviews, telephone interviews, and mail questionnaires with respect to (a) time and cost, (b) complexity and sensitivity of questions asked, and (c) quality of sample (coverage and response rate).

5. Give two examples of how researchers may use more than one survey mode in the same study.

6. Explain how the choice of a survey mode affects the choice of a sampling frame.

7. What is the purpose of field pretesting a survey instrument?

8. What are the principal strengths and weaknesses of surveys?

EXERCISES

1. Exercise 2 in Chapter 4 introduced you to a website for analyzing data from the General Social Survey (GSS): http://sda.berkeley.edu/sdaweb/analysis/?dataset=gss16. Return to this website to answer the following questions.

   (a) Examine the distribution of responses to an item in the 2016 GSS. Using the shaded column on the left, click on "PERSONAL AND FAMILY INFORMATION," click on a variable, and then click on a GSS questionnaire item. Now click "Copy to: Row." To examine the distribution of responses to this item, move to the right side of the page, type "Year(2016)" opposite "Selection Filter(s)"; opposite "Weight:" choose "No weight"; click on "Output Options" and check Percentaging "Column" (if it is not already checked) and "Confidence intervals" just below that; and then click "Run the Table." Report the percentage of respondents in the first variable category and the confidence interval for this percentage.

   (b) Examine the *relationship* between two questionnaire items in the GSS. Begin again on the left side of the Web page. Select the same GSS item as you did in Question (a), but this time "Copy to: Column" rather than "Row." Now select a question from the category "CONTROVERSIAL SOCIAL ISSUES." Copy to Row, delete "Year (2016)" from the "Selection Filter(s)" box you put in as part (a) of the exercise, check Percentaging "Column" if it is not already checked, and then click "Run the Table." Carefully describe the relationship between the two items (or variables) by comparing percentages across each row of the table.

   (c) Perform a trend analysis of a "controversial social issue." Select the same GSS item that you inserted as the "Row" variable in Question (b). Now type "year" as your "Column" variable. Check Percentaging "Column" and click "Run the Table." Reading across the table, report how the percentage has changed over time.

2. Box 8.2 identifies several common wording problems in constructing survey questions. Using the box as a guide, identify the wording problem(s) in each of the following questions and then rewrite the questions to make them more satisfactory.

(a) How many siblings do you have?
   ( ) 0–2
   ( ) 3–7
   ( ) 8 or more
(b) Do you think the man should initiate and pay for the first date?
(c) In divorce or separation cases, the man has just as much right as the woman to have custody of the children.
   ( ) Strongly agree
   ( ) Agree
   ( ) Disagree
   ( ) Strongly disagree
(d) Because women are less aggressive than men, a woman's place is in the home.
   ( ) Strongly agree
   ( ) Agree
   ( ) Disagree
   ( ) Strongly disagree
(e) Do you hold traditional sex-role attitudes?
(f) Does your mother work?
(g) Is the leadership in your family matriarchal, patriarchal, or egalitarian?

3. Suppose you are constructing a questionnaire for the purpose of conducting a survey of sex-role attitudes. What would be the best placement (beginning, middle, end) of the following questions?

   (a) How many sisters do you have?
   (b) Does your mother work outside the home?
   (c) Mothers should put their children before themselves.
      ( ) Strongly agree
      ( ) Agree
      ( ) Disagree
      ( ) Strongly disagree
   (d) Would you say that women nowadays are more likely to work outside the home than they were when you were growing up?

4. Imagine that you want to conduct a campus survey on extracurricular participation. Specifically, you are interested in who participates in extracurricular activities, what kind of extracurricular activities they participate in, how often they participate, and why they choose to participate. To reduce costs, assume you choose to do either a mail questionnaire survey or Web survey and you need to construct a survey instrument.

   (a) Outline the question topics to be covered.

(b) Write at least one question or find an existing question for each topic.

(c) Give an example of a good opening question.

(d) Identify possible sensitive questions. Where will you place them in the questionnaire?

5. Once you have developed questions for your campus survey (Exercise 4), field pre-test your questions on a small sample of potential respondents.

Field Research and In-Depth Interviews

Systematic People-Watching and Listening

STUDENT LEARNING OBJECTIVES

By the end of this chapter, you should be able to

1. Describe the six general features of qualitative research.

2. Explain variations in qualitative research with respect to how observations and interviews are conducted.

3. Describe the steps in the process of planning and conducting field research and apply them to a research topic.

4. Describe the steps in the process of planning and conducting in-depth interviews and apply them to a research topic.

5. Evaluate qualitative research, identifying its strengths and weaknesses.

249

Think back to the first day of your first-ever college course. You probably entered the classroom with some trepidation, not knowing what to expect. You may have checked to make sure you were in the right location. As you entered the classroom, you probably scoped it out: Was it a big lecture hall, a smaller classroom, or a more intimate seminar room? Who was in the class? Did you know anyone? Maybe you asked a friend or a stranger: "Is this Introduction to Sociology?" "What have you heard about this professor?" You also might have wondered what others were thinking and feeling: Are the other students as nervous as I am? Is the professor nervous too? In watching and questioning others, you better understood what was going on.

This example captures the essence of qualitative research as discussed in this chapter: to make sense of our sociocultural surroundings by keenly observing others, interacting with them, posing questions, and analyzing people's experiences, including our own. This is not to say that everyone is a researcher or that common sense is all there is to it. The ultimate goal of qualitative research is not personal but scientific—to build a general, abstract understanding of social phenomena. To gain this understanding, qualitative researchers have developed special skills and techniques for observing and asking questions as well as describing and analyzing everyday life and culture.

In Chapter 4 we identified methodological approaches designed to address qualitative research questions, which focus on social context, cultural meanings, and processes. In this chapter, we discuss two of these approaches: field research and in-depth interviews. (The qualitative analysis of existing data is discussed in Chapter 10.)

While the first approach, field research, can be conducted on a variety of topics and in many settings, it has one distinguishing characteristic: It is carried out "in the field"—in a social setting familiar to the people being observed—with the goal of not disturbing the naturalness of the setting. When it focuses on the culture of a group of people, whether near or afar, field research is often referred to as **ethnography**, a term derived from cultural anthropology. The second approach, in-depth interviewing, may be used to complement observations in field research or as a stand-alone method of data collection. In contrast to survey interviews, in-depth interviews provide a deeper, more comprehensive understanding of interviewees' experiences and interpretations, as reported in their own words.

We begin the chapter by describing two contemporary research examples: a field research study and an in-depth interview study. Based on these examples, we discuss the general features of qualitative research, followed by a discussion of its variations. We then outline the separate processes of conducting field research and in-depth interviews. We conclude by discussing the strengths and weaknesses of qualitative research.

ethnography An alternate word, derived from cultural anthropology, to describe field research, especially when it focuses on the culture of a group of people.

INTRODUCTORY FIELD RESEARCH EXAMPLE: *MEXICAN NEW YORK*

▲ Robert Courtney Smith

We live in an increasingly globalized society, where our lives are affected by local conditions in our own countries and conditions in the world more broadly. *Globalization* refers to the cultural, political, and economic interconnectedness of nations and people. One driving force of globalization is the migration, or movement, of people across national borders. As people move from one country to live in another, they have to negotiate at least two cultural worlds: their home country (where they were born) and their host country (where they are currently living). One potential response to this is *assimilation*, which refers to migrants adopting the culture of the host country. Another response is *transnationalization*, which is the process by which migrants and their children remain linked to their home countries through regularly observed rituals and practices (Smith 2006:6–7). Wanting to gain an insider's perspective on globalization and transnationalization, political scientist Robert Courtney Smith (2006:3) asked what these "processes mean in people's everyday lives," why migrants and their children are interested in "maintaining relations with their home towns and countries," and how participation in these processes affects migrants' "experiences of assimilation in the United States."[1]

To address these questions, Smith drew on 15 years of field research in the community of "Ticuani," a pseudonym for a 2,000-person town in southern Puebla, Mexico, near Mexico City (see Figure 9.1 for the general location). During the time he studied the Ticuanenses—that is, people from Ticuani—about half of the population left for the United States, with New York the most common destination. Smith's research was carried out in Ticuani, Mexico, and New York. It began in 1988 in Ticuani and a neighboring town, El Ganado; continued in New York while interspersed with "five-or six-week trips [to Ticuani] from 1991 to 1993"; focused on women and the second generation (that is, the children of people born abroad) as part of another research project between 1994 and 1997; and concluded with a second round of intensive field work (with other researchers) in Ticuani and New York between 1997 and 2002 (Smith 2006:5). Smith continues his research on this and related topics today (e.g., see Smith 2014).

Smith (2006:9–10) focused on transnational life "in politics in the first generation, in gender relations in the first and second generations, and in the assimilation experiences

---

[1] Our description of this study draws on Smith's book, *Mexican New York*, as well as detailed information about his research that he graciously provided (personal communication 2013).

UNITED STATES

GULF OF
MEXICO

MEXICO

Mexico City

PUEBLA

PACIFIC
OCEAN

GUERRERO

OAXACA

FIGURE 9.1
General Location of
the Mixteca, Southern
Mexico

of teenage students and gang members." As he indicates, he drew upon a variety of data collected over a long period of time:

> My own work involved long interviews, usually more than one, with at least sixty adult or young adult Ticuanenses and twenty-five to thirty of their U.S.-raised children, as well as extensive longitudinal work with a smaller group who are most actively involved in its transnational life. It also draws on more than one hundred life-history interviews for the second-generation project; seven long group interviews; and ethnographic fieldwork in schools, public places, and homes, as well as countless hours of supervision of more than a dozen students during three years of fieldwork in New York and Mexico. (Smith 2006:357)

Smith found that living in New York is not easy for Ticuanenses, nor for other Mexicans. Not only do they face discrimination similar to that encountered by other racial/ethnic minority and immigrant groups, but they also are forced to compete with these groups for jobs, education, housing, and other resources. Many first-generation migrants—that is, people who were born abroad—worked in low-wage jobs, such as in the garment and restaurant industries, which made some of them feel "inferior." While a small minority of first-generation migrants were upwardly mobile, most were not. This had consequences for their children, some of whom got "their first jobs in the same industry as their parents" (Smith 2006:27). Second-generation migrants' life chances also depend on their education, and large numbers of Mexicans do not complete high school. Some migrants became involved with drugs and gangs, partly as a reaction to an unfulfilled "American dream." Yet others, particularly those involved in a Ticuani youth group Smith studied, went on to achieve higher levels of education. Overall, Smith (2006:36) estimates that "about a fifth of the second-generation boys and a third of the girls are upwardly mobile in terms of occupation and education."

Many Ticuanense migrants remained connected to Ticuani and Mexico. One of the primary ways they did so is through the Ticuani Solidarity Committee of New York.

"The Committee," as Smith refers to it, funded public works projects in Ticuani, using money collected from the Ticuanense community in New York. Over time, the Committee also became increasingly involved in local Ticuani politics, and helped to organize numerous cultural events, the most prominent being the Feast of Padre Jesús, an annual eleven-day religious and secular celebration (Smith 2006:151). Whether for the Feast or vacation, many migrants return to Ticuani over the course of their lifetime, sometimes sending their children there to learn more about the culture.

Living transnationally, however, often produces cultural conflict. A case in point is how men and women attempt to "negotiate the different meanings of gender in New York and Ticuani" (Smith 2006:2). Migration to the United States presented a challenge to "ranchero masculinity," a gender ideology that "legitimize[s] men's dominant and women's subordinate positions" (96). While some first-generation men clung to this ideology, others adapted some of its elements to US conditions. Similarly, first-generation women alternated between acceptance and adaptation of "ranchero femininity," an ideology that stresses deference to men. Still, most first-generation women did *not* embrace what Smith calls the "New York woman" model, which is "an Americanized vision of independent womanhood who works, supports herself, and does not really need a man but would be prepared to marry one who shares her egalitarian vision" (97).

Second-generation migrants also deal with cultural conflicts. For example, while second-generation women are more likely to embrace the "New York" woman model than their mothers, they often find themselves in "lockdown" mode in New York, as their parents will not let them go out alone. When these women return to Ticuani, they have more freedom to go out than in New York. However, some are still under the watchful eyes of their brothers or boyfriends, who believe that it is their responsibility to protect them. Second-generation women and men also struggle with a different kind of conflict, which one immigrant poignantly described: "In New York, you don't fit in because you're Mexican. In Ticuani, you don't belong because you're not Mexican enough" (Smith 2006:147). A general lack of belonging, in fact, was something commonly expressed by male gang members. Gangs, particularly Mexican-only gangs, sometimes filled this void, especially in the absence of strong family ties and in the face of real or perceived danger.

According to Smith (2006:277), a common theme is the Ticuanenses' search for recognition and respect. Transnationalization provides both opportunities and constraints in this search. On the one hand, it is an alternative to mere assimilation, as staying connected to Ticuani helps migrants retain elements of their culture, which can serve as a source of pride in both the United States and Ticuani. On the other hand, transnationalization produces cultural conflicts, which, if not successfully resolved, can cause strain between Ticuanense migrants and locals, between

▲ Jessica Vasquez

men and women, and between children and their families. This conflict can also result in what Smith calls "negative assimilation," such as downward mobility and gang violence.

INTRODUCTORY IN-DEPTH INTERVIEW EXAMPLE: *MEXICAN AMERICANS ACROSS GENERATIONS*

Like Robert Smith, sociologist Jessica Vasquez was interested in the assimilation experiences of Mexican Americans.[2] These experiences, according to Vasquez (2011), are especially important to understand in light of the US backlash against immigration. While studies such as Smith's provide an understanding of the experiences of first-and second-generation immigrants, Vasquez also wanted to know about the experiences of the third generation (i.e., the grandchildren of people born abroad). In particular, she asked, "How do first-, second-, and third-generation Mexican Americans come to their sense of racial identity?" (Vasquez 2011:3). Her focus was on the roles the family and other institutions play in shaping this identity. Her most recent research continues to focus on race and family (e.g., see Vasquez 2015).

To address her research question, Vasquez conducted interviews with 67 Mexican Americans in 29 three-generation families in California. California, Vasquez (2011:23) notes, has the "second largest percentage of Hispanics . . . of all fifty states" and "has by far the largest Hispanic population in the United States." She recruited interviewees from northern and southern California—specifically, in the San Francisco Bay Area, Santa Barbara County, and Los Angeles County. Her recruitment efforts focused on second-and third-generation immigrants, who often introduced Vasquez to the rest of their families. The individuals she interviewed were predominantly middle class, as defined by a higher-than-average income, college education, or white-collar occupation.

Vasquez finds variation in the extent to which Mexican identity and heritage are salient for these families. On the one hand, some families tend to have "thinned attachment," whereby their "commitment to and familiarity with their Mexican heritage wanes over time" (Vasquez 2011:4). "Cultural maintenance," on the other hand, "describes those families that continue Mexican cultural practices, Catholicism, and the Spanish language through all three generations" (4).

The Montes-Rosenberg family exemplifies the thinned attachment tendency. In response to Vasquez's question, "How important is the Spanish language to you?" Maria Montes—a first-generation immigrant—says, "It is really important that we continue to . . . maintain

<hr>

[2]Our description of this study draws on Vasquez's book, *Mexican Americans Across Generations*, as well as detailed information about her research that she generously provided (personal communication 2014).

our language ... I wish with all my heart that my kids would know it more and would pass it on to their kids..." (Vasquez 2011:36). Maria further highlights the significance of Mexican heritage by relating the following advice to her children and grandchildren:

> We're Mexican and we have to be proud of the fact that we come from Mexico and never be ashamed that you are from Mexico. I said, "I know there are lots of people that look down on Mexicans, but you have to be proud. That's what we are." (Vasquez 2011:34)

Yet, Maria's daughter Tamara (second generation) does not share this commitment to the same degree: "I don't know that I identify with being an American or Mexican," she remarks (Vasquez 2011:40). Tamara recounts her experiences of being the first woman in her extended family to go to college, her marriage to a non-Mexican (Jewish) man, and her discontent with the Catholic church, all of which are indicative of a thinned attachment to Mexican heritage. This attachment is even "thinner" for Tamara's daughter Jillian (third generation), who previously held negative stereotypes of Mexicans: "I had really awful stereotypes of what Mexican people were like too, like all Mexican people are gardeners and maids" (49–50). She notes that Spanish "was my first language and I lost it" (55). When asked about how she sees herself today, Jillian identifies as white and has only partly accepted Mexican identity.

The Lopez family, by contrast, typifies what Vasquez calls cultural maintenance tendencies, particularly in the second and third generations. For Marcus Lopez (second generation), the prejudice he faced in the military made him acutely aware of his Mexican identity:

> My first exposure to prejudices was in the company I was assigned to because I came across [white] Texans. To them I was a bean-burner, a wetback, "come take my boots off, boy," "did your mom teach you how to make tortillas? Because I like tortillas." That was the first time I was exposed to actual prejudices and racism. I was kinda hurt by it. You know, I'm an American. (Vasquez 2011:69)

Through his participation in the Chicano Movement and college courses, Marcus became more aware of his heritage, which he also wants his children to take pride in: "I tell them ... to remember who you are and be proud of it" (Vasquez 2011:74). Marcus's son Tony learned about Mexican heritage especially from his maternal grandparents, who helped raise him. Growing up in "the traditional old-world family" and speaking Spanish with his grandparents allowed Tony to retain elements of his culture (77–78). In his current job at the county sheriff's department, which serves a community that is more than one-third Hispanic, Tony's language skills are prized and other elements of his identity remain salient, as he notes: "[I am] representing the Hispanic community.... I want to be a good role model and be available to help everybody. I want to carry my people up to the next level" (80).

Despite differences in their identification with Mexican heritage, interviewees reported sharing a common experience of facing discrimination, particularly among the second and third generation. A second-generation, "light-skinned" couple, Adele and Ruben Mendoza, experienced discrimination while hunting for an apartment. When they found an apartment they liked, the manager agreed to let them go home and get cash so that they could put down a deposit and a month's rent. They then recorded their names in a register and left. When they returned, however, they were told, "Sorry, it's already been rented." It appeared that recording "Ruben Mendoza" in the register identified them as Mexican and not "white," which evoked discrimination, because when they asked friends to check out the apartment, it was still vacant (Vasquez 2011:127).

This and other experiences of discrimination had one thing in common: They persisted in spite of Mexican Americans' entry into middle-class life or other forms of assimilation, or what Vasquez calls "racialization despite assimilation."

Synthesizing these findings, Vasquez argues that her study provides an important critique of early migration theory, which assumed that assimilation occurs in a "straight line" across successive generations. Rather, the road to assimilation is "bumpy," as racial identity is influenced by a host of factors. Primary among these factors are spouse/partner, gender, social position, and personal traits (such as name and phenotype) (Vasquez 2011:232–35). These and other factors, such as religion, Spanish language, and social context, are also related to whether individuals express thinned attachment or cultural maintenance tendencies.

GENERAL FEATURES OF QUALITATIVE RESEARCH

Qualitative research lends itself best to understanding the social context of people's lives, people's interpretations of their experiences, and social processes. Smith's and Vasquez's questions addressed this kind of understanding. To differing extents, their studies had six features common to qualitative research: (1) observation; (2) interviews; (3) supplementary archival and other data; (4) nonprobability sampling; (5) qualitative data analysis; and (6) reflexivity.

Observation

Observation in qualitative research generally differs from observation in other forms of social research in two ways. First, it is direct, usually with the naked eye, rather than the sort of indirect observation that characterizes respondents' reports in questionnaires or interviews. Second, in field research especially, it takes place in a natural setting, not a laboratory or other contrived situation.

Field researchers, for whom observation is the primary method of data collection, record their observations in notes. In *Mexican New York*, Smith (2006:138) presents notes from an exchange between a couple, Julia and Toño, at the cockfights (*los gallos*) in Ticuani:

Running out of money to bet on the *gallos*, Toño turned to Julia and said, "You got my back, right?" to which she responded, "What?!" impatiently. They spoke more, and Julia ended the conversation by saying loudly to him, "Don't ask me for money for *los gallos*. If you lose your money and don't have any more, that's your problem!" He turned away sullenly from her without saying anything and went back to the hangout with the guys he was drinking with.

Observations are often accompanied by the researcher's direct experience (Lofland et al. 2006). Unlike experiments and surveys, this experience is an integral part of field research and other qualitative research designs. Smith's study provides a particularly poignant example of how his experience shed further light on his observations. In Ticuani, when approached by a young man at a wedding, Smith (2006:249) noted:

> He was very friendly at first, but then became more aggressive. He asked me repeatedly, "You understand me?" a question often implying that the speaker will *make* you understand if you disagree. He seemed to be trying to find in my conversation some form of disrespect for him, for Ticuani, or for Mexico that would give him a pretext for attacking me, verbally or otherwise. For example, he asked me if I liked Ticuani, "even though" I was from New York, and his manner suggested he suspected I did not.

Smith ultimately defused the situation, but he points out that "the encounter was sometimes tense, and I felt myself getting angry at this young man but also getting nervous about what he might do" (Smith 2006:250). Smith had observed similar confrontations between second-generation Ticuanenses returning from New York and those living there, and he had heard of many such experiences from participants in his research. This experience, however, helped him to better understand the "emotional work" that goes into defusing a confrontation without appearing angry.

Observation and direct experience may also enrich the interpretation of data drawn mainly from interviews. After her interviews, Jessica Vasquez (2011:28) attempted "to capture intonation, speed of speech, body language, and [her] own rapport with and reaction to the respondent." An example of this is the "wry tone" that Jillian Rosenberg used when mentioning that Mexican identity is "cool" (54). Another example occurred prior to interviewing the Benavidas family. Vasquez was given a tour of their house, which she describes as being "immaculately decorated, boasting art on the walls from Spain, Mexico, and Ecuador, as well as southwestern art hand crafted by Melissa's [the host's] father" (64). She took these observations as further evidence of the "cultural maintenance" tendencies of the Benavidas family—that is, their strong attachment to Mexican heritage.

Interviews

A second general characteristic of qualitative research is interviewing. As Johnny Saldaña (2011:46) explains, "observation is primarily the researcher's take on social action, whereas the interview is the participant's take." Most interviewing in field research occurs informally, in ordinary conversations and as a natural extension of observation. Field interviewing may begin with questions that orient the researcher to the setting or group, such as: "Where can I find this?" "What is that?" "Who is she?" "What does she do?" Eventually, questions are aimed at expanding information about specific actions and events as well as probing their deeper meanings. Indeed, field researchers devote much of their time to asking questions such as "What do you think she meant by that?" "What are they supposed to do?" "Why did she do that?" "Why is that done?" (Lofland and Lofland 1995:70).

After researchers have been in the field for a while and have begun to develop an understanding of the setting, they may conduct formal interviews to secure more detailed information on individuals and to round out and check information already obtained. Unlike spontaneous informal questioning, researchers schedule and prepare questions in advance of formal interviews. This was the primary method of data collection in Vasquez's study, and Smith also did extensive formal interviewing. Characteristically, Vasquez's interviews lasted between an hour and two and a half hours and were tape recorded and transcribed.

Formal qualitative interviews, particularly when used as a stand-alone method, are synonymous with in-depth interviews, sometimes called "intensive" interviews (Lofland et al. 2006). According to Herbert Rubin and Irene Rubin (2012:29), **in-depth interviews** share three characteristics: (1) they are intended to yield rich and detailed information on participants' experiences and interpretations; (2) they primarily make use of open-ended questions, which require interviewees to answer in their own words (see Chapter 8); and (3) they are generally flexible. In order to yield "deep" responses characteristic of in-depth interviews, it is centrally important that the researcher establish rapport and trust with the interviewee (Johnson and Rowlands 2012:101). The interviewer and interviewee are said to be "conversational partners" (Rubin and Rubin 2012), responsible for the "co-generation of data" (Schwartz-Shea and Yanow 2012: Chapter 5). The interpersonal nature of in-depth interviews also makes face-to-face interviewing by far the primary mode of data collection.

In final reports of in-depth interview research, the data take the form of interviewees' verbatim statements, sometimes vividly describing their thoughts, feelings, or experiences. Consider, for example, Samantha Diaz's response to Vasquez's question about "whether she felt her physical appearance had helped her or barred her from gaining entrance to any social or occupational arena":

> I don't know if it's reality, but I feel like it's restricted me. I got the feeling that I'm jinxing myself or something, but when I tell people my last name, I wonder what reaction they're going to have. Because "Diaz" is very Mexican. . . . When I'm talking to people or interviewing for things [jobs] . . . it's like I'm back in high school again and I have to pretend I'm white again. . . . The sad thing, in high school too, I wanted to be a lighter color. I actually put Clearasil on my face to get it a lighter skin tone. (Vasquez 2011:131)

in-depth interview
A type of formal interview intended to yield deep responses through open-ended questions and a flexible format.

Just as interviews may serve as a cross-check on observations and vice versa, so too may interviews with different individuals serve as a cross-check of one another. An important feature of Vasquez's research design, for instance, was her decision to interview different generations who provided different—and sometimes conflicting—perspectives. In the Vargas family, for example, she reports, "the first-and second-generation women . . . were very strongly identified as Mexican and immersed in the Mexican community." But to her "surprise, the third-generation descendant had virtually nothing to report in the way of family stories or events that highlighted her Mexican identity" (Vasquez 2011:250). In this case, "the differences between generations were stark." "Yet," she states, "that is valuable data that is a benefit of conducting interviews with multiple family members about the same topic" (Vasquez 2011:250–51).

Supplementary Archival and Other Data

Qualitative researchers may also make use of a variety of other supplementary data, such as archival records and documents. While some of these data—for example, time diaries and logs—may be generated by participants, researchers tend to use publicly accessible information (Bailey 1996; Lofland et al. 2006; Saldaña 2011). The usefulness and choice of supplementary data depend on the understanding that the researcher wants to achieve and the setting, group, or participants being studied. Documents and archival records may further establish the context of a study and serve as a cross-check of other data.

One common source of supplementary data is governmental records. Smith used a variety of statistics compiled by the US and Mexican governments, New York City Planning Department, and Emergency Immigrant Census. He used these data to provide an overview of Mexican immigration and to document the educational and occupational outcomes of Mexicans in the United States. Similarly, Vasquez used US governmental data, such as the statistics on the Hispanic population in California, to establish the context of her research.

There are a variety of other supplementary data that researchers may use. When studying a group or organization, for example, researchers may examine organizational charts, brochures, electronic communications, and official records. An interesting example in Smith's study was his use of international telephone records, which were recorded by hand in local (Ticuani) operators' notebooks before the mid-1990s. Smith realized that these records may further his understanding of the connection between Ticuani and New York. When he counted the number of calls to specific area codes, he found that:

> [d]uring a typical month in 1992, there were roughly ten times as many calls placed to the United States as to all long-distance destinations in Mexico—288 versus 28. Of these, 209 were to New York City and 36 to other parts of the New York metropolitan area (New York, New Jersey, and Connecticut). (Smith 2006:44)

These data from Ticuani, according to Smith (44), "indicate its orientation to New York."

Finally, photos, videos, and visual materials can facilitate a researcher's understanding (Lofland et al. 2006). For example, videos of Ticuanense cultural and political activities, such as Committee meetings and events, were another source of data in Smith's study.

Nonprobability Sampling

Qualitative research is also characterized by nonprobability sampling. It frequently involves the nonrandom selection of settings or groups of people. Furthermore, the time required to carry out observations and interviews tends to restrict the possible sample size to a small number of cases.

Like much of field research, Smith's research represents a case study, where the "case" is the Ticuani community. As discussed in Chapter 6, cases may be selected because they (1) are conveniently located, (2) fit the research topic, (3) represent extreme or deviant instances of phenomena, and/or (4) provide relevant theoretical comparisons. Smith's selection of Ticuani as a case study was based on these and other considerations. His previous research on another Mexican community, El Ganado, afforded him entrée into the Ticuani community. His selection of Ticuani was "strategic" because of its relevance to transnational theory (Smith 2006:10). And as he points out, "Ticuani represents one of the strongest instances of local-level transnational life documented thus far . . ." (15). In this sense, Ticuani is an extreme case, which allows for theoretical comparisons with other cases, such as El Ganado and other communities Smith has studied.

Beyond the selection of a setting or group of people, qualitative researchers must decide what to observe. In field research, the delicate operation of entering the field tends to necessitate the nonrandom selection of observation sites. Smith conducted observations at different sites in the field, where he observed people, interactions, and events. He explicitly selected the Committee for observation given its relevance to transnational politics. Smith (2006:352) attended at least one of the Committee's all-day, Sunday meetings per month in the early 1990s and attended them weekly "during times of high or particularly interesting activity."

The decision about whom to interview also tends to follow nonrandom selection. To select her interviewees, Vasquez used multiple forms of nonprobability sampling. Using theoretical sampling, she intentionally selected people based on characteristics—namely, race/ethnicity and immigration status—that were relevant to her research. Furthermore, Vasquez made use of snowball sampling, whereby her interviewees referred others to her.

Qualitative Data Analysis

In qualitative research, data generally consist of written text from field notes and interview transcriptions, which require qualitative methods of analysis. Unlike researchers conducting experiments or surveys, qualitative researchers do not necessarily wait until all of the data have been collected to begin analysis. Rather, the hallmark of qualitative data analysis is an ongoing, iterative process in which data are compared across cases, time, and other relevant dimensions.

Illustrative of this process is Smith's analysis of observational and interview data regarding two Committee members, Don Emiliano and Don Gerardo. In analyzing these data, Smith (2006:95–96) finds many similarities:

> Both men have worked hard and steadily in Ticuani public life for more than thirty years in New York. Both describe their central identity as Ticuanense, and both are well known for their public service. Both men have worked extensively with the Committee. . . . Both have worked in restaurants in New York, where their late hours interfered with their ability to spend time with their families but paid good wages that supported a middle-class lifestyle.

Other data indicated notable differences, particularly in how these men's absences are viewed. For example, in separate interviews with the men's wives, Smith got contrasting views. When he asked Doña Selena, the wife of Don Emiliano, "What was it like when Don Emiliano went out so much for so many years . . . ?" she reported that her husband's absence bothered her at times, but she praised her husband's public service and said she had become more accustomed to his being away. Yet, Doña Talia, the wife of Don Gerardo, reacted quite differently to her husband's absence. Without even being asked about this in an interview, she pointed out that her husband was currently at a soccer game with friends, that he had not asked her or their children to join him, and that "he always is doing things with the Committee or drinking or playing" (Smith 2006:101–2).

Still other data indicate that Don Emiliano recognizes his wife's sacrifices and helps with the kids and around the house, whereas Don Gerardo does not act in the same way. Given the similarities between Don Emiliano and Don Gerardo, Smith concludes that the differences in how their absences are viewed are partly due to how these men and their wives negotiate gender ideology in the United States:

> Whereas Don Gerardo has tried to impose a marriage of respect on his family while Doña Talia unsuccessfully demands a companionate marriage, Don Emiliano and Doña Selena have renegotiated a type of companionate marriage, one that retains some elements of ranchero masculinity consistent with a respect for marriage. (Smith 2006:111)

In coming to these conclusions, Smith alternated between using an approach that he calls "dead reckoning," which relies on his own knowledge of the setting and its members, and an approach that uses existing theory to a greater extent, or what he calls "sailing with instruments." He describes his analysis as follows:

> Per this analogy, my analysis of gender and of coconstitution of masculinity and Mexicanness in emergent space drew first on a dead reckoning with the data

and then on an explicit engagement with the instruments, the theories. While this overstates the case—one always works with theories and ideas in mind when gathering and engaging data—my experience in, for example, comparing the meaning of Don Gerardo's and Don Emiliano's absences was really one of discovery. I had no explicit intention to write such a comparison when I was hanging out with or interviewing them. It was only later that the comparative insights emerged as I reread the notes and interviews with members of the two families. Having these insights into these two cases enabled me to go back and wrestle again with theories on gender and migration, to gain some purchase on them, and to guide further research. . . . In the end, my analysis emerged from my repeated readings of the fieldnotes and interviews and my own personal, but visceral and almost preconceptual, sense of what was going on. (Smith 2006:357–58)

In this instance, Smith's initial analysis followed the inductive logic of inquiry, typical of qualitative research. We'll have more to say about the process of analyzing qualitative data later in this chapter, and we devote the entirety of Chapter 13 to qualitative analysis.

Reflexivity

As discussed in Chapter 4, qualitative research relies on a different way of knowing than quantitative research. The qualitative researcher is an "instrument" of the research itself (Saldaña 2011:22). The researcher's understandings are greatly shaped by his/her relationships with the people being studied, which themselves are a product of the researcher's experiences and personal characteristics, such as race, class, gender, and sexuality. **Reflexivity** refers to the researcher's reflections on how these factors influence his or her knowledge of what is being studied. Reflexivity occurs throughout the research process, and in final reports of the study, researchers' reflections are intended to promote transparency and help the reader evaluate findings (Schwartz-Shea and Yanow 2012). You have already read one example of reflexivity, whereby Smith's direct experience with a local Ticuani man helped him understand the emotional work of diffusing a confrontation.

Qualitative researchers often reflect on their status as an *insider* or *outsider* in the setting or group being studied and how this shapes what they know. An insider is someone who, by virtue of their personal characteristics or experiences, is similar to the people being studied; an outsider is dissimilar (Merton 1972). Vasquez's part-Mexican heritage provided her with insider status, which, she acknowledges, shaped her research: "Being an 'insider' lets me pass the first test of authenticity and prompts acquiescence to the interview" (Vasquez 2011:255). In contrast, Smith was an outsider by virtue of the combination of his nationality (American) and race (white). For instance, when he first ran in the Antorcha, a 6- to 7-mile run commemorating the saint during the Feast of Padre Jesús, "everyone vigilantly noted my reactions at each stage. I was hyperaware

reflexivity A common practice in qualitative research, whereby a researcher reflects on how his or her characteristics and presence shape the research process.

BOX 9.1

CHECKING YOUR UNDERSTANDING

The "Nacirema" and Reflexivity

A classic field study would surely have to be Horace Miner's research on a group he called the "Nacirema." Before looking at or answering the questions below, read Miner's (1956) short article entitled "Body Ritual Among the Nacirema" (*American Anthropologist* 58, no. 3:503–7), which you can obtain easily online by doing a Web search for the article title. STOP. Spoiler alert! Have you read the article? If so, answer the following questions.

1. What do you think of the Nacirema's body-ritual practices? Do you find them in any way disgusting or repugnant?

2. As you may have realized, "Nacirema" is simply "American" spelled backward. Many aspects of US culture are disguised in the article by reversing the spelling (e.g., *latipso* = hospital) or giving them a different name (e.g., "holy mouth men" = dentist). Knowing this, how did your cultural background shape your response to the first question?

3. How does this exercise illustrate the importance of reflexivity in qualitative research?

---

of being watched . . ." (Smith 2006:182). As he continued to immerse himself in Ticuani life, how he related to others (and himself) changed:

> My own reflections on embodied experience and social proprioception reflect my in-between status as a fictive Ticuanense and an American ethnographer. My experience changed over time as I came to feel like, and by many to be seen as, an honorary Ticuanense. (Smith 2006:182)

These reflections are integrally important for the kind of understanding qualitative researchers hope to achieve. As we elaborate on Smith and Vasquez's studies, we provide other examples of how they practiced reflexivity. To practice this yourself, see Box 9.1, CHECKING YOUR UNDERSTANDING: The "Nacirema" and Reflexivity.

SUMMARY

Qualitative research is directed toward answering research questions focused on understanding social context, cultural meanings, and processes. It is characterized by six general features: (1) observation (and, often, direct experience) in natural settings; (2) interviews, which may be informal or formal and in-depth; (3) use of supplementary archival and other data; (4) small non-probability samples of cases, settings, and people; (5) the iterative and often inductive analysis of qualitative data; and (6) reflexivity, which refers to a researcher reflecting on how his or her characteristics and other factors shape the research.

VARIATIONS IN QUALITATIVE RESEARCH METHODS

Our description of the general features of qualitative research glosses over variations in how these methods are applied. The most significant variations involve the primary methods of data collection: observation and interviews. Observation differs in the extent to which the researcher (1) participates in the social setting and (2) reveals his or her identity as a researcher. In addition to the level of formality, qualitative interviews vary in (1) structure and (2) whether research participants are interviewed individually or as a group. Let's examine the Smith and Vasquez studies as well as other research examples to understand these important variations.

Degrees of Participation and Observation

Traditionally, in field research, a distinction is made between **participant** and **nonparticipant observation**. The participant observer is actively and intentionally involved in the phenomena being observed; the nonparticipant is a passive and intentionally unobtrusive observer. It is more accurate, however, to think of the two types of observation as poles of a continuum.

PARTICIPANT OBSERVATION

A primary goal of field research is to gain an insider's view of reality. Often the best way to do this, as the old adage says, is to walk a mile in another person's shoes—in other words, to participate actively, for an extended period of time, in the daily lives of the people and situations under study. This may require that the observer live or work in an area; it clearly assumes that the observer will become an accepted member of the group or community, able to speak informally with the people—to "joke with them, empathize with them, and share their concerns and experiences" (Bogdan and Taylor 1975:5). Robert Smith certainly participated at least to this degree: throughout the 15 years he studied the Ticuanenses, he was in the field for two rounds of intensive fieldwork. He attended cultural events, such as the Feast of Padre Jesús, and participated in rituals, such as the Antorcha.

Becoming a participant observer carries some risks. It can be an emotionally stressful experience for the researcher. In the early days in the field, before learning the ropes, researchers are likely to experience awkward and embarrassing encounters. Smith (2006:183) recalls one such gaffe when he referred to the "statue of Padre *Jesús*

participant observation A form of observation in which the field researcher participates to some degree in the activity or group being studied.

nonparticipant observation A form of observation in which the field researcher does not participate in the activity or group being studied.

as la muñeca grande (the big doll) instead of el icón (the icon)," which elicited "a smile and then a loud, snorting laugh" from his host in Mexico. Field researchers may also become sensitive to suspicious or hostile challenges to their intentions and "observer" role, as Smith did when he first ran in the Antorcha and in his near confrontation with a local Ticuani youth.

Balancing the requirements of both participating and observing can be challenging. To gain an insider's view, you need to gain the acceptance of those you are studying; to be accepted, you need to become actively involved in others' activities. However, it often is difficult to know where to draw the line. In fact, it is not unusual for fieldworkers to witness and to be pressured to participate in physically dangerous or morally and legally questionable activities. In a field study of a Chicago gang, Sudhir Venkatesh (2008) observed violence and other illegal activities such as the distribution of crack cocaine. He also participated in gang violence directed toward a man, who allegedly had beaten a woman, by kicking him (Venkatesh 2008:65–77). Although this example is extreme, it illustrates the difficulties of observing and participating, particularly when studying a deviant group.

NONPARTICIPANT OBSERVATION

The nonparticipant observer is, in effect, an eavesdropper, someone who attempts to observe people without interacting with them and, typically, without their knowing that they are being observed. A good example of nonparticipant observation is Lyn Lofland's study (1971, 1973) of how people in cities—strangers in public places—relate to one another in terms of appearance and spatial location. Although Lofland drew upon other materials, her study was based largely on hundreds of hours of observations. She made the observations in and around Ann Arbor and Detroit, Michigan, in bus depots, airports, libraries, stores, restaurants, bars, theaters, and parks; aboard buses; and on the streets. In most of these settings, she was able to "blend into the scenery," even for periods of several hours. Imagining herself viewing others through a one-way mirror, Lofland attempted to record everything within her line of vision. As the study progressed, she concentrated at times on certain kinds of behavior—for example, seating patterns and entrance behavior—but in general she simply recorded as much as she could.

One of Lofland's observation sites was a glass-walled hallway, called the "Fishbowl," between two buildings on the University of Michigan campus. Here, she became sensitized to the "grooming" actions of people as they are about to enter a public setting. Lofland (1971:303) describes how she made this discovery:

> One wall of the Fishbowl, the one which contains the doors, is solid glass, so that whenever I happened to be observing from a bench close to the doors, I could not fail to be struck by the preparation behavior that occurred over and over again as student after student neared the door, stopped, groomed himself

[or herself], and then entered. There were many instances of this behavior recorded in my notes before I ever "recognized" it as a pattern, but once I did, I was led to look for similar activities in other settings and eventually to "see" the full entrance sequence.

Lofland notes that some of her discoveries were made possible by her prolonged periods of observation in only a few sites. This provided sufficient familiarity with the settings to enable her to recognize faces and to make important distinctions among the different inhabitants, such as residents, patrons, customers, and newcomers.

As a separate, inclusive method, nonparticipant observation is comparatively little used in research to address qualitative research questions. Rather, it is often combined with some degree of participation.

BETWEEN PARTICIPATION AND OBSERVATION

Despite the tidiness of the descriptions of participant and nonparticipant observation, there is a rather fine line—or a fuzzy one—between the two. Indeed, some would argue that even a relatively unobtrusive observer sitting at a table in a restaurant taking notes influences the situation by virtue of his or her mere presence; thus, however unwittingly, such an observer is also a participant. Furthermore, one's role may vary across sites and situations within the research field. During his research Smith participated in cultural events and activities, but he assumed more of an observer role in Committee meetings and in other situations. Smith explains, "When different factions in the Ticuani community were openly fighting," for instance, "I tried to be invisible and have everyone forget that I was there" (Robert Smith, personal communication 2013). It is thus useful to view participation as a matter of degree.

Overt Versus Covert Observation

Another variation in field observation concerns whether the researcher reveals or conceals his or her identity as a researcher to those who are being observed. In **overt observation**, the researcher's status as a researcher is made known to others; in **covert observation**, it is not. (To help remember the difference, think of it like this: **overt** = **open**; **covert** = **closed**.)

OVERT OBSERVATION

Most field research involves overt observation. In many cases, assuming an overt observer role may be a prerequisite for gaining access to a setting or group (Lofland et al. 2006). It also may be necessary to let participants know they are being observed when the researcher's presence would elicit questions or arouse suspicion. An example of overt observation from Chapter 2 is Annette Lareau's (2011) research on social class and educational inequality in which Lareau and her assistants observed families in their homes. Whenever possible, Robert Smith informed participants of his research

overt observation A form of observation in which the researcher identifies himself or herself as a researcher to those who are being observed.

covert observation A form of observation in which the researcher conceals his or her identity as a researcher.

or otherwise made it clear that he was observing their activities. Below, he describes a particular instance of this in a Ticuani town meeting in New York:

> I . . . set up my tape recorder—a big lumpy, state of the art (in 1990s) tape re-corder with a microphone that captured sound 360 degrees—before a Ticuani town meeting in New York, and then periodically change[d] tapes, in the middle of the meeting. I was seen as a kind of unofficial historian, I think. People knew what I was doing and knew me. (personal communication 2013)

In other settings where people were unaware of Smith's research, they asked about his presence. During his field work in Mexico, for instance, Smith recounts: "People would see me—a white guy, six feet tall, who would always be running in the morning and went to all of the events—and want to know what my deal was. Who was I? Whose friend was I? Did I speak Spanish?" (personal communication 2013).

A limitation of overt observation is that participants may change their behavior when they know they are being observed, just as in laboratory experiments (see Chapter 7). Lareau (2011:9) acknowledges these *reactivity effects* in her study: "Unquestionably, our presence changed the dynamics as we were sitting in living rooms watching television, riding along in the backseat of the car to a soccer game, watching children get into their pajamas, or sitting in church with them." Lareau describes the first few family visits, in particular, as "very awkward"—not just for the family, but for Lareau and her assistants as well (Lareau 2011:355).

Such reactivity may be mitigated as field researchers establish trust and rapport with the participants. With time, participants can become habituated to the researcher's presence. In Lareau's study, for example, she and her assistants noticed that there was more yelling and cursing during the latter versus earlier stages of the research, suggesting that families had adjusted to the researchers' presence with time (Lareau 2011:9). Robert Smith reports that as a result of establishing rapport and trust with participants, they viewed him as a confidante. Many of them opened up to him, sometimes sharing things they had not shared with many others (personal communication 2013).

COVERT OBSERVATION

The major strength of covert observation is that it overcomes the problem of reactivity effects in overt observation. When people do not know they are being observed, they may act more "naturally." This strength, however, can be offset by a serious ethical weakness: covert observations may invade privacy and, by definition, prevent the observed from providing their informed consent. The extent to which this is ethically questionable depends on the nature of the research setting and the researcher's role in the setting. For example, nonparticipant, covert observation in public settings such as a restaurant or waiting room rarely is a problem. However, when the researcher gains access to a private setting such as home, private office, or closed meeting, without divulging his or her role as a researcher, this is clearly an invasion of privacy. Laud Humphreys' (1970:2009) field research on sexual behavior in public restrooms was considered ethically questionable (see Chapter 3) largely because he misrepresented himself as a voyeur and gained access to observational data as a result of this misrepresentation. Another example of ethically questionable covert observation is presented in Box 9.2, READING SOCIAL RESEARCH: Getting an Insider's View of Students by Passing as One.

BOX 9.2

READING SOCIAL RESEARCH

Getting an Insider's View of Students by Passing as One

Sometimes, it seems like professors just don't know what it's like to be a student these days. Right? Well, one professor "went back to school," as it were, to find out. A cultural anthropologist writing under the pseudonym "Rebekah Nathan" took a sabbatical and enrolled in classes at her own university, "AnyU" (also a pseudonym), for an academic year, lived in a dorm, hung out with and interviewed fellow students, and participated in student life. Published as a book aptly titled *My Freshman Year: What a Professor Learned by Becoming a Student* (2005), Nathan's study is an account of college culture and how students negotiate it. It earned praise for providing an in-depth view of student life usually hidden from the "gaze" of researchers. Yet, the study also raises ethical concerns related to its use of covert observation.

Wanting to provide a naturalistic account of student life, Nathan decided that she would not tell students that she was a researcher during the course of her observations unless they asked. Although many students were surprised to see a middle-aged, first-year student at their school, only one student in the study explicitly asked Nathan about this. To other students, Nathan was assumed to be a student, "albeit a 'returning' older student" (Nathan 2005:8). As a student, she was privy to the experiences and thoughts of fellow students at

AnyU, including students' interactions with one another and with their professors; students' comments about professors, courses, and college more generally; and other aspects of students' personal lives. In one instance, Nathan completed a group project with fellow students that involved interviewing one another about their sexual activities (162). However, she divulged her identity to her group members in this case and also refrained from publishing the accounts she heard.

As is typical in field research, Nathan supplemented her observations with interviews of students. In all of these interviews, she identified herself as a researcher, noting that the interview was *not* for a class project and that the findings might be published. She also had the students complete a signed consent form. In interviews with international students, Nathan explicitly identified herself as a professor.

Nathan's findings on AnyU college life—from how students cut academic corners to how administrative policies are out of touch with students—generated wide interest. *The New York Times* reported that Nathan's book quickly went through five hardback printings and sold out of 14,500 paperback copies in a week (Schemo 2006). The book was featured in columns in publications from *USA Today* (Marklien 2005) to *Inside Higher*

Ed (Jaschik 2005). One review of the book concluded that Nathan's observations "should help guide both faculty and administrators as they create the American university of today and tomorrow" (Pocock 2006:171). In fact, some of Nathan's observations led to changes at her own school (Schemo 2006).

Nathan anticipated that her study would generate ethical controversy. She secured approval of the study from AnyU's Institutional Review Board and took a number of steps to protect student privacy and avoid harm: She used pseudonyms for the school and students (as well as herself); she did not publish detailed information on sensitive topics, such as on academic cheating, because she had gained this information through friendships and believed that disclosing this information may be viewed as a betrayal (Nathan 2005:165); and she divulged her identity in several instances "in which the simple act of withholding information about [herself] threatened to harm, or at least disturb, other people who had a relationship to" her (161).

However, Nathan acknowledges that she can't be sure students wouldn't feel betrayed. After her research ended, for example, she saw a female student with whom she had worked on a course project. The student asked Nathan where she was going, which led to this exchange:

> *"To class," I answered.*
> *"What is it?" she asked.*
> *"Oh, an anthropology class ... actually I'm teaching it."*
> *"No kidding!" she exclaimed. "How did you get to do that? I want to take it!"*
> *"Well," I answered sheepishly, "it's 'cause I'm actually a professor too. I was a student last year to do some research, but now I'm back to being a professor."*
> *"I can't believe that," she responded and then paused. "I feel fooled." (Nathan 2005:167)*

Nathan (168) notes that this student's views about the research have since "evolved," but other students may share her initial reaction. A year after her book was published, Nathan was "outed" by a reporter and her true identity and institutional affiliation came to light (Schemo 2006), making the question of how students felt more than just hypothetical.

BETWEEN OVERT AND COVERT OBSERVATION

Just as the "participant" and "nonparticipant" observers are ideal descriptions of a researcher's role, so too are descriptions of the overt and covert observer. Even under the most overt form of observation, the emergent and flexible nature of field research often results in the researcher being in settings, situations, or groups when *not all* participants know they are being observed. Similarly, it may not be possible to completely conceal one's identity, for practical and ethical reasons. In Nathan's study (Box 9.2), a student's persistent questioning led Nathan to reveal her true identity; she also revealed her identity to others because of the possibility of harm.

At any given moment, a field researcher's level of participation and overtness can be located in the two-dimensional space shown in Figure 9.2. The figure represents the extent to which the researcher (1) acts as a scientific observer or participant and (2) conceals his or her identity as a researcher. Most social research is overt or located

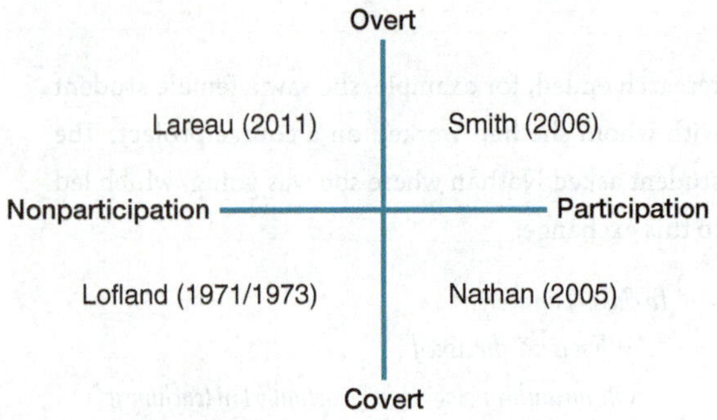

Overt

Lareau (2011)   Smith (2006)

Nonparticipation ——————————————————— Participation

Lofland (1971/1973)   Nathan (2005)

Covert

FIGURE 9.2
Levels of Participation
and Overtness in Field
Research

above the line, with varying degrees of participation. Much of Smith's fieldwork can be placed in the upper right quadrant; Lareau's observation of families falls in the upper left quadrant. Nonparticipation observation studies in public spaces, such as Lofland's, can be placed in the lower left corner of the figure. Studies such as Nathan's fall in the lower right quadrant.

A researcher's level of participation and overtness is also related to the functional role she or he may assume in a group. We will discuss this when we outline the process of conducting field research. For now, we turn to variations in qualitative interviews.

Interview Structure

One of the ways qualitative interviews vary is in their structure. Recall from Chapter 8 that structured interviews have very specific objectives, the same questions are asked in the same order for all interviewees, and interviewers have very little freedom in how the interview is conducted. Surveys use structured interviews, whereas interviews in qualitative research are usually unstructured or semi-structured. An unstructured interview is guided by broad objectives in which questions are developed as the interview proceeds; a semi-structured interview has more specific objectives, but permits the researcher flexibility in whether and how they are pursued. In both types of interviews, rather than follow a pre-established script, the interviewer is free to adapt the interview to capitalize on the special knowledge, experience, or insights of respondents. The informal, casual conversations typical of field research are examples of unstructured interviews. In-depth interviews tend to be unstructured or semi-structured.

Vasquez describes her in-depth interviews as semi-structured. Each interview was guided by a list of topics with specific, open-ended questions. At the beginning, she asked "for a narrative about the individual's biography, and then asked about his or her family's history." Other parts of her interview "focused on issues of family and racial identity" (Vasquez 2011:27). By contrast, an unstructured interview may be guided merely by a set of broad topics. But in either case, topics and questions may be covered in a different order for interviewees and may be skipped for some interviewees but not others (Rubin and Rubin 2012).

There are strengths and weaknesses related to each type of interview. The primary advantage of unstructured interviews is their spontaneity. In fact, as Vasquez (2011:251) suggests, researchers may inadvertently limit interviewees' responses by interrupting with questions and being overly concerned with following a script. The advantage of a more structured interview is that it helps keep the researcher and interviewee on topic. This is particularly important for novice researchers, as we discuss later.

Individual Versus Group Interviews

Interviews also vary in the number of participants. In addition to conducting individual interviews, both Smith and Vasquez conducted group interviews. Smith sometimes interviewed family members together: his interview with Doña Selena included her husband Don Emiliano and their daughter Mia, and he interviewed Don Gerardo's wife Talia with their children. Vasquez also conducted group interviews, such as with the Mendoza family discussed earlier, when families requested them. Recounting this process, she points out:

> These interviews were exciting because of the dynamism inherent in three-way (or more) conversations: people prod each other's memory, interject their own interpretations that might conflict with the story being told, and push each other to tell me certain stories that the original speaker did not initially volunteer. (personal communication 2014)

One special type of group interview is a **focus group**, defined as "a research technique that collects data through group interaction on a topic determined by the researcher" (Morgan 1996:130). In focus groups, the researcher typically takes the role of "facilitator" or "moderator" by posing questions and encouraging discussion from members of the group. Focus groups are conducted with people who may or may not already know one another, and may range in size from as few as 4 or 5 participants to as many as 10 or 12. The participants in a focus group respond not only to the interviewer's questions, but also to one another's responses. The data thus consist of participants' verbatim statements and their interactions with one another, which are recorded in notes, audio files, and/or on video. Focus groups may be used as a sole data collection method or in combination with other methods, such as individual, in-depth interviews (King and Horrocks 2010; Krueger and Casey 2015; Morgan 1996, 2012).

Mignon Moore (2011) used focus group interviews in a study on gay black women in New York. Specifically, she convened four groups, which varied in size from 9 to 12 participants. Characteristically, each of Moore's focus groups emphasized a particular topic: One group, for example, sought to understand the women's experiences as lesbians; another group, comprising women with children, "focused specifically on relationships in their home lives, what their relationships were like with the fathers of their children, and the quality of their partner's relationship with their children" (Moore 2011:231). As a way of eliciting reactions and stimulating discussion on gender displays in black lesbian communities, Moore began another focus group by showing the participants a documentary on African-American masculine-identified women. She convened this focus group, in particular, to attempt to reconcile conflicting information about the presentation of gender she had gathered through other data collection methods, including field research and individual, in-depth interviews (231).

focus group An interview method in which a researcher collects data from a group by moderating a group discussion on a particular topic.

An advantage of a group interview, as opposed to an individual one, is that it allows the researcher to observe social interaction among participants (King and Horrocks 2010; Morgan 1996, 2012). A practical benefit is that a researcher can gather information from a greater number of participants at one time. Methodologically, the biggest limitation of group interviews is that they add an extra layer of reactivity. Interviewees may provide responses that are not only socially desirable to the interviewer, but also to the other participants in the interview; similarly, participants may tend to go along with what others say. A final limitation concerns ethics: group interviews, by their nature, do not protect participants' confidentiality. As such, researchers need to ask participants to sign a disclosure statement asking them to protect one another's confidentiality (King and Horrocks 2010).

SUMMARY

Qualitative research varies in how observations and interviews are conducted. In observational research, researchers may participate in what they are observing (participant observation), merely observe without participating (nonparticipant observation), or participate to some degree in between. Furthermore, observation may be overt (open), covert (closed), or somewhere in between. Interviews may be more or less formal and structured; they may also be conducted individually or with groups of different sizes.

THE PROCESS OF CONDUCTING FIELD RESEARCH

Now that you know the general features of qualitative research and its major variations, are you ready to "go get the seat of your pants dirty in real research?" as University of Chicago Professor Robert Park reportedly told his students (McKinney 1966:71). Before you begin, remember that the general process for answering qualitative research questions is different than the process for answering quantitative research questions. The research questions themselves tend to be broader—sometimes called **guiding questions**—than those posed in surveys and experiments. In addition, these guiding questions are usually accompanied by a set of more focused research questions, which may emerge during the course of research. Recall, for example, that Smith's guiding question concerned the meaning of transnationalization processes in migrants' lives, while his more focused questions concentrated on the intersections among transnationalization, politics, gender, and migrant status.

guiding question
A relatively broad research question that guides the initial stages of qualitative research.

Initially, qualitative researchers may rely on a literature review to a lesser extent than researchers working from a deductive logic of inquiry. Because preconceived images can be very misleading, researchers may attempt to avoid preset hypotheses and instead let their observations and interviews guide the course of the research.

As outlined in Figure 9.3, the major steps in conducting field research are to select a research setting/group, gain access, establish roles and relationships, decide what to observe/whom to interview, gather and analyze data, leave the field, and write the report. Note that many of the arrows in the figure are bi-directional. This is because the steps in field research are interrelated; they may not be completed in the same order; and the researcher may move back and forth between them (Bailey 1996:xiv). As an example, a researcher may select a setting or group to study and then gain access; alternatively, he or she may gain access first and then choose to conduct a study.

Select Setting/Group

The most important considerations in selecting a setting or group are that it should speak to the research question at hand and should allow the researcher to better understand meaning, process, and/or actors' points of views (Lofland et al. 2006). Smith, for example, argued that the case of Ticuani provided unusual clarity about the globalization and transnationalization processes in which he was interested. But his selection of Ticuani was also rooted in his previous experiences. As an undergraduate student, he taught English in a migrant labor camp in Pennsylvania, where he met members of the Ticuani and other Mexican communities. This experience sparked an interest in Mexican communities that continued into graduate school, where he completed his PhD dissertation on three transnational communities including Ticuani (Smith, personal communication 2013).

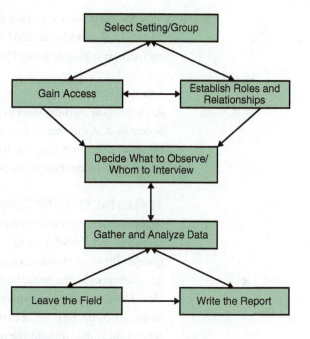

FIGURE 9.3
The Process of Conducting Field Research

Researchers have different opinions on where to start in selecting a setting or group. On the one hand, John Lofland and colleagues (2006) recommend "starting where you are"—that is, in a setting with which you are familiar. The advantage of starting where you are is that it facilitates entry. Examples of field researchers "starting where they are" include Patricia and Peter Adler's (1998) study of the peer groups to which their children belonged, David Karp's (1996) study of depression as a "sufferer of depression" himself, and Mitch Duneier's (1999) study of street vendors near where he lived (Lofland et al. 2006:11). For our student readers, examples of starting where you are might include your college or university, where you live or work, student groups with which you are involved, or a place where you volunteer.

On the other hand, Saldaña advises against "starting where you are," at least for novices who want to study their friends. For one thing, according to Saldaña (2011:34), you may lose valuable insight into the process of "gaining entry." In familiar settings, especially where researchers have a direct personal or professional stake, they may also experience problems in overcoming their own particular views of reality and of holding their feelings in abeyance (Taylor and Bogdan 1998).

Wherever you start, you need to evaluate sites for their appropriateness, access, risks, and ethics (Lofland et al. 2006:Chapter 2). You should also document why you selected a particular setting or group (Bailey 1996:37).

Gain Access

An important consideration in selecting a setting or group may be your ability to gain access to it. A number of factors shape a researcher's ability to gain access, including personal characteristics, the nature of the setting, and gatekeepers and others from whom permission may be needed.

PERSONAL CHARACTERISTICS

A researcher's personal characteristics, such as gender, class, race/ethnicity, religion, sexuality, and disability status, may shape her or his ability to access certain settings and groups. The most obvious instance of this is when a setting or a group is explicitly closed to certain people. The public bathrooms for men studied by Laud Humphreys (1970) were closed to women. Some groups and institutions also are largely closed to outsiders. For example, it may not be possible to study an elite high school, in the manner Shamus Rahman Khan (2011) did, without the necessary educational prerequisites and other resources: he assumed a job as a teacher at his former alma mater St. Paul's School to understand the transmission of inequality through observations of students, faculty, and staff.

Smith's personal characteristics shaped access in his research. His knowledge of Spanish was essential to study a predominantly Spanish-speaking community. However, Smith's status as a male posed challenges in conducting interviews with women alone. In one instance, this evoked reflexivity. Reflecting on an interview of a woman he conducted with a female researcher, Smith (2006:105) wondered if the interviewee's openness was a function of another female's presence or the rapport he had established with the interviewee and her family.

As you prepare to conduct your own study, it is worth reflecting on how your personal or other characteristics may shape your access. Yet, these characteristics do not necessarily *determine* access, as Lofland and colleagues (2006:24) advise: "Just because you do not share certain characteristics with the persons you wish to study, you should not automatically conclude that such research is impossible or even unusually difficult." As an example, Sandra Meike Bucerius (2013) studied an all-male group of Muslim immigrants in Germany. Although her status as a female, Christian, and German with a middle-class background made her an "outsider" to the group, she was able to gain access partly because the immigrants wanted their stories told, typical of some marginalized groups (Bucerius 2013:698).

NATURE OF THE SETTING

A researcher's ability to gain access to a setting varies according to whether the setting is public, private, or something in between. A *public setting* is one that is open to everyone, such as a park, street corner, or a public restroom, thus making entrée relatively easy (Lofland et al. 2006). Observations in public settings typically do not require formal permission, although it can be a good idea to inform relevant authorities of the study. As an example, David Snow negotiated and legitimated access to a number of settings for his partner Leon Anderson in a study of the homeless in Austin, Texas. Letting police know proved useful later, as Anderson was arrested and jailed for violation of an open-container ordinance with two homeless men one evening. He was bailed out the same night, and as a result of prior negotiations with the local police, "his arrest record was subsequently expunged from the police file and the arresting officer was reprimanded" (Snow, Benford, and Anderson 1986:395).

Examples of *semi-public settings* include movie theaters, stores, and for adults, bars. A semi-public setting is open to the public, but there is generally an expectation that people in these settings will purchase an item or "do" something. Conducting observations in a movie theater's lobby for an extended period of time, for example, may arouse suspicion about the researcher, who also may be accused of loitering. As such, it is generally a good idea to speak with the owner or manager before you begin your research. Formal permission may also be required.

Private settings such as a person's home and a private club deny access to all but acknowledged members and invited guests; others may be considered intruders (Lofland 1973:19). These settings typically require formal permissions and may be the most challenging to access. In recruiting families for in-home observations, Annette Lareau (2011:351) sent each family a letter, which she followed up with a telephone call. But knowing the imposition of her research on the families, she found the process of securing permissions highly stressful.

GATEKEEPERS AND OTHER PERMISSIONS

The process of gaining access, according to Peregrine Schwartz-Shea and Dvora Yanow (2012:58), is like negotiating passage through "gates of various sorts." "Gates" refer to authorities in charge of a setting or group—traditionally called **gatekeepers** in field research—who can grant or deny permissions for entry. Some examples of gatekeepers include the family members living in a home to be visited and owners or managers of movie theaters. The concept of "gates" also refers to institutions or organizations from which permission may be needed to gain access (Schwartz-Shea and Yanow 2012). For example, depending on the topic of research, legal permissions may be required, or at least sought, as in Snow's contact with the local police in the homeless study.

gatekeeper Relevant authority whose permission is needed to gain access to a setting or group.

Researchers may need multiple permissions, as illustrated in Smith's study. He obtained permissions from a Ticuani youth group and the Committee. At a Committee meeting he was invited to attend, Smith (2006:351–52) explains:

I summarized my research and asked for their approval. The discussion was vigorous, with Committee members wanting to know how it would benefit the community, what I would use it for, and other questions. Younger Ticuanenses in the Youth Group [another group Smith studied] gave me their blessing and urged the Committee to do the same, which in the end they did, even giving me a letter of introduction to the Ticuani president.

Obtaining formal permission from gatekeepers, however, does not guarantee interpersonal access (Schwartz-Shea and Yanow 2012:60). In Smith's study, the authority of the New York-based Committee over Ticuani affairs was contested, and in some cases resented, making interpersonal access to local Ticuani politicians more challenging. Given permission from the Committee to study Ticuanense politics, Smith was taken aback when he delivered the letter of introduction to the Ticuani municipal president: "I expected him [the president] to ask how he could help. Instead, he looked at the letter, placed it in a drawer without commenting on it, and sat stiffly" (Smith 2006:352). The president was unimpressed by the Committee's approval because it was interpreted as undermining his power. What occurred subsequently, however, facilitated Smith's interpersonal access:

> Sensing that doors were closing, I told him that I had met only once with the Committee and that they had okayed my project, and then I excitedly told him that I was going to run in the Antorcha. I inquired if perhaps we could speak in two days, when I got back. He smiled, remarking that it was good that I was doing the Antorcha. (Smith 2006:352)

Smith further reported that the "initially reticent" president ultimately helped his research "a great deal in the end." Part of the reason the president and others helped is that "People liked the fact that I really wanted to learn about Ticuani life and to actively participate in its rituals and collective life in New York and Ticuani" (352).

Finally, gaining access is a process that requires negotiation and *re-negotiation* throughout the time one spends in the field (Bailey 1996). Gatekeepers and other actors change; so do you and your research. As an example, Smith (2006:5) notes that changes in his personal life after his first round of intensive fieldwork affected his relationships when he re-entered Ticuani for a second round:

> I had been making my own journey from graduate student to professor, and from engagement to marriage to my wife, Maura, and the birth of my two children, Liam and Owen. Meeting my wife and children led Ticuanense to see me as more real and gave us more in common.

Establish Roles and Relationships

When field research involves a degree of participation, the researcher must balance the requirements of the roles of *scientific observer* and *participant* in a group or community, as discussed earlier. In addition, as a participant, the researcher must work out how he or she will relate to those in the field, which often amounts to assuming a particular role in the group or setting being observed. Forming relationships is important as this will determine the level of rapport and trust that can be developed with others and the extent and type of information that can be gathered.

You are likely to have the broadest access to information if you can become a fully accepted member of the group or community. This would be possible if you could join the group you were studying. For instance, if you were studying a charitable organization, you could become a volunteer member of that organization. At other times, you might assume a functional role in the setting. In his study of a college basketball team, for example, Peter Adler (Adler and Adler 1991) could not become a member of the team or member of the coaching staff. However, Adler was able to become an informal consultant to the team, which evolved into the formally defined university role of Academic Advisor to the entire intercollegiate athletic program. Although not a member of the team or staff, in this role Adler could more easily relate to the players and coaches in a businesslike as well as personal way.

As an outsider, Robert Smith could not become a full member of the Ticuani community. But he thoroughly immersed himself in the community, so that he formed close relationships, many of which continue to the present day. There also were situations, such as in an instance of fending off dogs with a Ticuani youth while running in the Antorcha, when, as Smith (2006:184) writes, "I seemed to my informants and felt to myself like a person who belongs in and with Ticuanense youth, even if I was not formally one of them." In this way, he was able to relate to and better understand the Ticuanenses. At times, Smith also could relate more easily to others because of the functional role he assumed in the setting. For example, when he attended meetings of the Committee, he was seen as an "unofficial historian," as described earlier.

In general, the more immersed you are in the setting and the closer you are to attaining full-member status, the greater the acceptance by others, and the more likely the opportunity to gather data on the most personal and intimate matters. In addition, gaining full membership in a group or community enables researchers "to supplement the data they gather with the greatest degree of their own subjective insight" (Adler and Adler 1987:81). On the other hand, full membership is intense and time-consuming, may have profound personal consequences, and can create a conflict between the member and researcher roles.

The role you assume in your research may be shaped by a self-conscious decision about how much you want to participate. However, it also can be influenced by personal characteristics and your ability to access certain settings and group members.

Decide What to Observe/Whom to Interview

Field researchers' decisions about what to observe or whom to interview are partly influenced by practical considerations. It can be challenging to locate suitable observation sites, make fruitful contacts, and access records. Convenience, accessibility, and happenstance shape where researchers can begin to make observations, whom they will meet there, and whom they will find most informative.

Research questions also influence what field researchers observe. Broader, guiding questions may lead researchers to simply observe as much as they can, as in Lyn Lofland's study of grooming behavior. More focused questions may direct researchers to particular types of observation. Smith explicitly selected Committee meetings and events for observation, given its relevance to the transnationalization processes in which he was interested. Similarly, your research question may focus on dimensions of the setting or particular actors, events, or processes (Miles and Huberman 1994; Schwartz-Shea and Yanow 2012).

key informant A person from whom field researchers acquire information who is selected on the basis of knowledge, expertise, or status within the group.

Traditionally, field researchers also have relied on information provided by **key informants**—also called key actors or insiders (Bailey 1996)—who are selected on the basis of their knowledge, expertise, or status within the group. For Smith, it was important to gather information from people with knowledge of the local and transnational processes in which he was interested. Hence, one of his key informants in Ticuani was Don Andrés, "a former municipal president and teacher in Ticuani" (Smith 2006:41). Similarly, in the United States, his key informants included members of the Committee and a Ticuani youth group. As often occurs in field research, Smith selected many of the persons he interviewed through a process of "serial selection" (Lincoln and Guba 1985) similar to snowball sampling (see Chapter 6), in which initial informants introduced him to others.

Gather and Analyze Data

The data that a field researcher collects are vast and varied, consisting of direct observations and experiences, interviews, and supplementary archival data. Observations, the primary data in field research, are recorded in a variety of ways. To begin, a researcher may make an effort to remember significant details of what is observed. Although these "mental notes" may serve as one source of the "record," memory is a poor substitute for a written record. During the course of observation, therefore, field researchers usually take **field jottings**—"little phrases, quotes, key words, and the like" (Lofland et al. 2006:109). As a general rule, jottings should be made as inconspicuously as possible, which may require that the researcher wait until participants are out of sight. Based on these jottings, field researchers then write a more complete set of **field notes**—that is, detailed written accounts of field observations—at the end of each day or as soon after the observations as possible (Lofland et al. 2006). Above all, these notes are intended to be descriptive of what the researcher observed. In addition, they may include what the researcher thought or felt at the time as well as some preliminary analysis of the situation or setting (Saldaña 2011).

field jottings Brief quotes, phrases, and key words that are recorded by field researchers while in the field.

field notes Detailed written accounts of field observations, which may also include a researcher's reflections and preliminary analyses.

To show you what field jottings look like and how they can be transformed to notes, examine the partial example of field jottings below. These are from observations of a trial court proceeding in which the claimant, Marcia Snow, is pursuing a temporary restraining order (TRO) from two landlords, Robert Thomas and Mike Murphy, the latter of whom is not in court due to illness (Emerson et al. 2011:30–31). The jottings mainly capture quotes and phrases, albeit with the speakers unidentified and unclear statements indicated in parentheses. Much of the dialogue concerns the health of the co-defendant.

[case number]

Snow, Marcia

Thomas

atty—   AIDS Mike

Murphy

legal guardian

_____

are you prepared to proceed against

the one individual—(both)

massive doses of chemother(apy)

I don't think he's ever going to come in here

I know he's well enough to walk—

came in (returned heater)—when?

you can call his doctor at UCLA and

he can verify all this

I just don't call people on the

telephone—courts don't operate that way—it has to be on paper or (in

person) (Emerson et al. 2011:54)

____

An abbreviated example of the field notes based on the above jottings and the research-er's memory is presented below (Emerson et al. 2011:55). They describe the claimant (Marcia Snow [MS]), one of the co-defendants (Robert Thomas [RT]), and parts of the court proceedings, especially concerning the health of the other co-defendant, Mike Murphy (MM):

Marcia Snow has longish, curly, dark brown hair, in her 20s, dressed informally in blue blouse and pants. No wedding ring, but with a youngish looking guy with glasses. Robert Thomas is in his 40s, light brown hair, shaggy mustache, jacket with red-black checked lining. Judge begins by asking RT if he has an atty; he does, but he is not here. He explains that his business partner, Mike Murphy, who is also named in the TRO, is not here today; he has AIDS and is very ill. "I'm his legal guardian," so I can represent his concerns. J asks MS: "Are you prepared to proceed against this one individual?" MS answers that she wants the order against both of them. RT then explains that MM has had AIDS for three years, has had "massive doses of chemotherapy," and adds: "I don't think he's ever going to come in here." J asks MS if from what she knows that MM is this sick. MS hesitates, then says: "I know he's well enough to walk." I saw him walking when he returned the heaters that they stole. J: When was this? (I can't hear her answer.) RT: He's had his AIDS for three years. He's very sick. "You can call his doctor at UCLA, and he can verify this." J: "I just don't call people on the telephone. Courts don't operate that way. It has to be on paper" or testified in person. RT repeats that MM is very ill, that he has to take care of him, and he is not getting better. . . .

analytic memo An adjunct to field notes, observations, and interviews that consists of recorded analyses that come to mind in going over data.

Data analysis usually begins in field notes. As field notes are recorded or reviewed, analysis may be aided by writing **analytic memo**s, which Saldaña (2013:41) vividly describes as "somewhat comparable to research journal entries or blogs—a place to 'dump your brain' about the participants, phenomenon, or process under investigation by thinking and thus writing and thus thinking even more about them." Analytic memo writing is intended to help the researcher identify emergent empirical patterns and concepts in the data. Qualitative analytic techniques, further discussed in Chapter 13, are used throughout the process of field research, both during and after one has left the field.

Leave the Field

Except in rare cases in which the researcher decides to permanently live in the setting or among the group being studied, he or she must leave the field at some point. Given that field researchers often develop close relationships, this can be an emotionally difficult step. Nevertheless, according to Lofland and colleagues (2006:78), the process is similar to saying good-byes in everyday life, and the same advice for how to do so applies to field research as well:

> Most generally, don't burn your bridges. And, more specifically in keeping with the etiquette of departures: inform people of your plans ahead of time; explain why and where you are going; say your good-byes personally insofar as it is possible; and, if appropriate, promise to stay in touch.

Throughout the research—and especially when the researcher leaves—an important question of reciprocity arises: Given that participants have shared their lives with the researcher, what is his or her responsibility to them? Answers to this question vary; so, too, do researchers' strategies. For example, in addition to paying participants to be in her study, Annette Lareau stayed in contact with the families, sending their children birthday cards and gifts. Not only has Robert Smith maintained relationships with his informants, but he has also advised the Mexican government on the issues they face and was a cofounder of the Mexican Educational Foundation of New York (personal communication 2013).

Just as gaining access to a setting or group involves considering how people will relate to your presence as a researcher, leaving the field involves considering how people will relate to your absence. Consistent with the ethical principles outlined in Chapter 3, it is important to be careful and deliberate in relating your plans to leave and to think about what happens afterward.

Write the Report

The last step is to write the report. In final reports of field research, data take the form of vivid descriptions and verbatim statements as well as analytic summaries. The former are intended to provide the reader with an understanding of what it feels like to be in the setting or among the people being studied. An excellent example comes from Smith's description of the Ticuanenses:

> Being in Ticuani during the Feast of Padre Jesús, when the migrants return, and afterward, when they have left, feels like being in two different towns: the first is a bustling town where young people dance late into the night, families eat and laugh together and money flows, and the second is a nursery and nursing home where the young and old await the return of their relatives in New York. (Smith 2006:39)

Analytic summaries include discussions of themes, patterns, and anomalies in the data. Smith's theme that the Ticuanenses were united in a search for recognition and respect is one such example. Another example is his analysis of Don Emiliano and Don Gerardo, which he calls a "paired comparison" because their similarities and differences aid in understanding the reasons for their different gender ideologies (Smith 2006:95).

Like other authors, Smith highlights the importance of writing as a way of clarifying analysis and deepening thoughts. Writing occurs throughout the research process, both in and out of the field. As you embark on field research, don't underestimate the power of writing at all stages of your study.

SUMMARY

The process of conducting field research involves selecting a setting or group, gaining access, establishing roles and relationships, deciding what to observe/whom to interview, gathering and analyzing data, leaving the field, and writing the report. This process is nonlinear; researchers may move back and forth between steps. For example, a researcher may first gain access to a setting or group and then decide to study it; data analysis may affect subsequent decisions about what to observe and whom to interview. Gaining access is shaped by the researcher's personal characteristics, the nature of the setting, and gatekeepers and others from whom permission may be needed. Given that field research often involves some degree of participation, an important consideration is establishing relationships with others, which may be facilitated by assuming a functional role within the group or setting.

Analysis begins in the field and continues afterward, resulting in a final written report that includes vivid descriptions of the setting/group and analytic summaries.

THE PROCESS OF CONDUCTING IN-DEPTH INTERVIEWS

The process of conducting in-depth interviews is outlined in Figure 9.4. This process parallels field research and involves the following steps: select and recruit interviewees, develop interview guide, gather data, and analyze data. The process may also be nonlinear, with the researcher moving back and forth between steps. To illustrate this process, we will frequently rely on Vasquez's study. Recall that her guiding question concerned how Mexican Americans "come to their sense of racial identity"; her more focused questions concentrated on the process of identity formation within the family and in "other social arenas" as well as the relationship between racial identity and assimilation (Vasquez 2011:5–6).

Select and Recruit Interviewees

The first step is to select and recruit interviewees, which Vasquez's study illustrates. Her identification of potential interviewees began with her research question, which focused on first-, second-, and third-generation Mexican Americans. Her interest in race/ethnicity, which was influenced by her own background as "both non-Hispanic white and Mexican American" (Vasquez 2011:x), was piqued when she attended college on the east coast and was seen as an "all-or-nothing-Mexican" (ix–x). The focus on three generations was a response to a "hole" in the literature. Previous research had examined the experiences of the first and second generation, but had largely neglected the third. The third generation also was of personal interest, as Vasquez noted: "I am third generation Mexican American on one side of my family and there was virtually nothing that illuminated or helped explain my experience" (personal communication 2014). Finally, she selected the Santa Barbara/Los Angeles counties and San Francisco Bay area as sites for her research because the former have historically been a major immigrant destination and the sites have large Hispanic populations (23–24).

To recruit interviewees who met the research profile, Vasquez began by contacting several organizations. At first she "sent letters of inquiry"; then she "followed up with phone calls to the principals of twenty-one high schools, heads of thirteen Hispanic chambers of commerce, and twelve priests

FIGURE 9.4
The Process of Conducting In-Depth Interviews

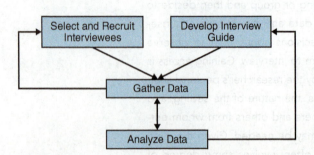

of Catholic churches" (Vasquez 2011:25). Upon the invitation of a contact, Vasquez also attended networking events through the chambers of commerce, where she was introduced to others. From these organizations, as well as through her colleagues at the University of California-Berkeley, she received names and contact information of potential interviewees.

Just as personal characteristics shape access in field research, they also shape recruitment efforts in interview research. Like Smith, Vasquez was reflexive about this. For example, she notes that her part-Latina identity and research topic "facilitated a bond with the people involved with the Hispanic chambers of commerce that allowed me to be quickly embraced" (Vasquez 2011:250). In e-mails, some potential interviewees expressed solidarity with Vasquez on the basis of their presumed common heritage or the topic of her research, which made them more inclined to want to participate (247).

As you embark on your own in-depth interview study, your research question will likely provide general guidance about whom to interview. For reasons of convenience and accessibility, however, you may need to limit your focus. Vasquez gives the following advice to novice researchers: "[D]on't be scared of your project. Understand that your project may morph as you proceed—you might sharpen your research question or revise your interview schedule—and that is *part* of the research process" (personal communication 2014).

Develop Interview Guide

The next step involves developing interview questions. As noted earlier, most in-depth interviews tend to be conducted individually (as well as face-to-face), using a semi-structured or unstructured format with almost exclusively open-ended questions. We suggest that novice interviewers begin with semi-structured interviews, making use of an **interview guide**. An interview guide, sometimes called an *interview protocol,* includes at least a list of topics and, depending on the planned structure of the interview, specific questions.

> **interview guide** A list of topics and specific questions to be asked in a qualitative interview.

To the extent that the interview guide includes specific questions, this requires writing out the questions beforehand. Figure 9.5 contains an abridged version of the interview guide that Vasquez used for the majority of her semi-structured interviews. Note how the guide is organized by broad topics but with specific questions. We refer to Figure 9.5 as we consider how to construct an interview guide.

To draft an interview guide, first consider the two primary types of questions asked in in-depth interviews: main questions and probes. The main questions are those most directly related to the research question. They are shaped by a researcher's knowledge or experience, the literature, or preliminary research (Rubin and Rubin 2012:134–35). In Vasquez's study, the main questions concerned people's family and immigrant histories as well as their experiences of race. **Probes** are follow-up questions used to gather additional detail and clarify responses. They may be written into an interview guide and/or asked spontaneously. An

> **probes** Follow-up questions used in surveys and in-depth interviews to gather more information about a respondent's answer.

FAMILY HISTORY & INTER-GENERATIONAL STORYTELLING

- KEY PEOPLE: Who were the key people in your family in your childhood?
- RELATIONSHIPS: Could you briefly describe your relationship with your: grandparents, parents, children, grandchildren (specifically those involved in this project)?
- LESSONS: What are some of the most important lessons your parents tried to teach you when you were growing up?
- FAMILY STORIES OR MEMORIES: Do you have any favorite "family stories or memories" from your youth?
- TRADITIONS: Are there any traditions or customs that stand out for you as you think about your youth?
- SAYINGS: What kinds of pithy sayings or quotations would your parents (or grandparents) commonly use?

IMMIGRATION

- **GEN 1:** Why did you decide to come to the U.S.? How did you come here?
- **GEN 1:** Were there any stories that you told your children and grandchildren about your move to the U.S.?
- **GEN 2 & 3:** Could you tell me how your (grand)parents came to the U.S.?

RACIAL LABELS & IDENTITY

- EARLIEST MEMORY OF RACE: Could you please tell me about the earliest memory you have about "something called race" (whether or not it was named at this point)?
- MIRROR: How do you think of yourself? When you look in the mirror, what do you see?
- FIRST TIME LABELED: Do you remember the first time someone told you that you were (Mexican) Mexican American?
  - o WHO?
  - o EXPLANATION & MEANING?
- [**ALL**] MEANING: What does it mean to you to be Mexican American?
- [**ALL**] KEY EVENTS: Are there any key events in your life that shaped your racial identity?

EXPERIENCES OF RACE

- ROLE OF RACE: What kind of "role" does race play in your life? (Does it matter? If so, how?)
- ACCESS/BARRED: Do you suspect that your race (or nationality) has helped you gain access to or, oppositely, barred you from a career opportunity or an area of social life you wanted to enter?
- DISCRIMINATION: Have you ever encountered discrimination?
  - o What happened and how did you react?
  - o *Did this affect how you saw yourself?*
- SPANISH: What is your Spanish language ability? How important is Spanish to you?
- IF NOT FLUENT: How do you feel about having limited Spanish ability?

MARRIAGE

- IF MARRIED: What is the racial/ethnic background of your spouse?
- [**ALL**] How important or unimportant to you is it to have your spouse be of a similar racial/ethnic background as yourself? Why?
- IF MARRIED: How has your affiliation to Mexican culture changed since marriage?
- [**ALL**] As you advise(d) (think about advising) your child(ren) in choosing a marriage partner, how important or unimportant would you say it is for a spouse to be of a similar racial/ethnic background?

CONCLUSION

Future

- PRESERVED: What about your culture or experience do you most want to see preserved and transmitted to the next generation?
- CHANGED: What about your culture or experience do you most want to see changed in the next generation?

Wrap-Up

- Apart from what we have already covered, are there other cultural experiences that are important to you or have significantly impacted your life?
- Would you like to add to or clarify anything we have discussed thus far?
- Is there anything I did not ask but that I should have?

FIGURE 9.5

Abridged Version of Interview Guide used for Mexican Americans across Generations

example of a probe in Vasquez's interview guide is the question asking for more information about experiences of discrimination: "What happened and how did you react?"

As you write drafts of questions, you should carefully consider their wording. Some of the tips for writing survey questions, discussed in Chapter 8, apply to in-depth interview questions as well: For example, the questions should be clear and unbiased, and should contain familiar words and avoid technical jargon. Yet, in-depth interviews allow researchers greater freedom in constructing questions because you need not specify response options, as in closed-ended questions, and you can make liberal use of probes to clarify and amplify the meaning of answers. Ordinarily, for example, it is not a good idea to ask too many either/or questions or questions that elicit one-word or brief responses; however, these can effectively set up probing follow-up questions. For example, Vasquez's interview guide includes some questions to which people may answer "yes" or "no" (e.g., "Do you remember the first time someone told you that you were (Mexican) Mexican-American?"). But note that these are often followed by probes intended to get richer and more detailed information (e.g., asking for an explanation and the meaning of Mexican heritage).

As in surveys, question order is also important. However, the more flexible nature of in-depth interviews makes the exact placement of questions less important than the overall "rhythm" of the interview: Ideally, the interview should begin with questions that are easy to answer and end on a neutral or positive note (Charmaz 2006; Rubin and Rubin 2012). Opening questions may include a few background questions or a **grand tour** (or simply, **tour**) question. A tour question asks interviewees for a broad description of the people, processes, or events being studied (Rubin and Rubin 2012). As the name implies, a tour question gives the interviewee an opportunity to "walk the interviewer around" the topic, as in Vasquez's question on family relationships: "Could you briefly describe your relationship with your: grandparents, parents, children, grandchildren...?" Also consistent with guidelines for survey interviews, she placed the potentially sensitive questions on the topic of race in the middle of the interview. Finally, her guide concludes with a wrap-up section, which includes a question asking if interviewees want to add or clarify anything.

Vasquez's interview guide and questions were refined throughout the process of conducting several interviews. A great way to refine a guide is by posing the question Vasquez asked at the end of her interview: "Is there anything I did not ask but that I should have?" Preparing for the interview involves other considerations beyond the construction of an interview guide. Some of these are discussed in Box 9.3, DOING SOCIAL RESEARCH: Preparing for an In-Depth Interview.

grand tour question
A broad opening question in in-depth interviews that asks for a general description of the people, processes, or events being studied. Also called *tour question*.

Gather Data

The next step is to gather data. In qualitative interviews, the quality and depth of the data partly depend on the rapport that the interviewer establishes with the interviewee. Although there is no recipe for establishing rapport (King and Horrocks 2010:48), you can do a few things to make the interviewee feel comfortable. For example, you should

---

BOX 9.3

Preparing for an In-Depth Interview

In final reports, researchers rarely recount every single step they take in carrying out research, and interview preparation is an area that often receives little or no attention. Yet the amount and type of preparation can have a major impact on the quality of the interview.

Unlike surveys, in which interviews begin immediately after interviewers contact and gain the cooperation of respondents, in-depth interviews are almost always scheduled in advance, after the successful recruitment of the person to be interviewed. So, to begin, you need to contact the person to schedule a time and place for the interview. Saldaña (2011:34–35) recommends scheduling the interview on a day and in a time block "in which the participant will not feel fatigued or rushed, if possible"; moreover, the location of the interview should be as comfortable, private, and free of distractions as is possible. If you are scheduling multiple interviews on the same day, you should give yourself ample time to rest in between (Rubin and Rubin 2012).

Prior to the scheduled date and time, you should remind the participant(s) of the interview. You also should prepare an informed consent form and be prepared to answer questions about how you will protect confidentiality.

On the day of the interview, it is a good idea to arrive early, make sure that the location is still well suited for interviewing, and check audio or video equipment, if used, for proper functioning. Some researchers may bring water to the interview for participants and themselves to prevent dry mouth; researchers may also provide candy or lozenges (Rubin and Rubin 2012; Saldaña 2011).

"enter the interview with an attitude of courtesy and respect," treating interviewees "as if they are important invited guests to [your] home" (Saldaña 2011:39). You also may "chitchat" with interviewees before the interview starts as a way of establishing a more relaxed atmosphere (Rubin and Rubin 2012).

Prior to beginning the formal interview, you should explain the nature of the study and acquire verbal or written consent; you also should ask permission to use an audio or tape recorder if that is part of the research. Here you might want to follow the procedure that Robert Weiss (2004:46) uses:

> I bring two copies of consent forms describing the study to my interviewees, both copies bearing my signature. After briefly explaining the study, I give both forms to the respondent, ask him or her to read one and, if comfortable with it, to sign one of the copies and keep the other. I usually have a tape recorder and ask if it is all right to turn it on.

As you begin to ask questions, recall that the purpose of the interview is often to obtain *in-depth* responses. Though probes may be written into an interview guide, you will likely need to ask for more information on the basis of people's responses. Weiss (2004:47) provides a good example of a spontaneous probe: "If a respondent says, 'We got along fine,' the interviewer should ask something like, 'When you say that, what are you thinking of?' or 'Can you tell me the last time that happened?' or 'Can you think of a time that really showed that happening?'"

The rest of the interview process largely depends on the type of interview being conducted—its focus, level of structure, and the number of participants. As is typical with in-depth interviews, Vasquez's questions were not rigid and each interview was "unique." She writes, "Even with an interview schedule, some questions were covered in depth while others were briefly touched on. Depending on interviewer-interviewee dynamic and rapport, an interviewee's life history, and personal style, the interview takes on its own form" (Vasquez 2011:251–52). With time, you may rely on your guide/schedule to a lesser extent, as Vasquez (251) did:

> In the course of an interview, I would juggle peering down periodically at my interview schedule while at the same time listening to the interviewee's narrative for thematic leads to follow. As I became comfortable with interviewing and my interview schedule became seared into my memory, I realized that I was conversationally delivering my questions.

Regardless of the type of interview, the interview typically ends with the researcher thanking the participant, exchanging contact information, and assessing the participant's feelings. As Rubin and Rubin (2012:89) state, "Your interviewees should be no worse off, and ideally should be better off, for having taken the time to talk to you." According to Vasquez (2011:245), "While some [of her] respondents found the interview difficult to the extent that it brought up sensitive topics, most ended their encounter with me with an expression of neutral or positive emotion." One of her interviewees found the interview particularly beneficial; as he said, "Wow, this is like therapy. I haven't been this open with anyone besides my close friends in a long time" (245). At the same time, researchers need to be particularly sensitive to potential risks to interviewees such as discomfort; they also should remind interviewees that they are not therapists and provide them with necessary resources after the interview is completed (Johnson and Rowlands 2012; Rubin and Rubin 2012).

Like observational data, interview data may be recorded in jottings and more detailed notes, but it is recommended to use audio or video devices, either alone or in combination with jottings and notes. Recall, for example, that Vasquez recorded her interviews in addition to taking notes. This gave her a complete verbatim record to which she could return again and again. On the other hand, interviews need to be transcribed, and in some cases—as in both Smith's and Vasquez's studies—translated. And this can take a great deal of time.

Table 9.1 Points of Divergence Between Thinned Attachment and Cultural Maintenance

	Thinned Attachment	Cultural Maintenance
Marriage	Exogamous	Endogamous
Gender Ideologies	Transitional/Egalitarian	Traditional/Transitional
Religion	Catholic or nonpracticing/Converted	Catholic
Spanish	English monolingual to bilingual	Bilingual
Personal Traits	Spanish surname or non; European phenotype or non	Spanish surname; Non-European phenotype
Social Context (Peers)	Heterogeneous/White	Heterogeneous/Mexican

Source: Table 3.1 in Vasquez (2011:65).

Analyze Data

Once interview data are transcribed, they need to be analyzed. A primary means of analysis is coding, or sorting data into categories, as was defined in Chapter 8. Qualitative interview data are sorted into categories represented by *words*, not *numbers* as in survey research. Moreover, codes are not usually predefined as in survey research, but rather emerge through an inductive analytic process. As further discussed in Chapter 13, the analyst often attempts to identify broader themes and patterns and discern how they relate to one another. Vasquez notes that she followed this general approach, using ATLAS.ti, a qualitative data analysis software program, to code and analyze her data. Initially, she coded her interviews in terms of keywords. Then, "working inductively," she coded emergent themes as she built her arguments (Vasquez 2011:263). She also attempted to discern exceptions in the data, such as where patterns broke down (personal communication 2014).

In the final research reports, the product of data analysis can take the form of rich description, as in field research, and theoretical conclusions. One product of Vasquez's data analysis was the previously described conceptual distinction between "thinned attachment" and "cultural maintenance" forms of identification with Mexican heritage. Table 9.1, from Vasquez's book, shows how these forms were related to other factors.

SUMMARY

The process of conducting in-depth interviews involves selecting and recruiting interviewees, developing an interview guide, gathering data, and analyzing data. Like the process of conducting field research, the steps may be completed in different orders. Selecting and recruiting interviewees is guided by the research question and ease of access. Developing an interview guide involves selecting good main questions and appropriate probes, and paying attention to question wording and order. Gathering data involves establishing rapport with interviewees, listening carefully, taking notes, and recording and transcribing interviewees' responses. Data analysis begins with coding in an attempt to find emergent patterns and themes as well as to understand how patterns and themes are related to one another.

STRENGTHS AND LIMITATIONS OF QUALITATIVE RESEARCH

Many social scientists favor qualitative research because they believe it addresses some of the limitations of experiments, surveys, and other quantitative methods. Of course, like all research methods, it has its own set of weaknesses. Understanding these strengths and limitations will help you not only to evaluate qualitative research, but also to decide if this is an appropriate method to use in your own research.

Naturalistic Approach

On balance, qualitative research is considered to be a more "naturalistic" approach than methods of quantitative data collection. Whereas experiments involve observing people in a lab or other contrived situations, field research involves observing people in their natural settings—in their homes, their places of work, where they volunteer, and so forth. Whereas surveys ask people to answer questions according to pre-constructed categories, qualitative interviews allow people to describe their feelings and experiences in their own words, similar to everyday conversation. In these ways, qualitative research better captures the naturally occurring elements of social life.

Subjective and Contextual Understanding

Another strength of qualitative research is that it can provide an in-depth understanding of social-cultural meanings, processes, and contexts. To a greater extent than other methods, this understanding is achieved through the development of relationships and interactions, which, as Robert Smith (2006:351) suggests, enable the researcher "to see social processes that might otherwise remain hidden." By participating in the activities of people being studied, field researchers especially can gain an insider's view of people's worlds that quantitative methods do not allow. Qualitative interviews can provide in-depth insights into people's thoughts, feelings, and experiences that may not be possible without establishing the kind of rapport and trust with participants characteristic of this method.

Furthermore, as sociologists know all too well, it is difficult to disentangle the effects of people's social context from their experiences. Experiments attempt to standardize the setting, while survey research sometimes employs statistical controls to capture some aspects of the context. By studying people *within* their sociocultural contexts, field research provides a view of people embedded within their environments.

Flexible Research Design

A final strength of qualitative research is its flexible research design. Because of its flexibility, qualitative research lends itself well to studies of dynamic situations and settings as well to studies of populations that otherwise may be difficult to access. Suppose, for example, you are interested in how people cope with the aftermath of a natural disaster. People's responses are likely to depend on the severity of the disaster and the length of time since the disaster occurred. To determine the immediate impact of a calamitous event, you would have to act quickly to get to the site, observe, and interview; otherwise, the opportunity to understand certain reactions may be lost. Drafting a questionnaire or designing a probability sample of households would result in the loss of valuable time and information. Similarly, there are many groups and sub-populations for which there is no sampling frame, which is the basis of probability sampling. Among them are homeless people (Snow and Anderson 1993), women in the hate movement (Blee 2003), and members of a gang (Venkatesh 2008). The non-probability sampling techniques characteristic of qualitative research design afford researchers the flexibility to find these populations "where they are."

Another important strength of the flexibility inherent in qualitative research design is well stated by Kathy Charmaz (2006:14): "Qualitative researchers have one great advantage over our quantitative colleagues. We can add new pieces to the research puzzle or conjure entire new puzzles—*while we gather data*—and that can even occur late in the analysis." Once beyond the pretesting stage of an experiment or survey, for example, quantitative researchers are fairly locked into their design. The standardization requisite of experiments and surveys does not afford quantitative researchers the opportunity to significantly change their data collection methods mid-course, although they may (and often do) conduct post-hoc statistical analyses to explore unanticipated findings.

Generalizability

Compared to surveys, which are characterized by probability sampling, qualitative research shares with experiments a similar weakness: an inability to generalize findings to a specific population. Qualitative research is particularly adept at providing *theoretical* generalizations, but the strength of these inferences is contingent upon the care and judgment of researchers in selecting cases. One way to improve theoretical generalizations is to select cases based on their similarities with and differences from other cases. Another strategy is to sample in a way that maximizes variation in the settings and groups observed (Schwartz-Shea and Yanow 2012:85–89). David Snow and Leon Anderson (1991:155) used this strategy in their study of the homeless by spending "time with as many homeless as possible in the range of settings most relevant to their daily lives."

Reliability and Validity

Another limitation that is the object of some debate concerns the quality of the data. On the one hand, as we noted above, qualitative research can yield an insider's view of reality and an in-depth, holistic understanding that is beyond the reach of quantitative approaches. In this sense, qualitative researchers argue, their data have greater validity. Because of the depth of the relationships qualitative researchers establish, they observe more honest behavior and get more truthful responses to their questions than the experimenter or survey researcher.

On the other hand, most qualitative research is carried out by a single observer or interviewer. The reliability and validity of the data, therefore, are highly dependent on the observational, interactive, and interpretive skills of the researcher; without the usual controls found in experiments and surveys, findings may be influenced more by the researcher's personal biases; and it is easy to imagine how another observer may see things quite differently. Furthermore, despite investigators' best efforts to blend into the setting and establish rapport as a way of encouraging participants to act and speak as they would "naturally," qualitative research may still be susceptible to reactive measurement effects. As discussed in Chapter 10, only some forms of existing/available data analysis are immune to this problem. Finally, just as surveys may not yield honest and accurate answers to questions, in-depth interviews may not either.

Researchers can effectively address some of these concerns. One of the simplest ways to enhance reliability is to conduct team research with two or more investigators. This was the approach taken by Snow and Anderson (1993) in their field research on the homeless in Austin, Texas. Smith also used this approach at times, conducting observations and interviews with students and other researchers. Qualitative researchers may also improve the quality of their data by comparing findings across different data sources: observations, interviews, and supplementary archival data. Cross-checking interviewees' accounts with other data, for instance, can assess the presence of reactivity effects as well as the tendency for interviewees to forget or misremember. This is the general model followed by field researchers, although it may not be used to the same extent in in-depth interviews as a stand-alone method. In both field research and qualitative interviews, however, interviewees' accounts of events sometimes can be cross-checked against one another, as in Vasquez's study.

Efficiency

Efficiency is an important consideration as you prepare to embark on your own research, likely with limited time and resources. So, it is important to realize that qualitative research can be labor-intensive and very time-consuming. To gain the kind of in-depth understanding that field research seeks to achieve, researchers must establish an accepted presence and develop relationships in the field, which can take a great deal of time and effort. And while in-depth interviews take considerably less time than field research to conduct, they tend to take longer than surveys because of the greater difficulty in selecting and recruiting interviewees and because of the greater investment made in each interview. Moreover, the amount and the form of the data often make qualitative analysis far more time-consuming than the analysis of quantitative data. On the other hand, if conducted at some nearby location, field research can be the least expensive approach. It does not require elaborate tools or equipment and, since it is typically conducted entirely by a single investigator, requires no additional personnel or training beyond the preparation of the investigator.

SUMMARY

The greatest strengths of qualitative research are its naturalistic approach, ability to provide subjective and contextual understandings, and flexible research design. However, qualitative research may have limited generalizability; the quality of the data depends heavily on the observational and interpretive skills of individual researchers; and it can be a relatively inefficient approach to gathering and analyzing data. Among the strategies that can strengthen field research are purposive case selection and sampling for maximum variation, employing a team approach, and comparing findings across different data sources and/or participants.

KEY TERMS

analytic memo, p. 280

covert observation, p. 266

ethnography, p. 250

field jottings, p. 278

field notes, p. 278

focus group, p. 271

gatekeeper, p. 275

grand tour question, p. 285

guiding question, p. 272

in-depth interview, p. 258

interview guide, p. 283

key informant, p. 278

nonparticipant observation, p. 264

overt observation, p. 266

participant observation, p. 264

probes, p. 283

reflexivity, p. 262

KEY POINTS

- The two principal methods of qualitative research are field research, which is based primarily on observation, and in-depth interviewing.
- In addition to observations and interviews, qualitative researchers tend to use supplementary archival data, nonprobability sampling, and qualitative data analysis.
- A unique feature of qualitative research is reflexivity, or researchers' reflections on how their experiences and personal characteristics influence the acquisition of knowledge.
- Observations in field research vary in the researcher's level of participation in the groups and settings under observation and the extent to which the researcher reveals his or her identity as a researcher.

- Interviews vary in structure, ranging from unstructured conversations to semi-structured in-depth interviews, and in number of interviewees.
- In focus group interviews, the researcher acts as a moderator or facilitator of group discussion and observes interaction among participants.
- The nonlinear process of conducting field research includes selecting a setting/group, gaining access, establishing roles and relationships, deciding what to observe/whom to interview, gathering and analyzing data, exiting the field, and writing a report.
- The nonlinear process of conducting qualitative interviews includes selecting and recruiting interviewees, developing an interview guide, gathering data, and analyzing data.
- The strengths of qualitative research include its naturalistic approach, ability to provide subjective and contextual understandings, and flexible research design.
- Qualitative research is highly dependent on the interpersonal and interpretive skills of the researcher, may be subject to reactive measurement effects, tends to be limited in generalizability, and is usually labor-intensive and time-consuming.

REVIEW QUESTIONS

1. What are the six general features of qualitative research?
2. How can observations and interviews complement one another in qualitative research?
3. Give an example of reflexivity from Smith's or Vasquez's study.
4. Using Figure 9.2 as a reference, describe the ways in which observations in field research vary.
5. What are the relative advantages and disadvantages of group interviews as compared to individual interviews?
6. Give an example of how a researcher's personal characteristics may affect (a) field research and (b) in-depth interviews.
7. How and when do field researchers record their observations?
8. Describe how the processes of conducting (a) field research and (b) in-depth interviews are "nonlinear."
9. What are the major strengths and limitations of qualitative research?

EXERCISES

1. In final reports of quantitative and qualitative research, authors rarely report all the details of their studies, especially problems they encountered or mistakes they made. A special issue of the *Journal of Contemporary Ethnography* (39, no. 5 [2010]) includes some of these "seldom told tales from the field." Read this issue and identify some of the challenges that qualitative researchers face.

2. In the January 1991 issue of the *Journal of Contemporary Ethnography* (19, no. 4: 423–49), David Snow, Cherylon Robinson, and Patricia McCall describe a participant observation study in which they examined the strategies women use to "fend off men and parry their advances" in public places. Read this article and then answer the following questions.

   (a) What are the two interconnected questions that the researcher's address? What is the "cooling out process" and how does it apply to these research questions?

   (b) Why do the researchers select singles bars, cocktail lounges, and other nightspots to study the cooling out process?

   (c) What three means of data collection do the researchers use?

   (d) How do the semi-structured interviews complement the data obtained from participant observation?

   (e) Based on the section entitled "Avoidance Tactics," provide one example of how data from participant observation and semi-structured interviews corresponded to one another.

   (f) What do the researchers claim about the generalizability of their findings to the cooling out process in other public settings?

3. As suggested earlier, there is more to observation than meets the eye. To better understand this, select a public setting, such as a cafeteria, coffee shop, library, or student lounge where you can unobtrusively observe others without anyone questioning your presence. Your research objective is to describe as fully as possible how people use this space. Are they alone or with others? In what sort of activities are they engaged? How long are they in the setting? And so forth. Before entering the field, you should consider what to observe and record: think about dimensions of the setting, actors, events, and processes. Plan to observe for at least an hour during a relatively busy time of the day and focus on a clearly delimited area such as a set of tables. Record your field notes as soon after leaving the field as possible, then go over your notes and develop a coding scheme for organizing the information.

4. Suppose you want to gain valuable qualitative interview practice by interviewing members of your own family about their cultural heritage. Using Vasquez's interview guide as a model (see Figure 9.5), develop an interview guide.

5. One of the best ways of learning is by doing—and, sometimes, making mistakes. To learn about some common challenges that students experienced in conducting in-depth interviews, read Kathryn Roulston, Kathleen deMarrais, and Jamie B. Lewis's "Learning to Interview in the Social Sciences" (*Qualitative Inquiry* 9, no. 4 [2003]: 643–68). Then, with the appropriate permissions, conduct a recorded interview yourself and analyze it, preferably with a seasoned researcher (as these authors analyze their students' interviews), to determine how you can improve your interviewing skills.

10

Existing Data Analysis

Using Data from Secondhand Sources

STUDENT LEARNING OBJECTIVES

By the end of this chapter, you should be able to

1. Give examples of the range and potential uses of existing data.

2. Explain the variations in existing data analysis, distinguishing among the analysis of existing statistics, content analysis, and comparative historical analysis.

3. Describe the steps in analyzing existing statistics and apply them to a research topic.

4. Describe the steps in content analysis and apply them to a research topic.

5. Describe the steps in comparative historical analysis and apply them to a research topic.

6. Evaluate existing data analysis as a general approach to social research, identifying its strengths and limitations.

Having discussed experiments, surveys, field research, and in-depth interviews in previous chapters, in this chapter we explore the analysis of existing data. What does existing data analysis have to do with you? You may have made a very important life decision on the basis of it. As you considered what college or university to attend, you might have examined four-year graduation rates presented in school brochures or posted on websites. You also may have researched the *U.S. News and World Report* Best Colleges rankings (see https://www.usnews.com/best-colleges). For the most part, *U.S. News* does not collect original data; rather, it relies on data that schools routinely collect and provide, which it supplements with information from other sources. *U.S. News* then compiles and analyzes these data to produce the numerical rankings, which are determined by several factors, including students' graduation rates, alumni giving, faculty resources, and overall financial resources.

This example captures the essence of *existing data analysis*. Existing data analysis departs from experiments, surveys, field research, and in-depth interviews in that it makes use of data produced by others, regardless of whether these data were intended for the purposes of research. Data can be found everywhere—death certificates, business personnel records, newspaper articles, Google trends, and even garbage. The sources are limited only by the researcher's imagination.

We begin the chapter by describing the diversity of data available to the imaginative researcher. Some existing data, such as statistics on births, deaths, marriages, and the like, are inherently quantitative; other data, such as letters and diaries, are best analyzed qualitatively. Thus, the diverse sources of existing data give rise to very different forms of analysis, with distinct research purposes. To illustrate the analysis of existing data, we consider three major methods: analysis of existing statistical data, content analysis, and comparative historical analysis. In each case, we present a research example that addresses a contemporary social issue, and describe the general process of carrying out the particular form of social research. We conclude by discussing general strengths and limitations of existing data analysis.

SOURCES AND EXAMPLES OF EXISTING DATA

The sources of existing data may be placed in five broad categories: (1) public documents and official records, including the extensive archives of the Census Bureau; (2) private documents; (3) mass media; (4) physical, nonverbal materials; and (5) social science data archives. Although these categories provide a useful summary of data sources, keep in mind that they overlap and that analysts may draw on more than one data source in any given study.

Public Documents and Official Records

Exemplifying the existing data approach is the historian who searches the written record for traces of events and processes from the past. A great deal of this record is public and can be found in **archives**—document collections located in physical and digital libraries. In addition, documents created to ensure the normal functioning of offices and departments are maintained at every level of government in every society throughout the world. These include the proceedings of government bodies, court records, state laws, and city ordinances. Many government agencies also maintain numerous volumes of official statistics. Add to this directories, almanacs, and publication indexes such as the *New York Times Index* and *Reader's Guide to Periodical Literature*, and one can imagine the massive information available from public records.

An especially rich data source is **vital statistics**: data on births, deaths, marriages, divorces, and the like. By state law, all births must be recorded, and death records must be filed before burial permits can be obtained. Birth records provide information not only on the child born but also on the parents, including their full names, address(es), ages, and usual occupations. Similarly, death records may contain, in addition to the usual biographical information, data on cause of death; length of illness (where applicable); whether injuries were accidental, homicidal, or self-inflicted; and the time and place of death. Ordinarily, the researcher obtains these records from an agency such as the Centers for Disease Control and Prevention (CDC), which compiles data for the nation as a whole, or from international organizations such as the United Nations, which compile such statistics for the world. One of the earliest sociological studies to make use of official records—in this case, statistics compiled from death records—was Émile Durkheim's classic study *Suicide* (1951), discussed at length in Chapter 2.

Perhaps the most widely used public storehouse of data is that collected and maintained by the US Bureau of the Census. According to the Constitution, every person in the nation must be counted at least once every 10 years. The censuses of population and housing gather information on the composition of every household in the country. In 2010, this included data on the age, gender, and race of each person, number of household members, and whether the residence was a house, apartment, or mobile home. Data from these decennial censuses, which began in 1790, are made available in two different forms: aggregate and individual. Aggregate data are released within months of their collection and describe various characteristics of the population of the states, counties, metropolitan areas, cities and towns, neighborhood tracts, and blocks.

Social scientists have used these data to study everything from the ecology of cities to residential mobility to racial segregation. In Chapter 5, we mentioned John Logan and Brian Stults's (2011) use of US censuses of the population to trace changes in racial/ethnic segregation from 1980 to 2010. The unit of analysis in this study is the census tract, which is a set of geographical boundaries somewhat comparable to what would be considered a neighborhood. By aggregating data to describe geographical units rather

archive A physical or digital library that contains a collection of historical documents or records.

vital statistics Data collected from the registration of "vital" life events, such as births, deaths, marriages, and divorces.

than individuals, the Census Bureau protects the privacy of individual persons, which it is sworn to do. However, after a period of 72 years, individual census records—known as the *manuscript census*—are released to the general public.

Beginning with the 1960 census, the bureau also has made available individual-level data (actual census responses) on a sample of the population, called the Public Use Microdata Sample (PUMS). A 1 percent PUMS sample is available for 1960 and 1970 and both 1 percent and 5 percent samples are available for subsequent censuses. To ensure confidentiality, the bureau removes names, addresses, and all other personal identifying information from these sample files. A project called IPUMS (the "I" is for "Integrated") is extending this series to other years and integrating the data over time by creating uniform codes for variables (IPUMS USA 2017). All IPUMS data are available free over the Internet at https://usa.ipums.org/usa/. In addition to the variables available through the Census, the IPUMS data include information such as people's wages, country of birth, and citizenship status. Quincy Thomas Stewart and Jeffrey Dixon (2010) used these data to analyze racial disparities in wages among native- and foreign-born men in 2000. Among their findings were that many of the well-known racial disparities in wages, such as that whites earn more than blacks and Latinos, extend to immigrants as well, even after statistically controlling for factors like citizenship status, English-speaking ability, and length of time in the United States.

Private Documents

A less accessible but no less important data source is private documents: information produced by individuals or organizations about their own activities that is not intended for public consumption. Diaries and letters long have been a favorite data source for the historian; other examples would be businesses' personnel and sales records, inventories, and tax reports; hospital patient records; and college transcripts.

An example of the use of private documents is Julie Kmec's (2007) study of the role of race and social networks in job turnover, which drew upon personnel records from a private business. The company maintained a database of job applicants and hires over 32 months, which was long enough for Kmec to observe routine turnover. In addition, the database contained information on the sex and race of applicants and, most importantly for examining network effects, on how applicants contacted the company. Examining persons hired for one entry-level position, Kmec found that, irrespective of race, workers recruited by a current employee of the company were less likely to leave voluntarily than workers recruited in other ways. Apparently, informal ties with a current employee provide social support and enrichment that bind workers to the company.

Institutional records also have been used to supplement survey data. In Chapter 12 we describe a survey in which undergraduate interviewees were asked for permission to access their college records, so that their grades, SAT scores, and high school class rank could be related to their self-reported level of alcohol consumption (Singleton 2007).

Mass Media

Also constituting part of the written record (as well as an oral and nonverbal record) are the mass media—books, newspapers, magazines, television, radio, films, the Internet. By analyzing the content of these sources, social researchers have addressed a variety of issues, from how fame is perpetuated in the media (van de Rijt et al. 2013) to cultural influences on Facebook photographs (Huang and Park 2013) to how news reports in the *New York Times* helped to define obesity as a social problem (Boero 2012).

The content of mass media may reflect as well as influence social relations in the larger society. Therefore, many researchers have analyzed media depictions of segments of society, particularly women and racial/ethnic minorities, as a way of gauging social structure and change. For example, in Chapter 4 we described a study that analyzed portrayals of blacks in children's picture books in the mid- to late-20th century and stories of racial conflict reported in the *New York Times* (Pescosolido, Grauerholz, and Milkie 1997). During this time, it was found, decreases and increases in blacks' visibility corresponded to the rise and fall of racial conflict.

Physical, Nonverbal Evidence

Although seldom used in the social sciences, nonverbal materials such as works of art, clothing, household items, and various artifacts constitute a rich source of evidence. Cave paintings, tools, and other artifacts are important data to archaeologists studying past civilizations, and historians find invaluable evidence in sculpture and other works of art.

One of the most interesting uses of physical evidence is the late William Rathje's Garbage Project, a long-term study of household refuse as a measure of consumer behavior (Rathje and Murphy 1992a, b). For over 30 years, Rathje studied garbage, mostly around Tucson, Arizona, but in several other areas as well. His analysis of refuse revealed much about contemporary culture and behavior that is of interest not only to social scientists but also to government, industry, and citizens concerned about the environment. Among Rathje's findings are that Americans waste about 15 percent of all solid food brought into the home; that they waste less now than in the past, probably as the result of improved refrigeration, transportation, processing, and packaging; and that in the 1980s the presence of plastics in garbage markedly increased, creating many environmental problems.

data archives
Repositories of survey, ethnographic, or qualitative interview data collected by various agencies and researchers that are accessible to the public.

Social Science Data Archives

Over the last 50 years, the social sciences have seen a tremendous proliferation of **data archives**, repositories of data collected by various agencies and researchers that are accessible to the public. Most of these archives contain survey data, but archives also exist for collections of ethnographies and in-depth interviews. Thus the use of data archives is an extension of survey research, field research, and in-depth interviews.

We already mentioned the analysis of existing survey data, called *secondary analysis,* in Chapter 8. A noteworthy example is the General Social Survey (GSS), whose data are deposited in several archives, including the ICPSR (Inter-University Consortium for Political and Social Research) and the Survey Documentation and Analysis Archive. Through these archives, you can find other survey datasets, such as the American National Election Studies, which is often used in studies on political attitudes and behaviors. In addition, GESIS (the Leibniz Institute for the Social Sciences) houses several international survey datasets, such as the European Values Survey (EVS) and the International Social Survey Programme (ISSP).

Social scientists also analyze data derived from studies of whole societies. One valuable archive of such data, called the Human Relations Area Files (HRAF), contains information recorded on microfiche and/or electronically on more than 350 cultures. These files, fully indexed with many available online, are in "raw data" form, with pages from ethnographic reports organized by topic. Two other sources of cross-cultural data available in "coded" form, with numeric codes on several variables for each society, are the *Ethnographic Atlas* (Murdock 1967) and the Standard Cross-Cultural Sample (SCCS) (Murdock and White 1969). The *Atlas* contains codes on approximately 40 variables for over 1,100 societies; the SCCS contains more extensive data on a smaller sample of 186 societies. Using all three of these data sources, Willie Pearson and Lewellyn Hendrix (1979) tested the hypothesis that divorce increases as the status of women increases. This follows from the theory that as women gain economic resources they become more autonomous and less dependent on their husbands. Based on data from 48 tribal societies, the findings showed that divorce rates were moderately correlated with female status as measured, for example, by the ability to inherit property and to achieve positions also held by men.

SUMMARY

As you can see, there is an abundance of existing data that may be used to address a wide range of research questions. Sources of these data include public documents and official statistics maintained by virtually every society throughout the world; private and personal records; mass media; physical, nonverbal materials; and social science data archives. In the remainder of the chapter, we focus on publicly accessible data and mass media, which comprise much of existing data research.

ANALYSIS OF EXISTING STATISTICAL DATA

Aside from the secondary analysis of surveys, the most widespread use of existing data in the social sciences is the analysis of existing statistics. In addition to vital statistics and census data, mentioned above, government agencies and international organizations publish a vast array of statistics. Table 10.1 presents a short, partial list of official-data sources and the kinds of statistics they provide. These statistics are the primary data sources for many studies. They also are used as supplementary information; as we saw in Chapter 9, for example, Robert Smith cited statistics on Mexican immigration to the United States and Jessica Vasquez presented data on the Hispanic population in California to establish the geographical and historical contexts of their research.

One area of social research that relies almost exclusively on official statistics is **demography**, the study of the structure of and changes in human populations. Demographers examine the size, composition, and geographical distribution of populations by using statistics on births, deaths, marriages, illnesses, migration, geographical mobility, and the like (Bogue 1969). To describe and explain population composition and change, demographers have developed various statistical indicators such as birth and death rates and the intercensal percent change (the relative

demography The study of the structure of and changes in human populations.

Table 10.1 Some Sources of Existing Official Statistics

Source	Sample Statistics
US Census Bureau www.census.gov	National, state, and local populations by age, sex, race, foreign-born, education, income
Bureau of Labor Statistics www.bls.gov	Employment, unemployment, inflation, earnings, time use
National Center for Education Statistics nces.ed.gov	Enrollment, racial/ethnic composition, dropout rate, expenditures from prekindergarten through graduate school
Bureau of Justice Statistics www.bjs.gov	Crime, criminal offenders, victims of crime
Centers for Disease Control and Prevention www.cdc.gov	Births, deaths, injuries, obesity, smoking, various diseases
UNESCO Institute for Statistics www.uis.unesco.org	National enrollment by gender, literacy, information technology in education
World Bank www.worldbank.org	Births, deaths, economic indicators, labor force participation, poverty
World Health Organization www.who.int	Life expectancy, infant mortality, causes of death, infectious diseases, physicians, hospitals

▲ Melissa Kearney

change in a population between two censuses). Logan and Stults's study of changes in US residential segregation, which applied the *dissimilarity index*, is an example of demographic analysis.

Another rich source of existing statistics, increasingly used by social scientists, is the Internet. The Internet contains numerous links to online data archives, article traffic for Wikipedia entries (see https://en.wikipedia.org/wiki/Wikipedia:Web_statistics_tool), and the public's online search habits (Google Trends). Moreover, many organizations compile data on the use of their websites, which may be accessed for research purposes. Such data can reveal not only online activity but also more general social behavior.

The use of existing statistics presents some unique methodological challenges. To understand the process of using existing data and the challenges it presents, let's first examine a study that used both vital statistics and data from Google Trends and Twitter.

Existing Statistics Example: The Impact of MTV's *16 and Pregnant* on Teen Childbearing

Teen pregnancy is an important social issue, especially in the United States, which has a teen birth rate that is much higher than in any other developed country in the world. In 2012, the US rate of 31 (births for every 1,000 women between the ages of 15 and 19) was four to five times greater than in France, Germany, Ireland, and Italy, all of which had rates of less than 10 (The World Bank 2014). Since the early 1990s, however, the teen birth rate has been falling steadily in the United States. The most rapid period of decline, according to economists Melissa Kearney and Phillip Levine (2015), occurred between 2008 and 2012. It just so happens that this period coincides with the introduction of MTV's *16 and Pregnant*, a documentary series that "shows the difficult reality of becoming a teen mother" (Kearney and Levine 2015:3597). This concurrence led Kearney and Levine to investigate whether exposure to the show influenced teens' interest in birth control and abortion and, in turn, influenced the decline in teen births.

▲ Phillip Levine

big data Unusually large datasets that are collected digitally and, because of their variety and structure, may require sophisticated computational methods.

As we pointed out in Chapter 4, it is very difficult to assess the impact of television programs and other media images on social attitudes and behavior. The effect of the media rarely can be separated from the effects of other events; causal direction is often ambiguous; and the timing of behavioral change is hard to pinpoint. New online data sources and statistical techniques, however, are making it possible to overcome some of these problems, as shown in Kearney and Levine's study. (For a description of these new online and other digitized data sources, see Box 10.1, READING SOCIAL RESEARCH: The Big Data Revolution.) Our description of this study omits its more complex statistical analyses, which are beyond the scope of this book, and focuses on the overall design and use of existing statistics.

READING SOCIAL RESEARCH

The Big Data Revolution

Kearney and Levine's study of the impact of *16 and Pregnant* uses two data sources—Google Trends and Twitter—that are part of an emerging "big data revolution." Fifteen years ago, "very few people were using the term 'big data'" (Kitchin 2014:67). Since then, it has become a buzzword in industry and academia. The term first appeared in academic publications in 2011, but its presence in the social sciences is even more recent, dating mostly from 2014 (Jenkins, Slomczynski, and Dubrow 2016).

The term **big data** refers to unusually large datasets that are generated digitally and require sophisticated computational methods (Lewis 2015:1). It is a product of the movement of organizations toward digital records (McFarland, Lewis, and Goldberg 2016:15) and the "digitization of social life" (Lazer and Radford 2017:19). You can appreciate the enormous growth in the digitization of social life when you realize that "we generate data whenever we go online, when we carry our GPS-equipped smartphones, when we communicate with our friends through social media or chat applications, and when we shop. You could say we leave digital footprints with everything we do that involves a digital transaction, which is almost everything" (Marr 2017).

A few examples illustrate the scope and variety of research using big data:

- Noting that exposure to news occurs increasingly through social media, political scientists Eytan Bakshy, Solomon Messing, and Lada Adamic (2015) examined the extent to which Facebook users were exposed to information that challenged their political views. The dataset included 10.1 million active users of Facebook who self-reported their ideological affiliation (liberal, moderate, and conservative). The data showed that an average of 20 percent of Facebook users had friends who report an opposing ideological affiliation.

- Racial bias in policing has been a highly controversial issue in recent years. Sociologist Joscha Legewie (2016) examined how incidents of extreme violence against police officers affect subsequent police treatment of residents. For data, he used "about 3.9 million time- and geocoded police stops of pedestrians in New York City between 2006 and 2012" (Legewie 2016:388). All stops were permitted by a stop-and-frisk program and recorded by the officer on a report worksheet, which included information on the timing, location, and circumstances of the stop, including the use of physical force. The main finding was an increase in the use of force against blacks but not against other residents following two fatal shootings of police officers by black suspects.

- With the increase in the number of people who identify themselves as multiracial, sociologists Celeste Vaughan Curington, Ken-Hou Lin, and Jennifer Hickes Lundquist (2015) examined how multiracial identity affects online dating. Their data came from a large US dating website in which users create a personal profile and search and view others' profiles. Among the basic profile information, users could identify with one or more of 10 ethnic/racial categories. Initially, the dataset consisted of "approximately 200 million messages exchanged among 9 million registered users" over an eight-year period (Curington et al. 2015:770).

continues

continued

Focusing on how monoracial users respond to initial messages sent by multiracial daters, the researchers found that multiracial daters generally are preferred over their minority counterparts.

As these examples show, big data present diverse opportunities for social research. At this early stage, a primary source of big data for social scientists is social media, especially Facebook and Twitter. Researchers have viewed these platforms in two ways: as a generalizable microcosm of society and a distinctive realm of human experience (Lazer and Radford 2017). Kearney and Levine's use of Twitter to trace teen interest in birth control and abortion is an example of the first view; the study of exposure to opposing political attitudes on Facebook is an example of the second. In either case, it is important to remember that "big data are almost always convenience samples" (Lazer and Radford 2017). In reality, "certain kinds of people are more likely than others to turn up in certain digital data sets"; even if the dataset contains "every phone call, every message, or every friendship," not everyone owns a cell phone, is on Twitter, or has a Facebook account (Lewis 2015:1–2).

The analysis of big data poses methodological challenges. One challenge is the varied and complex structure of the data. Unlike a simple subject × variable matrix of data (see Chapter 12), which can be analyzed with standard computer software and statistics, big data often have a different structure (e.g., with Facebook data, subject × subject) or format (narrative text and photos) that are not easily combined or analyzed. The analysis of data of such variety (and scale) requires advanced technical training, which is why "the first wave of studies" of big data "has been dominated by physical, computer, and information scientists" (Golder and Macy 2014:145).

There also are major ethical issues regarding the use of big data. For example, ordinarily, obtaining informed consent and anonymizing data protect privacy. But both of these processes may be inadequate in the age of big data. Aside from typically unread use agreements, there are no protections for human participants on the Internet. Further, there are several examples of big-data research in which attempts to anonymize the data failed to prevent the identification of individuals (Zook et al. 2017). In Chapter 3, we described a study using Facebook data in which the college and some student identities could be inferred from the data. (See Box 3.1 for a demonstration of how this could occur.) According to current federal regulations, research using public datasets is exempt from IRB review, the assumption being that "public" data are inherently low risk. But big data are forcing scientists to reconsider the ethical rules. Several proposed changes in the Common Rule are geared to big data, including altering the definition of "human subjects research" and requiring some projects to register plans for protecting privacy (National Research Council 2014).

The social sciences are just beginning to take advantage of the opportunities afforded by big data, but many challenges lie ahead.

Kearney and Levine used four types of existing statistics to answer questions about the impact of *16 and Pregnant*: Nielsen ratings, Google Trends, Twitter records, and Vital Statistics birth microdata.

1. The Nielsen ratings, which we mentioned in Chapter 5, are the well-known measures of the television viewing audience. They are based on meters attached

to the television sets or diaries kept by viewers of a large, random sample of US households. Ratings points indicate the percentage of the population that watched an episode of a show. Kearney and Levine were able to obtain ratings of *16 and Pregnant* broken down by 205 geographical areas. This breakdown was critical to their analysis, insofar as they could examine whether relatively larger declines in teen birth rates occurred in areas with a large viewership of *16 and Pregnant*.

2. Google Trends is a web facility that provides indexes of the frequency with which specific terms are entered on Google Search. The index varies from 1 to 100, where a value of 100 is assigned to the highest search frequency for a given time and place. Kearney and Levine used Google Trends to obtain search data on the term "*16 and Pregnant*" and on terms related to contraceptive use (e.g., "how get birth control") and abortion demand ("how get abortion").

3. Twitter records all tweets, maintaining a library of past tweets. Kearney and Levine analyzed the frequency of tweets that contained the same search terms as in their use of Google Trends.

4. Microdata for every live birth in the United States between January 2005 and December 2010 were obtained from the National Vital Statistics System, maintained by the CDC. These data enabled Kearney and Levine to break down counts of births for precise age groups and by county. Because month of birth and length of pregnancy were available, they also were able to approximate the month of conception.

Using these data, Kearney and Levine addressed three questions. For the show to have had an influence, teens had to watch it. So, the first question concerned the show's popularity: Was exposure to *16 and Pregnant* substantial? The Nielsen ratings revealed that the show was very highly rated, especially among young women. In addition, the pattern of Google searches and tweets for "*16 and Pregnant*" was consistent with exposure to the show, peaking during periods when the show was on the air. (Figure 10.1 presents Google Trends data for the show. The figure shows the peaks of interest. The first peak corresponds to the first season, when the show ran from June 11, 2009, to July 16, 2009. Notice that interest waned in 2013, when the show was not aired. Also notice the final peak, beginning in April 2014, when the show was revived for a fifth season.)

The second question concerned the show's impact on teen pregnancy: Did the show lead to a decrease in teen childbearing? Kearney and Levine's analysis showed that birth rates for young women declined significantly beginning in the third quarter after the show was first aired, but birth rates did not decrease for older age groups. Overall, they estimated that viewing the show *16 and Pregnant* accounted for 24 percent of the reduction in teen births from June 2009, when the show began, to December 2010.

The third question asked about the impact of the show on activities that could account for the decline in teen pregnancy: Did exposure to *16 and Pregnant* influence teens' interest in birth control and abortion? Kearney and Levine examined the Google Trends and Twitter datasets from January 1, 2009, five months before *16 and Pregnant*

FIGURE 10.1

Google Search Interest over Time for the Television Program *16 and Pregnant.* Numbers represent search interest relative to the highest point on the chart for the given region and time. A value of 100 is the peak popularity for the term. A value of 50 means that the term is half as popular. A score of 0 means there was not enough data for this term. Data source: Google Trends (www.google.com /trends).

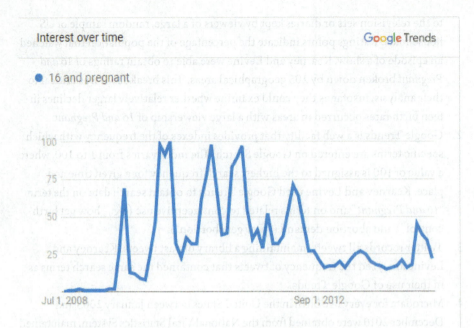

first aired, to December 31, 2012. Searches and tweets related to contraceptive use and abortion increased immediately after the show was aired; and, given that the show preceded the increase, Kearney and Levine assumed that the show was the cause. Although the relative impact of abortion and contraception on teen birth rates could not be evaluated, other data showing a decline in teen abortions during this period suggested to them that "a reduction in pregnancy is the likely mechanism" accounting for the decline in teen births (Kearney and Levine 2015:3626).

The Process of Analyzing Existing Statistics

Using existing statistics eliminates some of the steps in designing a study and collecting data. As shown in Figure 10.2, there are four major steps in this approach: (1) search for and obtain data, (2) measure variables, (3) evaluate and adjust the data, and (4) analyze the data. Below we consider the first three steps, each of which presents unique challenges.[1] We examine the analysis of quantitative data in Chapter 12.

SEARCH FOR AND OBTAIN DATA

The first challenge in analyzing existing statistics is finding and procuring data relevant to the research question. How do you know what to look for? And how do you find it, acquire it, and/or gain permission to use it? Perhaps the best advice is to let the research question serve as a guide to appropriate sources. In one sense, this is obvious.

---

[1]The discussion of the teen pregnancy study in this section relies on additional information graciously provided to us by Melissa Kearney and Philip Levine (June 4, 2014).

For example, researchers who are interested in job turnover will readily entertain the possibility of using company personnel records. But this advice holds true in another way. Aimlessly searching through records or dredging up data from archives is unlikely to yield anything of value. Even though the data pre-exist, that does not mean the researcher should reverse the research process by analyzing the data and then developing some rationale for the analysis after the fact. More than likely, the outcome will be a trivial and flawed study. It is far better to let your research question dictate your methodology than to let your method override the substantive and theoretical focus of your research.

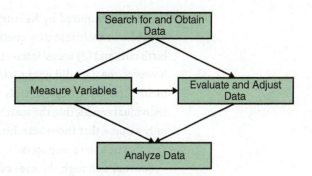

FIGURE 10.2
The Process of Analyzing Existing Statistics

Kearney and Levine knew from their own past research that a sudden and rapid decline in teen births had occurred and that none of the standard explanations for the teen birth rate could account for it. They became motivated to study the impact of *16 and Pregnant* when they heard someone suggest that the show might explain the decline (personal communication 2014). To answer their research question, they needed to link variation in viewing the show to variation in teen births and other indicators of the show's impact. Although they immediately considered using Nielsen data on viewership, they also learned that acquiring these data would be costly. Therefore, the first data source Kearney and Levine tapped was Google Trends, which other economists had used. Indeed, this strategy suggests a second guide to locating pertinent data: search the literature for relevant studies to see the data sources used by other researchers.

Kearney and Levine's initial analysis showed an association between the show's airing and Google search indicators of its impact. Therefore, they sought to acquire additional data to test the show's impact. The birth data maintained by the CDC were easily acquired. Access to public sources varies among the archives and agencies holding the data. But many of these data, including those compiled by government agencies such as the CDC, are mandated for public use without restrictions. The greatest access problems pertain to private and confidential records, such as those held by the Nielsen organization. To obtain the Nielsen data, Kearney and Levine paid thousands of dollars and signed a contract that prevented them from sharing the data with others (personal communication 2014). Acquiring the Twitter data was also difficult. Although Twitter maintains a library of tweets, Kearney and Levine (2015:3618) point out that these data are hard to work with and obtaining the data "requires the use of a third party vendor that has a contract with Twitter to process searches."

MEASURE VARIABLES

Locating data that can address the research question means that the data can provide measures of relevant variables. Still, there are many considerations about the measures that need to be taken into account, as Kearney and Levine's study shows.

The data acquired by Kearney and Levine enabled them to measure the three key variables in their research questions: (1) level of teen exposure to the show, (2) teen birth rate, and (3) teens' interest in birth control and abortion. Typical of existing data, however, the data did not provide a perfect fit between each variable and its measurement. First, the Google Trends and Twitter data lacked information on the age of the individual conducting the search or sending the tweet. Therefore, the researchers could only assume that those searching or tweeting about the show and about birth control and abortion were teenagers.

Second, although the uses of birth control and/or abortion could account for the impact of the show on teen birth rates, it was not possible to directly measure teen *use* of these methods. And so, Kearney and Levine settled on indirect measures of actual use, namely, *interest* in birth control and abortion, as revealed by Google searches and tweets.

Third, Kearney and Levine draw conclusions about individual behavior based on aggregate data, which summarize data from individuals to describe *social* units. The data from the *16 and Pregnant* study were in the aggregate, describing program ratings, Google searches, tweets, and birth rates for geographical areas and/or given points in time. The researchers draw conclusions, however, about the individual actions of teens within those areas and time periods. For example, the association between Nielsen ratings of the show and birth control searches and tweets following a given episode led them to infer that those who watched the show sought information about birth control. Such inferences often are reasonable, as they appear to be in this study. But as we pointed out in Chapter 4 (Box 4.2), it is not always safe to draw conclusions about one unit of analysis (e.g., individuals) on the basis of information about another unit (e.g., areas or time).

The use of multiple measures of a given variable is always a good practice in social research. This is even more imperative in existing data research that uses indirect and approximate indicators. Demographers often use several data sources and different estimation procedures. Similarly, Kearney and Levine were able to strengthen their findings by using three data sources on exposure to the show and two data sources on teen interest in birth control and abortion.

EVALUATE AND ADJUST DATA

Perhaps the most important general rule that applies to the use of existing data, irrespective of the source, is that the researcher must reconstruct the process by which the data were originally assembled. If you gather the data yourself, you generally are aware of their limitations, possible errors, and biases; you can adapt your analyses accordingly. But such adaptations may also be required of existing data. Therefore, it is crucial to try to determine, as far as possible, how, when, where, and by whom the data were collected. Only then can you begin to assess the validity of the data.

Kearney and Levine paid particular attention not only to how the data were collected but also to technological changes that could affect the process of measurement. For example, they noted that the measurement of viewing habits is complicated by viewers' ability to record shows and watch them later and to stream shows over the Internet. Data from Nielsen indicate, however, a high correlation in ratings of shows watched live versus recorded; moreover, other data indicate that watching television shows live is still the primary way that people watch shows. Kearney and Levine further note that the Nielsen data on exposure to the show included information on the age of viewers *only for households that complete diaries*, which may introduce bias if groups vary in their propensity to complete the diaries.

Once the data have been evaluated, it may become necessary to refine measures. If measurement errors or changes in definitions are detected, the researcher must make the necessary adjustments to allow for proper interpretation. For example, prior to the 2000 Census people could use only one racial category to describe themselves, but beginning in 2000 people were allowed to check multiple racial categories. Therefore, to compare racial segregation in 2000 and 2010 with segregation in 1980 and 1990, Logan and Stults had to recombine the 2000 and 2010 racial categories; for example, they operationally defined black or African American as the combination of black with any other race.

Kearney and Levine also had to make various adjustments to their data. When they broke down the Nielsen ratings by month, they discovered that they had too few viewers per geographical area. Therefore, they generated an average estimate of viewership in each area across the entire period that the show aired.

SUMMARY

Existing statistics come from a variety of sources, including government agencies, international organizations, and the Internet. They may be used as supplementary information to establish the temporal and geographical context of a study, but are also the primary data for many studies. The process of analyzing existing statistics begins with the challenge of finding and obtaining data that can adequately address the research question. In addition, researchers need to evaluate the fit between a variable and its measurement; they should carefully examine how the data were collected; and they may have to refine or adjust the data for purposes of analysis.

CONTENT ANALYSIS

The second analytic technique, **content analysis**, is not a single method but a set of procedures for systematically analyzing the symbolic content of recorded communications. In all communications, a sender conveys a message to an audience. The aim

content analysis
Systematic analysis of the symbolic content of communications in which the content is reduced to a set of coded variables or categories.

of content analysis is to make valid inferences about the sender, the message itself, or the intended audience (Weber 1990). Although the inferences depend on the research question, the basic approach is the same: to reduce the total content of a communication (e.g., all of the words or all of the visual imagery) to a set of coded variables or categories. This approach differs from the analysis of existing statistics in two important ways: it generates its own statistics and it analyzes the *content* of communications. Although the *16 and Pregnant* study concerned the effect of a recorded communication (i.e., a television show), it was not a content analysis: the researchers used existing Nielsen ratings and did not measure the show's content.

The definition of content analysis encompasses a great deal. First, it indicates that the "data" or "content" of the analysis includes printed matter and oral recordings as well as visual communications and works of art. Second, content analysis is not limited to existing data; it also may be applied to the analysis of responses to open-ended questions in survey research and to the coding of field notes in field research. Third, content analysis may be either qualitative or quantitative. In this chapter, we focus on content analysis of existing data as a form of deductive, quantitative research.

Content analysis may involve either manual or computer coding of message content. (Recall from Chapter 8 that *coding* is the assignment of a number or label to a piece of textual data.) Manual coding is more common and may be applied to a broader range of content than computer coding, which is used almost exclusively to analyze transcribed verbal materials. Therefore, we focus on manual coding. We begin by describing one study in detail. Then, as we discuss the process of content analysis, we introduce additional examples, including one that uses computer coding.

Content Analysis Example: Journalistic Accounts of the Iraq War

At the onset of the Iraq War (2003–2011), the US military introduced a new program in which journalists covering the war could become embedded with the troops. The embedded reporters wore military-issue camouflage uniforms and lived with and were protected by the troops. While the military and some journalists saw this as a unique opportunity to witness the troops' experience of the war, others criticized embedding as constraining access to the war and its consequences. To Andrew Lindner (2009), this criticism raised an important sociological question: How does the vantage point of journalists affect the types of stories that they write?

Lindner (2009:28) defines a vantage point as the "perspective resulting from the collective constraints and sanctions of a reporter's social location." In addition to the *embedded journalists*, he identified two other distinct journalistic vantage points on the Iraq War. One consisted of *Baghdad-stationed journalists* who were present and remained in two major hotels in the city of

▼ Andrew Lindner

Baghdad; the other were *independent journalists* who entered northern Iraq through Iran or Turkey and followed the action from there. All three vantage points were limited, albeit in different ways: embedded reporters had access to US troops on the front line in return for restrictions on their freedom of movement; Baghdad-stationed reporters had access to civilians with the support and accompaniment of Iraqi officials; and independent reporters were free to roam but had no immediate access to official sources. Given these circumstances, Lindner hypothesized that (1) embedded reporters were more likely than Baghdad-stationed journalists to report the coalition soldier's experience of the war; (2) Baghdad-stationed journalists were more likely than embedded reporters to report the Iraqi civilian's experience of the war; and (3) independent journalists were likely to fall between the other two vantage points in covering the coalition soldier's and Iraqi civilian's experience, hence producing the most balanced reporting.

▲ During the Iraq War, some journalists were embedded with American troops, some were stationed in Baghdad, and some entered Iraq through Turkey and Iran.

To test these hypotheses, Lindner analyzed the content of 742 English-language, print articles written by 156 journalists. All the articles were written by journalists present in Iraq during the major combat period, between March 19, 2003, and May 1, 2003. Lindner (2009:30) used a three-step process in selecting the articles: first he identified the relevant journalists by using "an online media map developed by the Poynter Institute" that tracked "the locations of journalists during the major combat period of the war." Then, he compiled a complete list of the articles produced by these journalists using various online sources, including news agency websites, Lexis-Nexis and Factiva. Finally, he randomly selected five articles written by each journalist.

Once the articles were selected, Lindner developed a coding scheme, which he and two other coders applied. To test his hypotheses, he coded 16 variables, shown in Table 10.2, for each article. The independent variable consisted of the journalist's wartime vantage point (*embedded, Baghdad-stationed, or independent*). Five dependent variables, representing news coverage of the war *from the coalition soldier's perspective*, consisted of whether the article made reference to combat, military movement, and soldier fatalities; whether it used a soldier in the field as a source; and whether it was a soldier human-interest story. An additional five dependent variables, representing coverage of the *Iraqi experience of the war*, included whether the article made reference to bombing, property damage, and civilian fatalities; whether it used an Iraqi civilian as a source; and whether it was an Iraqi human-interest story. Finally, the five control variables were the journalist's gender and nationality, prominence of news agency, article length, and article publication date.

Table 10.2 Key Variables Coded in Lindner's Content Analysis

INDEPENDENT VARIABLE	Journalist's vantage point
DEPENDENT VARIABLES	Combat
	Military movement
	Soldier fatalities
	Soldier in the field as a source
	Soldier human-interest story
	Bombing
	Property damage
	Civilian fatalities
	Use of Iraqi civilian as a source
	Iraqi human-interest story
CONTROL VARIABLES	Gender of journalist
	Nationality of journalist
	Prominence of news agency
	Length of article
	Publication date

The analyses consistently supported Lindner's hypotheses. On all five of the first set of dependent variables, articles by embedded journalists were significantly more likely than articles by Baghdad reporters to cover the soldier's military experience. Likewise, on every measure of the Iraqi experience of the war, articles written by embedded reporters were significantly less likely to contain Iraqi stories. By contrast, the coverage of articles by independent journalists ranked between that of the other two vantage points on 9 of 10 dependent variables. For example, one of the sharpest differences was the reporting of civilian fatalities: these were mentioned by 49.6 percent of Baghdad-stationed reporters, 29.7 percent of independent reporters, and 11.5 percent of embedded reporters. Moreover, all differences remained when controlling for the five control variables.

The Process of Content Analysis

Now that you are familiar with a research example, let's take a closer look at the steps in carrying out a content analysis. Figure 10.3 shows the major steps. Some of the steps may be skipped, depending on whether human or computer coding is used. For example, without the need for human coders, computer coding does not entail coder training or checks for reliability. In addition, although we present the steps as separate methodological decisions, some steps may be interdependent, depending on the type of communication—for example, text or visual images—being analyzed.[2]

SELECT RECORDED COMMUNICATION

As in all forms of social research, the initial steps in content analysis depend on the research question, which determines what content will be examined and why (Neuendorf 2002). Broadly speaking, Lindner asked how differences among message senders are related to message content. Content analysis also may be applied to describe patterns and trends in content, and to examine the association between communication content and social behavior. The sources of analyzable content include print and broadcast media, Web pages, photos, videos, music, interviews, and any other communication that has been or can be recorded.

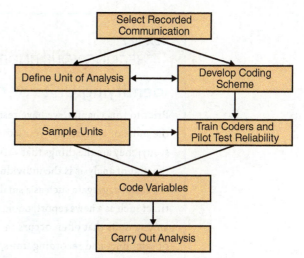

FIGURE 10.3
The Process of Content Analysis

DEFINE UNIT OF ANALYSIS

In much social research, the units of analysis are whole elements that cannot be subdivided. Each individual interviewed in survey research, for example, is an integral unit, and in sampling, collecting, and analyzing survey data, the unit is the same. By contrast, the units of content analysis often can be segmented and may differ for purposes of sampling, coding, and analysis. For example, the text of a news article can be broken down into words, sentences, paragraphs, or some other grammatical unit.

The segmentation of units gives rise to two primary types of units in content analysis: sampling units and recording units. Sampling units serve as the basis for identifying and sampling the target population (Neuendorf 2002). Lindner's (2009:30) target population consisted of all "English-language, print articles produced by journalists in Iraq during the major combat period." His sampling unit, therefore, was the whole article. **Recording units** (also called **coding units**) refer to that part of a communication that is the basis for coding; in an analysis of text, it is that element of the text described by the coded variables. Lindner's recording unit was the same as his sampling unit: the article. By comparison, in a content analysis of the depiction of women in magazine advertisements, the sampling unit was magazines and the recording unit was advertisements that featured women (Stankiewicz and Rosselli 2008). To further clarify this distinction, see Box 10.2, CHECKING YOUR UNDERSTANDING: Identifying Units of Analysis.

recording units The units of analysis in content analysis, such as words, sentences, paragraphs, and whole articles. Also called *coding units.*

---

[2]The discussion of the Iraq War study in this section relies on additional information graciously provided to us by Andrew Lindner (April 24, 2014).

BOX 10.2

CHECKING YOUR UNDERSTANDING

Identifying Units of Analysis

Prior to this chapter, we have restricted ourselves almost exclusively to individuals as the units of analysis. As you will recall, units of analysis are the cases or entities you study; they are the things that variables describe. In nearly all experiments and surveys, the unit of analysis is the individual. But in much research using existing data, the unit is a social aggregate such as a small group, formal organization, or nation, or a social artifact such as a news report, book, or magazine. Now we have added another distinction among units that often occurs in content analysis: sampling units, which are the basis of sampling, and recording units, which are the basis for analyzing content. To check your understanding of these concepts, we ask you to identify the relevant units in the following two studies.

1. In Chapter 3, we discussed a controversial study that examined the claim, made by opponents of same-sex marriage, that children with same-sex parents fare worse than children with opposite-sex parents. A study using existing statistics tested another argument of opponents of same-sex marriage: allowing same-sex couples to marry reduces the value of marriage to opposite-sex couples. For example, couples may be less apt to marry if new laws allow them to enter into domestic partnerships that grant the same rights as marriage. Marcus Dillender (2014) tested the impact of laws extending legal recognition for same-sex couples with data from the CDC and Current Population Survey. The data measuring the main outcome of interest consisted of the marriage rate per 1,000 individuals for each state from 1995 to 2010. When Dillender compared states that did and did not institute laws allowing same-sex couples to marry, he found no difference in opposite-sex marriage rates across this time period.

   a. What is the unit of analysis in this study?

2. Some Facebook users have received unfavorable news coverage concerning their posting of illegal, risqué, and embarrassing material. To examine this issue, Ashleigh Shelton and Paul Skalski (2013) conducted a content analysis to determine the prevalence of controversial content on Facebook. After randomly selecting 208 Facebook profiles from the University of Minnesota network in 2006, they measured controversial content in two ways. First, on the front profile page, which included Interests and Wall posts, they coded for the presence or absence of words of profanity and words or phrases making reference to partying, alcohol use, and drug use. Second, for all photographs drawn from the "view more photos of" option, they coded depictions

of partying, alcohol and drug use, sexually suggestive acts, and nudity, among other controversial content.

   a.   What is the sampling unit in this study?

   b.   There are two recording units. What are they?

   c.   When the researchers examined gender differences in the amount of controversial content disclosed on Facebook, one of the few differences was that males were significantly more likely than females to have profanity on their front page (on their Walls). What is the unit of analysis for this finding?

Answers: 1a. Marriage rates describe *states*; the researcher is comparing rates for states with and without new laws allowing same-sex couples to marry; therefore, states are the primary units of analysis. You also might infer that time is a unit insofar as the rates are examined within each state for several points in time. 2a. Facebook profile is the sampling unit. 2b. One recording unit is the "front profile page" on Facebook, which includes personal information and nonphoto Wall posts; the other recording unit consists of photographs drawn from the "view more photos of" option. 2c. The unit of analysis is the front profile page (or, more precisely, Wall posts).

DEVELOP CODING SCHEME

Developing a coding scheme is a matter of operationalizing the variables in the researcher's hypothesis. The key variables in Lindner's hypotheses were journalistic vantage point and coverage of the war. He operationalized vantage point by identifying three sets of journalists. Then he identified a set of variables that captured the variation in what journalists covered. To get an idea of this variation, Lindner did a preliminary reading of articles representing a range of coverage. Based on this reading, he decided to code the variables presented in Table 10.2 in addition to several other variables that were not included in his primary analysis (Lindner, personal communication 2014).

The coding scheme consists of all the variables to be coded together with the codes for each variable. To the extent that human coders are used, selecting and coding the variables in content analysis is analogous to deciding on a set of closed-ended questions in survey research. Instead of giving the questions to respondents who provide the answers, the content analyst applies them to a document or image. The "questions" applied to the document should be adequate for the research purpose, and the codes should be clearly defined, exhaustive, and mutually exclusive. Thus, for each article, Lindner asked questions relating to all of the variables described in Table 10.2. Taking the dependent variables at the top of the table as examples, he asked: "Was there any mention of combat? Was there any mention of military movements? Was there any mention of soldier fatalities?" And so forth. For every question, he decided to code 1 for "yes" and 0 for "no."

Lindner's coding of the dependent variables enabled him to arrive at a quantitative summary of the "message," or article content, which is the objective of content analysis. The way researchers code variables determines *how* the data may be quantified. Below is a list of the most common ways of measuring and quantifying the data:

1. *Appearance.* The simplest method is to code the presence or absence of message content. Lindner applied this method: he recorded whether specific content, as defined by his variables, *appeared* in each article. Although appearance measures tend to be rather imprecise, they can be applied to a large range of content.

2. *Intensity.* When attitudes and values are the objects of the research, the content analyst may use measures of intensity. An example would be the coding of the "valence" of drug and alcohol references in song lyrics—whether the lyrics presented substance abuse as negative, neutral, or positive.

3. *Time–space measures.* Early content analysts of (physical) newspapers often measured the space devoted to certain topics. Using column inches as their measure, for example, Janet Lever and Stan Wheeler (1984) found that sports coverage in the *Chicago Tribune* increased from 9 percent of the newsprint in 1900 to 17 percent in 1975. Analogously, television content has been measured in time (e.g., the number of hours of televised violence). Space-time measures may appropriately describe gross characteristics of the mass media, but they are too imprecise to serve as indicators of most verbal content.

4. *Frequency.* In computer analyses of textual content, variables often are defined and measured in terms of the frequency with which a given category of words appears. In an analysis of sex bias in letters of recommendation for faculty positions, Toni Schmader, Jessica Whitehead, and Vicki Wysocki (2007) used a computer program to count the number of words in several categories, including achievement words (e.g., goal), tentative words (e.g., perhaps), certainty words (e.g., always), and standout adjectives (e.g., superb). We'll tell you more about this study, including the main findings, below.

codebook A guide for coding that consists of a list of the variables together with definitions, codes, and instructions for applying the codes.

Once key variables have been identified and operationalized, the content analyst constructs either a codebook (for manual coding) or dictionary (for computer coding). A content analysis **codebook** consists of a list of the variables to be coded together with definitions, codes, and guidelines for applying the codes. Codebooks guide coders in locating and coding variables. Figure 10.4 presents an excerpt from Lindner's codebook. The first column contains a variable label; the second column provides a description of the variable and/or what to code. Other codebooks may contain more elaborate information and guidelines.

dictionary In computerized content analysis, the set of words, phrases, or other word-based indicators (e.g., word length) that is the basis for a search of texts.

A **dictionary** for computer text analysis "is a set of words, phrases, parts of speech, or other word-based indicators (e.g., word length, number of syllables) that is used as the basis for a search of texts" (Neuendorf 2002:127). In any given study, there are usually several dictionaries, each representing the measurement of a variable. For example, to content analyze letters of recommendation, one of the dictionaries that Schmader and colleagues (2007:514) created was the following list of words representing the use of "standout adjectives" (the asterisk is a stand-in for different forms of the word): excellen*, superb, outstanding, unique, exceptional, unparalleled, *est, most, wonderful, terrific*, fabulous, magnificent, remarkable, extraordinar*, amazing, supreme*, unmatched. Like

Variable Label	Description
NEWSID	Article i.d. (LASTFIRST##)
ARTDATE	Date of article
ARTSRCE	Where was the article published?
FOREIGN	Foreign (United States = 0, Foreign = 1)
BYLINE	Article Author
VANTG	Embedded = 1, Baghdad = 2, Independent = 3 (pre-coded in database, but verify coding)
PAGE	Page on which article **begins**
NLENGTH	Length of Story (Do NOT Count Headlines) Record # of words for print using the following scheme: **Count** # of words in 4 lines from the MIDDLE of a paragraph. Divide this sum by four to get an average # of words per line. Multiply this number by the # of lines in the article.
HEADLN	Record article headline
	Code for coverage of any of the following topics (yes = 1, no = 0)
CONFLICT	Close-range violence/conflict between soldiers and Iraqi combatants (includes close-range helicopter-combatant exchanges)
LGBOMB	Long range bombing
MOVMT	Military movements
IPERSN	Iraqi human interest story (e.g., family issues)
SPERSN	U.S./coalition human interest story (e.g., soldiers' personal stories)
MILISRC	Any mention of a U.S. or coalition military source (yes = 1, no = 0)
FLDSRC	Was this person a soldier in field? (e.g., private, sergeant, lieutenant, major, low level general, etc.) (yes = 1, no = 0)

FIGURE 10.4
Excerpt from Codebook for Lindner's Content Analysis

codebooks, a set of content analysis dictionaries usually contains variable or category names, rules for assigning text, and the specific text (e.g., words) to be assigned. Researchers may construct their own dictionaries, use standard dictionaries that accompany the computer program being used, or use dictionaries developed for specific content areas.

SAMPLE UNITS

Because content analysis is a labor-intensive activity for human coders, it is seldom possible to analyze all of the typically large volume of available texts and images. Yet, sampling is complicated for several reasons: there may be more than one unit to sample; not all text and images may be equally relevant to the research question; and, unlike survey researchers, content analysts are seldom interested in making precise statistical inferences about the population of texts or images (Krippendorff 2004). In general, when sampling in content analysis, you should aim to select a manageable amount of content-analyzable material that provides a valid answer to the research question.

Three populations are relevant to content analysis: communication sources (e.g., types of newspapers), documents (e.g., specific newspaper issues), and text and images within documents (e.g., pages, photographs). Lindner did not sample his sources—the journalists who reported on the war. But he did sample the documents (articles) they produced, randomly selecting five articles from each of 156 journalists. The number of articles written by these journalists varied from 2 to 70, so his sample is not representative of all the *articles* that were written. The sample does, however, provide representative coverage of each journalist, which is consistent with the aims of his research. For his research focus was on the effect of journalistic vantage point on the content of the reporting rather than on "the way in which the media [coverage of the war] was received by the consumer" (Linder 2009:31).

Many content analyses of the media *do focus* on text and images that are most likely to reach the consumer. Some of these studies purposefully select units to address the research question. For example, to study portrayals of alcohol and drugs in popular songs, Peter Christenson, Donald Roberts, and Nicholas Bjork (2012:126) aimed "to examine the songs most likely to reach the ears of young listeners over an extended period of time." Therefore, they selected the top 100 *Billboard* songs from each of the years 1968, 1978, 1988, 1998, and 2008. Other studies use probability sampling to provide statistically accurate estimates of media content. The National Television Violence Study (Wilson et al. 1997), which measured the amount of violence on television, constructed a sampling frame consisting of all television programs aired between 6 a.m. and 11 p.m. for 20 weeks between October 1994 and June 1995 in the Los Angeles market. Then the researchers randomly selected two half-hour time slots for each channel during each week that the sampling covered.

One development that has facilitated content analysis is the creation of a wide array of message archives, many available online, which can serve as sampling frames for selecting content. Lindner used several online sources, including Lexis-Nexis, a database of popular newspapers and magazines and other publications, to compile a complete list and access full text of the articles he analyzed. Christenson and colleagues (2012) used several Internet lyric sites to compile lyrics for the top 100 *Billboard* songs they analyzed. Other content analysts may draw on archives of television news and programs, political ads, and films.

TRAIN CODERS AND PILOT-TEST RELIABILITY

Although content analysis may be undertaken by a sole researcher, most often it involves multiple coders. To assure reliable and valid measurement, it is important to train coders. Lindner's training protocol involved a discussion of the aims of the research, the coding scheme, and a strategy for reading the journal articles, followed by a couple of group coding sessions in which he and his research assistants read and coded articles together (personal communication 2014). Optimally, content analysis should involve two checks for reliability, each based on separate subsamples (Neuendorf 2002). The first check serves as a pilot test of reliability before full coding of the data; the second provides a final check on the reliability of the coding scheme. Lindner used this procedure. Initially, he and his assistants coded three rounds of 10 articles each and progressively refined the codebook until they achieved a reliability of 95 percent or higher. Then he checked inter-coder reliability based on a coding of 10 percent of the articles (Lindner 2009).

CODE VARIABLES AND CARRY OUT ANALYSIS

The final two steps are to code the sampled material and analyze the message content. With human coding, the coders often use a coding form that corresponds to the codebook. The form typically lists variables with codes to check and/or space to enter the data. Lindner did not use a coding form; instead, based on the codebook, coders entered data directly into an Excel file. Several computer programs are available for content analysis, and most include pre-set dictionaries (Neuendorf 2011). Schmader and colleagues used the program Linguistic Inquiry Word Count (LIWC) after transcribing 886 letters written on behalf of 235 male and 42 female candidates for two faculty positions at a large research university.

Finally, the content analyst summarizes the message content and relates content variables to one another or to some other variable. As you may recall, Lindner found that the content of print news coverage of the war varied according to the journalistic vantage point. Schmader and colleagues found that letters of recommendation were similar for male and female candidates for a faculty position, with one major exception: recommenders used significantly more standout adjectives to describe male candidates compared to female candidates. These studies and other quantitative content analyses apply statistical methods that we discuss in Chapter 12. It is also possible to conduct content analyses using the qualitative data analysis techniques that are the topic of Chapter 13.

Now that you know the steps in content analysis, Box 10.3, DOING SOCIAL RESEARCH: Analyzing the Content of Cell Phone Use, will guide you through an analysis that will help you learn something about yourself.

BOX 10.3

DOING SOCIAL RESEARCH

Analyzing the Content of Cell Phone Use

Cell phones have become an integral part of our daily lives. For many young people, they are the primary means of communicating with others. How you use your cell phone reveals much about yourself: With whom do you communicate? What do you communicate about? What is important enough to put in a phone message? We propose that you conduct a content analysis of your own cell phone use. What makes this possible is that cell phones store communications, so that you can analyze the stored data. To guide your analysis, we've identified a series of decisions that you'll need to make:

1. What specific messages will you analyze? Text messages, voice messages, or something else? Will you analyze sent and/or received messages? How will you decide?

2. Whatever type of communication you analyze, we suggest that you obtain a sample of at least 100 communications. What is your sampling unit? How will you select your sample? What is your recording unit?

3. What will you code? You probably ought to code the date and time of each message. But then think about characteristics of the sender/receiver and of the communication content. How will you decide what to code? Once you've decided, develop a coding scheme or form.

4. How will you summarize the communication content? Will you relate communication content to other variables?

SUMMARY

Content analysis consists of a set of procedures for summarizing the content of recorded human communications, including both printed matter and visual imagery. After selecting a particular communication, researchers define the unit of sampling and coding, and develop an appropriate coding scheme. They then select a sample and, in human coding, train coders and pilot test the reliability of the coding scheme. Finally, the communication content is coded and analyzed.

COMPARATIVE HISTORICAL ANALYSIS

The third method of analyzing existing data originates with many of the founders of modern social science. In an effort to understand large-scale social processes such as industrialization and modernization, scholars such as Alexis de Tocqueville, Karl Marx, and Max Weber combined the systematic comparison of a small set of cases with in-depth historical analysis. To this day, comparative historical analysis is often used to develop causal explanations of real-world social transformations: for example, "the dissolution of colonial empires," the civil rights movement in the United States, and "the eruption of revolutions, wars, international terrorism, and ethnic conflicts" (Skocpol 2003:409).

Comparative historical analysis is comparative insofar as it involves a comparison of the similarities and differences between cases and between historical periods; it is historical in that it "considers events that occurred in the past" (Arthur 2011:175). In this section, we consider comparative historical studies that follow in the tradition of Marx and Weber. In addition to using existing data, these studies have three distinct features (Mahoney and Rueschemeyer 2003; also see Lange 2013). First, they are concerned with developing causal explanations. Second, they analyze historical sequences to understand how events unfold over an extended period of time. Third, they systematically compare a small number of similar and contrasting cases. Comparative historical analysis is like quantitative social research in its emphasis on causal explanations. On the other hand, the systematic comparison of in-depth historical narratives generally limits this approach to the qualitative analysis of a small number of carefully selected cases (Lange 2013). As you will see, case selection is of critical importance, and the tools for establishing causality differ from experimental and survey methods.

Although comparative historical research most often uses existing data, we should note that it might utilize oral history and interviewing as data sources (Arthur 2011). It also is not used exclusively to study large-scale social change; for example, it can be used to study organizations. Finally, comparative historical research is not limited to the study of a small number of cases (sometimes called "small-*N*" studies); in recent years it has been applied increasingly to large-*N* studies.

We begin with the description of a study that examined a major transformation in America's criminal justice system in the last quarter of the 20th century.

> **comparative historical analysis** The development of causal explanations of social change by describing and comparing historical processes within and across cases.

An Example of Comparative Historical Analysis: The Emergence of Mass Imprisonment

For 100 years, incarceration rates in the United States hovered around 100 inmates imprisoned per 100,000 population. Then, in the last quarter of the 20th century, there was a sudden and massive increase. By 2000, the incarceration rate had more than doubled in every state in the union, with an average increase of 285 percent (Campbell and Schoenfeld 2013). Moreover, this punitive turn was unique to the United States; no other Western democracy experienced a similar increase in imprisonment. What accounts for this extreme shift? Given that both the United States and other Western democracies experienced the same broad socioeconomic changes, sociologists Michael Campbell and Heather Schoenfeld (2013:1383) believe that the answer lies in the US political system, or, more specifically, in the "interaction between national politics and policy and state-level politics and policy."

Michael Campbell

Heather Schoenfeld

To develop a detailed explanation of widespread transformation in the US penal system, Campbell and Schoenfeld conducted a comparative historical analysis of penal development and politics from 1960 to 2001 in a sample of eight states: Arizona, California, Florida, Oregon, Minnesota, New York, Texas, and Washington. In addition, they examined national-level politics and penal policy during the same period.

As a general analytic strategy, Campbell and Schoenfeld followed a three-step process that they call "inductive periodization." The first step was to simplify the historical analysis by breaking down the 41-year history into three distinct periods. Their second step was to analyze the state and national data to explain the underlying causes of dominant patterns and policy outcomes within each period. The third step was to explain how politics and policy solutions in one period influenced changes that occurred in subsequent periods.

Table 10.3 identifies the three historical periods: *destabilization* (~1960–1975), *contestation* (~1975–1992), and *reconstruction* (~1992–2001). The table also shows the key defining characteristics of each period as indicated by "type of crime politics" (the political use of crime control), "definition of policy problem" (how policymakers defined the crime problem), and "policy outcome" (the types of penal policies that were formulated). Campbell and Schoenfeld's explanation of dominant patterns within each period and of changes over time is complex and detailed, and we cannot hope to do justice to their analysis here. What we will do is highlight some of the major developments that led to mass imprisonment so that you can understand how national and state-level politics influenced penal policy.

During the destabilization period, crime entered the national spotlight partly in reaction to the civil rights movement and other social unrest in the 1960s, as presidential candidates, including Richard Nixon and George Wallace, introduced "law-and-order" rhetoric to appeal to anti-black sentiment. Congress passed an omnibus crime act in 1968, which established a federal agency to make grants to states for crime control. Meanwhile, the federal courts focused on the rights of defendants and prisoners, which became a matter of concern to the states. At the state level, California gubernatorial candidate Ronald Reagan emphasized the link between social protest and crime to overwhelmingly defeat his opponent in 1966. In many states, new federal funding was used to hire and train police and helped to create victims' rights groups and law enforcement associations, and reformers advocated new sentencing guidelines and other changes to strengthen the criminal justice system. In short, this period was characterized by "questioning and challenges to the penal status quo" at both the national and state level (Campbell and Schoenfeld 2013:1389).

Events in the first period opened up a period of "contestation" in which policymakers had to figure out how to reform their penal systems. The key national event ushering in

Table 10.3 Periodization in the Transformation of the Penal Order

	Destabilization	Contestation	Reconstruction
Dates	~1960–1975	~1975–1992	~1992–2001
Description	Questioning and challenges to the penal status quo	Political contestation over the direction of penal policy	Solidification of a new penal order
Type of crime politics	Emergent crime politics	High crime politics	Captured crime politics
Definition of policy problem	Ineffective criminal justice response	Crisis in confidence	Leniency
Policy outcome	Capacity-building/ Reform	Constrain discretion/ Build prisons	Lengthen sentences/ Equip law enforcement

Source: Table 3 in Campbell and Schoenfeld (2013:1389).

mass incarceration during this period was the 1980 election of Ronald Reagan as president. Not only did the Reagan presidency emphasize crime (even though serious crime rates were stable or falling), it also launched the "war on drugs," which led to anti-drug abuse laws in 1986 and 1988. These laws established lengthy mandatory prison terms for drug sales and possession and provided generous funds that "increased the incentives for the state and local enforcement of drug laws" (Campbell and Schoenfeld 2013:1396). Another important consequence of Reagan's election was that Republican gubernatorial candidates in the 1980s, especially in the South, also adopted his "law and order" rhetoric to win election. In the short run, the crime politics of this period resulted in debates over penal policy; in the long run, states tended to expand prison capacity and introduce mandatory minimum sentences that limited judges' power to decide the length of imprisonment. Playing a key role in these developments were law enforcement and victims' interest groups, which helped frame the crime problem in the media as a need to keep violent criminals off the streets.

The developments in the first two periods, according to Campbell and Schoenfeld, helped establish a "new penal order" between about 1992 and 2001. The final period, reconstruction, is characterized "by relentless political pressure to toughen criminal sanctions and a dominance of ideas and politics that demonized offenders and privileged victims and law enforcement" (Campbell and Schoenfeld 2013:1401). During this period, state initiatives influenced federal policy. For example, provisions of the Violent Crime Control and Law Enforcement Act of 1994 included stricter liability for juveniles, "three strikes and you're out," and "truth in sentencing," all of which began at the state level. "Three strikes and you're out" statutes impose harsher sentences for repeat offenders convicted of three or more serious crimes; "truth in sentencing" refers to policies designed to maximize sentence terms and eliminate or restrict parole. Also, by this time, the federal courts upheld lengthy sentences for minor crimes and generally gave state legislatures free rein in establishing penal policy regulations. Both Democrats and Republicans aggressively supported punitive anticrime policies. As Campbell and Schoenfeld (1408) note, "a new political culture" had evolved "where 'law and order' politics became sacred pillars of state government, consuming a growing share of state resources, regardless of their effectiveness and relative utility in an era of declining crime and fiscal crisis."

The Process of Comparative Historical Analysis

Characteristic of comparative historical analysis, Campbell and Schoenfeld's study explains the development of mass imprisonment as a complex interaction of multiple causal factors operating at the national and state levels. Also characteristic, the research process is less apparent than in content analysis and the analysis of existing statistics. This is due partly to the dynamic interplay between theory and data as researchers apply both inductive and deductive logics to arrive at a configuration of factors that interact to produce particular outcomes (Ragin 1987). Figure 10.5 captures the general process of comparative historical research. The process combines two complementary sets of methods: within-case methods for analyzing individual cases and comparative methods to systematically compare cases (Lange 2013).[3]

FIGURE 10.5
The Process of
Comparative Historical
Analysis

SPECIFY ANALYTIC FRAMEWORK

Comparative historical research begins by establishing an analytic or theoretical framework for addressing the research question. To understand real-world transformations, for example, scholars invariably theorize about the causes of such transformations, and it is to this literature that comparative researchers turn to guide their research.

Campbell and Schoenfeld examined several theoretical explanations for mass incarceration. For example, socioeconomic changes in the late 20th century increased crime and "produced public anxiety that caused a dramatic shift in society's approach to crime control" (Campbell and Schoenfeld 2013:1376); "politicians, aided by the media, created and exploited crime as a proxy for a more explicit politics of

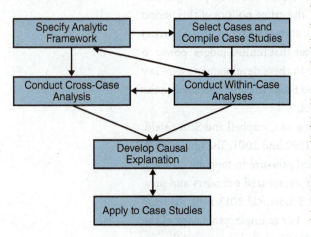

[3]The discussion of the mass incarceration study in this section relies on additional information graciously provided to us by Michael Campbell and Heather Schoenfeld (June 7, 2014).

race" (1376–77); and "the nature of the political system and the policy-making process in the United States create[d] incentives for tough-on-crime politics and policy" (1377). None of these explanations, however, accounts for a central paradox of mass incarceration in the United States: "If incarceration rates are first and foremost the result of decisions at the local level (arrests, prosecutions, and sentencing) and state level (sentencing policy, prison capacity), how is it that imprisonment grew in every state during roughly the same time period?" (1376).

In light of this paradox, Campbell and Schoenfeld (personal communication 2014) used a combination of extant theories and data from state cases to create their analytic framework, as outlined in Table 10.3. The literature pointed to politics as a source of incarceration growth, but the meaning of "politics" was not always clear. Since they "knew from examining [their] cases that politicians used crime control differently at different points in time," they first named the type of crime politics they observed in the cases: emergent crime politics, high crime politics, and captured crime politics (second row of Table 10.3). Second, to link politics with policies that increased imprisonment, they needed to have "policy outcomes" in their framework (last row of Table 10.3). Third, to incorporate a problem-solving model in which policy changes were a response to recurring problems, they decided to examine policymakers' definitions of the crime problem (third row of Table 10.3).

SELECT CASES AND COMPILE CASE STUDIES

The object of case selection varies by approach. Quantitative methods often assume that the "primary goal is to explain variation in dependent variables" (Ragin 2006:637). Therefore, the researcher wants cases to vary on the dependent variable; otherwise, there is nothing to explain. By contrast, comparative researchers tend to ask why particular transformations occur, which focuses attention on the presence of an outcome. Consequently, they often start by *selecting on the dependent variable*—by studying cases with the same outcome to "search for causally relevant commonalities" (Ragin 2006:638). This is essentially what Campbell and Schoenfeld did insofar as all of the states they selected had undergone, to varying degrees, a marked increase in the number of people imprisoned in the late 20th century. To strengthen inferences about "causally relevant commonalities" that produced this shift, they also selected cases that varied in size, by region, and by political and penal history. In short, their case selection was driven by the research topic (or outcome of interest) and analytic framework.

As Charles Ragin (2006:638) points out, sometimes researchers, like Campbell and Schoenfeld, limit their search to "positive cases to identify potential necessary [causal] conditions." But "[m]ore often, the identification of *relevant* negative cases follows from the study of positive cases, and researchers use these cases to validate the findings from the positive cases" (Ragin 2006:638). Ultimately, this second phase of case selection is crucial for testing theories. For although studying cases selected on the dependent variable can generate insights into causal processes and can contribute to theory building, it also can bias conclusions (Geddes 1990).

Campbell and Schoenfeld's choice of states was theory-driven, but also a practical matter of the availability of case studies. For each state selected, they needed detailed historical data on key actors and events in politics and penal policy from 1960 to 2001. Constructing in-depth case studies of this type, however, is an arduous task requiring extensive archival research. Consequently, comparative researchers frequently use the historical narratives of others, especially historians (Lange 2013). Campbell and Schoenfeld drew upon one or more data sources for each of the eight states. Three of the case studies were written by one of the co-authors based largely on original data such as "legislative bill files, internal communications between various actors in the penal and political field . . . , constituent letters, press releases, public testimonies, legal files . . . , and news articles pertaining to crime, prisons, and politics" (Campbell and Schoenfeld 2013:1384). The remaining case studies were secondary sources, which were drawn from similarly in-depth archival research.

CONDUCT WITHIN-CASE ANALYSES

The first analytic step in comparative historical analysis is to analyze sequences of events *within each case*. If you were studying countries, for example, you'd begin by effectively creating a timeline, or narrative, for each country based on your case studies.

Having compiled narratives for eight states, Campbell and Schoenfeld proceeded to analyze them case by case. As they read the cases, they report (personal communication, 2014), "we created a shared Google document where we kept a running narrative for each state that we could each add to, comment on, and code for relevant information." Each narrative provided a chronological account or story of the events and processes that led to changes in penal policy. Following their general framework, they coded national-level factors that seemed relevant for each state, and they coded state developments that seemed to be changing policy. Based on their coding, they uncovered similarities across cases that generated the three time periods identified in Table 10.3 (personal communication 2014). They then used two primary methods to identify causal sequences within cases: inductive periodization, which we described earlier, and process analysis.

process analysis
A within-case method of comparative historical analysis that examines possible intervening mechanisms that link an observed or theoretical association between events. Also called *process tracing*.

Process analysis (also called **process tracing**) examines the specific mechanisms through which one phenomenon has an effect on another (Mahoney 2004). In general, the analyst starts with an observed or theoretical association between events and then looks for intervening mechanisms linking these events within each case. This is analogous to identifying and testing the effects of intervening variables in a statistical association, discussed in Chapter 4. And like the quantitative analysis of intervening variables, it strengthens the inference that a relationship is causal (Mahoney 2004). Campbell and Schoenfeld's general framework theorized an association between politics and penal policy. Through process analysis, they uncovered recurring intervening links between national politics and state policy. One of these was interest group activity. The election of tough-on-crime politicians like President Reagan facilitated the organizational strength and activism of crime-related interest groups such as prosecutor's associations, correctional officers' unions, and victims' organizations, which influenced crime policy.

CONDUCT CROSS-CASE ANALYSIS / DEVELOP CAUSAL EXPLANATION / APPLY TO CASE STUDIES

The comparison of cases actually begins with the analysis of each case study, as investigators make note of similarities and differences. However, comparative historical analysts have developed more formal methods of cross-case analysis. We briefly discuss two of these methods below. For overviews of other methods, see James Mahoney (2004) and Matthew Lange (2013).

One set of methods is based on *Boolean algebra*, a mathematical logic in which variables are coded as dichotomies representing the presence or absence of some property. Instead of performing mathematical operations such as addition and subtraction, as in quantitative analysis, researchers examine combinations of causal variables that produce particular outcomes. A basic feature of Boolean techniques, as developed by Charles Ragin (1987), is the construction of "truth tables" to represent and analyze the data. A **truth table** consists of a data matrix that represents all possible combinations of values for a set of causal variables.

To show you how to use truth tables to make causal inferences, we adapt Charles Ragin and Lisa Amoroso's (2011:146–61) example of a study that examines causes of "ability tracking" (i.e., whether school districts track students based on their ability). Table 10.4 presents a truth table for this study with hypothetical data. The first step in creating this table is to identify all variables and place them in the columns of a matrix. In the school district study, the outcome variable is ability tracking (column 4); some possible causes of tracking include the racial diversity of the school district (column 1), "whether or not the school board elections in the district are open and competitive with good voter turnout " (column 2), and whether or not the teachers are unionized (column 3) (Ragin and Amoroso 2011:153).

The second step is to use the rows of the table to represent every possible combination of values on the independent variable—in other words, every possible combination of *causes* of ability tracking. Notice that, with three variables, the table has $2^3 = 8$ rows, and in each row we have dichotomized the variable to indicate its presence ($= 1$) or absence ($= 0$). Also note the various combinations: for example, the first row represents the combination in which racial diversity, competitive elections, and unionized teachers are all *absent* from school districts; the last row is the combination in which all three of these conditions are *present*. Other rows represent the other possible combinations.

truth table A table that presents all possible combinations of values, coded 0 (absent) or 1 (present), for a set of causal variables.

Table 10.4 Truth Table for Hypothetical Data on Tracking in School Districts

Row	Racial diversity	Causal Variable or Condition			Outcome	Number of cases
		Competitive elections	Unionized teachers			
1	0	0	0		0	3
2	0	0	1		0	3
3	0	1	0		0	1
4	0	1	1		0	1
5	1	0	0		0	1
6	1	0	1		0	1
7	1	1	0		1	3
8	1	1	1		1	3

Source: Adapted from Table 6.2 in Ragin and Amoroso (2011:155).

The third step is to code the outcome variable as 1 or 0, based on data from all cases, which in this example consists of a number of school districts. Although coded as 0 (absent) or 1 (present), this outcome is not always clear from the data. Rather, it is a summary of outcomes for all school districts with a particular combination of conditions. Indeed, the final column, which shows the frequency of each combination (number of cases), emphasizes this point, even though this column is not a necessary feature of a truth table.

Although Table 10.4 is a greatly simplified version of a larger and more complex analysis, it should give you an idea of how researchers may apply a Boolean approach to compare cases. Based on this table, you should be able to determine which configurations of conditions are associated with ability tracking (rows 7–8 = 1) and which are not (rows 1–6 = 0). Which two causal conditions are present whenever ability tracking occurs? (Answer: racial diversity and competitive elections.) Which condition is both present and absent when ability tracking occurs, and therefore can be eliminated as a cause of ability tracking? (Answer: unionized teachers.) The Boolean approach thus enables researchers to examine complex sets of causes holistically in terms of different combinations, which is an objective of comparative historical analysis. (For more information about this approach, see Ragin 1987, 2000, 2008; Ragin and Amoroso 2011.)

Campbell and Schoenfeld did not apply Ragin's Boolean approach. Rather, to begin to develop a general causal understanding of mass incarceration that applied to all states, they used a technique that Matthew Lange (2013) calls **narrative comparison** (also see Mahoney 2000; Rueschemeyer and Stephens 1997). With this approach, the

narrative comparison
A method of causal inference in which historical narratives of cases are analyzed to develop a general cross-case causal pattern and to validate it within each case.

analyst compares sequences of events across cases to determine if the cases follow a similar causal process. Campbell and Schoenfeld's comparison of historical sequences across states revealed the general causal pattern shown in Figure 10.6. They arrived at this model through an inductive, iterative process of data analysis and interpretation, as they describe (personal communication 2014):

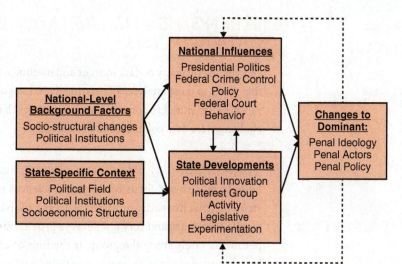

FIGURE 10.6
General Causal Model of Penal Transformation

> In our first round of analysis of the cases, we coded for national factors that seemed to influence the states and state factors that seemed to change politics and policies on the ground. We then went back to the data to try to determine what common national influences the cases shared and what exactly was changing at the state-level (the center boxes [Figure 10.6]). Here we found broad similarity across the cases. . . . [However,] we had cases that were not entirely consistent. That is, while all states trended toward mass incarceration, it happened at slightly different speeds and intensities. So we went back to the data a third time to code for state-level factors that may have influenced this process (the bottom left box).

Thus, Campbell and Schoenfeld worked back and forth between their evolving model and the case studies, developing a general model of the causal process that produced mass imprisonment and checking it against the case studies. By considering each case as whole, they could attend to causal complexity and determine the combinations of conditions, as presented in Figure 10.6, which led to increasingly punitive crime policy across all eight states.

SUMMARY

Traditionally, comparative historical analysis has consisted of the in-depth study of a small number of cases to determine the causes of historical change. Working from a theoretical framework that drives the search for causes, the analyst applies two complementary sets of methods: one set entails the construction and analysis of detailed historical narratives; the other involves the systematic comparison of cases. Both methods are strategic in developing explanations that identify configurations of causes of particular outcomes.

STRENGTHS AND LIMITATIONS OF EXISTING DATA ANALYSIS

Despite the diversity of data sources and methods, there are advantages and limitations that apply to most analyses of existing data. Like other approaches, existing data analysis is better suited to some research questions than others, and provides benefits and challenges for data collection and analysis.

Studying Social Structure, History, and Social Change

Despite the avowed focus of the social sciences on properties and changes in social structure, much of social research focuses on individual attitudes and behavior. Surveys are of individuals, and very few surveys provide direct measures of social relations; experiments rarely study the group as the unit of analysis; qualitative research often is based on interviews or observation of individual behavior. Existing data, however, often enable the researcher to analyze larger social units. You can see this most clearly in comparative historical research, with its emphasis on global and national transformations. The use of whole nations and states as units of analysis also characterizes demographic analyses such as Durkheim's study of suicide and research on racial segregation.

Similarly, existing data provide the social researcher with the best and often the only opportunity to study the past. To study some aspect of American society 50 or more years ago, it might be possible to conduct a survey of people who were alive at the time. But to do so presents several methodological problems, from the inaccuracy of respondents' memories to survivor bias in the sample. To study periods before the 20th century necessitates the search for existing data.

Most other approaches are also ill equipped to study social changes. Experiments, qualitative interviews, and field research have limited time spans, and longitudinal surveys rarely were undertaken until the last quarter of the 20th century. The analysis of existing data, however, is well suited to studies of social and cultural change. The sole object of comparative historical research is the study of social change. Trend studies such as the analysis of racial segregation have a long tradition among social demographers. Content analysis has been applied to numerous forms of communication to track changes in cultural images of women and minorities.

Nonreactive Measurement

A major problem in much social research is *reactive measurement*: changes in behavior that occur because of research participants' awareness that they are being studied or observed. Research with existing data also encounters this problem to the extent that the data sources are surveys or documents like autobiographies in which the author is clearly aware that the public will have access to what is said. Still, many existing data sources are nonreactive. With physical evidence and many other existing data sources, there is simply no reasonable connection between a researcher's use of the material and the producer's knowledge of such use. Lindner's content analysis of the influence of journalistic viewpoint on news reports on the Iraq War is nonreactive, as it occurred after the reports were written. Kearney and Levine's study of the impact of *16 and Pregnant* on teen childbearing is similarly nonreactive. Imagine, however, the kind of self-censorship that might have occurred if they had examined this relationship by asking teens in an interview survey whether they watched the show and about their sexual habits, including the use of contraceptives.

Cost Efficiency

Insofar as research using existing data bypasses the stage of data collection, it can economize greatly on cost, time, and personnel. This is most apparent in the secondary analysis of survey data, but other existing data sources also tend to be less costly than experiments, surveys, qualitative interviews, and field research. These costs vary depending on the nature of the data source and the time, money, and personnel required to obtain and to analyze the data. The tasks of the researcher using existing data, such as searching for and coding relevant information, often are tedious and time-consuming. Imagine, for example, the efforts of Lindner and his assistants in locating and coding numerous variables for 742 print articles. Yet, the cost per case in such studies is generally quite small compared with the cost of interviewing a respondent or running a single participant through an experiment.

Data Limitations

A major challenge that we noted about the analysis of existing statistics applies to all forms of existing data: finding data appropriate to answer a research question. This obstacle may seem less apparent to you than it is because of the numerous studies cited in this chapter that address a wide range of research questions. Using existing data, however, is a bit like wearing someone else's shoes. They may fit perfectly well. But more likely they will either be too small, pinching your toes, or too large, causing you to stumble. Data to address a research question simply may not exist. If available, the data may not be ideally suited to the researcher's purposes, may provide only indirect measurement, or may not be complete.

The completeness or representativeness of the data is especially problematic for researchers studying the remote past. Often, they must rely on whatever traces of information they can find, which are almost certain to be incomplete and are probably biased. Physical evidence is invariably subject to selective survival and selective deposit. **Selective survival** refers to the fact that some objects survive longer than others. The fact that pottery and bone survive the elements better than wood and paper has long been a problem for the archaeologist. A more serious problem for users of the written record is **selective deposit**—systematic biases in the content of the evidence that is available. Records may be selectively destroyed; other information may be edited.

selective survival
Incompleteness of existing historical data due to the fact that some objects survive longer than others.

selective deposit
Systematic biases in the content of existing historical data due to actions such as selective destruction or editing of written records.

Eugene Webb and associates (2000) note that members of Congress are allowed to edit proofs of the *Congressional Record*, a transcript of the speeches and activities of the US Congress, which means that this document hardly serves as a spontaneous account of events. As another example, these authors cite a study of the longevity of the ancient Romans based on evidence from tombstones. Wives who died after their husbands may have been underrepresented insofar as they were less likely to get a tombstone than wives who died before their husbands. Also, middle-class and upper-class Romans were more likely to have tombstones than the lower classes of Roman society. And the fact that mortality rates are likely to have varied across classes could bias estimates of longevity.

SUMMARY

Compared with other approaches to social research, existing data analysis is better suited for studying social structure, history, and social change; much of existing data tends to be less subject to reactive measurement effects; and using existing data tends to be more cost effective. On the other hand, it may be difficult to find data that fit a research question, the data may provide only approximate and indirect indicators of variables, and the data may be incomplete and unrepresentative of actions and events.

KEY TERMS

archive, p. 297

big data, p. 302

codebook, p. 316

comparative historical
  analysis, p. 321

content analysis, p. 309

data archives, p. 299

demography, p. 301

dictionary, p. 316

narrative comparison,
  p. 328

process analysis, p. 326

recording units, p. 313

selective deposit, p. 331

selective survival, p. 331

truth table, p. 327

vital statistics, p. 297

KEY POINTS

- Existing data analysis encompasses a variety of methods in which researchers make use of data produced by some other person or organization.
- Existing data are everywhere; they may be found in public documents and official statistics; private and personal records; mass media; physical, nonverbal materials; and social science data archives.

- A huge volume of statistical data is readily available from the official statistics of government agencies and international organizations and from the Internet.
- The biggest challenge to using existing statistics for social research is locating data that can adequately address a research question.
- Content analysis involves the analysis of verbal or visual communications by systematically summarizing their symbolic content.
- Content analysts develop coding schemes to record the content of a sample of communications.
- Traditionally, comparative historical analysis has addressed large-scale social transformations by systematically comparing the historical narratives of a small number of cases.
- To infer complex causal configurations, comparative historical researchers develop or use existing historical narratives of cases, and then use both within- and cross-case methods of analysis.
- Existing data analysis is the best approach for studying social structure, history, and social change; it tends to be more cost effective than other approaches; and much of existing data is nonreactive.
- It is often a challenge, however, to find data that fit a research question, the data may provide only indirect evidence of variables, and may be incomplete or a biased sample.

REVIEW QUESTIONS

1. Give an example of social research that uses each of the following data sources: (1) public documents, (2) private documents, (3) mass media, and (4) physical artifacts.
2. In what forms does the Census Bureau release information from the decennial census?
3. What do the authors mean when they say that "the use of data archives is an extension of survey research, field research, and in-depth interviews"?
4. Name two sources of *official* statistics and give examples of the data they provide.
5. Identify common units of analysis in the content analysis of textual data. What is the difference between a recording unit and a sampling unit?
6. What are the three defining characteristics of traditional comparative historical research?
7. What are the principal advantages of using existing data?

EXERCISES

1. To familiarize yourself with the data sources and tools available online from the US Census Bureau, visit the home page www.census.gov. Using this site as a point

of departure, find the table or data that will answer the following questions (unless otherwise indicated, provide the most recent estimates and specify the date):

(a) What percentage of the US population has income below the poverty level?

(b) What percentage of the US population is foreign born?

(c) Which states have the highest and lowest median household incomes?

(d) What is the average price of new single-family homes?

(e) What percentage of the US population who commute to work drive alone?

(f) What percentage of the population in your state are college graduates?

(g) What was the growth rate of the world population in 1970? What is it estimated to be in 2020?

2. In the December 2000 issue of *Social Psychology Quarterly* (63:352–64), Matthew Hunt and associates report a content analysis of the attention given to race and ethnicity in a leading social psychology journal. Read the article and answer the following questions.

(a) What general assumption of social psychological theory and research is called into question by the researchers, as reflected in the main title of the article, "Color Blind"?

(b) What is the researchers' unit of analysis (i.e., the recording unit)?

(c) One aspect of attention to race/ethnicity is whether race/ethnicity was "seriously considered" in the analysis. How is this operationally defined?

(d) What evidence is given regarding the reliability of the coding scheme?

(e) As indicated in Table 1, what changes occurred between 1970–74 and 1995–99 with respect to each type of attention to race/ethnicity?

(f) When a similar coding scheme was applied to the attention given to gender in the same journal, what did the researchers find? Compare changes in attention to *gender* between 1970–74 and 1995–99 with changes in attention to *race/ethnicity*.

(g) Were certain methodological approaches (e.g., surveys, experiments) more conducive to the examination of race/ethnicity than others? Briefly explain.

3. An advantage of much existing data is the ability to measure social change. Often you can measure change by replicating previous research. Older content analyses

in particular are well suited to this task. Find a study using content analysis that was published in the 1970s or 1980s and replicate it by extending the period of observation from the end date in the original study until the present. Examples of studies that could be replicated are Leslie Zebrowitz McArthur and Beth Gabrielle Resko's (1975) study of the portrayal of men and women in television advertisements, Neil Malamuth and Barry Spinner's (1980) analysis of sexual violence in best-selling erotic magazines (*Playboy* and *Penthouse*), and Ruth Thibodeau's (1989) analysis of the depiction of blacks in *New Yorker* cartoons.

11

Multiple Methods

Two or More Approaches Are Better Than One

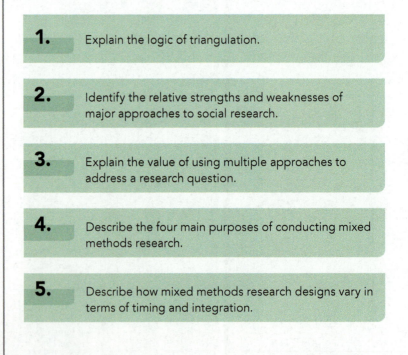

STUDENT LEARNING OBJECTIVES

By the end of this chapter, you should be able to

1. Explain the logic of triangulation.

2. Identify the relative strengths and weaknesses of major approaches to social research.

3. Explain the value of using multiple approaches to address a research question.

4. Describe the four main purposes of conducting mixed methods research.

5. Describe how mixed methods research designs vary in terms of timing and integration.

The preceding chapters have described a variety of approaches to social research. Much of the time investigators use only one of these approaches. In the long run, though, the best strategy is to address a research question with multiple methods. Indeed, people often adopt this strategy to solve problems in their everyday lives.

Consider, for example, the simple problem of waking up early to catch a flight. Let's say you normally awaken by means of an electric clock radio set for 7:30 a.m. To make sure that you are awake by 6:00, you might employ several methods. You might set the clock radio for 5:55, set your cell phone alarm for 6:00, and ask an early-rising friend to phone you at 6:05. You would then have three independent and somewhat dissimilar methods for solving the problem. If the electricity should go off, the cell phone alarm would work. If your cell phone battery dies, the friend should come through. If the friend proves unreliable, one of the other methods should work. By using multiple methods that do not share the same inherent weaknesses, we enhance our chances of solving the problem.

The value of using multiple methods is conveyed by the concept of **triangulation**, a term social scientists have borrowed from the field of navigation. To understand its conventional usage, imagine that you are lost deep in the woods of Maine and need to pinpoint your location for the local rescue team. Assume you have an old cell phone *without* GPS. Using your phone, you could call members of the team stationed at two different places, A and B. The team member at each position would then use a directional antenna to get a bearing on your location, which is represented by each of the dashed lines running from A and B in Figure 11.1. Neither direction by itself would provide enough information because you could be located anywhere along the A or B lines. But the point where the lines intersect would pin down your location. (Incidentally, GPS is based on a more sophisticated form of triangulation from satellites.)

Triangulation in social research refers to the use of two or more dissimilar methods to address the same research question. Each method is analogous to the different vantage points in Figure 11.1. As you have seen, all research procedures are subject to limitations and biases; however, dissimilar methods are not likely to share the same weaknesses. Therefore, we become more confident when different methods separately zero in on the same findings. In effect, the strengths of one method offset the weaknesses of the other.

The logic of triangulation applies to many different research activities, some of which we have described in previous chapters. These activities include the use of multiple measures of the same underlying concept; construct validation, in which researchers consider a variety of evidence to assess the validity of measurement; experimental replications to enhance external validity; and the use of two or more observers to record observations in field research.

This chapter extends these examples of multi-method research in two ways. First, we focus here on the use of different approaches (e.g., surveys and field observation) or kinds of data (e.g., field notes and statistical records).

triangulation
Addressing a research question with multiple methods or measures that do not share the same methodological weaknesses.

FIGURE 11.1
Triangulating the Location of a Cell Phone from Two Points, A and B

Cell phone

A   B

mixed methods research A research study that combines two or more approaches to data collection and analysis.

Combining different approaches or data, especially quantitative and qualitative, is known as **mixed methods research**; it has emerged as a new field in the social sciences, with a distinct history and methodology (Greene 2007; Pearce 2012; Small 2011; Tashakkori and Teddlie 2010).[1] Second, multiple methods may be applied to achieve purposes other than the convergence or confirmation of findings, which is the principal aim of triangulation. As we show, different approaches may be used to address complementary questions that clarify or deepen our understanding about a phenomenon; one research approach may be used to develop another approach; or different research approaches may be combined to expand the breadth or range of the research.

To begin, we compare the relative strengths and weaknesses of four basic approaches to social research. Next we present four examples of mixed methods research, which involve different combinations of approaches and serve different purposes. Then we outline the basic purposes and designs for conducting mixed methods research.

A COMPARISON OF FOUR BASIC APPROACHES TO SOCIAL RESEARCH

The principle of triangulation emphasizes the value of testing hypotheses with different methods that do not share the same methodological weaknesses. In this way, we build confidence in our assertions about the social world. An important implication of triangulation is that social researchers need to know the relative strengths and weaknesses of each approach in order to decide which methods to select and how best to combine them when possible.

In the concluding sections of Chapters 7–10, we discussed the strengths and weaknesses of each of the major approaches to social research. Table 11.1 summarizes these discussions by identifying the strengths and weaknesses of four main approaches on eight dimensions. To simplify the comparisons, the table focuses attention on specific ideal forms of these four strategies: laboratory experiments, surveys, field research, and analysis of existing statistics. It is important to recall, however, the variations within each basic strategy. Experiments may be conducted in the field as well as in the laboratory; surveys vary in mode (e.g., telephone interviews and mail questionnaires); field research may involve varying degrees of participation in the research setting and in-depth interviewing (which also serves as a stand-alone method); and existing data come in many forms that may be analyzed in markedly different ways. Furthermore, there are other research strategies that do not fit neatly into this fourfold typology,

---

[1]The term "mixed methods" generally refers to research that combines quantitative and qualitative methods or data; the term "multi-methods" refers more broadly to the combined use of different methods, whether exclusively quantitative, exclusively qualitative, or mixed. This chapter focuses on research that involves any possible combination of approaches or methods of data collection; however, we prefer to call this "mixed-methods research" and to use the literature on mixed methods as a guide to thinking about how methods may be combined.

which we ignore or touch on only lightly in this book, such as structured observation, life history interviews, ethnomethodology, and conversation analysis.

The entries in the table summarize the relative strength of each approach on each of eight dimensions. "W" means that the approach is relatively weak; "M" means that it is of "medium" strength or weakness; and "S" indicates that the dimension is a strength of the approach. As the first row of the table shows, none of the basic strategies is highly flexible with regard to the topics or research questions that it may address. The relative inflexibility of experiments and existing data analysis stems from analogous limitations: experimentation depends on what it is practically and ethically possible to manipulate; existing data research depends on the availability of the data. Beyond its general accessibility to research questions, each approach is uniquely suited to obtaining particular kinds of information. Thus, surveys are best for estimating population characteristics and describing the distribution of attitudes and opinions; field research affords access to actors' definitions of complex situations and events; and the analysis of existing data often provides the best and/or only means of studying the past and larger social units.

Table 11.1　Strengths and Weaknesses of Approaches on Eight Study Dimensions

| | Relative Strength* | | | |
DIMENSIONS OF ASSESSMENT	Lab Experiment	Survey	Field Research	Existing Data
Content restrictions: What is and is not feasible or practical to study	W	M	M	W
Internal validity: Control over extraneous variables	S	M	W	M
Ease of measurement: Ability to measure or perform checks on reliability and validity	S	S	W	M
Nonreactive measurement: Control for effects of awareness of being observed	W	W	M	S
Contextual understanding: Ability to study actions in relation to the social context	W	W	S	M
Control for investigator bias: Control for effects of researcher characteristics and behavior	W	W	M	S
External validity: Ability to generalize from sample results	W	S	W	M
Ability to replicate	S	S	W	M

*W, weak; M, medium; S, strong.

Experiments are strong in establishing internal validity because they provide the strongest inferences about cause and effect. Statistical controls possible in surveys and some existing data research allow for partial control of extraneous variables (hence the "M" in the table); however, the absence of such formal controls generally makes field research least acceptable for testing causal hypotheses.

Although it is easier to create measures and assess reliability and validity in experiments and surveys, these approaches are most vulnerable to methodological artifacts stemming from participants' awareness of being tested and experimenter or interviewer effects. Nonreactive measurement is a major strength of much existing data research. On the other hand, the extent to which field research is vulnerable to these artifacts depends on how well the investigator becomes accepted by others in the field setting and on how well he or she is able to perform simultaneously the roles of participant and observer. The greater the trust the investigator is able to develop, the less the likelihood of reactive measurement; the more adept he or she is at managing the participant and observer roles, the less the likelihood of investigator bias.

By observing social life in naturalistic settings, field research is best able to provide a holistic and contextual understanding of social actions. By comparison, experiments—whether in the laboratory or the field—isolate one or a few variables at a time, making it difficult to study complex interactions; surveys study what people say in the unique context of an interview or questionnaire, which may not indicate how they will act and feel in everyday life; and available data may provide limited contextual information.

Survey research affords the greatest control over error and bias associated with sampling and therefore provides strong sample generalization. The susceptibility of some existing data to selective deposit makes this approach moderate on sampling generalization. By contrast, external validity is a major weakness of experiments insofar as they typically take place in highly restricted settings with small, nonrandom samples of research participants. And while the quality of sampling is generally better in field research than in experiments, field studies are nonetheless based on isolated settings and nonrandom sampling procedures.

Experiments and survey studies are the easiest to replicate. Indeed, replication is fairly common in experiments, and surveys such as the GSS and various polls repeatedly ask the same questions to measure trends. The time-consuming nature of and lack of standardization in field research make this approach very difficult to replicate. Replication with alternative measures or with respect to different time periods is sometimes possible with existing data research, but this depends again on the availability of the data.

As Table 11.1 shows, patterns vary across the four main approaches, and no two research strategies share the same strengths and weaknesses. As our mixed methods examples will show, this is what makes the approaches complementary and strengthens inferences based on a triangulation of methods.

SUMMARY

The principle of triangulation implies that researchers should weigh the strengths and weaknesses of each approach to determine the best approach or best combination of approaches to address a research question. That no two approaches share the same strengths and weaknesses underscores the value of using a combination of approaches.

EXAMPLES OF MIXED METHODS RESEARCH

Mixed methods research may occur with many different combinations of approaches. In the following examples, researchers mixed a survey with in-depth interviews and participant observation, a field experiment with a survey, and a field experiment with field observation; in the final example, they used four different approaches or sources of data.

Effect of Abuse on Marriage and Cohabitation

An excellent example of research combining survey and field research is Andrew Cherlin and associates' (2004) study of the influence of physical and sexual abuse on marriage and cohabitation among low-income women. The investigators carried out their two-pronged study in low-income neighborhoods in Boston, Chicago, and San Antonio. In each neighborhood, the survey sample was randomly selected from households with children in which a female was the primary caregiver and the income was below 200 percent of the federal poverty line. In all, 2,402 women were interviewed, with questions about sensitive topics such as abuse and sexual activity asked using audio computer-assisted self-interviews to ensure confidentiality. Families in the field research, who were not in the survey, were recruited nonrandomly from the same neighborhoods as the survey. Data from these 256 families were drawn from a combination of in-depth interviews and participant observation that took place over a four-year period. For the first 18 months, the families were visited once or twice a month as researchers interviewed caregivers and accompanied them and their children "to the welfare office, doctor, grocery store, or workplace" (Cherlin et al. 2004:773). Thereafter, they were seen every six months.

Previous theory and research as well as preliminary analyses led the investigators to expect parallel sets of associations in the field and survey data. In their field research, they discovered a pattern that they called "abated unions," in which women had withdrawn from serious relationships with men altogether. Reasoning that experiences with abusive men might lead women to avoid intimate relationships, they expected the fieldwork data to show that women who have been abused as adults, but not as children, will be more likely to have abated unions than other women. The cross-sectional survey could measure only union status at the time of the survey—whether the woman was married, cohabiting, or single—and unlike the field research data, it did not contain enough information to construct the history of the unions. Cherlin and associates reasoned, however, that these status categories should correspond to fieldwork expectations in predictable ways. Women classified as having abated unions, for example, should be more likely to be single than married or cohabiting at the time of the survey; therefore, they hypothesized that women who have experienced abuse as adults are more likely to be currently single than married or cohabiting compared with women who have not been abused as adults.

Table 11.2 shows the parallel results from the field research and the survey. Table 11.1A breaks down union patterns observed in the field by the timing of reported abuse; Table 11.1B breaks down current union status, recorded in the survey, by the timing of reported abuse. As the field data show, women in abated unions were more likely to have been abused in adulthood (46 percent) than only as children (15 percent). And as inferred from the field data, single women in the survey were more likely to have been abused as adults only (74 percent) than as children (64 percent).

Table 11.2 Union Patterns (A) and Current Union Status (B) by Abuse Categories

	Experience of Abuse			
A. UNION PATTERNS (FIELD RESEARCH)	No Abuse	Childhood Only	Adulthood Only	Childhood and Adulthood
Sustained or Transitory Unions	97%	85%	54%	90%
Abated Unions	4	15	46	10
Total	101%	100%	100%	100%
Number of respondents	(81)	(13)	(63)	(71)
B. CURRENT UNION STATUS (SURVEY)				
Married or Cohabiting	46%	35%	26%	33%
Single	54	64	74	67
Total	100%	99%	100%	101%
Number of respondents	(1,139)	(224)	(539)	(494)

Note: Percentages may not sum to 100 due to rounding. Adapted from Tables 2 and 3 in Cherlin et al. (2004:775 and 777).

In a similar fashion, the investigators developed other expectations and hypotheses about the impact of a history of abuse on marriage and cohabitation. In every instance, both fieldwork expectations and survey hypotheses were supported by the data.

What Employers Say versus What They Do

Surveys are a very good strategy for measuring what people think and how they feel about something; however, they are less effective in measuring actual behavior. Still, researchers continue to use verbal reports of what people say they would do as indicators of what they actually do. To determine whether this is appropriate, Devah Pager and Lincoln Quillian (2005) compared a field experiment with a survey. Their findings show that using verbal reports of what people say they would do may be particularly problematic in studies of discriminatory behavior.

▲ Devah Pager

We described the field experiment (referred to as an "audit study") in Chapter 7. Recall that Pager (2003) sent matched pairs of confederates, called testers, to apply for real job openings in Milwaukee, Wisconsin. To test for hiring discrimination, the testers were similar except for two characteristics: race and criminal record. Pager manipulated race by having one white pair, which applied for 150 jobs, and one black pair, which applied for 200 jobs. All of the testers were men, and within each same-race pair one tester presented himself as having a criminal record and the other did not. Pager measured employment opportunity by whether the applicant received a callback for an interview, finding evidence of discrimination on the basis of both race and criminal record: blacks received fewer callbacks than whites, and men with criminal records received fewer callbacks than their counterpart without criminal records.

The second study, a telephone survey, was conducted several months after the field experiment. Each of the 350 employers who had been contacted in the field experiment was called and asked to participate in an interview about hiring preferences and practices. During the survey, interviewers read a "vignette describing a job applicant with characteristics" that closely matched the profile of the testers in the field experiment who indicated that they had a criminal record (Pager and Quillian 2005:362). Thus, if the tester had been white, the vignette described a hypothetical white applicant, and if the tester had been black, the hypothetical applicant in the vignette was black. Below is the wording of the vignette (Pager and Quillian 2005:362):

> Chad is a 23-year-old [black/white] male. He finished high school and has steady work experience in entry-level jobs. He has good references and interacts well with people. About a year ago, Chad was convicted of a drug felony and served 12 months in prison. Chad was released last month and is now looking for a job. How likely would you be to hire Chad for an entry-level opening in your company?

To answer the question in the vignette, employers were asked whether they would be "very likely, somewhat likely, somewhat unlikely, or very unlikely" to hire the applicant.

In almost every way, the vignette presented in the survey corresponded to the profile of the tester whom the employer encountered in the field experiment. The hypothetical applicant Chad had similar levels of education, experience, and personal qualities, and the type of crime was identical. And so, Pager and Quillian were able to compare employers' self-reported willingness to hire with how they actually responded to an applicant with nearly identical characteristics. Of the 350 employers contacted in the field experiment, 199, or 58 percent, responded to the survey. The results of the survey were not at all comparable to the field experiment. In the survey, irrespective of an applicant's race, slightly more than 60 percent of employers said they would be "somewhat likely" or "very likely" to hire a drug offender. In the field experiment, the callback rate was 17 percent for white testers with a criminal record and 5 percent for black testers with a criminal record.

To take into account the fact that some testers may not receive a callback for reasons unrelated to race or criminal record, Pager and Quillian calculated "the likelihood that a tester with a criminal record will receive a callback *relative to* a white tester without a criminal record" (2005:365). Thus, since 34 percent of white applicants with no criminal record received a callback and 17 percent of white applicants with a criminal record received callbacks, the adjusted percentage of the latter group was 17/34 or 50 percent.

Figure 11.2 presents the results of this calculation, comparing the employers' self-reported likelihood of hiring with the adjusted percentage of testers with criminal records who received callbacks. The figure shows a marginally significant difference between survey and audit results for white applicants ($p < .06$) and a significant difference for black applicants ($p < .05$). As Pager and Quillian (2005:365) point out, "the callback rate for black ex-offenders (14.7) [is] far short of the survey estimates of hiring likelihoods (61.7)."

Why the large disparity between what employers say they would do in a survey and what they actually did in the field experiment? Pager and Quillian (2005) provide several possible methodological explanations. One possibility is that attitude measures are susceptible to the *social desirability effect*, a problem we discussed in Box 5.4. This refers to the tendency of respondents to conceal their true feelings by giving answers that project a more favorable image of themselves. Thus, if employers perceive that racial

FIGURE 11.2
Expressed Willingness to Hire a Drug Offender According to Employer Survey and Field Experiment (Audit Study). Survey results include employers who said they were "very likely" or "somewhat likely" to hire the hypothetical applicant (with "very" at bottom of columns). Audit results represent the ratio of the percentage of callbacks for each group to the percentage of callbacks for white nonoffenders.

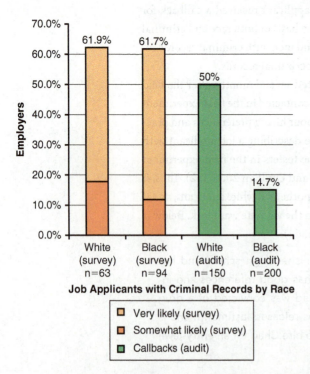

discrimination will not be viewed favorably, they may consciously suppress their negative reaction to a black applicant by falsely reporting their feelings.

A second possibility is that employers may be indicating their "genuine willingness to consider hiring an applicant with a criminal record *in the abstract*" (Pager and Quillian 2005:371), as in response to the hypothetical applicant in the survey. However, in real hiring situations, many factors may come into play, and "the presence of a criminal record may become a salient criterion by which to weed out less-qualified applicants" (371). Thirdly, the "priming" of characteristics such as race and criminal record may not elicit the same intensity of response in a phone interview as they do in person. Of course, it is possible that all of these processes as well as others may have produced the observed discrepancy.

Explaining Discrimination in a Low-Wage Labor Market

In 2004, Devah Pager, Bruce Western, and Bart Bonikowski (2009) conducted a second audit study in New York City. Whereas the Milwaukee study examined the impact of a criminal record on job discrimination, controlling for race, the New York study focused directly on racial discrimination. In addition, the new study examined the experiences of three racial/ethnic groups: black, Latino, and white. Thus, the researchers formed two teams, each consisting of a black, Latino, and white tester, who were men of similar ages and height, carefully matched in verbal skills, and underwent rigorous training. In one of the teams, the white tester had a criminal record and in the other team he did not; therefore, unlike the Milwaukee study, the impact of race could be compared directly with the impact of a criminal record. Finally, all testers took extensive field notes of their interactions with employers, which enabled the researchers to explore the process of discrimination.

To select job openings, each week over a period of nine months, the researchers drew a simple random sample of job listings from the classified sections of major New York newspapers and the online service Craigslist. Sampled job listings were limited to "entry-level positions, defined as jobs requiring little previous experience and no more than a high school degree. Job titles included restaurant jobs, retail sales, warehouse workers, couriers, telemarketers . . . and a wide range of other low-wage positions" (Pager et al. 2009:782). Testers were assigned fictitious résumés and presented themselves "as high school graduates with steady work experience in entry-level jobs" (781). The dependent variable was measured as any positive response consisting of either a callback for a second interview or a job offer.

Each team performed a separate experiment, so there are two sets of results. Figure 11.3 shows the positive response rates for the first team, consisting of equally qualified white, Latino, and black male applicants. Based on applications to 171 employers, white testers received a callback or job offer 31 percent of the time, compared with 25.1 percent for Latinos and 15.2 percent for blacks. Statistical tests indicate that the

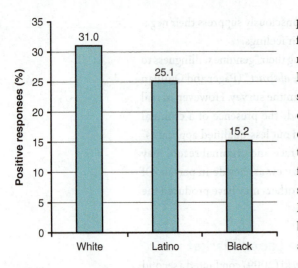

FIGURE 11.3
Percent of Callbacks
or Job offers by Race/
Ethnicity

FIGURE 11.4
Percent of Callbacks
or Job offers by Race/
Ethnicity and Criminal
Record

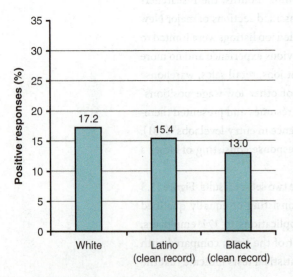

positive response rate for blacks differs significantly from the rates for both whites and Latinos, but there is no significant difference between whites and Latinos. Figure 11.4 shows the positive response rates for the second team, in which the white tester was assigned a criminal record. In this case, white testers received a callback or job offer for 17.2 percent of 169 job applications, compared with 15.4 percent for Latinos and 13.0 for blacks. These positive response rates do not differ significantly, essentially replicating the results of the Milwaukee study. That is, New York employers treated black and Latino applicants as equivalent to whites with a criminal record.

Together, the Milwaukee and New York audit studies provide clear evidence of "the continuing significance of race" in hiring decisions. These data do not tell us, however, the processes through which racial discrimination takes place. To uncover differential treatment, the researchers turned to testers' field notes to determine how interactions with employers differed by race/ethnicity. Although in many cases the discrimination was so subtle that differential treatment was difficult to detect, the researchers were able to identify three consistent patterns of discrimination in employers' behavior, which generally occurred at different points in the hiring process.

The first type of discrimination, which occurred at the initial point of contact, was "categorical exclusion": "an immediate or automatic rejection of the black (or minority) candidate in favor of a white applicant" (Pager et al. 2009:787). This pattern was revealed in several cases when minority applicants were told that the "position has already been filled," but the white tester, who applied later, was offered the job.

The second pattern of discrimination, labeled "shifting standards," occurred after initial contact as employers assessed the qualifications of applicants. In these cases, "similar qualifications or deficits" took on "varying relevance depending on the applicant's race" (Pager et al. 2009:787). For example, in the case of a job at a moving company, identical qualifications were evaluated differently for minority and white applicants. All three candidates pointed out their prior experience as stockpersons (albeit in different companies). But whereas both the black and Latino testers were told that they were looking for someone with moving experience, the employer told the white tester: "To be honest, we're looking for someone with specific moving experience. But because you've worked for [a storage company], that has a little to do with moving" (789). The tester was then asked "to come in tomorrow."

The third pattern of discrimination, "race-coded job channeling," occurred at the stage of job placement. This pattern "represents a process by which minority applicants are steered toward particular job types, often those characterized by greater physical demands and reduced customer contact" (Pager et al. 2009:787). For example, the black tester described the following interaction when he applied for a sales position at a lighting store:

> When she asked what position I was looking for I said I was open, but that since they were looking for a salesperson I would be interested in that. She smiled, put her head in her hand and her elbow on the table and said, "I need a stock boy. Can you do stock boy?" (Pager et al. 2009:790)

The Latino and white testers, by contrast, were able to apply for the advertised sales position.

Testers' field notes revealed 53 cases of job channeling. When these cases were coded as downward (e.g., from sales to stock boy) or upward (e.g., dishwasher to wait staff), the researchers found in the majority of cases that all testers on a team were channeled in the same direction. In the remaining 23 cases, however, channeling was strongly related to race. When channeling varied across testers, nine black testers, five Latino testers, and one white tester (who presented a criminal record) were channeled into lower positions, and no black testers, two Latino testers, and six white testers were channeled up.

Unpredictability and Unequal Control of Work Schedules and Time

What are you looking for in a job? According to a 2015 Harris Poll, 50 percent of job seekers are attracted to jobs with flexible hours (Indeed 2015). It seems likely that this desire is a response to what sociologists Dan Clawson and Naomi Gerstel (2014) describe as the increasing unpredictability in work hours and schedules. Unpredictability occurs because of ordinary disruptions in people's lives such as a sick child or parent and because employers ask or require people to stay at work late or arrive early. Clawson and Gerstel (2014:3) studied how people deal with this unpredictability, showing that "control over time is a crucial resource for keeping a job and having a family" and that this control is "shaped by gender and class inequalities."

To examine the joint effects of gender *and* class on schedules and hours, Clawson and Gerstel chose four linked health care occupations: doctors, nurses, emergency medical technicians (EMTs), and nursing assistants. Nurses and nursing assistants are almost exclusively women; physicians and

▼ Dan Clawson

▲ Naomi Gerstel

EMTs are mostly men. Physicians and nurses are relatively advantaged in terms of class: their occupations require more education and training, and they earn significantly more than their gender counterparts, EMTs and nursing assistants. Thus, the investigators looked at "two groups of women and two groups of men—each divided by class" (Gerstel and Clawson 2014:402). The choice of health care was strategic because it is a large part of the growing service industry and issues of time are salient, as many health care jobs must be filled around the clock.

In comparing unpredictability and control of time in these four occupations, Clawson and Gerstel used multiple methods to gather four types of data in two counties in the northeastern United States. First, they conducted a mail survey with a random sample of 200 people in each occupation. Second, they carried out 208 in-depth interviews, one-quarter of which were with individuals who managed schedules in the four occupations. Third, they observed eight sites for a total of 615 hours at four kinds of medical work organizations: two hospitals, two nursing homes, two doctors' offices, and two EMS centers (a fire department and a private ambulance service). Fourth, they obtained several documents, including union contracts and, at the observational sites, work schedules, handbooks given to new employees, and posted policies.

Rather than report results separately for each data source, Clawson and Gerstel seamlessly draw on all sources to describe variations in unpredictability among the four occupations. To measure unpredictability, all respondents were asked in the survey to report how many hours they worked last week at their main job; then they were asked, "Is this the number of hours that you usually work?" The survey data showed a negligible gender difference but significant class difference, with 26 percent of EMTs and 28 percent of nursing assistants, as compared with 15 percent of doctors and 17 percent of nurses, not working their usual hours in the previous week (Clawson and Gerstel 2014:93). In addition, at one of the two nursing homes they observed, the researchers obtained the official schedule as well as information on who actually worked for a six-month period. The results, as they report, were "stunning" (96). Even though the nursing home had a high occupancy rate and low staff turnover, 34 percent of the shifts were not worked as scheduled in advance.

Clawson and Gerstel defined any deviation from the official schedule as "churning." Churning occurred when employees added time to their official schedules and took time off from work for sick leaves and vacations. Their analysis of churning showed sharp differences among the occupations in how people deal with unpredictability and in the amount of control they have over it. With respect to added time, for example, there was a gender difference: both EMTs and doctors worked a lot of extra time, albeit for different reasons—EMTs for the money and doctors for peer respect and other reasons. EMTs were granted overtime often, with very little conflict between them and their employers, and doctors felt that their profession demanded long hours. By contrast, nurses and nursing assistants tended to work fewer hours but for very different reasons. Nurses sought to avoid extra time in union contracts, and were in conflict with supervisors about extending their workdays. Nursing assistants wanted to work more hours to pay the bills, but were constrained by employers who hired part-time workers or restricted positions to 24 to 32 regular weekly hours to avoid paying overtime.

As expected, Clawson and Gerstel found that families influenced the unpredictability of work hours and schedules, as changes were often created by family contingencies such as the need to care for a sick child. Thus, it is not surprising that their analysis of the nursing home schedule showed that mothers were more likely to call in to report that they could not work and to swap scheduled work times. Less expected, however, Clawson and Gerstel (2014:160) also found an intersection of class and gender in families' responses to the unpredictability of work hours and schedules. On the one hand, "advantaged male and female employees use their class privilege to uphold conventional gender expectations." With greater control over their schedules, doctors devoted long hours on the job and expected their spouses or paid caregivers to take care of the household and children, while nurses used their favorable market position and control to resist hours and "schedules that interfered with what they viewed as their primary responsibility to give care at home" (173). On the other hand, "class disadvantage pushes men and women to weaken gender expectations" (160). Nursing assistants, who often were the primary family breadwinner and lacked the power and control to resist schedule demands, worked extra shifts and unpredictable hours that forced them to rely on extended family for childcare. And, unlike doctors, EMTs were less likely to prioritize career over family. Dependent on their wives' incomes and able to modify their schedules "because of responsive employers and cooperative coworkers" (205), EMTs devoted a significant amount of time to domestic work and childcare.

In general, Clawson and Gerstel (2014:14) argue, "the allocation, experience, and control of time is collective," creating a "web of time":

> Because people are linked, changes in one person's schedule often create changes in the schedule of another person, both in the workplace and outside of it. Sometimes relations in the web create problems by increasing unpredictability; sometimes they provide solutions. The web leads to both since it depends on cooperation and accommodation. But it also creates struggles for control and other conflicts in and between occupations and organizations.

One solution to unpredictability and a key part of the web of time is coworkers who swap hours and schedules with one another. Coworker schedule swaps benefited both employees and employers, and happened in every occupation. However, they were most important for EMTs and especially nursing assistants, who face rigid schedules.

In the end, Clawson and Gerstel's research compels us to reconsider the meaning of flexibility. People who value job flexibility usually have in mind the ability to adjust work hours to deal with unexpected problems. In this sense, flexibility is one way of handling the unpredictable disruptions in our routines; another way "is to have a flexible family willing (and able) to adjust to our job demands" (Clawson and Gerstel 2014:8). Yet, both sources of flexibility, as their study shows, are unequally distributed by class and gender. Further, "as unpredictability has increased," Gerstel and Clawson (2015:65–66) contend, "employers are rebranding the term, demanding that workers show the 'flexibility' to adjust to uncertain schedules and last-minute changes employers impose. The increasing deployment of the rhetoric of flexibility indicates a trend toward unpredictability but also masks a struggle to control it."

PURPOSES OF MIXED METHODS RESEARCH

As our examples show, researchers may conduct mixed methods research for various purposes. This begs the question: When should you use multiple approaches? In the broadest sense, you should consider choosing mixed methods when this is likely to result in "a *better understanding* of the phenomenon being studied" (Greene 2007:98). While a variety of more specific purposes have been proposed (e.g., Greene, Caracelli, and Graham 1989; Mark 2015; Mark and Shotland 1987), four categories seem to capture most of mixed methods research: triangulation, complementarity, development, and expansion. We now discuss each of these purposes.

Triangulation

Research for the purpose of triangulation seeks to use one approach to verify or confirm the findings of another approach. Cherlin and colleagues' three-city study achieved this purpose. Through in-depth interviews and fieldwork, the investigators discovered that many low-income women had withdrawn altogether from relationships with men. Moreover, the women in this category (abated unions) were more likely to have experienced abuse as adults. Although the survey data did not identify women in abated unions, these data showed that single women were more likely than married or cohabiting women to report abuse as adults, which is consistent with the qualitative results.

The convergence of findings in the three-city study increases confidence because each approach lends a different perspective to the relationship between abuse and the formation of intimate relationships, and each has distinctive strengths and weaknesses. The survey measured abuse with a series of specific questions that respondents answered in confidence, whereas in the field, participants disclosed that they had been abused at various points—when they trusted the researcher enough to share such sensitive information. The survey data presented a cross-sectional view of respondents' union status; by contrast, the field research provided detailed observations on union histories. For example, about one-third of the women in the field study who were classified as having abated unions had not been married or cohabiting for at least one year prior to the research. These women were not in a sustained relationship during the fieldwork period, and indicated that they had no interest in forming such a relationship. Based on a relatively small, nonrandom sample, the field research also provided concrete examples of abuse–union patterns. By comparison, the survey was based on a large random sample and contained measures of several variables that were controlled in the statistical analysis. Thus, the fieldwork and survey complemented one another well, cross-validating and providing a multilayered understanding of the impact of abuse on unions among low-income families.

Pager and Quillian's comparison of experimental audit results with those of a survey of employers contacted in the audit study also was an attempt to triangulate. Although this study failed to cross-validate results from different approaches, its conflicting results further demonstrate the value of mixed methods designs with the aim of triangulation. On the one hand, the study shows the importance of applying methods that will provide the most valid answers to a research question. It clearly demonstrates that self-reports in surveys may not be appropriate to address questions about discriminatory *behavior*; more generally, it alerts us to the limitations in drawing inferences about behavior from what people say they will do. On the other hand, the discrepant findings led the researchers to theorize about why people may not always do what they say they will do. By producing discrepant results, mixed methods research thus can create empirical puzzles that raise new questions and prompt new insights and interpretations (Mark 2015).

Complementarity

Whereas triangulation designs use different approaches to address the same research question, complementary mixed methods designs address different but related research questions. The approaches are "complementary" in the sense that they "serve to elaborate, enhance, deepen, or broaden the overall interpretations and inferences from the study" (Greene 2007:101). Most complementary designs either use qualitative data to interpret the results of a quantitative study or quantitative data to test hypotheses derived from a qualitative study (Small 2010:65). A good example of the former purpose is Pager, Western, and Bonikowski's audit study in which the auditors recorded extensive field notes. The field experiment addressed the question, "Is there racial discrimination in the low-wage labor market in New York City?" However, the experimental data alone, which showed discrimination based on whether applicants received a callback or job offer, could not answer the question, "When and how did racial bias occur in the hiring process?" To address this question and provide a deeper, more comprehensive understanding, the researchers relied on the auditors' field observations.

In Chapters 4 and 5, we described a study that illustrates how quantitative data may be used to test a hypothesis derived from qualitative data. Jessica Calarco's (2011) study of help-seeking among elementary school children was based primarily on field observations. For much of the two years she spent in the field, Calarco kept jottings of classroom interactions that she expanded into detailed field notes. As she interpreted her field notes, she began to focus on help-seeking behaviors, and she noticed consistent class differences in students' interactions with teachers: middle-class students were more proactive in seeking help and, as a consequence, were more likely to get help and to spend less time waiting than working-class students. To provide a systematic test of this observed pattern, Calarco performed a quantitative analysis of help-seeking during the last six months of fieldwork as a supplement to her qualitative data. As we discussed in Chapter 5, she first defined four types of help-seeking, then she counted students' help-seeking during 16 class periods. Supporting the qualitative data, middle-class students were more likely to make all types of requests than working-class students.

In these two mixed methods designs, the methods are complementary insofar as one method fills in a gap or makes up for the weaknesses of another. Audit studies provide evidence of racial discrimination but fail to reveal the processes by which discrimination occurs. This gap was filled in the New York audit study through field observations that showed how employer–applicant interactions differed by race/ethnicity. Similarly, based on an inductive logic of inquiry, Calarco's field research allowed the topic of help-seeking to emerge and enabled her to observe social class differences in help-seeking; however, inductive inferences from unstructured field observations do not provide a test of the observed patterns. This requires structured and systematic data collection based on a deductive logic of inquiry.

Development

A mix of methods also may be used for the purpose of development, wherein one method helps in the development or implementation of another method. You have encountered this process in previous chapters even though we have not applied the term "mixed methods." For example, pretests of experiments and survey instruments usually involve qualitative observation or interviews with a small number of participants. Experimenters may interview pretest participants to probe their interpretation of procedures; survey researchers may use focus groups to create or check the wording of survey items, and they may conduct preliminary interviews to identify problematic questions and instructions. Survey pretests also may include open-ended questions to develop closed questions.

In each of these examples, qualitative research informs the design of quantitative research (experiments and surveys). But other combinations also are possible for developmental purposes. In developing scales to measure attitudes (see Chapter 5), a long-standing practice for creating multiple items is to review relevant written materials such as magazines, books, and speeches (Mark 2015). For example, Lannutti and Lachlan (2007) developed 12 of the items in their attitude toward same-sex marriage scale based on protections for same-sex couples defined by the National Gay and Lesbian Task Force. Qualitative researchers also use survey and other statistical data to guide sample selection. When designing a study of how people think and feel about different forms of community, David Hummon (1990) conducted in-depth interviews with people living in four types of community in California: a city (San Francisco), a middle-class suburb, a working-class suburb, and a rural small town. To make sure that the selected communities were typical of cities, suburbs, and towns, he examined "census data to compare each community to state and community norms for twenty-four selected social, economic, and demographic variables" (Hummon 1990:186).

The latter examples involved the intentional and planned use of one method or data source for the development of another. In some mixed methods studies, however, development may occur more or less unexpectedly. This was true of the study of unequal time, where different methods helped to implement other methods. For example, a question at the end of the survey asked respondents if they "might be interested in being interviewed." Clawson and Gerstel began the interview process with those who responded positively, and these respondents ultimately constituted one-quarter of the in-depth interviews. These early interviews, in turn, helped them identify key organizations for their fieldwork. And, as they describe (personal communication 2017), "Fieldwork put us in contact with many doctors, nurses, nursing assistants, and EMTs, as well as administrators, union staff, and schedulers. We used those contacts to set up additional interviews; ultimately almost three-quarters of our interviews came from contacts made through fieldwork."

Expansion

The fourth purpose for mixed methods research is to expand the scope and range of the study (Greene 2007). Although the methods in the unequal time study were often complementary, Clawson and Gerstel report that in the early phases of their research, they decided to use multiple methods because they thought, "each method would tell us part of the story that other methods would not" (personal communication 2017). Much of the research on time use consists of surveys, which focus on individuals. These data indicate individual factors associated with work hours and schedules; however, they fail to examine the social contexts—in particular family and organizational processes—that explain *why* people work the hours they do. Moreover, survey data do not examine the "gendered and classed processes embedded in and shaping an occupation or organization" (Gerstel and Clawson 2014:404). To understand these processes, Clawson and Gerstel needed in-depth interviews and field observations.

In discussing their fieldwork, for example, Clawson and Gerstel point out (personal communication 2017):

> Our observations allowed us to watch relationships and interactions—both on and off the floor. . . . The organization of time and the chain of command embedded in it became especially visible not only during periods of activity but during the many periods of waiting—whether it was patients in a "waiting room," nurses waiting for a doctor, EMTs or CNAs [certified nursing assistants] waiting for a nurse. Such observations and subsequent questions about them allowed us to analyze and understand class and gender as relational and sometimes (though not always)

conflictual: Not only did workers talk almost incessantly about time but we could see that when one person's schedule changed, so did the schedules of others—typically those with more power led to changes in the schedules of those with less. But we could also see that some changes were embedded in exchanges among equals: We saw that a permanent change in a low wage worker's regular schedule always required a manager's approval, but for last-minute responses to unpredictable events what mattered most were co-workers agreeing to cover the shift.

SUMMARY

Mixed methods may fulfill various purposes, both planned and unplanned. One methodological approach may verify or confirm the findings of another approach (triangulation); enhance the interpretation or inferences of another approach (complementarity); and facilitate the development or implementation of the methods of another approach (development); or different approaches may be used to examine different but related phenomena (expansion). While "theory suggests simplistic mixing of two or more methods for one purpose" (Greene 2007:129), in practice a mixed methods study may satisfy multiple purposes as in the study of unequal time.

MIXED METHODS RESEARCH DESIGNS

In addition to research purpose, mixed methods research may be classified in terms of various design features (Creswell et al. 2003; Greene 2007; Tashakkori and Teddlie 2003). Here we discuss two of the most important design decisions: timing and integration. Timing refers to whether the approaches are implemented sequentially or concurrently; integration pertains to whether they are carried out independently of one another or integrated throughout the process of data collection and analysis. Our four examples illustrate each of these design choices.

Sequential Designs

sequential design
A mixed methods design in which data collection and analysis with one approach precedes data collection and analysis with another approach.

In **sequential designs**, the collection and analysis of data by one approach precedes the collection and analysis of data by another. Pager and Quillian's study was sequential in design: the telephone survey of employers was carried out several months after the field experiment in which the same employers were first contacted. Only a sequential design could provide a direct comparison between what employers did (in the field experiment) and what they said they would do (in the survey) in terms of hiring job applicants. Calarco's study also entailed a sequential design as a hypothesis about social class and help-seeking that emerged from her fieldwork was subsequently tested with a quantitative analysis based on structured observation.

Sequential designs are implicit in mixed methods research that is conducted for the explicit purpose of development, and they often are used when one method is intended to complement another. In addition to using quantitative data to test ideas derived inductively from qualitative research, Mario Small (2011) cites several studies that followed up surveys with in-depth interviews to interpret and understand the mechanisms behind statistical associations. Thus, the strength of sequential designs lies in "their ability to resolve specific questions that emerge in the process of data collection with additional data collection" (Small 2011:68).

This strength was clearly demonstrated in the study of unequal time, which was both sequential and overlapping (or concurrent) in design. Clawson and Gerstel began by conducting the mail survey at the end of 2004; they then completed the in-depth interviews between 2006 and 2008; carried out their fieldwork over two years beginning in the summer of 2007; and collected and coded union contracts in 2010 and 2011. We noted earlier how this sequencing served the purpose of implementing the interviewing and fieldwork phases of data collection. In addition, Clawson and Gerstel found that survey responses helped them to develop questions for the in-depth interviews, and the interviews sensitized them to "places to be [and] things to observe" in their fieldwork. At one point in their fieldwork, they discovered the actual edited schedules at one nursing home, which led them to ask for the schedules at another site. Fieldwork further led them to observe union meetings and obtain union contracts, which they content analyzed for clauses on time. "These additional methods," they point out, "helped us flesh out the answer to our first and most basic question that cut across methods: Who controls work hours and schedules both in and outside the workplace?" (personal communication 2017).

Concurrent Designs

In **concurrent designs**, data collection with different approaches is carried out more or less simultaneously. Both the study of the effect of abuse on marriage and cohabitation and the New York audit study of discrimination in the low-wage labor market were concurrent. This type of design may be used for practical reasons or when the order of the data collection is not relevant to the research question, as in many triangulation studies. As Small (2011) points out, whether you decide on a concurrent or sequential design may depend, in part, on whether you must determine the nature of the design before you begin a study. Many qualitative researchers, especially those in the grounded theory tradition, believe that the type of data collected at any point should be based on what is being continuously discovered.

concurrent design
A mixed methods design in which data collection with different approaches is carried out at the same time.

Component Designs

By definition, the approaches chosen in mixed methods designs are connected or "mixed" in some way. An important distinction can be made, however, between designs in which the approaches are connected only at the concluding stage, when comparing findings, and designs in which the approaches are integrated at prior stages of data collection and analysis (Caracelli and Greene 1997; Greene 2007). In the former, called **component designs**, the approaches are implemented relatively independently without having one inform the other except to compare findings. Pager and Quillian's research could be considered a component design insofar as the field experiment and telephone survey were carried out and analyzed separately before connections were made between the two sets of results.

component design
A mixed methods design in which findings from different approaches are compared after each approach is carried out independently.

Integrated Designs

Mixed methods may be integrated in many ways during the stages of data collection and analysis. The Milwaukee audit study comparing the results of a survey and field experiment was an **integrated design** because employers in the survey were the same employers who were contacted in the field experiment. In the study of abuse and union formation, investigators used an iterative process of gathering and analyzing data that integrated the two approaches. Thus, they began with analyses of basic associations in the survey data; these associations provided useful leads for identifying and exploring more detailed patterns of abuse and intimate relations through the field research. Then, they used their deepened understanding from the fieldwork to develop hypotheses that could be tested with the survey data.

integrated design A mixed methods design in which different approaches are connected or merged during the process of data collection and analysis.

There also was substantial integration of methods in the study of unequal time. Interviews and fieldwork overlapped considerably, and "interviews . . . informed subsequent fieldwork and fieldwork enriched subsequent . . . interviews" (personal communication 2017). At one point in their fieldwork, for example, Clawson and Gerstel (personal communication 2017)

> observed numerous (what seemed almost constant) conversations about time between workers and supervisors and among co-workers; they talked about breaks, sudden extensions of work hours, about clauses concerning mandatory overtime in union contracts, the benefits of being able to exchange hours with some responsive ("nice") co-workers or the "unfair" demands that differential family obligations put on other less responsive co-workers.

These observations led them to expand the work areas where they observed and to discuss these issues "in interviews not only with the direct care workers on the floor but with the managers who alerted us to the importance of flexibility and meaning of flexibility for these occupational groups" (personal communication 2017).

nesting A process in mixed methods research whereby different kinds of data are collected from the same individuals or groups by embedding one approach within another.

Many integrated designs involve **nesting**, in which data collection with one approach is embedded within another approach, so that different kinds of data are collected from the same actors, organizations, or entities (Lieberman 2005; Small 2011). The inferential power of nesting (and integration) can be seen in the New York audit study, in which the collection of qualitative data on employer–applicant interactions was nested within the field experiment. Without this nested design, it is doubtful that the various patterns of differential treatment could have been identified. Carefully matched testers in the field experiment provided clear evidence of discrimination when they applied for entry-level positions. But these data revealed nothing directly about how and why one applicant received a callback or job offer and another did not. As Pager and colleagues point out (2009:793), their testers "rarely perceived any signs of clear prejudice." It was only by comparing field observations of employer interactions with black, Latino, and white applicants that patterns of differential treatment were revealed.

According to Small (2011), the most common nested designs are surveys in which some respondents are selected for in-depth interviewing. As we noted, one-quarter of the interviews in the Clawson and Gerstel study were carried out with respondents who agreed to be interviewed at the conclusion of the mail survey. Other studies have selected particular groups of survey respondents for follow-up interviews to address more focused research questions. Lisa Pearce (2002), for example, first conducted a survey of approximately 1,800 people in Nepal that examined the influence of religion on family size preferences. Then, to gain a deeper understanding of this relationship, she carried out field observations and in-depth interviews with 28 "anomalous cases" who desired far more children than her statistical model predicted. The in-depth study of these cases revealed, among other things, that the religious identity of young people was a reflection of their parents' and grandparents' beliefs. And when Pearce added measures of household religious environment to her analysis, she obtained a better predictive model for the younger age group.

It is important to note that Pearce's follow-up qualitative research was only possible because she had identifying information that enabled her to recontact survey respondents. Access to this kind of information is one of several obstacles for doing mixed methods research that we discuss in Box 11.1, DOING SOCIAL RESEARCH: Limitations and Guidelines for Doing Mixed Methods Research.

BOX 11.1

DOING SOCIAL RESEARCH

Limitations and Guidelines for Doing Mixed Methods Research

This chapter emphasizes the benefits of mixed methods research, but we would be remiss if we didn't point out the obstacles and limitations in using mixed methods. With these in mind, you should be in a better position to decide if a mix of methods provides the best means, considering your resources, of addressing your research question.

One obstacle is that using mixed methods is more time-consuming and expensive than a single approach. It requires more resources and places more demands on the researcher, who *continues continued*   must be knowledgeable about a range of approaches as well as how to mix them effectively. Given the training necessary to develop expertise and remain up to date in one research method, most researchers specialize. To overcome this problem, some scholars (Pearce 2012; Yoshikawa et al. 2008) recommend a team approach for mixed methods research that brings together researchers with different methodological training and expertise.

Not only may the use of mixed methods be more difficult for researchers, but it also can be more burdensome for participants, especially with regard to time. Mixed methods invariably create a greater burden when the same participants are involved in more than one method of data collection, such as when survey respondents are asked to participate in in-depth interviews.

Besides the additional burden placed on research participants, mixed methods designs that begin with a survey and follow up with qualitative research present other problems (Leahey 2007). For the follow-up to be possible, researchers must have access to identifying information to do fieldwork in the area of the original research site or to recontact participants. But to protect privacy, this kind of information is generally removed after data collection and is always stripped from surveys available for secondary analysis. Therefore, a practical limitation of this type of mixed methods research is that the researchers must have conducted the surveys themselves and must have the foresight to obtain the information necessary to contact respondents and get IRB approval to do so. Clawson and Gerstel, for example, requested contact information from survey respondents who indicated that they might be interested in being interviewed (personal communication 2017). And in her study of religion and childbearing preferences in Nepal, Pearce (2002) had unusually detailed information about every respondent partly because the researchers planned to combine these data with other surveys.

Finally, similar to the use of big data (see Box 10.1), mixed methods research may pose a threat to invasion of privacy whenever data from different sources are linked (Brewer and Hunter 1989). As you may recall, this was an ethical issue in Laud Humphreys' study, in which he observed homosexual acts and then, in disguise, later contacted and interviewed the participants.

Now that you're aware of both the benefits and limitations of mixed methods research, we offer a few guidelines for doing your own research. For the novice researcher, who may be undertaking a small-scale project, we recommend:

1. Determine whether a mix of approaches can best address your research question.

2. Take a team approach by having different people carry out each method.

3. If time is short (say, less than a semester), use a concurrent mixed methods design.

4. Limit integration to a comparison of basic findings.

5. Obtain informed consent and protect privacy for each method of data collection.

SUMMARY

The timing and level of integration of different methods creates four different types of mixed methods designs. In sequential designs, data collection and analysis with one approach precedes that of another approach, whereas in concurrent designs, data collection and analysis with different approaches occur simultaneously. In component designs, different approaches are linked only after each approach is independently implemented, whereas in integrated designs, there is a blending of approaches during the process of data collection and analysis. Neither of these distinctions is hard and fast, however, as mixed methods may involve both sequential and concurrent methodological components, and integration is a matter of degree.

KEY TERMS

component design, p. 356

concurrent design, p. 355

integrated design, p. 356

mixed methods research, p. 338

nesting, p. 356

sequential design, p. 354

triangulation, p. 337

KEY POINTS

- Triangulating, or applying different methods and research strategies to address the same research question, enhances the validity of study results.
- In selecting a research approach and in combining approaches, researchers should carefully consider the strengths and weaknesses of alternative research strategies.
- Mixed methods research combines more than one method of data collection or analysis in the same investigation.
- Methods of data collection may be combined to examine the convergence of research findings (triangulation), to interpret or test the knowledge gained from one method with data from another method (complementarity), to facilitate the development or implementation of the methods of data collection (development), or to broaden the scope and range of a study (expansion).
- Mixed methods designs vary along two main dimensions: timing and integration.
- Sequential designs gather data from one approach before or after another approach; in concurrent designs, data collection occurs at the same time.
- Component designs gather data independently from different approaches and compare findings; integrated designs blend the methods during data collection and analysis.

REVIEW QUESTIONS

1. Explain how the principle of triangulation applies to convergent validity assessment, discussed in Chapter 5.
2. Each approach to social research applies the principle of triangulation in different ways. Explain how triangulation typically is applied in experiments, surveys, field research, and the analysis of existing data.
3. Describe the relative strengths and weakness of the four basic approaches with respect to: (a) internal validity (or the ability to determine cause and effect), (b) nonreactive measurement, and (c) external validity.
4. What are the two principal ways of combining methods for the purpose of complementarity?
5. Give two examples of how mixed methods may be used for the purpose of development.
6. What are two basic dimensions of mixed methods research designs?
7. Identify the purposes and designs of (a) Pager and Quillian's Milwaukee audit study ("What Employers Say Versus What They Do") and (b) Pager, Western, and Bonikowski's New York audit study ("Explaining Discrimination in a Low-Wage Labor Market").

EXERCISES

1. What basic approach to social research would you use to address each of the following research objectives? In each case, explain the advantages of this approach over others.

   (a) A 2000 film *Pay It Forward* popularized the idea that people who are the beneficiaries of a favor or good deed should "pay it forward" by doing a favor for others rather than pay back the original benefactor. Suppose you want to test the more general proposition that experiencing success or good fortune increases a person's willingness to help others. For example, will someone who receives an award or, say, happens to find a dollar bill in the street, be more likely to help others than someone who does not experience such good fortune?

   (b) Suppose a student task force is asked to document the current state of formal volunteering on a college campus: How many students volunteer? Where do current students volunteer? What kinds of volunteer work do they do?

   (c) In a comparative study of 15 European nations, Kieran Healy (2000) showed that how blood is collected and distributed in a society affects who gives blood and how much or how often they donate. Suppose you decide to investigate the relationship between blood-collection practices and blood donation in the United States from World War II to the present.

2. In an article in the July 2000 issue of the *American Journal of Sociology* (106:1–39), Sandra Smith and Mignon Moore examined the extent to which black students at a predominantly white university were close to one another. Read this article and answer the following questions.

    (a) What two methods of data collection did the researchers use?

    (b) Identify the type of mixed methods research design.

    (c) How did the researchers select respondents for in-depth interviews?

    (d) Table 2 reports survey results showing that "socially distant students participate in fewer informal activities with other black students [and in] . . . fewer minority-oriented and black-specified student activities compared to close-feeling students." How did the in-depth interviews elaborate this finding?

    (e) Table 2 also shows that socially distant black students were less likely to disapprove of interracial friendships and interracial dating. What did the in-depth interviews reveal about the frequency with which interracial dating and friendships were discussed and the degree to which these behaviors were sanctioned in the black community on campus?

    (f) Table 3 shows that biracial students were less likely than monoracial students to feel close to other blacks on campus. What factors identified in the in-depth interviews help explain this finding?

    (g) What general purpose was served by this mixed methods research?

Quantitative Data Analysis

Using Statistics for Description and Inference

STUDENT LEARNING OBJECTIVES

By the end of the chapter, you should be able to

1. Distinguish between descriptive and inferential statistics.

2. Identify the steps in quantitative data analysis.

3. Describe and apply the steps in processing survey data.

4. Explain how to read tables and graphs depicting univariate and bivariate distributions.

5. Differentiate tests of statistical significance from measures of association.

6. Explain how multivariate testing is used to statistically control for extraneous variables.

So far you have learned about methods of measurement, sampling, and data collection. Throughout this book, we also have presented many research findings. Here is a sampling from quantitative research:

- Broh found a statistically significant association between athletic participation and high school grades (Chapter 4).
- Rosenberg found a strong association between self-esteem and depression (Chapter 5).
- As hypothesized, participants in the murder condition withheld more questions, on average, than participants in the assault condition (Chapter 7).
- Compared with exclusionists and moderates, inclusionists were more often women than men, were more likely to be college educated, and were less religious (Chapter 8).

Although we have not always presented the data in detail, all of these findings are based on statistics. For example, Beckett Broh (2002:76) reported: "Net of controls, participating in interscholastic sports throughout high school is related to improved math ($b = .044, p < .01$) and English grades ($b = .073, p < .001$)." What you have not yet learned, and what we want to show you in this chapter, is how these statistics are produced and what they mean.

The analysis and interpretation of data is often the final step in the research process. As we illustrated in Chapter 2, however, data analysis is part of a cycle of inquiry that takes place whenever theory and data are compared. This comparison occurs continually in qualitative research when an investigator struggles to bring order to, or make sense of, his or her observations and interviews. In quantitative research such as surveys and experiments, the researcher typically brings theory and data together when testing a hypothesis once the data have been gathered and processed. Thus, data analysis consists of the "dynamic interplay between theory and data" (Rosenberg 1968:217): Theory guides the analysis of data, and data analysis contributes to the development of theory.

This chapter covers quantitative data analysis; Chapter 13 is devoted to qualitative data analysis. By quantitative data, we mean observations that have been transformed into counts or numbers. These are the data most typically generated in experiments, surveys, and some forms of research using existing data. Quantitative analysis is synonymous with statistical analysis. A *statistic* is a summary statement about a set of data; statistics as a discipline provides techniques for organizing and analyzing data.

Researchers draw upon two broad types of statistics: descriptive and inferential. **Descriptive statistics** organize and summarize data to make them more intelligible. The high and low scores and average score on an exam are descriptive statistics that readily summarize a class's performance. **Inferential statistics** are used to estimate population characteristics from sample data (discussed in Chapter 6) and to test

descriptive statistics Procedures for organizing and summarizing data.

inferential statistics Procedures for determining the extent to which one may generalize beyond the data at hand.

hypotheses. In this chapter, we describe these different types of statistics and elaborate on the logic underlying their application in quantitative analysis.

Because much of quantitative research follows the deductive model of inquiry, we focus on the process by which investigators perform statistical tests of hypotheses. The most elaborate forms of analysis are done with survey data and with some forms of existing (quantitative) data. Given the widespread use of surveys in social research, we concentrate on survey data in this chapter. We begin with a description of a survey. Using data from this survey and the General Social Survey (GSS), we then describe the key steps in quantitative data analysis.

INTRODUCTORY EXAMPLE OF SURVEY DATA ANALYSIS: DRINKING AND GRADES

In Chapter 6 we mentioned a series of campus surveys conducted by students in Royce Singleton's methods classes. As we noted, the surveys consisted of face-to-face interviews with random samples of enrolled students. Modeled after the GSS, each campus survey focused on a specific topic but also contained questions that were repeated over time. In particular, the fall 2003 survey focused on health behaviors, including students' sleep and eating habits, how often they exercise, and how often they drink alcoholic beverages.

Like many surveys, the campus survey yielded data enabling researchers to address numerous research questions. For purposes of illustration, we will consider one: Does students' consumption of alcoholic beverages affect their academic performance? Research evidence on this question is mixed. For example, some studies have found that "heavy" drinkers are more likely than "nonheavy" drinkers to report missing class, falling behind in their schoolwork, and doing poorly on tests (Presley and Pimentel 2006; Wechsler et al. 2000). Other studies have found a negative association between alcoholic consumption and self-reported grade point average (GPA) (Core Institute 2006; Wolaver 2002).

FIGURE 12.1
Questions on Alcohol Consumption from the Interview Schedule, 2003 Campus Survey

Still others have failed to find a significant association between these variables when controlling for several other variables (Wood and Sher 1997; Paschall and Freisthler 2003).

Data from the campus survey provide a solid basis for examining the relationship between drinking and grades. The data on grades were obtained from official college records rather than students' self-reports. The survey contained many background variables that might influence alcohol consumption, academic performance, or both. Moreover, the questions about alcohol consumption as well as measures

---

34. How would you describe your consumption of alcohol? Do you abstain from drinking altogether or would you describe yourself as a light, moderate, or heavy drinker?

Abstain . . . . (GO TO QUESTION 39)	1
Light	2
Moderate	3
Heavy	4

35. About how often do you drink alcoholic beverages? (HAND CARD F TO RESPONDENT.)

Almost every day	1
Three to four times a week	2
Once or twice a week	3
Two to three times a month	4
About once a month	5
Several times a year	6
About once a year	7

36. On a typical weekend night when you choose to drink, about how many drinks do you consume? Consider one drink as a bottle of beer, a glass of wine, a wine cooler, a shot glass of liquor, or a mixed drink.

☐☐ drinks

of academic performance were repeated in three subsequent campus surveys, conducted in spring and fall of 2004 and spring of 2005. After randomly selecting a single interview from students who were interviewed in more than one survey, the total sample size was 754. Thus, combining data from all four surveys produced an unusually large and rich dataset with which to address the research question.

Figure 12.1, from the 2003 survey questionnaire, shows the three questions that were asked about drinking. The first question (34) asks students to describe themselves as drinkers. Nonabstainers were then asked how often they drink alcoholic beverages, with seven possible responses ranging from "about once a year" to "almost every day" (question 35). Finally, they were asked how much they drink "on a typical weekend night" (question 36).

To measure academic performance, interviewers asked respondents at the conclusion of the interview for permission to retrieve information from official college records, including grades, SAT scores, and high school class rank. Two measures of academic performance then were added to the datafile at the end of the semester during which the survey was conducted: a student's average grade during the semester of the survey (semester GPA) and his or her cumulative grade-point average at that time (cumulative GPA).

Finally, all campus surveys contained additional measures of background variables. Of particular relevance to the research question, these included sex, academic class, race/ethnicity, athletic status, parents' level of education, and parents' annual income.

Singleton's (2007) quantitative analysis of data from the four campus surveys showed that the amount of alcohol that students reported consuming on a typical weekend night was negatively associated with their cumulative GPA, even after statistically controlling for key background variables. In other words, the more drinks a student consumed, the lower his or her grades. Below we describe in detail how Singleton analyzed the data to reach this conclusion. But first we provide an overview of the steps involved in quantitative analysis.

INTRODUCTORY OVERVIEW: THE PROCESS OF QUANTITATIVE ANALYSIS

Figure 12.2 outlines the steps involved in analyzing quantitative data. While some of these steps apply to all forms of quantitative analysis, the process as a whole is most applicable to the analysis of survey and existing (quantitative) data. Just like the other steps of research, there are variations depending on the data collection approach; moreover, there are substeps within each step.

The first step of preparing data for computerized analysis, called **data processing**, overlaps with data collection. To conduct quantitative analyses,

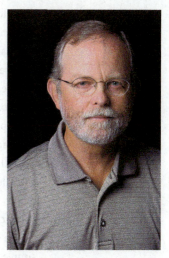

▲ Royce A. Singleton, Jr.

data processing The preparation of data for analysis.

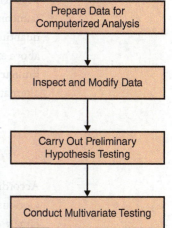

FIGURE 12.2
The Process of Quantitative Data Analysis

Prepare Data for Computerized Analysis

Inspect and Modify Data

Carry Out Preliminary Hypothesis Testing

Conduct Multivariate Testing

the information gathered in a survey, for example, must be quantified and transcribed to a computer-readable datafile. In addition, the datafile should be as error-free as possible.

Researchers analyzing existing data—whether from a survey, such as the GSS, or another source—begin their analysis at the second step: data inspection and data modification. The goal of inspection is to get a clear picture of the data in order to determine appropriate statistical analyses and necessary data modifications. The reasons for data modification are many: for example, a researcher may want to combine the responses to several items in order to create an index or scale (see Chapter 5), change one or more of the values for a variable, or combine categories for purposes of analysis. As we describe below, Singleton combined answers to two survey questions to create a measure of alcohol consumption.

The analysis then turns to empirical testing of the hypothesized relationships. For simple two-variable (bivariate) hypotheses, the analyst determines whether the association between the independent and dependent variables confirms theoretical expectations. For example, Singleton found that alcohol consumption was negatively associated with GPA, as predicted. In a true experiment, assessing the relationship between the independent and dependent variables is often the final analysis step because an adequate design effectively controls extraneous variables.

In nonexperimental designs, some extraneous variables may affect a hypothesized bivariate relationship. Therefore, the quantitative analyst conducts multivariate testing as a final step by statistically controlling for extraneous variables. If preliminary hypothesis testing supports theoretical expectations, the analyst formulates and tests multivariate models to rule out, to the extent possible, that the initial results are a spurious consequence of uncontrolled antecedent variables. Singleton had to examine the possibility, for example, that students' academic aptitude creates a spurious association between drinking and grades. Conversely, if hypothesized relationships are not supported in preliminary testing, the researcher designs multivariate models to determine if uncontrolled extraneous variables are blocking or distorting the initial results. While quantitative data analysis often proceeds from the deductive logic of inquiry, as in the above examples, it may also follow the inductive logic of inquiry. For example, the preliminary testing step may reveal unanticipated (serendipitous) findings that suggest alternative multivariate models.

PREPARE DATA FOR COMPUTERIZED ANALYSIS: DATA PROCESSING

According to James Davis and Tom Smith (1992:60), data preparation is the "least glorious" step of survey research. But, as they also note, the quality of the data rests largely on data processing: many errors may be introduced into the data, and many checks and safeguards should be incorporated to avoid such errors. To make this step more manageable, data processing can be broken down into four smaller steps: coding, editing, entering data into a datafile, and checking data for errors (cleaning). The accomplishment of each data-processing task depends on the type of data and how they were collected.

Coding

In quantitative research, coding consists of transforming data into numbers, if it is not already in this form. As we described in Chapter 8, coding survey responses generally occurs as part of the process of data collection. Actually, most surveys are precoded; that is, prior to data collection, each response category of closed-ended questions is assigned a number, which may be specified directly on the interview schedule. Figure 12.1 shows the numerical codes assigned in questions 34 and 35. In conducting the survey, interviewers either circle the numbered response or, in computer-assisted interviewing, enter the numbered response directly into a datafile.

Coding answers to closed-ended survey questions is straightforward: there are relatively few categories, and you simply assign a different code to each category. However, the coding of responses to open-ended survey questions with large numbers of unique responses and textual data more generally, as in in-depth interviews and some forms of content analysis, is much more complicated. We'll have more to say about this type of coding in Chapter 13 on qualitative analysis.

Editing

Editing involves checking for errors and inconsistencies in the data. An error in the campus survey, for example, would be the recording of a student's birth date as 4/11/1899; an inconsistency would have occurred if a respondent who reportedly "abstains" from drinking (question 34) also drinks alcoholic beverages "almost every day" (question 35). Most editing is programmed into computer-assisted and online surveys; for instance, if an interviewer entered "1" ("abstain") on question 34, the program would prompt the interviewer to skip questions 35 and 36.

For the campus survey, interviewers checked over each completed form for errors and omissions soon after each interview was conducted. Respondents were recontacted if necessary, or corrections were made from memory. In addition, the instructor (or survey supervisor) went over each completed survey to check for omitted questions and to verify that answers were recorded legibly, the correct forms were used, and so forth.

Entering the Data

Once data are coded and edited, they need to be entered into a computer datafile. As with editing, data entry into a computer file occurs automatically in computer-assisted interviews. For some paper-and-pencil surveys, data may be entered using software programmed to detect some kinds of erroneous entries; this is called computer-assisted data entry (CADE). Data from the campus surveys were entered by hand into a statistical software package without the aid of a data-entry program that checks for errors. The software, originally named Statistical Package for the Social Sciences and known today by the acronym SPSS, is widely used in the social sciences. (Other popular statistical software packages are Stata, SAS, and R, the latter of which is free. In addition, programs such as Microsoft Excel and Google Sheets [which is also free] may be used for data entry and some forms of analysis.)

data matrix The form of a computer datafile, with rows as cases and columns as variables; each cell represents the value of a particular variable (column) for a particular case (row).

When data are entered, they are stored in a **data matrix** or spreadsheet, with observations as rows and variables as columns. Figure 12.3 presents a partial data matrix for the 2003 campus survey. The figure shows the typical form of data storage. The rows represent respondents, who are identified by unique ID codes (first column). The remaining columns contain the coded responses to each question or variable. Carefully look over the matrix. As you do, take note of the following:

- Notice that the columns are headed by abbreviated variable names. To facilitate data analysis, the campus survey used mnemonic labels. For example, the labels FREQALC and NUMDRNKS, which represent questions 35 and 36, respectively, stand for "frequency of alcohol consumption" and "number of drinks consumed."
- Numerical codes in the matrix cells identify question responses or variable categories. For respondent's sex (sixth column), a code of 1 was used for males and 2 for females. Thus the first four listed respondents are females, and the next two are males.

ID	ALCCONS	FREQALC	NUMDRNKS	RACE	SEX	CLASS	CUMGPA
001	2	6	3	1	2	1	2.34
002	2	4	7	1	2	3	3.31
003	4	2	12	5	2	2	3.33
004	3	3	6	1	2	2	3.03
005	1	9	97	3	1	4	99
006	3	3	10	1	1	3	3.37
007	2	3	3	1	2	3	99
008	2	6	2	1	1	4	3.23
009	3	2	8	1	1	4	2.47
010	3	3	10	1	1	1	2.61

FIGURE 12.3
Partial Data Matrix for 2003 Campus Survey

- Distinct codes are used to identify respondents to whom the question does not apply or missing data. The term **missing data** refers to the absence of substantive information on a variable for a respondent. In the campus survey, "don't know" responses and refusals to answer the question were treated as missing data. Thus, the code "9" in column 3 (FREQALC) and the code "97" in column 4 (NUMDRNKS) opposite ID 005 indicate that these questions were skipped and did not apply to this respondent (because a code of "1" [for "abstain"] was entered in column 2 [ALCCONS]). The code "99" in column 8 (CUMGPA) for IDs 005 and 007 indicates that these data are missing (because these respondents did not grant permission to have their GPAs obtained from the Registrar).

missing data Refers to the absence of information on a variable for a given case.

In addition to the datafile, most researchers create a codebook. Like a codebook for content analysis, described in Chapter 10, a survey codebook serves as a guide for coding and data entry and as a detailed record of the electronic layout of the data. Codebooks are essential to researchers who are analyzing available survey data such as the GSS. Whether you are analyzing one of the numerous datasets available online or creating a codebook for your own survey, Box 12.1, DOING SOCIAL RESEARCH: Codebook Documentation, will familiarize you with the information contained in a codebook.

BOX 12.1

DOING SOCIAL RESEARCH

Codebook Documentation

A survey codebook is like a dictionary in that it defines the meaning of the numerical codes for each named variable, such as the codes for sex in the campus survey. Codebooks also may contain question wording, interviewer directions, and coding and editing decision rules. Examining a codebook and other study documentation, such as information about the sample and data collection procedures, should help you decide if a given dataset will be useful for your research.

Figure A is a codebook entry from the GSS Cumulative Data file 1972–2016 (Smith et al. 2017). Look over this entry and see if you can find the following information:

1. Variable name and label.

2. Exact wording of the survey question.

3. Values and value labels (i.e., numerical and textual response options) for valid or legitimate responses.

continues

continued

GUNLAW	FAVOR OR OPPOSE GUN PERMITS

Description of the Variable
86. Would you favor or oppose a law which would require a person to obtain a police permit before he or she could buy a gun?

Percent	N	Value	Label
76.4	30,936	1	FAVOR
23.6	9,536	2	OPPOSE
	21,165	0	IAP
	722	8	DK
	107	9	NA
100.0	62,466		Total

Properties	
Data type:	numeric
Missing-data codes:	0,8,9
Mean:	1.24
Std Dev:	.42
Record/column:	1/576

BOX 12.1 FIGURE A
Codebook entry from GSS Cumulative Data File, 1972–2016

4. Codes for missing data.

5. Record and column locations (i.e., the electronic location of these data in the datafile).

Answers: 1. GUNLAW, FAVOR OR OPPOSE GUN PERMITS. 2. Would you favor or oppose a law which would require a person to obtain a police permit before he or she could buy a gun? 3. 1 = FAVOR; 2 = OPPOSE. 4. 0 = IAP (Inapplicable); 8 = DK (Don't know); 9 = NA (No answer). 5. Record = 1; column = 576.

Cleaning

data cleaning The detection and correction of errors in a computer datafile that may have occurred during data collection, coding, and/or data entry.

After the data have been entered into a computer file, the researcher "cleans" the data. **Data cleaning** refers to detecting and resolving errors in coding and in transmitting the data to the computer.

Data entry can introduce errors when entry operators misread codes, transpose numbers, skip over or repeat responses to survey questions, and so on. The first step in data cleaning is to check for these kinds of errors by verifying data entries whenever feasible. One procedure is to have two persons independently enter the information into separate computer files and then use a software program to compare the two files for noncomparable entries. Another procedure, which was used in the campus surveys and which we recommend for small-scale student projects, is to have one person enter the information and then have another person compare on-screen data entries with the completed survey.

Beyond verification, two cleaning techniques generally are applied. These techniques check for the same kinds of errors that could occur during data collection, except that they screen data entries in a computer file rather than responses recorded on a questionnaire or interview schedule. The first of these, called **wild-code checking**, consists of examining the values entered for each item to see whether there are any illegitimate codes. In Singleton's study, for example, any code other than 1 ("male") or 2 ("female") for the variable "sex" is not legitimate. The second cleaning technique, used in most large-scale surveys, is called **consistency checking**. The idea here is to see whether responses to certain questions are related in reasonable ways to responses to particular other questions. Checks for consistency thus require comparisons across variables, such as comparing data entries for ALCCONS and FREQALC to see if respondents who "abstain" from drinking are correctly coded as "9" (for "not applicable") on the frequency of consumption item.

Once you have entered and cleaned the data, you are ready to inspect, modify, and analyze them.

> **wild-code checking**
> A data-cleaning procedure involving checking for out-of-range and other "illegal" codes among the values recorded for each variable.

> **consistency checking**
> A data-cleaning procedure involving checking for unreasonable patterns of responses, such as a 12-year-old who voted in the last US presidential election.

SUMMARY

Preparing data for quantitative analysis entails four steps: coding, editing, data entry, and cleaning. Coding consists of assigning numbers to the categories of each variable. Editing is designed to ensure that the data to be entered into the computer are as complete, error-free, and readable as possible. When data are entered into the computer and stored in a datafile, they are organized as a matrix or spreadsheet, with observations as rows and variables as columns. After entry, the data are cleaned for errors in coding and transmission to the computer. This is a multistep process, usually beginning with a verification procedure and continuing with checks for "illegal" codes (wild-code checking) and inconsistent patterns (consistency checking).

INSPECT AND MODIFY DATA

Starting with a cleaned dataset, the next analysis step is to inspect the data to decide on subsequent data modifications and statistical analyses. The goal of inspection is to get a clear picture of the data by examining one variable at a time. The data "pictures" generated by **univariate analysis** come in various forms—tables, graphs, charts, and statistical measures. These pictures allow us to see how much the data vary and where they are mainly concentrated or clustered. The nature of the techniques depends on whether the *level of measurement* of the variables you are analyzing is nominal/ordinal

> **univariate analysis** The statistical analysis of one variable at a time.

or interval/ratio. Recall from Chapter 5 that we cannot add, subtract, multiply, or divide the numbers assigned to the categories of nominal and ordinal variables, whereas we can perform basic mathematical operations on the values of interval and ratio variables. Consequently, different forms of analysis and statistics are applied to variables measured at different levels. Following data inspection, the researcher may want to change one or more variable codes, rearrange the numerical order of variable codes, combine variable categories, estimate values for missing data, add together the codes for several variables to create an index or scale, and otherwise modify the data for analysis.

Nominal- and Ordinal-Scale Variables

At first, Singleton performed univariate analyses to observe the amount of variation in the variables to be analyzed. It is generally a good idea, for example, to see if there is sufficient variation in responses to warrant including the variable in the analysis. As a rule, the less variation, the more difficult it is to detect how differences in one variable are related to differences in another variable. To take an extreme example, if almost all of the students in the campus survey identified their race as white, it would be impossible to determine how *differences* in race were related to differences in alcohol consumption or in academic achievement.

Suppose we wanted to inspect the responses to the question on "race" in the campus survey. To measure "race," students in the campus survey were asked the following open-ended question: "What is your racial or ethnic background?" The questionnaire contained the five most likely response categories, given the racial/ethnic composition of the college (see codes 1–5 in Table 12.1). Interviewers were instructed to use these categories to record answers, and to write down, verbatim, the respondent's answer if it did not fit into one of the five categories. In addition, interviewers circled more than one response category for those respondents who identified themselves as having mixed racial/ethnic identity.

frequency distribution A tabulation of the number of cases falling into each category of a variable.

percentage distribution A norming operation that facilitates interpreting and comparing frequency distributions by transforming each frequency to a common yardstick of 100 units (percentage points) in length; the number of cases in each category is divided by the total and multiplied by 100.

One means of data inspection is to organize responses into a table called a **frequency distribution**. A frequency distribution is created by adding up the number of cases that occur for each coded category. When we used SPSS to do this for the race/ethnicity question, our output looked like that in Table 12.1.

As you can see from the table, the number of "whites" in the combined sample is 642. This is important information; however, this number by itself is meaningless unless we provide a standard or reference point with which to interpret it. To provide an explicit comparative framework for interpreting distributions, researchers often create **percentage distributions**, which show the size of a category relative to the size of the sample. To create a percentage distribution, you divide the number of cases in each category (White, African American, Asian American, etc.) by the total number of cases overall and multiply by 100. This is what we have done in Table 12.2. Now you can see more clearly the relative difference in responses. For example, we see that whites constitute 85 percent of the sample and that fewer than 4 percent of the respondents identified with any other single racial/ethnic group.

Table 12.1 Frequency Distribution of Race/Ethnicity for the Campus Survey*

Code	Label	Frequency
1	White	642
2	African American	25
3	Asian American	29
4	Puerto Rican	10
5	Other Latino	22
6	Other	8
7	White/African American	1
8	White/Asian American	6
9	White/Puerto Rican	1
10	White/Latino	2
11	African American/Puerto Rican	2
12	Arab American	5
13	No answer	1
Total		754

Question: What is your racial or ethnic background?

In Table 12.2, the percentages are based on the total number of responses, *excluding* missing data—those in the "no answer" category. Only one student ("no answer") either was not asked the question (interviewer error) or did not respond. Since this is not a meaningful variable category, it would be misleading to include it in the percentage distribution. The total number of missing responses is important information. If this information is not placed in the main body of a table, then it at least should be reported in a footnote to the relevant table or in the text of the research report. Also notice that the base number for computing percentages, 753, is given in parentheses below the percentage total of 100 percent. It is customary to indicate in tables the total number of observations from which the statistics are computed. This information may be found elsewhere—at the end of the table title or in a headnote or footnote to the table; often it is signified with the letter **N**.

Univariate analysis is seldom an end in itself. One important function mentioned earlier is to determine how to combine or recode categories for further analysis.

N An abbreviation representing the number of observations on which a statistic is based (e.g., N = 753).

Table 12.2 Percentage Distribution of Race/Ethnicity for the Campus Survey

Response	%
White	85.3
African American	3.3
Asian American	3.9
Puerto Rican	1.3
Other Latino	2.9
Other	1.2
White/African American	.1
White/Asian American	.8
White/Puerto Rican	.1
White/Latino	.3
African American/Puerto Rican	.3
Arab American	.7
Total	100.0
(Number of responses)	(753)
(Missing data)	(1)

The decision to combine (or collapse) categories may be based on theoretical criteria and/or may hinge on the empirical variation in responses. Thus, years of education might be collapsed into "theoretically" meaningful categories (grade 8 or lower, some high school, high school graduate, some college, college graduate) based on the schooling deemed appropriate for qualifying for certain occupations in the United States. Alternatively, one might collapse categories according to how many respondents fall into each category. If the sample contains only a handful of respondents with less than a college education, these respondents may be placed in one category for purposes of analysis.

One problem with the race/ethnicity data is that there are too few respondents in several categories to provide reliable bases of comparison. To resolve this problem, Singleton applied both theoretical and practical criteria. Prior research and theory indicate that there is an association between being white and heavy alcohol use among US college students. In addition, no racial identity other than "white" had more than

29 respondents. Therefore, Singleton created a "new" variable by collapsing all of the categories other than "white" into a single "nonwhite" category. This produced a two-category variable for race/ethnicity: white and nonwhite.

Interval- and Ratio-Scale Variables

Creating frequency or percentage distributions is about as far as the univariate analysis of nominal- and ordinal-scale variables usually goes. On the other hand, data on interval and ratio variables may be summarized not only in tables or graphs, but also in terms of various statistics. Consider question 36 from the campus survey, which asks respondents, "On a typical weekend night when you choose to drink, about how many drinks do you consume?" (see Figure 12.1). Since respondents' answers were recorded in number of drinks, this variable may be considered a ratio-scale measure. We could get a picture of the number of drinks consumed, as we did with the race/ethnicity variable, by generating a distribution of the responses. Table 12.3 presents a computer-like output for the number of drinks students reported consuming. Notice that Table 12.3 presents two kinds of distributions: frequency and percentage. Notice also that abstainers (who were not asked this question) were coded as "97," for "not applicable." Can you tell from the table what percentage of nonabstaining respondents report that they typically consume *one drink* on a weekend night?

We also can get a picture of a distribution by looking at its various statistical properties. Three properties may be examined. The first consists of measures of central tendency—the mean, median, and mode. These indicate various "averages" or points of concentration in a set of values. The **mean** is the arithmetical average, calculated by adding up all of the responses and dividing by the total number of respondents. It is the "balancing" point in a distribution because the sum of the differences of all values from the mean is exactly equal to zero. The **median** is the midpoint in a distribution—the value of the middle response; half of the responses are above it and half are below. You find the median by ordering the values from low to high and then counting up until you find the middle value. In an odd-numbered dataset with $N = 3$, the second ordered value would be the median. For example, if we had a dataset with three respondents who respectively say they consume 7, 10, and 12 drinks on a typical weekend night, the median would be 10. In an even-numbered dataset with $N = 4$, the median would be the average of the second and third ordered values. For instance, if we had a dataset of four respondents who respectively say they consume 7, 10, 12, and 15 drinks on a typical weekend night, the median would be 11 ($= [10 + 12]/2$). The **mode** is the value or category with the highest frequency. For the data in Table 12.3, the mean is 6.51 (drinks), the median is 6, and the mode is 6.

A second property that we can summarize statistically is the degree of variability or dispersion among a set of values. The simplest dispersion measure is the **range**. Statistically, this is the difference between the lowest and highest values, but it is

mean The average value of a dataset, calculated by adding up the individual values and dividing by the total number of cases.

median The midpoint in a distribution of interval- or ratio-scale data; indicates the point below and above which 50 percent of the values fall.

mode The value or category of a frequency distribution having the highest frequency; the most typical value.

range The difference between the lowest and highest values in a distribution, which is usually reported by identifying these two extreme values.

Table 12.3 Number of Drinks Consumed on a Typical Weekend Night, Campus Survey

Code	Label	Frequency	Percent
00	0 drinks	1	.2
01	1 drink	20	3.1
02	2 drinks	44	6.7
03	3 drinks	74	11.3
04	4 drinks	82	12.5
05	5 drinks	81	12.4
06	6 drinks	83	12.7
07	7 drinks	56	8.5
08	8 drinks	57	8.7
09	9 drinks	18	2.7
10	10 drinks	58	8.9
11	11 drinks	5	.8
12	12 drinks	36	5.5
13	13 drinks	8	1.2
14	14 drinks	2	.3
15	15 drinks	21	3.2
16	16 drinks	1	.2
18	18 drinks	4	.6
20	20 drinks	2	.3
23	23 drinks	1	.2
25	25 drinks	1	.2
97	Not applicable	97	Missing
98	No answer	2	Missing
Total		754	100.0
(Valid cases) (655)			
(Missing cases) (99)			

usually reported by identifying these end points, such as "the number of drinks consumed ranged from 0 to 25." Of several other measures of dispersion, the most commonly reported is the **standard deviation**. As we saw in Chapter 6, this is a measure of the "average" spread of observations around the mean.

With respect to the variable of number of drinks consumed, the standard deviation could be used to compare the degree of variability in drinks consumed among different subgroups or in samples from different populations. The standard deviation of number of drinks consumed for the campus survey was 3.68. Among male respondents, the standard deviation was 3.97, revealing more variability among men than women, for whom the standard deviation was 2.23. As a further example, the ages of GSS respondents in 2016 ranged from 18 to 89, with a standard deviation of 17.69 years. By comparison, the standard deviation for age in the campus survey, which ranged from 17 to 24, was 1.3 years.

A third statistical property of univariate distributions is their shape. This property is most readily apparent from a graphic presentation called a **histogram**. Figure 12.4 presents a histogram for the data in Table 12.3. The figure reveals that the distribution has a cluster of high points (4–6 drinks), with the data lopsided or "skewed" mostly to the right of this cluster. Superimposed on the histogram is a "bell-shaped" distribution, so called because it has the general shape of a bell. In a bell-shaped distribution, the three measures of central tendency (mean, median, and mode) are identical. In a positively skewed distribution like Figure 12.4, the mean has a higher value than the mode and median. One particular type of bell-shaped distribution is the *normal distribution*, which we described in Chapter 6. The normal distribution describes the shape of many variables and statistics, such as the sampling distribution of the mean.

Collectively, these three statistical properties—central tendency, dispersion, and shape—provide a good picture of quantitative data. Many investigators, in fact, describe their data in terms of a mean or median, an index of dispersion, and occasionally the overall form (for which there are also statistical indices).

Inspecting the frequency distribution also enables you to spot extreme values or **outliers** that can adversely affect some statistical procedures. Apparent outliers in Table 12.3 and Figure 12.4, for example, are students who report consuming 20 or more drinks on a typical weekend night. Various analytic procedures, which are beyond the scope of this book, exist for identifying outliers. When Singleton used the "Explore" function in SPSS, he detected 9 data points that were outliers in the distribution of number of drinks consumed: namely, values of 16 or more drinks. If such

standard deviation
A measure of variability or dispersion that indicates the average "spread" of observations about the mean.

histogram A graphic display in which the height of a vertical bar represents the frequency or percentage of cases in each category of an interval/ratio variable.

outliers Unusual or suspicious values that are far removed from the preponderance of observations for a variable.

FIGURE 12.4
Histogram of Data in Table 12.3

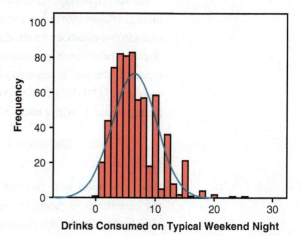

Drinks Consumed on Typical Weekend Night

outliers are the product of interviewer errors, it is probably best to exclude these data from the analysis. However, because these extreme values appeared to be exaggerated reports of drinking behavior, Singleton assigned each a value of 15.

Data inspection can also reveal the prevalence of missing values. The simplest way to handle cases with missing values, which we did in percentaging Table 12.2, is to remove them from the statistical calculations. This method, called **listwise deletion**, often is used when there are relatively few missing cases. Excluding cases with missing data on *any* of the variables in a planned multivariate analysis, however, can lead to a much smaller, biased sample that is unrepresentative of the target population. Paul Allison (2002) relates a hypothetical illustration of a sample of 1,000 that shrinks to only 360 respondents after excluding the 5 percent of missing values on each of the 20 variables. Consequently, researchers typically use various procedures for replacing or otherwise handling missing data.

For almost all the variables in the campus survey, there were few missing values. A major exception was parents' income: 148 respondents either refused to report their parents' income or, more commonly, did not know. Because eliminating these 148 cases would produce a smaller and possibly less representative sample, Singleton did not apply listwise deletion. Instead, he used one of the formal statistical solutions, called **imputation**, that have been devised to replace missing values with a typical value calculated from the available ("nonmissing") data. For example, one procedure would be to assign the mean income of nonmissing values to the missing values. Another procedure, which Singleton applied in the multivariate analysis below, predicts missing values from known values of other variables. In this case, missing values for income were predicted based on the regression of income on race and parents' education for respondents with nonmissing values on income. (We discuss regression later in this chapter. For a thorough discussion of imputation procedures, which are beyond the scope of this textbook, see McKnight et al. [2007].)

Another important function of data modification is to reduce data complexity by combining variables into indexes, scales, or other composite measures. Singleton combined answers to two questions for the final operational definition of number of drinks consumed. Because the research question asks about *all* students, not just nonabstainers, those who reported "abstain" in question 34 (ALCCONS) were recoded as "0" on "number of drinks consumed" (NUMDRNKS). After recoding and correcting for outliers, this variable had a range of 0 to 15 with a mean of 5.61 and a standard deviation of 3.90.

listwise deletion A common procedure for handling missing values in multivariate analysis that excludes cases which have missing values on any of the variables in the analysis.

imputation A procedure for handling missing data in which missing values are assigned based on other information, such as the sample mean or known values of other variables.

SUMMARY

Having entered and cleaned the data, the researcher is ready to inspect and modify the data for the planned analysis.

The goal of inspection is to get a clear picture of the data by examining each variable singly (univariate analysis). At first, the categories or values of each variable are organized into frequency and percentage distributions. If the data constitute interval-level measurement, the researcher will also compute statistics that define various properties of the distribution. Statistical measures of central tendency include the most typical value (mode), the middle value (median), and the average (mean). Common measures of dispersion are the difference between the lowest and highest values (range) and an index of the spread of the values around the mean (standard deviation). Distributions also may be described in terms of their shape. Data modifications include changing one or more variable codes, collapsing variable categories, imputing estimated values for missing data, and adding together the codes for several variables to create an index or scale.

CARRY OUT PRELIMINARY HYPOTHESIS TESTING

Having collected, processed, inspected, and modified the data, a researcher is finally in position to carry out preliminary hypothesis testing. For novice researchers, this can be an exciting—but also potentially disappointing—stage in the research process. This is because whenever we formulate a hypothesis, it is possible that the hypothesis is "wrong" (and it's hard not to take this personally!).

The object of **bivariate analysis** is to assess the relationship between two variables, such as between the independent and dependent variable in a hypothesis. As in the previous section, we begin by showing how tables and figures can be used to depict the joint *distribution* of two variables. "Eyeballing" the data helps, but there are more precise ways of assessing bivariate relationships. And so, we also introduce two types of statistics for determining whether one variable is associated with the other: tests of statistical significance and measures of association. In general, this amounts to determining, first, whether the relationship is likely to exist (or whether it might be a product of random error) and, second, the strength of the relationship between the variables. Finally, as with univariate analysis, the way in which bivariate analysis is done depends on the level of measurement.

bivariate analysis The statistical analysis of the relationship between two variables.

Nominal- and Ordinal-Scale Variables

When the variables analyzed have only a few categories, as in most nominal- and ordinal-scale measurement, bivariate data are presented in tables. The tables constructed are known as *cross-tabulations* or *contingency tables*. A cross-tabulation requires a table with rows representing the categories of one variable and columns representing the categories of another. When a dependent variable can be identified, it is customary to make this the row variable and to treat the independent variable as the column variable.

Let us first consider the cross-tabulation of two nominal-scale variables from the 2016 GSS shown in Table 12.4. The row variable consists of "attitude toward gun control" or, more precisely, whether the respondent favors or opposes a law that would require a person to obtain a police permit before he or she could buy a gun (see Box 12.1). The column variable is "sex." Sex is clearly the independent variable in this relationship.

What sort of information does this table convey? First, notice that the last column and the bottom row, each labeled "Total," show the total number of respondents with each single characteristic, for example, 828 males. Because these four numbers (1,330, 528, 828, 1,030) are along the right side and the bottom margin of the table, they are called **marginal frequencies**, or *marginals*. The row marginals (1,330, 528) are the univariate frequency distribution for the variable "attitude toward gun control"; the column marginals (828, 1,030) are the univariate frequency distribution for the variable "sex." Also, the number at the lower right-hand corner (1,858) is *N*, the total sample size excluding missing cases. *N* equals either the sum of the row or column marginals or the sum of the four numbers (548 + 782 + 280 + 248) in the body of the table.

The body of the table where the categories of the two variables intersect contains the bivariate frequency distribution. Each intersection is called a *cell*, and the number in each cell is called a **cell frequency**. Cell frequencies in a *bivariate* table indicate the numbers of cases with each possible combination of *two* characteristics; for example, there were 548 *males* who *favored gun control*. Because Table 12.4 has two rows and two columns, it is referred to as a 2 × 2 table.

Now that we know the meaning of the numbers in a cross-tabulation, how do we analyze these numbers to assess the relationship between the variables? With sex as the independent variable in Table 12.4, we can assess the relationship by examining whether males or females are more likely to favor (or oppose) gun control. To determine the "likelihood" that a male or female either supports or opposes gun control, we need to create separate percentage distributions for males and females. Doing this converts each column "total" to 100 percent, so that the cell values are based on the same total.

marginal frequencies
Row and column totals in a contingency table (cross-tabulation) that represent the univariate frequency distributions for the row and column variables.

cell frequency
The number of cases in a cell of a cross-tabulation (contingency table).

Table 12.4 Attitude toward Gun Control by Sex, 2016 General Social Survey

ATTITUDE TOWARD GUN CONTROL*	Sex		Total
	Male	Female	
Favor	548	782	1,330
Oppose	280	248	528
Total	828	1,030	1,858

*Would you favor or oppose a law which would require a person to obtain a police permit before he or she could buy a gun?

The result is a *bivariate percentage distribution*, presented as Table 12.5. Now when we compare responses across sex, we see clearly that males are less likely to favor gun control by a percentage of 66.2 to 75.9 and, conversely, more likely to oppose (33.8 percent to 24.1 percent).

A bivariate percentage distribution enables one to compare the distribution of one variable across the categories of the other. In Table 12.5, we created such a distribution by percentaging *down* so that the column totals, corresponding to the categories of the independent variable, equaled 100 percent. The rule that we followed in deriving this table is to *compute percentages in the direction of the independent variable* (i.e., based on the categories of the independent variable). If sex had been the row variable and attitude toward gun control the column variable, we would have run the percentages in the other direction—across rather than down.

To interpret the relationship in Table 12.5, we compared percentages by reading *across* the table. In so doing, we followed a second rule: *Make comparisons in the opposite direction from the way percentages are run*. Having percentaged down, we compared across; had we percentaged across, we would have compared down. These are extremely important rules to follow, because cross-tabulations may be percentaged in either direction and are easily misinterpreted.

As you read across Table 12.5, you see that there is a difference of 9.7 percent (75.9–66.2) in females relative to males who favor gun control. This "percentage difference" indicates that a relationship exists for these data; if there were no difference between the percentages, we would conclude that no relationship exists. Remember, however, that these are *sample* data. The important question is not whether a relationship exists in these data; rather, do the observed cell frequencies reveal a true relationship between the variables in the *population*, or are they simply the result of sampling and other random error? To answer this question, you need to understand the logic of tests of statistical significance.

Table 12.5 Attitude toward Gun Control by Sex, 2016 General Social Survey

	Sex	
ATTITUDE TOWARD GUN CONTROL	Male	Female
Favor	66.2%	75.9%
Oppose	33.8	24.1
Total	100.0%	100.0%
(*N*)	(828)	(1,030)

TESTS OF STATISTICAL SIGNIFICANCE

test of statistical significance
A statistical procedure used to assess the likelihood that the results of a study could have occurred by chance.

To determine whether a relationship is due to chance factors, researchers use **tests of statistical significance**, which you read about in Chapter 4 (see Box 4.4). The way that such tests work is that we first assume what the data would look like if there were no relationship between the variables—that is, if the distribution were completely random. The assumption of no relationship or complete randomness is called the **null hypothesis**. The null hypothesis in Singleton's research is that there is *no* relationship between alcohol consumption and academic performance (i.e., Singleton is wrong). Based on the null hypothesis, we calculate the likelihood that the observed data could have occurred at random. If the relationship is unlikely to have occurred randomly, we reject the null hypothesis of no relationship between the variables. In such cases, researchers generally interpret this as supportive of the hypothesis that there *is* a relationship.

null hypothesis
The hypothesis, associated with tests of statistical significance, that an observed relationship is due to chance; a test that is significant rejects the null hypothesis at a specified level of probability.

Psychologist David Lane (2014) provides an interesting example of this logic based on James Bond's insistence that he could tell whether a martini has been shaken or stirred:

> Suppose we gave Mr. Bond a series of 16 taste tests. In each test, we flipped a fair coin to determine whether to stir or shake the martini. Then we presented the martini to Mr. Bond and asked him to decide whether it was shaken or stirred. Let's say Mr. Bond was correct on 13 of the 16 taste tests. Does this prove that Mr. Bond has at least some ability to tell whether the martini was shaken or stirred?
>
> This result does not prove that he does; it could be he was just lucky and guessed right 13 out of 16 times. But how plausible is the explanation that he was just lucky? To assess its plausibility, we determine the probability that someone who was just guessing would be correct 13/16 times or more.

According to the probability distribution of random guessing, the probability of being correct 13 of 16 times is very low: 0.0106. "So, either Mr. Bond was very lucky, or he can tell whether the drink was shaken or stirred" (Lane 2014). Given the low probability of his being lucky, we would conclude that Mr. Bond can tell the difference between a stirred and a shaken martini.

chi-square test for independence (χ^2)
A test of statistical significance used to assess the likelihood that an observed association between two variables could have occurred by chance.

Which statistics can be used to determine the probability that a relationship does not exist? For cross-tabulations, the most commonly used statistic is the **chi-square** (*or* χ^2) **test for independence**. The chi-square test is based on a comparison of the observed cell frequencies with the cell frequencies one would expect if there were no relationship between the variables. Table 12.6 shows the expected cell frequencies, assuming no relationship, and the derived bivariate percentage distribution for the data in Table 12.4. Notice that the cell percentages in Table 12.6 (reading across) are the same as the marginals; this indicates that knowing whether a respondent is male or female is of no help

Table 12.6 Attitude Toward Gun Control by Sex, Assuming No Relationship, 2016 General Social Survey

ATTITUDE TOWARD GUN CONTROL	Frequencies			Percentages		
	Male	Female	Total	Male	Female	Total
Favor	609	758	1,367	73.6%	73.6%	73.6%
Oppose	219	272	491	26.4	26.4	26.4
Total	828	1030	1,858	100.0%	100.0%	100.0%
(*N*)				(828)	(1,030)	(1,858)

in predicting attitude toward gun control, precisely the meaning of the null hypothesis of "no relationship" between the variables. The larger the differences between the actual cell frequencies and those expected assuming no relationship, the larger the value of chi-square, the less likely the relationship occurred randomly, and the more likely that it exists in the population.

The chi-square value (18.68)[1] for the data in Table 12.4 is statistically significant ($p < .01$), which indicates that there is a significant difference between the observed cell frequencies in Table 12.4 and the cell frequencies one would expect if there were no relationship between the variables (Table 12.6). Recall from Chapter 4 that the lowercase *p* stands for "probability"; for example, "$p < .01$" means that the probability is less than .01, or 1 in 100, that the association could have occurred randomly, assuming there is no relationship in the larger population from which the sample was drawn. With odds this low, we can be confident that the result would not have occurred by chance. Therefore, we can conclude that in the American adult population, females are more likely than males to favor gun control.

Knowing that this relationship is likely to exist in the population, however, does not tell us the strength of the relationship between the independent variable and the dependent variable. It is possible for a relationship to exist when changes in one variable correspond only slightly to changes in the other. The degree of this correspondence, or association, is a second measurable property of bivariate distributions.

MEASURES OF ASSOCIATION

In a 2 × 2 table, the percentage difference provides one indicator, albeit a poor one, of the strength of the relationship: the larger the difference, the stronger the relationship.

---

[1]The chi-squared tests of GSS data in this chapter are based on the Rao-Scott-P statistic.

However, researchers prefer to use one of several other statistics to measure relationship strength. These **measures of association** are standardized to vary between 0 (no association) and plus or minus 1.0 (perfect association). One such measure, which can be used for 2 × 2 tables, is Cramer's phi coefficient, which varies from 0 to 1; this equals .15 for the data in Table 12.4. Although the choice of labels is somewhat arbitrary, this magnitude suggests a "low" association between sex and attitude toward gun control (Davis 1971:49).

Although some measures of association may vary from –1 to +1, for variables with nominal categories, the sign, – or +, does not reveal anything meaningful about the nature of the relationship. However, when both variables have at least ordinal-level measurement, the sign indicates the direction of the relationship. Statistically, *direction* refers to the tendency for increases in the values of one variable to be associated with systematic increases or decreases in the values of another variable. Both variables may change in the same direction (a positive relationship) or in opposite directions (a negative relationship).

In a positive relationship, lower values of one variable tend to be associated with lower values of the other variable, and higher values of one variable tend to go along with higher values of the other. Table 12.7 shows a positive relationship between two ordinal variables from the campus survey: self-description as a drinker (question 34) and frequency of alcohol consumption (question 35). To make the table easier to "read," we have recoded the latter variable to create three categories. Carefully examine this table before reading further. We will treat frequency of consumption as the dependent variable, although there is probably a reciprocal influence here: that is, how much you drink affects your description of yourself as a drinker and vice versa. Notice that, as in the previous examples, Table 12.7 is percentaged

Table 12.7 Frequency of Alcohol Consumption by Self-description as Drinker, Campus Survey

SELF-DESCRIPTION AS DRINKER**	Frequency of Alcohol Consumption*		
	Less than Once a Week	1 or 2 Times a Week	3 or More Times a Week
Light	82.6	31.3	7.0
Moderate	17.4	65.8	59.9
Heavy	0.0	2.9	33.1
Total	100.0%	100.0%	100.0%
(*N*)	(155)	(345)	(157)

How often do you drink alcoholic beverages?

**How would you describe your consumption of alcohol . . . would you describe yourself as a light, moderate, or heavy drinker?*

Table 12.8 Number of Hours per Day Watching TV by Highest Degree Received, 2016 General Social Survey

NUMBER OF TV HOURS	Highest Degree				
	Less Than High School	High School	Associate/Jr College	Bachelor Degree	Graduate Degree
0–1	18.6	23.4	27.0	38.3	44.8
2–3	36.2	42.7	42.1	40.6	44.3
4 or more	45.2	33.9	30.9	21.1	10.9
Total	100.0%	100.0%	100.0%	100.0%	100.0%
(N)	(221)	(956)	(152)	(350)	(201)

down for each category of the independent variable, frequency of consumption; thus, comparisons should be made across. The percentage of students who describe themselves as "light" drinkers (first row) falls with increasing frequency of consumption: 82.6 to 31.3 to 7.0 percent. Similarly, the percentage describing themselves as "heavy" drinkers (third row) consistently rises as frequency of consumption increases: 0.0 to 2.9 to 33.1 percent. It is this sort of pattern (self-described heavier drinking associated with more frequent consumption) that suggests a clearly positive relationship.

In a negative (inverse) relationship, there is a tendency for *lower* values of one variable to be associated with *higher* values of the other variable. Table 12.8, based on GSS data, reveals such a relationship between education and the number of hours of television watched on an average day: as education increases, television-viewing time decreases. (There are many possible explanations here: perhaps higher-income persons are more apt to be exposed to and can better afford other, more expensive forms of entertainment, or perhaps more highly educated people have less leisure time.)

One ordinal measure of the strength of association is the statistic *gamma*. The value of gamma is .84 for the data in Table 12.7 and −.29 for the data in Table 12.8. Thus, there is a high positive association between self-description as a drinker and frequency of alcohol consumption and a moderate negative association between television viewing and years of schooling. The statistical significance of a relationship between two ordinal-scale variables also may be tested with the chi-square statistic. The chi-square test for both tables is statistically significant.

So far we have restricted ourselves to variables having only 2 to 5 categories and to tables with 4 to 15 cells. This is not unusual because most cross-tabulation analyses in

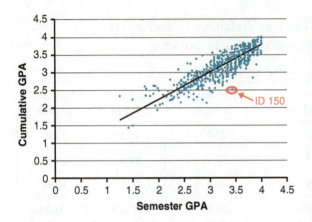

social research are limited to variables with relatively few categories. There are three important reasons for this. First, the size of the table increases geometrically as the number of categories for each variable increases. And the larger the table, the more difficult it is to discern the pattern of the relationship, which can be much more complex than the positive or negative relationships we have described. Second, the finer the breakdown of one's sample into various categories, the fewer cases there will be for any given breakdown (or cell of the table). Hence, larger tables may require impractically large samples for reliable assessments. Finally, variables with a relatively large number of categories either constitute or tend to approximate interval-scale measurement. With interval-scale variables, we can use a more precise and more powerful form of statistical analysis known as "correlation" and "regression."

Interval- and Ratio-Scale Variables

The analysis of the relationship between two interval/ratio variables begins by plotting the values of each variable in a graphic coordinate system, which may take you back to high school geometry. Researchers then use a statistical method called **regression analysis** to determine the mathematical equation that most closely describes the data. Through this equation, they identify statistics that show the relationship between two variables. For the purposes of illustration, we begin here by performing a regression analysis on two variables that we expect to have a strong relationship: cumulative GPA and GPA for the semester when the survey was conducted. Then we apply the same analysis to test the hypothesis that students who drink heavily tend to have low GPAs.

Let us begin our analysis by looking at a **scatterplot** of data from the campus survey on cumulative GPA and semester GPA (Figure 12.5). Each plot or point in the graph represents the values of one of the 710 students for whom we have data on both of these variables. With the vertical axis as our reference, we can read the value of the dependent variable (cumulative GPA); and with the horizontal axis as our reference, we can read the value of the independent variable (semester GPA). The respondent identified in the figure as ID 150, for example, has a semester GPA of 3.5 and a cumulative GPA of 2.5.

The scatterplot gives the researcher a rough sense of the form of the relationship: whether it is best characterized with a straight or a curved line and whether it is positive or negative. This is crucial information because regression analysis assumes that the data have a particular form. If a straight line provides the best fit with the data, we should do linear regression; if a curve provides the best fit, we should use special techniques for fitting curvilinear relationships (which are beyond the scope of this book).

regression analysis A statistical method for analyzing bivariate (simple regression) and multivariate (multiple regression) relationships among interval- or ratio-scale variables.

scatterplot A graph plotting the values of two variables for each observation.

The overall form of the data in Figure 12.5 clearly shows a linear trend from the lower left corner to the upper right corner. The trend of the data also shows, as expected, that cumulative GPA increases as semester GPA increases.

Having decided to fit a straight line to the data, and therefore to do *linear* regression analysis, we need to know two things: (1) the mathematical equation for a straight line and (2) the criterion for selecting a line to represent the data.

The general form of the equation for a straight line is $\hat{Y} = a + bX$, where $\hat{Y}$ is the predicted value of the dependent variable and X is the corresponding value of the independent variable. Thus, an equation for a straight line relating cumulative GPA, as the dependent variable, and semester GPA, as the independent variable, is:

Cumulative GPA $= a + b$ (Semester GPA)

The value a, called the **Y-intercept**, is the point where the line crosses the vertical axis (where Semester GPA $= 0$). The value b, called the **slope** or **regression coefficient**, indicates how much $\hat{Y}$ increases (or decreases) for every change of one unit in X. In our example, the slope indicates how much increase (or decrease) occurs in cumulative GPA for every change of 1 grade point in semester GPA. To get the line of best fit, then, we could simply draw a line on the scatterplot that seems to best reflect the trend in the data and then determine the values of a and b from the graph. Of course, there are many lines that we could draw—a and b can take on an infinite number of values. How, then, do we know when we have obtained the best fit?

Regression analysis uses the method of least squares as the criterion for selecting the line that best describes the data. According to this method, the best-fitting line *minimizes* the sum of the *squared* vertical distances from the data points to the line. We have drawn the **regression line**, also called the least squares line, on the scatterplot. Now imagine a dashed line showing the vertical distance, as measured by cumulative GPA, between a specific data point, say ID 150, and the regression line. The regression line represents the equation for predicting Y from X; the vertical distances between data points and this line represent prediction errors (also called **residuals**). Thus, by finding the line that minimizes the sum of the squared distances from it, we are, in effect, finding the best linear predictor of the cumulative GPA from knowledge of a student's semester GPA.

The precise equation generated by the method of least squares can be found via a mathematical formula with the aid of a computer program. When we applied this formula to the data in Figure 12.5, we got the following equation:

Cumulative GPA $= .695 + .768$ (Semester GPA)

This equation indicates that students with a hypothetical 0.0 semester GPA would be predicted to have an average cumulative GPA of 0.695 (i.e., $.695 + [.768 \times 0] = .695$). For every one-unit increase in semester GPA (e.g., from a semester GPA of 0

Y-intercept The predicted value of the dependent variable in regression when the independent variable or variables have a value of zero; graphically, the point at which the regression line crosses the Y-axis.

slope/regression coefficient A bivariate regression statistic indicating how much the dependent variable increases (or decreases) for every unit change in the independent variable; the slope of a regression line.

regression line A geometric representation of a bivariate regression equation that provides the best linear fit to the observed data by virtue of minimizing the sum of the squared deviations from the line; also called the *least squares line.*

residuals The difference between observed values of the dependent variable and those predicted by a regression equation.

to a semester GPA of 1), an increase of about three-quarters of a grade point (.768) is expected in cumulative GPA. The regression equation gives the best linear prediction of the dependent variable based on the data at hand. ID 150, for example, has a predicted cumulative GPA of 3.383 (.695 + [.768 × 3.5]), which is .883 greater (the residual) than his or her current 2.5 cumulative GPA. Can you spot the largest residuals in Figure 12.5?

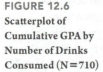

correlation coefficient
A measure of the strength and direction of a linear relationship between two variables; it may vary from −1 to 0 to +1.

The strength of the association between two interval/ratio variables is frequently measured by the **correlation coefficient** (symbolized as *r*), which may vary between −1 and +1. The sign of the coefficient, which is always the same as the sign of the regression coefficient, indicates the direction of the relationship. The magnitude of its value depends on two factors: (1) the steepness of the regression line and (2) the variation or scatter of the data points around this line. If the line is not very steep, so that it is nearly parallel to the X-axis, then we might as well predict the same value of Y for every unit change in X; in other words, there is very little change in our prediction (as indicated by *b* in the equation) for every unit change in the independent variable. By the same token, the greater the spread of values about the regression line (regardless of the steepness of the slope), the less accurate are predictions based on the linear regression. The scatterplot for the regression of cumulative GPA on semester GPA shows that the line is fairly steep in relation to the horizontal axis and that the data points cluster fairly close to the line. Not surprisingly, therefore, the correlation coefficient indicates a strong positive association of .88.

Statistics also exist for testing whether the correlation coefficient and the regression coefficient are significantly different from zero. These may be found in most statistics textbooks. Both of these coefficients are significant ($p < .001$) for the data in Figure 12.5.

Now that we have illustrated regression analysis and introduced its key concepts, let's examine the bivariate relationship between number of drinks consumed and cumulative GPA. Figure 12.6 shows the scatterplot for these variables. How would you describe the form of the relationship? Does it seem to show a positive or negative association? Would a straight or curved line best fit the data? The overall pattern is somewhat difficult to discern; however, the trend seems to indicate that as the number of drinks consumed increases, cumulative GPA decreases. Also, since the relationship does not appear to be sharply curvilinear, we can assume that a straight line offers as good a fit as a curved line.

When we applied the method of least squares to the data in Figure 12.6, we obtained the following regression equation:

FIGURE 12.6
Scatterplot of Cumulative GPA by Number of Drinks Consumed (N=710)

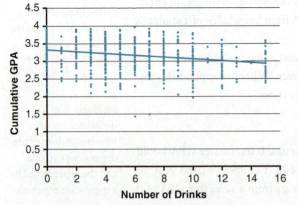

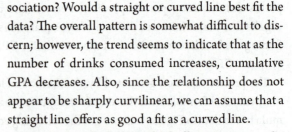

Cumulative GPA = 3.311 − .026 (Number of drinks consumed)

The equation thus shows that a student's cumulative GPA decreases by .026 for every drink consumed. For students who abstain from drinking, the average predicted cumulative GPA is 3.311; by comparison, students who consume 5 drinks on a typical weekend night would have an average predicted cumulative GPA of 3.181 (3.311 − [.026 × 5]). The correlation between alcohol consumption and grades was −.24, which was statistically significant at $p < .001$. Thus, a preliminary test of the bivariate relationship supports the hypothesis that students who drink more heavily tend to have lower cumulative GPAs. Before you read further, be sure to read Box 12.2, CHECKING YOUR UNDERSTANDING: The Meaning of Statistical Significance and Strength of Association.

BOX 12.2

CHECKING YOUR UNDERSTANDING

The Meaning of Statistical Significance and Strength of Association

As you have seen, two types of statistics can be used to assess bivariate relationships: tests of statistical significance and measures of strength of association. Each of these statistics provides different information, and even seasoned researchers sometimes misinterpret what they can and cannot tell us about the relationship between two variables (Shaver 1993). So, let's consider each statistic as it relates to tests of the hypothesis that drinking is associated with cumulative GPA.

Suppose researchers at three other colleges conduct surveys in which they use the same questions on alcohol consumption and also request permission to obtain data on cumulative GPA from official records. Each survey is based on a random sample of the undergraduate student population; however, because of different resources, the surveys have markedly different sample sizes. Below are hypothetical findings.

College A:	$r = -.28$	$p < .10$	$N = 30$
College B:	$r = -.11$	$p < .001$	$N = 795$
College C:	$r = -.20$	$p < .01$	$N = 196$

1. At which college is the relationship between number of drinks consumed and cumulative GPA strongest?
2. Is the association statistically significant at all three colleges?
3. What do these data tell us about the theoretical and practical importance of the association between drinking and grades?

continues

continued

To answer the first question, we use the correlation coefficient r. This is a *descriptive* statistic that indicates strength of association, or how well we can predict one variable from knowledge of another. The absolute value of r (ignoring the plus or minus sign) is the measure of strength. The coefficient is largest, and therefore the relationship is strongest, for College A.

To answer the second question, we need to examine the p-values, which are based on tests of statistical significance. Tests of significance are *inferential* statistics that determine the probability (at some specified level p) of a particular result, assuming the null hypothesis is true. The null hypothesis here is $r = 0$. If the null hypothesis is rejected, we can be reasonably confident that there is a relationship between alcohol consumption and GPA in the population from which the sample was drawn. Using the traditional level of significance of .05, the association is significant at College B and College C, but not at College A.

Comparing the findings, you can see that the association is strongest ($r = -.28$) at College A, whereas the association is least likely to occur by chance ($p < .001$) at College B. This suggests that the level of statistical significance (or p-value) tells us nothing about strength of an association. The reason is that p-values depend not only on the magnitude of the correlation coefficient but also on the size of the sample. If the sample is big enough, even very weak correlations are unlikely to occur by chance and, therefore, are likely to differ from 0 in the population from which the sample was drawn. For example, given the sample size of 795 at College B, a correlation of .06 would be significant; and with a sample size of 10,000, a correlation of .02 would be significant.

Just as statistical significance tells us nothing about strength of association, or the magnitude of a result, it also reveals nothing about its theoretical or practical importance. In fact, neither of these judgments can be based on statistics alone. For example, statistical significance is insufficient to establish causality, which often determines whether a finding is theoretically important. Further, practical importance depends on the magnitude of the result as well as an assessment of human values and costs (Shaver 1993).

If we were to replicate the survey and produce the above results, this would enhance the theoretical importance of the association between drinking and GPA. Although the size of the coefficient varies, it is consistently a negative nonzero correlation. How important this result is theoretically depends on subsequent multivariate analysis. As for practical importance, we'll let you be the judge. Let's assume that the direction of influence is from drinking to grades. Based on real data from the campus survey, students at this college who consume 10 drinks on a typical weekend night are estimated to have, on average, a cumulative GPA that is a quarter of a point lower than those who abstain from drinking, which is just about the difference between a B and B^+ average.

SUMMARY

Bivariate analysis examines the relationship between two variables. For relationships involving exclusively nominal- or ordinal-scale variables, such analysis begins with the construction of cross-tabulations. Tests of statistical significance and measures of association are then applied to determine, respectively, whether the relationship is likely to have occurred by chance and the strength of the association. For relationships involving interval- or ratio-scale variables, the data are plotted in a scatterplot and characterized in terms of a mathematical equation. Linear regression analysis identifies the straight-line equation that provides the best fit with the data by virtue of minimizing the sum of the squared deviations from the line. The slope of the line reveals the predicted change in the dependent variable per unit change in the independent variable, and the correlation coefficient indicates the strength of the association.

CONDUCT MULTIVARIATE TESTING

Once you've conducted bivariate analyses on nonexperimental data, all is not said and done. If you've found a statistically significant relationship, there is reason to hold your excitement in abeyance. The regression analysis in the previous section shows that there is a bivariate *association* between cumulative GPA and number of drinks consumed. However, if the goal is to test the causal hypothesis that drinking lowers grades, our analysis cannot end here. As we have emphasized repeatedly, causal inferences are based not only on association but also theoretical assumptions and empirical evidence about *direction of influence* and *nonspuriousness*.

In a cross-sectional survey such as the campus survey, for example, a correlation between X and Y may imply that X causes Y, Y causes X, X and Y mutually cause each other, or that X and Y are causally unrelated (spurious association). Multivariate analysis can help the researcher to choose among such possible interpretations. But it is important to realize that *statistical analyses by themselves do not provide a basis for inferring causal relationships*. Instead, a researcher starts with a theoretical model of the causal process linking X and Y and then determines if the data are consistent with the theory.

The theoretical model (or hypothesis) linking alcohol consumption and GPA can be summarized simply in an arrow diagram with a line connecting the variables, as shown in Figure 12.7A. This model assumes that the direction of influence is from alcohol consumption to GPA. It is possible, however, that the reverse direction holds—doing poorly academically leads to heavy drinking—or that these variables mutually cause each other (not shown in the figure). In this section, we use data from the campus survey to test Model A, leaving tests of alternative directional models to future research.

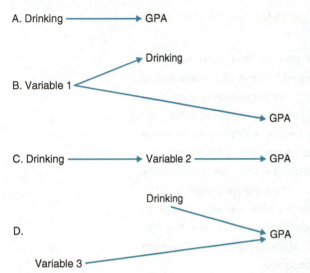

FIGURE 12.7
Arrow Diagrams for Different Causal Models of the Relationship between Drinking and GPA

Another shortcoming of Model A is that there are many other, extraneous variables that may be a cause of drinking or grades or both. Of the many possible alternative models, we will briefly describe three. Model B in Figure 12.7 illustrates an outcome in which the original relationship is spurious. Notice that an antecedent variable (variable 1) is a cause of both drinking and GPA and there is no direct causal link (arrow) between these variables. Model C presents a second alternative in which an intervening variable (variable 2) is causally positioned between drinking and GPA; that is, drinking influences variable 2, which in turn influences GPA. Finally, Model D represents an outcome in which an extraneous variable is neither antecedent nor intervening, but rather has an independent effect on GPA.

The figure represents models with generic extraneous variables. Which variables are actually in the data? Data from the campus survey include several antecedent variables: sex, race, parents' education, parents' income, whether a student is an intercollegiate athlete, and academic aptitude as measured by total score on the Scholastic Aptitude Test (SAT). Any one of these variables might create a spurious association between drinking and GPA (Model B) or be an independent cause of GPA (Model D). To test for spuriousness (Model B) as well as independent effects on GPA (Model D), we now introduce two of the several strategies for multivariate analysis: elaboration of contingency tables and multiple regression. Furthermore, to show how these strategies are based on the same logic of analysis, we use the same data, albeit in different forms.

Elaboration of Contingency Tables

The multivariate analysis of contingency tables introduces a third control variable (and sometimes additional variables) into the analysis to enhance or "elaborate" our understanding of a bivariate relationship. To illustrate the logic of this elaboration, we first created a contingency table of the *bivariate* relationship between cumulative GPA and number of drinks by dichotomizing each of these variables. That is, for each variable, we collapsed all the values into two categories with an approximately equal proportion of cases in each category. For cumulative GPA, the split occurred at less than 3.2 and 3.2 or greater; for number of drinks, the split occurred between 5 or fewer drinks and 6 or more drinks.

Table 12.9 shows the bivariate association between the dichotomized variables cumulative GPA and number of drinks consumed. The data indicate that there is an association: by a difference of 18.5 percent, students who report consuming 6 or more

Table 12.9 Cumulative GPA by Number of Drinks Consumed, Campus Survey

	Number of Drinks Consumed	
CUMULATIVE GPA	5 or Less	6 or More
Less than 3.2	40.0%	58.5%
3.2 or greater	60.0	41.5
Total	100.0%	100.0%
(*N*)	(355)	(323)

drinks on a typical weekend night are more likely to have a cumulative GPA below 3.2 than are students who report consuming 5 or fewer drinks. Moreover, the chi-square test is significant at $p < .001$; so, an association is likely to exist among all students at the college from which this sample was drawn.

The objective of elaboration is to examine the impact of additional "third" variables on a bivariate relationship. We are especially interested in understanding the impact of antecedent variables that might create a spurious relationship, as in theoretical Model B. For example, researchers have speculated that the association between drinking and GPA might be spurious due to precollege factors such as academic aptitude. That is, students with a relatively low aptitude might be likely to drink more *and* to do less well academically than students with a relatively high aptitude. To explore this possibility, we introduce a measure of respondents' aptitude—SAT total score—into the analysis by holding it constant. In contingency table elaboration, third variables are held constant by means of subgroup classification. Each category of the third variable constitutes a distinct subgroup, and the original two-variable relationship is recomputed separately for each subgroup. Table 12.10 does this for the variables of cumulative GPA, number of drinks consumed, and dichotomized SAT total score. However, the percentages in the table are hypothetical and used only for the purpose of illustrating Models B and C.

Notice that we now have two "tables," one for each category of the variable "SAT total score." These are called **partial tables** or **partials**, because each shows the association between alcohol consumption and GPA for part of the total number of observations. SAT total score is held constant, because in each partial table all respondents are alike with respect to their SAT scores. Look over the partial tables carefully. What do they reveal about the relationship between alcohol consumption and GPA when SAT score is controlled?

Reading across each partial table, we find no association between alcohol consumption and GPA (e.g., in the first partial, 62.3 – 62.3 = 0). Thus, the original relationship

partial table A table in elaboration analysis which displays the original two-variable relationship for a single category of the control variable, thereby holding the control variable constant.

Table 12.10 Cumulative GPA by Number of Drinks Consumed and SAT Total Score, Hypothetical Data

	SAT Total Score Less than 1270		SAT Total Score 1270 or Greater	
CUMULATIVE GPA	5 or Less	6 or More	5 or Less	6 or More
Less than 3.2	62.3%	62.3%	36.1%	36.1%
3.2 or greater	37.7	37.7	63.9	63.9
Total	100.0%	100.0%	100.0%	100.0%
(N)	(170)	(159)	(185)	(164)

(shown in Table 12.9), which indicated that heavier drinkers had lower GPAs than lighter drinkers, has disappeared when SAT score is controlled. These hypothetical data, therefore, support Model B in Figure 12.7. The relationship is spurious, produced by a common association with SAT score, an indicator of academic aptitude. We draw this inference not only on the basis of the data, however, but also on the basis of prior theoretical assumptions about the causal ordering of these variables. These same data might just as well have been generated by Model C:

Number of drinks ⟶ SAT total score ⟶ Cumulative GPA

Here "SAT total score" is an *intervening* variable between "drinks consumed" and "cumulative GPA," whereas in Model B, SAT total score is an *antecedent* variable with respect to these variables. We prefer Model B as an interpretation because it makes no sense that the number of drinks that students reported consuming at the time of the survey determined the scores they obtained on the SAT while in high school. But it is crucial to realize that this interpretation rests on theory; the data in Table 12.10 are consistent with either theoretical model.

The outcomes of elaboration analysis are seldom this tidy. Recall that the data in Table 12.10 are hypothetical. As the real data in Table 12.11 show, the relationship between cumulative GPA and number of drinks consumed does not reduce to zero in either partial. Rather, it exists in both partial tables, although it is somewhat stronger in one than in the other. For which subgroup of students is the relationship stronger? Students who consume greater amounts of alcohol are more likely to have a cumulative GPA less than 3.2, but the percentage difference is 13.3 (55.9 − 69.2) among those with relatively low SAT scores (less than 1270), as compared with 22.8 percent (25.4 − 48.2) among those with relatively high SAT scores (1270 or greater). So, alcohol consumption appears to have a somewhat greater effect on GPA among those with high SAT scores.

Table 12.11 Cumulative GPA by Number of Drinks Consumed and SAT Total Score, Campus Survey

	SAT Total Score Less than 1270		SAT Total Score 1270 or Greater	
CUMULATIVE GPA	5 or Less	6 or More	5 or Less	6 or More
Less than 3.2	55.9%	69.2%	25.4%	48.2%
3.2 or greater	44.1	30.8	74.6	51.8
Total	100.0%	100.0%	100.0%	100.0%
(N)	(170)	(159)	(185)	(164)

Showing that the relationship between drinking and GPA is maintained when controlling for SAT total score eliminates the possibility that academic aptitude produced a spurious relationship. This conclusion is limited, however, and it is subject to three criticisms that pertain to much analysis of contingency tables: (1) Collapsing variables such as amount of alcohol consumed, GPA, and SAT scores into two categories may eliminate important information and distort the results; (2) several other variables (e.g., sex, race, parents' income) might produce a spurious association between alcohol consumption and GPA; and (3) controlling for one variable at a time ignores the possibility that spuriousness may be created by the simultaneous action of two or more extraneous variables.

We can never be absolutely certain that alcohol consumption lowers grades. Ultimately, our confidence in this causal relationship depends on our holding constant all antecedent variables that might reasonably be expected to produce a spurious relationship. Multiple regression, described in the next section, is generally better when we want to analyze the simultaneous effects of several independent variables on a dependent variable.

Multiple Regression

Multiple regression is simply an extension of bivariate regression to include two or more independent variables. Like the partial tables of elaboration analysis, it provides information about the relationship between an independent variable and a dependent variable while controlling for the effects of other independent variables. Unlike partial tables, control is not limited to a few variables nor is information lost from collapsing variables into fewer categories.

multiple regression
A statistical method for determining the simultaneous effects of several independent variables on a dependent variable.

The general formula for a multiple-regression equation is like the formula for the linear equation in bivariate regression except that it includes additional independent variables:

$$\hat{Y} = a + b_1 X_1 + b_2 X_2 + b_3 X_3 + \ldots$$

In this equation, $\hat{Y}$ is the predicted value of the dependent variable, each X represents an independent variable, the b values are **partial regression coefficients** or **partial slopes**, and a is the Y-intercept (the predicted value of the dependent variable when all of the X values are equal to zero). The slopes in this equation differ from those in bivariate regression in that each represents the impact of the independent variable when *all other variables in the equation are held constant*. This tells us the effect of a given variable beyond the effects of all the other variables included in the analysis.

When researchers report the results of multiple regression, they present the intercept and the regression coefficient for each variable in a table. Table 12.12 shows the outcome for the campus survey of the regression of cumulative GPA on selected independent variables. Model 1 includes seven independent variables; Model 2 adds an eighth: number of drinks consumed, which is the independent variable of theoretical interest. To interpret the results of this analysis, we need to explain several features of the variables and the statistics presented in the table.

partial regression coefficient/partial slope Coefficients in a multiple-regression equation that estimate the effects of each independent variable on the dependent variable when all other variables in the equation are held constant.

- Three of the variables—"male," "white," and "intercollegiate athlete"—represent dummy variables. A **dummy variable** is a variable that is recoded into two categories that are assigned the values of 1 and 0. Dummy coding enables the researcher to manipulate the variable numerically, as in multiple regression. Thus, for the campus survey data, 1 = male and 0 = female; 1 = white and 0 = nonwhite; 1 = intercollegiate athlete and 0 = not an intercollegiate athlete.
- All other independent variables are treated as interval/ratio level measures. This includes academic class, which is highly correlated with age ($r = .88$) and essentially serves as a proxy for age at this college.
- The statistics opposite each independent variable in the first and third columns are *unstandardized* regression coefficients. The second and fourth columns display estimated standard errors, which are used to compute significance tests.
- The last row of the table contains a statistic, R^2, which indicates how well the data fit the model or how well we can predict the dependent variable based on this set of independent variables. R^2 may vary from 0 to 1. It is particularly useful for comparing models containing the same dependent variable but different sets of independent variables, such as Models 1 and 2 in Table 12.12.
- Asterisks (*,**) next to the coefficients indicate which independent variables are significantly related to cumulative GPA. The levels of significance are specified in a footnote to the table.
- In addition to levels of significance, the footnote shows the number of cases upon which the statistics are based. It also indicates that values of "0" in the table mean that the statistic has been rounded to 0.

dummy variable A variable or set of variable categories recoded to have values of 0 and 1. Dummy coding may be applied to nominal- or ordinal-scale variables for the purpose of regression or other numerical analysis.

R^2 A measure of fit in multiple regression that indicates approximately the proportion of the variation in the dependent variable predicted or "explained" by the independent variables.

Now that you know the meaning of the statistics reported in Table 12.12, let's examine the outcome of the multiple regression. To begin, we'll pose some questions:

Table 12.12 Regression of Cumulative GPA on Selected Independent Variables, Campus Survey

INDEPENDENT VARIABLES	Model 1		Model 2	
	Coefficient Estimate	Standard Error	Coefficient Estimate	Standard Error
SAT total score	.001**	.000	.001**	.000
Male	−.202**	.028	−.121**	.030
White	.183**	.046	.209**	.045
Intercollegiate athlete	−.065*	.032	−.053	.032
Academic class	.008	.012	.016	.012
Parents' education	.013	.009	.014	.008
Parents' income	−.000	.000	−.000	.000
Number of drinks			−.025**	.004
Intercept	1.608	.163	1.681	.159
Adjusted R^2	.228		.265	

$N = 678$; $*p < .05$; $**p < .001$; values of .000 indicate that the statistic has been rounded to zero.

1. Is number of drinks significantly related to GPA when controlling for all of the other independent variables in the equation?
2. Which variables in Model 2 have a significant impact on cumulative GPA?
3. In Model 1, what does the coefficient for "male" mean?
4. What happens to the regression coefficient for male when number of drinks is added to the equation (Model 2)? What does this imply about the relationship among sex, number of drinks, and cumulative GPA?
5. In both models, which variable has the biggest impact on cumulative GPA?

Now, on to the answers:

1. To answer the first question, the coefficient for number of drinks is statistically significant when controlling for all the other independent variables in the model. Moreover, the coefficient (−.025) is nearly identical to the regression coefficient we obtained in the bivariate regression (−.026). So, the relationship between drinking and cumulative GPA appears to be unaffected by these other variables, and the data support the hypothesis that drinking is associated with GPA.

2. In addition to number of drinks, three other variables in Model 2 are significant predictors of cumulative GPA: SAT total score, sex ("male"), and race ("white").

3. The coefficient of −.202 for "male" means that on average, when controlling for all other variables in the model, males have a cumulative GPA that is .202 lower than females. (To control the other variables, just assign each variable a value of 0.)

4. When number of drinks is added to the equation, the coefficient for sex reduces in absolute magnitude from −.202 to −.121. This difference shows the effect of number of drinks on the *relationship* between sex and cumulative GPA. It suggests that number of drinks may be an intervening variable between sex and cumulative GPA: sex affects drinking behavior, which in turn affects cumulative GPA. In other words, one of the reasons males have lower grades than females is that they consume more alcohol.

5. To determine which variable has the greatest impact on cumulative GPA, we need to compare the coefficients. There is a problem, however, in comparing the unstandardized slope coefficients in Table 12.12. As you may recall, regression coefficients (or slopes) indicate the amount of change in Y that is associated with each change of one unit in X. For example, the *unstandardized* regression coefficient of −.025 for number of drinks means that cumulative GPA decreases by .025 with each drink that is consumed. The problem with unstandardized regression coefficients, however, is that the units differ for each independent variable. For SAT total score, it is a point; for income, the unit is dollars; for amount of alcohol consumed, it is a single drink; and so on. Because the units differ, you cannot compare the slopes to determine their relative impact on the dependent variable. After all, what sense does it make to compare the impact of a single point on the SAT test with a single drink of alcohol? To compare slopes, they should be "standardized" in a way that expresses the effects in terms of a common unit; a standard deviation is a unit common to both independent variables and the dependent variable. One way of calculating a standardized regression coefficient is to multiply the unstandardized regression coefficient (presented in Table 12.12) by the ratio of the standard deviation of the independent variable to the standard deviation of the dependent variable. This is what we have done in creating the coefficients in Table 12.13.

standardized regression coefficients Coefficients obtained from a norming operation that puts partial-regression coefficients on common footing by converting them to the same metric of standard deviation units.

The statistics opposite each independent variable in Table 12.13 are **standardized regression coefficients**. Notice that we have not included the Y-intercept in this table. The reason is that, when standardizing the coefficients, the Y-intercept is set to 0. Notice also that the *standardized* regression coefficient for number of drinks in Model 2 is −.233. This means that for every increase of one standard deviation in number of drinks, there is a decrease of .233 standard deviation in cumulative GPA. With each variable now standardized, we can compare coefficients to see which has the biggest impact. The variable with the biggest impact is SAT total score, followed by number of drinks.

Table 12.13 Standardized Regression Coefficients for Regression of Cumulative GPA on Selected Independent Variables, Campus Survey

Independent Variables	Model 1	Model 2
SAT total score	.325**	.314**
Male	−.245**	−.147**
White	.150**	.170**
Intercollegiate athlete	−.070*	−.057
Academic class	.023	.044
Parents' education	.060	.064
Parents' income	−.054	−.023
Number of drinks		−.233**
Adjusted R^2	.228	.265

$N = 678$; $^*p < .05$; $^{**}p < .001$.

Now that you see how we could use multivariate analysis to test theoretical models, we hasten to add that we have barely scratched the surface of multivariate modeling. What we have tried to do is give you a sense of the logic of statistical control and the kinds of inferences that can be made from various statistics. But there are many methods of multivariate analysis other than elaboration and multiple regression. For example, there are special techniques for modeling different types of dependent variables (e.g., dichotomous, nominal, and ordinal measures), for straightening or transforming nonlinear relationships into a form suitable for linear modeling, for modeling mutual causation, processes occurring over time, and so forth. In addition, we have ignored the process of model testing, which usually involves the consideration of a series of models of varying complexity. In short, our presentation is quite superficial and cannot be substituted for formal coursework in statistics.

Finally, we also should point out that our presentation generally ignores the assumptions that underlie multiple regression as well as other forms of statistical analysis. Box 12.3, READING SOCIAL RESEARCH: The Impact of Statistical Assumptions in Quantitative Data Analysis, alerts you to a few of the more important assumptions.

BOX 12.3

The Impact of Statistical Assumptions in Quantitative Data Analysis

All statistics make certain assumptions about the data, and researchers often apply these statistics even though the assumptions are not met. Fully understanding how the violation of assumptions may affect an analysis requires an advanced knowledge of statistics. Still, it is important to understand the critical role of a few basic assumptions in the interpretation of quantitative data analysis.

The most fundamental assumption of inferential statistics is that the data are based on a random process—either random sampling or random assignment. As we saw in Chapter 6, the ability to estimate the margin of error in a sample depends on a known sampling distribution, which is produced by repeated random sampling. Similarly in tests of statistical significance, we compare results from a random sample against a randomly generated statistical distribution, such as chi-square, to determine the likelihood that the result occurred by chance. If the sample is nonrandom, the test statistic does not apply because there is no basis for estimating the chance occurrence of the result.

Another important assumption in linear regression and correlation analysis is that a straight line provides the best fit for the data. As we pointed out, researchers often make this determination by examining a scatterplot. This method is far from foolproof, however, and if the best-fitting straight line is calculated for data that

are nonlinearly related, statistical predictions based on the sample data may be seriously in error.

Multiple regression makes an additional assumption about the correlations among independent variables: a regression equation should not contain two or more variables that are highly correlated. If two variables are highly correlated, then we cannot estimate the independent effects of the variables, and the inclusion of both variables in the equation can distort estimates of coefficients. If two highly correlated variables (e.g., academic class and age in the campus survey) are found, then the easy solution is to drop one from the regression equation. A far more difficult problem is *multicollinearity*, which arises when combinations of two or more variables are highly related with each other.

Finally, all forms of regression analysis are subject to what is called a *specification error*. All regression analysis involves the specification of a model containing a set of variables. A specification error occurs when the equation leaves out important variables. For example, if an equation fails to contain an antecedent variable that is a common cause of a bivariate relationship, the results of a bivariate analysis may be misleading because the relationship is spurious. To the extent that a model is misspecified, a regression analysis will produce biased estimates of coefficients.

SUMMARY

We introduced two methods of model testing that are used to examine the effects of an independent variable on a dependent variable while controlling for other relevant independent variables. In elaboration of contingency tables, we begin with a two-variable relationship and then systematically reassess this relationship when controls are introduced for a third variable (and sometimes additional ones). Variables are controlled, or held constant, by computing partial tables, which examine the original two-variable relationship separately for each category of the control variable. Of the numerous possible outcomes, one is of particular interest: if the model specifies the control variable as causally antecedent to the other two variables and the original relationship disappears in each partial table, then the original relationship is spurious. A better technique for analyzing the simultaneous effects of several independent variables on a dependent variable is multiple regression. The partial-regression coefficients in a multiple-regression equation show the effects of each independent variable on the dependent variable when all other variables in the equation are held constant. Comparison of partial-regression coefficients may be facilitated by standardizing them to the same metric of standard deviation units.

KEY TERMS

bivariate analysis, p. 379

cell frequency, p. 380

chi-square test for independence (χ^2), p. 382

consistency checking, p. 371

correlation coefficient, p. 388

data cleaning, p. 370

data matrix, p. 368

data processing, p. 365

descriptive statistics, p. 363

dummy variable, p. 396

frequency distribution, p. 372

histogram, p. 377

imputation, p. 378

inferential statistics, p. 363

listwise deletion, p. 378

marginal frequencies, p. 380

mean, p. 375

measures of association, p. 384

median, p. 375

missing data, p. 369

mode, p. 375

multiple regression, p. 395

N, p. 373

null hypothesis, p. 382

outliers, p. 377

partial regression coefficient/ partial slope, p. 396

partial table, p. 393

percentage distribution, p. 372

R^2, p. 396

range, p. 375

regression analysis, p. 386

regression line, p. 387

residuals, p. 387

scatterplot, p. 386

slope/regression coefficient, p. 387

standard deviation, p. 377

standardized regression coefficients, p. 398

tests of statistical significance, p. 382

univariate analysis, p. 371

wild-code checking, p. 371

Y-intercept, p. 387

KEY POINTS

- To prepare quantitative data for computerized analysis, the data must be processed by coding and editing the data, entering them into an electronic datafile, and cleaning for errors.

- Once processed, the data are inspected by examining the univariate distribution of each variable.
- Data inspection is facilitated by creating percentage distributions and, for interval/ratio variables, by calculating statistics that describe the central tendency, variation, and shape of a distribution.
- Data inspection may lead to data modification, such as imputing missing values and combining data from two or more variables.
- After univariate analysis comes bivariate analysis, in which the statistical significance and degree of association between two variables are examined.
- Bivariate relationships of nominal/ordinal variables are depicted in contingency tables.
- Examining the relationship of two interval/ratio variables often involves regression analysis: plotting the variables in a graph and then determining the best-fitting line.
- Various statistics are available to test for significance (e.g., chi-square for contingency tables) and to measure degree of association (e.g., the correlation coefficient).
- The analysis of three or more variables involves applying statistical procedures that test specified theoretical models.
- Elaboration of contingency tables systematically controls for third variables by creating partial tables in which categories of the third variable are held constant.
- Multiple regression can examine the effect of an independent variable by controlling simultaneously for several other variables.

REVIEW QUESTIONS

1. What is the purpose of editing and data cleaning? When does editing occur? When does data cleaning occur?
2. What are some reasons for inspecting the data prior to analysis?
3. Explain the difference between descriptive and inferential statistics by providing examples of each.
4. What are the rules for percentaging and reading contingency tables to determine the relationship between variables?
5. What does the chi-square test for independence tell you about the association between variables?
6. Consider the following regression equation based on 2016 GSS data:

   Respondent's years of education = 10.50 + .31 (Father's years of education)

   (a) How much change in respondent's education is associated with each increase of one year in father's education?

   (b) What is the predicted years of education of a respondent whose father has completed 16 years of education?

7. Describe the difference between a regression coefficient and a correlation coefficient.

8. Explain the difference between the regression coefficient in bivariate regression and the partial-regression coefficients in multiple regression.

EXERCISES

1. In Chapter 4, Exercise 2, we asked you to examine a contingency table and a correlation based on data from the GSS. In accessing and analyzing the GSS data, you used a website maintained by the University of California Berkeley (http://sda.berkeley.edu/sdaweb/analysis/?dataset=gss16). Now we want you to repeat these analyses, but answer additional questions about various statistics. Go to this website, generate the statistics specified below, and answer the following questions.

   (a) First, opposite "Row:" enter DRUNK; opposite "Column:" enter SEX; opposite "Selection Filter(s):" enter YEAR (1994), and opposite "Weight:" use the dropdown menu to find and click "No weight." Now click on the "Output Options" tab and under "Cell Contents," you will see "Percentaging": check "Column." Below that you will see "Other options," where you should check "Summary Statistics" and "Question text." Finally, click "Run the Table." Compare the percentages in the first row of the table. Who is more likely to say that they sometimes drink more than they think they should? What is the value of gamma (a measure of association that may vary from −1 to +1)? What is the significance of the first Rao-Scott test (which is a modified version of the chi-square test)? What does each of these statistics tell you about the relationship between DRUNK and SEX?

   (b) At the top of the page, click the "Regression" Tab. Opposite "Dependent" enter REALRINC (which stands for respondent's income in constant dollars); below "Independent," enter EDUC; opposite "Selection Filter(s)," enter YEAR(2016), and opposite "Weight:" use the dropdown menu to find and click "No weight." Now click "Run Regression." Write out the regression equation. (Note that the "constant" is the Y-intercept, which in this case is negative because it is an estimate for someone with 0 years of education—a highly unlikely occurrence in the contemporary United States.) What is the value of the *un*standardized regression coefficient (B)? What does it tell you about the relationship between years of education and annual income? In a bivariate regression, the correlation is the same as the standardized regression coefficient (Beta). What is the correlation between highest year of education completed and annual income?

2. Now that you know how to use the Berkeley website, go to the website and test a bivariate hypothesis using GSS data. First, formulate a hypothesis by selecting one independent variable and one dependent variable from the following lists. (Note that all variables have nominal- or ordinal-level measurement.)

Independent Variable	Mnemonic Label
Respondent's sex (male/female)	SEX
Respondent's race (white/nonwhite)	RACE(1,2)
Level of education	
(high school or less/ > high school)	DEGREE(r:0–1;2–4)

Dependent Variable	Mnemonic Label
Support for legalization of marijuana (should/should not be legal)	GRASS
Attitude toward homosexuality (sexual relations between same-sex adults is always or almost always wrong/ sometimes wrong or not wrong at all)	HOMOSEX(r:1–2;3–4)
Whether or not one has seen an X-rated movie	XMOVIE

3. Conduct an elaboration analysis by repeating the test of your hypothesis in Exercise 2 using either SEX or RACE(1,2) as a control variable. (Note: If SEX is the independent variable in your hypothesis, then use RACE; if RACE is the independent variable, then use SEX.) Carefully explain what happens to the original relationship in each of the partial tables.

4. Surveys typically report that residents of large cities are more tolerant of deviant behavior than are resident of smaller cities and rural areas. Suppose that data are available for three variables: (1) respondent's tolerance of deviant behavior (let's label this TOLERANCE), (2) size of current place of residence (CURRENT RESIDENCE), and (3) size of place in which the respondent was living at age 16 (AGE16 RESIDENCE). For each of the following hypotheses, draw arrow diagrams to specify an appropriate causal model: (a) the social environment of the current residence renders people more or less tolerant; (b) tolerance is learned during adolescence and remains relatively constant thereafter; (c) both AGE16 and CURRENT residential environments affect tolerance of deviant behavior.

5. Repeat the steps in Exercise 1(b) with REALRINC as the dependent variable and EDUC as an independent variable, and then add the following independent variables to the equation: RACE(d:1), a dummy variable with "white" = 1; and

SEX(d:1), a dummy variable with "male" = 1. Recall that B = unstandardized regression coefficient and Beta = standardized regression coefficient.

(a) Write out the multiple regression equation using the *unstandardized* partial regression coefficients. Based on this equation, what is the estimated income, on average, of a white male with a bachelor's degree (i.e., 16 years of education)? How much less, on average, does a white female with the same education earn?

(b) Which variable—EDUC, RACE, or SEX—has the biggest impact on income? Which variable is not statistically significant?

13

Qualitative Data Analysis
Searching for Meaning

STUDENT LEARNING OBJECTIVES

By the end of this chapter, you should be able to

1. Identify and apply the steps in qualitative data analysis.

2. Describe how textual data are prepared for analysis.

3. Explain the purposes of different types of coding, memo-writing, and data displays.

4. Explain how researchers may draw and evaluate conclusions from qualitative data.

5. Give examples of major variations in qualitative data analysis.

What do the following findings have in common?

- Based on observation and interviews with families, Annette Lareau (2011) concluded that middle-class parents and working-class/poor parents tend to engage in different childrearing strategies (Chapter 2).
- Through in-depth interviews, Kathleen Blee (2002) found that women in racist groups did not conform to many of the popular beliefs about them (Chapter 6).
- Jane Hood's (1983) in-depth interview study found that women who worked out of economic necessity developed a more equal division of household labor in their marriage than women who returned to work for self-fulfillment (Chapter 6).
- Robert Courtney Smith's (2006) extended field research found that transnationalization processes can both aid and constrain Ticuanenses' search for recognition and self-respect (Chapter 9).
- Jessica Vasquez's (2011) in-depth interview study found that Mexican American families differ in their levels of attachment to Mexican heritage, with some expressing "thinned attachment" and others a more firmly attached pattern of "cultural maintenance" (Chapter 9).

If you answered that these findings are based on qualitative research designs, you are correct. Now note the process by which you came to this conclusion: you read the text of the examples and made comparisons. This is similar to the process of analyzing qualitative data, the subject of this chapter. Qualitative analysis is largely an inductive process that involves grouping together specific pieces of usually nonnumerical data, such as text, that share similarities to formulate more general and abstract conclusions. As we've mentioned before, the inferences generated through this process are subject to *multiple interpretations* and *vary in strength*. Hence, if you answered that the above findings are similar in that they are all reported in this book, you'd also be correct. And while this and the previous inference may be strong, a weaker inference, as you'll see, would be that these studies followed the same qualitative analysis techniques.

In this chapter, we outline a general process by which qualitative data can be analyzed. But note the tentative nature of this statement: "*a general process by which qualitative data *can be* analyzed.*" There are few agreed-upon standards about how researchers *should* analyze qualitative data, as numerous authors suggest (Charmaz 2006; Corbin and Strauss 2008; Emerson, Fretz, and Shaw 2011; Gibbs 2007; Lofland et al. 2006; Miles, Huberman, and Saldaña 2014; Saldaña 2013). Drawing on these authors' work, we present a process model that integrates common features of qualitative data analysis. We then illustrate the steps in this model with data from a research study of homelessness in Austin, Texas. We conclude with a discussion of some of the major variations in qualitative data analysis.

INTRODUCTORY EXAMPLE: HOMELESSNESS IN AUSTIN, TEXAS

▲ David Snow

▲ Leon Anderson

Beginning in the mid-1970s, evidence of increasing homelessness in America generated much public interest and debate. Correspondingly, social researchers began conducting studies of homelessness in communities throughout the country. The vast majority of these studies shared two characteristics: (1) they were based on questionnaire surveys and (2) they were concerned primarily with describing personal characteristics and disabilities of the homeless, such as mental illness and alcoholism. For nearly a year and a half in the mid-1980s, David Snow and Leon Anderson (1987, 1993) conducted a field study of homeless individuals living in or passing through Austin, Texas.[1] In contrast to most other studies of homelessness, they were more interested in the "material, interpersonal, and psychological strategies" of "street life" from the perspective of the homeless themselves (Snow and Anderson 1993:20).

Field observations of the homeless were made over a period of one year, from September 1, 1984, to August 31, 1985, with Anderson as the principal ethnographer. His strategy was to "hang out" with as many homeless "individuals as possible on a daily basis, spending time with them in varied settings (e.g., meal and shelter lines, under bridges, in parks, at day-labor pickup sites), over the course of the 12 month period" (Snow and Anderson 1987:1342). In the end, he spent over 400 hours in many different settings with 168 homeless individuals. In addition, Snow spent another 200 hours negotiating access to records and interviewing police officers, local political officials, and personnel of agencies serving the homeless. As part of their study, Snow and Anderson (1993) also tracked a random sample of homeless individuals, although this will not be the focus of our discussion.

The principal data were based on direct observation of and interaction with the homeless, especially listening to their conversations. While Anderson asked questions and probed from time to time, mostly he engaged in relatively unobtrusive listening that took two basic forms: (1) eavesdropping (e.g., listening to others while waiting in meal lines) and (2) ordinary conversational listening when interacting with two or more homeless individuals (Snow and Anderson 1987:1343).

Data from observations and conversations were recorded in two steps. First, while in the field, Anderson took mental notes and jotted down key phrases and words to aid his recall of particular events. Second, as soon as possible after leaving the field, he elaborated this information into a detailed narrative account. As an aid to this process,

[1]Our discussion of Snow and Anderson's data analysis draws on their published work (Snow and Anderson 1987, 1993), discussions of it in Lofland et al. (2006), and personal communications with Anderson (2014), for which we are very grateful.

Anderson routinely met with Snow to review his field experiences, discuss their methodological and theoretical implications, and make plans for subsequent observations (Snow and Anderson 1987:1344).

Snow and Anderson's findings broadly concerned homeless people's lifestyles and sense of self and identity. One set of findings focused on "identity talk": the ways in which the homeless constructed and negotiated their personal identities (Snow and Anderson 1987:1336). Snow and Anderson identified several different patterns of identity talk. One of these, called "distancing," consists of disassociating oneself from homeless persons as a social category. For example, one individual who had been on the streets for less than two weeks said, "I'm not like the other guys who hang out down at the 'Sally' [Salvation Army]. If you want to know about street people, I can tell you about them; but you can't really learn about street people from studying me, because I'm different" (1349). Another pattern, labeled "fictive storytelling," involves recounting stories about one's experiences and accomplishments that are clearly embellished to some degree, such as (1) exaggerated claims regarding past or current wages and (2) fantasies about the future. For example, some homeless persons fantasized about becoming rich. As one said, "You might laugh and think I'm crazy, but I'm going to be rich. I know it. I just have this feeling. I can't explain it, but I am" (1361).

On the basis of homeless people's material survival strategies, patterns of identity talk, other interpersonal factors, and time on the street, Snow and Anderson (1993) classified them into three generic types: the "recently dislocated," "straddlers," and "outsiders." The recently dislocated often think back to their lives before they became homeless; they are afraid to socialize with other homeless people; they tend to seek employment; and they are especially likely to seek services from organizations such as the Salvation Army. "Straddlers" are a type in between the "recently dislocated" and "outsiders," having "one foot planted in street life" and another in their former lives (52). These individuals socialize with other homeless people and make use of survival strategies beyond formal organizations like the Salvation Army, showing some adaptation to the streets. Finally, "outsiders" are "individuals for whom street life has become taken-for-granted . . . [and] . . . they rarely talk about getting off the street" (57–58). Within these three generic types of homeless street people, there is further variation and subtypes: as an example, the "mentally ill"—a subtype of "outsiders"— constitute a very small percentage of homeless street people that Snow and Anderson encountered during their field research.

Based on their findings, Snow and Anderson questioned the assumption that the need for self-esteem is secondary to the satisfaction of physiological survival needs. Maintaining a sense of meaning and self-worth, they contend, may be especially critical for the survival of homeless and other marginal members of society. Moreover, homeless people's paths on and off the streets are varied and shaped by interpersonal, institutional, and other factors.

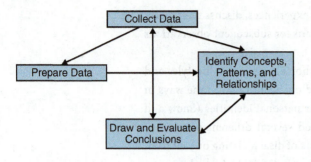

FIGURE 13.1
A Process of Analyzing Qualitative Data

OVERVIEW: A PROCESS OF ANALYZING QUALITATIVE DATA

The qualitative methods discussed in this book—field research, in-depth and focus group interviews, and comparative historical analysis—use different kinds of data. Field research, for example, prizes observational data; interviews primarily yield verbal reports; existing data may come in the form of text and visual imagery. In this chapter we focus on the analysis of textual data, based on field notes and interviews. Figure 13.1 outlines a general process of analyzing these data. As the figure indicates, the steps in this process overlap with one another and are not linear, reflecting the iterative nature of qualitative research.

In much qualitative research, data analysis begins during data collection. The next step, *preparing the data*, is similar to quantitative analysis, except the data to be prepared are primarily text, which need to be transformed into a more readable form, checked for errors and corrected, and organized and managed using a physical filing system or an electronic database.

Analysis incorporates the inductive process of measurement, discussed in Chapter 5, whereby researchers *identify concepts, patterns,* and *relationships* in the data through operationally defining the phenomena they are studying. This is facilitated by coding, memo-writing, and other analytic strategies.

The *conclusions researchers draw* from their analysis range from the descriptive to the theoretical and need to be *evaluated* for their strength and quality. This is a back-and-forth process in which inferences from an early stage of the analysis may be discarded, modified, or replaced through additional analysis or data collection.

We now elaborate on each of these steps using the homelessness study and other research examples. We caution, however, that these studies do not always follow the process in the order in which we present their analysis.

PREPARE DATA

An initial step is to prepare the data. To do so, researchers transform the data into readable form, edit and clean the data, and manage, or store, the data. These are not just mechanical processes; they also involve analysis (Gibbs 2007:11).

Transform the Data to Readable Text

Field jottings alone may not provide the necessary detail for analysis, and as you might imagine, starting and stopping an audio or video device in order to analyze its content may prove difficult. As such, these data are typically prepared by transforming them into more readable text.

Field jottings, as you'll recall from Chapter 9, are brief quotes, phrases, and key words that are recorded by researchers in the field. After the researcher has left the site or is otherwise inconspicuous to the participants, he or she expands upon the jottings to form a more complete set of field notes. In the homeless study, Anderson began by writing field jottings, which were turned into a complete set of field notes shortly after leaving the field (Anderson, personal communication 2014). In total, the notes were over 600 double-spaced typed pages. Field researchers today most often enter their notes directly into word-processing programs.

> 1 BARRY
> 2 Well, the only thing that we've really given up is—well we used to
> 3 go dancing. Well she can't do it now so I have to go on my own,
> 4 that's the only thing really. And then we used to go indoor bowling
> 5 at the sports centre. But of course, that's gone by the board now. So
> 6 we don't go there. But I manage to get her down to works club, just
> 7 down the road on the occasional Saturdays, to the dances. She'll sit
> 8 and listen to the music, like, stay a couple of hours and then she's
> 9 had enough. And then, if it's a nice weekend I take her out in the
> 10 car.

FIGURE 13.2
Partial Transcript from a Qualitative Interview

To prepare interview data, researchers often transcribe interviewees' words into text. There are many questions to consider about *how* to transcribe interview data (Gibbs 2007:Chapter 2). For example, should you transcribe the data yourself or hire someone to do so (assuming you have resources)? Should you use a digital voice recorder or voice recognition software to transcribe your data? Should you correct any grammatically incorrect remarks by your interviewees? Should the transcribed data include every utterance, pause, or "filler" (e.g., "uh," "um")? We address some of these questions below. For other questions that are beyond the scope of this chapter, you may want to consult Graham Gibbs's *Analyzing Qualitative Data* (2007) for guidance.

The transcript often appears as a series of numbered lines, with an interviewee's pseudonym or identification number noted somewhere on the transcript. An example of a partial transcript is presented in Figure 13.2, in which "Barry"—who looks after his wife with Alzheimer's disease—is asked, "Have you had to give anything up that you enjoyed doing that was important to you?" (Gibbs 2007:42).

Check for and Resolve Errors

Transformations of data in any form—numerical or textual—may introduce errors. Although field researchers strive to accurately capture observed reality, recorded observations involve interpretations that can vary from one observer to another. Therefore, researchers may check their field notes with participants and other sources to identify and resolve errors. When research is conducted in a team, observers may compare notes. Snow and Anderson used a variation of this approach, whereby they regularly met to review Anderson's notes. As you conduct your research, it is a good idea to have someone else look over your notes, provided that ethical considerations allow for this. A common "error" that novices make is simply one of omission—that is, they do not include pertinent information or enough detail in their notes (Emerson et al. 2011; Rossman and Rallis 2003).

Table 13.1 Examples of Transcription Errors

Transcriber's Typed Phrase	What Interviewee Actually Said
DIFFERENT INTERPRETATIONS	
reflective bargaining	collective bargaining
certain kinds of ways of understanding	surface kinds of ways of understanding
and our	and/or
mixed service	lip service
denying neglect	benign neglect
OPPOSITE MEANINGS	
ever meant to	never meant to
it just makes sense	it doesn't make sense
formal	informal
there's one thing I can add	there's nothing I can add
there's more discernible actions	there aren't discernible factions

Source: Adapted from Table 2.1 in Gibbs (2007:19).

Errors are especially likely to occur in the transcription of interview data. Regardless of whether you transcribe the data yourself, have someone else transcribe it, or use voice recognition software, it is possible that what the interviewee said will not be accurately recorded. This could occur because the interviewee was simply misheard, because the quality of the recording was poor, or for some other reason (Gibbs 2007:18–19). To get an idea of how easy it would be to make a mistake, look at Table 13.1 for examples of transcription errors provided by Carl Cuneo in a study of trade union activities (quoted in Gibbs 2007:19).

Some errors, such as those in Table 13.1, can be detected by comparing the audio/video recording to the transcription. Other errors, such as typos and misspelled words, can be detected by reading over the transcript or using a word processing spell-checking function. While it is important to correct these and other such "input" errors, researchers generally are not advised to correct an interviewee's grammar (Gibbs 2007).

Manage the Data

Field notes can fill a book, especially if they encompass years of research; interview transcripts can run several pages just for a single interview; and pages of archival records may number in the thousands. It is thus important to find a means of managing your data, which involves organizing and storing it.

A basic strategy as you begin to organize qualitative data is to label it. Called **attribute coding**, this differs from the coding discussed later in that its primary intent is to manage the data by labeling characteristics of fieldwork settings, participants, and so forth on the top of a set of field notes or interview transcript, or typing them into a word-processing or **Computer-Assisted Qualitative Data Analysis Software (CAQDAS)** program (Saldaña 2013:69–70). Below is an example of attribute-coded field notes (Saldaña 2013:71), which identifies primary features of the participants, setting, and activities observed:

> PARTICIPANTS: 5TH GRADE CHILDREN
> DATA FORMAT: P.O. FIELD NOTES/SET 14 OF 22
> SITE: WILSON ELEMENTARY SCHOOL, PLAYGROUND
> DATE: 6 OCTOBER 2010
> TIME: 11:45 a.m.–12:05 p.m.
> ACTIVITIES INDEX [a list of the field notes' major contents]:
>> RECESS
>> BOYS PLAYING SOCCER
>> BOYS ARGUING
>> GIRLS IN CONVERSATION
>> GIRLS PLAYING FOUR-SQUARE
>> TEACHER MONITORING
>> DISCIPLINE

When applied to transcribed interviews, this method resembles the coding of variables in survey research, as evidenced in another example from Saldaña (2013:70–71):

> PARTICIPANT (PSEUDONYM): BARRY
> AGE: 18
> GRADE LEVEL 12
> GPA: 3.84
> GENDER: MALE
> ETHNICITY: WHITE
> SEXUAL ORIENTATION: HETEROSEXUAL
> SOCIAL CLASS: LOWER-MIDDLE
> RELIGION: METHODIST
> DATA FORMAT: INTERVIEW 4 OF 5
> TIME FRAME: MARCH 2011

In addition, John Lofland, David Snow, Leon Anderson, and Lyn Lofland (2006) recommend creating "coding files" into which data can be categorized. In the case of fieldwork, they advise, "Initially, you should develop coding files for every actor you encounter, every major setting-relevant activity and/or event, and the range of places

attribute coding A method of coding that identifies the characteristics of participants, settings, and other phenomena of interest, largely as a means of managing the data.

Computer-Assisted Qualitative Data Analysis Software (CAQDAS) Software packages that aid in the management and analysis of data.

in which the actors have been encountered and the activities/events observed. . ." (Lofland et al. 2006:206). Snow and Anderson (1993) ultimately created coding files for 25 "focal settings," which were places relevant to the lives of homeless street people in Austin. They also created files for the 168 homeless individuals they encountered as well as for 30 "cultural domains," or aspects of homeless culture, which we discuss later.

To store qualitative data, you need to decide whether to use a physical filing system, electronic system, or some combination. This decision has implications for the rest of your analysis. On the one hand, the physical filing system helps novice researchers to gain intimate familiarity with the data. Moreover, software programs cannot do all the work of the researcher. On the other hand, basic and more specialized software programs can increase efficiency (Gibbs 2007; Lofland et al. 2006; Miles, Huberman, and Saldaña 2014; Saldaña 2013).

Snow and Anderson used a physical filing system, whereby they placed their typed notes into files. In doing so, they were able to see that some files "bulged" with data (Snow and Anderson 1987:1345). According to Anderson, some were "a couple of inches thick" (personal communication 2014).

With data today invariably in electronic form, researchers use word-processing and spreadsheet programs for organizing and storing data (Miles, Huberman, and Saldaña 2014; Saldaña 2013). These programs allow one to save different files; place comments, notes, and labels within a file; and cut and paste text. In addition, several CAQDAS programs allow researchers to manage, code, and display their data. At the time of Snow and Anderson's data collection, these programs were not widely available or used (Anderson, personal communication 2014). Vasquez (2011) used one of them, ATLAS.ti, to analyze her interviews, as you may recall from Chapter 9. Some other programs include NVivo, MAXQDA, and the Qualitative Data Analysis Program (QDAP), the latter of which is free.

SUMMARY

Data preparation involves transforming the data into more readable text, usually in electronic form. An important function of data preparation is to check for and correct errors. To manage the potentially vast amount and array of textual data, you need to organize it and decide whether to use a physical filing system, an electronic system, or some combination for storage.

IDENTIFY CONCEPTS, PATTERNS, AND RELATIONSHIPS

If you are sitting in front of pages of field notes or interview transcripts, you're likely wondering how to move from the bits and pieces of data to the kinds of inferences you read in research reports. Coding, memo-writing, and creating data displays are different ways of doing so. Coding emerged as part of the grounded theory tradition, as its founders Barney Glaser and Anselm Strauss (1967:102) sought to utilize the techniques of quantitative research to develop strategies that would enhance theoretical development. Coding is often accompanied by memo-writing (see Chapter 9). While contemporary versions of grounded theory inform our discussion of coding and memo-writing in this section (Charmaz 2006; Corbin and Strauss 2008), we describe these strategies in more general terms and reserve our discussion of grounded theory methods for a later section.

Coding

Coding begins with the selection of a unit of textual data, which is shaped by the specific form of data collection. First, consider field notes: Snow and Anderson had over 600 double-spaced typed pages. They initially organized/coded these data broadly, as indicated earlier, in terms of coding files such as focal settings and cultural domains. For some parts of their analysis, they extracted from their field notes "data entries," which "varied from a single sentence to several pages in length" (Snow and Anderson 1987:1345). In semi- and unstructured interviews, data can span many transcript pages, sometimes without any discernible "break." Kathy Charmaz (2006) suggests initially selecting transcript lines as units. Whatever unit you choose, it is important that you document your decision. When there are more than two coders, it is also essential that they agree on the standard unit in order to achieve *inter-coder reliability* (Campbell et al. 2013).

Beyond organizing/managing the data, coding is used to summarize and condense the data as well as raise it to a more conceptual and abstract level. Many types of coding, which are often "mixed and matched," are applied for these purposes (Saldaña 2013); Johnny Saldaña's *The Coding Manual for Qualitative Researchers* (2013) profiles more than 30 such methods. What researchers code depends on their research question, the form (and units) of their data, and other considerations. Emerson and colleagues (2011:177) recommend asking the following questions of field notes:

- What are people doing? What are they trying to accomplish?
- How, exactly, do they do this? What specific means and/or strategies do they use?
- How do members [participants] talk about, characterize, and understand what is going on?

These and similar questions may be asked of different kinds of data, including transcripts.

To illustrate the coding process, let's return to Snow and Anderson's study. Recall that they organized their field notes into files representing focal settings, homeless individuals, and cultural domains. Cultural domains, which will be our focus here, refer to "categories of meaning, events, and problems that constitute the social world and life-style of the homeless." Among the 30 cultural domains they identified were identity and self-concept, "drinking and alcohol, drugs, food and eating, sleeping and shelter, social relationships, and work" (Snow and Anderson 1987:1345). Files relating to identity and self-concept, which became the basis of one part of their analysis, were among those that bulged with data entries, with 202 statements made by 42 percent of the field sample (1345). For example, consider the following two statements:

- "[I'm] the tramp who was on the first page of yesterday's newspaper" (1355).
- "...I'm a bum and I know who my friends are" (1356).

In each of these statements the individual is verbally asserting who they are, which Snow and Anderson ultimately referred to as "identity talk."

As they extracted, further coded, and analyzed these data, Snow and Anderson found three generic patterns of identity talk, which they called "distancing," "embracement," and "fictive story telling." Distancing is a way of disassociating oneself from other people or places; embracement refers to acceptance of a particular identity; and fictive story telling refers to relating stories that are clearly exaggerated to some degree. To get an idea of the different data entries for each pattern, look at the six statements below, some of which you've already read. Preceding them are codes we derived from Snow and Anderson's (1987) published work, although they may not have used these labels to begin:

- DISTANCING: "I'm not like the other guys who hang out down at the 'Sally' [Salvation Army]. If you want to know about street people, I can tell you about them; but you can't really learn about street people from studying me, because I'm different" (1349).
- DISTANCING: "If you spend a week here [at the Salvation Army], you'll see how come people lose hope. You're treated just like an animal" (1352).
- EMBRACEMENT: "[I'm] the tramp who was on the first page of yesterday's newspaper" (1355).
- EMBRACEMENT: "...I'm a bum and I know who my friends are" (1356).
- FICTIVE STORY TELLING: "You might laugh and think I'm crazy, but I'm going to be rich. I know it. I just have this feeling. I can't explain it, but I am" (1361).
- FICTIVE STORY TELLING: "Tomorrow morning I'm going to get my money and say, 'Fuck this shit.' I'm going to catch a plane to Pittsburgh and tomorrow night I'll take a hot bath, have a dinner of linguini and red wine in my own restaurant... and have a woman hanging on my arm" (1362).

This gives you an idea of how Snow and Anderson coded a portion of their data, but their analysis did not end there. In fact, they further distinguished among different types of distancing, embracement, and fictive story telling, which they related to the characteristics of homeless street people. As part of the process, they conceptually defined "identity talk" as a means of asserting one's own *personal identity*, which may or may not correspond to one's *social identity* (i.e., the largely negative labels society uses for homeless people) (Snow and Anderson 1987:1347–48). Still other parts of their analysis will be highlighted in later sections. Before reading about this, see Box 13.1, DOING SOCIAL RESEARCH: Coding Textual Data.

Memo-Writing

In Chapter 9 we noted that researchers write analytic memos as a way of "dumping their brains" about their research (Saldaña 2013). Memos may include personal reflections on the research experience, a discussion of methodological issues, or thoughts about what is going on in the data. Memo-writing is often used in conjunction with coding. Saldaña (2011:99) writes, "think of codes and their consequent categories as separate picture puzzle pieces, and their integration into an analytic memo as the assembly of the picture."

There are many different types of memos; here we highlight what Lofland and colleagues (2006:210) call a **code memo** (also called a **code note** [Strauss and Corbin 1990]). Code memos are written as a means of elaborating the basis of coding categories and have a form similar to a *codebook* (see Chapters 10 and 12); they are effectively the *operational definitions* of a concept. Although he doesn't call it a code memo, Saldaña (2013:44–45) similarly recommends that you should "[r]eflect on and write about your code choices and their operational definitions," using the following memo as an illustration of this:

code memo A type of memo written explicitly for describing the basis of one's operational definitions. Also called a *code note*.

13 November 2011
CODE DEFINITION: TWEEN ANGST

Since Barry is in sixth grade, he's a "tween." The word "tween" is almost limbo-like: in-between; not quite a child, not quite a teen—you're a "tween." This almost has a condescending tone to it. When you're in-between, you're in parentheses. When you're in-between, you're neither here nor there. It's a transition, a phase, a stage, a place where you can get lost, where you can lose yourself if you're not careful.

Angst, the second part of the code phrase, is another choice that is my own word. The mother did not say it directly, but that is what it seems her son experienced. Angst—or anxious tension—is what so many adolescents go through, but I wonder if they are ever taught that word? Will knowing that what they are going through has a label ease the pain or make it any better? To be rejected is one of the most devastating acts for a tween (and a child and a teenager and an adult). Was he rejected because he was a "people pleaser"? I know I was. It sucks to be good—at least when you are a tween.

Use TWEEN ANGST whenever Barry experienced this state, as described by himself or his mother, during his sixth through eighth grade school years.

BOX 13.1

DOING SOCIAL RESEARCH

Coding Textual Data

Now that you are familiar with coding textual data, try your hand at it. At the beginning of this chapter, we presented findings and asked what they had in common. Let's consider the "findings" as the sentence-length units to be coded (which are also demarcated by bullet points). To refresh your memory, they are:

- Based on observation and interviews with families, Annette Lareau (2011) concluded that middle-class parents and working-class/poor parents tend to engage in different childrearing strategies (Chapter 2).

- Through in-depth interviews, Kathleen Blee (2002) found that women in racist groups did not conform to many of the popular beliefs about them (Chapter 6).

- Jane Hood's (1983) in-depth interview study found that women who worked out of economic necessity developed a more equal division of household labor in their marriage than women who returned to work for self-fulfillment (Chapter 6).

- Robert Courtney Smith's (2006) extended field research found that transnationalization processes can both aid and constrain Ticuanenses' search for recognition and self-respect (Chapter 9).

- Jessica Vasquez's (2011) in-depth interview study found that Mexican American families differ in their levels of attachment to Mexican heritage, with some expressing "thinned attachment" and others a more firmly attached pattern of "cultural maintenance" (Chapter 9).

If we assume that the answer mentioned at the outset is a commonality—the findings are all based on qualitative research designs—then how do they differ?

One way to code these data is to ask what *kind* or *type* of qualitative research design each finding is based on. For example, you might code Lareau's as "field research," Blee's as "in-depth interviews," Hood's as "in-depth interviews," Smith's as "field research," and Vasquez's as "in-depth interviews." Note that these codes stick close to the data (and are also quite literal), which is a practice Charmaz (2006:49) recommends. If you coded this way, the preliminary outcome would look like this:

- Qualitative research design
    o Field research
    o In-depth interviews

This should help you to understand the basics of coding textual data. We'll see a similar outcome/data display later.

You see in this memo an attempt to conceptually define "tween angst" and a rule about when to use this code. Also included are questions and reflections, characteristic of memos.

Snow and Anderson wrote what would be considered memos. Anderson notes that he and Snow included in their written materials citations to previous research, such as Erving Goffman's; the clarification of concepts, such as "identity" and "role embracement"; and a discussion of "theoretical issues" (personal communication 2014).

Data Displays

Qualitative analysts need to summarize the vast amount of text with which they are working. To do so, they may create different "data displays" (Miles, Huberman, and Saldaña 2014) or "diagrams" (Lofland et al. 2006). Displays help researchers differentiate among concepts and identify patterns or relationships in the data. In this section, we focus on taxonomies, data matrices, typologies, and flowcharts, drawing heavily on the work of Lofland et al. (2006) and using Snow and Anderson's study as an illustration.

taxonomy A system of classification that is usually ordered in some way.

TAXONOMIES

A **taxonomy** is a system of classification in which objects are placed into ordered categories, which may be arranged hierarchically. Examples of taxonomies are the table of contents of a book and the outline of a book chapter (Saldaña 2013:157). The outcome of coding presented in Box 13.1 is an example of a preliminary taxonomy in which "field research" and "in-depth interviews" were classified as components of "qualitative research designs."

Snow and Anderson (1993) generated taxonomies by asking what kinds or types of phenomena are represented in the data. Figure 13.3 illustrates a taxonomy derived from their data on the material survival strategies of the homeless (Lofland et al. 2006:147). You may recognize its general structure from our discussion of conceptualization in Chapter 5 (see Figure 5.3), as the taxonomy distinguishes among the types and dimensions of concepts.

FIGURE 13.3
Taxonomy of Material Survival Strategies among the Homeless

DATA MATRICES

You're familiar with the notion of a data matrix from Chapter 12. Data matrices are particularly effective in helping researchers to understand relationships. They may be populated with numbers or text. To help you further understand Snow and Anderson's (1993) analysis and the importance of data displays, we derive a partial data matrix from their study below.

1. **Institutionalized Assistance**
   - 1A. Institutionalized Labor (Working for Street Agencies)
   - 1B. Income Supplements
     - 1B.1. Public Assistance
     - 1B.2. Assistance from Family and Friends
2. **Wage Labor**
   - 2A. Regular Work
   - 2B. Day Labor
3. **Shadow Work**
   - 3A. Selling/Peddling/Vending (Informal Sales Work)
     - 3A.1. Selling Junk and Discarded Items
     - 3A.2. Selling Illegal Goods and Services
       - 3A.2a. Selling Drugs
       - 3A.2b. Prostitution
     - 3A.3. Selling Plasma
   - 3B. Soliciting Public Donations
     - 3B.1. Panhandling
     - 3B.2. Performing in Public
   - 3C. Scavenging
     - 3C.1. Scavenging for Food
     - 3C.2. Scavenging for Salable Goods
     - 3C.3. Scavenging for Money
   - 3D. Theft

Snow and Anderson (1993:41) compared all 168 homeless individuals across eight "dimensions of contrast":

1. Work/livelihood
2. Range/mobility
3. Sleeping arrangements
4. Substance use
5. Identity talk
6. Daily routines taken for granted
7. Talk/plans about getting off the street
8. Time on the street.

We already have mentioned work/livelihood (see their taxonomy) and identity talk. These and other dimensions were usually further classified into different types; for example, one type of work/livelihood was wage/day labor. Snow and Anderson (1993:46) describe how they compared homeless individuals across dimensions, which in this case involves using numerical codes:

> Each of the 168 individuals in the field sample was assigned a numerical value of 0 to 2 depending on the relative frequency with which it was determined that he or she engaged in each of the dimensional activities. The determination of relative frequency was made on the basis of observed behaviors and conversational encounters. If we acquired, on the basis of these two data sources, a sense that an individual was an extensive user of day labor, for example, then he or she was assigned a value of 2. If day-labor use was a less frequent but still salient feature of an individual's street life-style, then a value of 1 was assigned. And if the individual rarely used day labor, as far as we could determine, then a value of 0 was assigned.

Now, using the first four dimensions, we derived the partial data matrix in Table 13.2. Note, first, that the matrix is *for illustrative purposes only.* The rows consist of four dimensions (**in capital letters**) and their types, corresponding to the table from which it is adapted (Snow and Anderson 1993:44–45).[2] The columns consist of homeless individuals, although we have included only four, for reasons of space. We also included *hypothetical* data for one type of the work/livelihood dimension: wage/day labor.

This matrix should give you a sense of the importance of displaying data to draw inferences. In a complete data matrix, researchers can see how text or numbers cluster together, the latter of which can be facilitated by quantitative data analysis. In fact, we

---

[2] Lofland et al. (2006:214) refer to this as a matrix, but we distinguish between a data matrix and a table in order to maintain consistency with Chapter 12.

Table 13.2 Partial Data Matrix with Hypothetical Data

	Homeless Individual #1	Homeless Individual #2	Homeless Individual #3	Homeless Individual #4
WORK/LIVELIHOOD				
Wage/day labor	0	0	1	2
Selling goods and services				
Selling plasma				
Begging and panhandling				
Scavenging				
Income supplements				
RANGE/MOBILITY				
Interstate				
Intercity				
Intracity				
SLEEPING ARRANGEMENTS				
Paid shelter				
Free shelter				
Sleeping rough				
Personal/private				
SUBSTANCE USE				
Alcohol use				
Drug use				

Source: Derived from first column of Table 2.2 in Snow and Anderson (1993:44–45).

derived Table 13.2 from Snow and Anderson's reported mean scores for different types of homeless individuals.

TYPOLOGIES

Typologies are displays "based on the cross-classification of two or more ideas, concepts, or variables" (Lofland et al. 2006:214). A typology differs from a taxonomy, which distinguishes among categories of "ideas, concepts, or variables," but not their interrelationships. Earlier in this book, you've seen examples of typologies, such as Jessica

typology A representation of findings based on the cross-classification of two or more concepts, variables, or ideas.

Table 13.3 Snow and Anderson's Typology of Homeless Individuals

Recently Dislocated	Straddlers		Outsiders				
	Regular	Adapted	Tramps		Bums		Mentally Ill
			Traditional	Hippie	Traditional	Redneck	

Source: Adapted from margin of Table 2.3 in Snow and Anderson (1993:48–49).

Vasquez's typology of "thinned attachment" versus "cultural maintenance" tendencies (Chapter 9) and Annette Lareau's typology of childrearing differences (Chapter 2).

In the homeless study, Snow and Anderson created several typologies. In one typology, shown in Table 13.3, they classified the homeless into three major types: "recently dislocated," "straddlers," and "outsiders." These types varied in terms of the eight dimensions of contrast identified above. One source of variation, for example, was how much time homeless individuals spent on the streets: the recently dislocated had spent less time on the streets than straddlers, who in turn spent less time on the streets than outsiders (Snow and Anderson 1993:40–41).

The typology divides straddlers and outsiders into different subtypes and further differentiates among subtypes of outsiders. Although straddlers occupy a status in between the recently dislocated and outsiders, a few homeless individuals had adapted to the life of the street, mainly by working for agencies serving the homeless (Snow and Anderson 1993:55). Thus, the typology distinguishes this type ("adapted") from "regular" straddlers.

Moving from left to right in this table, outsiders were classified as tramps, bums, and the mentally ill. As Snow and Anderson note, they did not use the terms "tramps" and "bums" in a pejorative sense; rather, they used these terms partly because some homeless individuals used them to refer to themselves and other homeless individuals (recall the quotes presented earlier). Tramps differ from others in three ways:

> They are highly migratory, with a much larger range than the other homeless. Their travels are typically patterned rather than random. And they possess a strong sense of independence and self-control that prompts them to look down both on street novices who have not yet learned the ropes and on those who subsist largely on handouts from organized charity and who accept substantial support from social services. (Snow and Anderson 1993:59)

The typology further distinguishes between two types of tramps: traditional and hippie tramps. The latter are "heirs of the 1960s counterculture … [and] they identify with counterculture values and the rock heroes of that period, practice arts and crafts, use and sell drugs, and hang out together on the streets in an almost communal fashion" (1993:60).

"Bums" are the next subtype of outsiders. They "consistently had two characteristics in common that clearly separated them from others: their limited range of travel, and their heavy use of alcohol" (Snow and Anderson 1993:62). Bums are further divided between "traditional" and "redneck." The latter, according to Snow and Anderson (1993:65),

> is a variant of the bum type that is probably peculiar to the Southwest . . . Their livelihood is based primarily on a mixture of selling plasma, peddling, and panhandling, whereas the traditional bum does little of the former. They also tend to hang out together, in an almost ganglike fashion, and they are noticeably proprietary, claiming as their own turf a former used car lot across the street from the Salvation Army.

The final subtype of outsiders is the mentally ill, which were classified based on evidence of at least two of three indicators of mental illness: "prior institutionalization; designation as mentally ill by other homeless individuals; and conduct that is so bizarre and situationally inappropriate that it would be likely to be construed as symptomatic of mental illness by most observers" (Snow and Anderson 1993:66).

Snow and Anderson's typology aids in understanding who the homeless people in Austin, Texas, are and how they survive. To further understand how researchers may construct displays and how you may evaluate them, see Box 13.2, READING SOCIAL RESEARCH: From Displays Back to Data.

BOX 13.2

READING SOCIAL RESEARCH

From Displays Back to Data

An excellent way to understand the process of analysis and evaluate research findings is to conduct "backward coding," a simplified adaptation of a teaching technique suggested to us by our colleague David Hummon. In final research reports, data are displayed as text (e.g., verbatim statements, observations), graphically, or both. When only text is used, it may be possible to infer categories, if not explicitly stated, from the organization of the article, such as the subheadings of a "findings" section; in graphic displays, categories tend to be labeled. Backward

coding involves: (1) creating a "code sheet" based on these categories; (2) placing the observations and verbatim statements within each major category; and (3) once the typology is filled with data, comparing the data entries and their corresponding categories to one another.

To better understand typologies, in particular, we recommend you practice with Annette Lareau's article, "Invisible Inequality: Social Class and Childrearing in Black and White Families" (*American Sociological Review* 2002). Lareau's typology distinguishes between

continues

continued

"concerted cultivation" and "accomplishment of natural growth" parenting styles along several dimensions. The first step in backward coding is to construct a "blank" form of this typology, as we have in Table A (see Table 2.1 for the original).

The next step is to place data entries in the categories: as examples, you could include the quotations from Alexander Williams and Harold McAllister on language use in the appropriate box under "concerted cultivation" and "accomplishment of natural growth," respectively. After placing the illustrative data entries from the article in their appropriate boxes, you can also evaluate the "fit" of the conceptual categories to the data.

Table A Lareau's Typology of Differences in Childrearing

	Childrearing Approach	
	Concerted Cultivation	Accomplishment of Natural Growth
Organization of daily life		
Language use		
Interventions in institutions		
Consequences		

Source: Adapted from Table 1 in Lareau (2011:31).

FIGURE 13.4
Flow Chart of
Homeless Careers

FLOWCHARTS

The final graphical form of presentation is a "flowchart." We have used flowcharts throughout this book because they are especially effective at displaying processes.

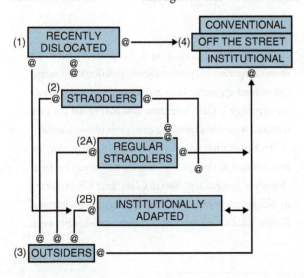

Snow and Anderson (1993) created a flowchart, presented in Figure 13.4, to map their typology onto pathways of different "homeless careers." Beginning with the "Recently Dislocated" in the figure, for example, you see that there are two paths: one, as represented by the arrow in the left-hand side of the figure, is to "Institutionally Adapted" (Straddlers); another, represented by the arrow on the right-hand side, leads to "extrication" from the streets, whether voluntarily (Conventional) or involuntarily (Institutional) (1993:273).

The path that homeless individuals take, according to Snow and Anderson (1993:277), is dependent on four major factors: "personal resource deficits, institutional factors, group-based ties, and cognitive factors." In their book, Snow and Anderson illustrate different paths and the factors that shape them with some of their key informants.

SUMMARY

To identify concepts, patterns, and relationships in their data, researchers may use coding, memo-writing, and/or other analytic techniques. Coding begins with the selection of a textual unit and involves comparing units to identify commonalities, which may be facilitated by writing memos about coded material and other aspects of the research. Creating visual displays or diagrams is another technique researchers use to summarize the data as well as identify patterns and relationships.

DRAW AND EVALUATE CONCLUSIONS

Matthew Miles, A. Michael Huberman, and Johnny Saldaña (2014, Chapter 11) suggest that the "final" step is to draw and verify conclusions, which we give a slightly different name: draw and *evaluate* conclusions. Researchers' conclusions range from the descriptive to the more theoretical. Description is fundamental to qualitative research and encompasses examples such as Robert Smith's observations of Ticuani in Chapter 9. Researchers may also infer *themes,* which are recurring threads or patterns that "summarize the manifest (apparent) and latent (underlying) meanings of data" (Saldaña 2011:108). An example is Snow and Anderson's theme that the homeless use various strategies to maintain a sense of meaning and self-worth. Inferences that are more theoretical attempt to connect patterns, themes, and concepts to develop propositions, which—as you'll recall from Chapter 2—are characteristic of theory (Miles, Huberman, and Saldaña 2014). It is important to note, however, that qualitative research may modify or extend existing theory (Lofland et al. 2006) or develop it from "the ground up" (known as *grounded theory,* discussed below).

Snow and Anderson's study shows the variety of conclusions one may draw from data. They described how homeless individuals talked and illustrated the paths they take. They identified numerous patterns in the data, as we demonstrated with their concept of "identity talk." Typical of the conceptualization process, they defined concepts, differentiated their dimensions and types, and showed relationships among concepts, including from previous research. They state that their research on identity talk "suggest[s] a modification of existing role identity theory" (Snow and Anderson 1987:1366). And, they conclude with theoretical *propositions.* The following examples are partly illustrated in their flowchart (Figure 13.4) on the paths that homeless street people take: first, "the longer a person is on the street, the more difficult extrication becomes" (Snow and Anderson 1993:300). Second, "the longer someone is on the streets, the more difficult it is for rehabilitative caretaker agencies to assist that person in extrication" (301).

But how can you evaluate—and perhaps even strengthen—the conclusions you draw? In Chapter 9 we discussed means of evaluating reliability, validity, and generalizability mainly as they pertain to aspects of research design. Some of the strategies we mentioned as means of strengthening conclusions were to use a team approach, multiple sources of data, and different sampling strategies, all of which characterize Snow and Anderson's research. They conducted research together and jointly coded their notes; they used multiple sources of data, including interviews and institutional data not discussed here; they used a sampling strategy designed to maximize variation; and they examined data from a random sample of homeless.

Beyond elements of research design, there are other ways of evaluating, or "verifying," conclusions (see Miles, Huberman, and Saldaña [2014] for a complete discussion). One is to look for *exceptions* to patterns in the data. As an example, Snow and Anderson (1987:1363) note that their findings concerning identity talk largely focused on the construction of *positive* personal identities, but an exception to this was "a longtime street person [who] lamented in a demoralized tone that he was 'nothing but a bum'." They indicate that such cases were relatively rare. Far from weakening their inferences, Snow and Anderson's discussion of this case and the rarity of similar cases lend credibility and trustworthiness to their conclusions, which is an overall goal of qualitative analysis (Schwartz-Shea and Yanow 2012). Snow and Anderson concluded that while homeless individuals may at times talk about themselves in the negative way the public at large tends to see them, there is far from a one-to-one correspondence with what the public thinks of them and what they think of themselves.

member checking A method of evaluating qualitative data in which researchers share their results with participants and ask them to comment on their accuracy and completeness.

You may also check with participants in your research. **Member checking** refers to asking participants if the findings make sense to them. Thus, they might be asked to read one's research report or portions thereof, which Lareau (2011) did in her follow-up field study of 12 families. Similarly, findings that make use of participants' own words are sometimes said to be more valid accounts of their experiences, especially from the perspective of grounded theory (Charmaz 2006). Snow and Anderson's typology was partly grounded in the "folk" terminology that homeless people used to describe themselves.

While some of the strategies for evaluating conclusions differ for qualitative and quantitative research, they ultimately serve the same overall goal: to see if the model "fits." In assessing fit, researchers move between data and theory, characteristic of the scientific process described in Chapter 2.

SUMMARY

Conclusions that may be drawn from qualitative analysis range from the descriptive to the more theoretical. They may be strengthened by aspects of research design and further evaluated by looking for exceptions to patterns, checking with members, and ensuring that they are grounded in participants' voices and experiences.

VARIATIONS IN QUALITATIVE DATA ANALYSIS

While we have presented a general process of qualitative data analysis, researchers vary in how they approach the data. This variation is partly a function of the form of the data and partly a reflection of different philosophical orientations to analysis. Below we discuss three variations in qualitative data analysis: grounded theory methods, narrative analysis, and conversation analysis.

Grounded Theory Methods

In its original form, as advanced by Glaser and Strauss (1967), grounded theory best epitomizes the inductive logic of inquiry, emphasizing the *discovery* of theory through data analysis. A strict interpretation of grounded theory suggests that the analysis should be made without reference to existing research. Researchers are advised, "at first, literally to ignore the literature of theory and fact on the area under study, in order to assure that the emergence of categories will not be contaminated by concepts more suited to different areas" (Glaser and Strauss 1967:37). Although this interpretation has been called into question and opinion is divided (Charmaz 2006; Corbin and Strauss 2008; Glaser 1978; Strauss and Corbin 1990), grounded theory retains at its core an emphasis on theoretical development and places a premium on research participants' voices and actions as sources of data in which a theory is rooted.

The primary grounded theory analytic technique is the **constant-comparative method**, by which the researcher makes comparisons throughout the process of analysis until theoretical *saturation* has occurred; theoretical sampling is part of this process (see Chapter 6). Comparisons are made through coding and memo-writing, which occur in *at least* two phases or steps (Charmaz. 2006:46; Charmaz and Belgrave 2012:356): the *initial/open* phase and the *focused/selective* phase. The following discussion identifies some specific types of coding and memos used by those working in grounded theory traditions (Saldaña 2013).

In the initial/open phase, units of data are compared with each other to develop codes. Common units of analysis in grounded theory are lines (for interview transcripts) and incidents (for field research). **In vivo coding**, which uses people's own words as codes, may be employed in this stage (Charmaz 2006; Corbin and Strauss 2008). This form of coding reflects grounded theory's emphasis on participants' voices. It can help the analyst understand the extent to which people are expressing their thoughts and feelings in the same language. For example, Charmaz (1991) found that many of the chronically ill people she interviewed talked about having "good days" and "bad days," which became in vivo codes in her study (Charmaz 2006:57).

constant-comparative method The general analytic strategy of grounded theory methods, which involves making comparisons at increasingly higher levels of abstraction through coding, memo-writing, and theoretical sampling.

in vivo coding A form of coding that uses participants' own words as labels.

Christine Danforth, a 43-year-old receptionist, had returned to work after eight recent hospitalizations and a lengthy convalescence from a flare-up of lupus erythematosus and Sjögren's syndrome (see Charmaz 1999). A statement from her interview and the initial coding of the statement appear below.

Initial Coding	Interview Statement
Recounting the events Going against medical advice Being informed of changed rules Suffering as a moral status Accounting for legitimate rest time Distinguishing between "free" and work time Receiving an arbitrary order Making a moral claim Finding resistance; tacit view of worth Having a devalued moral status because of physical suffering Taking action Learning the facts Making a case for legitimate rights Trying to establish entitlement Meeting resistance Comparing prerogatives of self and other Seeing injustice Making claims for moral rights of personhood	And so I went back to work on March 1st, even though I wasn't supposed to. And then when I got there, they had a long meeting and they said I could no longer rest during the day. The only time I rested was at lunchtime, which was my time, we were closed. And she said, my supervisor, said I couldn't do that anymore, and I said, "It's my time, you can't tell me I can't lay down." And they said, "Well you're not laying down on the couch that's in there, it bothers the rest of the staff." So I went around and I talked to the rest of the staff, and they all said, "No, we didn't say that, it was never even brought up." So I went back and I said, "You know, I just was talking to the rest of the staff, and it seems that nobody has a problem with it but you," and I said, "You aren't even here at lunchtime." And they still put it down that I couldn't do that any longer. And then a couple of months later one of the other staff started laying down at lunchtime, and I said, you know, "This isn't fair. She doesn't even have a disability and she's laying down," so I just started doing it.

FIGURE 13.5
Action/Process Coding in an Interview Transcript

action coding A form of coding that uses gerunds (-ing words) to signal activity in the data. Also called process coding.

Another form that may be used in the initial phase is called **action coding** or **process coding**. This technique uses gerunds (-ing words) to refer to processes or action in the data (Charmaz and Belgrave 2012:356–57; Saldaña 2013:96). Figure 13.5 presents an example from a transcript of Charmaz's interview with Christine Danforth. As you can see from this transcript, the use of gerunds as codes keeps Christine active. Both action/process coding and in vivo coding can be used in combination with other forms of coding (Saldaña 2013). The key to this phase of coding is to "remain open," as Charmaz (2006:49) suggests.

The focused/selected phase of the analysis uses "the most significant and/or frequent earlier codes to sift through large amounts of data" (Charmaz 2006:57). Here the analyst applies the constant-comparative method by comparing selected codes and their associated data developed during the initial/open phase to data collected later (e.g., through theoretical sampling); comparing codes to one another to develop concepts and their dimensions and properties; and integrating concepts into a theory (Charmaz 2006; Corbin and Strauss 2008; Glaser and Strauss 1967).

Charmaz (2006) cites Hood's (1983) interview study of wives working outside the home as illustrative of some of these comparison processes. As noted in Chapter 6, Hood's initial coding of women who returned to work out of *self-fulfillment* showed that they were not getting much help from their husbands, which led her to wonder if this would be different for women who returned to work out of *economic necessity*. When she used theoretical sampling to expand her sample, subsequent coding confirmed an important concept in her study: bargaining power over the household division of labor varied by whether women worked out of self-fulfillment versus economic necessity.

Much of advanced analysis of grounded theory methods is facilitated by memo-writing, which is done throughout the process (Saldaña 2013:52–53). As Juliet Corbin and Anselm Strauss (2008:118) note, there are memos for:

- Open data exploration
- Identifying/developing the properties and dimensions [of] concepts/categories
- Making comparisons and asking questions
- Elaborating the paradigm: the relationships between conditions, actions/interactions, and consequences
- Developing a story line

As ordered, these memos roughly reflect the progression from data to theory, characteristic of grounded theory methods. In open data exploration, researchers write memos about the data. They also write memos that identify properties and dimensions, similar to the code memos described earlier; write memos that ask questions about the data; and so on.

To give you an idea of what a memo focused on more theoretical concerns looks like, Figure 13.6 presents one that Corbin and Strauss (2008:137–38) use to "elaborate the paradigm" of a study on the pain experience. This memo integrates many parts of the analysis, as it identifies patterns (e.g., concerning pain experiences), specifies some relationships (e.g., between searching for relief and the outcome of such a search), and has elements of conceptualization (e.g., "pain tolerance"). As Corbin and Strauss (2008:118) caution, it is important not to get caught up on which type of memo you are writing; "more important is just to get into the habit of writing."

This gives you an idea of some specific techniques used in the grounded theory tradition, which may be adopted more widely. Researchers working in this tradition may use still other techniques, such as data displays/diagrams discussed earlier. For more in-depth guidance in using grounded theory methods for analysis, we recommend Kathy Charmaz's (2006) *Constructing Grounding Theory* and Juliet Corbin and Anselm Strauss's (2008) *Basics of Qualitative Research*.

> After months of collecting data and immersing myself in the pain stories of others, what is the overall pain story to be told? I think the story is somewhat as follows. Pain is a difficult experience unless the pain is "very mild" and of very "short duration." Every time I did an interview, I could feel the "intensity" of "suffering" of people who were experiencing "severe pain," as they spoke about their experience. These people are driven to find "relief" but relief is often "elusive" (dimension of the ability to relieve pain which can vary from relief being "obtainable" to being "elusive"). The search for relief often takes them down dead end paths with emotions ranging from "anger" to "depression" for many reasons (property of emotional response to pain). . . . It seems to me that "pain tolerance," which is an interesting concept, diminishes when the pain is of "long duration" and people are "fatigued" or worn down by its "constancy." "Searching for relief" can be compared to being lost in a dark forest at night, as one is trying to find a way through, an escape, but the escape path is blocked and difficult to locate in the dark. People sometime[s] become "desperate" wondering if the suffering will ever end and sometimes wishing for death as an "escape" from their pain. . . . I do see some patterns emerging. There are those persons who experience "acute temporary pain." Their pain experience may have been intense but for the moment that intensity is forgotten when the situation has passed. . . . There are those who suffer from "chronic pain." They have developed management strategies for controlling its intensity and impact on daily life. . . . Then there is the group in which "every day" is a "pain experience," the "constant pain sufferers." Suffering defines their lives. Everyday activities are severely limited. Depression is moderate to severe, as one would expect. There is little hope that the situation will improve. Their stories are touching.

FIGURE 13.6
Advanced Memo Used to Elaborate the Paradigm of a Study on the Pain Experience

Narrative Analysis

A narrative is essentially a story, which often has an internal structure. The stories we tell about ourselves, for example, may be organized chronologically or topically. They may be told for a variety of reasons: to recount events, to affirm our identity, and so forth (Gibbs 2007:59–62). **Narrative analysis** examines the structure and meaning of stories. It may be used to analyze literary works, interviews, and other data (Franzosi 1999; Gibbs 2007; Riessman 2012; Wertz et al. 2011). The primary focus of this section will be on interview data.

Narrative analysis begins in a similar way to the analysis of other interview data: Interviews are transcribed and read. But in narrative analysis it is the narrative, or story line, that constitutes the primary focus. Narratives are compared to one another within a case (i.e., a single interview participant telling multiple stories), across cases

narrative analysis The qualitative analysis of narratives, including literary texts and stories derived from interviews and other sources, which examines their structure, meaning, and other characteristics.

(i.e., multiple interviewees), or both. The analytic techniques vary depending on whether the relative emphasis is on structure, meaning, or other considerations. One of these considerations concerns whether narratives should be analyzed as a whole or broken down into parts, as you do when you code text (Wertz et al. 2011:226).

A traditional way of analyzing the structure of narratives is to classify the parts of the story as follows (Saldaña 2013:133, citing Patterson 2008:25):

1. ABSTRACT—what is the story about?
2. ORIENTATION—who, when, where?
3. COMPLICATING ACTION—then what happened?
4. EVALUATION—so what?
5. RESULT—what finally happened?
6. CODA—a "sign off" of the narrative

Although this may seem complicated, you'd probably recognize the structural elements of a narrative event in your daily life. "Let me tell about this one time . . ." might signal an abstract. "That's all I have to say about that," a phrase uttered by actor Tom Hanks in the title role of the 1994 movie *Forrest Gump*, is an explicit coda or "sign off." The "essential" element of a narrative is the "complicating action," according to William Labov, who developed this classification scheme (Franzosi 1999:522, citing Labov 1972:370). You're likely familiar with "complicating actions" from movies: this is what happens to set up plots and subplots. To return to *Forrest Gump*, which is especially appropriate given that the film is told as a series of biographical narratives, a complicating action in Forrest's childhood narrative is that he is not able to run. Similarly, one may analyze narratives by classifying their parts into scenes (Riessman 2012).

Another way of analyzing narratives is to focus on meaning. To do so, researchers may identify *themes*. Common themes in people's biographies are related to their trajectories in life (where they've been and where they are now), their careers, and their relationships with others (Gibbs 2007:62–63). The interview questions asked by researchers may also help to identify themes (Rubin and Rubin 2012:195).

An example of narrative analysis comes from Kathleen Blee's (1996, 2002) study of women in racist organizations, discussed in Chapter 6. To understand why women join these groups and how it affects them, Blee conducted *life history interviews* with 34 female leaders and activists in racist organizations. Typical of life history interviews, she began in an open-ended way by asking women to tell their life stories. After this, she asked a series of questions intended to construct "a precise chronological account of the respondent's life, especially the sequence of events prior and immediately subsequent to her first affiliation with an organized racist group" (Blee 1996:688). Blee (1996:687) notes several advantages of life history interviews in studying these women:

> respondents are less likely to present group dogma as personal sentiment. The focus on life histories is particularly well-suited to understanding the sequence

and patterning of life events and thereby untangling causes and effects of affiliation. Also . . . life histories can capture the rhythm of social movement participation and withdrawal over an individual's lifetime.

Blee made use of narrative analysis to understand both the meaning and structure
of the women's lives. Her narratives revealed how women racist activists "'make sense'
of their world and their place in that world—how they identify themselves [and] what
they perceive as major events and significant turning points of their lives . . ." (Blee
1996:687). Importantly, she did not take women's stories as literal accounts of their
histories, but rather focused on how they *constructed* these histories, which can be
contradictory and incomplete. She conducted *within-case* and *cross-case* narrative
analysis: within-case analysis, in this context, refers to analyzing the multiple narratives of a single woman; cross-case analysis involves comparing the narratives across
the 34 women.

One set of findings centered on women's conversion, selective adoption, and resig-
nation to the goals of the racist organizations. Blee (1996:689–90) found that nearly
all of the women she interviewed explained their conversion to racist ideas and goals
in terms of a "single dramatic life event—a near-death experience, loss of a loved
one, even the death of a pet . . ." As an example, she discusses Alice, "a 23-year-old
racist skinhead, interviewed on death row," who "cited a car accident as her personal
turning point":

> "Since the day I was born," Alice recalled, she had been taught racist attitudes
> by her parents, but, like them, she had never felt the inclination to act on those
> beliefs until she awoke from a coma after her car accident. In Alice's narrative,
> descriptions of the loss of control she felt as a hospital patient—"IVs in my
> arms, tubes in my nose"—blurred together with images of African American
> nurses surrounding her bedside, probing and invading her body. Assertions
> of self against institutional dehumanization and bodily invasion thus took on a
> racialized cast for which her earlier belief system served as an ideological tem-
> plate: "I said [to the African American nurses] 'don't touch me. Don't get near
> me . . . leave me alone.'" It was this incident, she concluded, that brought her
> into permanent "racial awareness" and that set the stage for her subsequent
> involvement in neo-Nazi gangs. (Blee 1996:690).

It is important to note that the women's accounts of their conversion reflect "how
they learned to think about their entry into organized racism; in fact (and according to
their later chronological accounts), their entry was more incremental and far less dramatic" (Blee, personal communication 2014). Also, the women did not believe in all of
the ideas of the organizations of which they are a part. Women selectively adopted ideas,
such as accepting the racist beliefs of the Ku Klux Klan, but rejecting its misogyny. In

some cases, women did not advocate the goals of the organization, but resigned themselves to accepting them (Blee 1996).

Conversation Analysis

conversation analysis The qualitative analysis of conversations, which are typically recorded, transcribed, and analyzed in terms of their structure, sequencing, word choice, and other characteristics.

Stop for a moment and think about a conversation you've recently had: How was it organized? Did you and your conversational partner take turns talking, responding in sequence to one another? If your conversation was with your professor in a college/university setting, how might that differ from one with your friends? Which words did you choose and why? Conversations—the focus of **conversation analysis**—are social interactions consisting of language, other "utterances," and nonverbal behavior. Conversation analysis is partly rooted in a tradition in sociology called ethnomethodology (Garfinkel 1967), the study of the methods people use to make sense out of everyday life, which posits that social life is patterned by norms that people may not recognize and take for granted. It is also grounded in Erving Goffman's work, which highlights the importance of roles and identity in shaping interactions. Conversation analysts have sought to understand the structure and sequence of a conversation, including how people take turns talking (Sacks et al. 1974) and the strategies people employ to achieve goals (Heritage 2004; Maynard and Clayman 1991; Rapley 2007).

Analyzing conversations is a somewhat different process than the general process of analyzing qualitative data outlined earlier. These differences begin with data collection, as conversation analysis is especially likely to be used with (field) observational data. When video is used to record conversations—for example, to capture important nonverbal interaction—narrative accounts may be added to the transcription to indicate observations. Regardless of whether video or audio recordings are used, transcriptions tend to be quite detailed (Rapley 2007; tan Have 2006).

Data may be transcribed using the Jeffersonian method, named after Gale Jefferson (Jefferson 2004; Sacks et al. 1974), which consists of a shorthand notation to indicate speakers' pauses, their length, and other such details. Below are a few examples of Jeffersonian transcribing conventions (Rapley 2007:59–60, based on Jefferson 2004):

0.6	Length of silence measured in tenths of a second
(.)	A micro-pause of less than two-tenths of a second
:::	Two or more colons indicate sound-stretching of the immediately prior sound
WORD	All capital letters convey a marked increase in volume

Based on these examples of the conventions, you can imagine how time-consuming transcription may be: the length of pauses is counted; overlaps are noted; and attention is paid to volume. As such, samples of conversations tend to be small. For more in-depth guidance on performing conversation analysis, we recommend Tim Rapley's (2007) *Doing Conversation, Discourse, and Content Analysis*.

The analysis of conversational data partly depends on its context. Whereas some research focuses on ordinary everyday conversations, other research focuses on "institutional talk," or how people converse and interact in formal settings, such as when making 911 calls, in their doctors' offices, and so forth (Heritage 2004). John Heritage (2004:120) cites Don Zimmerman's (1984) research on emergency calls as an example of institutional talk. Zimmerman's analysis of the structure of these calls identified five phases: (1) An opening, (2) Request, (3) Interrogative series, (4) Response, and (5) Closing. Figure 13.7 identifies these phases by number in an example of an emergency call transcript. The phases indicated in the transcript are effectively patterns repeated across data.

In an analysis of calls from three dispatch centers, including observation at two of them, Zimmerman (1992:434–35) found that the structure of emergency calls is different from ordinary calls in that the callers and call takers are usually anonymous and the traditional "How are you?" opening is skipped. The conversation moves along certain sequences, similar to those noted above, but not without variation and "work" on the part of the caller and call taker, as callers may give frantic or incomprehensible descriptions of what the problem is, which the call taker then needs to discern and respond to (461). In instances where the caller is distraught, for example, "this may involve such things as [issuing] directives ('stop shouting' or 'answer my questions') or reassurances ('help is on the way')" (430).

These examples represent some ways to analyze conversational data in terms of its structure and sequencing. Yet, there are many more strategies for analyzing conversations (see Heritage [2004] for a discussion), some of which are similar to the strategies used for analyzing narratives.

| 1 | 911: | Midcity Emergency::, | |
| 2 | | (.) | **1** |
3	C:	U::m yeah (.)	
4		somebody just vandalized my car,	**2**
5		(0.3)	
6	911:	What's your address.	
7	C:	three oh one six maple	
8	911:	Is this a house or an apartment.	
9	C:	I::t's a house	**3**
10	911:	(Uh-) your last name.	
11	C:	Minsky	
12	911:	How do you spell it?	
13	C:	M I N S K Y	
14	911:	We'll send someone out to see you.	
15	C:	Thank you.=	**4**
16	911:	=Mmhm=	
17	911:	=bye.=	
18	C:	=Bye.	**5**

FIGURE 13.7
An Emergency Call Transcript with Phases Identified

SUMMARY

Among major variations in qualitative data analysis, grounded theory follows the general strategy of the constant-comparative method and uses various types of coding and memo writing in different phases of the analysis to generate theory "grounded" in data. Narrative analysis focuses on narratives, or stories, to examine the structure and/or meaning of existing textual data and interviews. Conversation analysis focuses on conversations, which are usually transcribed in detail and analyzed in terms of their structure, sequencing, word choice, and other characteristics.

KEY TERMS

action coding, p. 428

attribute coding, p. 413

code memo, p. 417

Computer-Assisted Qualitative Data Analysis Software (CAQDAS), p. 413

constant-comparative method, p. 427

conversation analysis, p. 432

in vivo coding, p. 427

member checking, p. 426

narrative analysis, p. 429

taxonomy, p. 419

typology, p. 421

KEY POINTS

- Beyond data collection, qualitative data analysis entails preparing the data; identifying patterns, relationships, and concepts; and drawing and evaluating one's conclusions.
- Data preparation involves transforming the data into readable text, checking for and correcting errors, and managing or organizing the data into physical and/or computer files.
- Qualitative analysts discover patterns in the data and develop concepts by means of coding, memo-writing, and data displays.
- Coding summarizes the data and invites comparison; memo-writing helps researchers record their thoughts about codes or other issues; and data displays create more abstract summaries that facilitate concept and theory development.
- The conclusions researchers draw range from the descriptive to the more theoretical. Evaluating them amounts to assessing their strength and quality, such as by checking for exceptions and through member checking.
- Grounded theory methods stress the discovery of theory largely through the constant-comparative method, which involves making comparisons at increasingly higher levels of abstraction through coding, memo-writing, and theoretical sampling.
- Narrative analysis is applied to stories, from literary works or from interviews, which may be analyzed in terms of their structure, meaning, type, and other characteristics.
- Conversation analysis focuses on conversations, usually from observations, which are recorded, transcribed in detail, and analyzed in terms of their structure, sequencing, word choice, and other characteristics.

REVIEW QUESTIONS

1. List some ways in which errors can occur in the transcription of interview data. How can interview transcripts be checked and corrected?
2. What are the two major forms of storing data? What are their relative advantages and disadvantages?
3. What is attribute coding and when does it occur in the process of qualitative analysis?
4. What is the general purpose of analytic memo-writing? In what ways may it be used?
5. Give an example of a (a) taxonomy, (b) typology, (c) data matrix, and (d) flowchart.
6. Compare and contrast in vivo and action/process coding. What purpose does each serve, and how are the codes generated?
7. Explain the difference between narrative analysis and conversation analysis.

EXERCISES

1. In Box 13.1, we asked you to practice coding data. What were you thinking as you considered how to code the data? Did you jot down any notes? Now that you understand memo-writing, return to the box and, using any notes you may have taken, write a memo. Ideally, of course, this should be completed as you are making the coding decisions, but this will help you to understand one of the purposes of memo-writing.
2. Earlier in this chapter, we asked you to evaluate published research by practicing backward coding on findings presented in a typology (see Box 13.2). Now, we want to give you some practice in constructing a typology based on the text of this chapter. To give you some direction, below we present a data display with the different approaches as the columns and two of the major steps in qualitative analysis as the rows. Filling out this data matrix should help you learn how to construct a typology (and study for the test!).

	"General"	Grounded Theory	Narrative Analysis	Conversation Analysis
Data preparation				
Analytic strategies for identifying concepts and patterns				

3. The best way of understanding qualitative data analysis is to analyze your own data. If you don't have any at this point, complete Exercise 2 in Chapter 9 by applying the steps outlined in this chapter. For example, transform your field jottings to notes and write a memo about your coding. You'll likely find that this process differs depending on whether you recorded observations, dialogue, or both.

4. To understand variations in qualitative data analysis, read *Five Ways of Doing Qualitative Analysis: Phenomenological Psychology, Grounded Theory, Discourse Analysis, Narrative Research, and Intuitive Inquiry* (Wertz et al. 2011), in which the authors analyze the same text from different perspectives. If you have collected interview data, you may want to try each approach on a segment of it just to see what you come up with.

Reading and Writing in Social Research

It's All About Communication

STUDENT LEARNING OBJECTIVES

By the end of this chapter, you should be able to

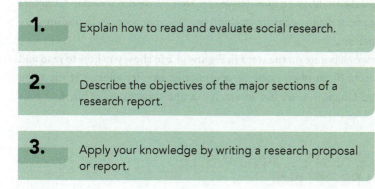

1.   Explain how to read and evaluate social research.

2.   Describe the objectives of the major sections of a research report.

3.   Apply your knowledge by writing a research proposal or report.

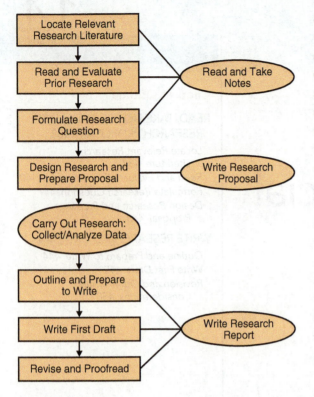

FIGURE 14.1
The Process of Reading and Writing Social Research

Science could not exist without communication. Only through communication can scientists learn about and contribute to the shared body of knowledge that defines each scientific discipline. Much scientific communication takes place orally, but the advancement of science is not based on the oral tradition; it ultimately depends on writing. Through written research reports, books, and articles, researchers communicate with others, who review, apply, and extend their work.

A major purpose of this chapter is to enhance research writing skills. Yet, we consider not only how to write about research but also how to read the research of others. This reading/writing interface is the essence of communication in everyday life. For communication is (or at least it is supposed to be!) a two-way street: one person speaks (or signs); the other listens (or sees) and responds. And so it is in social research: we read prior research to understand what others have done; we write reports to accurately communicate our findings.

Like conducting research, there is an underlying process of communication—or reading and writing—in social research. Figure 14.1 presents an idealized model of this process. In quantitative research, the reading phase typically comes first, leading to the formulation of a research question and a proposal, and the writing phase generally follows data analysis. In qualitative research, as we discussed in Chapters 9 and 13, reading and writing occur throughout the research process, including data collection and analysis.

In this chapter we elaborate on the steps in Figure 14.1 to show you how to read and write social research. Because you may be reading this chapter after or at the same time that you read Chapter 4, we use research examples discussed in the first four chapters.

READ, TAKE NOTES, AND WRITE RESEARCH PROPOSAL

Reading social research entails understanding and evaluating studies reported in the social science literature. Throughout this book, you have encountered "Reading Social Research" boxes designed to aid your reading. In this section, we provide tips on how to locate relevant studies, evaluate them, and use them as a basis for formulating a research question and developing a research proposal.

Locate Relevant Research Literature

Research begins with the selection of a topic. However, topics must be transformed into answerable research questions, which researchers are expected to relate to existing theory and research. The first step in "reading," therefore, is to locate the social science literature that is relevant to your topic. Box 4.1, How to Search the Literature, provides guidelines for using the library's electronic databases to *search* the scientific literature. Here we elaborate on how to *read* the literature to formulate a research question.

As a first step, you should identify relevant articles and books by examining titles and

American Sociological Review
76(6) 862–882
© American Sociological
Association 2011
DOI: 10.1177/0003122411427177
http://asr.sagepub.com

"I Need Help!" Social Class and Children's Help-Seeking in Elementary School

Jessica McCrory Calarco[a]

Abstract

What role do children play in education and stratification? Are they merely passive recipients of unequal opportunities that schools and parents create for them? Or do they actively shape their own opportunities? Through a longitudinal, ethnographic study of one socioeconomically diverse, public elementary school, I show that children's social-class backgrounds affect when and how they seek help in the classroom. Compared to their working-class peers, middle-class children request more help from teachers and do so using different strategies. Rather than wait for assistance, they call out or approach teachers directly, even interrupting to make requests. In doing so, middle-class children receive more help from teachers, spend less time waiting, and are better able to complete assignments. By demonstrating these skills and strategies, middle-class children create their own advantages and contribute to inequalities in the classroom. These findings have implications for theories of cultural capital, stratification, and social reproduction.

FIGURE 14.2
Title and Abstract of a Journal Article

abstracts. Titles provide clues about the research topic, but abstracts are much more helpful in judging the relevance of the research to your topic. An **abstract**, usually only included in research articles, is a capsule version of the full report that briefly describes the research question, hypotheses (if applicable), data and methods, and the major findings or results. In Chapter 4, we discussed Jessica McCrory Calarco's (2011) study, which was published as a journal article. A portion of the first page of her article, in which the abstract is located, is reprinted as Figure 14.2.

Note how Calarco's abstract briefly summarizes questions that the study addresses, the methods (ethnography, a term that is sometimes used interchangeably with field research), the setting/source of data (a diverse public elementary school), and the main findings. Reading an abstract, such as Calarco's, helps to determine whether the study may be relevant for your research. If so, you may skim the "introduction" and the "methods" sections of the article for keys to the author's perspective, then dwell on the "findings"/"results" and their implications.

Books, which are often the publication venue of qualitative research, do not have abstracts. A good way to get an overview of the study is to skim the introductory and concluding chapters of the book. The introduction is likely to frame the research and the conclusion is likely to summarize major findings or results. Regardless of whether the study is quantitative or qualitative, the methods section may be reported in an appendix, rather than in the main text of the book.

abstract A capsule version of a research report that briefly describes the research question or hypothesis, data and methods, and the major findings or results.

Read and Evaluate Prior Research

At step two, you decide what to read in detail; keep a separate record of references; evaluate the credibility of each reference; take notes and ask questions about the research. As you read, you should ask two kinds of questions: (1) How does the study contribute substantively to research on the topic? and (2) Is the study credible and methodologically sound?

If you are interested in the topic of social class and children, for example, you may decide to read Calarco's article in detail. Assuming it's relevant for your research, you should keep a record of this reference. To do so, you need to locate the pertinent publication details, which usually can be found on the first page of journal articles such as Calarco's. In addition, reference management programs mentioned in Chapter 4 (i.e., *EndNote, Zotero, Mendeley, RefWorks*) can automatically find and import these details. Look closely at Figure 14.2 and you will see the publication details that are necessary for many reference formats:

- Author(s): Jessica McCrory Calarco
- Article Title: "'I Need Help!' Social Class and Children's Helping-Seeking Behavior in Elementary School"
- Year of Publication: 2011 (located in the top right-hand corner)
- Journal Title: *American Sociological Review* (also in the top right-hand corner)
- Volume and Issue: 76 and 6 (sometimes journals only list one number, which is the volume; if the issue number is listed, it's usually enclosed in parentheses)
- Page Numbers: 862–82

For books, you can usually find the pertinent publication details on the first few pages. These include the name of the author, the title of the book, the year in which it was published, the publisher, and the place of publication (e.g., city/state and country). For a study of social class and children, you may decide to read Annette Lareau's book *Unequal Childhoods*, which we discussed in Chapter 2. The second edition of this book was published in 2011 in Berkeley, California, by the University of California Press.

Knowing the publication details can help you evaluate the credibility of the reference. One such detail, a relatively hard and fast standard that is provided in many databases, is whether a research publication is peer-reviewed. **Peer review** is a system in which researchers' reports are evaluated by other scholars in the field. These scholars, or peers, read the reports, provide comments and critiques, and offer an overall evaluation of the research concerning whether it should be accepted or rejected for publication. An important part of the peer review system is that it is usually double blind, which means that the authors do not know who the reviewers are and the reviewers do not know who the authors are. Although we believe it is sufficient for your purposes to determine whether a reference is peer-reviewed, there are other ways to gauge the credibility of the reference. For example, there are measures to evaluate the impact of a journal on the field, which are often taken as signs of journals' prestige. For books, there are no such measures of

peer review A system in which researchers' reports are evaluated by fellow academics and researchers.

Table 14.1 Matrix of Studies and Their Key Features

	Calarco (2011)	Lareau (2011)	Study #3
Research question(s)			
Argument/ Hypothesis			
Data			
Method(s)			
Results/Findings			
Conclusions			

which we are aware, but a general rule of thumb is that university presses, such as the University of California Press, are more highly regarded than nonuniversity presses.

Having evaluated the credibility of the reference, you can proceed to understand how a study contributes substantively to a research topic. You will find a researcher's claims about a study's contribution in the literature review and discussion sections of journal articles. And by reading the latest references, you can begin to trace the line of inquiry on a topic and identify the key studies. Then, as you read and take notes, you should begin to see similarities and differences and thus determine what each study distinctively contributes. One way to facilitate comparison is to make a matrix with the names of the studies (i.e., the citations) on one axis and key features of studies on another axis as we have done in Table 14.1.

In addition to identifying key features and substantive findings, you also should evaluate each study's claims. Throughout this book, we describe methods of assessing the quality of research, and we identify the relative strengths and weaknesses of various approaches, which we summarize in Chapter 11. Box 14.1, READING SOCIAL RESEARCH: Questions to Ask in Evaluating a Research Report, provides a guide for reading and critiquing research. We present this box, however, with a word of caution: understanding and applying all of these questions require that you read all of this book.

Formulate Research Question

Reading the literature prepares you for the next step: transforming your general topic into an answerable research question. In Chapter 4 we mentioned that research questions often attempt to fill a "gap" in the literature. For example, Jeff Dixon and Michael Rosenbaum (Chapter 2) found that research on contact theory (which posits that interracial contact reduces prejudice) had focused almost exclusively on black–white contact and had not adequately accounted for the impact of contact in various settings. So, they examined the effect of contact between whites and non-Hispanic whites in

---

BOX 14.1

READING SOCIAL RESEARCH

Questions to Ask in Evaluating a Research Report

The questions below are presented in the order in which they are most likely to be answered in a research report, such as a journal article. Keep in mind, however, that the information needed to answer a question may be found in one or more parts of the report.

1. Has the researcher posed a question or problem that can be addressed through social research? (Chapter 4)

2. How is the research question/hypothesis related to prior research and theory? Is the theoretical foundation of the research clear? If there is a hypothesis, does it clearly follow from the theory that is presented? (Chapter 4)

3. Which general methodological approach (e.g., experiment, survey, field research, etc.) is taken? Is the approach or combination of approaches well suited to addressing the research question or testing the hypothesis? (Chapters 7–11)

4. Does the author adequately address ethical concerns? Are procedures implemented that adequately protect participants' rights and welfare? (Chapter 3)

5. For quantitative studies, what are the independent and dependent variables? What other key variables are identified? (Chapter 4)

6. How are central concepts defined and operationalized? Does the author present prior evidence regarding the reliability and validity of measures?

Does the present study assess reliability and validity? (Chapter 5)

7. What is the unit of analysis? Is probability or non-probability sampling used to select units? How many are selected and from where? What inferences does the author make from his or her observations? If population characteristics are estimated, what is the margin of error? Do the author's generalizations about research results seem reasonable? (Chapter 6)

8. What other evidence is reported regarding the quality of the data? In an experiment, does the design contain appropriate means of control? In a survey, what is the response rate and does the author address the issue of nonresponse bias? In field research and in-depth interviews, does the author discuss relationships with participants and reflexivity? For existing data analysis, what is the quality and source of the data and how well does it fit the research question? (Chapters 7–10)

9. For quantitative studies, does the author describe the statistical analyses that are applied to the data? Are the findings clearly presented, with appropriate inferences about the strength and direction of association and statistical significance of hypothesized relationships? Does the author make causal inferences? What evidence is presented regarding direction of influence and nonspuriousness? (Chapter 12)

10. For qualitative studies, what form of qualitative analysis (e.g., grounded theory, narrative analysis) does the author apply? Are the analytic techniques (e.g., coding) adequately described? Does the analysis lead to an in-depth understanding of the topic? Does the author discuss member checking and/or negative cases? (Chapters 9 and 13)

11. What substantive conclusions are drawn from the study? Does the author discuss alternative explanations of research findings or results? Does the author discuss limitations of the study and the implications of study results for future research?

addition to contact between whites and blacks and the effect of contact in the community, school, family, and workplace.

Although finding "holes" in the literature is a worthy goal, sociologist Mark Edwards (2012) points out that it can be difficult to find them or to have the resources to fill them, especially for beginning researchers. On the other hand, it is worthwhile for small-scale projects to replicate previous studies. In so doing, the project may contribute to the literature simply by confirming prior research. Additionally, it may expand the literature by improving on the methodology or by showing how findings apply to different settings, time periods, or populations.

Design Research and Prepare Proposal

Once researchers come up with a research design to address their research question, they may prepare a research proposal. You may be asked to write a proposal to gain the approval of an instructor or thesis chair to carry out research, or you may submit a proposal to request funding to support your research. A research proposal is a written description of how the researcher intends to address the research question. The outline of a proposal is essentially the same as the first three parts of a research report, which we discuss in detail in the next section: an introduction, literature review, and description of methods and data to be used to address the research question. The difference is that a proposal describes what the researcher plans to do rather than what he or she did. In addition, it is usually shorter than the parallel parts of the final report; in fact, funding agencies usually have word and/or page limits.

In preparing to do research, you also may be required to submit a proposal to the Institutional Review Board (IRB). As we pointed out in Chapter 3, this usually means completing a form that asks you to describe the aims and methods of your proposed research and to specify how participants' rights are to be protected. Although requirements vary somewhat across institutions, Chapter 3 outlines a set of issues that you will likely need to address. These include the potential risks and benefits of the research, as well as the steps you will take to gain informed consent, protect confidentiality, and otherwise secure the data, and, if deception is involved, to debrief participants.

SUMMARY

The initial aim of reading social research is to locate relevant social science literature, so that you can transform a general topic into a researchable question and place your research in the context of prior research and theory. Reading the abstracts of journal articles and the opening and concluding chapters of books should indicate whether a study warrants further attention. Once relevant works are identified, you should record bibliographic information, determine how the study contributes to the topic, and evaluate its methodology. Determining the contributions of previous studies can be aided by forming a matrix that compares key features across each reference. From this comparison, you can decide how your research may contribute to a line of inquiry and then formulate a research question and develop a research proposal.

WRITE RESEARCH REPORT

Either during or after the collection and analysis of your data, you turn your attention to writing—to communicating what you did and what you found. The objective is to communicate precisely and accurately what questions framed the research, what literature informed it, what you did, what you found, and what conclusions might be drawn. When this is done well, the report clearly conveys what was learned and others are able to make an informed evaluation of the study.

Outline and Prepare to Write

Before you begin to write, you should have a conception of the overall organization of the research report. Although there are differences in the organization of reports based on quantitative and qualitative research, as discussed below, we recommend writing an outline that organizes the paper in terms of the following sections:

- An introduction that includes a statement of the problem under investigation
- A literature review that summarizes and places the problem in the context of related theory and research
- A description of the design and execution of the study
- A presentation of the data analysis that identifies the method of analysis and the specific results/findings of the study
- A discussion that offers a broad interpretation of the results/findings.

Within each of these major headings you should list subtopics and important points. As you may discover, outlining frequently brings out the recognition of new ideas and the necessity for transition topics that lead from one point to the next. You should ask the following continually as the outline becomes detailed: How can I move logically from this point to that point? Does the organization make sense? Have I left out anything essential? A report-length paper of 15 to 20 pages requires an outline of at least one and possibly two or more single-spaced pages.

Write First Draft

With your outline in hand, the next step is to write a draft of your research report. As you begin to write, we have a few recommendations:

1. Avoid so-called "writer's block" by **free writing**—recording your thoughts quickly, without regard to grammar and punctuation and without referring to your notes, data, or other information. As experienced writers, we know how difficult it is to write. More often than we care to count, our minds have been blank as we faced a blank document on our computer screen. Sociologist Howard Becker (2007) is one of many advocates of free writing; when his students were having trouble getting started, he advised them to simply sit down and write whatever came into their heads without pausing to look at notes, books, data, or other aids. In free writing, the idea is to write continuously as quickly as you can for a time without worrying about grammar, spelling, and so forth. Although the topics in free writing may be completely open, Becker seems to suggest—and we agree—that it is important to at least stay on the research topic.

2. Related to the first point, consider your first draft a "draft" and not the final report. Too often, because of time and other constraints, students treat writing as a kind of test in which a paper is a problem that they get one shot at answering (Becker 2007). All professionals who write fully expect to go through multiple drafts; they know that their first draft is not the finished product. Rather, they see writing as a form of thinking, in which early drafts may show some confusion and lack coherence. As Becker (2007:17) notes, "the rough draft shows you what needs to be made clearer"; rewriting and editing "let you do it." (We have more to say about revision below.)

3. Make sure you have a clear grasp of the audience's level of knowledge and sources of interest. For the social science reader familiar with the area of study, the report may include technical language, an abbreviated presentation of previous research, and a detailed presentation of methods and findings. For lay readers, in contrast, it should omit technical terms and provide a more detailed presentation of the background of the research and a more general presentation of methods and findings. Because students commonly err in providing too little information about research methods and using too many technical terms, we recommend that you gear your writing to a lay audience.

free writing An exercise to overcome the difficulty in beginning to write by quickly recording thoughts, without regard to grammar and punctuation or reference to notes, data, books, and other information.

4. Use the active voice. The use of active rather than passive verbs is standard advice in writing texts. Becker believes this practice is particularly important for sociologists. The reason, as he explains, is that:

> Active verbs almost always force you to name the person who did whatever was done. . . . We seldom think that things just happen all by themselves, as passive verbs suggest, because in our daily lives people *do* things and *make them happen*. Sentences that name active agents make our representations of social life more understandable and believable. "The criminal was sentenced" hides the judge who, we know, did the sentencing and, not incidentally, thus makes the criminal's fate seem the operation of impersonal forces rather than the result of people acting together to imprison him or her. (Becker 2007:79–80)

In addition to using the active voice, unless you are instructed otherwise, we recommend that you write in the first person. Like Johnny Saldaña (2011), who recommends the first person when writing about qualitative research, we think this makes the writing more personal and engaging.

5. Communicating accurately and clearly requires proper grammar, punctuation, and style. The principles of being concise and direct, of avoiding unnecessary jargon, of providing examples to clarify points, and so forth apply just as strongly to technical as to any other form of writing.

6. Finally, we agree with Edwards (2012:5) that no matter how much advice we may impart about writing, "there is no substitute for reading sociological texts [i.e., journal articles and monographs] as a way of learning how to write." Reading publications "by sociologists and noting how they say it" will help you gain a sense of "good sociological writing."

With these points in mind, let us consider in some detail the topical outline suggested above. It is important to note that this is only one of many possible outlines. It applies best to quantitative research. Moreover, considerations of length, subject matter, purpose, and audience may influence the organization and elaboration of this outline in the actual report. A report may emphasize measurement, sampling, or something else depending on the study. No perfect outline exists ready to be adopted for every research report. The important point is that the outline should be functional and should facilitate your writing.

INTRODUCTION TO THE REPORT

This section sets up the rest of the paper. It is the place, Edwards (2012:43) points out, "where you try to hook the reader with an answer to the question, 'Why should I care?'" To answer this question requires a clear statement of the problem and why it is of general interest and importance. General interest and importance may be demonstrated by relating the problem briefly to the theoretical context of the study or by pointing to its social and practical significance. For example, Beckett Broh opens her article in *Sociology of Education* (see Chapter 4) by noting that despite the widespread practice and costs of extracurricular programming, particularly sports, in American schools, there is very little scientific information about its academic benefits. Her research, she then points out, addresses two questions (Broh 2002): (1) Does participation in inter-scholastic sports promote academic achievement? (2) Does participation in nonsport activities improve achievement?

In some ways, the introduction can be the most difficult part of the report to write. In fact, we have struggled at times to introduce chapters in this book. In these cases, we have followed some sage advice that Becker received while in graduate school: write the introduction last, after you have a complete draft of the report. You can never be certain when you begin a report of exactly what you'll write. So, it is often easier and more effective to write the introduction after you know how the paper turns out.

LITERATURE REVIEW

The literature review is where you are expected to present the theoretical context of the problem under investigation and how it has been studied by others. The idea is to cite relevant literature in the process of presenting the underlying theoretical and method-ological rationale for the research. This means providing a "selective but fair treatment of the state of current knowledge about a topic" (Edwards 2012:21) rather than trying to report every study ever done on the topic.

In studies designed to test specific hypotheses, the aim of this section should be to show, if possible, how the hypotheses derive from theory or previous research. When this is not possible—for example, because the research question or hypothesis is based on everyday observations and experiences—one should still show the relevance of the study to previous research and theory, if only to show how it contradicts existing evidence or fills a gap in scientific knowledge.

Finally, it is a good idea, especially for lengthy literature reviews, to end this section with (1) a concise restatement of the research question or hypothesis, (2) a presentation of the theoretical model in a figure, such as an arrow diagram (see Chapter 12), and/or (3) a brief overview of the study.

METHODS

In the Methods section you should state clearly and accurately how the study was done. The following subtopics may help you to accomplish this objective.

DESIGN First you must state what type of study you have done: experiment, survey, field research, or some other approach. The particular approach determines the primary design and procedural issues that must be addressed. Key issues for the different approaches are as follows:

1. In the case of an experiment, the type of experimental design and the procedures of its implementation
2. In a survey, the type of survey instrument, its length, and the sampling design
3. In field research, the nature of the setting(s) and the researcher's relationship to informants
4. In in-depth interviews, the type of interviews conducted (in terms of structure, number of participants, and content) and the extent of rapport established
5. In research using existing data, the sources of data and their completeness.

SAMPLE This section should make clear who participated in the study, how many cases were sampled, how they were selected, and whom or what they represent. It is necessary to discuss sampling procedures, the limitations of the sample data (including nonresponse bias for surveys), and types of inferences that it is possible to make from the data.

MEASUREMENT Here, operational definitions are described. In quantitative research, you should define concepts and describe how variables were measured. In an experiment, this means specifying the procedures for manipulating the independent variable and measuring the dependent variable. In a survey, this should include the specific questions that were asked as measures of each variable in the theoretical model. In field research, you should describe fully the kinds of observations that were made and, if relevant, other sources of information such as documents and in-depth interviewing. Longer reports may contain appendixes with some of these materials, such as copies of the complete questionnaire or interview guide.

In addition, this section should include any evidence on reliability and validity that is not presented in other sections, such as the outcome of manipulation checks and tests for measurement reliability and validity.

PROCEDURES This section, which may be a part of the description of sampling and measurement, presents a summary of the various steps in the conduct of the research. This is especially important for an experiment and in qualitative research. Experiments should include a step-by-step account of the study from the participant's point of view. Qualitative researchers often give a chronological account of the research, telling how they selected and gained entry into the setting, how they met and developed relationships with informants or interviewees, and how long they were in the setting. In fact, the research report of a field researcher usually follows a narrative, from either the researcher's or informant's point of view, which begins with a discussion of these methodological issues.

FINDINGS/RESULTS

The heart of the research paper is the findings/results section, toward which the entire report should be aimed. This is where questions or hypotheses that framed the research are answered. In quantitative analyses, the researcher should describe what sort of statistical analyses were performed on the data. This description should be very specific with regard to the kind of analysis (e.g., "three-way analysis of variance," "paired *t*-tests," "ordinary least squares regression"), and it may include (which we recommend for the student researcher) descriptions of the statistical techniques or references to the computer software package (e.g., SPSS) used to carry out the analysis. Furthermore, the researcher often constructs tables, charts, and graphs to facilitate the presentation of findings. Here, we have some specific recommendations.

1. Use tables and figures sparingly, to summarize large amounts of information. During the course of research, investigators usually generate many more tables than they can possibly present in the research report. These interim tables guide the researcher in determining the course of the analysis, but more often than not they contain single facts that can be reported in the text of the report.

2. Organize this section around the major hypotheses or theoretical questions and/or major findings. If there is a single main hypothesis, then a single table may suffice to summarize the findings.

3. Discuss the data in terms of what they show about the research problem or hypothesis. Do not let the data speak for themselves, and do not discuss the data merely in terms of the variables or the numbers in a table. In other words, subordinate the data to the arguments presented and use the data and tables to help tell a story.

This last point also applies to qualitative research. The data in such studies are usually not numbers but quotations, concrete observations, and historical events. As we saw in Chapter 13, various visual displays (e.g., typologies, taxonomies) may be used to communicate findings. Still, the data should be used in the same way as in quantitative analysis: organized around the thesis of the report and presented to support arguments. More generally, the presentation of data should convey an understanding of how research participants think and act within their social contexts.

DISCUSSION

Research reports end with a summary of the major findings and a general interpretation of the study results. The summary serves as a sort of "caboose abstract," reviewing the highlights of the report. This is particularly useful in cases in which the paper is long or necessarily complex. It is important to avoid excessive repetition in the summary: do not lift passages from earlier parts of the paper but, rather, restate the basic problem and basic findings.

Beyond summarizing, the discussion section may accomplish several goals. First, it provides a place to point out the shortcomings of the research. For example, the data may be drawn from populations or under conditions that limit the generalizability of the findings. Honesty regarding such limitations is important in preventing readers from making more from the research than is warranted. Second, it provides a chance to point out inconsistencies, account for anomalies, and suggest improvements in the research design. Third, the discussion section allows the writer an opportunity to place the whole project into broader perspective, to mention the theoretical and practical implications of the study, and to discuss possible future work.

Finally, researchers often conclude reports with a succinct statement of the major point of the study. For example, having examined class differences in help seeking in an elementary school, Calarco (2011:879) used part of her article title to tell readers what they should take away: "In repeatedly saying 'I need help!' middle-class children gain advantages that help reinforce existing social and educational opportunities."

REFERENCES

Finally, the report needs to include some sort of bibliography or reference list. Although the usual practice is to list only works cited in the body of the report, uncited works that were important in the development of the study may also be included. The format of the references varies slightly from one discipline to another. Box 14.2, DOING SOCIAL RESEARCH: ASA Guidelines for In-Text Citations and References, should help you understand and apply the style guide used in this book and often used in sociology courses.

Revision and Other Writing Considerations

Finally, your draft should go through multiple revisions, and when the final draft is completed, you should carefully proofread it. As noted earlier, many students make the mistake of treating the first draft as the only draft. Most professional writers, on the other hand, assume that the first draft will be one in a series of drafts designed to sharpen and improve the final product. The purpose of a first draft is to transfer ideas, thoughts, and facts from the mind of the writer into some material form that can be reflected on by the author. We cannot put a number on how many subsequent drafts should be written; however, it is hard to imagine a polished report that is not the product of numerous drafts. Good writing requires attention to detail; it means writing as if every word and sentence should be taken seriously. And that requires extensive rewriting.

For many people the best time to revise a paper is after taking some time away from the work. Writers who wait until the last few hours or days to write a paper will not produce a good paper—among other reasons, because they simply will not have time

BOX 14.2

DOING SOCIAL RESEARCH

ASA Guidelines for In-Text Citations and References

The American Sociological Association (ASA) has established formal guidelines that apply to articles published in journals and books sponsored by the association. Many instructors ask their students to use the *American Sociological Association Style Guide* (2014). Below are a few of its rules. If you plan to major in sociology or pursue graduate studies in sociology, we recommend that you read the complete *Style Guide*.

Whenever a publication or presentation is the source of claims or ideas, you must give credit to the source. Giving credit begins with citations inserted in the text that include the author(s) and year of publication. If you are quoting directly from a work, you must also include page numbers. Below are examples that show how these rules apply under different conditions:

1. Author's name in the text.

    Lareau (2011) highlights class differences . . .

2. Author's name not in the text.

    Research indicates . . . (Lareau 2011).

3. First citation for a work with three authors.

    Seeking help . . . bolsters learning (Ryan, Hicks, and Midgley 1997).

4. Subsequent citations for works with three authors and citations of works with more than three authors: use et al.

    . . . (Ryan et al. 1997).

5. Citations with more than one reference: use semicolon to separate and list alphabetically.

    . . . (Gall 1985; Newman 2000; Ryan, Hicks, and Midgley 1997).

6. Direct quotation or reference to specific passage: follow year with page number(s).

    As Stevenson (1991:128) suggests, reprimands "clarify the rules . . ."

All names cited in the text should be placed in a reference list following the text and footnotes. This section is headed "References," and all references are listed alphabetically by the first author's last name. The ASA includes surnames and first names for all authors, as in the following examples.

7. References for books.

    Adler, Patricia A. and Peter Adler. 1998. *Peer Power: Preadolescent Culture and Identity.* New Brunswick, NJ: Rutgers University Press.

continues

continued

8. References for journal articles with one author.

Calarco, Jessica McCrory. 2011. "'I need help!' Social Class and Children's Help-Seeking in Elementary School." *American Sociological Review* 76(6):862–82.

9. References for journal articles with more than one author.

Pescosolido, Bernice A., Elizabeth Grauerholz, and Melissa A. Milkie. 1997. "The Portrayal of Blacks in U.S. Children's Picture Books Through the Mid- and Late-Twentieth Century." *American Sociological Review* 62(3):443–64.

10. References for chapters in edited volumes.

Charmaz, Kathy. 2002. "Qualitative Interviewing and Grounded Theory Analysis." Pp. 675–94 in *Handbook of Interview Research: Context and Method,* edited by Jaber F. Gubrium and James A. Holstein. Thousand Oaks, CA: Sage.

11. References to websites.

American Sociological Association. 1999. *Code of Ethics and Policies and Procedures of the ASA Committee on Professional Ethics.* Washington, DC: ASA. Retrieved November 8, 2014 (http://www.asanet.org/images/asa/docs/pdf/CodeofEthics.pdf).

to "sleep on it" and reread their work in a refreshed frame of mind. Authors' judgments about the quality of their work may vary directly with the recency of the effort. The passage of time tends to bring perspective and a renewed energy to tackle a job that perhaps did not seem necessary earlier. Much revision, of course, can be of the "cut and paste" variety. This job usually involves the revision of what is unclear, the deletion of what is extraneous, and the addition of what had been omitted.

Finally, at some point in the successive drafting of a report, you will have a "working" draft ready to be shown to others who can provide critical feedback. We realize that much of the writing students do, with its rigid time constraints, does not allow for this. But there is no better way of judging the clarity of your writing than asking others if they understand what you are saying. Professionals know this and often develop a circle of friends who will read their work. We encourage students to do the same.

LENGTH

Probably the most frequently asked question regarding student papers is: How long should it be? The most appropriate but usually unsatisfying answer is, As long as it needs to be. Many students make the mistake of underestimating the length that thoroughness demands; they may omit vital information and thus seriously weaken the impact of the report. On the other hand, some students make the mistake of thinking that the longer a report is, the better it is. The techniques of "padding" a paper through overuse of citations, excessive use of full quotations instead of summarizing the findings of cited sources, and reliance on vocabulary and jargon intended to "impress" the audience are mistakes that experienced readers usually see through. Jeffrey Katzer, Kenneth Cook, and Wayne Crouch (1998) refer to these smoke screens as "paraphernalia of pedantry" and conclude that they are more likely to be distracting than to facilitate communication. And it is communication that is the essence of the research process.

AVOIDING PLAGIARISM

One form of scientific misconduct is plagiarism. Plagiarism, according to the US Department of Health and Human Services, is "the appropriation of another person's ideas, processes, results, or words without giving appropriate credit" (Steneck 2007:21). Plagiarism in any form, whether intentional or accidental, is a serious and often punishable offense. As you write your report, therefore, you must be careful to properly cite all work that is the source of the ideas presented.

Leonard Rosen and Laurence Behrens (1992:582) believe that much plagiarism is unintentional, occurring because of writers' carelessness or ignorance about the conventions of quotation and citation. They offer two general rules for avoiding unintentional plagiarism. First, "whenever you quote the exact words of others, place these words in quotation marks and properly cite the source." To quote a source is to extract a word, phrase, sentence, or passage from the original and insert it into the text. Quoted material should be enclosed within double quotation marks or, if lengthy (more than 40 words, according to the *ASA Style Guide*), indented as a block quote. Second, "whenever you paraphrase or summarize the ideas of others, do not use whole phrases, many of the same words, or sentence structures similar to the original," and be sure "to identify the source of the paraphrased or summarized material." To summarize is to condense the original into a sentence or two in your own words; to paraphrase is to follow the original statement more closely but still restate it in your own words. In general, your report will be easier to read and better convey your understanding of what you read if you summarize or paraphrase others' ideas rather than present a stream of quotations. Use direct quotations only when the original words are particularly well chosen—clear, incisive, and powerful.

SUMMARY

Writing the research report is facilitated greatly by preparing an outline, keeping in mind the intended audience and how they will read the report, and writing several drafts as well as soliciting others' critical comments on early drafts. Most research reports contain the following components: (1) an introduction to the problem pointing out its theoretical, practical, and/or social significance; (2) a literature review relating the research problem to previous theory and research; (3) a methods section outlining precisely how the research was done, including the overall approach and design and methods of sampling and measurement; (4) a findings/results section; (5) a discussion of the limitations and anomalies as well as the broader theoretical and practical implications of the research; and (6) a list of references cited in the report.

KEY TERMS

abstract, p. 439   free writing, p. 445   peer review, p. 440

KEY POINTS

- The process of reading and writing social research usually begins by identifying relevant literature, reading and evaluating it, and formulating one or more research questions.
- Writing often begins with the development of a research proposal, which synthesizes relevant literature, poses one or more research questions or hypotheses, and describes the methods and data to be used to address the question.
- Research reports typically include an introduction, literature review, a description of data and methods, presentation of results or findings, a discussion/conclusion, and references.
- In writing a research report, researchers may develop an outline, write a draft, and revise it multiple times based on proofreading and comments from others.
- Ultimately, writing requires attention to detail, including the careful citation of sources.

REVIEW QUESTIONS

1. What does the textbook recommend as the primary means of evaluating the credibility of published articles?
2. Besides identifying gaps in research on a topic, what does the textbook recommend as a worthwhile research question?

3. For whom or for what purpose may a research proposal be written?
4. What are the major components of a research report?
5. What is an effective way of overcoming the difficulty in beginning to write?
6. In a sentence, describe the objective of each of the following sections of a research report: (a) introduction; (b) literature review; (c) results/findings.
7. Identify two rules for avoiding unintentional plagiarism.

EXERCISES

1. To practice locating literature relevant to a research topic, suppose that you are interested in the household division of labor among same-sex couples. More specifically, you want to know how this differs from the division of labor among heterosexual couples. First, following the guidelines presented in Box 4.1, use the comprehensive sociology database SocINDEX (which should be available in your library's online research databases) to conduct a search on this topic. What keywords seem to produce the most relevant list of references? Second, begin reading the titles and abstracts that you find. List the first five references that you believe are relevant to your topic.

2. Choose a topic and repeat the steps in Exercise 1. For the first five journal articles that you deem relevant to your topic, determine whether the article is peer-reviewed. Now summarize the contents of each reference using Table 14.1 as a framework.

3. Addressing the questions outlined in Box 14.1, write a critique of the following article: Stack, Steven, and Jim Gundlach. "The Effect of Country Music on Suicide." *Social Forces* 71, no. 1 (1992):211–18.

Glossary

Note: The numbers at the end of each definition indicate the chapters in which the term is most prominent.

abstract A capsule version of a research report that briefly describes the research question or hypothesis, data, and methods, and the major findings or results. (14)

action coding A form of coding that uses gerunds (*-ing* words) to signal activity in the data. Also called *process coding*. (13)

analytic memo An adjunct to field notes in field research that consists of recorded analyses that come to mind in going over notes and observations. (9, 13)

anonymity Ethical safeguard against invasion of privacy in which data cannot be identified with particular research participants. (3)

antecedent variable A variable that occurs before, and may be a cause of, both the independent and dependent variables in a causal relationship. (4, 12)

archival records A source of operational definitions that consists of existing documents and institutional records. (5, 10)

archive A physical or digital library that contains a collection of historical documents or records. (10)

attribute coding A method of coding that identifies the characteristics of participants, settings, and other phenomena of interest, largely as a means of managing the data. (13)

audit study A study that examines racial and other forms of discrimination by sending matched pairs of individuals to apply for jobs, purchase a car, rent an apartment, and so on. (7, 11)

beneficence The Belmont principle that researchers have an obligation to secure the well-being of participants by maximizing possible benefits and minimizing possible harms. (3)

big data Unusually large datasets that are collected digitally and, because of their variety and structure, may require sophisticated computational methods. (10)

bivariate analysis The statistical analysis of the relationship between two variables. (12)

case study The holistic analysis of a single person, group, or event by one or more research methods. (6)

causal relationship A relationship in which it is theorized that changes in one variable produce or bring about changes in another variable. (4, 12)

cell frequency The number of cases in a cell of a cross-tabulation (contingency table). (12)

chi-square (χ^2) test for independence A test of statistical significance used to assess the likelihood that an observed association between two variables could have occurred by chance. (4, 12)

closed-ended question Survey questions that require respondents to choose responses from those provided. (8)

cluster sampling A probability sampling design in which the population is broken down into natural groupings or areas, called clusters, and a random sample of clusters is drawn. (6)

code memo A type of memo written explicitly for describing the basis of one's operational definitions. Also called *code note*. (13)

code note *See* **code memo**. (13)

codebook A guide for coding that consists of a list of the variables together with definitions, codes, and instructions for applying the codes. (10, 12)

coding The sorting of data into numbered or textual categories. (8, 9, 10, 13)

coding units *See* **recording units**.

Common Rule Label given to the federal policy for the protection of human subjects. (3)

comparative historical analysis The development of causal explanations of social change by describing and comparing historical processes within and across cases. (10)

component design A mixed methods design in which findings from different approaches are compared after each approach is carried out independently. (11)

computer-assisted personal interviewing (CAPI) A software program, usually on a portable computer, that aids interviewers by providing appropriate instructions, question wording, and data-entry supervision. (8)

Computer-Assisted Qualitative Data Analysis Software (CAQDAS) Software packages that aid in the management and analysis of data. (13)

computer-assisted self-administered interviewing (CASI) An electronic survey in which a questionnaire is transmitted on a computer disk mailed to the respondent or on a laptop computer provided by the researcher. (8)

computer-assisted telephone interviewing (CATI) A set of computerized tools that aid telephone interviewers and supervisors by automating various data-collection tasks. (8)

concept Terms scientists use to group together phenomena that have important things in common. (4, 5)

conceptual definition A verbal definition of a concept that is derived from theory and directs the search for appropriate measures. Also called *theoretical definition*. (5)

conceptualization The development and clarification of concepts. (5)

concurrent design A mixed methods design in which data collection with different approaches is carried out at the same time. (11)

confidence interval A range (interval) within which a population value is estimated to lie at a specific level of confidence. (6)

confidentiality Ethical safeguard against invasion of privacy by which data obtained from participants are not shared with others without their permission. (3)

conflict of interest In science, a conflict between the goal of producing accurate, unbiased knowledge and other motives such as financial gain, professional advancement, or political interests. (3)

consistency checking A data-cleaning procedure involving checking for unreasonable patterns of responses, such as a 12-year-old who voted in the last US presidential election. (12)

constant-comparative method The general analytic strategy of grounded theory methods, which involves making comparisons at increasingly higher levels of abstraction through coding, memo-writing, and theoretical sampling. (13)

construct validation Measurement validation based on an accumulation of research evidence indicating that a measure is related to other variables as theoretically expected. (5)

content analysis Systematic analysis of the symbolic content of communications in which the content is reduced to a set of coded variables or categories. (10)

control variable A variable that is not allowed to vary or is otherwise held constant during the course of data collection or analysis. (4, 12)

convenience sampling The selection of cases that are conveniently available. (6)

convergent validation Measurement validation based on the extent to which independent measures of the same concept are associated with one another. (5)

conversation analysis The qualitative analysis of conversations, which are typically recorded, transcribed, and analyzed in terms of their structure, sequencing, word choice, and other characteristics. (13)

correlation coefficient A statistical measure of the strength and direction of a linear relationship between two variables; it may vary from -1 to 0 to $+1$. (4, 12)

cover story An introduction presented to research participants to obtain their cooperation while disguising the research hypothesis. (7)

coverage error The error that occurs when the sampling frame does not match the target population. (6, 8)

covert observation A form of observation in which the researcher conceals his or her identity as a researcher. (9)

Cronbach's alpha A statistical index of internal-consistency reliability that ranges from 0 (unreliable) to 1 (perfectly reliable). (5)

cross-sectional design The most common survey design, in which data are gathered from a sample of respondents at essentially one point in time. (8)

data Information recorded from observation; may be in numerical or nonnumerical form. (2)

data archives Repositories of survey, ethnographic, or qualitative interview data collected by various agencies and researchers that are accessible to the public. (10)

data cleaning The detection and correction of errors in a computer datafile that may have occurred during data collection, coding, and/or data entry. (12)

data matrix The form of a computer datafile, with rows as cases and columns as variables; each cell represents the value of a particular variable (column) for a particular case (row). (12, 13)

data processing The preparation of data for analysis. (12)

debriefing A session at the end of a study in which an investigator meets with a participant to impart information about the study, including its real purpose and the nature and purpose of deception (if used), and to respond to questions and concerns. (3)

deductive logic Reasoning in which the conclusion necessarily follows if the evidence is true. (2)

demography The study of the structure of and changes in human populations. (10)

dependent variable The variable that the researcher tries to explain or predict; the presumed effect in a causal relationship. (4, 12)

descriptive statistics Procedures for organizing and summarizing data. (12)

descriptive survey A survey undertaken to provide estimates of the characteristics of a population. (8)

dictionary In computerized content analysis, the set of words, phrases, or other word-based indicators (e.g., word length) that is the basis for a search of texts. (10)

disproportionate stratified sampling A sampling procedure in which strata are sampled disproportionately to population composition. (6)

double-barreled question A question in which two separate ideas are presented together as a unit. (8)

double-blind experiment An experiment in which neither research participants nor research personnel know participants' treatment condition during the running of the experiment. (7)

dummy variable A variable or set of variable categories recoded to have values of 0 and 1. Dummy coding may be applied to nominal- or ordinal-scale variables for the purpose of regression or other numerical analysis. (12)

ecological fallacy Erroneous use of data describing an aggregate unit (e.g., organizations) to draw inferences about the units of analysis that comprise the aggregate (e.g., individual members of organizations). (4)

editing Checking data and correcting for errors in completed interviews or questionnaires. (8, 12)

empirical indicator A single, concrete proxy for a concept such as a questionnaire item in a survey. (5)

empirical pattern A relationship among phenomena usually inferred from data. (2)

ethics Standards of moral conduct that distinguish right from wrong. (3)

ethnography An alternate word, derived from cultural anthropology, to describe field research, especially when it focuses on the culture of a group of people. (9)

exhaustive The measurement requirement that a measure includes all possible values or categories of a variable so that every case can be classified. (5, 8)

existing data analysis Analysis of data from existing sources of information that were not produced directly by the researcher who uses them. (1, 10, 11)

experiment Basic approach to social research that entails manipulating an aspect of the environment to observe behavior under different, controlled conditions. (1, 7, 11)

explanatory survey A survey that investigates relationships between two or more variables, often attempting to explain them in cause-and-effect terms. (8)

external validity The extent to which experimental findings may be generalized to other settings, measurements, populations, and time periods. (7)

extraneous variable A variable that is not part of a hypothesized relationship. (4, 12)

face-to-face (FTF) interview A type of interview in which the interviewer interacts face to face with the respondent. (8)

factorial design An experiment in which two or more variables (factors) are manipulated. (7)

field experiment An experiment conducted in a natural setting. (7)

field jottings Brief quotes, phrases, and key words that are recorded by field researchers while in the field. (9)

field notes Detailed written accounts of field observations, which may also include a researcher's reflections and preliminary analyses. (9, 13)

field pretesting An evaluation of a survey instrument that involves trying it out on a small sample of persons. (8)

focus group An interview method in which a researcher collects data from a group by moderating a group discussion on a particular topic. (9)

free writing An exercise to overcome the difficulty in beginning to write by quickly recording thoughts, without regard to grammar and punctuation or reference to notes, data, books, and other information. (14)

frequency distribution A tabulation of the number of cases falling into each category of a variable. (12)

gatekeeper Relevant authority whose permission is needed to gain access to a setting or group. (9)

grand tour question A broad opening question in in-depth interviews that asks for a general description of the people, processes, or events being studied. Also called *tour question*. (9)

guiding question A relatively broad research question that guides the initial stages of qualitative research. (9)

Hawthorne effect A change in behavior, such as an improvement in performance, that occurs when research participants know they are being studied. (2)

histogram A graphic display in which the height of a vertical bar represents the frequency or percentage of cases in each category of an interval/ratio variable. (12)

history A threat to internal validity that refers to events other than the manipulation of the independent variable. (7)

hypothesis An expected but unconfirmed relationship among two or more phenomena. (2, 4, 12)

imputation A procedure for handling missing data in which values are assigned based on other information, such as the sample mean or known values of other variables. (12)

in vivo coding A form of coding that uses participants' own words as labels. (13)

independent variable A presumed influence or cause of a dependent variable. (4, 12)

in-depth interview A type of formal interview intended to yield deep responses through open-ended questions and a flexible format. (9)

index A composite measure of a concept constructed by adding or averaging the scores of separate indicators; differs from a scale, which uses less arbitrary procedures for combining indicators. (5)

inductive logic Reasoning in which the conclusion is implied by, but goes beyond, the evidence at hand and, hence, may or may not be true. (2)

inferential statistics Procedures for determining the extent to which one may generalize beyond the data at hand. (12)

informed consent The ethical principle that individuals should be given enough information about a study,

especially its potential risks, to make an informed decision about whether to participate. (3)

Institutional Review Board (IRB) A committee formed at nearly all colleges and universities that is responsible for reviewing research proposals to assess provisions for the treatment of human (and animal) subjects. (3)

integrated design A mixed methods design in which different approaches are connected or merged during the process of data collection and analysis. (11)

inter-coder reliability *See* **inter-rater reliability**. (5, 10)

internal consistency A form of reliability assessment; the consistency of "scores" across all the items of a composite measure (i.e., index or scale). (5)

internal validity Evidence that rules out the possibility that factors other than the manipulated independent variable are responsible for the measured outcome. (7)

inter-rater reliability The extent to which different observers or coders get equivalent results when applying the same measure. Also called *inter-coder reliability*. (5, 10)

interval measurement A level of measurement that has the qualities of the ordinal level plus equal distances (intervals) between assigned numbers. (5, 12)

intervening variable A variable that is intermediate between two other variables in a causal relationship; it is an effect of one and a cause of the other. (4, 12)

interview guide A list of topics and specific questions to be asked in a qualitative interview. (9)

interview schedule A survey form used by interviewers that consists of instructions, the questions to be asked, and, if they are used, response options. (8)

judgmental sampling *See* **purposive sampling**. (6)

justice The Belmont principle that the benefits and burdens of research should be fairly distributed, so that the group selected for research also may benefit from its application. (3)

key informant A person from whom field researchers acquire information who is selected on the basis of knowledge, expertise, or status within the group. (9)

laboratory experiment An experiment conducted in a controlled environment. (7)

leading question A question in which a possible answer is suggested, or some answers are presented as more acceptable than others. (8)

listwise deletion A common procedure for handling missing values in multivariate analysis that excludes cases which have missing values on any of the variables in the analysis. (12)

longitudinal design Survey design in which data are collected at more than one point in time. (8)

manipulation check Procedure used to provide evidence that participants interpreted the manipulation of the independent variable in the way intended. (7)

marginal frequencies Row and column totals in a contingency table (cross-tabulation) that represent the univariate frequency distributions for the row and column variables. (12)

maturation A threat to internal validity that refers to psychological or physiological changes taking place within participants. (7)

mean The average value of a dataset, calculated by adding up the individual values and dividing by the total number of cases. (6, 12)

measurement error A lack of correspondence between a concept and measure that is due to problems with an operational definition or with its application. (5)

measurement validity The goodness of fit between an operational definition and the concept it is purported to measure. (5)

measures of association Descriptive statistics used to measure the strength and direction of a bivariate relationship. (12)

median The midpoint in a distribution of interval- or ratio-scale data; indicates the point below and above which 50 percent of the values fall. (12)

member checking A method of evaluating qualitative data in which researchers share their results with participants and ask them to comment on their accuracy and completeness. (13)

missing data Refers to the absence of information on a variable for a given case. (12)

mixed methods research A research study that combines two or more approaches to data collection and analysis. (11)

mixed-mode survey A survey that uses more than one mode of data collection, either sequentially or concurrently, to sample and/or collect the data. (8)

mode The value or category of a frequency distribution having the highest frequency; the most typical value. (12)

multiple regression A statistical method for determining the simultaneous effects of several independent variables on a dependent variable. (12)

multistage cluster sampling A sampling design in which sampling occurs at two or more steps or stages. (6)

mutual exclusivity The measurement requirement that each case can be placed in one and only one category of a variable. (5, 8)

N An abbreviation representing the number of observations on which a statistic is based (e.g., $N = 753$). (12)

narrative analysis The qualitative analysis of narratives, including literary texts and stories derived from interviews and other sources, which examines their structure, meaning, and other characteristics. (13)

narrative comparison A method of causal inference in which historical narratives of cases are analyzed to develop a general cross-case causal pattern and to validate it within each case. (10)

nesting A process in mixed methods research whereby different kinds of data are collected from the same individuals or groups by embedding one approach within another. (11)

nominal measurement A level of measurement in which numbers serve only to label categories of a variable. (5, 12)

nonparticipant observation A form of observation in which the field researcher does not participate in the activity or group being studied. (9)

nonprobability sampling Methods of case selection other than random selection. (6, 9)

nonresponse bias See **nonresponse error**. (6)

nonresponse error In survey sampling, the error that occurs when nonrespondents (sampled individuals who do not respond or cannot be contacted) differ systematically from respondents. Also called *nonresponse bias*. (6)

normal curve A bell-shaped distribution of data that characterizes many variables and statistics, such as the sampling distribution of a proportion or mean. Also called *normal distribution*. (6, 12)

normal distribution See **normal curve**. (6, 12)

null hypothesis The hypothesis, associated with tests of statistical significance, that an observed relationship is due to chance; a test that is significant rejects the null hypothesis at a specified level of probability. (12)

open-ended question A survey question that requires respondents to answer in their own words. (8)

operational definition A detailed description of the research procedures necessary to assign units of analysis to variable categories. (5)

operationalization The process of identifying empirical indicators and the procedures for applying them to measure a concept. (5)

ordinal measurement A level of measurement in which different numbers indicate rank order of cases on a variable. (5, 12)

outliers Unusual or suspicious values that are far removed from the preponderance of observations for a variable. (12)

overt observation A form of observation in which the researcher identifies himself or herself as a researcher to those who are being observed. (9)

panel study A longitudinal design in which the same individuals are surveyed more than once, permitting the study of individual and group change. (8)

paper-and-pencil questionnaire survey A survey form filled out by respondents. (8)

partial regression coefficient Coefficients in a multiple-regression equation that estimate the effects of each independent variable on the dependent variable when all other variables in the equation are held constant. Also called *partial slope*. (12)

partial slope *See* **partial regression coefficient**. (12)

partial table A table in elaboration analysis which displays the original two-variable relationship for a single category of the control variable, thereby holding the control variable constant. (12)

participant observation A form of observation in which the field researcher participates to some degree in the activity or group being studied. (9)

peer review A system in which researchers' reports are evaluated by fellow academics and researchers. (4, 14)

percentage distribution A norming operation that facilitates interpreting and comparing frequency distributions by transforming each frequency to a common yardstick of 100 units (percentage points) in length; the number of cases in each category is divided by the total and multiplied by 100. (12)

population The total membership of a defined class of people, objects, or events. (6)

posttest-only control group design The most basic experimental design in which the dependent variable is measured after the experimental manipulation. (7)

pretest A trial run of an experiment or survey instrument to evaluate and rehearse study procedures and personnel. (7, 8)

pretest-posttest control group design An experimental design in which the dependent variable is measured both before and after the experimental manipulation. (7)

probability The likelihood that something will occur, which may vary from 0 to 100 percent. (6)

probability distribution A distribution of the probabilities for a variable, which indicates the likelihood that each category or value of the variable will occur. (6)

probability proportionate to size sampling The selection of cases in cluster sampling so that the probability of selection is proportionate to the size of (i.e., the number of cases in) the cluster. (6)

probability sampling Sampling based on a process of random selection that gives each case in the population an equal or known chance of being included in the sample. (6)

probes Follow-up questions used in surveys and in-depth interviews to gather more information about a respondent's answer. (9)

process analysis A within-case method of comparative historical analysis that examines possible intervening mechanisms that link an observed or theoretical association between events. Also called *process tracing*. (10)

process coding *See* **action coding**. (13)

process tracing *See* **process analysis**. (10)

proportionate stratified sampling A sampling procedure in which strata are sampled proportionately to population composition. (6)

purposive sampling Sampling that involves the careful and informed selection of typical cases or of cases that represent relevant dimensions of the population. Also called *judgmental sampling*. (6)

qualitative research Basic approach to social research that involves directly observing and often interviewing others to produce nonnumerical data. (1, 4, 9, 11, 13)

qualitative research question A question that asks about social processes or the meaning and cultural significance of people's actions. (4, 9)

quantitative research question A question that asks about the relationship between two or more variables. (4, 12)

R^2 A measure of fit in multiple regression that indicates approximately the proportion of the variation in the dependent variable predicted or "explained" by the independent variables. (12)

random assignment The assignment of research participants to experimental conditions by means of a random device such as a coin toss. (7)

random selection A selection process that gives each element in a population an equal or known chance of being selected. (6)

random-digit dialing (RDD) A sampling-frame technique in which dialable telephone numbers are generated (sampled) randomly. (8)

range The difference between the lowest and highest values in a distribution, which is usually reported by identifying these two extreme values. (12)

ratio measurement The highest level of measurement, which has the features of the other levels plus an absolute (nonarbitrary) zero point. (5, 12)

reactive measurement effect An effect in which participants' awareness of being studied produces changes in how they ordinarily would respond. (7, 10)

recording units The units of analysis in content analysis, such as words, sentences, paragraphs, and whole articles. Also called *coding units*. (10)

reflexivity A common practice in qualitative research, whereby a researcher reflects on how his or her characteristics and presence shape the research process. (9)

regression analysis A statistical method for analyzing bivariate (simple regression) and multivariate (multiple regression) relationships among interval- or ratio-scale variables. (12)

regression coefficient *See* **slope**. (12)

regression line A geometric representation of a bivariate regression equation that provides the best linear fit to the observed data by virtue of minimizing the sum of the squared deviations from the line; also called the *least squares line*. (12)

reliability The stability or consistency of an operational definition. (5)

replication The repetition of a study using a different sample of participants and often involving different settings and methods. (7)

research design The overall plan of a study for collecting data. (4)

residuals The difference between observed values of the dependent variable and those predicted by a regression equation. (12)

respect for persons The Belmont principle that individuals must be treated as autonomous agents who have the freedom and capacity to decide what happens to them, and researchers must protect those with diminished autonomy. (3)

response rate In a survey, the proportion of people in the sample from whom completed interviews or questionnaires are obtained. (6, 8)

sample A subset of cases selected from a population. (6)

sampling distribution A theoretical distribution of sample results for all possible samples of a given size. (6)

sampling error The difference between an actual population value (e.g., a percentage) and the population value estimated from a sample. (6)

sampling frame An operational definition of the population that provides the basis for drawing a sample; ordinarily consists of a list of cases. (6)

sampling with replacement A sampling procedure whereby once a case is selected, it is returned to the sampling frame, so that it may be selected again. (6)

sampling without replacement A sampling procedure whereby once a case is selected, it is NOT returned to the sampling frame, so that it cannot be selected again. (6)

saturation In purposive and theoretical sampling, the point at which new data cease to yield new information or theoretical insights. (6, 13)

scale A composite measure of a concept constructed by combining separate indicators according to procedures designed to ensure unidimensionality or other desirable qualities. (5)

scatterplot A graph plotting the values of two variables for each observation. (12)

secondary analysis Analysis of survey or other data originally collected by another researcher, ordinarily for a different purpose. (8, 10)

selection A threat to internal validity that is present whenever participants are not randomly assigned to experimental conditions. (7)

selective deposit Systematic biases in the content of existing historical data due to actions such as selective destruction or editing of written records. (10)

selective survival Incompleteness of existing historical data due to the fact that some objects survive longer than others. (10)

self-report *See* **verbal report**. (5, 8)

semi-structured interview A type of interview that, while having specific objectives, permits the interviewer some freedom in meeting them. (8, 9)

sequential designs A mixed methods design in which data collection and analysis with one approach precedes data collection and analysis with another approach. (11)

serendipity pattern Unanticipated findings that cannot be interpreted meaningfully in terms of prevailing theories and, therefore, give rise to new theories. (2)

simple random sample A probability sampling design in which every case and every possible combination of cases has an equal chance of being included in the sample. (6)

slope A bivariate regression statistic indicating how much the dependent variable increases (or decreases) for every unit change in the independent variable; the slope of a regression line. Also called *regression coefficient*. (12)

snowball sampling A sampling procedure that uses a process of chain referral, whereby each contact is asked to identify additional members of the target population, who are asked to name others, and so on. (6)

social desirability effect A tendency of respondents to bias answers to self-report measures so as to project socially desirable traits and attitudes. (5)

spurious relationship A noncausal statistical association between two variables produced by a common cause (i.e., an antecedent variable). (4, 7, 12)

standard deviation A measure of variability or dispersion that indicates the average "spread" of observations about the mean. (6, 12)

standard error A statistical measure of the "average" sampling error for a particular sampling distribution, which indicates how much sample results will vary from sample to sample. (6)

standardized regression coefficients Coefficients obtained from a norming operation that puts partial-regression coefficients on common footing by converting them to the same metric of standard deviation units. (12)

statistical significance The likelihood that the results of a study, such as an association between variables, could have occurred by chance. (4, 12)

stratified random sample A probability sampling design in which the population is divided into strata (or variable categories) and independent random samples are drawn from each stratum. (6)

structured interview A type of interview with highly specific objectives in which all questions are written beforehand and asked in the same order for all respondents, and the interviewer's remarks are standardized. (8)

survey Basic approach to social research that involves asking a relatively large sample of people direct questions through interviews or questionnaires. (1, 8, 11)

survey-based experiment An experiment embedded in a survey in which respondents are given different, randomly assigned versions of survey questions. (7)

target population The population to which the researcher would like to generalize his or her results. (6)

taxonomy A system of classification that is usually ordered in some way. (13)

telephone interview A type of interview in which interviewers interact with respondents by telephone. (8)

test of statistical significance A statistical procedure used to assess the likelihood that the results of a study could have occurred by chance. (4, 12)

test-retest reliability The association between repeated applications of an operational definition. (5)

theoretical definition *See* **conceptual definition**. (5)

theoretical sampling A sampling process used in qualitative research in which observations are selected in order to develop aspects of an emerging theory. (6, 13)

theory An interconnected set of propositions that shows how or why something occurs. (2)

threats to internal validity Types of extraneous variables that pose alternative explanations of an experimental outcome, thereby threatening the validity of the experimental manipulation. (7)

tour question *See* **grand tour question**. (9)

trend study A longitudinal design in which a research question is investigated by repeated surveys of independently selected samples of the same population. (8)

triangulation Addressing a research question with multiple methods or measures that do not share the same methodological weaknesses. (11)

truth table A table that presents all possible combinations of values, coded 0 (absent) or 1 (present), for a set of causal variables. (10)

typology A representation of findings based on the cross-classification of two or more concepts, variables, or ideas. (13)

unidimensionality Evidence that a scale or index is measuring only a single dimension of a concept. (5)

units of analysis The entities such as people, nations, and artifacts that are studied, which are described and compared in terms of variables. (4, 10)

univariate analysis The statistical analysis of one variable at a time. (12)

unstructured interview A type of interview guided by broad objectives in which questions are developed as the interview proceeds. (8, 9)

variable A measured concept that may vary across cases or across time. (4)

verbal report An operational definition based on respondents' answers to questions in an interview or questionnaire. Also called *self-report*. (5, 8)

vital statistics Data collected from the registration of "vital" life events, such as births, deaths, marriages, and divorces. (10)

weighting A procedure that corrects for the unequal probability of selecting one or more segments (e.g., strata) of the population. (6)

wild-code checking A data-cleaning procedure involving checking for out-of-range and other "illegal" codes among the values recorded for each variable. (12)

Y-intercept The predicted value of the dependent variable in regression when the independent variable or variables have a value of zero; graphically, the point at which the regression line crosses the Y-axis. (12)

References

Adcock, Robert, and David Collier. 2001. "Measurement Validity: A Shared Standard for Qualitative and Quantitative Research." *American Political Science Review* 95(3):529–46.

Adler, Patricia A., and Peter Adler. 1987. *Membership Roles in Field Research.* Newbury Park, CA: Sage.

Adler, Patricia A., and Peter Adler. 1991. *Backboards & Blackboards: College Athletes and Role Engulfment.* New York: Columbia University Press.

Adler, Patricia A., and Peter Adler. 1998. *Peer Power: Preadolescent Culture and Identity.* New Brunswick, NJ: Rutgers University Press.

Ainlay, Stephen C., Royce A. Singleton, Jr., and Victoria L. Swigert. 1992. "Aging and Religious Participation: Reconsidering the Effects of Health." *Journal for the Scientific Study of Religion* 31(2):175–88.

Alford, Robert R. 1998. *The Craft of Inquiry: Theories, Methods, Evidence.* New York: Oxford University Press.

Allison, Paul D. 2002. *Missing Data.* Thousand Oaks, CA: Sage.

Allport, Gordon. [1954] 1979. *The Nature of Prejudice.* Reading, MA: Addison-Wesley.

American Anthropological Association. 2012. *Statement of Ethics: Principles of Professional Responsibility.* Arlington, VA: American Anthropological Association. Retrieved June 2, 2017 (http://ethics.americananthro.org/category/statement/).

American Association for Public Opinion Research (AAPOR). 2017a. An Evaluation of 2016 Election Polls in the United States. Released May 4, 2017. Retrieved September 6, 2017 (http://www.aapor.org/Education-Resources/Reports/An-Evaluation-of-2016-Election-Polls-in-the-U-S.aspx).

American Association for Public Opinion Research. 2017b. Question Wording. Retrieved July 6, 2017 (http://www.aapor.org/Education-Resources/For-Researchers/Poll-Survey-FAQ/Question-Wording.aspx).

American Political Science Association (APSA). 2012. *A Guide to Professional Ethics in Political Science.* Retrieved June 2, 2017 (http://www.apsanet.org/portals/54/Files/Publications/APSAEthicsGuide2012.pdf).

American Political Science Association. 2013. Senate Delivers a Devastating Blow to the Integrity of the Scientific Process at the National Science Foundation. Retrieved June 3, 2017 (http://www.prnewswire.com/news-releases/senate-delivers-a-devastating-blow-to-the-integrity-of-the-scientific-process-at-the-national-science-foundation-199221111.html).

American Psychological Association (APA). 2017. *Ethical Principles of Psychologists and Code of Conduct.* Washington, DC: APA. Retrieved February 1, 2018 (http://www.apa.org/ethics/code/ethics-code-2017.pdf).

American Psychological Association. 2012. About APA. Retrieved September 24, 2014 (http://www.apa.org/about/index.aspx).

American Sociological Association (ASA). 1999. *Code of Ethics and Policies and Procedures of the ASA Committee on Professional Ethics.* Washington, DC: ASA. Retrieved September 22, 2014 (http://www.asanet.org/images/asa/docs/pdf/CodeofEthics.pdf).

American Sociological Association. 2003. *How Does Your Department Compare? A Peer Analysis from the 2000–2001 Survey of Baccalaureate and Graduate Programs in Sociology.* Washington, DC: American Sociological Association. Retrieved August 13, 2012 (www.asanet.org/images/research/docs/pdf/DepartmentSurveyReportComplete.pdf).

American Sociological Association. 2004. Epstein Elected 97th President of the American Sociological Association; Marriage Amendment Opposed. Press release, June 16. Retrieved February 4, 2014 (http://www.asanet.org/press/20040616.cfm).

American Sociological Association. 2012a. Minutes of ASA Council Meeting. August 21, 2012. Retrieved February 4, 2014 (http://www.asanet.org/documents/asa/pdfs/council_minutes_aug_21_2012.pdf).

American Sociological Association. 2012b. Mission. Retrieved September 24, 2014 (www.asanet.org).

American Sociological Association. 2014. *American Sociological Association Style Guide,* 5th ed. Washington, DC: ASA.

Appelbaum, Lauren D. 2001. "The Influence of Perceived Deservingness on Policy Decisions Regarding Aid to the Poor." *Political Psychology* 22(3):419–42.

Aquilino, William S. 1994. "Interview Mode Effect in Surveys of Drug and Alcohol Use." *Public Opinion Quarterly* 58(2):210–40.

Arthur, Mikaila Mariel Lemonik. 2011. "The Neglected Virtues of Comparative-Historical Methods." Pp. 172–92 in *New Directions in Sociology: Essays on Theory and Methodology in the 21st Century,* edited by I. Zake and M. DeCesare. Jefferson, NC: McFarland and Company.

Babbie, Earl. 2010. *The Practice of Social Research,* 12th ed. Belmont, CA: Wadsworth, Cengage Learning.

Bailey, Carol A. 1996. *A Guide to Field Research.* Thousand Oaks, CA: Pine Forge Press/Sage.

Bailey, Sarah Pulliam. 2016. "White Evangelicals Voted Overwhelmingly for Donald Trump, Exit Polls Show." *The Washington Post,* November 9. Retrieved July 23, 2017 (https://www.washingtonpost.com/news/acts-of-faith/wp/2016/11/09/exit-polls-show-white-evangelicals-voted-overwhelmingly-for-donald-trump/?utm_term=.4dc56444ddbd).

Baker, Reg, et al. 2013. *Report of the AAPOR Task Force on Non-Probability Sampling.* Retrieved September 24, 2014 (http://www.aapor.org/Reports1.htm#.Uld2vbbkARM).

Bakshy, Eytan, Solomon Messing, and Lada A. Adamic. 2015. "Exposure to Ideologically Diverse News and Opinion on Facebook." *Science* 348(June 5):1130–32.

Barrera, Davide, and Brent Simpson. 2012. "Much Ado About Deception: Consequences of Deceiving Research Participants in the Social Sciences." *Sociological Methods and Research* 41(3):383–413.

Barrett, Don. 2012. "Presentation, Politics, and Editing: The Marks/Regnerus Articles." *Social Science Research* 41(6):1354–56.

Baumrind, Diana. 1985. "Research Using Intentional Deception: Ethical Issues Revisited." *American Psychologist* 40(2):165–74.

Becker, Gary. 1964. *Human Capital.* New York: National Bureau of Economic Research.

Becker, Howard S. 1967. "Whose Side Are We On?" *Social Problems* 14(3):239–47.

Becker, Howard S. 2007. *Writing for Social Scientists: How to Start and Finish Your Thesis, Book, or Article,* 2nd ed. Chicago: University of Chicago Press.

Berger, Peter. 1963. *Invitation to Sociology: A Humanistic Perspective.* New York: Doubleday.

Bertrand, Marianne, and Sendhil Mullainathan. 2004. "Are Emily and Greg More Employable than Lakisha and Jamal? A Field Experiment on Labor Market Discrimination?" *American Economic Review* 94(4):991–1013.

Biernacki, Patrick, and Dan Waldorf. 1981. "Snowball Sampling: Problems and Techniques of Chain Referral Sampling." *Sociological Methods and Research* 10(2):141–63.

Blalock, Hubert M., Jr. 1964. *Causal Inferences in Non-experimental Research.* Chapel Hill: University of North Carolina Press.

Blascovich, Jim, and Joseph Tomaka. 1991. "Measures of Self-Esteem." Pp. 115–60 in *Measures of Personality and Social Psychological Attitudes,* edited by J. P. Robinson, P. R. Shaver, and L. S. Wrightsman. San Diego: Academic Press.

Blee, Kathleen M. 1996. "Becoming a Racist: Women in Contemporary Ku Klux Klan and Neo-Nazi Groups." *Gender and Society* 10(6):680–702.

Blee, Kathleen M. 2002. *Inside Organized Racism: Women in the Hate Movement.* Berkeley: University of California Press.

Boas, Franz. 1911. *Handbook of the American Indian Languages.* Washington, DC: Government Printing Office.

Boero, Natalie. 2012. *Killer Fat: Media, Medicine, and Morals in the American "Obesity Epidemic."* New Brunswick, NJ: Rutgers University Press.

Bogdan, Robert, and Steven J. Taylor. 1975. *Introduction to Qualitative Research Methods: A Phenomenological Approach to the Social Sciences.* New York: Wiley.

Boggle, Kathleen A. 2008. *Hooking Up: Sex, Dating, and Relationships on Campus.* New York: New York University Press.

Bogue, Donald J. 1969. *Principles of Demography.* New York: Wiley.

Brewer, John, and Albert Hunter. 1989. *Multimethod Research: A Synthesis of Styles.* Newbury Park, CA: Sage.

Brief of ASA. 2013. Brief of American Sociological Association (ASA) as Amicus Curiae Supporting Respondents, *Hollingsworth et al. v. Perry et al.* and *U.S. v. Windsor* (February 28, 2013) (Nos. 12–144, 12–307).

Brief of Social Science Professors. 2013. Amici Curiae Brief of Social Science Professors in Support of Hollingsworth, *Hollingsworth et al. v. Perry et al.*, and Bipartisan Legal Advisory Group, *U.S. v. Windsor* (January 29, 2013) (Nos. 12–144, 12–307).

Broh, Beckett A. 2002. "Linking Extracurricular Programming and Academic Achievement: Who Benefits and Why?" *Sociology of Education* 75(1):69–91.

Bucerius, Sandra Meike. 2013. "Becoming a "Trusted Outsider": Gender, Ethnicity, and Inequality in Ethnographic Research." *Journal of Contemporary Ethnography* 42(6):690–721.

Bunge, Mario A. 1979. *Causality and Modern Science,* 3rd ed. New York: Dover.

Burawoy, Michael. 2004. "2004 Presidential Address: For Public Sociology." *American Sociological Review* 70(1):4–28.

Calarco, Jessica McCrory. 2011. "'I Need Help!' Social Class and Children's Help-Seeking in Elementary School." *American Sociological Review* 76(6):862–82.

Caldwell, John C. 1986. "Routes to Low Mortality in Poor Countries." *Population and Development Review* 12(2):171–220.

Campbell, John L., Charles Quincy, Jordan Osserman, and Ove K. Pedersen. 2013. "Coding In-Depth Semistructured Interviews: Problems of Unitization and Intercoder Reliability and Agreement." *Sociological Methods & Research* 42(3):294–320.

Campbell, Michael C., and Heather Schoenfeld. 2013. "The Transformation of America's Penal Order: A Historical Political Sociology of Punishment." *American Journal of Sociology* 118(5):1375–423.

Carey, Alex. 1967. "The Hawthorne Studies: A Radical Criticism." *American Sociological Review* 32(3):403–16.

Carmines, Edward C., and Richard A. Zeller. 1979. *Reliability and Validity Assessment.* Beverly Hills, CA: Sage.

Charmaz, Kathy. 1991. *Good Days, Bad Days: The Self in Chronic Illness and Time.* New Brunswick, NJ: Rutgers University Press.

Charmaz, Kathy. 2001. "Grounded Theory." Pp. 335–52 in *Contemporary Field Research: Perspectives and Formulations,* 2nd ed., edited by R. M. Emerson. Prospect Heights, IL: Waveland Press.

Charmaz, Kathy. 2002. "Qualitative Interviewing and Grounded Theory Analysis." Pp. 675–94 in *Handbook of Interview Research: Context and Method,* edited by J. F. Gubrium and J. A. Holstein. Thousand Oaks, CA: Sage.

Charmaz, Kathy. 2006. *Constructing Grounded Theory: A Practical Guide Through Qualitative Analysis.* Thousand Oaks, CA: Sage.

Charmaz, Kathy, and Linda Liska Belgrave. 2012. "Qualitative Interviewing and Grounded Theory Analysis." Pp. 347–66 in *The Sage Handbook of Interview Research: The Complexity of the Craft,* 2nd ed., edited by J. F. Gubrium, J. A. Holstein, A. B. Marvasti, and K. D. McKinney. Los Angeles: Sage.

Cheng, Simon, and Brian Powell. 2015. "Measurement, Methods, and Divergent Patterns: Reassessing the Effects of Same-Sex Parents." *Social Science Research* 52:615–26.

Cherlin, Andrew J., Linda M. Burton, Tera R. Hurt, and Diane M. Purvin. 2004. "The Influence of Physical and Sexual Abuse on Marriage and Cohabitation." *American Sociological Review* 69(6):768–89.

Christenson, Peter, Donald F. Roberts, and Nicholas Bjork. 2012. "Booze, Drugs, and Pop Music: Trends in Substance Portrayals in the Billboard Top 100—1968–2008." *Substance Use and Misuse* 47(2):121–29.

Church, Allan H. 1993. "Estimating the Effect of Incentives on Mail Survey Response Rates: A Meta-Analysis." *Public Opinion Quarterly* 57(1):62–79.

Cialdini, Robert B. 2009. *Influence: Science and Practice*, 5th ed. Boston: Allyn and Bacon.

Cialdini, Robert B., and Noah J. Goldstein. 2004. "Social Influence: Compliance and Conformity." *Annual Review of Psychology* 55:591–621.

Citro, Constance F. 2010. "Legal and Human Subjects Considerations in Surveys." Pp. 59–79 in *Handbook of Survey Research, edited by P. V. Marsden and J. D. Wright*. Bingley, UK: Emerald Group.

Clawson, Dan, and Naomi Gerstel. 2014. *Unequal Time: Gender, Class, and Family in Employment Schedules*. New York: Russell Sage Foundation.

Code of Federal Regulations (CFR). 2009. *Title 45—Public Welfare, Part 46—Protection of Human Subjects*. Office of the Federal Register. Washington, DC: US Government Printing Office.

Cohen, Philip N. 2014. "Regnerus Study Controversy Guide." Family Inequality, August 15. Retrieved February 4, 2014 (http://familyinequality. wordpress.com/2012/08/15/regnerus-study-controversy-guide/).

Coleman, James S. 1988. "Social Capital in the Creation of Human Capital." *American Journal of Sociology* 94(Supplement):S95–S120.

Coleman, James S. 1990. *Foundations of Social Theory*. Cambridge, MA: Belknap Press of Harvard University Press.

Converse, Jean M., and Stanley Presser. 1986. *Survey Questions: Handcrafting the Standardized Questionnaire*. Newbury Park, CA: Sage.

Cook, Karen S., and Toshio Yamagishi. 2008. "A Defense of Deception on Scientific Grounds." *Social Psychology Quarterly* 71(3):215–21.

Cooley, Charles Horton. 1912. *Human Nature and the Social Order*. New York: Charles Scribner's Sons.

Corbin, Juliet, and Anselm Strauss. 2008. *Basics of Qualitative Research*, 3rd ed. Los Angeles: Sage.

Core Institute. 2006. Data from the 2005 CORE and Alcohol Drug Survey. December 2006. Carbondale: Core Institute, Southern Illinois University.

Couper, Mick P. 2011. "The Future of Modes of Data Collection." *Public Opinion Quarterly* 75(5):889–908.

Couper, Mick P., Michael W. Traugott, and Mark J. Lamias. 2001. "Web Survey Design and Administration." *Public Opinion Quarterly* 65(2):230–53.

Curington, Celeste Vaughan, Ken-Hou Lin, and Jennifer Hickes Lundquist. 2015. "Positioning Multiraciality in Cyberspace." *American Sociological Review* 80(4):764–88.

Curtin, Richard, Stanley Presser, and Eleanor Singer. 2005. "Changes in Telephone Survey Nonresponse Over the Past Quarter Century." *Public Opinion Quarterly* 69(1):87–98.

Davis, James A. 1971. *Elementary Survey Analysis*. Englewood Cliffs, NJ: Prentice-Hall.

Davis, James A., and Tom W. Smith. 1992. *The NORC General Social Survey: A User's Guide*. Newbury Park, CA: Sage.

de Leeuw, Edith D. 2005. "To Mix or Not to Mix Data Collection Modes in Surveys." *Journal of Official Statistics* 21(2):233–55.

de Leeuw, Edith W. 2008. "Choosing the Method of Data Collection." Pp. 113–35 in *International Handbook of Survey Methodology*, edited by E. D. de Leeuw, J. J. Hox, and D. A. Dillman. New York: Lawrence Erlbaum.

Demo, David H. 1985. "The Measurement of Self-Esteem: Refining Our Methods." *Journal of Personality and Social Psychology* 48(6):1490–502.

Deutscher, Irwin, Fred P. Pestello, and H. Frances G. Pestello. 1993. *Sentiments and Acts*. New York: Aldine De Gruyter.

Diener, Edward, and Rick Crandall. 1978. *Ethics in Social and Behavioral Research*. Chicago: University of Chicago.

Dillender, Marcus. 2014. "The Death of Marriage? The Effects of New Forms of Legal Recognition on Marriage Rates in the United States." *Demography* 51(2):563–85.

Dillman, Don A. 2007. *Mail and Internet Surveys: The Tailored Design Method*, 2nd ed. New York: Wiley.

Dillman, Don A., Jolene Smyth, and Leah Melani Christian. 2009. *Internet, Mail, and Mixed-Mode Surveys: The Tailored Design Method*, 3rd ed. New York: Wiley.

Dixon, Jeffrey C., and Michael S. Rosenbaum. 2004. "Nice to Know You? Testing Contact, Cultural and Group Threat Theories of Anti-Black and Anti-Hispanic Stereotypes." *Social Science Quarterly* 85(2):257–80.

Dixon, John, and Clyde Tucker. 2010. "Survey Nonresponse." Pp. 593–630 in *Handbook of Survey Research*, 2nd ed., edited by P. V. Marsden and J. D. Wright. Bingley, UK: Emerald Group.

Doyle, Sir Arthur Conan. 1894. *The Memoirs of Sherlock Holmes*. New York: Harper and Brothers.

Duneier, Mitchell. 1999. *Sidewalk*. New York: Farrar, Straus & Giroux.

Durkheim, Émile. [1897] 1951. *Suicide: A Study in Sociology*, translated by John A. Spaulding and George Simpson, edited by George Simpson. New York: Free Press.

Edwards, Mark. 2012. *Writing in Sociology*. Los Angeles: Sage.

Ellison, Nicole B., Charles Steinfield, and Cliff Lampe. 2007. "The Benefits of Facebook 'Friends': Social Capital and College Students' Use of Online Social Network Sites." *Journal of Computer-Mediated Communication* 12(4):1143–68.

Ellison, Nicole B., Jessica Vitak, Rebecca Gray, and Cliff Lampe. 2014. "Cultivating Social Resources on Social Network Sites: Facebook Relationship Maintenance Behaviors and Their Role in Social Capital Processes." *Journal of Computer-Mediated Communication* 19(4):855–70.

Emerson, Robert M., Rachel I. Fretz, and Linda L. Shaw. 2011. *Writing Ethnographic Fieldnotes*, 2nd ed. Chicago: University of Chicago Press.

Erikson, Kai T. 1966. *Wayward Puritans: A Study in the Sociology of Deviance*. New York: Wiley.

Farrell, Henry. 2013. "Blogs, the Conversation: Tom Coburn Doesn't Like Political Science." *The Chronicle of Higher Education* (March 22). Retrieved January 14, 2014 (http://chronicle.com/blogs/conversation/2013/03/22/tom-coburn-doesnt-like-political-science/).

Fausto-Sterling, Anne. 1992. "Why Do We Know So Little About Human Sex?" *Discover* 13(6):28–30.

Fienberg, Stephen E. 1971. "Randomization and Social Affairs: The 1970 Draft Lottery." *Science* 171(January 22):255–61.

Firebaugh, Glenn. 1978. "A Rule for Inferring Individual-Level Relationships from Aggregate Data." *American Sociological Review* 43(4):557–72.

Firebaugh, Glenn. 2008. *Seven Rules for Social Research*. Princeton, NJ: Princeton University Press.

Fischer, Claude. 2009. "The 2004 GSS Finding of Shrunken Networks: An Artifact?" *American Sociological Review* 74(4):657–69.

Fleming, James S., and Barbara E. Courtney. 1984. "The Dimensionality of Self-Esteem: II. Hierarchical Facet Model for Revised Measurement Scales." *Journal of Personality and Social Psychology* 46(2):404–21.

Ford, Thomas E. 1997. "Effects of Stereotypical Television Portrayals of African-Americans on Person Perception." *Social Psychology Quarterly* 60(3):266–78.

Fowler, Floyd J., Jr. 1995. *Improving Survey Questions: Design and Evaluation*. Thousand Oaks, CA: Sage.

Franzosi, Roberto. 1998. "Narrative Analysis—or Why (and How) Sociologists Should Be Interested in Narrative." *Annual Review of Sociology* 24:517–54.

Frey, William H. 2012. New Racial Segregation Measure for Large Metropolitan Areas: Analysis of the 1990–2010 Decennial Censuses. Population Studies Center, University of Michigan. Retrieved January 21, 2013 (http://www.psc.isr.umich.edu/dis/census/segregation2010.html).

Garfinkel, Harold. 1967. *Studies in Ethnomethodology*. Englewood Cliffs, NJ: Prentice-Hall.

Gates, Gary J., et al. 2012. "Letter to the Editors and Advisory Editors of *Social Science Research*." *Social Science Research* 41(6):1350–51.

Gerstel, Naomi, and Dan Clawson. 2014. "Class Advantage and the Gender Divide: Flexibility on the Job and at Home." *American Journal of Sociology* 120(2):395–431.

Gerstel, Naomi, and Dan Clawson. 2015. "Normal Unpredictability and the Chaos in Our Lives." *Contexts* 14(4):64–66.

Gibbs, Graham R. 2007. *Analyzing Qualitative Data*. Los Angeles: Sage.

Gieryn, Thomas. 1999. *Cultural Boundaries of Science: Credibility on the Line*. Chicago: University of Chicago Press.

Glaser, Barney G. 1978. *Theoretical Sensitivity*. Mill Valley, CA: Sociology Press.

Glaser, Barney G., and Anselm L. Strauss. 1967. *The Discovery of Grounded Theory: Strategies for Qualitative Research*. Chicago: Aldine.

Glazer, Myron. [1972] 2009. "Impersonal Sex." Pp. 213–22 in *Tearoom Trade: Impersonal Sex in Public Places*, Enlarged Edition with a Retrospect on Ethical Issues, by Laud Humphreys. New Brunswick, NJ: Aldine Transaction.

Goffman, Erving. 1959. *The Presentation of Self in Everyday Life*. Garden City, NY: Doubleday.

Golder, Scott A., and Michael W. Macy. 2014. "Digital Footprints: Opportunities and Challenges for Online Social Research." *Annual Review of Sociology* 40:129–52.

Gorman, Michele. 2017. "It's Too Easy to Buy Guns, A Majority of Americans Say." *Newsweek*, June 30. Retrieved July 23, 2017 (http://www.newsweek.com/too-easy-buy-guns-united-states-630490).

Grant, Naomi K., Leandre R. Fabrigar, and Heidi Lim. 2010. "Exploring the Efficacy of Compliments as a Tactic for Securing Compliance." *Basic and Applied Social Psychology* 32(3):226–33.

Gray-Little, Bernadette, Valerie S. Williams, and Timothy D. Hancock. 1997. "An Item Response Theory Analysis of the Rosenberg Self-Esteem Scale." *Personality and Social Psychology Bulletin* 23(5):443–51.

Greene, Jennifer C. 2007. *Mixed Methods in Social Inquiry*. San Francisco: Jossey-Bass.

Greene, Jennifer C., Valerie J. Caracelli, and Wendy F. Graham. 1989. "Toward a Conceptual Framework for Mixed-Method Evaluation Designs." *Educational Evaluation and Policy Analysis* 11(3):255–74.

Groves, Robert M. 2006. "Nonresponse Rates and Nonresponse Bias in Household Surveys." *Public Opinion Quarterly* 70(5):646–75.

Groves, Robert M. 2011. "Three Eras of Survey Research." *Public Opinion Quarterly* 75(5):861–71.

Groves, Robert M., and Mick P. Couper. 1998. *Nonresponse in Household Interview Surveys*. New York: Wiley.

Groves, Robert M., Floyd J. Fowler, Jr., Mick P. Couper, James M. Lepkowski, Eleanor Singer, and Roger Tourangeau. 2009. *Survey Methodology*, 2nd ed. New York: Wiley.

Groves, Robert M., Stanley Presser, and Sarah Dipko. 2004. "The Role of Topic Interest in Survey Participation Decisions." *Public Opinion Quarterly* 68(1):2–31.

Guest, Greg, Arwen Bunce, and Laura Johnson. 2006. "How Many Interviews Are Enough? An Experiment with Data Saturation and Variability." *Field Methods* 18(1):59–82.

Guttman, Louis. 1974. "The Basis for Scalogram Analysis." Pp. 142–71 in *Scaling: A Sourcebook for Behavioral Scientists*, edited by G. M. Maranell. Chicago: Aldine.

Gwartney, Patricia A. 2007. *The Telephone Interviewer's Handbook*. San Francisco: Jossey-Bass.

Hadaway, C. Kirk, Penny Long Marler, and Mark Chaves. 1993. "What the Polls Don't Show: A Closer Look at U.S. Church Attendance." *American Sociological Review* 58(6):741–52.

Hagan, John, and Alberto Palloni. 1998. "Immigration and Crime in the United States." Pp. 367–87 in *The Immigration Debate: Studies on the Economic, Demographic, and Fiscal Effects of Immigration*, edited by J. P. Smith and B. Edmonston. Washington, DC: National Academy Press.

Hainmueller, Jens, and Michael J. Hiscox. 2010. "Attitudes Toward Highly Skilled and Low-Skilled Immigration: Evidence from a Survey Experiment." *American Political Science Review* 104(1):61–84.

Hancock, Mark S., and Krista J. Gile. 2011. "Comment: On the Concept of Snowball Sampling." *Sociological Methodology* 41:367–71.

Haney, Craig, W. Curtis Banks, and Philip Zimbardo. 1973. "Interpersonal Dynamics in a Simulated Prison." *International Journal of Criminology and Penology* 1:69–97.

Hart Research Associates. 2015. Falling Short? College Learning and Career Success. Retrieved May 22, 2017 (https://www.aacu.org/sites/default/files/files/LEAP/2015employerstudentsurvey.pdf).

Healy, Kieran. 2000. "Embedded Altruism: Blood Collection Regimes and the European Union's Donor Population." *American Journal of Sociology* 105(6):1633–57.

Henry, P. J. 2008. "College Sophomores in the Laboratory Redux: Influences of a Narrow Data Base on Social Psychology's Views of the Nature of Prejudice." *Psychological Inquiry* 19(2):49–71.

Heritage, John. 2004. "Conversation Analysis and Institutional Talk." Pp. 103–47 in *Handbook of Language and Social Interaction*, edited by K. L. Fitch and R. E. Sanders. Mahwah, NJ: Erlbaum.

Hertwig, Ralph, and Andreas Ortmann. 2008. "Deception in Social Psychological Experiments: Two Misconceptions and a Research Agenda." *Social Psychology Quarterly* 71(3):222–27.

Hofferth, Sandra L., Gregory J. Welk, Margarita S. Treuth, Suzanne M. Randolph, Sally C. Curtin, and Richard Valliant. 2008. "Validation of a Diary Measure of Children's Physical Activities." *Sociological Methodology* 38:133–54.

Holbrook, Allyson L., Melanie C. Green, and Jon A. Krosnick. 2003. "Telephone Versus Face-to-Face Interviewing of National Probability Samples with Long Questionnaires: Comparisons of Respondent Satisficing and Social Desirability Response Bias." *Public Opinion Quarterly* 67(1):79–125.

Holbrook, Allyson L., Jon A. Krosnick, and Alison Pfent. 2008. "The Causes and Consequences of Response Rates in Surveys by News Media and Government Contractor Survey Research Firms." Pp. 499–528 in *Advances in Telephone Survey Methodology*, edited by J. M. Lepkowski et al. New York: Wiley.

Hood, Jane C. 1983. *Becoming a Two-Job Family*. New York: Praeger.

Huang, Chih-Mao, and Denise Park. 2013." Cultural Influences on Facebook Photographs." *International Journal of Psychology* 48(3):334–43.

Hulbert, Ann. 2004. "The Gay Science: What Do We Know About the Effects of Same-Sex Parenting?" *Slate* (March 12). Retrieved January 24, 2014 (http://www.slate.com/articles/life/sandbox/2004/03/the_gay_science.html).

Hume, David [1748] 1951. "An Enquiry Concerning Human Understanding." In *Theory of Knowledge*, edited by D. C. Yalden-Thomson. Edinburgh: Nelson.

Hummon, David M. 1990. *Commonplaces: Community Ideology and Identity in American Culture*. Albany: State University of New York Press.

Humphreys, Laud. [1970] 2009. *Tearoom Trade: Impersonal Sex in Public Places*, Enlarged Edition with a Retrospect on Ethical Issues. Chicago: Aldine Transaction.

Hyman, Herbert H. 1955. *Survey Design and Analysis*. Glencoe, IL: Free Press.

Igo, Sarah E. 2007. *The Averaged American: Surveys, Citizens, and the Making of a Mass Public*. Cambridge, MA: Harvard University Press.

Indeed. 2015. Talent Attraction Study: What Matters to the Modern Candidate. Retrieved August 20, 2017 (http://offers.indeed.com/rs/699-SXJ-715/images/TalentAttractionStudy.pdf).

IPUMS USA. 2017. IPUMS USA. Retrieved July 29, 2017 (https://usa.ipums.org/usa/).

Irvine, Janice. 2012. "Can't Ask, Can't Tell: How Institutional Review Boards Keep Sex in the Closet." *Contexts* 11(2):28–33.

Jaschik, Scott. 2005. "Undercover Freshman." *Inside Higher Ed* (July 13). Retrieved December 16, 2013 (http://www.insidehighered.com/news/2005/07/13/frosh).

Jefferson, Gail. 2004. "Glossary of Transcript Symbols with an Introduction." Pp. 13–23 in *Conversation Analysis: Studies from the First Generation*, edited by G. H. Lerner. Philadelphia: John Benjamins.

Jenkins, J. Craig, Kazimierz M. Slomczynski, and Joshua Kmerulf Dubrow. 2016. "Political Behavior and Big Data." *International Journal of Sociology* 46(1):1–7.

Johnson, Alan G. 1988. *Statistics*. San Diego: Harcourt Brace Jovanovich.

Johnson, Byron, et al. 2012. "Letter to the Editor." *Social Science Research* 41(6):1352–53.

Johnson, John M., and Timothy Rowlands. 2012. "The Interpersonal Dynamics of In-Depth Interviewing." Pp. 99–114 in *The Sage Handbook of Interview Research: The Complexity of the Craft*, 2nd ed., edited by J. F. Gubrium, J. A. Holstein, A. B. Marvasti, and K. D. McKinney. Thousand Oaks, CA: Sage.

Jones, James H. 1981. *Bad Blood: The Scandalous Story of the Tuskegee Experiment—When Government Doctors Played God and Science Went Mad*. New York: Free Press.

Junco, Reynol. 2015. "Student Class Standing, Facebook Use, and Academic Performance." *Journal of Applied Developmental Psychology* 36(January):18–29.

Junco, Reynol, and Shelia Cotten. 2012. "No A 4 U: The Relationship Between Multitasking and Academic Performance." *Computers and Education* 59(2):505–14.

Kalleberg, Arne L. 2000. "Nonstandard Employment Relations: Part-time, Temporary, and Contract Work." *Annual Review of Sociology* 26:341–65.

Kalsbeek, William D., and Robert P. Agans. 2008. "Sampling and Weighting in Household Telephone Surveys." Pp. 29–55 in *Advances in Telephone Survey Methodology*, edited by J. M. Lepkowski et al. New York: Wiley.

Karp, David A. 1996. *Speaking of Sadness: Depression, Disconnection, and the Meanings of Illness.* New York: Oxford University Press.

Karpinski, Aryn C. 2009a. A Description of Facebook Use and Academic Performance Among Undergraduate and Graduate Students. Paper presented at the Annual Meeting of the American Educational Research Association, San Diego.

Karpinski, Aryn C. 2009b. "A Response to Reconciling a Media Sensation with Data." *First Monday* 14(5), 4 May. Retrieved May 21, 2017 (http://www .uic.edu/htbin/cgiwrap/bin/ojs/index.php/fm /article/view/2503/2183).

Karpinski, Aryn C., Paul A. Kirschner, Ipek Ozer, Jennifer A. Mellott, and Pius Ochwo. 2013. "An Exploration of Social Networking Site Use, Multitasking, and Academic Performance Among United States and European University Students." *Computers in Human Behavior* 29(3):1182–92.

Katz, Jay. 1972. *Experimentation with Human Beings: The Authority of the Investigator, Subject, Professions, and State in the Human Experimentation Process.* New York: Russell Sage Foundation.

Katzer, Jeffrey, Kenneth H. Cook, and Wayne W. Crouch. 1998. *Evaluating Information: A Guide for Users of Social Science Research*, 4th ed. New York: McGraw-Hill.

Kearney, Melissa, and Phillip Levine. 2015. "Media Influences on Social Outcomes: The Impact of MTV's *16 and Pregnant* on Teen Childbearing." *American Economic Review* 105(12): 3597–632.

Kelman, Herbert C. 1968. *A Time to Speak: On Human Values and Social Research.* San Francisco: Jossey-Bass.

Kendall, Patricia L. 1986. "Attending an Ivy League College and Success in Later Professional Life." Pp. 394–96 in *The Practice of Social Research*, 4th ed., by Earl Babbie. Belmont, CA: Wadsworth.

Khan, Shamus Rahman. 2011. *Privilege: The Making of an Adolescent Elite at St. Paul's School.* Princeton, NJ: Princeton University Press.

King, Gary, Robert D. Keohane, and Sidney Verba. 1994. *Designing Social Inquiry: Scientific Inference in Qualitative Research.* Princeton, NJ: Princeton University Press.

King, Nigel, and Christine Horrocks. 2010. *Interviews in Qualitative Research.* Thousand Oaks, CA: Sage.

Kinsey, Alfred C., Wardell B. Pomeroy, and Clyde E. Martin. 1948. *Sexual Behavior in the Human Male.* Bloomington: Indiana University Press.

Kinsey, Alfred C., Wardell B. Pomeroy, Clyde E. Martin, and Paul H. Gebhard. 1953. *Sexual Behavior in the Human Female.* Bloomington: Indiana University Press.

Kirschner, Paul A., and Aryn C. Karpinski. 2010. "Facebook® and Academic Performance." *Computers in Human Behavior* 26(6):1237–45.

Kitchin, Rob. 2014. *The Data Revolution: Big Data, Open Data, Data Infrastructures and Their Consequences.* London: Sage.

Kmec, Julie A. 2007. "Ties that Bind? Race and Networks in Job Turnover." *Social Problems* 54(4): 483–503.

Kriner, Douglas L., and Francis X. Shen. 2012. "How Citizens Respond to Combat Casualties: The Differential Impact of Local Casualties on Support for the War in Afghanistan." *Public Opinion Quarterly* 76(4):761–70.

Krippendorff, Klaus. 2004. *Content Analysis: An Introduction to Its Methodology*, 2nd ed. Thousand Oaks, CA: Sage.

Krosnick, Jon A., and Stanley Presser. 2010. "Question and Questionnaire Design." Pp. 263–313 in *Handbook of Survey Research*, 2nd ed., edited by P. V. Marsden and J. D. Wright. Bingley, UK: Emerald Group.

Krueger, Richard A., and Mary Anne Casey. 2015. *Focus Groups: A Practical Guide for Applied Research*, 5th ed. Los Angeles: Sage.

Krumpal, Ivar. 2013. "Determinants of Social Desirability Bias in Sensitive Surveys: A Literature Review." *Quality & Quantity* 47(4):2025–47.

Krupnik, Igor, and Ludger Müller-Willie. 2010. "Franz Boas and Inuktiut Terminology for Ice and Snow: From the Emergence of the Field to the 'Great Eskimo Vocabulary Hoax.'" Pp. 377–400 in *SIKU: Knowing Our Ice*, edited by I. Krupnik et al. Netherlands: Springer.

Krysan, Maria, and Reynolds Farley. 2002. "The Residential Preference of Blacks: Do They Explain Persistent Segregation?" *Social Forces* 80(3):937–80.

Kubrin, Charis E., and Scott A. Desmond. 2015. "The Power of Place Revisited: Why Immigrant Communities Have Lower Levels of Adolescent Violence." *Youth, Violence and Juvenile Justice* 13(4):345–66.

Kuhn, Thomas. 1970. *The Nature of Scientific Revolutions,* 2nd ed. Chicago: University of Chicago Press.

Labov, William. 1972. *Language in the Inner City.* Philadelphia: University of Pennsylvania Press.

Lane, David M. 2014. Logic of Hypothesis Testing. Introduction. Online Statistics Education: An Interactive Multimedia Course of Study. Retrieved March 5, 2014 (http://onlinestatbook.com/2/logic_of_hypothesis_testing/intro.html).

Lange, Matthew. 2013. *Comparative-Historical Methods.* London: Sage.

Lannutti, Pamela J., and Kenneth A. Lachlan. 2007. "Assessing Attitude Toward Same-Sex Marriage: Scale Development and Validation." *Journal of Homosexuality* 53(4):113–33.

Lareau, Annette. 2011. *Unequal Childhoods: Class, Race, and Family Life,* 2nd ed. Berkeley: University of California Press.

Laumann, Edward O., John H. Gagnon, Robert T. Michael, and Stuart Michaels. 1994. *The Social Organization of Sexuality: Sexual Practices in the United States.* Chicago: University of Chicago.

Lavrakas, Paul J. 2010. "Telephone Surveys." Pp. 471–98 in *Handbook of Survey Research,* 2nd ed., edited by P. V. Marsden and J. D. Wright. Bingley, UK: Emerald Group.

Lazarsfeld, Paul F., Bernard Berelson, and Hazel Gaudet. 1948. *The People's Choice.* New York: Columbia University Press.

Lazer, David, and Jason Radford. 2017. "Data ex Machina: Introduction to Big Data." *Annual Review of Sociology* 43:19–39.

Leahey, Erin. 2007. "Convergence and Confidentiality? Limits to the Interpretation of Mixed Methodology." *Social Science Research* 36(1):149–58.

Leavitt, Fred. 2001. *Evaluating Scientific Research: Separating Fact from Fiction.* Long Grove, IL: Waveland Press.

Lee, Yun-Suk, and Linda J. Waite. 2005. "Husbands' and Wives' Time Spent on Housework." *Journal of Marriage and the Family* 67(2):328–36.

Legewie, Joscha. 2016. "Racial Profiling and Use of Force in Police Stops: How Local Events Trigger Periods of Increased Discrimination." *American Journal of Sociology* 122(2):379–424.

Lever, Janet, and Stan Wheeler. 1984. "The Chicago Tribune Sports Page, 1900–1975." *Sociology of Sport Journal* 1(4):299–313.

Lewis, Kevin. 2015. "Three Fallacies of Digital Footprints." *Big Data and Society* 2 (July–December):1–4.

Lewis, Kevin, Jason Kaufman, Marco Gonzalez, Andreas Wimmer, and Nicholas Christakis. 2008. "Tastes, Ties, and Time: A New Social Network Dataset Using Facebook.com." *Social Networks* 30(4):330–42.

Lieberman, Evan S. 2005. "Nested Analysis as a Mixed-Method Strategy for Comparative Research." *American Political Science Review* 99(3):435–52.

Lieberson, Stanley. 1985. *Making it Count: The Improvement of Social Research and Theory.* Berkeley and Los Angeles: University of California Press.

Lincoln, Yvonna S., and Egon G. Guba. 1985. *Naturalistic Inquiry.* Beverly Hills, CA: Sage.

Lindner, Andrew M. 2009. "Among the Troops: Seeing the Iraq War Through Three Journalistic Vantage Points." *Social Problems* 56(1):21–48.

Lindsay, D. Michael. 2008. "Evangelicals in the Power Elite: Elite Cohesion Advancing a Movement." *American Sociological Review* 73(1):60–82.

Lofland, John, and Lyn H. Lofland. 1995. *Analyzing Social Settings: A Guide to Qualitative Observation and Analysis,* 3rd ed. Belmont, CA: Wadsworth.

Lofland, John, David Snow, Leon Anderson, and Lyn H. Lofland. 2006. *Analyzing Social Settings: A Guide to Qualitative Observation and Analysis,* 4th ed. Belmont, CA: Wadsworth/Thompson Learning.

Lofland, Lyn H. 1971. *A World of Strangers: Order and Action in Urban Public Space.* PhD Diss., University of California, San Francisco.

Lofland, Lyn H. 1973. *A World of Strangers: Order and Action in Urban Public Space.* New York: Basic Books.

Logan, John R., and Brian Stults. 2011. The Persistence of Segregation in the Metropolis: New Findings from the 2010 Census. Census Brief prepared for Project US2010. Retrieved January 21, 2013 (http://www.s4.brown.edu/us2010/Data/Report/report2.pdf).

Lucas, Jeffrey W., Corina Graif, and Michael J. Lovaglia. 2006. "Misconduct in the Prosecution of Severe Crimes: Theory and Experimental Test." *Social Psychology Quarterly* 69(1):97–107.

Mahoney, James. 2000. "Strategies of Causal Inference in Small-N Analysis." *Sociological Methods and Research* 28(4):387–424.

Mahoney, James. 2004. "Comparative-Historical Methodology." *Annual Review of Sociology* 30:81–101.

Mahoney, James, and Dietrich Rueschemeyer. 2003. "Comparative Historical Analysis: Achievements and Agendas." Pp. 3–38 in *Comparative Historical Analysis in the Social Sciences,* edited by J. Mahoney and D. Rueschemeyer. Cambridge, UK: Cambridge University Press.

Malamuth, Neil M., and Barry Spinner. 1980. "A Longitudinal Content Analysis of Sexual Violence in the Best Selling Erotic Magazines." *Journal of Sex Research* 16(3):226–37.

Manfreda, Katja Lozar, and Vasja Vehovar. 2008. "Internet Surveys." Pp. 264–84 in *International Handbook of Survey Methodology,* edited by E. D. de Leeuw, J. J. Hox, and D. A. Dillman. New York: Lawrence Erlbaum.

Mark, Melvin M. 2015. "Mixed and Multimethods in Predominantly Quantitative Studies, Especially Experiments and Quasi-Experiments." Pp. 21–41 in *The Oxford Handbook of Multimethod and Mixed Methods Research Inquiry,* edited by S. Hesse-Baber and R. B. Johnson. New York: Oxford University Press.

Mark, Melvin M., and R. Lance Shotland. 1987. "Alternative Models for the Use of Multiple Methods." Pp. 95–100 in *Multiple Methods in Program Evaluation,* edited by M. M. Mark and R. L. Shotland. San Francisco: Jossey-Bass.

Marklien, Mary Beth. 2005. "Professor Explores Her College." *USA Today* (August 22). Retrieved December 16, 2013 (http://usatoday30.usatoday.com/life/books/news/2005–08–22-freshman-year_x.htm).

Marr, Bernard. 2017. "The Complete Beginner's Guide to Big Data in 2017." *Forbes* (March 14). Retrieved August 11, 2017 (https://www.forbes.com/sites/bernardmarr/2017/03/14/the-complete-beginners-guide-to-big-data-in-2017/#49cc6bc17365).

Marshall, Martin N. 1996. "Sampling for Qualitative Research." *Family Practice* 13(6):522–25.

Martinez, Ramiro, Jr., and Matthew T. Lee. 2000. "On Immigration and Crime." Pp. 485–524 in *Criminal Justice 2000. The Nature of Crime: Continuity and Change,* Vol. 1, edited by G. LaFree. Washington, DC: US Department of Justice, Office of Justice Programs, National Institute of Justice.

Massey, Douglas S. 2012. "Comment." *Social Science Research* 41(6):1378.

Maynard, Douglas W., and Steven E. Clayman. 1991. "The Diversity of Ethnomethodology." *Annual Review of Sociology* 17:385–418.

McArthur, Leslie Zebrowitz, and Beth Gabrielle Resko. 1975. "The Portrayal of Men and Women in American Television Commercials." *Journal of Social Psychology* 97(2):209–20.

McCarthy, Justin. 2017. "US Support for Gay Marriage Edges to New High." Gallup: Politics, May 15. Retrieved July 23, 2017 (http://www.gallup.com/poll/210566/support-gay-marriage-edges-new-high.aspx).

McFarland, Daniel A., Kevin Lewis, and Amir Goldberg. 2016. "Sociology in the Era of Big Data: The Ascent of Forensic Social Science." *American Sociologist* 47(1):12–35.

McGonagle, Katherine A., Robert F. Schoeni, Narayan Sastry, and Vicki A. Freedman. 2012. "The Panel Study of Income Dynamics: Overview, Recent Innovations, and Potential for Life Course Research." *Longitudinal and Life Course Studies* 3(2):268–84.

McKinney, John C. 1966. *Constructive Typology and Social Theory.* New York: Appleton-Century-Crofts.

McKnight, Patrick E., Katherine M. McKnight, Souraya Sidani, and Aurelio Jose Figueredo. 2007. *Missing Data: A Gentle Introduction.* New York: Guilford.

McPherson, Miller, Lynn Smith-Lovin, and Matthew Brashears. 2006. "Social Isolation in America: Changes in Core Discussion Networks over Two Decades." *American Sociological Review* 71(3):353–75.

McPherson, Miller, Lynn Smith-Lovin, and Matthew Brashears. 2008. "ERRATA: Social Isolation in America: Changes in Core Discussion Networks over Two Decades." *American Sociological Review* 73(6):1022.

McPherson, Miller, Lynn Smith-Lovin, and Matthew Brashears. 2009. "Models and Marginals: Using Survey Evidence to Study Social Networks." *American Sociological Review* 74(4):670–81.

Mead, George Herbert. 1934. *Mind, Self, and Society.* Chicago: University of Chicago Press.

Merton, Robert K. 1972. "Insiders and Outsiders: A Chapter in the Sociology of Knowledge." *American Journal of Sociology* 78(1):9–47.

Merton, Robert K. 1996. *On Social Structure and Science.* Chicago: University of Chicago Press.

Mervis, Jeffrey. 2013. "Congress Limits NSF Funding for Political Science." *Science* 339 (March 29):1510–11.

Michael, Robert T., John H. Gagnon, Edward O. Laumann, and Gina Kolata. 1994. *Sex in America: A Definitive Survey.* Boston: Little, Brown.

Miles, Matthew B., and A. Michael Huberman. 1994. *Qualitative Data Analysis: An Expanded Sourcebook,* 2nd ed. Thousand Oaks, CA: Sage.

Miles, Matthew B., A. Michael Huberman, and Johnny Saldaña. 2014. *Qualitative Data Analysis: An Expanded Sourcebook,* 3rd ed. Thousand Oaks, CA: Sage.

Milgram, Stanley. 1974. *Obedience to Authority: An Experimental View.* New York: Harper and Row.

Moore, Mignon. 2011. *Invisible Families: Gay Identities, Relationships and Motherhood Among Black Women.* Berkeley: University of California Press.

Morgan, David L. 1996. "Focus Groups." *Annual Review of Sociology* 22:129–52.

Morgan, David L. 2012. "Focus Groups and Social Interaction." Pp. 161–76 in *The Sage Handbook of Interview Research: The Complexity of the Craft,* 2nd ed., edited by J. F. Gubrium, J. A. Holstein, A. B. Marvasti, and K. D. McKinney. Thousand Oaks, CA: Sage.

Morris, John B. 2016. "First Look: Internet Use in 2015." National Telecommunications & Information Administration, March 21. Retrieved July 23, 2017 (https://www.ntia.doc.gov/blog/2016/first-look-internet-use-2015).

Murdock, George P. 1967. "Ethnographic Atlas: A Summary." *Ethnology* 6(2):109–236.

Murdock, George P., and Douglas R. White. 1969. "Standard Cross-Cultural Sample." *Ethnology* 8(4):329–69.

Nathan, Rebekah. 2005. *My Freshman Year: What a Professor Learned by Becoming a Student.* Ithaca, NY: Cornell University Press.

National Commission for the Protection of Human Subjects of Biomedical and Behavioral Research. 1979. *The Belmont Report.* Retrieved January 24, 2014 (http://www.hhs.gov/ohrp/humansubjects/guidance/belmont. html).

National Opinion Research Center (NORC). 2013. *GSS General Social Survey.* Retrieved July 23, 2017 (http://www.norc.org/Research/Projects/Pages/general-social-survey.aspx).

National Research Council. 2014. *Proposed Revisions to the Common Rule for the Protection of Human Subjects in the Behavioral and Social Sciences.* Washington, DC: The National Academies Press.

National Science Foundation (NSF). 2013. FY 2018 Budget Request to Congress, Directorate for Social, Behavioral, and Economic Sciences (SBE). Retrieved June 1, 2017 (https://www.nsf.gov/about/budget/fy2018/pdf/24_fy2018.pdf).

Neuendorf, Kimberly A. 2002. *A Content Analysis Guidebook.* Thousand Oaks, CA: Sage.

Neuendorf, Kimberly A. 2011. "Content Analysis—A Methodological Primer for Gender Research." *Sex Roles* 64(3-4):276–89.

Owens, Timothy J. 1993. "Accentuate the Positive—and the Negative: Rethinking the Use of Self-Esteem, Self-Deprecation, and Self-Confidence." *Social Psychology Quarterly* 56(4):288–99.

Owens, Timothy J. 1994. "Two Dimensions of Self-Esteem: Reciprocal Effects of Positive Self-Worth and Self-Deprecation on Adolescent Problems." *American Sociological Review* 59(3):391–407.

Pager, Devah. 2003. "The Mark of a Criminal Record." *American Journal of Sociology* 108(5):937–75.

Pager, Devah, and Lincoln Quillian. 2005. "Walking the Talk? What Employers Say Versus What They Do." *American Sociological Review* 70(3):355–80.

Pager, Devah, Bruce Western, and Bart Bonikowski. 2009. "Discrimination in a Low Wage Labor Market: A Field Experiment." *American Sociological Review* 74(5):777–99.

Pager, Devah, Bruce Western, and Naomi Sugie. 2009. "Sequencing Disadvantage: Barriers to Employment Facing Young Black and White Men with Criminal Records." *Annals of the American Academy of Political and Social Sciences* 623(1):195–213.

Paik, Anthony, and Kenneth Sanchagrin. 2013. "Social Isolation in America: An Artifact." *American Sociological Review* 78(3):339–60.

Palys, Ted, and John Lowman. 2002. "Anticipating Law: Research Methods, Ethics, and the Law of Privilege." *Sociological Methodology* 32:1–17.

Paschall, Mallie J., and Bridget Freisthler. 2003. "Does Heavy Drinking Affect Academic Performance in College? Findings from a Prospective Study of High Achievers." *Journal of Studies on Alcohol* 64(4):515–19.

Pasek, Josh, eian more, and Eszter Hargittai. 2009a. "Facebook and Academic Performance: Reconciling a Media Sensation with Data." *First Monday* 14(5), 4 May. Retrieved May 22, 2017 (http://www.uic.edu/htbin/cgiwrap/bin/ojs/index.php/fm/article/view/2498/2181).

Pasek, Josh, eian more, and Eszter Hargittai. 2009b. "Some Clarifications on the Facebook-GPA Study and Karpinski's Response." *First Monday* 14(5), 4 May. Retrieved May 22, 2017 (http://www.uic.edu/htbin/cgiwrap/bin/ojs/index.php/fm/article/view/2504/2187).

Patterson, Wendy. 2008. "Narratives of Events: Labovian Narrative Analysis and Its Limitations." Pp. 22–40 in *Doing Narrative Research*, edited by M. Andrews, C. Squire, and M. Tamboukou. London: Sage.

Paxton, Pamela. 2000. "Women's Suffrage in the Measurement of Democracy: Problems of Operationalization." *Studies in Comparative International Development* 35(3):92–111.

Pearce, Lisa D. 2002. "Integrating Survey and Ethnographic Methods for Systematic Anomalous Case Analysis." *Sociological Methodology* 32(1):103–132.

Pearce, Lisa D. 2012. "Mixed Methods Inquiry in Sociology." *American Behavioral Scientist* 56(6):829–48.

Pearl, Judea. 2010. "The Foundations of Causal Inference." *Sociological Methodology* 40:75–149.

Pearson, Willie, Jr., and Lewellyn Hendrix. 1979. "Divorce and the Status of Women." *Journal of Marriage and the Family* 41(2):375–85.

Perrin, Andrew J., Philip N. Cohen, and Neal Caren. 2013. "Responding to the Regnerus Study: Are Children of Parents Who Had Same-Sex Relationships Disadvantaged? A Scientific Evaluation of the No-Differences Hypothesis." *Journal of Gay & Lesbian Mental Health* 17(3):327–36.

Pescosolido, Bernice A. 1990. "The Social Context of Religious Integration and Suicide: Pursuing the Network Explanation." *Sociological Quarterly* 31(3):337–57.

Pescosolido, Bernice A., and Sharon Georgianna. 1989. "Durkheim, Suicide, and Religion: Toward a Network Theory of Suicide." *American Sociological Review* 54(1):33–48.

Pescosolido, Bernice A., Elizabeth Grauerholz, and Melissa A. Milkie. 1997. "The Portrayal of Blacks in U.S. Children's Picture Books Through the Mid- and Late-Twentieth Century." *American Sociological Review* 62(3):443–64.

Phillips, David P., Todd E. Ruth, and Sean MacNamara. 1994. "There Are More Things in Heaven and Earth: Missing Features in Durkheim's Theory of Suicide." Pp. 90–100 in *Emile Durkheim: Le Suicide One Hundred Years Later*, edited by David Lester. Philadelphia: Charles Press.

Pielke, Roger A. Jr. 2007. *The Honest Broker: Making Sense of Science in Policy and Politics.* New York: Cambridge University Press.

Pierce, Albert. 1967. "The Economic Cycle and the Social Suicide Rate." *American Sociological Review* 32(3):457–62.

Pocock, Sharon. 2006. Book Review of *My Freshman Year: What a Professor Learned by Becoming a Student. Perspectives: Teaching Legal Research and Writing* 14(3):169–71.

Popper, Karl R. [1959] 1992. *The Logic of Scientific Discovery.* London: Routledge.

Portes, Alejandro. 1998. "Social Capital: Its Origins and Applications in Modern Sociology." *Annual Review of Sociology* 24:1–24.

Powell, Brian. 2003. *Constructing the Family Survey 2003.* Bloomington: Indiana University Center for Social Research.

Powell, Brian, Catherine Bolzendahl, Claudia Geist, and Lala Carr Steelman. 2010. *Counted Out: Same-Sex Relations and Americans' Definitions of Family.* New York: Russell Sage Foundation.

Presley, Cheryl A., and Edgardo R. Pimentel. 2006. "The Introduction of the Heavy and Frequent Drinker: A Proposed Classification to Increase Accuracy of Alcohol Assessments in Postsecondary Educational Settings." *Journal of Studies on Alcohol* 67(2):324–31.

Prewitt, Kenneth. 2013. "Is Any Science Safe?" *Science* 340(May 3):525.

Putnam, Robert. 2000. *Bowling Alone: The Collapse and Revival of American Community.* New York: Simon and Schuster.

Ragin, Charles C. 1987. *The Comparative Method: Moving Beyond Qualitative and Quantitative Strategies.* Berkeley: University of California Press.

Ragin, Charles C. 2000. *Fuzzy-Set Social Science.* Chicago: University of Chicago Press.

Ragin, Charles C. 2006. "How to Lure Analytic Social Science Out of the Doldrums: Some Lessons from Comparative Research." *International Sociology* 21(5):633–46.

Ragin, Charles C. 2008. *Redesigning Social Inquiry: Fuzzy Sets and Beyond.* Chicago: University of Chicago Press.

Ragin, Charles C., and Lisa M. Amoroso. 2011. *Constructing Social Research: The Unity and Diversity of Method,* 2nd ed. Los Angeles: Sage/Pine Forge.

Rapley, Tim. 2007. *Doing Conversation, Discourse and Document Analysis.* Los Angeles: Sage.

Rathje, William, and Cullen Murphy. 1992a. "Garbage Demographics." *American Demographics* 14(5): 50–54.

Rathje, William, and Cullen Murphy. 1992b. *Rubbish! The Archaeology of Garbage.* New York: HarperCollins.

Redding, Richard E. 2013. "Politicized Science." *Society* 50(5):439–46.

Regnerus, Mark. 2012a. "How Different Are the Adult Children of Parents Who Have Same-Sex Relationships? Findings from the New Family Structures Study." *Social Science Research* 41(4):752–70.

Regnerus, Mark. 2012b. "Parental Same-Sex Relationships, Family Instability, and Subsequent Life Outcomes for Adult Children: Answering Critics of the New Family Structures Study with Additional Analyses." *Social Science Research* 41(6):1367–77.

Regnerus, Mark. 2012c. "Queers as Folk: Does It Really Make No Difference If Your Parents Are Straight or Gay?" *Slate,* June 11. Retrieved February 6, 2014 (http://www.slate.com/articles/double_x/doublex/2012/06/gay_parents_are_they_really_no_different_.html).

Resnick, Sofia. 2013. "New Family Structures Study Intended to Sway Supreme Court on Gay Marriage, Documents Show." *Huffington Post.* Retrieved February 3, 2014 (http://www.huffingtonpost.com/2013/03/10/supreme-court-gay-marriage_n_2850302.html).

Reynolds, William M. 1988. "Measurement of Academic Self-Concept in College Students." *Journal of Personality Assessment* 52(2):223–40.

Riessman, Catherine Kohler. 2012. "Analysis of Personal Narratives." Pp. 367–79 in *The Sage Handbook of Interview Research: The Complexity of the Craft,* 2nd ed., edited by J. F. Gubrium, J. A. Holstein, A. B. Marvasti, and K. D. McKinney. Los Angeles: Sage.

Robinson, John P., and Geoffrey Godbey. 1997. *Time for Life: The Surprising Ways Americans Use Their Time.* University Park: Pennsylvania State University.

Robinson, W. S. 1950. "Ecological Correlations and the Behavior of Individuals." *American Sociological Review* 15(3):351–57.

Robson, David. 2013. "There Really Are 50 Eskimo Words for 'Snow.'" *Washington Post,* January 14. Retrieved September 26, 2014 (http://articles.washingtonpost.com/2013-01-14/national/36344037_1_eskimo-words-snow-inuit).

Roethlisberger, Fritz J., and William J. Dickson. 1939. *Management and the Worker: An Account of a Research Program Conducted by the Western Electric Co. Hawthorne Works, Chicago.* Cambridge, MA: Harvard University Press.

Rosen, Leonard J., and Laurence Behrens. 1992. *The Allyn & Bacon Handbook.* Boston: Allyn and Bacon.

Rosenberg, Milton J. 1979. *Conceiving the Self.* New York: Basic Books.

Rosenberg, Morris. 1965. *Society and the Adolescent Self-Image.* Princeton, NJ: Princeton University Press.

Rosenberg, Morris. 1968. *The Logic of Survey Analysis.* New York: Basic Books.

Rosenfeld, Michael J. 2015. "Revisiting the Data from the New Family Structure Study: Taking Family Instability into Account." *Sociological Science* 2: 478–501.

Rossman, Gretchen, and Sharon F. Rallis. 2003. *Learning in the Field: An Introduction to Qualitative Research.* Thousand Oaks, CA: Sage.

Roth, Wendy D. 2010. "Racial Mismatch: The Divergence Between Form and Function in Data for Monitoring Racial Discrimination of Hispanics." *Social Science Quarterly* 91(5):1288–311.

Rowe, Ian. 2015. "Civility 2.0: A Comparative Analysis of Incivility in Online Political Discussion." *Information, Communication & Society* 18(2):121–38.

Rubin, Herbert J., and Irene S. Rubin. 2012. *Qualitative Interviewing: The Art of Hearing Data,* 3rd ed. Los Angeles: Sage.

Rubin, Zick. 1970. "Measurement of Romantic Love." *Journal of Personality and Social Psychology* 16(2):265–73.

Rueschemeyer, Dietrich, and John Stephens. 1997. "Comparing Social Historical Sequences: A Powerful Tool for Causal Analysis." *Comparative Social Research* 17:55–72.

Rydell, Robert J., Allen R. McConnell, and Sian L. Beilock. 2009. "Multiple Social Identities and Stereotype Threat: Imbalance, Accessibility, and Working Memory." *Journal of Personality and Social Psychology* 96(5):949–66.

Sacks, Harvey, Emanuel A. Schegloff, and Gail Jefferson. 1974. "A Simplest Systematics for the Organization of Turn-Taking for Conversation." *Language* 50(4):696–735.

Saldaña, Johnny. 2011. *Fundamentals of Qualitative Research: Understanding Qualitative Research.* New York: Oxford University Press.

Saldaña, Johnny. 2013. *The Coding Manual for Qualitative Researchers,* 2nd ed. Thousand Oaks, CA: Sage.

Salt-N-Pepa. 1991. "Let's Talk About Sex." *Blacks' Magic.* New Plateaus Records, August 27.

Savin-Williams, Ritch C. and Gail A. Jaquish. 1981. "The Assessment of Adolescent Self-Esteem: A Comparison of Methods." *Journal of Personality* 49(3):324–36.

Scarce, Rik. 1999. "Good Faith, Bad Ethics: When Scholars Go the Distance and Scholarly Associations Do Not." *Law and Social Inquiry* 24(4):977–86.

Scarce, Rik. 2005. "A Law to Protect Scholars." *Chronicle of Higher Education* 51(August 12):B24–B25.

Schemo, Diana Jean. 2006. "What a Professor Learned as an Undercover Freshman." *New York Times,* August 23. Retrieved December 16, 2013 (http://www.nytimes.com/2006/08/23/education/23FACE.html?pagewanted=all).

Schmader, Toni, Jessica Whitehead, and Vicki H. Wysocki. 2007. "A Linguistic Comparison of Letters of Recommendation for Male and Female Chemistry and Biochemistry Job Applicants." *Sex Roles* 57(7-8):509–14.

Schuman, Howard, and Graham Kalton. 1985. "Survey Methods." Pp. 635–97 in *Handbook of Social Psychology,* 3rd ed., vol. 1, edited by G. Lindzey and E. Aronson. New York: Random House.

Schumm, Walter R. 2012. "Methodological Decisions and the Evaluation of Possible Effects of Different Family Structures on Children: The New Family Structures Survey (NFSS)." *Social Science Research* 41(6):1357–66.

Schwartz, Howard, and Jerry Jacobs. 1979. *Qualitative Sociology: A Method to the Madness.* New York: Free Press.

Schwartz-Shea, Peregrine, and Dvora Yanow. 2012. *Interpretive Research Design: Concepts and Processes.* New York: Routledge.

Sears, David O. 1986. "College Sophomores in the Laboratory: Influences of a Narrow Data Base on Social Psychology's View of Human Nature." *Journal of Personality and Social Psychology* 51(3):515–30.

Sell, Jane. 2008. "Introduction to Deception Debate." *Social Psychology Quarterly* 71(3):213–14.

Shamoo, Adil E., and David B. Resnik. 2009. *Responsible Conduct of Research*, 2nd ed. New York: Oxford University Press.

Shaver, James P. 1993. "What Statistical Significance Testing Is, and What It Is Not." *Journal of Experimental Education* 61(4):293–316.

Shelton, Ashleigh K., and Paul Skalski. 2014. "Blinded by the Light: Illuminating the Dark Side of Social Network Use Through Content Analysis." *Computers in Human Behavior* 33(April):339–48.

Sherkat, Darren E. 2012. "The Editorial Process and Politicized Scholarship: Monday Morning Editorial Quarterbacking and a Call for Scientific Vigilance." *Social Science Research* 41(6):1346–49.

Shih, Tse-Hua, and Xitao Fan. 2008. "Comparing Response Rates from Web and Mail Surveys: A Meta-Analysis." *Field Methods* 20(3):249–71.

Silver, Howard J. 2006. "Science and Politics: The Uneasy Relationship." *Open Spaces.* Retrieved January 24, 2014 (http://open-spaces.com/article-v8n1-silver.pdf).

Simmel, Georg. 1972. *On Individuality and Social Forms*, edited by Donald N. Levine. Chicago: University of Chicago Press.

Simon, Julian L., and Paul Burstein. 1985. *Basic Research Methods in Social Science: The Art of Empirical Investigation,* 3rd ed. New York: Random House.

Singer, Eleanor. 2002. "The Use of Incentives to Reduce Nonresponse in Household Surveys." Pp. 163–77 in *Survey Nonresponse,* edited by R. M. Groves et al. New York: Wiley.

Singleton, Royce, Jr. 1969. An Empirical Study of Selective Exposure and Selective Perception Relative to Television Programs with Negro Stars. Master's thesis, Oklahoma State University. Stillwater, OK.

Singleton, Royce A., Jr. 1998. Is Sociology a Science? A Classroom Exercise for Promoting Discussion. Presented at the Annual Meetings of the American Sociological Association, San Francisco.

Singleton, Royce A., Jr. 2007. "Collegiate Alcohol Consumption and Academic Performance." *Journal of Studies on Alcohol and Drugs* 68(4):548–55.

Singleton, Royce A., Jr., and Bruce C. Straits. 2018. *Approaches to Social Research, 6th ed.* New York: Oxford University Press.

Sjoberg, Gideon. 1967. "Introduction." Pp. xi–xvii in *Ethics, Politics, and Social Research,* edited by G. Sjoberg. Cambridge, MA: Schenkman.

Sjoberg, Gideon, Norma Williams, Ted R. Vaughan, and Andree F. Sjoberg. 1991. "The Case Study Approach in Social Research: Basic Methodological Issues." Pp. 27–79 in *A Case for the Case Study,* edited by J. R. Feagin, A. M. Orum, and G. Sjoberg. Chapel Hill: University of North Carolina Press.

Skocpol, Theda. 2003. "Double Engaged Social Science: The Promise of Comparative Historical Analysis." Pp. 407–28 in *Comparative Historical Analysis in the Social Sciences,* edited by J. Mahoney and D. Rueschemeyer. Cambridge, UK: Cambridge University Press.

Small, Mario Luis. 2011. "How to Conduct a Mixed Methods Study: Recent Trends in a Rapidly Growing Literature." *Annual Review of Sociology* 37:57–86.

Smith, Christian. 2012. "An Academic Auto-da-fé." *The Chronicle of Higher Education,* July 23. Retrieved February 6, 2014 (https://chronicle.com/article/An-Academic-Auto-da-F-/133107/).

Smith, Oliver. 2016. "Mapped: The 58 Countries That Still Have the Death Penalty." *The Telegraph,* Travel|Maps and Graphics section. Retrieved September 5, 2017 (http://www.telegraph.co.uk/travel/maps-and-graphics/countries-that-still-have-the-death-penalty/).

Smith, Robert Courtney. 2006. *Mexican New York: Transnational Lives of New Immigrants.* Berkeley: University of California Press.

Smith, Robert Courtney. 2014. "Black Mexicans, Conjunctural Ethnicity, and Operating Identities: Long-Term Ethnographic Analysis." *American Sociological Review* 79(3):517–48.

Smith, Tom W. 1987. "That Which We Call Welfare by Any Other Name Would Smell Sweeter: An Analysis of the Impact of Question Wording on Response Patterns." *Public Opinion Quarterly* 51(1):75–83.

Smith, Tom W., Michael Davern, Jeremy Freese, and Michael Hout,. 2017. *General Social Surveys, 1972–2016: Cumulative Codebook [machine-readable data file].* Principal Investigator, Tom W. Smith, Co-Principal Investigators, Peter V. Marsden and Michael Hout, NORC ed. Chicago: National Opinion Research Center. 1 data file (62,466 logical records) and 1 codebook (3,689 pp).

Sniderman, Paul M., and Douglas B. Grob. 1996. "Innovations in Experimental Design in Attitude Surveys." *Annual Review of Sociology* 22:377–99.

Sniderman, Paul M., Louk Hagendoorn, and Markus Prior. 2004. "Predisposing Factors and Situational Triggers: Exclusionary Reactions to Immigrant Minorities." *American Political Science Review* 98(1):35–49.

Snow, David A., and Leon Anderson. 1987. "Identity Work Among the Homeless: The Verbal Construction and Avowal of Personal Identities." *American Journal of Sociology* 92(6):1336–71.

Snow, David A., and Leon Anderson. 1991. "Researching the Homeless: The Characteristic Features and Virtues of the Case Study." Pp. 148–73 in *A Case for the Case Study*, edited by J. R. Feagin, A. M. Orum, and G. Sjoberg. Chapel Hill: University of North Carolina Press.

Snow, David A., and Leon Anderson. 1993. *Down on Their Luck: A Study of Homeless Street People.* Berkeley: University of California Press.

Snow, David A., Robert D. Benford, and Leon Anderson. 1986. "Fieldwork Roles and Information Yield: A Comparison of Alternative Settings and Roles." *Urban Life* 14(4):377–408.

Sorokin, Pitirim. 1937. *Social and Cultural Dynamics*, vol. II. New York: American Book Company.

Spencer, Bruce D., Martin R. Frankel, Steven J. Ingels, Kenneth A. Rasinski, Roger Tourangeau, and Jeffrey A. Owings. 1990. *National Educational Longitudinal Study of 1988: Base Year Sample Design Report.* Washington, DC: US Department of Education, Office of Educational Research and Improvement.

Stacey, Judith, and Timothy J. Biblarz. 2001. "(How) Does the Sexual Orientation of Parents Matter?" *American Sociological Review* 66(2):159–83.

Stankiewicz, Julie M., and Francine Rosselli. 2008. "Women as Sex Objects and Victims in Print Advertisements." *Sex Roles* 58(7-8):579–89.

Steiger, Darby Miller, and Beverly Conroy. 2008. "IVR: Interactive Voice Response." Pp. 285–98 in *International Handbook of Survey Methodology*, edited by E. D. de Leeuw, J. J. Hox, and D. A. Dillman. New York: Lawrence Erlbaum.

Steneck, Nicholas H. 2007. *ORI Introduction to the Responsible Conduct of Research.* Washington, DC: US Government Printing Office. Retrieved November 9, 2014 (http://ori.hhs.gov/sites/default/files/rcrintro.pdf).

Stevens, S. S. 1951. "Mathematics, Measurement, and Psychophysics." Pp. 1–49 in *Handbook of Experimental Psychology*, edited by S. S Stevens. New York: Wiley.

Stewart, Quincy Thomas, and Jeffrey C. Dixon. 2010. "Is It Race, Immigrant Status, or Both? An Analysis of Wage Disparities among Men in the United States." *International Migration Review* 44(1):173–201.

Stratford, Michael. 2014. "Poli Sci Victory, For Now." *Inside Higher Ed,* January 24. Retrieved June 1, 2017 (https://www.insidehighered.com/news/2014/01/24/wake-coburn-amendment-repeal-social-science-groups-plot-path-forward).

Strauss, Anselm, and Juliet Corbin. 1990. *Basics of Qualitative Research: Grounded Theory Procedures and Techniques.* Newbury Park, CA: Sage.

Sudman, Seymour. 1976. *Applied Sampling.* New York: Academic Press.

Sudman, Seymour, and Norman M. Bradburn. 1982. *Asking Questions: A Practical Guide to Questionnaire Design.* San Francisco: Jossey-Bass.

Sudman, Seymour, and Graham Kalton. 1986. "New Developments in the Sampling of Rare Populations." *Annual Review of Sociology* 12:401–29.

Sudman, Seymour, Monroe G. Sirken, and Charles D. Cowan. 1988. "Sampling Rare and Elusive Populations." *Science* 240(May 20):991–96.

Tashakkori, Abbas, and Charles Teddlie. Eds. 2010. *Sage Handbook of Mixed Methods in Social and Behavioral Research,* 2nd ed. Los Angeles: Sage.

Taylor, Steven J., and Robert Bogdan. 1998. *Introduction to Qualitative Research Methods: A Guidebook and Resource,* 3rd ed. New York: Wiley.

ten Have, Paul. 2006. "Conversation Analysis Versus Other Approaches to Discourse. Review of Robin Wooffitt (2005). *Conversation Analysis and Discourse Analysis.*" *Forum: Qualitative Social Research.* Retrieved June 29, 2014 (http://www.qualitative-research.net/index.php/fqs/article/view/100/209).

Thibodeau, Ruth. 1989. "From Racism to Tokenism: The Changing Face of Blacks in *New Yorker* Cartoons." *Public Opinion Quarterly* 53(4):482–94.

Thomas, Gary. 2011. *How to Do Your Case Study: A Guide for Students and Researchers.* Los Angeles: Sage.

Thomas, Quincy T., and Jeffrey C. Dixon. 2010. "Is it Race, Immigrant Status, or Both? An Analysis of Wage Disparities among Men in the United States." *International Migration Review* 44(1):173–201.

Tourangeau, Roger, Lance J. Rips, and Kenneth A. Rasinski. 2000. *The Psychology of Survey Response.* Cambridge, UK: Cambridge University Press.

Tourangeau, Roger, and Ting Yan. 2007. "Sensitive Questions in Surveys." *Psychological Bulletin* 133(5):859–83.

US Census Bureau. 2006. *Current Population Survey: Design and Methodology.* Technical Paper 66.

US Centers for Disease Control and Prevention. 2016. US Public Health Service Syphilis Study at Tuskegee: The Tuskegee Timeline. Retrieved June 2, 2017 (http://www.cdc.gov/tuskegee/timeline.htm).

US Department of Health and Human Services. 2012. Informed Consent Checklist—Basic and Additional Elements. Retrieved January 24, 2014 (http://www.hhs.gov/ohrp/policy/consentckls.html).

Van Belle, Gerald. 2008. *Statistical Rules of Thumb.* Hoboken, NJ: Wiley.

Van de Rijt, Arnout, Eran Shor, Charles Ward, and Steven Skiena. 2013. "Only 15 Minutes? The Social Stratification of Fame in Printed Media." *American Sociological Review* 78(2):266–89.

Vasquez, Jessica M. 2011. *Mexican Americans Across Generations.* New York: New York University Press.

Vasquez, Jessica M. 2015. "Disciplined Preferences: Explaining the (Re)Production of Latino Endogamy." *Social Problems* 62(3):455–75.

Vaughan, Diane. 1992. "Theory Elaboration: The Heuristics of Case Analysis." Pp. 173–202 in *What Is a Case? Exploring the Foundations of Social Inquiry,* edited by C. C. Ragin and H. S. Becker. Cambridge, UK: Cambridge University Press.

Vaughan, Diane. 1996. *The Challenger Launch Decision: Risky Technology, Culture, and Deviance at NASA.* Chicago: University of Chicago Press.

Vaughan, Ted R. 1967. "Governmental Intervention in Social Research: Political and Ethical Dimensions in the Wichita Jury Recordings." Pp. 50–77 in *Ethics, Politics, and Social Research,* edited by G. Sjoberg. Cambridge, MA: Schenkman.

Venkatesh, Sudhir. 2008. *Gang Leader for a Day: A Rogue Sociologist Takes to the Streets.* New York: Penguin.

Von Hoffman, Nicholas. [1970] 2009. "Sociological Snoopers." Pp. 177–81 in *Tearoom Trade: Impersonal Sex in Public Places,* Enlarged Edition with a Retrospect on Ethical Issues, by L. Humphreys. New Brunswick, NJ: Aldine Transaction.

Wallis, W. Allen, and Harry V. Roberts. 1956. *Statistics: A New Approach.* New York: Free Press.

Walther, Joseph B., Brandon Van Der Heide, Kim Sang-Yeon, David Westerman, and Stephanie Tom Tong. 2008. "The Role of Friends' Appearance and Behavior on Evaluations of Individuals on Facebook: Are We Known by the Company We Keep?" *Human Communication Research* 34(1):28–49.

Warwick, Donald P. [1973] 2009. "Tearoom Trade: Means and Ends in Social Research." Pp. 191–212 in *Tearoom Trade: Impersonal Sex in Public Places,* Enlarged Edition with a Retrospect on Ethical Issues, by L. Humphreys. New Brunswick, NJ: Aldine Transaction.

Webb, Eugene J., Donald T. Campbell, Richard D. Schwartz, and Lee Sechrest. 2000. *Unobtrusive Measures,* rev. ed. Thousand Oaks, CA: Sage.

Weber, Max. 1949. *The Methodology of the Social Sciences,* translated by Edward A. Shils and Henry A. Finch. New York: Free Press.

Weber, Max. [1905] 1998. *The Protestant Ethic and the Spirit of Capitalism,* 2nd ed., translated by Talcott Parsons. Los Angeles: Roxbury Publishing Company.

Weber, Robert Philip. 1990. *Basic Content Analysis,* 2nd ed. Newbury Park, CA: Sage.

Wechsler, Henry, Andrea Davenport, George Dowdall, Barbara Moeykens, and Sonia Castillo. 1994. "Health and Behavioral Consequences of Binge Drinking in College: A National Survey of Students at 140 Campuses." *Journal of the American Medical Association* 272(21):1672–77.

Wechsler, Henry, Jae Eun Lee, Meichun Kuo, and Hang Lee. 2000. "College Binge Drinking in the 1990s: A Continuing Problem. Results of the Harvard School of Public Health 1999 College Alcohol Study." *Journal of American College Health* 48(5): 199–210.

Wechsler, Henry, and Toben F. Nelson. 2008. "What We Have Learned from the Harvard School of Public Health College Alcohol Study: Focusing Attention on College Student Alcohol Consumption and the Environmental Conditions that Promote It." *Journal of Studies on Alcohol and Drugs* 69(4):481–90.

Weiss, Robert S. 2004. "In Their Own Words: Making the Most of Qualitative Interviews." *Contexts* 3(4):44–51.

Wertz, Frederick J., Kathy Charmaz, Linda M. McMullen, Ruthellen Josselson, Rosemarie Anderson, and Emalinda McSpadden. 2011. *Five Ways of Doing Qualitative Analysis: Phenomenological Psychology, Grounded Theory, Discourse Analysis, Narrative Research, and Intuitive Inquiry.* New York: Guilford Press.

Whyte, William Foote. 1993. *Street Corner Society: The Social Structure of an Italian Slum,* 4th ed., rev. and enl. Chicago: University of Chicago Press.

Willard, J. C., and C. A. Schoenborn. 1995. "Relationship Between Cigarette Smoking and Other Unhealthy Behaviors Among Our Nation's Youth: United States, 1992." Advance Data from *Vital and Health Statistics,* No. 263. Hyattsville, MD: National Center for Health Statistics.

Wilson, Barbara J., et al. 1997. *National Television Violence Study, Vol. 1, Part I: Violence in Television Programming Overall. University of California, Santa Barbara Study.* Newbury Park, CA: Sage.

Wilson, William Julius, and Richard P. Taub. 2006. *There Goes the Neighborhood: Racial, Ethnic, and Class Tensions in Four Chicago Neighborhoods and Their Meaning for America.* New York: Alfred A. Knopf.

Wolaver, Amy M. 2002. "Effects of Heavy Drinking in College on Study Effort, Grade Point Average, and Major Choice." *Contemporary Economic Policy* 20(4):415–28.

Wood, Phillip K., and Kenneth J. Sher. 1997. "Predicting Academic Problems in College from Freshman Alcohol Involvement." *Journal of Studies on Alcohol* 58(2):200–10.

World Bank. 2014. Adolescent Fertility Rate (Births per 1,000 Women Ages 15–19). Retrieved June 5, 2014 (http://data.worldbank.org/indicator/SP.ADO.TFRT).

Wray, Matt, Cynthia Colen, and Bernice Pescosolido. 2011. "The Sociology of Suicide." *Annual Review of Sociology* 37:505–28.

Wright, James D., and Peter V. Marsden. 2010. "Survey Research and Social Science: History, Current Practice, and Future Prospects." Pp. 3–25 in *Handbook of Survey Research,* 2nd ed., edited by P. V. Marsden and J. D. Wright. Bingley, UK: Emerald Group.

Wyche, Susan P., Sarita Yardi Schoenebeck, and Andrea Forte. 2013. "'Facebook is a Luxury': An Exploratory Study of Social Media Use in Rural Kenya." Pp. 33–44 in *Proceedings of the 2013 Conference on Computer Supported Cooperative Work.* New York: ACM.

Yoshikawa, Hirokazu, Thomas S. Weisner, Ariel Kalil, and Niobe Way. 2008. "Mixing Qualitative and Quantitative Research in Developmental Science: Uses and Methodological Choices." *Developmental Psychology* 44(2):344–54.

Zimbardo, Philip G. 1973. "On the Ethics of Intervention in Human Psychological Research: With Special Reference to the Stanford Prison Study." *Cognition* 2(2):243–56.

Zimbardo, Philip G., Craig Haney, W. Curtis Banks, and David Jaffe. 1973. "The Mind Is a Formidable Jailer:

A Pirandellian Prison." *New York Times Magazine*, Section 6, April 8:38, ff.

Zimmer, Michael. 2010. "'But the Data is Already Public': On the Ethics of Research in Facebook." *Ethics and Information Technology* 12(4):313–25.

Zimmerman, Don H. 1984. "Talk and Its Occasion: The Case of Calling the Police." Pp. 210–28 in *Meaning, Form and Use in Context: Linguistic Applications Georgetown Round-table on Languages and Linguistics*, edited by D. Schiffrin. Washington, DC: Georgetown University Press.

Zimmerman, Don H. 1992. "The Interactional Organization of Calls for Emergency Assistance." Pp. 418–69 in *Talk at Work; Interaction in Institutional Settings*, edited by Paul Drew and John Heritage. Cambridge, UK: Cambridge University Press.

Zook, Matthew, et al. 2017. "Ten Simple Rules for Responsible Big Data Research." *PLoS Computational Biology* 13(3):e1005399. Retrieved August 12, 2017 (http://journals.plos.org/ploscompbiol/article?id=10.1371/journal.pcbi.1005399).

Zuberi, Tukufu. 2003. *Thicker Than Blood: How Racial Statistics Lie*. Minneapolis: University of Minnesota Press.

Zuberi, Tukufu, and Eduardo Bonilla-Silva. Eds. 2008. *White Logic, White Methods: Racism & Methodology*. Lanham, MD: Rowman and Littlefield.

Credits

PHOTO CREDITS

Chapter 1
p. 2: Monkey Business Images/Shutterstock.

Chapter 2
p. 15: Alexander Raths/Shutterstock; p. 16: 500 Prime/Narin Sapaisarn; p. 26: John Buckingham, College of the Holy Cross; p. 26: Courtesy of Michael Rosenbaum; p. 27: Wendy Concannon; p. 31: Pictorial Press Ltd/Alamy Stock Photo; p. 34: Women in the Relay Assembly Test Room, ca. 1930. Western Electric Company Hawthorne Studies Collection, Baker Library, Harvard Business School.

Chapter 3
p. 42: PHILIP G. ZIMBARDO, INC.; p. 44: Alexandra Milgram. From the film OBEDIENCE © 1968; p. 60: Everett Collection Historical/Alamy Stock Photo; p. 77: Photography by Brian Kellett; p. 77: Daniel Calarco.

Chapter 4
p. 78: Lightspring/Shutterstock; p. 100: Ermolaev Alexander/Shutterstock.

Chapter 5
p. 113: Meredith Corporation, Photography by Ken Burris; p. 132: Martin Shields/Alamy Stock Photo.

Chapter 6
p. 164: James Steidl/Shutterstock; p. 173: Tony Altany.

Chapter 7
p. 183: Photo by James Levin, The Diamonback; p. 183: Courtesy of Corina Graif; p. 183: Courtesy of Michael Lovaglia; p. 194: Mark Poprocki/Shutterstock.

Chapter 8
p. 213: Courtesy of Brian Powell; p. 222: Yemen Polling Center.

Chapter 9
p. 251: Courtesy of Robert Smith; p. 254: Courtesy of Jessica Vasquez.

Chapter 10
p. 302: Courtesy of Melissa S. Kearney; p. 302: Courtesy of Philip Levine; p. 310: Andre Camp, Skidmore College; p. 311: pavalena/Shutterstock; p. 322: Courtesy of Michael Campbell; p. 322: Courtesy of Heather Schoenfeld.

Chapter 11
p. 343: Devah Pager; p. 347: Courtesy of Dan Clawson; p. 348: Courtesy of Naomi Gerstel.

Chapter 12
p. 365: John Buckingham, College of the Holy Cross.

Chapter 13
p. 408: Courtesy of David Snow; p. 408: Courtesy of Leon Anderson.

FIGURE CREDITS

Chapter 3
Figure 3.1: 1933 letter to "subjects" in Tuskegee Syphilis Experiment, National Archives; commentary at side from *Tuskegee Truths* (Reverby, 2000:187).

Chapter 4
Box 4.1, Figures A and B: Google and the Google logo are registered trademarks of Google Inc., used with permission; Figure 4.7: Jaromir Chalabala/Shutterstock.

Chapter 5
Figure 5.4: Krysan, M., & Farley, R. "The Residential Preference of Blacks: Do They Explain Persistent Segregation?" *Social Forces*, Vol. 80 (3) pp. 937–980; Figure 5.5: Adapted from Figure 5.2, p. 155 in Babbie, *The Practice of Social Research*, 12e. Cengage; Figure 5.6: Lang, C.E., et al., "Assessment of upper extremity impairment, function, and activity after stroke: foundations for clinical decision making," *Journal of Hand Therapy*, Vol. 26 (2), Table 2, pp. 104–115. Copyright © 2013 Elsevier.

Chapter 6
Figure 6.7: Survey Research Center, 1976. *Interviewer's Manual*, rev. ed., p. 36. Ann Arbor: Institute for Social Research.

Chapter 7
Figure 7.1: Pager, D., "The Mark of a Criminal Record," *American Journal of Sociology*, Vol. 108, No. 5, Fig. 3, p. 948.

Chapter 8
Figure 8.1: Powell, B., et al., *Counted Out: Same-Sex Relations and American's Definitions of Family*. New York: Russell Sage Foundation, 2010; Figure 8.4: Adapted, with slight revisions, from Groves et al., 2009: Figure 2.4.

Chapter 10
Figure 10.4: Permission granted by researcher (Lindner); Figure 10.6: Campbell, Michael C., and Heather Schoenfeld, 2013. The transformation of America's penal order: A historical political sociology of punishment. *American Journal of Sociology* 118:1375–1423.

Chapter 11
Figure 11.2: Pager, Devah, and Lincoln Quilligan. 2005. Walking the talk? What employers say versus what they do. *American Sociological Review* 70:355–80; Figure 11.3: Figure 1a in Pager, Devah, Bruce Western, and Bart Bonikowski. 2009. Discrimination in a low wage labor market: A field experiment. *American Sociological Review* 74:777–99; Figure 11.4: Figure 2a in Pager, Devah, Bruce Western, and Bart Bonikowski. 2009. Discrimination in a low wage labor market: A field experiment. *American Sociological Review* 74:777-99.

Chapter 13
Figure 13.3: Figure 2a in Pager, Devah, Bruce Western, and Bart Bonikowski. 2009. Discrimination in a low wage labor market: A field experiment. *American Sociological Review* 74:777–99; Figure 13.4: Snow, David A., and Leon Anderson. 1993. *Down on Their Luck: A Study of Homeless Street People*. Berkeley: University of California Press; Figure 13.5: Original source is Charmaz 2002: *Handbook of Interview Research*, p. 685; Figure 13.6: Advanced Memo Used to Elaborate the Paradigm, ~325 words, Corbin and Strauss 2008:137–38; Figure 13.7: Adapted from Zimmerman (1984).

TABLE CREDITS

Chapter 2
Table 2.1: Lareau, Annette, 2011. *Unequal Childhoods: Class, Race, and Family Life*, 2nd ed. Berkeley: University of California Press.

Chapter 7
Table 7.1: Adapted from Table 1, p. 103, in Lucas, J.W., et al., "Misconduct in the prosecution of severe crimes: theory and experimental test." *Social Psychology Quarterly*, 69, 97–107; Table 7.2: OUP. Kriner, D., and F. X. Shen. 2012. "How Citizens Respond to Combat

Casualties: The Differential Impact of Local Casualties on Support for the War in Afghanistan." *Public Opinion Quarterly.* 76: 761–770.

Chapter 8
Table 8.1: Powell, B., et al, *Counted Out: Same-Sex Relations and American's Definitions of Family.* New York: Russell Sage Foundation, 2010.

Chapter 9
Table 9.1: Vasquez, Jessica M. 2011. *Mexican Americans Across Generations.* New York: New York University Press.

Chapter 8
Table 10.3: Campbell, Michael C., and Heather Schoenfeld, 2013. The transformation of America's penal order: A historical political sociology of punishment. *American Journal of Sociology* 118:1375–1423; Table 10.4: Adapted from Table 6.3, p. 155 in Ragin and Amoroso (2011).

Chapter 11
Table 11.2: Adapted from Tables 2 and 3 in Cherlin et al. (2004:775 and 777).

Chapter 13
Table 13.1: Gibbs, Graham R. 2007. *Analyzing Qualitative Data.* Los Angeles: Sage; Table 13.2: Snow, David A., and Leon Anderson. 1993. *Down on Their Luck: A Study of Homeless Street People.* Berkeley: University of California Press; Table 13.3: Snow, David A., and Leon Anderson. 1993. *Down on Their Luck: A Study of Homeless Street People.* Berkeley: University of California Press.

TEXT CREDITS

Chapter 1
p. 10: Computer-Supported Cooperative Work, CSCW '13 Proceedings of the 2013 conference on Computer supported cooperative work (http://dl.acm.org/citation.cfm?id=2441783).

Chapter 2
pp. 27, 28, 29, 30: Lareau, Annette. 2011. *Unequal Childhoods: Class, Race, and Family Life*, 2nd ed. Berkeley, University of California Press (316 words).

Chapter 3
pp. 48, 49, 50, 51, 52, 53, 58: CFR (Code of Federal Regulations), 2009; pp. 62, 63, 65. Stacey, Judith, and Timothy J. Biblarz. 2001. (How) does the sexual orientation of parents matter? *American Sociological Review* 66:159–83; p. 64: Becker, Howard S. 1967. Whose side are you on? *Social Problems* 14:239–47.

Chapter 4
pp. 76, 77, 82: Broh, Beckett A. 2002. Linking extracurricular programming and academic achievement: Who benefits and why? *Sociology of Education* 75:69–91; pp. 83, 98, 99, 100, 101, 102: Calarco, Jessica McCrory. 2011. "I need help!" Social class and children's help-seeking in elementary school. *American Sociological Review* 76:862082; pp. 116, 137, 138: Calarco, Jessica McCrory. 2011. "I need help!" Social class and children's help-seeking in elementary school. *American Sociological Review* 76:862082.

Chapter 7
pp. 182, 183, 184, 187, 194, 195, 196, 198, 203: Lucas, Jeffrey W., Corina Graif, and Michael J. Lovaglia. 2006. Misconduct in the prosecution of severe crimes: Theory and experimental test. *Social Psychology Quarterly* 69:97–107.

Chapter 9
pp. 241, 252, 253, 254, 256, 257, 259, 260, 261, 262, 263, 264, 274, 275, 276, 277, 278, 281, 289: Smith, Robert Courtenay. 2006. *Mexican New York: Transnational Lives of New Immigrants.* Berkeley: University of California Press. 1159 words; pp. 254, 255, 256, 257, 258, 259, 262, 266, 267, 270, 271, 273, 274, 282, 283, 286, 287, 288: Vasquez, Jessica M. 2011. *Mexican Americans Across Generations.* New York: New York University Press (1580 words); p. 286: Weiss, Robert S. 2004. In their own words: Making the most of qualitative interviews. *Contexts* 3(4):44–51; pp. 257, 259, 262, 273, 278, 280, 286, 287: Saldaña, Johnny. 2013.

The Coding Manual for Qualitative Researchers, 2nd ed. Thousand Oaks, CA: Sage; p. 279: Emerson, Robert M., Rachel I Fretz, and Linda L. Shaw. 2011. *Writing Ethnographic Fieldnotes*, 2nd ed. Chicago: University of Chicago Press.

Chapter 10

pp. 321, 322, 323, 324, 326: Campbell, Michael C., and Heather Schoenfield. 2013. The transformation of America's penal order: A historical political sociology of punishment. *American Journal of Sociology* 118:1375–1423.

Chapter 11

pp. 343, 344, 345: Pager, Devah, and Lingoln Quillian. 2005. Walking the talk? What employers say versus what they do. *American Sociological Review* 59:391-407. American Sociological Association; pp. 345, 346, 347, 357: Pager, Devah, Bruce Western, and Bart Bonikowski. 2009. *Discrimination in a low wage labor market: A field experiment*. American Sociological Association;

pp. 347, 348, 349, 350, 353: *Unequal Time: Gender, Class, and Family in Employment Schedules*. New York: Russell Sage Foundation.

Chapter 12

p. 382: Lane, David M. Logic of hypothesis testing. Introduction. Online Statistics Education: An Interactive Multimedia Course of Study.

Chapter 13

pp. 408, 409, 414, 415, 416, 418, 425, 426: Snow, David A., and Leon Anderson. 1987. Identity work among the homeless: The verbal construction and avowal of personal identities. *American Journal of Sociology* 92:1336–71; pp. 408, 409, 414, 419, 420, 421, 422, 423, 424, 425: Snow, David A., and Leon Anderson. 1993. *Down on Their Luck: A Study of Homeless Street People*. Berkeley: University of California Press; pp. 430, 431, 432: Blee, Kathleen M. 1996. Becoming a racist: Women in contemporary Ku Klux Klan and neo-Nazi groups. *Gender and Society* 10:680–702.

Index

Note: Page numbers followed by *t* refer to tables; page numbers followed by *f* refer to figures; and italicized page numbers refer to photos.

AAA. *See* American Anthropological Association
AAPOR. *See* American Association of Public Opinion Research
abated unions, 341–42
abstract, of research reports, 439, 439*f*
abuse and cohabitation study, 341–43, 342*t*, 350–51
academic performance
  Facebook and, 2, 3, 4
  multitasking and, 226
academic performance and alcohol study, 364–65. *See also* Singleton, Royce
  bivariate regression in, 386-89, 386*f*, 388*f*
  cross-tabulation in, 384–85, 384*t*
  data processing in, 367–71
  elaboration analysis in, 392–95, 393*t*, 394*t*, 395*t*
  imputation in, 378
  modeling relationships in, 391–92, 392*f*
  multiple regression in, 396–99, 397*t*, 399*t*
  null hypothesis of, 382
  partial data matrix for, 368*t*
  SPSS and, 372, 377
  univariate analysis in, 372–79, 373*t*, 374*t*, 376*t*, 377*f*
academic performance and sports participation study. *See also* Broh, Beckett
  causal relationships in, 85
  conceptualization of variables, 87–88, 108–9, 110*t*
  correlation coefficient for, 93
  direction of influence in, 94
  hypothesis of, 106
  intervening variables for, 95
  introduction of research report for, 447
  NELS and, 85, 87, 93, 112, 115, 125, 157
  nominal measurement in, 119
  operational definitions of variables, 112
  ordinal measurement in, 119–20

research questions of, 82–83
Rosenberg Self-Esteem Scale and, 128
secondary analysis, 243
self-reports for variables, 115
social capital and, 108–9, 112, 129
statistical control in, 95
target population for, 157
variables in, 88–89
accelerometers, 134
action coding, 428, 428*f*
active voice, for writing research report, 446
Adamic, Lada, 303
Adler, Patricia, 273
Adler, Peter, 273, 277
Afghanistan war, opposition to, study, 192–93, 192*t*
African Americans
  dissimilarity index for segregation of, 117–18
  focus group on, 271
  interracial contact and stereotypes of, 26–27
  racial conflict and images of, 87
  racism toward, 35
  on television, 75
  in Tuskegee study, 43, 43*f*, 47
aggregate data, 86
aging and religion study
  sampling frame for, 158
  stratified random sampling in, 160–62, 161*t*
  target population for, 157
AIDS
  snowball sampling for, 174
  social research on, 61
Ainlay, Stephen, 157, 160. *See also* aging and religion study
alcohol and academic performance study. *See* academic performance and alcohol study
Allison, Paul, 378
Allport, Gordon, 26–27
American Anthropological Association (AAA)
  Code of Ethics of, 70
  on social responsibility, 68–70
  Statement on Ethics: Principles of Professional Responsibility of, 48, 56

American Association of Public Opinion Research (AAPOR)
  Code of Professional Ethics and Practices of, 56
  on 2016 pre-election polls, 156
American Political Science Association (APSA), 61–62
  A Guide to Professional Ethics in Political Science of, 56
American Psychological Association (APA)
  on deception, 41, 51, 57
  Ethical Principles of Psychologists and Code of Conduct of, 48, 56
American Sociological Association (ASA)
  Code of Ethics of, 41, 48, 51–53, 56, 68
  on conflict of interest, 68
  on deception, 41, 51-52
  on private information, 53
  same-sex marriage and, 65
  same-sex parenting and, 66–67
  on social responsibility, 68–69
American Sociological Association Style Guide, 452
  on block quotes, 451
Amoroso, Lisa, 64, 327
analytic notes, for field research, 280
Analyzing Qualitative Data (Gibbs), 411
Anderson, Leon, 275, 290, 291, 408, 408–9. *See* homelessness in Austin, Texas, study
Annual Review of Sociology, 80
anonymity, of research participants, 52–53
antecedent variables, 88, 89*f*
  in theoretical models, 392–95
APA. *See* American Psychological Association
appearance, for content analysis, 316
APSA. *See* American Political Science Association
archival records
  for content analysis, 318
  for existing data analysis, 296–97
  for operational definitions, 117–18
  for qualitative research, 259–60
  for qualitative research questions, 98–99
arrow diagrams, 391–92, 392*f*
ASA. *See* American Sociological Association